From Muskets to Missiles: Politics and Professionalism in the Chinese Army, 1945–1981

Also of Interest

The Chinese Military System: An Organizational Study of the Chinese People's Liberation Army, Second Edition, revised and updated, Harvey W. Nelsen

China Briefing, 1981, edited by Robert B. Oxnam and Richard C. Bush

China Briefing, 1980, edited by Robert B. Oxnam and Richard C. Bush

Technology, Defense, and External Relations in China, 1975-1978, Harry G. Gelber

China, the Soviet Union, and the West: Strategic and Political Dimensions for the 1980s, edited by Douglas T. Stuart and William T. Tow

China: A Political History, 1917-1980, fully revised and updated edition, edited by Richard C. Thornton

China in World Affairs: The Foreign Policy of the PRC Since 1970, Golam W. Choudhury

China's Quest for Independence: Policy Evolution in the 1970s, edited by Thomas Fingar and the Stanford Journal of International Studies

The Chinese Communist Party in Power, 1949-1976, Jacques Guillermaz

Chinese Communist Power and Policy in Xinjiang, 1949-1977, Donald H. McMillen

Perspectives on a Changing China: Essays in Honor of Professor C. Martin Wilbur, edited by Joshua A. Fogel and William T. Rowe

The People's Republic of China: A Handbook, edited by Harold C. Hinton

China's Four Modernizations: The New Technological Revolution, edited by Richard Baum

Military Power and Policy in Asian States: China, India, Japan, edited by Onkar Marwah and Jonathan D. Pollack

Cadres, Commanders, and Commissars: The Training of the Chinese Communist Leadership, 1920-45, Jane L. Price

*Available in hardcover and paperback.

Westview Special Studies on China and East Asia

*From Muskets to Missiles:
Politics and Professionalism
in the Chinese Army, 1945-1981*

Harlan W. Jencks

This book provides a detailed description and evaluation of the military, political, economic, and social context within which PLA officers have functioned since the civil war (1945-1949). Its aim is to evaluate the personal commitments and professional implications of a military career in the People's Republic of China. Focusing on the crucial factors of military function and technology, Dr. Jencks describes and analyzes the various post-1949 crises in the high command; his emphasis is on the import of these events for the officer corps rather than on the details of the events themselves. A wealth of information on the force structure, equipment, and military capability of the PLA provides an up-to-date assessment of Chinese military power. At the same time, the information depicts the life and work of Chinese soldiers and is central to the "biography" of the post-1945 generations of PLA officers.

Dr. Jencks is a postdoctoral research associate at the Center for Chinese Studies at the University of California, Berkeley. He is also a Major in the U.S. Army Reserve and a consulting faculty member of the U.S. Army School of International Studies at Fort Bragg, North Carolina.

Published in Cooperation with
THE CENTER FOR CHINESE STUDIES
University of California
Berkeley, California 94720

The Center for Chinese Studies, supported by the Ford Foundation, the Institute of East Asian Studies (University of California, Berkeley), and the State of California, is the unifying organization for social science and interdisciplinary research on contemporary China.

PUBLICATIONS

Schurmann, Franz. *Ideology and Organization in Communist China* (Second Edition, 1968)

Wakeman, Frederic, Jr. *Strangers at the Gate: Social Disorder in South China, 1839-1861* (1966)

Townsend, James. *Political Participation in Communist China* (1967)

Potter, J. M. *Capitalism and the Chinese Peasant: Social and Economic Change in a Hong Kong Village* (1968)

Schiffrin, Harold Z. *Sun Yat-sen and the Origins of the Chinese Revolution* (1968)

Van Ness, Peter. *Revolution and Chinese Foreign Policy: Peking's Support for Wars of National Liberation* (1970)

Larkin, Bruce D. *China and Africa, 1949-1970: The Foreign Policy of the People's Republic* (1971)

Schneider, Laurence A. *Ku Chieh-kang and China's New History: Nationalism and the Quest for Alternative Traditions* (1971)

Rice, Edward E. *Mao's Way* (1972)

Wakeman, Frederic, Jr. *History and Will: Philosophical Perspectives of Mao Tse-tung's Thought* (1973)

From Muskets to Missiles: Politics and Professionalism in the Chinese Army, 1945-1981

Harlan W. Jencks

Westview Press / Boulder, Colorado

Westview Special Studies on China and East Asia

All rights reserved. No part of this publication may be reproduced or transmitted in any form or by any means, electronic or mechanical, including photocopy, recording, or any information storage and retrieval system, without permission in writing from the publisher.

Copyright © 1982 by Westview Press, Inc.

Published in 1982 in the United States of America by
    Westview Press, Inc.
    5500 Central Avenue
    Boulder, Colorado 80301
    Frederick A. Praeger, Publisher

Library of Congress Catalog Card Number: 81-19863
ISBN: 0-86531-301-6

Composition for this book was provided by the author
Printed and bound in the United States of America

In Memoriam

*Captain George Patrick O'Toole
United States Army*

Contents

Tables and Figures xiii
Foreword by Harvey Nelsen xv
Preface xvii
Abbreviations xxi

1 MILITARY PROFESSIONALISM 1

   Introduction 1
   Military Professionalism Defined 2
   Civil-Military Relations 7
   Civil-Military Relations and Technology 12
   Civilian Institutions and Military Professionalism . 13
   Soviet Marxism and Militarism 15
   Modernization and Professionalization in China and the USSR . 25
   Convergence 29
   Notes 31

2 PLA MODERNIZATION AND PROFESSIONALISM 37

   Introduction 37
   The Early Years: 1921-37 38
   The Anti-Japanese War: 1937-45 41
   The Civil War: 1945-49 45
   The Professional Trend: 1950-59 46
   The "Red-Expert" Balance: 1959-65 54
   The Case of Lo Jui-ch'ing 58
   Foreign Military Involvement in the 1960s 62
   Notes 63

3 "MAOISM" 69

   Mao and "Maoism" 69
   Domestic Roles of a "Maoist" Army 78
   Notes 86

4	PROFESSIONALISM ON TRIAL	89
	Introduction	89
	The PLA in Crisis: 1966-68	91
	The PLA in "Control": 1969-71	103
	The Perennial Problems: Succession and Revisionism: 1971-75	110
	Mao's Death and the Succession	122
	Notes	127
5	THE FORCE STRUCTURE	135
	The Central Military Structure	135
	The General Departments	140
	Schools and Research Institutions	146
	Main Force Ground Combat Units	146
	Main Force Support Units	152
	The Air Force	154
	Nuclear Forces	158
	The Navy	160
	The Military Regions	162
	The Militia	169
	Regimental Reclamation Farms	172
	Some Observations on the Chinese Military System	174
	Notes	179
6	THE MILITARY INDUSTRIAL SYSTEM	189
	Introduction	189
	Defense Industry	194
	Research and Development	202
	The Impact of Politics	207
	Current Developments and the Future	209
	Notes	213
7	PERSONNEL MANAGEMENT IN THE PLA	223
	Introduction	223
	Personnel Management	223
	Motivation	231
	Command	234
	Conclusions and Projections	244
	Notes	247
8	CONCLUSION	253
	The Debate Over Military Line	253
	Persistant "Professionalism"	255
	Trends	258
	Unresolved Issues	265
	The Future	266
	Notes	268

Appendices

- A. Organization and Equipment of Type "A" Units of the PLA ... 271
  - Major Items of Equipment and Weapons, Type "A" Corps ... 272
  - Infantry Corps Organization ... 274
  - Infantry Division Organization ... 275
  - Infantry Regiment Organization ... 276
  - Infantry Battalion Organization ... 277
  - Infantry Company Organization ... 278
  - Armored Division Organization ... 279
- B. PLA Ground Forces Weapons and Equipment in Service ... 281
- C. Main Force Deployment: 1980 (Map) ... 285
- D. PLA Air Force Equipment ... 287
- E. Missiles of the Second Artillery Command ... 295
- F. The PLA Navy and Its Equipment ... 297
- G. The Military Regions and Districts (Maps) ... 301
  - The Eleven Military Regions: 1981 ... 301
  - Military Districts and Major Garrisons: 1980 ... 302

Selected Bibliography ... 303
Name Index ... 313
Subject Index ... 315

Tables and Figures

Tables

3.1	Total PLA Economic Labor, 1957-79	82
3.2	Total PLA Economic Labor, 1957-79 (Excluding Railroad Engineers, Construction Engineers, Telecommunications Troops, and Motor Transport Units)	84
4.1	Military Representation in the Chinese Power Structure, 1969-71	106
4.2	Major "Rehabilitated" PLA Men: 1971-72	113
4.3	Military Region Command Reassignments in December 1973-January 1974	114
4.4	Major PLA Figures "Rehabilitated" in 1973-74	116
5.1	PLA Ground Forces Strength	147
5.2	PLAAF Strength: 1979	155
6.1	The Ministries of Machine Industry--1981	195
7.1	Kwangtung Provincial Conscription Quotas: 1968	226

Figures

5.1	The Command Structure of the PLA: 1980	136
5.2	The General Staff Department	142
5.3	The General Political Department	143
5.4	The General Rear Services Department	145
5.5	Estimated Military Regional Organization	164
5.6	The Militia Administrative & Supervisory System: 1980	168
6.1	Trends in Military Procurement: 1964-79	191
6.2	The Chinese Military-Industrial and Research Systems: 1979	205
7.1	PLA Political Organization	237

Foreword

Next to the party, the People's Liberation Army (PLA) is the most important institution in China. Western scholarship achieved a working knowledge of the party-government system prior to the Cultural Revolution in the 1960s, while studies on the military lagged far behind. This was due to three factors: First, socio-political analysis of armed forces was a relatively new field with important conceptual breakthroughs being made by Samuel Huntington and Morris Janowitz in the late 1950s and early 1960s; secondly, China's security consciousness rendered secret even routine information on the military; and finally, the elite status of the PLA resulted in almost no refugees in Hong Kong with military backgrounds. A handful of North American and British scholars wrote histories and monographs on the PLA, gradually moving the field forward. These are surveyed by Harlan Jencks in his preface. The Cultural Revolution breached China's security wall around its military, offering the possibility of more rigorous political analysis. In the years since Mao's death in 1976, the media of the People's Republic have become much more open in discussing the topic.

By taking full advantage of the data and of earlier studies, Jencks has brought our understanding of the PLA up to par with our knowledge of Chinese civilian politics and history. He also provides a dimension which has been heretofore lacking—an in-depth knowledge of the armed forces of the USSR. All too commonly, China scholars (including this one) have treated the PLA as *sui generis*. However, in the 1950s, it was totally reorganized on the Soviet model, and while great changes have since taken place, elements of that influence persist. Finally, Jencks' own years in the US Army certainly add to his understanding of force building and military capabilities issues, though at some risk of parochialism regarding the feasibility of radically different management systems.

Neither the title nor the table of contents do proper justice to the scope of this work. It is the most comprehensive analysis yet attempted of civil-military relations in the People's Republic of China. Professionalization is merely a central, continuing issue within a matrix of political, social, economic, national, and international security issues which are all carefully analyzed. This is certainly the most important book yet published on the PLA and one which sets new standards of scholarship on the topic for the 1980s.

Harvey Nelsen

Preface

In the mid-1960s, John Gittings, Samuel Griffith, and Alexander George published the first comprehensive English-language studies of the Chinese People's Liberation Army (PLA).[1] These books were accompanied by shorter studies of military professionalism in the PLA by Davis Bobrow, and especially by Ellis Joffe, who continues to write perceptively on the subject.[2]

Two events of the 1960s provided enough data to permit foreign scholars to begin applying the tools of social science to the PLA, as opposed to "China watching" or "Sinology." First was the fortuitous acquisition of the secret PLA Work Bulletins for 1961.[3] Second was the Great Proletarian Cultural Revolution, with its flood of unofficial Red Guard publications. An upsurge of scholarship filled in biographical and organizational details. Pictures began to form of the PLA's place in policy making, of divisions among various military groups, and of the line-up of those groups with civilian interest groups. The Cultural Revolution and the subsequent fall of Defense Minister Lin Piao also provided glimpses into the considerable slippage from policy formulation to propaganda to implementation.

In 1972 and 1973, William W. Whitson published two landmark volumes on Chinese military affairs. In *The Military and Political Power in China in the Seventies*, he assembled a collection of essays by a diverse group of highly qualified scholars. A number of the individual studies (for example, Gillespie and Sims on the General Rear Services Department, and Harvey Nelsen on paramilitary organizations) are still the basic descriptive and analytical works on those subjects. Collectively, Whitson and his contributors set the standards and direction for virtually all subsequent PLA scholarship. In his *The Chinese High Command*, Whitson boldly put forward the "field army elite" thesis, based on a long-standing interpretation of the PLA used by Nationalist military observers on Taiwan. Debunking the "Whitson Thesis" became something of a preoccupation among students of the PLA, and it has been killed and overkilled repeatedly. Unfortunately, and quite unfairly, this has tended to overshadow Whitson's immense and enduring contributions. For one thing, he conceptualized and defined China's "military generations"—an analytical tool which has stood up to hard use. With his collaborator Chen-hsia Huang, Whitson also provided a meticulously detailed institutional and biographical history. Whatever its flaws, "The Whitson Book" remains both the definitive history of the PLA and the most useful English-language biographical reference on its high command.

There was still plenty left to do. In 1974, Jonathan Pollack surveyed PLA scholarship and posed a comprehensive list of questions which, for the most part, had not even been addressed: "Can lines of authority and patterns of communications be identified within and across ... bureaucratic hierarchies?" "At what levels are conflicting pressures and responsibilities of military officials most evident?" "To what extent did the PLA's activation as a political force during the 1960s undermine or alter more formal lines of command and control?" What are the PLA's political resources and how is military influence exerted? What voice does the PLA have in economic matters? Comparative work on issues like professionalization and military attitudes toward political participation were still lacking, as well.[4]

Harvey Nelsen made a good start on many of these issues in 1977 with his *The Chinese Military System*, and Jonathan Adelman broke new ground with his comparative study of the Soviet and Chinese officer corps.[5]

To date, the only attempt to deal with Chinese military professionalism in a comparative social science perspective is in Amos Perlmutter's *The Military and Politics in Modern Times*, also published in 1977. Perlmutter is not a China scholar, and I find his characterization of PLA officers as "revolutionary professionals" dissatisfying. Yet Perlmutter put a *definition* of "military professionalism" and a discussion of the PLA into the same book—something which no China scholar has yet done. The present book is, among other things, a China scholar's attempt to do just that.

Pollack also called for consideration, in a comparative perspective, of the "consequences of changing military technology and professionalization for political control, the economic context of military affairs, and the more general military role in foreign and domestic policy formulation." Further, he noted that, "No sense now exists of the personal commitments and professional implications involved in the pursuit of the military occupation in contemporary China." This book tries to address that set of issues. This has required detail and depth to fill in the organizational data so ably provided by Gittings, Whitson et al., and Nelsen. I have tried to construct the context within which officers of the post-1945 "military generations" have functioned, not in the high command, but down in the regiments, battalions, and companies. I have focused upon military function and technology—two aspects heretofore neglected. These lower ranks are disciplined and obedient, so they cannot be considered entirely apart from their commanders. Accordingly, the formulation of national security policy has been addressed, and there is description and analysis devoted to the high command at and above division level. This is not the main focus of the study, however, so there is little new regarding the mystery still surrounding such crises as the fall of P'eng Te-huai, the flight of Lin Piao, and the overthrow of the "gang of four." It is the impact of these events, rather than the events themselves, which concerned the lower ranks.

I am convinced that if we are to understand the younger officers who will enter the high command in the coming decade, we need to understand their career experiences so far. Inevitably, the picture is incomplete, based as it is on occasional glimpses provided by the official and nonofficial press, by the intelligence community, and by an occasional refugee.

There is a great deal of detail here on force structure, equipment, and military capability. This is provided for two reasons. First, the academic community, as well as military and governmental professionals, need an up-to-date book on the state of Chinese military power. Second, these details form the environment within which Chinese soldiers live and work, and are therefore central to the "biography" of the post-1954 generations of PLA officers.

Chapter 1 presents a theory of military professionalism and a discussion of the compromised professionalism of the Soviet officer corps. Chapters 2 and 4 trace the development of the PLA, emphasizing the influences which have either hindered or encouraged professionalization. Chapter 3 deals with the military implications of radical "Maoism," in theory and practice. Chapters 5, 6, and 7 are devoted to detailed studies of military structure and function, politics, and technology in 1975-81, emphasizing the influences in and on the lower and middle ranks of the officer corps.

Specialists will quickly note that descriptive details in chapters 5, 6, and 7 are often at variance with Nelsen's coverage in 1977. In virtually all cases, the variance is because of rapid change in the PLA, rather than any failure by Nelsen. As this is written, I am painfully aware that further developments inside China are likely to overrun portions of this book before it even goes to press. If we were to wait for contemporary China to "settle down," however, we would know little and publish nothing.

As this study neared completion the PRC officially converted all its transliterations of Chinese words to the Pin-Yin system, and most foreign scholars and publishers followed suit. This presented a dilemma, particularly regarding source titles and quotations using other systems. The dilemma was compounded for me because I hope to reach beyond China scholars to professional military readers who fairly cannot be expected to recognize that "Peking," "Pei-ching," and "Beijing" are all the same place, nor to easily shift among different systems. Accordingly, I have used the Wade-Giles system throughout, except for place names, which are in the standard postal system used by virtually everybody until 1979. The only exceptions are titles of certain publications, (e.g., *Beijing Review*) which are alphabetized using Pin-Yin. My use of Wade-Giles even extends to source citations as, for example, "Peking Domestic Service," even when an entry in a translation service may actually say "Beijing." This, again, is to avoid confusing non-China specialists. I assume that a China scholar looking up a reference to "Canton Kwangtung Provincial Service" will recognize that he has found it on the cited page which says "Guangzhou Guangdong Provincial Service."

Abbreviations that refer to sources can confuse most military men, and military abbreviations can confuse most China scholars. Accordingly, I have provided one all-inclusive glossary where a soldier can find *"SCMP"* and a China scholar can find "ECM."

In preparing this book, I have been generously assisted by so many people and organizations that it is quite impossible to list them all. I must acknowledge a special few, however. In Hong Kong, the Universities Service Centre, directed by John Dolfin, provided vital research facilities, resources, and assistance, as well as a stimulating scholarly environment. The Hong Kong Defense Liaison Office of the US Consulate General, under Colonel Richard E. Gillespie, was extremely helpful. I am especially grateful to Major William McMurdy and Captain Richard Latham for sharing their time, expertise, and open sources.

The undertaking was financially possible thanks to a research fellowship grant from the Center for Chinese Studies at the University of California at Berkeley. The center, under the guidance of Frederic Wakeman, Lowell Dittmer, and Joyce Kallgren, provided an exciting, challenging, and happy workplace. I am especially grateful to C. P. Chen and Annie Chang for their invaluable library assistance, to Peter Ray for help with translation, and to Therese Pipe and Karen Tulis for administrative and clerical support. Cheryl Fortie prepared the final typescript with speed, accuracy, common sense, and unfailing equanimity.

Others who have read and commented on various drafts include Thomas

Robinson, Daniel Lev, George Modelski, Lowell Dittmer, Joyce Kallgren, and John Service. Military colleagues at Fort MacArthur, California; Fort Bragg, North Carolina; and the National War College have also contributed both research assistance and criticism. I also wish to thank Colonel Monte Bullard, Lieutenant-Colonel Jack Leide, Major Dannen Mannschreck, Major Robert Walz, Captain Thomas Menza, the members of the University of Washington China Colloquium, and the Contemporary China Study Group at Berkeley. I am grateful to the Regents of the University of California, publishers of *Asian Survey*, for permission to reprint much of chapter 6, which first appeared in my "The Chinese 'Military-Industrial Complex' and China's Defense Modernization," *AS*, 20, No. 10 (October 1980).

My stay at the Universities Service Centre happily coincided with that of Harvey Nelsen. He generously took me under his intellectual wing, and has devoted countless hours to discussion, criticism, correspondence, and encouragement.

Finally, I am grateful to Professor James Townsend, who supervised the doctoral dissertation from which this book developed. His insistence upon objective scholarship has been matched only by his patience and kindness.

To all of you, named and unnamed, and especially to Professors Townsend and Nelsen, please accept my profound gratitude. Ultimately, of course, the final responsibility for the merits and defects of this study must be my own.

NOTES

1. John Gittings, *The Role of the Chinese Army* (New York: Oxford UP, 1967); Samuel B. Griffith, *The Chinese People's Liberation Army* (New York: McGraw-Hill, 1967); and Alexander George, *The Chinese Communist Army in Action* (New York: Columbia UP, 1967).

2. Davis B. Bobrow, "The Good Officer: Definition and Training," *CQ*, No. 18 (April-June 1964), 141-152; and Ellis Joffe, "The Conflict Between Old and New in the Chinese Army," *CQ*, No. 18 (April-June 1964), 118-140.

3. *Kung-tso T'ung-hsun* [*Bulletin of Activities*] (Peking: General Political Department of the PLA, 1961), trans. by J. Chester Cheng in *The Politics of the Chinese Red Army* (Stanford, CA: Stanford UP, 1966). Cited throughout as *KTTH*.

4. Jonathan D. Pollack, "The Study of Chinese Military Politics: Toward a Framework for Analysis," in Catherine McArdle Kelleher, ed., *Political Military Systems: Comparative Perspectives* (Beverly Hills and London: Sage, 1974). this discussion is based especially on pp. 259-263.

5. Jonathan R. Adelman, "Origins of the Difference in Political Influence of the Soviet and Chinese Armies: The Officer Corps in the Civil Wars," *Studies in Comparative Communism*, 10, No. 4 (Winter 1977), 347-369.

Abbreviations

Listed here are all abbreviations appearing more than once in the text, notes, charts, tables or appendices.
Bibliographic sources are italicized.

AA	Anti-Aircraft
AAHMG	Anti-Aircraft Heavy Machinegun
AFD	Air Force District (same as AFDD)
AFDD	Air Force Defense District (Same as AFD)
AFP	*Agence France Presse*
AMS	Academy of Military Sciences of the PLA
APC	Armored Personnel Carrier
APSR.	*American Political Science Review*
AS	*Asian Survey*
ASW	Antisubmarine Warfare
AT	Antitank
AWST	*Aviation Week and Space Technology*
BR.	*Beijing Review* (formerly *Peking Review*, changed January 1979).
CAAC	Civil Air Administration of China
CAS	Chinese Academy of Sciences
CB.	*Current Background* (Hong Kong, US Consulate General)
CBR	Chemical, Biological, Radiological (Warfare)
CC.	Central Committee (of the Chinese Communist Party)
CCP	Chinese Communist Party
CFCP	*Chieh-fang Chün Pao* [*Liberation Army Daily*] (Peking)
CFCHP.	*Chieh-fang Chün Hua-pao* [*Liberation Army Pictorial*]
China Report . . .	*China Report: Political, Sociological and Military Affairs* (JPRS, formerly *TPRCP*, changed July 1979).
CIA	Central Intelligence Agency (US)
CKCNP.	*Chung-kuo Ch'ing-nien Pao* [*China Youth News*] (Peking)
CKYCYK	*Chung-kung Yen-chiu Yueh-k'an* [*Studies of Chinese Communism Monthly*] (Taipei)
CNA	*China News Analysis* (Hong Kong)
CNS	*China News Summary* (Hong Kong)
CofS	Chief of Staff
CP	*China Pictorial* (Peking)

xxi

CPSU	Communist Party of the Soviet Union
CPV	Chinese People's Volunteers (Korean War period)
CQ	*China Quarterly*
CRG	Cultural Revolution Group (GPCR period)
CSM	*Christian Science Monitor*
CYL	Communist Youth League of China
CYTFH	*Chu-ying Tung-fang-hung* [*Pearl River East is Red*] (Canton; Red Guard Headquarters of Organs of Joint Committee of Red Rebels in the Pearl River Film Studio)
DOSAAF	Voluntary Association for Cooperation with the Army, Air Force, and Navy (Soviet)
ECM	Electronic Countermeasures
EW	Electronic Warfare
F and F	*Facts and Features* (Taipei)
FBIS	*Foreign Broadcast Information Serivce: People's Republic of China* (National Technical Information Service, US Department of Commerce)
FCYP	*Fei-ch'ing Yueh-pao* [*Communist Affairs Monthly*] (Taipei)
FEER	*Far Eastern Economic Review* (Hong Kong)
FLP	Foreign Languages Press (Peking)
FLPH	Foreign Languages Publishing House (Moscow)
GLF	Great Leap Forward
GNP	Gross National Product
GPCR	Great Proletarian Cultural Revolution
GPD	General Political Department of the PLA
GPO	US Government Printing Office
GRSD	General Rear Services Department of the PLA (also known as the General Logistics Department)
GSD	General Staff Department of the PLA
HC	*Hung Ch'i* [*Red Flag*] (Peking)
HE	High Explosive
HMG	Heavy Machinegun
HOW	Howitzer
HSPT	*Hung-se Pao-tung* [*Red Riot*] (Canton; Red Rebels of Central-South Institute of Forestry, Canton Red Guard Headquarters)
HTCS	*Hsien-tai Chün-shih* [*Contemporary Military Affairs, CONMILIT*] (Hong Kong)
HTJP	*Hsing-tao Jih-pao* [*Star Island Daily*] (Hong Kong)
I and S	*Issues and Studies* (Taipei)
ICBM	Intercontintinental Ballistic Missile
IRBM	Intermediate-Range Ballistic Missile
JMJP	*Jen-min Jih-pao* [*People's Daily*] (Peking)
JPRS	Joint Publication Research Service (Washington, DC)
KGB	Committee of Public Safety (Soviet)
KMJP	*Kuang-ming Jih-pao* [*Bright Daily*] (Peking)
KMT	Chinese Nationalist Party (Kuomintang)
KT	Kiloton (explosive power equal to 1,000 tons of TNT)
KTTH	*Kung-tso T'ung-hsun* [*Bulletin of Activities, 1961*] (Peking)
LMG	Light Machinegun
MAC	Military Affairs Commission (of the CCP Central Com-

	mittee)
MCC	Military Control Committee
MD	Military District (sometimes called PMD)
MF	Main Force
MG	Machinegun
MMI	Ministry of Machine Industry (numbered one through eight)
MND	Ministry of National Defense/Minister of National Defense
MPA	Main Political Administration (of the Soviet Army)
MPS	Ministry of Public Security/Minister of Public Security
MR	Military Region
MRBM	Medium-Range Ballistic Missile
MSD	Military Subdistrict
MT	Megaton (explosive power equal to one million tons of TNT)
MVD	Ministry of the Interior (USSR)
NCNA	*New China News Agency [Hsin Hua]*
NCO	Non-commissioned Officer
NDIC	National Defense Industrial Committee
NDIO	National Defense Industrial Office
NDSTC	National Defense Science and Technology Commission
NPC	National People's Congress
NYT	*New York Times*
PAD	People's Armed Department (Same as PAFD)
PAFD	People's Armed Forces Department (Same as PAD)
PAP	People's Armed Police
PC	Political Commissar
PCC	Production and Construction Corps
PLA	People's Liberation Army
PLAAF	People's Liberation Army Air Force
PLAN	People's Liberation Army Navy
PLANAF	People's Liberation Army Naval Air Force
PMD	Provincial Military District (an MD which coincides with a province)
PR	*Peking Review*
PRC	People's Republic of China
PSB	Public Security Bureau
PSF	Public Security Forces
PW	Prisoner of War
R&D	Research and Development
RC	Revolutionary Committee
RF	Regional Force (or Local Force)
RL	Rocket Launcher
RSC	Revolutionary Servicemen's Committee
SAM	Surface-to-Air Missile
SCMM	*Survey of China Mainland Magazines* (Changed to *SPRCM* in March 1974) (Hong Kong, US Consulate General)
SCMP	*Survey of the China Mainland Press* (Changed to *SPRCP* in March 1974) (Hong Kong, US Consulate General)
SDC	Self-Defense Corps (Yenan era)
SEG	Science and Education Group of the State Council

SLBM	Submarine-Launched Ballistic Missile
SMR	*Soviet Military Review* (Moscow)
SMW	Mao Tse-tung, *Selected Military Writings*, Peking: FLP, 1967.
SP	Self-Propelled
SPRCM	*Survey of People's Republic of China Magazines* (formerly *SCMM*)
SPRCP	*Survey of the People's Republic of China Press* (formerly *SCMP*)
SSTC	State Science and Technology Commission
SWI	Mao Tse-tung, *Selected Works*, Volume I, Peking: FLP, 1967.
SWII and SWIII	Mao Tse-tung, *Selected Works*, Volumes II and III, Peking: FLP, 1965.
SWIV	Mao Tse-tung, *Selected Works*, Volume IV, Peking: FLP, 1961.
TCC	*Translations on Communist China* (JPRS, Washington, DC)
TCC:P&S	*Translations on Communist China: Political and Social* (JPRS, Washington, DC)
TFYL	*Tsao-fen Yu-li [Rebellion is Justified]* ("916" Revolutionary Rebels of the Seventh Ministry of Machine Industry)
TPRC	*Translations on the People's Republic of China* (formerly TCC, changed in March 1974)
WSJ	*Wall Street Journal*
UP	University Press
URI	Union Research Institute (Hong Kong)
US or USA	United States of America
USCGDLO	United States Consulate General (Hong Kong) Defense Liaison Office
USSR	Union of Soviet Socialist Republics
YCL	Young Communist League (Komsomal) of the USSR
Yearbook '73	*Yearbook on Chinese Communism, 1973 [Chung-kung Nien-pao]* (Taipei: Chung-kung Yen-chiu Publishers, 1973)

From Muskets to Missiles:
Politics and Professionalism
in the Chinese Army, 1945–1981

1
Military Professionalism

INTRODUCTION

The purpose of this study is to examine the extent, nature, and political implications of professionalization in the Chinese People's Liberation Army (PLA). Heretofore, this subject has been addressed by a number of scholars,[1] but typically the reader has been left to provide his own intuitive definition of "military professionalism." This lack of definition has led to the identification of certain figures as "military professionals" simply because they wore PLA uniforms and opposed certain policies of Mao Tse-tung.

This study seeks to provide a more rigorous definition of military professionalism and to apply it to the Chinese case. We will find that an armed force's technological complexity bears directly upon the professionalism of its officers. We will therefore devote considerable attention to the pattern and timing of technical modernization in the PLA, in an effort to ascertain where and to what extent there are likely to be professional Chinese officers.

As Thomas Etzold has written, and as current events continue to show, there is no doubt that the PLA must and will modernize.[2] Rather, the questions include the following: When and with what urgency and priorities will modernization proceed? With what combination of domestic and imported technology? With what force structures and capabilities as ultimate goals? We must also ask what the impact will be, both within the PLA and within the political system and society in general. With respect to the military's role in China, three major issues have long been identified:[3] (1) PLA behavior as a political elite and its relationship with other sectors; (2) The resource and technological demands of the military sector and their impact on the rest of the economy; (3) The economic and administrative responsibilities assumed by the PLA in society.

We will also consider the "generation gap" with respect to professionalization--a gap accentuated by the continuing domination of the military by aging veterans of the Long March and Yenan eras. There is an important differentiation within the PLA at about the level of regimental commander. At that level and above, the officer corps consists of men who joined a struggling revolutionary movement and led it to victory. Below that level are officers who (like their American, British, or Soviet counterparts) joined the officer corps of an existing national army. The older group will die off or retire fairly rapidly over the next decade, to be replaced by these younger men, about whom little is known. We will attempt to piece together, in general terms, the career experiences of these younger officers in order to make some projections about how the Chinese high command will behave a decade hence.

The "generation gap" factor should not be overstated. As we shall see, there have been advocates of technical modernization and relatively professional military officership since the 1920s. Several have held influential posts for decades. In fact, PLA behavior during the Great Proletarian Cultural Revolution (GPCR) of 1966-69 indicated that, even then, many top leaders tended to act in remarkably "professional" ways. The influence of such leaders, which has waxed and waned over the decades, must be evaluated.

This first chapter will be devoted to an examination of the concept of military professionalism, and to a review of the emergence of professional characteristics in the Soviet Army. Soviet influence has been a significant factor in PLA history, and the Soviet experience provides useful insights into the interplay of advanced military modernization with authoritarian politics.

MILITARY PROFESSIONALISM DEFINED

From earliest times, certain persons have been accorded special status because they benefited society with specialized knowledge or skills. Priests and medical healers already enjoyed such status in primitive societies. In classical antiquity, sea captains were accorded special status and authority. Over the centuries, groups of these and other specialists evolved into what we today identify as "professions."

Until very recently, however, the leadership of armed forces was an undifferentiated aspect of political leadership--on whatever scale. Kings, freebooters, adventurers, landholders--all who exercised power and authority over others--had to be brave, strong, and cunning in battle, or they stood to lose their followings and their lives. The industrial revolution and the advent of the modern bureaucratic nation-state, however, created the need for specialists in the military art and military science.[4]

The modern state made it possible to raise and finance mass armies of conscripted citizens, which replaced the small mercenary armies of the past. As Western armies assumed this mass character, it became increasingly difficult for aristocratic part-time officers to handle them.

> In the eighteenth-century army, the rank and file formed an outcast group, isolated and distrusted, with no roots in, or connection with, the rest of society. The officers, on the other hand, had definite status in society by virtue of their aristocratic position. In the reversal of roles which took place in the nineteenth century, the enlisted men became a cross-section of the national population--citizens at heart—and the officers became a separate professional group living in a world of their own with few ties to outside society.[5]

Thus, the officer corps became the continuing hard core of the new national mass armies.

Not only could aristocratic amateurs not handle the troops, they found it impossible to cope with the march of military technology. Artillery gunnery, railway movement, and a host of complex new organizational and technical problems made it imperative that armies be led by full-time specialists rather than part-time generalists. Solid scientific staff work replaced intuitive "genius." By mid-twentieth century, professional officers in industrialized states were spending about one-third of their total careers in formal schools—probably the highest ratio of any profession.

A professional soldier, however, is necessarily more than a mere technician, for his functions border on economics, sociology, religion, and politics as much as they do on physics and mathematics. This is most apparently true of those high-ranking officers who must make representation to, and advise, the state's political leaders. It is true to a certain degree of any officer, however, for the organization of violence is intimately related to the cultural patterns of a society. Professional officers in the West have therefore been expected to have a broad background of general culture, usually symbolized by a university-level education.[6]

The degree of professionalism in a military organization is closely related to the characteristics of the polity it serves. For a variety of historical reasons, military professionalism first appeared, and became highly developed, in the nineteenth-century Prussian general staff system, which first applied to the waging of war the now-familiar bureaucratic principles of hierarchy, specialization, education, and promotion based on merit.[7]

The truly revolutionary aspect of the Prussian system "was its assumption that genius was superfluous, and even dangerous, and that reliance must be placed upon average men succeeding by superior education, organization, and experience. This approach ... subordinated the individual to the collective will and intelligence of the whole, and yet guaranteed to the individual wide freedom of action so long as he remained upon his proper level and within his sphere of responsibility. It was the antithesis of the eighteenth-century theory of the military genius." It represented, in a word, the triumph of well-trained mediocrity.[8]

This first truly professional officer corps emerged within the context of the struggle between the rising bourgeoisie and the declining aristocracy. Ambitious commoners and impoverished nobility alike found in military officership an honorable calling with a future. More important, because neither class was strong enough, after the disaster at Jena in 1806, to gain control of the army, a grudging compromise was adopted: The army would remain outside of politics altogether. Noble and burger alike came to accept the doctrine of military apoliticism, rather than risk having the army fall into the "wrong" hands. In practice, however, since the state remained in aristocratic hands, the meritocratic ideal was not fully implemented. Even in the heyday of Prussian professionalism, the landed *Junker* class dominated the upper levels of the officer corps. Thus, even this "purest" example of military professionalism was "contaminated."[9]

It should perhaps be emphasized that our use of the Prussian model does not imply that it was long-lasting, for it was not; nor that it was (or is) good or desirable. It is used herein as a "benchmark." We will be asking the question, "How, and to what extent, if at all, is the Chinese officer corps approaching the Clausewitzian military-professional ideal?"

The first comprehensive rationale for the modern profession of arms was set down by Karl von Clausewitz in his *Vom Krieg*, published in 1831. It contained the seminal conceptions of the role of the professional soldier in society and of the dual nature of war. Like medicine or law, wrote Clausewitz, war is, on the one hand, a unique and autonomous science with its own methods and goals. On the other hand, war is a subordinate science whose ultimate purposes come from outside itself.

The profession of officership, characterized by Lasswell as "the management of violence," is characterized, like other professions, by *expertise, responsibility* and *corporativeness*.

The expertise of a profession is based upon universal standards "which inhere in the knowledge and skill and are capable of general application irrespective of time or place." This expertise is largely reducible to writing, has a history which is studied, and a future which is researched. Formal institutions usually exist to teach, preserve, and develop this body of professional knowledge. Contact between the practical and the academic sides of the profession is maintained by journals, conferences, and the circulation of personnel between academic and practical pursuits.[10]

The conception of war as an "autonomous and yet instrumental science implies a similar theory with respect to the specialist in war." Because the management of violence has a grammar of its own, the military professional must be permitted to develop expertise at this grammar without extraneous interference. The ends for which military forces are employed, however, are outside his competence to judge. Clausewitz's assertion that "war is a continuation of politics by other means" clearly established the subordination of the soldier to the statesman. Huntington observes that, "Virtually all the other aspects of professionalism must necessarily follow" for "in formulating the first theoretical rationale for the military profession, Clausewitz also contributed the first theoretical justification for civilian control."[11] Clausewitz was quite explicit on this point when he asserted, "The political object of war really lies outside of war's province." War has no logic or purpose of its own, but these are found rather in the realm of the statesman's expertise, not the soldier's. Policy, he wrote, may well "take a wrong direction, and prefer to promote ambitious ends, private interests, or the vanity of rulers," but the military man must always simply assume that policy is "the representative of all interests of the whole community."[12]

Clausewitz therefore held that the professional soldier's behavior in relation to society is "guided by an awareness that his skill can only be utilized for purposes approved by society through its political agent, the state .... The principal responsibility of a military officer is the security of the state." Professional behavior is guided by an explicit code, expressed in law, and also is guided by custom and tradition. Unlike a doctor or a lawyer, however, the officer serves only one client—the state, which monopolizes the military profession on behalf of society.[13]

Because his profession is thus "monopolized," the professional officer's compensation is only partially determined by the market. He is neither a citizen-soldier nor a mercenary; and he tends to be poorly paid compared with other professionals. He is also motivated by tradition, prestige, technical pride, and a sense of social obligation. As Morris Janowitz has written, "As long as there are dangerous and irksome tasks to be done, an engineering philosophy cannot suffice as the organizational basis of the armed forces .... Heroism is an essential part of the calculations of even the most rational and self-critical military thinker."[14]

The professional officer bears three distinct responsibilities. First, he *represents* to the government the claims of the military security of the state. Second, he *advises* the government on the military implications of alternative courses of state action. Third, he *implements* state policy decisions which require his particular services. His job at this implementation level is the practical application of the resources at his disposal to the attainment of the policy object directed—whether or not he agrees with the policy, or even considers the object to be reasonably attainable at all.[15] At that point, his duty is quite literally to do or die.

The corporativeness of a profession lies in its members' consciousness of themselves as a group apart from laymen. In the final analysis, a profession defines itself, and specifies its own boundaries. These boundaries vary somewhat from society to society, but are generally recognized universally. The medical profession, for example, generally refuses to consider naturopaths, chiropractors, or faith healers as members of the medical profession. Similarly, professional military officers generally refuse to recognize mercenaries, security guards, or policemen as military professionals. Frequently, such borderline groups claim membership in the profession but continue, sometimes indefinitely, to be "defined out" by the professional "establishment." Membership in a professional organization is usually as much a criterion of professional status as competence and acceptance of special responsibilities. "The interest of the profession requires it to bar its members from capitalizing upon professional competence in areas where that competence has no relevance, and likewise to protect itself against outsiders who would claim professional competence because of achievements or attributes in other fields."[16] In the case of the professional officer, a public bureaucracy is the only context within which he is legally permitted to practice his profession. "His commission is to the officer what his license is to a doctor."

But the officer corps is "more than a creature of the state. The functional imperatives of security give rise to complex vocational institutions which mold the officer corps into an autonomous social unit." For one thing, entry is restricted to those with the proper education and training, and entry is usually restricted to the lowest commissioned rank. Levels of competence are distinguished by *ranks* within the profession, and by *office* within the bureaucracy. Assignment to office may be more or less subject to influence from outside the profession, but appointments to rank are normally made by the officer corps itself. This rank inheres in the individual himself, and "reflects his professional achievement measured in terms of experience, seniority, education, and ability." While an officer's bureaucratic authority derives from his office, his eligibility for that office derives from his rank.[17]

The military professional devotes an unusually high percentage of his life to professional activities. "He normally lives and works apart from the rest of society; physically and socially he probably has fewer nonprofessional contacts that most other professional men. The line between him and the layman or civilian is publicly symbolized by uniforms and insignia of rank."[18] He is similarly separated from the enlisted soldier, whose trade is the application of violence, rather than its management.

The corporativeness of the military profession, as of other professions, is quite consciously felt across political boundaries and across time. Since military expertise is "universal in the sense that its essence is not affected by change in time or location ... the same standards apply in Russia as in America, and in the nineteenth century as in the twentieth. The possession of a common professional skill is a bond among military officers cutting across differences."[19] Perlmutter regards this officer corps corporativeness as the most crucial issue in civil-military relations (see below).

The military professional is characterized by a set of attitudes and attributes that may fairly be labeled "the military mind," and he holds to a professional *ethic*. Of course, there are variations in the adherence of individuals and of officer corps to this archetypical professional ethic, but the ethic itself is "non-dated and non-localized." It is no more altered by technological change than medical ethics were altered by the discovery of penicillin.[20]

A major aspect of this ethic is *nationalism*. Since the soldier's responsibility is for the military security of the state, he views the state (not class, nor party, nor religion, etc.) as the fundamental political entity. He stresses the on-going nature of threats to the military security of the state, and the continuing likelihood of war. These beliefs lead him to hold that military preparedness ought to be a continuous priority of the whole society. He stresses tradition, esprit, unity, community, and social discipline because he places a premium on hierarchy, order, division of labor, public safety, and the supremacy of society over the individual. the professional soldier, in brief, is a philosophical conservative.

His stress upon the continuing likelihood of war is grounded in a fundamental pessimism. From the earliest days of his training, the professional officer is taught to plan and provide for the "worst possible case" --to always overestimate the threat and underestimate his own preparedness whenever he is in any doubt. He therefore looks not so much at enemy (or potential enemy) intentions, but rather at capabilities; and he always assumes the worst with respect to both. His pessimism applies to himself and his own countrymen as well: Normal human beings are not heroes, so it is up to the military to organize them so as to "overcome their inherent fears and failings."[21] Furthermore, human nature is viewed as universal and changeless, for the professional soldier sees the history of mankind as the history of war. His Hobbesian view of man and his belief in the nation-state lead the military man to regard efforts at achieving world peace as "utopian." He is, he will assert, a "realist."

His stress on the constant threat to the state leads the professional officer to press for constant preparedness. His desire is for more military forces and a higher state of readiness. He believes that military resources need to be converted into actual military strength. "He wants force in being, not just latent force. He desires forces capable of meeting virtually every possible contingency."[22] Because of his consciously pessimistic evaluations of enemy capabilities and intentions, he can conjure up all sorts of horrendous contingencies for which he must then devise counter-measures.

There will, of course, be disagreements about which threats, and therefore which counter-measures, are most critical. An infantry general, for example, will usually conceive the most critical threats to be those requiring more infantry divisions as counter-measures; but he will readily agree that a huge and flexible submarine fleet is also very necessary and that, ideally, the state ought to maintain both. The list of priorities of an admiral in the submarine service will naturally be the reverse; but again, he will believe that ideally there ought to be lots more of both. The general and the admiral share an identical world view; they disagree only about priorities.

Since he favors any and all measures to protect the state, the military professional favors the conclusion of treaties and alliances provided they really increase state security. Alliance with weak, adventurous, or erratic states is to be avoided, and alliances ought to be based upon mutuality of interest rather than upon ideological views. (He lives, remember, in a very Hobbesian world.) Similarly, the expansion of the state's territory or the establishment of foreign bases are only assets if they represent real aids to security, and not overcommitment. "Grand political designs and sweeping political goals are to be avoided, not because they are undesirable, but because they are unpractical. The military security of the state must come first. Moral aims and ideological ends should not be pursued at the expense of the state."[23]

It follows that, popular assumptions to the contrary notwithstanding, the professional officer rarely favors the actual resort to war, or policies which unnecessarily risk war. He "normally opposes reckless, aggressive, belligerent state action." Under certain circumstances, he may advocate "preventative war," but he generally "recognizes the impossibility of predicting the future with certainty."

> He will always argue that the danger of war requires increased armaments; he will seldom argue that increased armaments make war practical or desirable. He always favors preparedness, but he never feels prepared. Accordingly, the professional military man contributes a cautious, conservative, restraining voice to the formulation of state policy. This has been his role in most modern states including fascist Germany, communist Russia, and democratic America. He is afraid of war. He wants to prepare for war. But he is never ready to fight a war.[24]

Far from being a "hawk," the professional officer tends to see himself as a victim of civilians (both leaders and populace) who glorify war, pursue adventurous designs, and then blame the military if they miscarry. "The tendency of the civilian politician is to court popular favor by curbing the arms budget and simultaneously pursuing an adventurous foreign policy. The military man opposes both tendencies."[25]

His pacifism is reinforced by a strong tendency, especially among senior officers, toward "institutional conservatism." Although fundamentally conservative in its view of history, the military ethic is not opposed to change per se. It is open to new and even radical developments in technology and tactics. Moltke the Elder stressed "the unchangeable fundamental conditions of good generalship in their relation to changeable tactical forms."[26] Furthermore, and despite all his meticulous planning and preparations, the soldier's pessimism counsels him to expect the unexpected once battle is joined. He must therefore value innovation, imagination, and flexibility to complement planning, for, as Moltke once remarked, "No plan survives contact with the enemy."[27] In practice, however, the professional military exhibits the widely noted tendency to "prepare for the last war," which results from the hesitancy of senior officers to shake up the military structure. War, of course, is likely to do just that, and to produce such drastic changes that the pre-war elite may well be displaced by young upstarts. Furthermore, professionals often come to view the accumulation of military power as an end itself; and oppose anything that might dissipate it—including war.[28]

To summarize then, the professional military ethic is "pessimistic, collectivist, historically inclined, power-oriented, nationalistic, militaristic, pacifist, and instrumentalist in its view of the military profession. It is, in brief, realistic and conservative.[29]

CIVIL-MILITARY RELATIONS

Prior to the emergence of industrialized nation-states, the problem of "civil-military relations" simply did not exist because the institutional separation between military and civil leadership was virtually non-existent. In the West, for example, it was landed aristocrats who led the armies and ruled the polities. This historical dimension is quite important since we must consider civil-military relations in any society as being one component of a complex and inter-dependent social, political, and economic system. A study of formal institutions may provide only a very small part of the total picture.

The principal components of such a system [of civil-military relations] are the formal, structural positions of military groups in politics and society at large, and the nature of the ideologies of military and nonmilitary groups. As parts of a total system, no one of these elements can change without producing further changes in the other elements. ... A system of civil-military relations thus involves a complex equilibrium between the authority, influence, and ideology of the military on the one hand, and the authority, influence, and ideology of nonmilitary groups on the other.[30]

National Security Policy

The national security policy of any state is characterized, according to Huntington, by "three forms and two levels." The *forms* are: (1) military (external) security policy, (2) internal security policy, and (3) "situational security policy [which] is concerned with the threat of erosion resulting from long-term changes in social, economic, demographic, and political conditions tending to reduce the relative power of the state." Theoretically, a perfectly rational-legal government would deal with external security using only the military and the foreign affairs bureaucracy; with internal security only with its police forces; and with situational security with various other specialized agencies.

Without going into a lengthy critique of "boundary maintenance" theory, we can certainly agree that if the military is deeply involved in making and implementing internal and situational security policy, the pattern of civil-military relations will differ profoundly from a state where the military is relatively confined to dealing with external security policy.

The two *levels* of national security policy are institutional policy and operating policy. The former "deals with the manner in which operational policy is formulated and executed." Civil-military relations are always the principal institutional component of military security policy, but may also become a critical institutional component of internal and situational security policy. In that situation, civil-military relations become centrally important to security policy in general, and to the entire political system.

The operating level of military policy involves, most obviously, the dynamic issues of when, where, how, and under what circumstances to utilize military force. Also included are quantitative issues such as size, recruitment, and supply of military forces, "including the fundamental question of the proportion of state resources devoted to military needs." Qualitative issues of operating policy include composition, organization, equipment, and development. These qualitative issues encompass such widely ranging subjects as types of weapons, the location of bases, and arrangements with military allies.[31]

At the institutional level, the military security policy of a state is influenced by a "complex balancing of power and attitudes among civilian and military groups." On one hand, soldiers press for the functional imperatives stemming from external threats. On the other hand, nonmilitary groups press the priority of "societal imperatives arising from the social forces, ideologies, and institutions dominant within society." Since these conflicting sets of imperatives are in constant flux, there is a continuing need to redefine the system of civil-military relations. "Military institutions which reflect only social values may be incapable of performing effectively their military function. On the other hand, it may be impossible to contain within society military institutions shaped purely by functional imperatives." The basic problem of civil-military relations then is to maximize the military security of the state at the least sacrifice of other social values. The political relationship of the officer corps to the state is the principal focus of this continuous counterbalancing of functional and societal imperatives.³²

As noted above, the archetypically professional officer considers politics to be outside the scope of military competence. He believes that an officer who becomes involved in politics is undermining his profession, most obviously because he is devoting less than full attention to military pursuits. More importantly, however, he thereby risks dividing the profession against itself by substituting extraneous values for professional values, and allowing political considerations to warp professional judgment. At the level of military grand strategy, of course, there will be an overlap with state policy where the two may come into conflict. The ideal professional will represent, advise, and then defer to the statesman's decisions.

Since the modern military profession exists only to serve the state, policy direction must necessarily come from the state's political leadership. As a consequence, a professional officer corps is organized into a hierarchy of obedience, without which military professionalism is impossible. Loyalty and obedience are necessarily the highest of professional military virtues. There are certain circumstances (e.g., receipt of clearly illegal or immoral orders) under which a professional officer might decide to disobey; but he is extremely loath to do so, and will always presume his orders to be proper in the absence of overwhelming evidence to the contrary.³³

Officer Corps Influence

All these considerations confine the formal authority of the professional officer corps strictly within military organizations. There are, however, a number of factors which may contribute to the officer corps having informal authority in the society at large.³⁴ Among the factors influencing the degree of informal authority of the officer corps, we may identify the following:

Group affiliations include unofficial affiliations within the military, and affiliations with nonmilitary groups. Preservice affiliations with a particular class or geographic area fall into the latter category. An obvious example in China is the origin of most of the top party, government and army leaders in the central and upper Yangtze valley. Inservice affiliations include informal ties which may exist, as a result of working together in the course of official duties, between and among various groups of officers, government officials, or civilians.³⁵ Whitson's "Field Army Elites" are a case of such an extra-legal grouping.³⁵ Other examples include the special relationship which may develop (in the US) between certain officers and a congressional committee, or (in China) between certain officers and a local party committee. Another example would be the special relationship that often exists between the officer corps and defense contractors. Postservice affiliations include private or governmental organizations or informal groups which contain many former officers. Veterans' organizations, certain defense contractors, and other groups fall into this category in the US. The extent of their importance in China is an open question, since virtually everybody in the communist movement was involved somehow with the PLA prior to 1949. This points up one of the basic reasons we would not expect to find a high degree of professionalism in the PLA: There simply hasn't been enough time for a distinctly *military* elite to separate itself from politics--even if the prevalent ideology encouraged it to do so.

Human and economic resources subject to officer corps authority are factors which can vary radically without any change at all in the unity, scope, or level of formal military authority. National involvement in an all-out war, for example, can bring virtually the entire economy under military authority without any change in formal military roles.

Hierarchical interpenetration: The penetration of officers into civilian hierarchies will increase the authority of the officer corps in society, but will tend to result in decreased military professionalism. Conversely, the authority of the military profession decreases when civilians penetrate the officer corps. The role of "reserve" or "militia" officers is quite important here. Modern armies make a clear legal distinction between "reservists" and the "regular" officer corps, since the main social roles of the former are elsewhere in society. Their "motivations, values, and behavior frequently differ greatly from those of the career professional," and tend to be much more political. An illustrative, if extreme, example was the behavior of reserve general Ariel Sharon, who commanded Israeli operations west of the Suez Canal in the October 1973 war. When ordered by his government to halt his advance into Egypt on 22 October, he ignored the order and proceeded to isolate the Egyptian Third Army by driving on to Suez City. He then reverted to his civilian role as leader of the rightest opposition Likud party during the December elections. His civilian role motivated him to defy military orders, and allowed him to get away with it.

The penetration of civilians into the officer corps reduces the authority of the officer corps, while the penetration of officers into civilian hierarchies increases it. In either case, however, the responsiveness of the military to central governmental control and the overall degree of professionalism in the officer corps are reduced. In the view of the professional officer, the military security of the state is endangered in either case.

Prestige and popularity are the most volatile of the factors affecting informal officer corps authority. The officer corps and its leaders tend to be more popular in time of war or crisis than in peacetime, and more popular at the beginning of a war than at the end. Their prestige and popularity are likely to fall sharply when a war is unsuccessful, even if it is unsuccessful for reasons beyond officer corps control. The generally high prestige and popularity of the PLA and its leaders have been a major reason for their great influence in China.

Intervention

Separate from the issue of officer corps influence is the possibility of intervention by military units in political, social, and economic life. This may be the result of praetorian intervention by military leaders, but not necessarily. Civilian leaders often intervene with military forces to control disorder or provide public services. The presence of armed soldiers in a public street, post office, or factory thus does not prove, in and of itself, anything about the civil-military relations of a country. The critical issue in such a situation is who is giving the soldiers their orders.

Civilian Control

Huntington describes ideal civil-military relations as "objective civilian control"--an optimum state of equilibrium between military imperatives and societal values.[36] This situation is only possible where the officer corps is thoroughly competent, obedient, and apolitical. Such a situation is impossible in the People's Republic of China because of the state ideology, the make-up of the military-political leadership, and the recent revolutionary history of China. Huntington describes the alternatives to "objective civilian control" as various types of "subjective civilian control."

This arrangement is an alternative which most civilians tend to prefer. The demand for "political control" or "civilian control" of the armed forces has historically been, in fact, a demand for subjective control. It has usually been overlooked, although it is perfectly obvious, that maximum (subjective) civilian control always and necessarily means maximum control by some civilians at the expense of others: Subjective civilian control always involves the power relations among civilian groups. Any discussion of "civilian control of the military" therefore must begin with the question: "Which civilians?"

The simplest, and historically recurrent, solution has been civilian control by a particular class or caste (e.g., European nobility, Japanese *Samurai*, Indian *Kshatryia*). The assumption that civilian control meant class control led to an interesting anomaly in the West. The perspective of Jacksonian liberal democracy led Americans to identify the rising phenomenon of military professionalism with aristocracy, since it challenged the dominance of subjective (liberal democratic) civilian control. On the other hand, Europeans (notably de Tocqueville) identified military professionalism with democracy, since it challenged subjective (aristocratic) civilian control. The institutions of military professionalism "were neither aristocratic nor democratic; they were military. But neither the aristocratic nor the democratic perspective could differentiate them from the socio-political enemy."[37]

A second pattern of subjective civilian control has been control by governmental institutions. The problem here has been that when different civilian institutions disagree on the proper role of the military (as they seem inevitably to do), then a struggle develops between them over just which civilian institutions ought to exercise control (the president or congress, the king or parliament, etc.).

A third possibility is subjective control by constitutional form: The armed forces may be controlled the same way everything else in society is controlled. This pattern has been especially evident under totalitarian regimes, where, contrary to popular belief, the officer corps does not necessarily have more power than in other states. In fact, it is often quite the opposite: In 1941-45, the American military, for example, had vastly more political power than did the military in either Germany or the Soviet Union.

Huntington writes that "terror, conspiracy, surveillance, and force" are the methods of government in a totalitarian state, and that these are the same means by which the civilians in such a state control their armed forces. "Subjective civilian control thus is not the monopoly of any particular consitititutional system."[38] Van Doorn, however, points out that subjective control is more frequently and efficiently implemented by means of political indoctrination. A "program of systematic and enduring politicization is aimed at the creation of a military officer who is a professional expert as well as a politically active citizen. The two roles are considered to be mutually supporting rather than being likely to cause personal and institutional tensions."[39]

To summarize Huntington's models then, "Subjective civilian control achieves its end by civilianizing the military, making them the mirror of the state. Objective civilian control achieves its end by militarizing the military, making them the tool of the state." Military participation in politics is antithetical to objective civilian control: It is an assumption of subjective civilian control.[40] In the case of the PRC, we will necessarily be concerned with a case of subjective civilian control.

CIVIL-MILITARY RELATIONS AND TECHNOLOGY

In a theory derived, but diverging, from Huntington's, Amos Perlmutter stresses the criticality of officer corps corporativeness in determining the political behavior of the military. Perlmutter characterizes three basic types of modern officers. The first is the "classical professional"--the same Clausewitzian type described by Huntington. Second is the "praetorian" soldier, and third is the "revolutionary."

The "praetorian" officer, who is widely observed in Latin America, Africa, and the Middle East, is described as highly "professional" but excessively corporative. The "degree of commitment to corporativism, rather than to professionalism, determines the level of political intervention by the military," which is quite high in the case of "praetorian" officers.[41] It is important to note that Perlmutter equates "professionalism" with "expertise."[42]

Huntington accepts Perlmutter's view that military corporativism can furnish a motive for political intervention. He holds, however, that such corporativism is a "perversion" of true military professionalism, "in which the corporativist element overbalances the components of expertise and responsibility."[43]

Perlmutter characterizes a third type of "professionalism," represented by the "revolutionary" soldier. This type of officer is "professional" (i.e., expert) but his "orientation, organization, and inclination ... are anticorporate or noncorporate."[44] This admittedly broad category is said to range "from anticorporate romantic revolutionaries at one end of the continuum, through national liberation fighters (Marxist and non-Marxist), to routinized revolutionary professionals."[45] Whereas this "revolutionary soldier" is committed to professional expertise, the "historical professional and the praetorian soldier are committed to the principle of exclusivity."[46] The Israeli and Chinese armies are cited as having this "professional revolutionary" officership. In both places, an undifferentiated group of leaders initially led both the military and political aspects of the revolutionary movements. They were intensely concerned with the indoctrination of the revolutionary army, and inculcating the doctrine that it was an army "of the people" and of the political movement or party.

Perlmutter's reference to routinization points up his important proviso that "although in the 1970s the revolutionary soldier is essentially noncorporate, he does exhibit some corporate characteristics. The institutionalization of the revolutionary professional in China and in Israel may orient him more firmly toward corporatism . . . ."[47] Routinization is indeed a critical issue, for it is a common phenomenon. Van Doorn writes that the political control pattern of the military is likely to be "reshaped after the first period of one-sided domination by the political regime. The now firmly-established system will be disposed to loosen its grip in the new situation which promotes moves to restructure the control mechanisms. In concrete terms, the armed forces attempt to increase their autonomy within the newly-built political context."[48]

The basic flaw in Perlmutter's argument is his contention that, "Professionalism, that is, the acquisition and manipulation of skill, is not a variable that explains a military's weltanschauung .... The convergence of skill and control produces military corporate intervention. Skills, or their acquisition, result in an occupational, not a *political*, orientation."[49] In fact, military skills do tend to produce certain social and political orientations, as outlined in our discussion of Huntington. The emergence of the military profession as a corporate entity was the direct result of the increased complexity of military skills which accompanied the industrial revolution and the bureaucratic national state. Specialized skill and technique give rise to a desire for professional autonomy and to a sense of group consciousness among those who wish to set and maintain standards.

In his comparative study of the "rate, scope, and direction of political change resulting from the impact of increased technology on the institution of the political officer" in the Polish and East German armies, Dale Herspring has empirically corroborated the routinizing and professionalizing influence of technology.[50] He notes that few modern officers are willing to act on their own initiative "if they fear that their every action is being monitored by a political officer. The safest approach is to act only when ordered and then in accordance with established procedure. Yet modern military technology places strong emphasis on initiative and quick reaction."[51] It therefore becomes necessary, according to Herspring, to find roles for political control personnel which will not interfere with those of the military command, and which will not appear irrelevant or competitive to the latter. "The Party thus comes under pressure to familiarize the political officer with the rudiments of military technology, while at the same time curbing his influence in the personal affairs of regular officers and replacing his propaganda function with one more acceptable to regular military officers." This redefinition of political officer roles "will emphasize his qualifications as a specialist in the socio-psychological problems associated with modern warfare. He will become a social scientist. Closely associated with this new emphasis ... will be a deemphasis on his role as a propagandist and personnel specialist." Herspring's premise is that as technological modernization proceeds, the ruling party will increasingly need to change the role of its political personnel, and to allow more professional autonomy by reducing overt political controls. He found that this was exactly what happened in both armies, and that it was more pronounced in Poland, where military modernization proceeded faster and reached a higher level. He also notes that, "Assuming a close relationship between technology and the role of the political officer, it would appear that a Communist regime has considerable capacity to control the tempo of political change by varying the amount of technology introduced."[52] He concludes that, although there are other socio-political factors involved, the relationship between technology and changes in military political controls is quite clear. Moreover, improved technology has been the official "justification for all changes made in the role of the political officer" in both armies.

CIVILIAN INSTITUTIONS AND MILITARY PROFESSIONALISM

The relationship between technological modernization and civil-military relations is a main theme of this study. It must be understood, however, that the stability of the civilian regime is a far more fundamental determinant. On this point, virtually all observers agree: Weak or instable political systems spawn military praetorianism.[53]

In imperial Germany, before 1914, the military stayed out of civilian politics largely because those areas into which it might have been tempted were occupied by vigorous officials of the civilian government. In Japan, however, the attempted transition from the Meiji oligarchy to parliamentary democracy led to a great deal of institutional upset. Various scandals discredited the tentative attempts at democracy, while under a succession of weak governments, civilian bureaucracies became increasingly demoralized and vulnerable to military penetration. The military had no professional compunctions about taking over more governmental functions, and civilian officials were too tied up in the vicissitudes of partisan strife to present a united barrier to military expansion.

Here is a pattern which is readily apparent in a great many countries--notably, but by no means only, in the "third world." In many of these politically developing states, the officer corps is by far the most well-organized, unified, and self-conscious elite. Frequently it is the best-educated and most modern national elite as well, at least in terms of technical and organizational expertise. Furthermore, "third world" officers, like Japanese officers in the 1870 to 1914 era, find inspiration in the military unifiers of Europe--men like Garibaldi and Bismark. William Whitson identifies this notion of a Bismarkian mission to unify the nation by force of arms as a key ingredient of the "warlord tradition" of Chinese military thought.[54]

Among officers almost everywhere, moreover, deeply felt nationalism tends to evoke the recurring theme that the military represents the "real nation." From French paratroopers to US Air Force generals to Bolivian military dictators, one encounters this notion of the *pur et dur* nation, as opposed to the corrupt and noisy minority in power. These latter invariably include intellectuals in general, plus most of the press and most civilian politicians. The military often thinks of itself as representing the views of the "real people." In the absence of strong civilian institutions and a high sense of professionalism, this belief can lead the military to the notion that it ought to act as the "guardian" of national virtue by exerting its purifying influence over society.[55]

A highly developed sense of military professionalism will inhibit an officer corps from expanding beyond its immediate concern with military defense, but strong civilian institutions are the only safeguard. Military professionalism presupposes a reasonably stable and institutionalized polity. If civilian institutions are weak, the professional military ethic will not long suffice to prevent praetorianism. On the contrary, some aspects of the professional ethic will encourage praetorianism under such circumstances: "Perceived and actual inefficiency, corruption, instability, or radical tendencies [in the state] reflect on professional corporate and organizational integrity and on the military's inclination to intervene. Thus, the propensity to intervene stems from *some* corporate orientations of the professional that under normal conditions (i.e., a stable, efficient, and nonradical regime) makes [the professional officer] a loyal noninterventionist and in most cases makes the military a subservient organization . . . . In sum, military corporatism is both a bulwark against intervention and, in different times and regimes, a stimulant for it."[56]

Thus, if there is a low degree of institutionalization, the officer corps will be highly politicized. In the absence of effective political institutions which are recognized as legitimate and authoritative means for resolving conflicts, social forces confront each other nakedly. In such a society, which Huntington characterizes as a "praetorian society," all self-conscious social groups are highly politicized, not just the officer corps.

In view of this, it will be instructive for us to review the behavior of the

PLA during the Cultural Revolution, when the previously stable and authoritative political structures of the PRC were in upheaval, and PLA military professionalism—to whatever extent it existed—was subjected to a severe prolonged trial.

SOVIET MARXISM AND MILITARISM

As we have already indicated, state ideology may be opposed to the emergence of a professional officer corps. Western liberalism, fascism, and Japanese *bushido* are examples of twentieth-century ideologies which are hostile to the conservative pessimistic rationalism of the professional officer. Marxism, too, holds that the military must be patterned upon non-military ideals, and be under subjective civilian control. Like the liberal and the fascist, the Marxist insists upon the duty of every citizen to bear arms; and like the liberal, he views a war as a moral crusade. Lenin and Trotsky both insisted, in 1917, upon the establishment of a militia army, for the same reasons—almost point for point—that Jefferson and Madison argued in 1787. Since Marxists stress social class as the ultimate basis of politics, it is hardly surprising that they have repeatedly condemned the military professional ethic as "the bourgeois military line." Like the aristocrats and democrats of the last century, Marxists have identified military professionalism with their principal socio-political enemy.

The Leninist "vanguard" doctrine has made Marx's dictatorship of the proletariat operative in highly politicized societies ruled by authoritarian regimes. "An 'unpolitical army' is an intolerable anomaly" in such a society, whether it be China, the USSR, or the Third Reich.[57] In all cases, military professionalism was suppressed and subjective civilian (party) control exerted. All three regimes attempted to fill the ranks of their officer corps with men who were primarily loyal to the ruling party, its discipline, and its doctrine, rather than to the military profession and its ethic.

Yet the technological imperative has been at work in both the Soviet and the Chinese communist armies from the beginning. Both regimes, and especially their military leaders, have sought to improve their arms and equipment. It appears to be inescapable that, whether one begins with a professional officer corps or with a technically sophisticated army, one will tend to end up with both, given stable civilian political institutions.

The Soviet Experience And Its Influence

Soviet influence on Chinese military theory and practice has varied considerably in both its strength and its content. It was very strong in the 1920s, and reflected the early revolutionary experience of the Soviet military. Soviet influence was considerably less important, and less "revolutionary" in the 1930s and 1940s. In the mid-1950s, Soviet military equipment and advisors succeeded to a certain degree in reshaping the PLA along Russian "professional" lines. During the long intervening periods, the Chinese military developed independently.

The Soviets have developed and vacillated considerably in their organization, technology, and philosophy since 1917. Any reference to Soviet influence on the Chinese military must, therefore, be dated. Whitson writes of the "Russian revolutionary model" as though it were the only Soviet influence.[58] It was not. In particular, the highly orthodox military influence of the 1950s was hardly "revolutionary." Whitson's brief discussion of the developments in

Soviet military thought in the 1920s is excellent, but leaves the impression that by the 1930s, the "Russian model" was set. In fact, the 1941-45 period saw the emergence of a much more professionally oriented Soviet military establishment.

The following pages briefly review the development of Soviet military doctrine and practice, to ascertain the impact of Soviet military influence on China, and to give us an idea of what the PLA may someday become.

On 15 January 1918, a decree of the Council of People's Commissars called for the formation of an army which was to be essentially a voluntary militia. The official birth of the Soviet Army, however, was marked by the "Scheme for Compulsory Military Training" published in *Izvestia* (No. 83) on 26 April 1918. The voluntary militia concept had already given way to universal conscription. All male workers were to be subject to the draft. Other classes were theoretically forbidden to bear arms but, in fact, Trotsky had already begun the wholesale incorporation of experienced cadres from the old Tsarist army. Fifty thousand officers and 200,000 NCOs were called into the service of the revolution. The initial attempt to form a voluntary workers' militia, governed by soldiers' councils and elected officers, had shown itself to be militarily impracticable, so Trotsky was moving to reestablish more orthodox forms of discipline and control.[59]

The need to insure political reliability in the Army was met on 6 April 1918, when Trotsky issued "Regulations for War Commissars." They stated in part:

> It is the duty of a War Commissar to prevent the army from showing disrespect to the Soviet authority and to prevent army institutions from becoming nests of conspiracy or employing weapons against workmen and peasants. A War Commissar takes part in all the activities of the commanding officer to whom he is attached; these two persons must receive reports and sign orders jointly.
>
> All work must be done under the eyes of the Commissar. The only work which he does not undertake is the special military leadership, which is the task of the military expert with whom he cooperates.[60]

The first war commissars took full advantage of their prerogatives, however, and by late 1918 some were even issuing orders on their own, without their commanders' signatures. Trotsky and Lenin took a rather ambivalent attitude toward this, torn as they were between their desires for military efficiency and political reliability. The result was that they also called upon commanders to take part in political work because it was closely related to military efficiency. The activities of commanders and commissars thus began to interpenetrate, and as Red Army units were welded together in battle, the commissars became increasingly superfluous.

The mass-militia concept did not die easily. As late as 1920, the Ninth CPSU Congress called for a complete military reorganization to create a true workers' and peasants' militia, based territorially. Units would be based near production centers so as to "give the workers the necessary military training while withdrawing them from productive labour as little as possible." The declaration asserted that, "The essence of the Soviet militia system, must be the closest association of the army with the process of production . . . ."[61]

The need for rapid military reaction and for border defense made it increasingly apparent that the militia would at least have to be supplemented by regular troop units. According to Trotsky, "The Red Army was created from the very beginning as a necessary compromise between the two systems, with the emphasis on the regular troops." The imperatives of military security seemingly made it inescapable. Writing in exile, with the benefit of hindsight, Trotsky ruefully observed that, "The correlation between [numbers and importance of] regular troops and militia can serve as a fair indication of the actual movement toward socialism."[62] If that is the case, then the USSR moved away from socialism rather quickly, and Trotsky himself was instrumental in setting the trend.

As regularization proceeded, the militia diminished in size and importance, while the separation of the military became complete. The commissar system was progressively abandoned, especially after Lenin's death in 1924. "One-man command" (*edinonachalie*) became a principle of "socialist military science."

By 1934, the commissars had been entirely replaced by "Deputy Commanders for Political Affairs" (*zampolity*), who functioned within an orthodox unified chain of command. The official Soviet view today is that the commissar system was a temporary requirement, necessitated by the political unreliability of many officers in the early years. As commanders became more reliable, and commissars became more technically proficient, their functions merged in practice and in theory. One-man command was therefore a progressive step, formally instituted during the military reforms of 1921-28.[63]

The guiding hand in the early stages of these reforms was M.V. Frunze (1885-1925), who was instrumental in establishing a centralized chain of command, formalized officer career training, and in rescinding the regulations which had required Red Army units to engage in economic production. He also persuaded the Central Committee to prohibit local party organizations from interfering in the military affairs of locally based army units. Before his death in October 1925, Frunze had carried out sweeping reforms which laid the firm foundation for a "professionalized" Soviet Army. His aim was to create an army which was militarily orthodox in terms of its organization and technology, but was still politically reliable and responsible to central civilian control. He achieved this by "communizing" the military, subjecting it to strict subjective civilian control by means of the regular military chain of command.[64] The essentials of Frunze's system remain intact today.

Frunze was succeeded as chief of the Red Army by M.N. Tukhachevsky (1893-1937), a former Tsarist lieutenant who had commanded the Military Academy since 1922. He energetically undertook the technical modernization of the Soviet armed forces, established military technical schools, and pressed for military-related industrial development.[65]

Neither Frunze nor Tukhachevsky should be thought of as some sort of Russian Moltke. Both were dedicated communists who fully advocated strict subjective political controls. Frunze formulated the doctrine of "unified strategy" as his answer to the troublesome "red versus expert" problem. "Unified strategy" called for a defensive strategy of mass mobilization, and reflected the military weakness of the USSR before 1925. In some respects it anticipated, and no doubt influenced, Mao Tse-tung's defensive strategy of "luring the enemy deep" and then defeating him by "people's war." Politics was to be very much in command of military operations, and mass mobilization was to be the basis of strategy and tactics. It was this doctrine that Frunze's appointee, V.K. Blücher (also known as Galen) brought to Whampoa in 1924, and which was successfully adapted during the Northern expedition.[66]

Tukhachevsky, although he was an early advocate of massed tanks, artillery, and paratroops, actually maintained that, in the offensive, the Red army needed to retain no reserves because "it would find allies among the liberated masses wherever it adanced."[67] Even so, after Tukhachevsky and his chief of staff, Boris Shaposhnikov, succeeded Frunze, the Soviet military increasingly turned toward the doctrine of "integral strategy." This doctrine held that the Army ought to be left to plan, organize, train, and fight, with mass support organized separately by central civilian authorities. The role of the military was to fight and prepare to fight--not to produce economic goods or engage in mobilization politics. As a result of this shift in Soviet thinking, cadets at Whampoa (like Hsu Hsiang-ch'ien, Lin Piao, and T'ao Chu) were learning "unified strategy," while their comrades in the Soviet Union were learning "integral strategy." Among these latter were Liu Po-ch'eng, Yeh Chien-ying, Chou En-lai, Teng Hsiao-p'ing, Hsu Kuang-ta, Hsiao Ch'ing-kuang, and Nieh Jung-chen.[68]

The trend toward one-man command, "integral strategy," and professionalized officership was dramatically symbolized by the establishment of military ranks on 22 September 1935. Tukhachevsky justified the move as creating "a more stable basis for the development of commanding and technical cadres."[69] From exile, Trotsky argued, as did "Maoists" in the 1960s, that only military *position* matters, and that rank is a reversion to old "bourgeois" ways. "The rank of major," declared Trotsky, "adds nothing to the commander of a battalion."[70] As we have seen, however, it adds a great deal, for it formalizes his membership in a corporate body--the officer corps.

The rise of the Nazi threat gave added impetus to the professionalization of the Red Army through the 1930s. It was completely reorganized and equipped, becoming a really modern army. By 1937, nearly eighty percent of the Red Army was regular troops. The officer corps emerged as a new social elite. At the same time, the vast majority of officers became party members. Nothing indicated military rebelliousness or disloyalty.[71]

Then, in May 1937, Stalin abruptly reestablished the dual-command system which required commissars to countersign all orders. On 11 June, Marshal Tukhachevsky was arrested, and the "great purge" of the army was on. Before the end of 1938, between 30,000 and 70,000 officers were purged, including three of the five Marshals of the Soviet Union, ninety percent of the generals, and eighty percent of the colonels.[72] In the short run, the purge led to the disastrous defeats of 1941-42, and to several spectacular mass-defections of units to the Germans. What has been largely overlooked is the important long-range effect: The Soviet Army entered World War II led largely by men who had little or no revolutionary experience. As an important result, the Soviet officer corps has not been dominated by an aging oligarchy of "old warriors" as has been the case in China. Twenty-five years after the October Revolution, most Soviet general officers were men who first saw combat in 1939-41. Thirty years after the proclamation of the People's Republic of China, there were still division commanders who made the Long March.

The dual-command system failed miserably in Finland, and the position and function of commissar were abolished once again in August 1940. The system was reintroduced for the third time in July 1941, but it was widely ignored in combat units. Finally, in October 1942, it was abolished for the last time. Even when Stalin reimposed stringent controls after V-E Day, one-man command continued to be a basic principle of Soviet military doctrine.[73]

World War II turned the Red Army decisively away from the last vestiges of "revolutionary" military doctrine. the Soviet Union might encourage and even assist "peoples' wars" elsewhere in the world--but that was the concern of the KGB and the Foreign Ministry. The armed forces were thoroughly committed to a relatively professional view of national military security.

The post-war Soviet officer corps has exhibited a high degree of expertise, specialized responsibility, and corporativeness. Although high-ranking officers continue to hold high positions in the party, and have been decisive in succession crises, the officer corps has become steadily more aloof from political activity other than prescribed routine indoctrination within military units. Also, the phenomenon of individuals holding multiple civil and military offices has disappeared except at the very highest levels.

The Soviet officer has come to accept the military professional ethic, described above, to a large degree. "Apoliticism" is, of course, rejected in theory, and a great deal of routine lip-service is paid to the party and to "proletarian internationalism." Just how strongly the officer corps is committed to the CPSU and its global aspirations, as opposed to the military imperatives of Soviet national defense, is a critical and open question.

Motivation in the Soviet Army

Since 1942, political work within the armed forces has been the responsibility of each unit commander who is assisted by his "Assistant Commander for Political Affairs" (*zampolit*).[74] The work of these *zampolity* is directed through the chain of command by the Main Political Administration of the Soviet Army and Navy (MPA) which is closely linked to the CPSU. It also directs the activities of political informers within the ranks of the armed forces.

Through the *zampolity*, the MPA controls the primary party organizations at all levels down to company/battery/air squadron. Although a *zampolit* might graduate from a special school, and is on a distinct "career track" from a commander, he is still very much part of the normal chain of command, with roughly the same role as the executive officer in a Western military organization. In the absence of the commander, he assumes full responsibility for operations, and the commander, conversely, assumes both roles in the absence of the *zampolit*. In any case, the ultimate responsibility rests solely upon the officer in command, including responsibility for political work.

In December 1973, twenty percent of all Soviet servicemen, and seventy percent of the officers, were party members. "Most" company-level (and presumably all higher-level) units had active CPSU groups.[75] *These party organs function, not only in fact but in theory, as tools of the commander in his exercise of military authority*: "The Party ... organizations are a reliable support of commanders in the struggle for stronger discipline."[76]

Political indoctrination primarily comes to the common soldier in regularly scheduled "political information" (*polinformatsia*) classes, conducted by a unit officer--as often as not, the commander or a staff officer rather than the *zampolit*. In contrast to the Chinese case, political work has long been regarded as a means to an end--not as a primary good in itself:

> The day-to-day life and activity of any Soviet Army subunit are subordinated to one goal--that of enhancing combat readiness.[77]

This is a straightforward statement of the "purely military" viewpoint which Mao Tse-tung consistently opposed.

In addition to political indoctrination, the Soviet armed forces utilize a variety of other means to motivate their personnel. The simple appeal of patriotism is probably the most important of these. The Marxist-Leninist doctrine of "proletarian internationalism" has been rationalized away, and the multinational composition of the USSR has been reconciled with "Soviet patriotism" rather neatly, at least in thory: since the USSR is a multi-national workers' state, the Soviet Army is held to be "internationalist both by its composition and by the missions which it had to discharge."[78]

The principle of "unity between the people and the army" is symbolized almost entirely by means of governmental and CPSU organizations. Local party groups sometimes sponsor mutual visitations of soldiers and workers. An enterprise or collective farm may "adopt" a particular military unit and become its "patron." Although the regular requirement for the military to engage in economic production was abandoned in the early 1920s,[79] the army still assists with the grain harvest and certain strategic construction projects.[80]

The people and the military are also linked by a unique paramilitary organization known as the Voluntary Society for Cooperation with the Army, Air Force, and Navy (*Dobravol'no obshchestvo sodiestvia armii, aviatsii, i flotii*), or DOSAAF.[81] The DOSAAF, which is said to have over 30 million members, is subordinate to the Defense Ministry but its organization parallels that of the CPSU. Members receive training in a variety of military-related skills and "technical sports" such as skiing, marksmanship, parachuting, driving, flying, gliding, radio and electronics, etc. In addition, members receive instruction in military history, drill, and ceremonies. The DOSAAF seems to bear responsibility for civil defense in the Soviet Union, and hence receives considerable training in anti-aircraft defense, fire-fighting, rescue, decontamination, first-aid, etc.[82]

In addition to these more or less uniquely "Soviet" measures, the Soviet serviceman is motivated by most of the same means employed in all modern armies. From the Tsarist Army have come elaborate uniforms, medals, and insignia, as well as the custom of designating certain units as "Guards" formations in honor of outstanding combat service. Frequent competitions lead to the awarding of the titles of "excellent unit" and "expert" individual soldier.

As in most armies, the pride of the individual in his unit is emphasized in symbol and ceremonial. Unit colors are presented to each unit by the Presidium of the Supreme Soviet, and must be "guarded at all cost." As in most European armies, a soldier normally remains in the same regiment throughout his military career. An effort is also made to place sons in the same regiments in which their fathers served, to emphasize the traditions and continuity of the combat heritage of the "Great Patriotic War" of 1941-45.[83]

The official Soviet military view of what it is that a man fights for, and why, recognizes the same basic factors that have been noted in other modern armies.[84] Colonel Kovalyov elaborates three important factors which motivate soldiers to perform well: First is "collective cohesion," especially the cohesion of small unit solidarity, and social pressures for mutual assistance. The soldier "will always try not to let his comrades down." Second, the "example of the commander" is "particularly important." Third, soldiers are encouraged by awards and commendations presented to both units and individuals.[85]

Centralism, One-Man Command, and the Party

A striking characteristic of Soviet military literature is its relentless emphasis on the theme of absolute unquestioning obedience to all orders and regulations. The Soviet officer is admonished to explain why orders must be obeyed to the letter, but the principle of absolute detailed obedience is never compromised under any circumstances.[86] The roots of this attitude are to be found both in the autocratic Russian tradition and in the Soviet experience. Unlike the Chinese, who won power through prolonged decentralized guerrilla warfare, the Soviets gained power relatively quickly with relatively conventional armies. Lenin is on record as fearing "like the plague the unruly guerrilla spirit, the arbitrary actions of isolated detachments . . . ."[87]

The Soviet officer functions within what is the most highly centralized military chain of command in the world. He receives from his superiors meticulously detailed orders which he obeys instantly and to the letter. He expects, and gets, the same obedience from his subordinates.

> The principle of *centralism* is of exceptional significance in Soviet military development. It finds expression in the fact that all formations of the Army and Navy with their staffs are completely subordinated to the government of the Soviet Union.[88]

This last phrase touches upon the important question of whether the Red Army is a party army or a national state's army. Soviet military literature strongly indicates the latter. The armed forces are repeatedly described as the tool and the guardian of the state, and it is the need to maximize the state's military security which justifies "one-man command":

> The need for one-man command is dictated above all by military experience. In combat conditions, when the situation changes rapidly, there is not time to discuss and take a decision in the framework of collegiality. Here, there must be a commander with full powers, whose order is an inviolable law for his subordinates.[89]

Since this is an accepted principle everywhere, the question arises as to whether there is any real difference between military command in the USSR and, say, the United States or Britain. This is obviously a troubling question, for the literature is filled with lengthy explanations of just how and why Soviet officership is somehow different. The official explanation is that the Soviet officer is different because Soviet society is different. A Soviet commander is of the same class as the soldiers, and obeys the workers' party and state. This theoretically changes everything, and is supposedly in sharp contrast to officership in non-socialist armies, which is held to be characterized by "a desire to turn the soldiers into blind executors of the will imposed on them."[90]

The unique feature of the Soviet military is indeed the role of the party, but the results of party control appear to be almost diametrically opposed to those claimed. In fact, blind obedience is demanded of the Soviet soldier to a far greater extent than it is of the British, American, or Chinese soldier. The arrogant disdain and rigid separation of the Soviet officer corps vis-a-vis enlisted soldiers is much more marked as well.

A curious ambivalence seems to characterize the relationship between

Soviet officers and the party. On one hand, an extreme degree of subjective civilian (CPSU) control is seen in the demand for absolute, almost slavish, obedience to all orders; as well as in the very high proportion of party members in the officer corps. On the other hand, it is remarkable to note the extent to which the CPSU groups within a military unit are quite explicitly relegated to the status of tools for the commander's use in exercising one-man command. This is in sharp contrast to the Chinese system, and to the early revolutionary Soviet practice as well. The commander represents the authority of the state *and* of the CPSU, and is solely and personally responsible for all the unit does or doesn't do—including its political training.

> The commander relies on the Party organization and uses its prestige and influence in the interests of enhancing combat readiness and strengthening military discipline.[91]

> The Commander acts in close contact with the Party organizations and political workers. This helps *them* avoid mistakes and ensures strict and undeviating implementation of all the measures adopted by the command, orders, and instructions. The closer the commander's link with the Party... organizations, with army activists, the firmer the discipline in the unit and the more successfully he exercises troop control.[92]

The party branch is regarded as a tool of the commander, and never as a means of restricting his actions.[93] It is also used as a means of applying peer pressure on the individual soldier to conform.

Since the days of Tukhachevsky, the rationale for "one-man command" and for the separation of army and people, has been the functional imperative of technical expertise. One-man command, in turn, has been the rationale both for slavish discipline and for the privileged status of the officer corps.

The Soviet Officer Corps Today

In countless ways, the Soviet military officer enjoys a highly privileged status, both as an individual and as a member of a sharply segregated social elite. The emphasis on the high status of officers has resulted in separation from, and arrogance toward, the enlisted ranks. The Soviets have even created a "qualitatively new category of commanders close in rank to officers" to help bridge the distance between officers and the ranks. The ranks of *Praporshchik* (ensign) in the army and *Mitchman* (warrant officer) in the navy were instituted in 1972. These men are very senior NCOs who are promoted to this new rank to act as "immediate assistants to officers," and fill the roles played by the first-sergeants and sergeants-major of most other armies.

The low status of NCOs and the creation of these quasi-officers are symptomatic of a marked "devaluation" of military rank in the USSR. Even before 1972, the Soviet Army was one of the few in the world to have three grades of lieutenants (Junior Lt., Lt., Senior Lt.) rather than the usual two. The advent of the *Praporshchik* in effect, adds what might be thought of as a "Fourth Lieutenant." In most armies, a company is supposed to be commanded by a captain or even by a major. In the Soviet Army, companies are commanded by senior lieutenants. Similarly, battalions are generally commanded by lieutenant-colonels, but are commanded by majors in the Soviet Army, and so forth. All this is symptomatic of a system which severely limits the initiative of the commander at each level, while giving him absolute detailed authority over his subordinates (with which, in turn, he limits *their* initiative). Soviet military formations of a given type tend to be much smaller than those of the other powers. Thus, a Soviet unit commander is not only of a lower rank than his Western counterpart, but he commands fewer people. He can exert tighter control as a direct result. Again, we can logically conclude that a Soviet commander is just not entrusted with much initiative or flexibility.

Despite all this, Soviet military doctrine with respect to command initiative is much like that of any modern army:[94] The commander should keep his mission and the intent of his superior commander foremost in mind, but be flexible in executing his orders, making such modifications as the situation demands, while keeping "next higher" informed. Yet, according to Lt. Gen. V. Merimsky, the prime virtue of a Soviet officer is not his imagination, judgment, or initiative, but his "iron will" in carrying out orders—no matter what. A Soviet commander leads by his exemplary "sense of duty ... self-control and irreproachable execution of orders."[95] The Soviets recognize the need for decentralized execution on the modern battlefield, but cannot bring themselves to allow it.

Subjective civilian control of the Soviet armed forces is handled much differently today than it was during the civil war. It is assured by a highly centralized and rigid command structure, rather than by a commissar system. This is basically the system Frunze set up in the 1920s. The officer corps itself has been coopted by, and subordinated to, the central leadership of party and state. The tight discipline and the narrow limits on his personal initiative make the Soviet officer highly responsive to this leadership. As Roman Kolkowicz has observed, this ideal still has not been achieved to the full satisfaction of the CPSU's civilian leaders.

> Most desirable from [the CPSU] point of view would be, of course, an officer corps that consisted only of dedicated and unquestionably loyal men, each of whom combined the best traits of the commander with those of the commissar. Whenever an attempt has been made, however, to realize this ideal ... the results have been disappointing; for it has proved difficult, if not impossible, for the officer to maintain with equal fervor the dual loyalty to his profession and to the Party, notwithstanding the theoretical principle that ideological motivation will govern both loyalties and preclude any possible conflict.
>
> The adherence of the Soviet military to the traditions and objectives, the values and symbols, that resemble those of other large military establishments reveals the simple truth that professional loyalties in such guild-like organizations are very intense and virtually proof against ideological onslaughts from outside the profession.[96]

The party, therefore, harbors a deep and abiding mistrust of the army which is manifested in a propensity, especially at higher levels of command, to interfere in military affairs and to infringe upon military prerogatives. The overall effect "has been to lower discipline, morale, and military effectiveness."[97]

In addition to this primary reliance on the chain of command, subjective civilian control is reinforced by a number of other means. Not only the MPA but also the KGB maintains a system of informers within the armed forces. The KGB itself maintains a separate "Army of Internal Security," and an operational air force. The KGB thus serves as a political and even military counterforce to the regular armed forces (much as the SS did in the Third Reich).[98] Van Doorn has observed of these "special party militias or military armed police forces" that "it is not only the individual officer who has a controlling party member [i.e.: commisar] at his side; the regular army as such also has to tolerate a rival organization."[99] The absence of such a formal "counter-army army" in the PRC contrasts significantly with the Soviet experience.[100] As we shall see in chapters four and five, however, the People's Militia, the airborne infantry of the PLA air force, and the military regional system have all tended to provide similar counterweights to the PLA main forces.

Still another device for assuring CPSU control is that of exploiting personal and factional rivalries within the armed forces. This practice is not unique to the Soviet Union, of course, for it seems to be used virtually everywhere civilians seek to gain or maintain subjective control.

The mainstay of party control continues to be the MPA, acting principally through the military chain of command. The MPA has almost always been headed by a "political general," frequently one with extensive civilian political experience. The only exception was the period from 1949 to 1962, when the MPA was headed by a succession of career commanders during the years of Stalin's death and the struggle for succession. As we would expect, the political power of military commanders varies inversely with the strength and unity of the CPSU. When the Party is deeply divided by internal struggles, the support of the armed forces is actively wooed by the factions involved, and top commanders are in a position to extract concessions. The absence of either constitutional-legal or traditional provisions for the transfer of power is an inherent problem in both the Soviet Union and the PRC. Succession crises periodically threaten institutional stability and "pare down the authority structure to the underlying frame of naked power."[101] The pivotal role of Marshal Zhukov in the ascent of Khrushchev was a case in point. As a reward, he became a full member of the Presidium of the CPSU Central Committee in July 1957. In consolidating his power, Khrushchev regarded Zhukov as a threat, however, and removed him after less than four months, accusing him of "Bonapartist policy."[102] In that same month, a decree of the Central Committee "Concerning the Improvement of Party and Political Work in the Soviet Army and Navy" reasserted the political controls Zhukov had sought to reduce.[103]

There is little, if any, evidence that Zhukov (or any other commander since the civil war) ever cherished dreams of a military coup d'etat. On the contrary, it is illuminating to enumerate the concessions Zhukov did extract for his support: First, he insisted that the military victims of the great purge be officially "rehabilitated," and that the history of World War II be rewritten to give the Red Army full credit for the victory—not Stalin. Second, he demanded and got a lessening of political control over military decision making. Third, he pressed for bigger arms budgets and more emphasis on heavy industry.[104] These concessions were the same sorts of things military professionals want everywhere: Prestige, resources, and autonomy.

Military Professionalism in the USSR

Marshal V.D. Sokolovsky, editor of the standard postwar work on Soviet military strategy, began his introduction to the volume with a cogent defense of Clausewitz. "It is well known," he wrote, "that the essence of war as a continuation of politics does not change with changing technology and armaments."[105] The entire first chapter of *Military Strategy*, in fact, is largely a restatement of many elements of the military professional ethic described above, embellished with occasional obligatory assertions of the class nature of war and strategy. In essence, Sokolovsky claims that it is the Soviet officer who is the real professional. He is scientific, peace-loving, and rational, whereas the officers of imperialist states are adventurous, bellicose, and "metaphysical." For every mention of class and party, there are five of the state. Entire paragraphs, notably the defense of Clausewitz, are almost interchangeable with Huntington.

Military professionalism is seen in many familiar guises in the Soviet Union. In the mid-1970s, for example, there has been controversy over the issues of "detente" and the Strategic Arms Limitation Talks (SALT). The leading opponents of the SALT negotiations have been Soviet generals whose arguments are the same as those of their opposite numbers in Washington: The only guarantee of security is armed strength in being, and arms limitation pacts are always scraps of paper.[106]

The generals are neither challenging party control nor trying to start a war. They are simply advocating the miltiary professional's perennial position of pessimistic "realism" vis-a-vis "utopian" schemes for world peace.

MODERNIZATION AND PROFESSIONALIZATION IN CHINA AND THE USSR

For many reasons, the Soviet and Chinese armies have not responded to the technological imperative the same way. Perhaps the most important single factor has been the makeup of the respective officer corps.[107] By the outbreak of the Chinese civil war, PLA officers were tested, experienced, and thoroughly reliable both politically and militarily. The Soviet Army, on the contrary, was led mainly by former Tsarist officers well into the 1930s.

During their civil wars, both the Soviet and Chinese communists engaged in a type of warfare which was more concerned with winning over populations than with destroying enemy forces. The "dual-command" system of a military commander and a coequal political commissar can work very well in such a situation.

Unlike the Chinese, however, the Soviets believed from the beginning that the best military forces are necessarily those armed with the most advanced weapons and equipment. Lenin himself said that technological superiority on the battlefield is just as important as organization, discipline, and even class consciousness: "In the final analysis, victory in any war depends on the spirit animating the masses . . . [but] even the best armies, even people most sincerely devoted to the revolutionary cause, will be immediately exterminated by the enemy if they are not adequately armed, supplied with food, and trained."[108] This contrasts with the "Maoist" dicta that "nuclear weapons are a paper tiger," and that class consciousness is "a spiritual atomic bomb."

A corollary of the Soviet emphasis on military hardware is emphasis on combined arms tactics and strategic offensive into enemy territory as the best means of defense. As Whitson points out, this approach to military defense tends to isolate the masses from the military. A further corollary is the discarding of the commissar system, the main justification for which, aside from providing political watchdogs, was its function of mobilizing local mass support for military operations. This function is vital to a primitive army operating within its own territory. The disastrous experiences in Finland and Korea, respectively, pointed up to the Soviets and the Chinese the need for a conventional logistical system in lieu of the popular support which was not forthcoming on foreign soil. Furthermore, while the local population can provide porters and food, and can even manufacture small arms ammunition, they cannot possibly provide gasoline or sparkplugs or laser range-finders. The commissar's logistical functions are thus rendered obsolete both by "forward defense" and by advanced technology.[109]

It has been Soviet doctrine since the 1930s, therefore, that the masses do not participate in combat nor even in service support roles. Rather, the role of the party is in coordinating the functions of the military and the masses from the top. What the industrialized masses must provide are newer and better weapons systems and the technically qualified recruits to man them.[110] The militia concept has been discarded for the same reasons: Modern arms simply can't be employed—especially beyond the frontiers—by part-time citizen-soldiers.[111]

As technological advancement and "regularization" of the Soviet Army proceeded, "one-man command" was almost bound to follow. Modern combined-arms tactics require centralized control and coordination, and a responsive logistical support system. "One-man command," in turn, impacted heavily upon civil-military relations. The technological level of an army is not an independent variable, nor is it merely dependent on the technical state of the industrial base. It is, rather, closely interrelated with the fundamental social and political arrangements of society. The present status of the Soviet officer corps presents a case in point, and has provided, no doubt, a warning to those Chinese leaders who wish to continue the revolutionalization of Chinese society, and to protect the "mass line" against "revisionism."

The Chinese began with a much more primitive industrial base, and still have far to go before they reach the Soviet level of industrialization. They have therefore sought to make a virtue of necessity by emphasizing foot infantry, militia, and political organization. They have also elected not to sacrifice everything else to the expansion of heavy industry—as the Soviets did under Stalin. The persistence of the "people's war" concept, of the commissar system, and, indeed, of the whole "Maoist" approach to military affairs, has been largely a result of China's relatively low level of industrial development.

Advanced technology has not evenly affected all parts of the Soviet armed forces.[112] Military opinions became polarized in the 1950s around two views of modern warfare: "Modernists" emphasized that future wars were likely to be short, with strategic nuclear missiles being decisive and conventional forces being virtually irrelevant. these tended to be young, technically educated officers assigned to the strategic missile and air forces, air defense forces, and the submarine service. Opposing their views were "Conservatives" who visualized a long war in which all arms and services remained necessary. These officers tended to be older and more senior, and to be assigned to the ground and tactical air forces and the surface navy. This polarization became politically relevant when Khrushchev announced a new, and highly "modernist," strategic doctrine in January 1960. This led to the demobilization of 250,000 officers, mainly from the conventional forces, and a shift of resources to nuclear missiles. This process was halted when "Conservative" resistance was reinforced by the 1961 Berlin crisis and the 1962 Cuban missile fiasco.

According to Kolkowicz, three distinct career patterns have emerged in the 1970s, each with characteristic attitudes toward technology, politics, and professionalism:

Political officers insist that nothing is apolitical, and that their role remains vital to a modern army. Yet they have been under precisely the same pressures as those described by Herspring in the Polish and East German armies, and their role is evolving in the same direction.

Technicians, engineers, and other specialists have tended to crawl into their technical shells, and successfully evade most political work. They regard themselves as indispensable, and hold non-technical officers in low regard.

Traditional troop commanders hold to the "conservative" views described above, and resent the privileged status of the technicians. While they recognize the importance of political work, they tend to see it as consuming too much training time, and they resent the surveillance and interference of the MPA system.

The recent conflicts generated by the influx of technology and technicians into the Soviet Army are not relevant to the PLA just yet. But the Soviet experience will be very instructive a few years hence. Indeed, inter-service rivalries may well be developing over the limited resources currently being devoted to military modernization in China.

Such a development would actually represent a step forward for Chinese military professionalsim, since inter-service rivalries have heretofore involved political power rather than mere resource allocation. The role of the air force in the 1971 Lin Piao affair is a case in point. "Whenever threatened by a challenge to its basic professional or institutional prerogatives and values" the Soviet Army "tends to close ranks and offer a fairly unified response to such a challenge."[113] The PLA, by contrast, has seldom closed ranks, even on such issues as the military budget or the corporate interests of the officer corps. "Almost always, national security issues have divided, rather than unified the PLA." As modernization and professionalization proceed, the PLA is likely to become a more effective interest group. That is to say, it will be more effective in uniting to resist threats to corporate military interests and to departures from military conceptions of national interest.

Technology is not the only factor, however, for military professionalism has not even kept pace with the rather significant strides that have been made in modernizing the PLA. Indeed, it must be admitted that there are less industrialized states than China (e.g., India) with more professional armies. We must therefore identify what other factors have retarded military professionalization despite the technological pressures.

Obviously, much of the answer lies in differences of historical background. In sharp contrast to the Soviet case, the CCP and its army "have formed throughout their history a single institutional system with a single elite performing simultaneously the functions of political and military leadership."[114] Furthermore, the leaders of the PRC appear to be committed to the traditional Chinese pattern of civil ideological and organizational control. "Rule over China has always required something stronger than armies."[115] China is still controlled by the "old warriors" who led the revolution.[116] They are a distinctly "modernizing elite," but they retain the traditional characteristic of combining both military and political roles.

Kolkowicz writes that the Soviet Communist Party has long ago sought to coopt a "certain number of prominent military leaders into the highest Party councils ... where, theoretically, they may present the military's point of view and look out for the military's interests."[117]

> For a time, this cooptation of top military leaders into positions of power and prestige had the desired effect of preventing the larger military establishment from developing a focus, direction, and institutional identity of its own. More recently, however, there has been a change, as the attack on the personality cult, the lessening charisma of individual Party leaders, and the doubts cast on some previously sacrosanct ideological tenents, combined with the evident importance of the military factor in the foreign policy of the Soviet Union, have favored the professionalization and heightened institutional loyalty of the officer corps in a manner that reaches into the upper layers of the military hierarchy.[118]

In contrast, the Chinese PLA *is* a powerful institution, and has been for decades. The PLA's leaders are not coopted into the top circles of the Chinese Communist Party—they were there from the outset. This lack of differentiation between military and civilian leadership is surely one reason why the PLA, at least at the upper levels, has tended to remain nonprofessional much longer than did the Soviet Army. In 1977-81, some of the senior PLA leaders most frequently identified as "professionally inclined" appear to be maintaining relatively revolutionary practices and ideals in the face of rampant "revisionism" in other sectors of society. In May 1978, Yeh Chien-ying, for example, called for a strengthening of PLA political work. "Otherwise," he said, "It would face the dangers of getting away from the party's leadership, of changing its proletarian character, of losing its combat strength, and having its leadership usurped by bourgeois careerists."[120] Clearly, Yeh remains a revolutionary as well as a soldier. Ironically, such revolutionary rhetoric must be viewed as "moderation" within the context of the "radical revisionism" of 1978. The Soviet experience should alert us to watch for important changes, however, once the Chinese "old warriors" leave the scene and younger officers take over the PLA high command, and younger civilians take over the party and state machinery.

Until now, the debates over the role of the PLA, and over "military line" have been subsidiary to the fundamental issues of power and ideology. Under Mao Tse-tung, the real issues involved his personal power and his commitment to continuing revolution and ideological purity. Mao was quite willing to have a technologically advanced PLA, provided those fundamental commitments were not compromised. The problems flowed from the inherent contradictions between military modernization and Mao's vision of ideological rectitude. He was not willing to sacrifice either his personal power or his ideological vision for modernization—either in the army or in the rest of society. He wanted modernization, but only on his own terms. Other members of the elite, at various times, attempted to enhance their own power at Mao's expense, and to reorder the priorities for what they viewed as overriding practical reasons.

The most practical reason for military modernization was the need to defend China against the modern forces of her enemies. Just as World War II had moved the Soviet Union toward professionalism, the Korean War—also a foreign war against a technically advanced foe—had the same effect on the

PLA. This reinforces one of our basic hypotheses: The objective characteristics of modern warfare give rise to a universal "professional" viewpoint among those charged with the military security of any state.

These technological pressures and Mao's counterpressures generated several distinct orientations among Chinese officers. The first of these can be identified as "radical Maoist." This orientation is examined in detail in Chapter 3. There appear to have been relatively few "radical Maoist" officers, but they profoundly affected the PLA and the country in the 1960s and early 1970s.

Second is the "professional" orientation. This characterizes a category similar to one Franz Schurmann labels "pure expert."[121] Schurmann's "pure expert" category contains most of the elements of what we have defined as "pure military professionalism." Schurmann specifically attributes to the "pure experts" "one main concern: that the army be provided with the most modern defense capabilities." This describes those within the PLA high command who have been most anxious to avoid political involvement, and proceed with doing their jobs. Among the top PLA commanders showing this orientation are Yeh Chien-ying, Nieh Jung-chen, Liu Po-ch'eng, and Su Yü. It is this type of officer to whom we will be referring, throughout this study, as "professional" or (more accurately) "professionally inclined."

There is a third orientation which we might call "bureaucratic careerist." Schurmann suggests a distinction between the "pure experts" described above, and another group he labels "red professionals." These latter, he says, are "more political than professional." Schurmann's definition of "red professional" emphasized those aspects of "pure military professionalism" that Mao found most objectionable: corporativeness and organizational autonomy.

The problem with Schurmann's distinction is that there is considerable overlap between his "pure experts" and "red professionals," as there is between our "professionals" and "bureaucratic careerists." "Professional" officers generally wish to be promoted, and "careerists" often value expertise and efficiency. Schurmann's desire to make a theoretical distinction between the two orientations is understandable, but impractical. He is quite correct, however, to suggest different manifestations of professionalism among different groups of officers. Indeed, a given individual may well act "expertly" on one issue and "bureaucratically" on another. Surely it is well to bear in mind the possible conflict between corporate and personal career considerations and the professional commitment to national defense. However, few military professionals anywhere are so selflessly dedicated that career considerations never influence their actions.

CONVERGENCE

Our discussion of "military professionalism" has been intended to provide a basis for asking some pertinent questions about the political and military development of the PLA, and especially of the Chinese officer corps. China's dominant anti-professional ideology, its recent history, the nature of the ruling revolutionary elite, and the institutional disruptions of the past two decades have all precluded a high degree of military professionalism. There is abundant evidence, however, that many of the same functional military imperatives have been at work in China which have led to professionalization elsewhere. The trend in that direction was particularly strong from the Korean War until the fall of Defense Minister P'eng Te-huai in 1959. It will be seen that there are many Chinese officers who incline toward something like

Soviet-style "professionalism"—not a "pure" professionalism to be sure, but one closer to Clausewitz than to Mao Tse-tung. The role of the PLA during the Great Proletarian Cultural Revolution, and since, suggests that the PLA is commanded by men who lean toward what Mao repeatedly condemned as the "purely military approach" or the "bourgeois military line." This tendency is even stronger among younger PLA officers, especially those recruited after about 1945.

This is not to say that the officer corps will wish to dispense with the Communist Party. As a focus for national political loyalty, it will probably remain unchallenged, as has been the case in the Soviet Union. However, as Kolkowicz observes, the Soviet officer corps has developed certain "universal traits" of military institutions which are often in opposition to Communist Party values. Soviet officers' military values or traits "reflect their natural drive toward autonomy and their inherent professionalism."[122] With the passing of Mao and the ascent of men like Yeh Chien-ying and Teng Hsiao-p'ing, the Chinese officer corps seems more than ever destined to approximate the Soviet situation in a few decades.

We have been presenting a somewhat specialized aspect of what is widely known as "convergence theory." Mao's notion of "modern revisionism" is, in fact, a sort of convergence theory: "Theories of convergence seem to suggest themselves easily to disillusioned Marxists, or at least, to Marxists who have become disillusioned about the Soviet Union. Consider the theories of Trotsky, Achminov, Djilas, Mao, and the European and American New Left."[123]

Alfred Meyer has suggested that there are two premises or assumptions upon which all convergence theories rest. First is a belief in irreversible progress. Second is a belief in technological-economic determinism. This study emphasizes the latter: Industrial technology (and the sort of warfare it gives rise to) leads to functionally corresponding social structures or systems of social relationships (including the professionalization of officership). The result, according to convergence theory, is that highly industrialized societies inevitably give rise to similar political systems.[124]

Mao Tse-tung clearly rejected the first premise: The very term "revisionism" (*hsiu-cheng chu-i*) indicates that Mao did not believe in irreversible progress—at least not in the short run. On the contrary, he emphasized the ever-present danger of "capitalist restoration."

The technological-economic determinism premise was much harder for Mao to reject. He always argued that hidden class enemies can cause "revisionism" by corrupting and then over-throwing the dictatorship of the proletariat from within. He never said that modern technology leads to revisionism and, indeed, basic Marxist doctrine holds quite the opposite. Interestingly, the current leadership has seen fit to steer a middle course by arguing that expertise, per se, has no class character at all—a stance clearly at variance with both Mao and Marx:

> Some comrades say that capitalism and revisionism follow the "expert line" .... This is ... wrong .... Otherwise, this absurd logic would be used: By raising everyone's scientific and cultural levels and by training more experts, we will only add to the factors leading to revisionism.[125]

This is precisely the "absurd logic" of convergence theory and of "Maoism." During the Cultural Revolution, and many other "rectification" campaigns as far back as the *cheng-feng* movement of 1942-44, cadres and young people were repeatedly sent away from the centers of modern industry and organization "down to the countryside" (*hsia-fang* or *hsia-hsiang*) to heighten their "proletarian" consciousness. This is fundamentally contradictory: People are sent away from factories to learn from *peasants* how to be "proletarian." One very plausible explanation is that Mao recognized the congeniality of scientific organization and "revisionism."

It is remarkable that the Soviet textbook definition of socialism is almost exactly the same as the Weberian and post-Weberian definition of bureaucracy: both defined as the imposition of rationality on the affairs of men through complex organization and scientific management.[126]

We might well add that with respect to the military affairs of men, this is a pretty good definition of military professionalism as well.

Perhaps Meyer identifies the key factor when he notes that some observers see a "psychological convergence" of systems which rely on bureaucratic organization and rational-legal authority. Such systems "... tend to attract people of similar personalities to elite positions .... Careerists, conformists, high achievers, people intellectually creative but capable of teamwork—will do well" in any such system.[127]

Such people certainly do well in the Soviet armed forces. They have filled the officer corps from top to bottom; assisted by the passage of time, the elimination of the old revolutionaries, and the imperatives of modern war and nuclear cold war. Mao's assertion that the "bourgeois military line" has triumphed in the USSR is true to the extent that the modern military professional ethic has been largely, but by no means completely, adopted by the Soviet officer corps. Over the coming decades, the same factors will probably produce the same general result in China.

NOTES

1. Davis B. Bobrow, "The Good Officer: Definition and Training," *CQ*, No. 18 (April-June 1964), 141-152; Ellis Joffe, "The Conflict Between Old and New in the Chinese Army," *CQ*, No. 18 (April-June 1964), 118-140; and James Jordan, "The Maoist vs. the Professional Vision of a People's Army," in *The Military and Political Power in China in the 1970's*, ed. William W. Whitson (New York: Praeger, 1972), pp. 25-45.
2. Thomas H. Etzold, "Analyzing Military Modernization: The State of the Art, 1978," *I and S*, 14, No. 7 (July 1978), p. 68.
3. Jonathan D. Pollack, "The Study of Chinese Military Politics . . .," in *Political-Military Systems*, ed. Catherine M. Kelleher (Beverly Hills and London: Sage, 1974), p. 241.
4. Samuel P. Huntington, *The Soldier and the State* (New York: Vintage, 1957), passim, especially p. 19.
5. Ibid., p. 39.
6. Ibid., pp. 13-14.
7. Walter Goerlitz, *The German General Staff: 1857-1945*, trans. B. Battershaw (New York: Praeger, 1953), Chapter II.
8. Huntington, p. 51.
9. Amos Perlmutter, *The Military and Politics in Modern*

Times (New Haven and London: Yale UP, 1977), pp. 42-46 and 48. Perlmutter's interpretation of the Prussian experience sharply differs with Huntington's.
10. Huntington, p. 8.
11. Ibid., pp. 56 and 58.
12. Clausewitz quoted by Huntington, pp. 57-58.
13. Huntington, pp. 15-]6.
14. Morris Janowitz, *The Professional Soldier* (New York: Free Press, 1960), p. 35.
15. Huntington, p. 72.
16. Ibid., p. 10.
17. Ibid., p. 10, 16-17.
18. Ibid., p. 16.
19. Ibid., p. 13.
20. Ibid., p. 62.
21. Ibid., pp. 63-65 and 79.
22. Ibid., pp. 66-67.
23. Ibid., p. 68. It is striking that these are almost exactly the terms in which Hans J. Morgenthau describes his "realist theory of international relations," in *Politics Among Nations*, 4th ed. (New York: Knopf, 1967), Chapter I, especially pp. 10 ff.
24. Huntington, pp. 68-69. For example, see the role of the US Air Force in dissuading President Kennedy from attacking Cuban missiles with a "surgical air strike" in October 1962: Graham T. Allison, *Essence of Decision* (Boston: Little, Brown, 1971).
25. Huntington, pp. 69-70.
26. Quoted in Huntington, p. 71.
27. Quoted in F.W. von Mellenthin, *Panzer Battles*, trans. H. Betzler (New York: Ballantine, 1973), p. 112.
28. Huntington, p. 69.
29. Ibid., p. 79.
30. Ibid., p. viii.
31. Ibid., p. 1.
32. Ibid., p. 2.
33. Ibid., pp. 73-78.
34. The following draws heavily on Huntington, pp. 88-89.
35. William W. Whitson, *The Chinese High Command* (New York: Praeger, 1973), passim.
36. Huntington, pp. viii and 85-86.
37. Ibid., p. 35.
38. Ibid., pp. 80-83.
39. Jacques van Doorn, "Political Change and the Control of the Military," in *The Military Profession and Military Regimes*, ed. Jacques van Doorn (Paris and The Hague: Mouton, 1969), p. 20.
40. Huntington, pp. 83-84.
41. Perlmutter, p. xvi.
42. Ibid., note pp. 312-313.
43. Samuel P. Huntington, "Forward," in Perlmutter, p. xi.
44. Perlmutter, p. 205.
45. Ibid., p. xv.
46. Ibid., p. 205.
47. Ibid., p. xv.
48. Van Doorn, pp. 22-23.
49. Perlmutter, note pp. 312-313 (emphasis in original).

50. Dale R. Herspring, "Technology and the Changing Political Officer in the Armed Forces," *Studies in Comparative Communism*, 10, No. 4 (Winter 1977), 371.
51. This, and the following quotations, are from Herspring, pp. 372-373.
52. Herspring, pp. 390-391. The quotations are from p. 391.
53. Ibid., p. 392 implies this. Also see Perlmutter, p. 9. The following discussion draws heavily on Samuel P. Huntington, *Political Order in Changing Societies* (New York: Yale UP, 1968), Chapter IV.
54. Whitson, p. 8.
55. A good American example is Curtis E. LeMay, with Dale O. Smith, *America is in Danger* (New York: Funk and Wagnalls, 1968). Also see John S. Ambler, *The French Army in Politics* (Columbus, OH: Ohio State UP, 1966), pp. 194-195. On "guardianship," see Huntington, *Political Order*, pp. 225-233. Perlmutter describes "arbitrater" praetorianism in similar terms on pp. 104-107 and 141-144.
56. Perlmutter, p. 25.
57. Huntington, p. 116. Also see Goerlitz, Chapters IX-XII.
58. Whitson, pp. 14-15.
59. David B. Ralston, ed., *Soldiers and States* (Boston: Heath, 1966), pp. 157-159. For an admirably detailed study of the composition of the Soviet officer corps in the civil war period, see Jonathan R. Adelman, "Origins of the Difference in Political Influence of the Soviet and Chinese Armies . . .," *Studies in Comparative Communism*, 10, No. 4 (Winter 1977), 347-369.
60. The full text is in Ralston, ed., p. 160.
61. Ninth CPSU Congress, "Scheme for the Transition of the Militia System" (Moscow, 1924); reprinted in Ralston, ed., pp. 163-164.
62. Leon Trotsky, *The Revolution Betrayed* (New York: Merit, 1937); reprinted in Ralston, ed., p. 165.
63. B. Borisov and V. Ryabov, *The Soviet Army* (Moscow: FLPH, n.d. [1960?]), p. 32.
64. Whitson, pp. 14-15.
65. Whitson, p. 15; and Colonel A. Orlov, "Marshal Tukhochevsky," *SMR*, February 1973, pp. 44-45.
66. Whitson, pp. 15-16.
67. Leonard Schapiro, "The Great Purge," in Ralston, ed., p. 172.
68. Whitson, pp. 15-16.
69. Quoted by Trotsky, p. 167; also see Schapiro, p. 170.
70. Trotsky, p. 167.
71. Ibid., pp. 160-167.
72. Schapiro, pp. 171-173.
73. John S. Reshetar, *The Soviet Polity* (New York: Dodd, Mead, 1971), p. 184.
74. The following discussion is drawn from Roman Kolkowicz, *The Soviet Military and the Communist Party* (Princeton, NJ: Princeton UP, 1967), pp. 28-29, 92, 374, and 377; Colonel A. Korkeshkin, "A Powerful Weapon," *SMR*, December 1973, pp. 52-53; Reshetar, pp. 184-185; V. Staritsyn, "A Political Worker's Talent," *SMR*, May 1973, pp. 24-25; and Lieutenant Colonel V. Zhukov, "The Enemy has Penetrated the Defenses," *SMR*, May 1973, pp. 34-36.
75. Korkeshkin, p. 53.
76. Colonel S. Titov, "Conscientiously and Scrupulously," *SMR*, September 1973, p. 45.

77. Colonel M. Korobeinikov, "The Soldier and War," *SMR*, February 1973, p. 29.
78. Colonel D. Diyev, Review of *The Armed Forces of the USSR*, by Marshal Andrei Grechko, *SMR*, November 1973, p. 40.
79. Major General V. Sulimov, "Principles of The Development of the Soviet Armed Forces," *SMR*, March 1973, pp. 12-13; and Colonel L. Yeremeyev and Lieutenant Colonel M. Svirdov, "True to Their Country," *SMR*, February 1973, pp. 7-9.
80. *CSM*, 26 August 1976, p. 26.
81. Reshetar, p. 176.
82. Reshetar, p. 176; and Major V. Amelchenko, "A Society of Millions," *SMR*, December 1973, pp. 2-3.
83. Major V. Aidarov, "Interior Service Regulations," *SMR*, May 1973, p. 42; and Yeremeyev and Svirdov, pp. 7-9.
84. Colonel V. Kovalyov, "Motives Behind Behavior in Battle," *SMR*, August 1973, pp. 36-37.
85. For concurring American views on battle motivation, see Edward A. Shils and Morris Janowitz, "Cohesion and Disintegration in the Wehrmacht in World War II," *Public Opinion Quarterly*, 12, No. 2 (Summer 1948), 280-315; and S.L.A. Marshal, *Men Against Fire* (New York: Morrow, 1966).
86. Colonel K. Amirov, "Under the Laws of Military Life," *SMR*, January 1973, p. 30.
87. V.I. Lenin, *Sochineniya*, 4th ed., Vol. 29 (Moscow: Gosizdat, 1941-65), p. 512, cited in Adelman, p. 356.
88. Sulimov, pp. 13-14.
89. Ibid., p. 14.
90. Colonel M. Goryachev, "Socialist Unity of Command," *SMR*, July 1973, p. 6.
91. Sulimov, p. 14.
92. Goryachev, p. 8 (emphasis added).
93. Senior Lieutenant Y. Chernyshov, "School of Education," *SMR*, May 1973, p. 47.
94. Colonel L. Korzun, "Commander's Initiative in Battle," *SMR*, October 1973, p. 14-15.
95. Lieutenant General V. Merimsky, "The Commander's Character," *SMR*, December 1973, p. 37.
96. Kolcowicz, p. 342.
97. Ibid., pp. 7-8, 21, 29, 340-346. The quotation is from p. 13.
98. Reshetar, pp. 176-188.
99. Van Doorn, p. 21.
100. Adelman, pp. 368-69.
101. Van Doorn, pp. 12-13; and Kolkowicz, p. 11.
102. Reshetar, pp. 185-187.
103. Marshal V. D. Sokolovsky, ed., *Military Strategy* (Moscow, 1962; trans. and reprinted New York: Praeger, 1963), p. 381.
104. Reshetar, pp. 187-188; Raymond Garthoff, "Introduction" to Sokolovsky, passim; and Kolcowicz, pp. 107-108.
105. Sokolovsky, ed., pp. 17-18 (see note p. 17 for Lenin's approving comments on *Vom Krieg*).
106. *CSM*, 5 June 1974, p. 1; *CSM*, 21 August 1975, p. 30; and *CSM*, 14 December 1973, p. 8.
107. Adelman, passim, especially pp. 351 ff.
108. Lenin (source not cited), quoted in Colonel K. Chermashentsev,

"Man and His Weapons," *SMR*, August 1973, p. 28.
   109.   Whitson, p. 476.
   110.   Colonel I. Barsukov, "Army of the Working People," *SMR*, February 1973, pp. 2-4.
   111.   Sulimov, p. 13.
   112.   The following is drawn from Rowan Kolkowicz, "The Impact of Modern Technology on the Soviet Officer Corps," in *Armed Forces and Society*, ed. Jacques van Doorn (Paris and The Hague: Mouton, 1968), pp. 162-166.
   113.   Roman Kolkowicz, "The Military," in *Interest Groups in Soviet Politics*, eds. Skilling and Griffith (Princeton, NJ: Princeton UP, 1971), p. 167. The following is drawn from Harry Harding, unpublished paper, 1978.
   114.   Andrew Nathan, "A Factionalism Model for CCP Politics," *CQ*, No. 58 (January-March 1973), 58.
   115.   Harold Z. Schiffran, "Military and Politics in China: Is the Warlord Model Pertinent?" *Asia Quarterly*, No. 3 (1975), 203.
   116.   This apt term was coined by Ross H. Munro in "China Turns to Its Old Warriors," *CSM*, 9 March 1977, p. 2.
   117.   Roman Kolkowicz, *The Soviet Military and the Communist Party*, p. 29.
   118.   Ibid., pp. 346-347.
   119.   Ibid., p. 347.
   120.   Yeh Chien-ying, Speech at the All-Army Political Work Conference on 29 May 1978, *NCNA*, 4 June 1978, trans. in *FBIS*, No. 108, p. E13.
   121.   Franz Schurmann, *Ideology and Organization in Communist China*, 2nd ed. (Berkeley and Los Angeles: University of California Press, 1968), pp. 562-565.
   122.   Kolkowicz, *The Soviet Military and the Communist Party*, p. 323.
   123.   Alfred G. Meyer, "Theories of Convergence," in *Change in Communist Systems*, Chalmers A. Johnson, ed. (Stanford, CA: Stanford UP, 1970), p. 319. In his supposed "Letter to Chiang Ch'ing," Mao wrote rather resignedly, in 1966, that China would become revisionist after his death. *I and S*, 9, No. 4 (January 1973), 96.
   124.   Meyer, pp. 322-323.
   125.   "Commenting on the So-Called 'Expert Line'," *KMJP*, 20 October 1978, trans. in *FBIS*, No. 213, pp. E6-E9.
   126.   Meyer, p. 326.
   127.   Ibid., p. 318.

2
PLA Modernization and Professionalism

INTRODUCTION

The purpose of this chapter is to trace the history of the PLA from its origins in the early 1920s to the eve of the Great Proletarian Cultural Revolution. We will also observe the development and interaction of Mao's military line and the much more professional military ideas advocated over the years by most of the PLA's top commanders. Despite these and other disagreements, however, the final authority of the Party Central Committee over the army was almost never questioned.

Propaganda to the contrary notwithstanding, there were long periods when the "military thought of Mao Tse-tung" did not guide the PLA. Moreover, Mao himself was quite willing to conduct rather conventional military operations when the situation seemed to demand it.

The PLA's pre-1949 experience is still a matter of interest today because the Chinese military is still dominated, at the top, by Yeh Chien-ying, Teng Hsiao-p'ing, and Hsu Hsiang-ch'ien—members of what Whitson calls the "first military generation." At the next level—all the way from the General Staff down into the divisions—the PLA is dominated by the "second generation," which entered the army in 1928-31. This second generation is rather poorly educated (formally) and nearly all were born into poor peasant families in the Yangtze Valley. Although they are superb conventional tacticians, they have very limited experience and training in the employment of modern weapons, and virtually none in combined arms operations. As of 1980, they were, on the average, about sixty-eight years old.

Within the next few years, the "third and fourth military generations" (1931-40) may take over the active direction of the PLA (although they may have another decade to wait, if the second generation proves as reluctant to retire as has the first). It is these men, who joined the Red Army in Kiangsi and during the Long March, who may turn the PLA away from its traditions. Like the first generation, they are much better educated and more cosmopolitan than the second generation, but they are less influenced by western Europe or by traditional China than any of the older men.[1]

As Joseph Heinlein has pointed out, the "traditions of the PLA" have been carried by these first four generations, whereas the impact of all later generations on PLA traditions has been relatively small.[2] For that reason, Whitson is probably correct when he asserts that the Soviet military influence on the PLA has never been much more than a veneer, since it has been almost entirely academic. This has been true owing to the lack of really advanced weapons systems, and to the lack (with the important exception of thirty-two months in Korea) of any really sophisticated and dedicated opponent.[3] But as Heinlein points out, the long-range impact of the Comintern on Chinese *politics*, and on the commissar system, was very great indeed. "It should be remembered, " to cite one good example, "that exhortation of the masses to emulate the military as the socialist model of altruism for the good of the state was introduced to China in the Whampoa classroom."[4]

Whitson probably overstates the case when he concludes that the "commanders have blended Russian and earlier warlord perspectives into a unique *professional* operational code," that he believes to have prevailed since 1950,[5] but it is certainly true that military "Maoism" has generally been in retreat since 1945, and that the trend toward professionalism continues. This trend is likely to accelerate as the "sixth military generation" (recruited during the civil war) begins to make itself felt. These men entered the PLA as it first acquired tanks, aircraft, and other modern weapons, and they ended the Korean War as company and battalion commanders. They might be the first generation to be a distinctly miltiary elite, and they will begin entering the top levels of the PLA in the coming decade.

THE EARLY YEARS: 1921-37

Although the People's Liberation Army celebrates its official birthday on the anniversary of the Nanchang Uprising (1 August 1927), its origins go back to the opening of the Whampoa Military Academy in 1924. As we saw in Chapter 1, when General Blucher arrived at Whampoa he brought with him Frunze's concept of "unified strategy," which was the result of Soviet revolutionary experience. "Unified strategy" had grown out of a series of crises in the USSR over many of the same issues of military ethic and style that were to "burden Chinese Communist military and political leaders for the next forty years."[6] As we have also seen, these issues continued to be controversial in the Soviet Union until World War II. One immediate result was that while the cadets at Whampoa were learning "unified strategy," Chinese students in Moscow were simultaneously being taught "integral strategy." The nascent Chinese Communist officer corps therefore tended to be split into those who adhered to "unified strategy"—with its decentralized control and intermixing of party, army, and government—and the adherents of "integral strategy"—which emphasized central control, but provided for greater autonomy of vertical chains of political, military, and governmental command. Thus, the stage was set for the "red-expert" split even before the PLA was officially born.

The Whampoa vision was of a "party army" within which political commissars played a key role, along with party organizations in all units. Under the supervision of the commissars, however, the military commanders were to be solely responsible for purely military functions. Furthermore, tactics were quite conventional indeed: Mass assaults with machinegun and artillery support were fixed as "the only proper form of battle. Anything less impressive was characterized as 'banditry.'"[7] Later on, guerrilla tactics were introduced into the controversy by Mao Tse-tung, who was neither at Whampoa nor in Moscow, but was laboring to organize peasants in his native Hunan.

According to Whitson, Mao's early military thought was an attempt to coalesce from the "Russian revolutionary" and "Chinese peasant" models—an attempt that increasingly took on the nature of "a modified peasant model." This model cast the political commissar in the role of the crafty leaders of the traditional peasant rebel bands. Mao's biographers have emphasized his fascination, since boyhood, with tales of such figures as Sung Chiang in *Water Margin* and Chu-ko Liang in *The Romance of the Three Kingdoms*. Early peasant recruits to the Red Army referred to the commissars as "little Chu-ko Liangs," and saw them as men who, like their namesake, were clever and tricky, and worked on the principle that the pen was often mightier than the sword. PLA "Chu-ko Liang meetings," to enlist the soldiers' ideas and to discuss military and political matters, have been reported as recently as the early 1970s. The "peasant tradition" blurred the distinction between commander and commissar, and cast both in the role of father figure (or, better yet, "sworn brother") to the soldiers, as in *Water Margin*. In either case, military comradeship was a horizontal rather than a vertical bond uniting leaders and led,[8] a notion reinforced by the Marxist doctrine of "class brotherhood."

In the 1920s, however, Mao was virtually a minority of one, for the Whampoa generation was led mostly by men who were heavily influenced by foreign military models. These men (Whitson's "first military generation") were generally well-educated, and some of them (e.g., Chou En-lai, Nieh Jung-chen, and Chu Teh) had studied in western Europe.[9]

Chu Teh is generally conceded to be the real "father of the PLA," although he was eclipsed by the Mao cult during the Cultural Revolution. Despite, or perhaps owing to, his early training in the warlord armies of Yunnan, Chu was the real founder of the emphasis on small unit operations and leadership which became the hallmarks of the PLA. It was also Chu, and not Mao, who first introduced the post-battle critique, and promulgated the "Three Rules of Discipline and Eight Points for Attention."[10] But Chu, like his colleague P'eng Te-huai, insisted that soldiers had to be soldiers first, and party members second.

Chou En-lai, one of the most sophisticated of the "first generation," was a proponent of the Soviet model from 1924, when he became political commissar at Whampoa. His eventual acceptance of Mao's strategy for a protracted anti-Japanese war of resistance (around the time of the Tsunyi conference in 1935) marked the beginning of Mao's dominance over CCP military doctrine. During the early years, however, Chou and Chang Kuo-t'ao profoundly influenced the soldiers of the Whampoa and Kiangsi periods along relatively "professional" lines; and Chou repeatedly turned to them for support in later years.[11]

It was Chu Teh, P'eng Te-huai, Chou En-lai, and Chang Kuo-t'ao whom Mao was attacking in his famous Kutien speech in 1929. It was they who were guilty of what Mao labeled the "warlord mentality" and the "purely miltiary approach."[12] During the seven years between the Autumn Harvest Uprising and the start of the Long March, Mao's views were often suppressed by the more conventionally minded commanders, while he increasingly became the spokesman for the political commissars.

Commissar Roles

The original system of "party representatives" instituted at Whampoa, and based on the Soviet system, was essentially a "defensive" means of gaining and assuring obedience and loyalty to the party. In other words, it did what the *zampolit* system does to this day in the Soviet Union. The commissar was, in Whitson's apt phrase, the "institutional conscience" of the revolutionary army.[13]

After 1928, as the "Chu-Mao" Army expanded, and later under the

Kiangsi Soviet, commissars steadily increased in importance, as they relieved commanders of virtually all work except strictly miltiary affairs. It appears that a pattern developed which has since recurrently been adopted and then condemned: Commanders came to view commissars not as co-commanders but as administrative assistants. The result, in practice as well as in theory, often was that the commissars came to control not only political training, but also personnel administration (loyalty, recruitment, assignment, transfer, and promotion), schools, theaters, libraries, literacy classes, sports, construction, and economic production. All this helped stabilize units which were recruited largely from among warlord armies and bandit gangs. Commissars were also called upon to set up governments in newly occupied areas. That, in turn, led them into the function of mobilizing the population for support of the army. Commissars thus took charge of supply, labor levies, medical evacuation, intelligence, and counterintelligence. That in turn led to their control over psychological warfare, sabotage, communications, and militia work. The intelligence and recruiting functions further led to commissar responsibility for handling prisoners of war.[14]

Although this relieved commanders of considerable administrative burden, they viewed commissars with mixed feelings. Whereas the commissar saw himself as the guardian of party authority over the army, and the guarantee against "warlordism" and banditry, the commander saw the commissar as an infringement upon command authority and military effectiveness. Commanders demanded the final say on grounds of military efficiency, while commissars demanded it based upon their better theoretical grasp of doctrine and their supposedly better understanding of the "big picture."[15]

The "Political Work Regulations" which Mao attempted to implement in 1929 explicitly gave a unit's commissar the last word in any disagreement with its commander.[16] Those regulations were not widely implemented, however, and the tension between commissars and commanders usually had to be worked out on a case-by-case basis. Arrangements as to the relative status and power of commanders vis-a-vis commissars varied considerably from unit to unit, and over time. The tension hardly ever seemed to result in any challenge to the overall leadership of the party, however. The issue was and is that "commanders tend to prefer a military organization that minimizes intermediate political authorities between themselves and available military power."[17] The need to recognize the overall direction and authority of the party was so generally accepted as to be really remarkable. Discontented leaders attempted repeatedly to increase their power at the center, but they almost never split away or renounced Marxist-Leninist theory. Chang Kuo-t'ao was the only important exception. To be sure, this left plenty of room for internal contention over just how and to what extent the Central Committee (CC) and its local representatives would participate in military affairs. Whitson's three models (Chinese peasant, Russian revolutionary, and Warlord) sidestep this critical issue of party loyalty.[18] The CCP was the central locus of political legitimacy from the beginning. Factionalism and infighting there were, and in plenty, but the party's ultimate authority over the army was never challenged by any significant miltiary faction.

After the Kutien Conference, civil party cadres, as well as commanders, argued that a clearer division of labor between the military (commanders and commissars) and the party was necessary. In November 1931 the anti-Mao forces were strong enough to carry through. Chou and the "Returned (Russian) Students" confined commissars to "purely military" functions; and in December, Mao was replaced as Party Secretary of the First Front Army. From then until December 1941, Mao's "guerrillaism" was in eclipse. Under the influence of Chu, Chou, P'eng, Yeh Chien-ying, the "Returned Students," and Comintern advisor "Li Teh" (Otto Braun), "integral strategy" dominated. After November 1931, with the exceptions of a few men at the very top of the CCP structure, commanders and commissars specialized in their respective roles. They have continued to do so, as a rule, ever since.[19]

Debates on Strategy and Tactics

The highly conventional strategy adopted to defend against the Fifth Encirclement Campaign (1933-34) called for preemptive attacks and the defense of "every inch of the Soviet." The results were disastrous, leading to the decision to undertake the Long March, and preparing the way for Mao's return to power at Tsunyi in 1935.[20]

In 1936, Yang Ch'eng-wu, newly appointed as a divison commander, asked his corps commander, Lin Piao, for his advice on how to do a good job.[21] Lin's nine-point response provides a striking illustration of the highly professional tendencies of the time—even in a Whampoa-trained soldier who was to become known, thirty years later, as a radical "Maoist." The necessary qualities of a commander, said Lin, were as follows:

1. Diligence
2. Clarifying the intent of the superior level.
3. Investigation and study: "One must guard against fighting a battle in a disorderly and confused manner."
4. Map study.
5. Thorough consideration of the problems.
6. Promptness in notifying the inferior levels of the decisions.
7. A good and unified leadership group.
8. A good combat style: "Whatever is said must be done, decisively, neatly, and thoroughly. The cultivation of a good style hinges on the cadres. A strong general has no weak soldiers under him. The style of the men follows the lead of the cadres."
9. Political work: Soldiers "must be properly trained in tactics and in skill . . . . Skill creates courage, and courage creates skill. With an advanced proletarian awareness, a good combat style, and hard combat skill, troops will be like winged tigers, and become invincible . . . . The military commander must not forget politics at any time . . . . Assigning a group of political cadres to serve as military cadres will not only not weaken political work, but, in fact, strengthen it."

Lin had a long way to go from this to the "spiritual atom bomb" of 1965.

THE ANTI-JAPANESE WAR: 1937-45

From 1937 to 1941, regular communist forces continued to expand and frequently engaged in conventional military operations. But the situation increasingly indicated that Mao's guerrilla strategy was more appropriate. The way was finally cleared for Mao's strategy by two disastrous military setbacks.

The first of these was the "Hundred Regiments Offensive," a rather conventional operation by the Red Army aimed at destroying Japanese communications and installations. Beginning in late August 1940 and ending on

5 December, the campaign achieved initial success, but ended with the Red Army on the defensive, and provoked the vicious Japanese "Three-all" campaign.[22]

The second disaster was the annihilation, in January 1941, of the New Fourth Army, one of the most "regularized" Communist forces.

The fundamental issue of the power struggle in Yenan was not military strategy, however. Rather it was the far more fundamental one of the Sinification of Marxism-Leninism. Mao and his "mass-line" style of political leadership won out in the spring of 1942.[23]

The Mass Line

Mao made a crucial political alliance with Liu Shao-ch'i, who represented a more orthodox Leninism.[24] Liu had worked mainly in enemy-held areas where organization and compartmentalization were necessary for survival. In the relative safety of the "red base areas" Mao was laboring to build the mass line, at the expense of bureacratic organization. The two men struck a balance, and "by unifying operational structures throughout the ... base areas the Yenan leadership attained central authority while preserving local autonomy...."[25]

While Liu glorified Mao, the latter increased his emphasis on the cadre apparatus, regulation, and discipline. This compromise was destined to hold together with the appearance of monolithic solidarity until it cracked under the strain of the Great Leap Forward and shattered in the Great Proletarian Cultural Revolution.

The "mass line" was a theory of leadership which Mao had worked out sufficiently well by this time that he was able to name and explicate it. The mass line is closely related to the Leninist concept of democratic centralism, but is meant to apply, not only within the party, but also to work with the masses, and within the army. It is frequently summarized in CCP literature with such slogans as "Combine the general with the specific," "Unite leadership with the masses," and "From the masses to the masses."[26] The mass-line concept calls for a continuous interchange of information, opinions, and initiative between the Party leadership and the masses. The mass line worked especially well during the Yenan period, because CCP goals and popular aspirations were largely complementary.[27]

The Cheng-feng Campaign

Mao's conception of mass-line leadership placed a premium on skill in mobilizing and coordinating the efforts of party, government, and people and directing the efforts of the mobilized groups in all-out assaults on specific goals--all at the expense of rule-abiding government and party departments. Cadres had to modify and adapt directives from above and then articulate and defend them in coordinating conferences and struggle meetings. "It was precisely these qualities which the party sought to foster in small group criticism" in the *cheng-feng* (rectification of work-style) movement of 1942-43. The result intended, and largely achieved, was creation of a corps of cadres whose loyalty to the party overruled personal ties and interests. They were able to persuade, motivate, and mobilize their peers--both within the party and among the masses--in group struggle sessions where traditional status and "face" were scorned.[28]

Mark Selden has pointed out that because one purpose of rectification was to break down old-style personal loyalties, there was a need for some central object to which personal loyalties could be redirected. Mao Tse-tung emerged as that object of loyal adoration in the course of the *cheng-feng* campaign. He was able to do so by eliminating all significant opposition within the party and establishing his thought (*szu-hsiang*) as the guiding light of the revolution.[29]

A number of subsidiary mass movements accompanied *cheng-feng*, of which the most spectacular was the great drive to increase production and achieve economic self-sufficiency. Although virtually all units and organizations of government, party, and military participated in this movement, it was the army that provided the greatest effort and achieved the best results.

Red military units had been engaged in various productive activities since the end of the Long March. In the rear base areas, especially, they had provided protection for the harvest and recaptured plundered crops from the Japanese. Army units had also provided labor during peak periods of agricultural activity, such as a harvest. these activities continued to be of particular importance in the base areas in the Japanese rear until 1945, and were instrumental not only in benefiting the base areas' economies, but in winning popular support.[30] But in 1943 under the two slogans, "Organize for Production" and "Move with Your Own Hands," unit production by all government, party, and army units began in earnest, with many regular army units engaged in production as a primary activity. They worked mainly in agriculture, but also engaged in small-scale commercial and transportation enterprises.[31]

In the two years after 1939, increased Kuomintang (KMT) and Japanese military pressure and blockade had caused a multitude of economic hardships in the border regions. Yet Mao was able to claim, by 1945, that "You can see that Kuomintang soldiers are pale and thin, while [ours] are healthy and strong."[32] By 1944, all unit budgets of the army were predicated on reduced government subsidies and increased self-sufficiency.[33] Mao wrote that military self-support also had several beneficial "by-products":[34]

1. The improvement in the relationship between officers and men brought about by their all laboring together.
2. Enhancement in the army of "the love of labor."
3. The strengthening of discipline.
4. The improvement of relations between the people and the army: First, due to mutual aid in production, and second, to the fact that the army's own production made it less of a burden on the people.
5. "The army complains less often about the government authorities, and the relationships between them are improved."
6. Army production served as a model to encourage and motivate production by the people.

Military-Political Organization in the Villages

The army also was instrumental in the process of integrating rural villages into the Communist political system. Army units in the countryside helped the local peasants organize Militia and Self-Defence Corps (SDC) units (*Tzu-wei chun*) and Local Guerrilla or Public Security Forces (*Pao-an tui*).[35] Local para-military units which had already existed without CCP connections were infiltrated and gradually taken into the overall Communist military organization. At the top of this organization were the regular army units themselves.

Political work was carried out at all levels of this para-military structure by army political commissars and local party cadres. In 1943 the CC ruled that the positions of political commissars in all garrison units of the regular army were to be held by secretaries of the local party committees. "Through the efforts of these commissars and Party branches organized at the lowest levels, the Red Armies became effective political as well as military forces."[36]

Party and army thus became so intertwined, in many areas, that the distinction became virtually meaningless.[37] This situation provided the means the CCP needed to penetrate the natural village; "to create organization from within a village rather than imposing it from the outside."[38] As the Yenan Period progressed, the SDC and guerrilla units increasingly became identical in membership with local "labor exchanges" and "mutual aid teams." Leaders of these para-military units—energetic young CCP cadres—displaced the leaders of the work teams, the traditional village elites.

>This "penetration of the natural village" was, in essence, the great achievement of the Yenan period. The work and battle teams had arisen on a traditional foundation of work cooperation, but, through their Party cadre leaders, had been transformed into a new type of organization that served the political-military and social-economic aims of the Chinese Communist Party. The team was indissolubly a part of the village, yet at the same time transcended it.[39]

The CCP had thus done what no state power had achieved in three thousand years of Chinese politics: It had created "an organization loyal to the state which was also solidly imbedded in the natural village," and had achieved it with "a new type of leader, the cadre."[40] The *cheng-feng* campaign and the great campaigns for rural cooperativization and production thus were closely interrelated, and the army was intimately involved in this entire process.[41]

Cheng-feng also produced such high quality cadres that, in April 1945, Mao could boast, "If only the leadership at the higher level sets tasks properly and gives those subordinate . . . to them free reign to overcome the difficulties through their own efforts, then the problem of supply will be solved in a satisfactory manner."[42]

The close connection that had been developed between the army and the population, greatly enhanced by army production, had established solidly the leadership of the CCP and gained extensive acceptance and active support in the countryside of north China.[43]

The Red Army provided the most spectacular demonstration of the effectiveness of the reconsolidation period. It was decided in mid-1944 to expand the army in order to prepare for the anticipated defeat of Japan. By incorporating the carefully nurtured guerrilla and militia forces, the regular army expanded from 470,000 in early 1944 to 900,000 in 1945. By the spring of 1946, regular forces numbered 1,500,000. No sacrifice in political purity was risked, either, for even after this expansion, CCP members in the army still made up close to the ideal ratio of one in three (400,000 members out of 1.5 million troops in May 1946).[44]

The 1942-44 period was thus the time when Mao's military-political line became fully formulated, and during which it was most extensively practiced. It was unquestionably what the Chinese Communist movement needed at the time. But it was, and is, debatable whether it remained applicable ever since.

THE CIVIL WAR: 1945-49

In the optimistic atmosphere of girding for the coming showdown with Chiang K'ai-shek, the PLA was reconsolidated and reorganized along regular lines, while the emphasis in Yenan shifted to modernization. Schools of artillery, aviation, engineering, and tank warfare were set up. The newly renamed Military Affairs Commission (MAC) was set up by 1946, with Yeh Chien-ying as Mao's vice-chairman. Yeh, P'eng Te-huai, and Chu Teh worked out the mobilization plans and the initial objectives for the civil war.

The MAC foresaw that Lin Piao's newly formed Fourth Field Army, in Manchuria, would fall heir to a great deal of modern equipment. Accordingly, Lin was given most of the graduates from the new technical schools. The Fourth thus became the largest and most modern of the PLA's five field armies.[45]

In all army areas, the civil war was conducted largely along the lines of "integral strategy." Mao himself, in *The Present Situation and Our Tasks* (25 December 1945), published his "Ten Principles of Operations," which were remarkably conventional in tone. The situation, Mao wrote, was taking a qualitative turn in favor of the Communists, and decisive mobile warfare was now called for. Since 1971, it even has been claimed that Lin Piao was dragging his feet, persisting in guerrilla warfare after Mao's call for the changeover to mobile warfare.[46]

The initial Communist offensives out of their base areas in August-November 1945 were preemptive attacks which may well have drawn Chiang into the fatal mistake of dispersing his forces and attempting to fight on all fronts at once. The overall conduct of PLA operations was generally characterized by decentralized execution and tactics within the context of a strategy of mobile warfare. The high command closely monitored operations, and did shift forces between field armies on occasion; but really centralized coordination only began in 1949. Tactics became increasingly conventional as more tanks, aircraft, artillery, and industrial capacity came under CCP control, and as increasing numbers of technically skilled soldiers defected to the PLA. Commissars continued to be charged with mobilization of popular support for the increasingly complex logistical system which was still based on village-level party and militia organizations. In 1946-48, many of the local organizations in north China which had borne the brunt of the anti-Japanese war were reduced to "little more than transport units."[47]

As the war moved south and west, commissars found they had increasing responsibilites. The Communists had less local political support there, so the PLA had to take over administrative and logistical functions which were being handled by local CCP cadres in the north and east. As a result, in the southwest and in Tibet, the army had to resort more to "unified strategy" and devote ever-increasing resources to administrative and political purposes.[48]

There were great variations in the civil-war experience, with respect to the political roles of the PLA, the level of technical sophistication achieved, and the degree of centralized control exercised. The overall trend, however, was toward regularization and technical complexity, and away from direct political involvement. PLA economic production was virtually non-existent. Mao's conceptions of guerrilla warfare, economic production, political involvement, and extreme decentralization had served the Communists well in 1942-44. But the civil war marked a decisive turn away from this "people's war" strategy advocated in Mao's military writings of the 1930s and early 1940s.

THE PROFESSIONAL TREND: 1950-59

Even before the official proclamation of the People's Republic of China (1 October 1949), the process of consolidating power and converting party and army to a peacetime footing was underway. Particularly in the established base areas of north China, demobilization of the PLA was well advanced before the conquest of Hainan Island was completed in the spring of 1950. Even as preparations for the invasion of Taiwan were intensified, hundreds of thousands of soldiers were demobilized.

PLA units which had been formed recently were generally the first to be demobilized, so former regional and guerrilla troops were the first to go. In this way, the regular PLA tended to slough off those troops that were closest to the people. Some of these latter units were "demobilized" only in the sense that they were converted to local garrison and police duties. They evolved, respectively, into the regional forces and the Public Security Forces of the PLA.

As civilian CCP and governmental cadres became available, the PLA disengaged itself from those non-military duties it had been forced to assume in the south and west. "Expert" criteria became predominant in PLA personnel actions, and formal military schools were established. In 1950-51, senior officers' schools were set up in Peking and Nanking, and an Air Force Academy was set up in Sian. In August 1950, the first jet pilot training began at Shenyang, with newly arrived Soviet instructors and aircraft.[49]

In October 1949, Hsu Hsiang-ch'ien was named to be the first Chief of the General Staff, with Nieh Jung-chen as his deputy. Nieh, trained in Europe as an engineer, had been a close associate of Liu Shao-ch'i and P'eng Chen during the anti-Japanese War. For decades Nieh had been an advocate of professional and technical specialization in both party and army. He was soon to prove his political and logistical skill with the procurement and allocation of Soviet weapons to troops in the Korean staging areas in Manchuria. He has been "one of the key architects of the modernized People's Liberation Army."[50] At the top of the military structure, the MAC continued to be dominated by Yeh Chien-ying, Chu Teh, and P'eng Te-huai. Thus, the General Staff and the MAC were run by professionally and technically oriented officers.

The Korean Intervention

PLA demobilization was halted abruptly by China's entry into the Korean War in late October 1950.[51] Just how and why the decision was made to enter the war remains subject to speculation, although the primary factor was certainly the desire to maintain North Korea as a buffer zone.[52] Despite Soviet pressure and their own supposed preference for "pre-emptive attack," PLA commanders did not necessarily favor intervention. Indeed, according to at least one 1967 Red Guard source, P'eng Te-huai personally opposed the decision.[53] As Gittings points out, the Korean War completely upset the PLA's two main tasks in 1950: demobilization and the conquest of Taiwan. The intervention of the US Seventh Fleet to "neutralize" the Taiwan Strait (25 June 1950) rendered the final showdown with Chiang Kai-shek impossible.

It has been argued, notably by Gittings, that Mao favored the Korean intervention as a means of undermining Kao Kang's "independent kingdom" in Manchuria by moving in large military formations from other regions.[54] Whitson makes a somewhat similar case for Mao's having welcomed the Korean War as a means of breaking up the "regional hegemony" of the five "field army elites" and of truly nationalizing the PLA. The war certainly did result in the movement of units from all over China, and, at least to some extent, must have reshuffled the military-political power constellations created by the civil war.[55]

In any event, the decision to intervene in Korea was inevitably influenced by internal political factors and Sino-Soviet relations, as well as by the obvious national security factor. The war itself, in turn, profoundly affected the nascent communist state, its relations with the USSR, and its army.

The Korean War

Perhaps the most immediate and drastic impact of the Korean fighting was felt by the PLA's internal political system. Alexander George has detailed the rapid erosion of commissar credibility during the first nine months in Korea.[56] During the civil war, commissars had fulfilled many useful roles, especially in recruiting, collecting intelligence, and organizing logistical support. But in Korea the commissars' usefulness was foreclosed by the fundamental fact of a non-Chinese population. The commissar system is just not very useful in foreign wars. Frustrated commissars evidently tried to find other tasks to justify their presence, and thereby encroached on the commanders, who became convinced that the commissars were excess baggage. There is some evidence that this clash between commanders and commissars tended to erode the authority of both, and caused both to resent the system of "committee decision" that was implicit in their theoretically co-equal status.[57]

As the PLA lost its initial advantages of surprise and momentum, UN forces dug in and began to bring their enormous firepower to bear. The impression on the PLA—amply documented by Alexander George and Samuel Griffith—was shattering, for it had faced nothing like this before.[58] The initial rush of "mobile warfare" tactics had stretched PLA supply lines dangerously thin across the bleak Korean mountains, where they were mercilessly pounded from the air. At the front, as the value of traditional political work came into question, the importance of firepower and logistics became painfully clear.

Exactly who was in command of the PLA (formally the "Chinese People's Volunteers" or CPV) during those first six months in Korea is subject to some doubt. It was long and generally assumed to have been Lin Piao, but the 1972-75 campaign to criticize Lin produced repeated assertions that he was never in Korea at all. At any rate, command of the CPV was passed to P'eng Te-huai in the early spring of 1951, and Chinese tactics, logistics, and politics all took on a decidedly new look. P'eng realized that the fluid tactics of the Civil War would not work against a well-armed and determined enemy—especially in restricted terrain and on foreign soil.

As early as April 1951, P'eng was complaining bitterly to Chou En-lai that his logistical support was grossly inadequate.[59] The PLA had crossed the Yalu with the same hodge-podge of weapons and equipment with which it had ended the civil war, apparently intending to resupply itself off the enemy, as it always had before. That source of supply dried up after the initial offensive was blunted, however. The logistical burden produced by the mixed bag of types and calibers of ammunition alone would have strained the most modern supply system, but the CPV had to depend on a trickle of supplies, laboriously brought over the mountains at night on the backs of Chinese and Korean porters. The system had to be modernized, and the PLA had to standardize its ordnance.

P'eng knew he needed help, and he knew where to get it: The General Staff had been pressing the Soviets for massive aid from the outset of the fighting, and Stalin's initial hesitancy had caused considerable Sino-Soviet friction. By late 1951, however, significant Soviet aid began to reach the front, and P'eng was able to somewhat stabilize his supply situation. The PLA was gradually reequipped with Soviet weapons.

UN airpower, however, continued to extract a terrible toll in troop morale and in lost supplies. In order to make up for his material inferiority, P'eng expended the only resource he had in abundance: manpower. The "human sea" attacks of 1952-53 were his only available counter to UN firepower.

Under the pressure of combat, military results became all-important. The tradition of commissar counter-signatures on operational orders was virtually ignored, and unit party branches began to disappear. The Korean experience was felt throughout the PLA, as units from all over China were rotated to the battle area.[60]

The Sino-Soviet Honeymoon

PLA commissars (presumably with Mao's support) attempted to reverse the decline in political work, and to reassert traditional commissar roles and prestige. A new set of "Draft Regulations on Political Work" was adopted in April 1954, in an effort to put politics back in command. "However, judging from the limited press coverage and the absence of a large-scale propaganda campaign in support of the Draft Regulations, the efforts to check the rise of professionalism were apparently not very successful."[61]

Within weeks of the Korean armistice, the United States provided P'eng and the "professionals" with a major justification for continuing wholesale regularization, by administering a humiliating demonstration of China's military vulnerability. A carrier task force steamed down the Chinese coast, conducting massive aerial instrusions over the coastal provinces to test defenses and photograph military installations. Not one Chinese interceptor rose to meet the intruders. This arrogant exercise of raw power convinced many Chinese that PLA modernization ought to be given top priority, so that no such flagrant violation of China would ever be allowed again.[62]

After Stalin's death, a "honeymoon period" in Sino-Soviet relations facilitated modernization. China strove to be "modern and Soviet." P'eng Te-huai became the PRC's first Minister of Defense in September 1954, assisted by Yeh Chien-ying. Working closely with Marshal Zhukov, his opposite number in the Soviet Union, P'eng presided over a far-reaching program of modernization. In 1954, with Soviet parts and assistance, the first Yak-18 primary trainers were assembled at the new National Aircraft Factory in Shenyang. By 1956, the first jet-fighters (MiG-17s) were produced, and by 1957 the Chinese were essentially self-sufficient in weapons up to about 90 millimeter.

The PLA officer corps was reoriented toward the Soviet model, while commissars were reduced to an all-time low in their power and prestige. Conscription began in September 1954 (six months before its formal legalization), thus abandoning the PLA's cherished "volunteer" tradition. Regularization, modernization, and strict discipline became the order of the day.

After the Korean armistice, PLA ground units began converting to a "triangular division" of 12,900 men, similar to the one used in the Civil War, but modified somewhat by Soviet influence. (In Korea CPV divisions had been unwieldy "four-cornered" giants of almost 17,000, to facilitate P'eng's labor-intensive tactics.) Half the PLA was converted to the new standard organization before the process was interrupted by the Great Leap Forward and the subsequent loss of Soviet aid. A result was that the PLA partly consisted of modified units with sub-standard equipment, a situation which still persists to some extent.[63]

As ever-increasing priority was given to military expertise, formal PLA schools proliferated in the early and mid-1950s. In addition to the Sian Air Force Academy, the PLA was operating eighteen flight training schools by the end of 1953. An Advanced Military Institute was established in Nanking in 1951, under Liu Po-ch'eng, a "devotee of Russian military theory."[64] It was by far the most prestigious officer's school, at least until the Senior War College (now called the PLA Military Academy) was opened in Peking in 1958—also under Liu's direction. Both of these academies emphasized the need to "study advanced Soviet experience" in the employment of armor, artillery, airpower, and "integral strategy."

> By 1961 at least seventy-five military training institutions had been established, sixty-four of them concentrated on logistics and military operations and eleven on the education of commissars. The General Staff and War College (Nanking), the General Military Academy (Harbin), the Miltiary Research Institute (Peking), and the Academy of Military Sciences (Peking) acted as "Graduate Schools" for the other military academies.[65]

P'eng also began a systematic assault on the militia system. He ordered a ten to thirty percent cutback in militia strength, and recalled most of its weapons, "to guard against the rise of problems." Meanwhile, he began to organize "army reserve divisions" along Soviet lines, with which he intended ultimately to replace the militia.[66]

The adoption of conscription and P'eng's "reserve army" program resulted in a major reduction in the size of the PLA. According to Franz Schurmann:

> There was strong dissent from this policy during the mid-1950s. Generals Liu Po-ch'eng and Yeh Chien-ying . . . argued against reduction of the armed forces and for "immediate development of well-trained and well-equipped forces in being . . . ." The policies advocated by Liu and Yeh appeared to be even more "expert" than those of P'eng.[67]

Alice Hsieh has argued that P'eng's policy was aimed at decreasing defense expenditures by heavy reliance on a trained reserve. The savings would then be invested in long-range heavy-industrial development. P'eng's policy implicitly meant that for the immediately foreseeable future, China would continue to rely on the USSR for technological aid and for its "nuclear umbrella."[68]

The Emergence of a "Regular" Officer Corps

By 1954, a "functional system" was emerging in all spheres of the Chinese government. In 1949, CCP members still frequently had been assigned multiple and overlapping functions. Conflicts had been ironed out within the established discipline and control practices of the party. But as the 1950s wore on, functional specificity developed to the point where identifiable governmental systems had created their own particular orientations and career patterns: The CCP "monolith" began to break up into various "power constellations or bases" which were rooted in organizational structures.[69]

The formal delineation of functional groups and subgroups within the military came with the promulgation of the "Regulations on the Service of Officers," on 8 February 1955.[70] These regulations, adopted "in order to further the building of the Chinese PLA as a modern, regular army" (article 1), did a great deal more than just establish a hierarchy of Soviet-style ranks and insignias. They also divided the officer corps into functionally specific groups. Article 4 specified the following classes of officers "in accordance with their professions":

1. Commanding Officers
2. Political Officers
3. Technical Officers
4. Quartermasters
5. Medical Officers
6. Veterinary Officers
7. Judge Advocates
8. Administrative Officers

P'eng Te-huai's "reserve army" system was explicitly included; and the distinction between regular and reserve officers was carefully drawn with regard to pay, titles, promotion criteria, uniforms, etc. (articles 3, 45-51).

Officer selection and promotion were to be based on "political quality and professional ability" (article 25). Entry into the officer corps was limited (articles 5 and 6) and, generally speaking, was possible only at the lowest rank (*Shao-wei*: Second Lieutenant). Exceptions might be made for those with expecially high examination marks or technical qualifications (articles 11-12, 47). No such exceptions applied, significantly, to new political officers.

Authority to appoint, remove, and promote officers was highly centralized and restricted to the military chain of command and (for top posts) the Standing Committee of the National People's Congress. The regulations made no mention of the MAC, nor indeed of the Party. A number of provisions (especially in article 8), imply that commanders held final authority over all of the other seven classes of officers, including commissars. At the highest levels (generals and marshals), however, no distinctions were made among the eight classes. At that level, military, political, and technical responsibility are presumably too closely interwoven to permit specialization. Implicit in the supremacy of commanders was the more professional system of "one-man command" which the Soviet advisors advocated, and which P'eng had always preferred.

"Ranks," according to article 22, "are life-long honorable titles of officers who may not be deprived of their ranks unless with court decision based on their crime." Article 24 required that: "Officers should wear shoulderboards and insignias conforming with their ranks. NCOs and privates are prohibited to wear shoulderboards and insignia of officers." Up to 1955, all PLA personnel had received food, clothing, and a small allowance in lieu of salaries, but that now changed dramatically. Although the regulations themselves did not mention differential salaries, they were adopted at that time. By 1964, monthly salaries would vary from US $2.50 for privates to US $192-236 for full generals.[71]

It is by no means certain that Mao Tse-tung was opposed to the technical modernization and regularization of the PLA, but he clearly opposed the introduction of rank titles and insignia. His disapproval can be inferred from a provision in article 9 of the regulations, which established the rank of "Supreme Marshal" (*Ta Yuan-shuai*). This rank was to be conferred on the one "Supreme Commander who has attained particularly outstanding merit in organizing the people's armed forces in revolutionary wars." That obviously was intended to be Mao's military title, since Chu Teh and P'eng Te-huai—the only other plausible candidates for the title—were among the ten men named to be Marshals (*Yuan-shuai*). If the title of "Supreme Marshal" was intended as an appeal to Mao's vanity, to secure his approval of the new system, it did not work. He never assumed any military title and did not, as far as is known, ever refer to anyone else by a military rank (unless he was being sarcastic about "great generals"). How vigorously Mao opposed the new system in the Central Committee is unknown, but he did avoid identifying himself with it publicly.

It should also be observed that the "Regulations on the Service of Officers" contained some provisions which were not "military professional" at all. Articles 39 and 41 dealt with "Officers in Active Service Detailed," defined as officers "invited by non-military departments and detailed by the Ministry of Defense to these departments to undertake military work." This provision made allowance for militia work, as well as for other military training in civilian organizations. It also probably applied to military personnel assigned to the schools, laboratories, and factories of China's emerging military-industrial complex. Officers on "Active Service Detailed" status continued to wear PLA uniforms, and could be recalled at any time by the Defense Ministry. On the other hand, their salaries were paid by the civilian agencies to which they were assigned, and might exceed (but not be less than) the normal pay for their military ranks. This provision, plus the preferred status of reserve and retired officers (article 38), meant that significant numbers of officers were in a sort of half-and-half status between the military and civilian spheres. This facilitated military contributions to China's overall technical and economic development, but significantly compromised the autonomy of the officer corps.

The Soviet Model Reconsidered

In September 1956, in his report to the Eighth Party Congress, P'eng said, "We must intensify our study of modern military science and technique, the art of commanding a modernized army in battle, and new military systems."[72] Radical "Maoists" subsequently claimed that P'eng's ultimate intention was to create an exact copy of the Soviet Army, and to "negate the Party's absolute leadership over the army to eliminate the system of collective leadership by Party committees and to enforce the system of one-man leadership."[73] Clearly, P'eng did oppose collective leadership within the PLA. But the Soviet model, which P'eng was selectively applying, provides for overall party control within a system of one-man command. The Soviet system works very nicely, provided the officer corps is thoroughly "communized" and coopted.

It is barely conceivable that, by 1955, Mao may have believed that PLA officers had become reliable enough politically to permit the transition away from the commissar system—just as Lenin and Stalin did in the 1920s. Mao himself made frequent references to "advanced Soviet experience" in the 1950s. It is well-known that the "Hundred Flowers" campaign, which led to a flood of criticism of the party and its ideology, shocked and disillusioned Mao.

His decision to launch a counterattack against P'eng and the Russianization of the PLA came at the same time, and for the same reasons, as the "Anti-Rightist" campaign of mid-1957. Mao realized that China was not nearly so unified behind the party and its ideology (and himself) as he had thought when he had called for "blooming and contending" in 1956. Although the PLA officer corps had not voiced any public criticism, Mao would probably have reconsidered any thoughts he ever had about allowing the commissar system to "wither away" in favor of one-man command. A purge of junior military officers was conducted in 1957.[74]

While Mao certainly objected to certain manifestations of Soviet influence, he was not opposed to modernization per se. He supported the development of modern industry, and reportedly called for nuclear research as early as 1955.[75] He recognized that nuclear weapons would strengthen his hand in world politics.

Mao's main criticism was directed against the "mechanical application of foreign experience." As Gittings notes, the officer corps had quickly adopted an elitist attitude which actually hindered real modernization.[76] The mid-1950s seem to have witnessed overly harsh discipline, and serious abuses of civilians and soldiers by officers and their families. This is not an unusual phenomenon during the early stages of military modernization, although it was something of a retrogression for the PLA. Rank-conscious officers in young armies are inclined to avoid getting their hands dirty, whereas real modernization requires them to do just literally that: Weapons and equipment must be inspected constantly, and hardships must be shared—especially by junior officers. PLA leaders had always been exemplary in these respects, but the combination of peace and Soviet-style uniforms, rank, and insignia apparently caused an overreaction away from the PLA's traditional egalitarianism. Chinese officers adapted, all too readily, to their new status as a favored elite, and began to exhibit some of the same bad habits that had damaged KMT and warlord armies. P'eng Te-huai has been officially blamed for all this, but it seems more likely that he recognized it for the serious obstacle to real professionalism that it was. It was under P'eng that a mass movement was launched in 1958 to send the haughty and pampered families of officers back to their home villages, thereby ridding PLA garrisons of a major source of officer-enlisted friction.

In September 1958, another movement was launched—for officers to "go down to the companies and soldier" (*hsia-lien tang-ping*). This movement required every officer to spend one month per year serving as a common soldier, and was "intended to demonstrate that no military man had an iron rice bowl."[77] The only difference between officers and enlisted men was their work, and to think otherwise was incorrect and non-communist. It has become conventional wisdom, reinforced by Red Guard sources in 1967, that P'eng opposed the *hsia-lien* movement. He no doubt disapproved of its extremism, but he may well have considered that something like it was a necessary means of chastening the officer corps without foregoing the benefits of a system of ranks and of strict (but just) discipline. The *hsia-lien* movement came at a time when nationwide movements were being launched against bureaucratism, dogmatism, subjectivism, and conservatism,[78] and the PLA was caught up in the larger extremist trend. An official statement in *August First Magazine* claimed that *hsia-lien* was a step in the transition to communism—a transition that was officially thought to be just around the corner during those first heady months of the Great Leap forward.[79]

P'eng was appalled by the disorder and the utopianism of the Great Leap, especially by its disruption of national defense industry. But his grip on the PLA was beginning to slip, and he couldn't resist the extremes of the *hsia-lien* movement. He had made bitter enemies among the political commissars, who saw the Great Leap as their chance to regain lost power and prestige. As *hsia-lien* sent more and more senior commanders down to "soldier in the companies," P'eng's credibility among "professional" commanders began to weaken dangerously as well.

The same month that saw the launching of *hsia-lien* (September 1958) also saw the creation of serious doubts about the reliability of the Sino-Soviet military alliance. Substantial US military and political backing for Chiang Kai-shek during the Taiwan Straits crisis was in marked contrast to the slow, cautious, and grudging Soviet support for Peking. If there had been any doubts, the Straits crisis must have convinced Mao and the Central Committee that they needed an independent nuclear capability. Soviet inaction weakened P'eng's political position considerably, since he had become closely identified with the Soviet alliance.

P'eng's position was further weakened by the terrible beating his air force took at the hands of Nationalist pilots.[80] If that was a sample of all the military efficiency P'eng could deliver, after seven years of Soviet tutelage, maybe the whole approach was as unreliable as the alliance had proven to be.

The Fall of P'eng Te-huai

A measure of P'eng's diminished power was the speed with which Mao's call for "Everyone a Soldier" sent PLA regional forces headlong into a massive crash program in militia training. It is especially indicative that, although carried out with PLA resources, the militia program was directly under local party control.[81] Mao had overruled P'eng on a military issue where the lines were clearly drawn. P'eng's "reserve army" was totally disregarded, while mass formations of workers and peasants drilled daily with bayonets and spears. On top of that, the PLA was blamed, late in 1959, when the militia expansion flopped. The agonizing reappraisal of 1958's overblown production statistics also revealed that the "Everyone a Soldier" movement had been a disaster. The program had resulted in paper militia units, corruption, and even some cases of units taking weapons and becoming bandits.[82]

At the same time, the military academies came under radical attack. Obviously, Soviet influence was a major fault, but there were others: Academy recruitment discriminated against peasants and workers, and encouraged caste-consciousness in the officer corps. Furthermore, the whole officer recruitment system prescribed by the 1955 regulations discouraged promotion from the ranks.

Finally, at the Lushan Plenum of August 1959, P'eng was removed. His opposition to the economic policies and disruptions of the Great Leap, and to the mass militia, had made enemies of Mao and his followers, as had his close identification with the Soviets. In fact, the Soviets may well have administered the coup de grace to P'eng by repudiating the nuclear power-sharing agreement in June. That action also confirmed the fears of men like Yeh Chien-ying, Su Yü, Nieh Jung-chen, and Liu Po-ch'eng, who had opposed P'eng's heavy reliance on the USSR, and had advocated the maintenance of more powerful Chinese forces-in-being to guard against surprise attack.

P'eng's military policy was probably seen as the basic cause of the PLA being humiliated by the "US puppets" on Taiwan. Moreover, he had publicly supported the *hsia-lien* movement. As Defense Minister he hardly could have done otherwise. The break with the Soviets, the humiliation in 1958, *hsia-lien*, and the militia fiasco all eroded the loyalty of the professionally inclined commanders to P'eng—and that loyalty had provided his bedrock support. Thus, P'eng lost their support partly because the blame for two of Mao's abortive radical movements (*hsia-lien* and the mass militia) was dropped in his lap.

This scenario is also indicated by the fact that as soon as Lin Piao took over as the new Minister of Defense, he instituted measures which relieved much of the pressure on commanders, but left the commissars with enhanced power. One of Lin's first acts was to abolish the mass militia, and to order the Military Districts to rebuild a sound, effective (and therefore much smaller) militia, using PLA men as the core. The militia began to come under greater PLA control—a trend that continued through the 1960s. Mao himself set the priorities for the new militia work as (1) Organization; (2) Political work; and (only then) (3) Military training[83]—just the priorities P'eng would have recommended in 1958, if he had been asked.

Lin also slackened off on *hsia-lien* in early 1960. Officers continued to "go down," but no longer were required to actually "soldier" as privates. Instead they were sent to the companies as observers and instructors (they "made contact with the masses" and "shared experiences").[84]

P'eng fell for a number of reasons, but not for pursuing regularization ("the bourgeois military line")—at least not directly. He had been creating an army which was more concerned with military effectiveness than with politics. Worse, the officer corps, dominated by the commanders, was organizationally and consciously differentiating itself from the rest of the party and government. Although the officer corps never showed signs of revolt, it was gradually becoming capable of revolt. It was making the transition from "opinion group" to "faction,"[85] a development *neither Mao nor Liu Shao-ch'i welcomed*.

It is just conceivable that Mao was willing to accept the emergence of a Soviet-style officer corps up to 1956. If so, the "Hundred Flowers" fiasco changed his mind. P'eng had to go, personally, because of his opposition to Mao's economic policies and his close association with the Soviets.

THE "RED-EXPERT" BALANCE: 1959-65

Exactly how and why Lin Piao was chosen to replace P'eng will probably remain uncertain. He was quite acceptable to the officer corps, since his credentials as a troop commander were impeccable. On the other hand, his "redness" was unsullied by the P'eng Te-huai years since he had been ill, and relatively inactive, during the mid-1950s. Given Lin Piao's "professional" training and career, and his past disagreements with Mao, he was probably as acceptable to Liu as he was to Mao.[86] In any event, Mao did not simply appoint Lin on his own. It must be recalled that Mao was very much on the defensive at Lushan because of the failures of the Great Leap. It is suggested here that P'eng Te-huai was eliminated by Mao *and* Liu, both as a potential rival and a convenient scapegoat for recent political, economic, and military setbacks. Lin was an acceptable replacement because he was red enough to suit Mao and expert enough to suit Liu. Moreover, he could speak to and for the PLA, since he held its confidence. The really intriguing question is just how and why Lin emerged as "Chairman Mao's best pupil and closest comrade-in-arms" during the ensuing six years.

Lin Piao's Consolidation of Control

The PLA was in considerable disarray in late 1959, and its prospects were grim, as China sank deeper into the hardships of the "three bad years" (1959-61). Lin's energy in attacking the army's problems proved to be more than equal to the task.

One of his most pressing problems was conflict within the PLA itself. Commissars were using the Great Leap to reestablish their power at the expense of the commanders. Their squabbling, as in Korea, was detracting from the authority of both. New cleavages were opening as well: The air force, the navy, and the main forces had been deprived of resources which were diverted to the militia and the regional forces. They were also suffering the greatest losses from the technological and industrial stagnation caused by the Great Leap.

Lin acted decisively to restore discipline, unity, and morale. In addition to moderating *hsia-lien* and revamping the militia program, he reemphasized training and the nuclear program.

Despite these and other concessions to the commanders, the influence of P'eng Te-huai apparently persisted. The derogatory references to P'eng in the secret 1961 *Bulletin of Activities* are indicative. P'eng continued to work "in the third rank," supervising military construction in Szechuan. He corresponded with Mao, Chou, and other leaders, and evidently retained a following in the civilian party as well as the PLA. In 1962, he reportedly made a strong bid for "reversal of verdict." The now-famous play by Wu Han, "Hai Jui Dismissed from Office" was attacked by Mao as an appeal for P'eng's reinstatement (although a recent study by Thomas Fisher casts considerable doubt on Wu Han's intention in that regard).[87] That the accusation was made indicates Mao's fears about the influence of P'eng and his ideas. It is entirely possible that the "P'eng Te-huai clique" was still a real influence in the PLA right through the Cultural Revolution.[88]

Lin set about reorganizing the PLA high command in the fall of 1959, using politically reliable former associates. Two career political commissars, Lo Jui-ch'ing and Ch'iu Hui-tso, took over as chiefs of the General Staff and General Rear Services Department (GRSD), respectively. Lo brought along the Public Security Forces from his former post as Minister of Public Security. The General Political Department (GPD) was ostensibly under the aged and ailing Marshal Lo Jung-huan, but was actually run by Lin's associate Hsiao Hua. Lo died in 1963, and Hsiao formally took over as GPD director in September 1964. The reorganization clearly subordinated the General Staff to the Ministry of National Defense (MND), and Lin's power to coordinate varying PLA commands and activities was notably greater than P'eng's had been.[89] The Mao-Lin alliance controlled the MAC fairly effectively, although Ho Lung, the senior vice-chairman, continued to exercise a great deal of influence.[90]

On 29 September 1959, in his first major policy speech, Lin set the tone for much of what was to follow. He called for reconstruction of the party organization in the PLA, stricter political education, and closer contact with the masses. He used a far more conciliatory tone than had been used toward the PLA in the previous few years, however, and even admitted certain shortcomings in the setting up of the communes. But he also sharply criticized those in the army who had rejected the mass movements and failed to engage enthusiastically in economic work. He redefined "military democracy" in terms much more acceptable to the "professional" commanders, emphasizing "democracy under centralized guidance." Although he was about to abolish the mass militia, Lin also paid lip-service to "participation for turning the whole population into fighting men."[91]

A subtle but significant modification was also made to Mao's doctrine that "men are superior to material."[92] Lin's new formulation was that "men and material form a unity with man as the leading factor." Later in the year, Lin also reinstated Su Yü as a Vice-Minister of Defense. Su had been fired in October 1958, for advocating all-out priority to PLA modernization. Here again, Lin was acting more "professionally" than had his villified predecessor. Military training was reemphasized, and sixty to seventy percent of the PLA's time was henceforth to be devoted to it, even though politics was supposed to become "the heart and soul of the army."

In the years that followed, Lin restored morale and discipline with many of the traditional PLA methods of the Yenan and Civil War periods. The party-branch system, which had atrophied badly since 1950, was restored, as were branches of the Communist Youth League and the company-level Revolutionary Servicemen's Committees. A series of political campaigns ensued, aptly described by Griffith as a "mathematical blitz." These included the "Three-Eight," "Four-Firsts," "Five-Good Soldier," "Two Recollections and Three Investigations," and "Four-Good Company" movements. In 1961, the GPD issued "Five Principles for PLA Management and Education at Company Level."[93] These contained a "critical but ponderous restatement of the complexities of the mass line as applied to army life."[94]

It was emphasized that, "Cadres and soldiers of our army are all class brothers. They are completely equal politically, the only difference being the work to which each has been assigned. there is no such designation as high or low in their status."[95] The "Eight Love the Soldier Demands" and the "Eight Respect the Cadre Demands" were promulgated to help the class brothers get along.[96]

In October 1961, the GPD issued a special "Selection of Mao Tse-Tung's Works" of seventy articles in twelve chapters, "in accordance with the practical needs of the armymen."[97] This became the principal text for PLA political study, and was apparently the immediate predecessor to *Quotations from Chairman Mao*, the famous "Little Red Book" published by the GPD in 1966.

Beginning in 1961, new training manuals were issued, to erase the "vestiges of dogmatism," emphasize the primacy of men over weapons, and to counter the blind application of foreign (i.e., Soviet) models.[98] In the popular publications of the time, the only technical expertise mentioned with any enthusiasm was rifle marksmanship. But this publicly "Maoist" posture belied much of the reality, for the regional forces were being upgraded and the militia continued to be deemphasized. Within the army, technical skill was accorded renewed status. The investment in missiles, aircraft, and nuclear weapons was increased. Lin was taking pains to maintain the "red-expert" balance.[99]

The air force (PLAAF) probably had the worst morale and discipline problems in the PLA. Air force officers had become a particularly arrogant elite during the 1950s, and had been subjected to special criticism in 1958-59. Then the PLAAF had been especially hard hit by the loss of Soviet aid and by the economic dislocation of the Great Leap. Many of the pilots had only defected from the Nationalist Air Force in the last months of the civil war. Because of the high educational requirements, air crewmen trained since 1949 still tended to be from urban bourgeois backgrounds. The reliability of air crews was apparently so questionable that, as early as 1959, the air force was forbidden to fly over water without special permission. The inevitable happened anyway: There was a spate of defection flights to Taiwan in 1960-63. In addition to a tightening of political and flight controls, the entire air force underwent a strict screening for loyalty and class background. Despite a shortage of trained pilots, a large number were grounded or dismissed outright.[100]

Because of his extreme concern with air force loyalty, Lin took special pains to consolidate his hold on its officers. One result was that by 1967, the air force high command was thoroughly "packed" with men who were personally loyal to Lin Piao. This was to have major political repercussions in 1971.

The PLA's political refurbishment was formalized when, in March 1963, new "Political Work Regulations for the Chinese People's Liberation Army" were promulgated by the CCP Central Committee. These regulations officially codified the formulae Lin had worked out since 1959, embodying the "Maoist," mass-line ideal. Far more than any previous document, the 1963 regulations not only collated and formalized, but dealt in great detail with basic issues of doctrine, organization, political work, and leadership methods. Yet little was new except the magnitude of political involvement. The regulations suggest that the all-pervasive political system envisioned by Mao and Lin was not fully operational, but it was by now an attainable goal which they were determined to achieve.[101]

The Mao-Lin Alliance

While the rest of China had been allowed to recover from the Great Leap Forward by Liu Shao-ch'i's "revisionism," the PLA had been inculcated with "Chairman Mao's Glorious Thoughts." By late 1963 there were, in effect, two Chinese Communist Parties: One was headed by Liu and Teng Hsiao-p'ing and operated through the civilian CCP apparatus. The other was the military party system, dominated by Mao and Lin Piao, and operating through the GPD and the unit party branches.

We will probably never know exactly when, and on what terms, Mao enlisted the support of Lin Piao in his effort to counter the civilian party and Liu's revisionism. By the end of 1963, Mao was satisfied that the PLA could be used as a model for the rest of China. On 1 February 1964, a *JMJP* editorial kicked off the movement to "Learn from the PLA in Political and Ideological Work." Chairman Mao desired to spread the "rich experience" of PLA political work throughout Chinese society.

As the popularity and organizational strength of the PLA increased during 1963-64, public criticism of the military virtually ceased, while soldiers (mainly regional force commissars) assumed many of the former functions of party and governmental cadres. While the latter allowed themselves to be overshadowed by the PLA, the CCP took increasingly strong exception to the PLA's preemption of influence in political decision making and in governmental operations. What was particularly galling to the civilian party was the formation of "political departments" in units of economic administration and management—political departments directly modeled on those in the army and run by active-duty PLA commissars.[102] Thus was much of the political ground cut from under Liu Shao-ch'i in 1963-64.

The PLA incursion into civilian politics created intra-military stresses as well. It was commissars who spearheaded the incursion, and they not only clashed with civilian cadres, but also began to overshadow PLA commanders—particularly in the regional forces.[103] Because local party organs and regional military units had worked closely together since 1949, or even earlier, close personal relations had developed between local CCP leaders and PLA commanders. Now both began to feel threatened by aggressive commissars. This situation set the stage for some bloody confrontations during the Cultural Revolution, when commissars and Red Guards, on the one hand, battled openly with commanders and local party organizations, on the other.[104] While Mao and Lin greased the skids for Liu Shao-ch'i, they also created an explosive situation in military and adminsitrative centers all over China.

THE CASE OF LO JUI-CH'ING

Despite all of the political preparations which have been described, the PLA and the militia proved to be a good deal less radical during the Cultural Revolution than might have been expected. One reason for this was undoubtedly the fact that behind the rhetoric, and parallel to the political retrenchment, the PLA devoted considerable effort to normal military tasks during the early 1960s. As noted earlier, Lin Piao maintained a balance of both military and political work in his refurbishment of the army. Military training and readiness were the responsibility of the General Staff Department and its chief, Lo Jui-ch'ing. Lo's contribution to the strengthening of the PLA was thus quite important, but it left him vulnerable to political attack when he and Lin began to clash over strategic policies and political power.

The Official Case Against Lo

Lo was actually stripped of his power in November 1965, and was officially purged on 16 May 1966. Public criticism did not begin until the summer of 1967, when Lo was characterized as "the jack-booted storm-trooper pushing the reactionary bourgeois military line." He was specifically accused of opposing political work in the PLA and of saying that "to regard Mao's works as the PLA's supreme directive does not conform to the system of our state." Worse still, he allegedly recommended that officers study Liu Shao-ch'i's *How to be a Good Communist*.[105]

Actually, there is little evidence that Lo underrated the importance of political work. He made frequent (and quite "Maoist") political statements in the 1961 *Bulletin of Activities*. To be sure, he did not take the "spiritual atom bomb" dogma literally; but then, neither did anyone else in the PLA high command, if we may judge by their actions throughout the 1960s.

Lo was not a military commander by training or experience. On the contrary, he had been a political commissar for years before he took over the Ministry of Public Security in the 1950s. In that capacity, he had served as the regime's top political policeman. Despite Lo's background, Western scholarship has generally accepted the official line that he was a "military professional." He was castigated in 1967-71 for saying "a red head is no harder than a steel tank," and "military affairs are the same as politics, and . . . should receive equal emphasis." He probably said such things, all right, but so did the rest of the PLA high command in 1959-64. Like P'eng Te-huai before him, Lo was attacked *ex post facto*, for backing the official line of the time: The same official line his attackers had backed, but subsequently repudiated.

The importance of military training is a case in point. In 1967, a major policy statement attacked Lo and P'eng as follows: "They clamoured that 'the conditions are different.' What conditions are different? The Imperialists do indeed have atomic bombs and nuclear weapons. But this is not so terrific! Marxists have at all times held that no matter what changes take place in technical equipment the basic laws of revolutionary war will never change."[106] Lo's opinion that modern conditions were different was hardly unique during the first years of Lin Piao's tenure in the MND, however. On 30 December 1960, Hsiao Hua told a telephone conference of the MAC Administrative Council that:

> Chief Lin emphasized that we must ideologically recognize the importance of military training. He said that we are carrying on our training under a new condition and a new situation. This differs from the conditions in the past periods of fighting . . . . At the time, the Army units could fight a battle without or with little training. Since techniques were relatively simple in those days, they were easy to learn—But the situation today is basically different. Most of the Army units have not fought battles for a very long time. Some soldiers and lower-level cadres have not even fought a single battle. Thus we must strengthen our training. Modern weapons are far more complicated than the old ones. Our men need full training before they can handle them. If our training is bad, incidents will occur in the time of peace, and defeat will follow in the time of war . . . . This is the basic change in the situation, a great not small difference between the present and the past.[107]

Lo Jui-ch'ing's "bourgeois military line" on the issue of "different conditions" was thus being advocated by the GPD, in 1961, and was attributed to Lin Piao himself.

Another aspect of Lo's "black line" which was heavily criticized later was a program of big contests in military skills which Lo inaugurated in 1964. This program had some fairly serious drawbacks: Unit commanders became so intent on winning competitions that they shifted men into "crack fighters squads," at the expense of overall combat readiness. The competitions also resulted in "training for show rather than for fighting, and . . . made for a great deal of formalism and empty display . . . waste and extravagance."[108] The big competitions undoubtedly did result in all these abuses, but Lo hardly deserves all the blame: The 1963 "Political Work Regulations" repeatedly encouraged commanders at all levels to use "competitions and contests" to enourage good political and military training. Moreover, "revolutionary contests and competitions" were encouraged in the Regulations on Political Work" written for the Eighth Route Army in 1939.[109] Lin Piao may not have originated the big competitions, but he must have approved of them. They were personally attributed to Lo Jui-ch'ing only after the shortcomings of the program had become obvious, and when Lo's purge had to be justified. Further indication that the competitions were a phony issue is seen in the fact that they continued to be held well into 1966—perhaps a full year after Lo was stripped of his power.[110]

Lo did oppose certain of the "Maoist" military policies which emerged in 1960-65. In particular, he seems to have persistently emphasized the main forces over regional forces and (especially) the militia.[111] As in the case of the competitions, however, this was a phony issue: No "corrective" action was taken after Lo was purged.

Lin, Lo, and the Vietnam Dilemma

The real cause of Lo Jui-ch'ing's fall from power was a bitter controversy over military security policy that evolved as the Sino-Soviet rift widened, and as American involvement in Indochina assumed threatening proportions. Peking had to decide upon a response to the American threat, and that necessarily begged reconsideration of the Sino-Soviet relationship. If the North Vietnamese were to be given full support, including the use of bases in Southern China, then it was imperative to repair the Sino-Soviet alliance to deter US reprisals. China's own nuclear deterrent was still years away from operational status. Lo Jui-ch'ing therefore advocated a *modus vivendi* with the USSR which would put China back under the Soviet "nuclear umbrella."

Whether Lo realized it or not, this strategy had domestic political implications which placed him among Mao's enemies. Liu Shao-ch'i was also trumpeting strong support for Hanoi and, implicitly, improved relations with Moscow.[112] Lo probably came to realize this, for he began an attempt to undercut and replace Lin Piao, Mao's closest ally. The official report on Lo's "mistakes" alleges some rather heavy-handed moves to enhance his own power at Mao's and (especially) Lin's expense.[113] Sometime in 1964, Lo launched what can only be described as a power grab: He began a campaign to convince the MAC and Lin himself that Lin was too ill to run the PLA, and ought to turn full control over to himself. Meanwhile, Lo made repeated, thinly veiled attacks on the Mao-Lin line of "politics in command." Most notably, he told graduating classes at top-level military academies that soldiers ought not to be controlled by "empty-headed politicians" (*k'ung-t'ou cheng-chih-chia*).

Despite Lo's efforts to displace Lin, the latter was confirmed as Minister of National Defense and First Vice-Premier by the National People's Congress in January 1965. In June, military rank titles and insignia were abolished. Soviet-style uniforms disappeared, and every soldier, from Lin Piao to the lowliest recruit, again wore the simple *Chung Shan* suit and cap of the civil war era.

Lin Piao's speech of September 1965 (*Long Live the Victory of the People's War!*) cannot be fully appreciated without reference to Lo Jui-ch'ing and the other Chinese advocates of active anti-American solidarity in Indochina. By emphasizing self-sufficiency as *necessary* to a successful people's war, Lin could justify a relatively low level of involvement in Vietnam, while maintaining an ideologically defensible position vis-a-vis the Soviet Union.[114] Lin was speaking for Mao, and for those other Chinese leaders who believed that embroilment in the Vietnam War was dangerous and unnecessary. Mao, moereover, had ideological and domestic political reasons for continuing the Sino-Soviet dispute. To end it, or even suspend it, would have been to concede ideological points to his domestic opponents.

The "people's war" strategy of the 1960s was not totally defensive by any means, but was applied variously in different situations. With respect to Vietnam, Chinese aid and construction troops made a very considerable contribution to Hanoi's war effort, but the official Chinese line deemphasized this.[115]

A close corollary of Lo Jui-ch'ing's preference for an "offensive defense" in Vietnam was his approach to force modernization. As Chief of Staff he was acutely aware of the PLA's badly weakened condition in the early 1960s. One logical option was to seek renewed Soviet assistance. By advocating that option, of course, Lo opened himself to charges of underrating the ability of the Chinese people to create a self-sufficient modern defense industry. Lo was in a position to fully appreciate the weakness of the PLA. A particularly glaring weakness was the air force, which was smaller and more obsolescent in 1965 than it had been in 1950.[116] The situation in the other technical service branches was comparable.

Lo viewed war over Vietnam as necessary, or at least inevitable, by 1965. He therefore considered it vital to increase forces in being, rather than devoting resources to research and development (R&D) on weapons that would not become available for years to come. Lo's criticism of the defense industry was just that it was concentrating on R&D rather than on production. The subsequent accusation, that he hindered R&D, is plausible if (as seems logical) he wanted to divert resources into "medium technology" areas like anti-aircraft artillery, aircraft, and field artillery to defend Southern China from American attack.[117] Thus, NCNA was half correct when it claimed in 1967 that: "In the whole field of the national defense scientific research institutions they [Lo and P'eng Te-huai] made it a definite principle that 'scientific research is for production and must suit its needs.'" Lo Jui-ch'ing did hold that position, but P'eng did not. The official "Report on Lo's Mistakes" criticized him specifically for having questioned the work of the National Defense Science and Technology Commission (under Nieh Jung-chen): "Even after the appearance of our atomic bomb, he still frantically attacked our national defense scientific research work as going from data to data, from design to design, without completing anything."[118] The problem with data and designs is that they are useless for waging war now, and that was Lo's primary concern. His advocacy of Soviet aid and his criticism of the defense research establishment were both derived from his overriding concern with preparing the PLA for imminent war with the United States. Mao and Lin demonstrated that it was both possible and advantageous to avoid such a war, and they seem to have had the support of defense research "experts" like Nieh Jung-chen and Su Yü.

"People's war" rhetoric not only avoided involvement in Indochina, but also bought time for the further modernization of China's defenses. Once Lo himself was gone, the policies he had advocated could be judged on their own merits. That helped pacify some of his remaining supporters as well. After 1965, many of his proposals were implemented, just as many of P'eng's had been in 1960-64. Defense preparations were not expanded on a "crash" basis at the expense of advanced research, as Lo had proposed, but, "paeans to People's War notwithstanding, there is evidence that some of Lo's other proposals for the improvement of China's defenses were ultimately accepted. Overall troop strength was increased, defenses in the south reinforced, and aircraft production expanded. But these measures were implemented more slowly and geographically more widely than Lo had originally proposed."[119] Although Lo was criticized for "worshipping" foreign technology, the PLA continued to purchase some European, Japanese, and even Soviet technology, and to hire foreign experts throughout the 1960s.

Mao and Lin Piao worked out a pragmatic strategic policy: Nuclear weapons development was accelerated dramatically, and technological modernization of air, sea, and land forces continued without Soviet assistance. Meanwhile, renewed emphasis was given to the officially stated defensive policy of "people's war." While conventional armaments advances were studiously downplayed—and often not publicized at all,[120] the nuclear program was held up as a "victory of Mao Tse-tung Thought." Jonathan Pollack's fascinating analysis of Chinese "detonations statements" shows their general emphasis on the nuclear program as a vindication of Mao's thought and of the

Cultural Revolution.[121] Secondary emphasis was placed on each test as "a further step in the modernization of China's defensive capabilities and as an even greater achievement in terms of scientific and technological sophistication." Every step in the nuclear and rocketry programs was played for maximum internal political impact—occasionally at the expense of real progress.

Since the purge of P'eng Te-huai, then, a "balanced policy" of "people's war" *and* modernization has been in effect, with propaganda emphasis generally on the former and resource priority on the latter.[122] The policy called for gradual improvement in all forces, from militia to nuclear missiles. Events since the Cultural Revolution indicate that the "balanced policy" is still in effect, although the emphasis has shifted much more toward modernization of the regular forces. The real virtue of the policy was, and is, that it can encompass such shifts. These shifts inevitably affect the militia and the ground forces more than the technically sophisticated branches of the PLA, which are more constrained by long lead-times in weapons programs. That such long-term programs continued through the 1960s refutes the notion that "people's war" was ever taken seriously as a long-term strategy—even during the Cultural Revolution.

Lin Piao seems to have been the architect of the "balanced policy." His fall in 1971 came partly because his support for that policy began to waver, as he became embroiled in radical politics and an attempted power grab at the center.

FOREIGN MILITARY INVOLVEMENT IN THE 1960s

Firing Lo Jui-ch'ing did not make the Vietnam war go away. Chinese involvement continued to grow, largely in a futile effort to counterbalance the ever-expanding influence of the USSR among China's Asian neighbors. Despite the official "people's war" line, the expansion of foreign military aid, begun under Lo in about 1963, continued at a modest pace. In 1965, PLAAF commander Liu Ya-lou toured air force facilities in Albania, Pakistan, Cambodia, North Vietnam, and Romania, and made or renewed aid agreements with all but the last. Chinese aircraft were the backbone of the North Korean and North Vietnamese air forces until late 1966, when Soviet aid surpassed China's in both countries. Although there was no proven case of North Vietnamese interceptors operating from Chinese bases, there were very close ties between the two air forces, especially in 1964-66. PLAAF installations, especially the complex at Mengtzu in Yunnan, became major maintenance and repair points for the North Vietnamese air force.

During the US "bombing pause" of January 1967, companies of PLAAF fighter planes were rotated between China and Vietnamese airfields. Perhaps these visits were just intended as morale-building gestures, since the PLAAF cleared out as soon as the American raids resumed.[123] On the other hand, the presence of the Chinese interceptors was known to US intelligence, and obviously implied a threat of Chinese involvement in Vietnam's air defense. The resumption of the raids was clear indication that the US was willing to call China's bluff. That failed bluff (if that was the intent) was the closest the PLA came to "formal" involvement in the war. The contributions made by PLA construction and anti-aircraft units were not openly acknowledged until after the war ended.

Geographical proximity made US-Chinese confrontations inevitable, however, and there were sporadic armed clashes for nearly a decade. As early as 1963, there were reported naval confrontations in the South China Sea.[124] *Peking Review* claimed that twenty US pilotless reconnaissance drones had been shot down over Chinese territory from 1964 through February 1970. US manned aircraft penetrated Chinese airspace continually in those years, often by accident, but sometimes intentionally.[125]

The PLAAF was careful to avoid combat unless it was definitely over Chinese territory, and unless conditions otherwise favored the defense. Most American intrusions were simply protested. There were several useful results: First, the US was given no reasonable pretext to attack China. Second, the "siege mentality" was maintained throughout the Cultural Revolution with reports of new US provocations. Third, occasional reports of air victories helped buoy up military and civilian morale, and reaffirm the "invincibility of Chairman Mao's Glorious Military Thought."

Aerial incidents were especially numerous during the bombing raids along the Chinese border in 1966-67. Many were the inevitable and accidental results of poor navigation or bad weather, but some were provoked. Despite strict orders from Washington, American pilots were aggressively "going in harm's way" at that time. There was only one unsubstantiated claim that US aircraft ever actually *attacked* China,[126] but there were lots of intrusions. The Chinese proved that by collecting American fuel "drop tanks" all over Southern China.

In mid-1966, the US military somewhat reduced tensions (and the impact of Chinese propaganda) by reversing its policy of flatly denying any intrusions over China. On 21 August, the US Navy announced that two A6-A attack bombers had been chased out of Vietnam by interceptors, and were "presumed lost over China." Only five hours later did Radio Peking announce the downing of two "intruders." The Americans finally defused the situation by imposing a "bomb-line" well south of the Chinese border in later 1967. That made it much harder to stray over China—accidentally or otherwise—and the incident rate dropped sharply.[127]

American reconnaissance aircraft continued to fly over China until at least 1971, however. The Chinese only protested over-flights by conventional aircraft and drones. Those protests and therefore, presumably, the intrusions, ceased after the 1971 Sino-American "thaw."

More sophisticated American surveillance continued. Satellite and electronic surveillance has become an accepted fact of international politics. The far more blatant overflights by American SR-71 "Blackbird" strategic surveillance aircraft have never been admitted by either side. The Chinese never protested, because to do so would be to admit that the PLA is helpless to stop them. This serves to symbolize the dilemma of radical "Maoist" military thinking: Such violations of Chinese airspace can be prevented only by a "professional" modern air force. Such pragmatic considerations forced Mao Tse-tung to moderate his "guerrillaism" frequently, especially after 1945. The important distinction, between the hard-headed realism of Mao's military writings and the "military thought" attributed to him during the Cultural Revolution, is examined in the following chapter.

NOTES

1. Whitson, pp. 416-432 and 552.
2. Joseph Heinlein, "The Ground Forces," in *The Military and Politi-*

cal Power in China in the 1970's, ed. William W. Whitson (New York: Praeger, 1972), pp. 153-156.
3. Whitson, p. 479.
4. Heinlein, p. 156.
5. Whitson, p. 539.
6. Ibid., p. 14.
7. Ibid., p. 18.
8. Ibid., pp. 20-21.
9. Ibid., pp. 15-16 and 30-31.
10. Evans F. Carlson, Twin Stars of China (New York: Dodd, Mead, 1941), passim. Chu Teh's role in evolving PLA tactics is regaining official recognition: See Su Yu in CFCP, 1 December 1978, trans. in FBIS, No. 233, pp. E13-E18.
11. Whitson, pp. 40, 51-53, and 60.
12. The history of the Kutien speech was rewritten in January 1981 to make Chou, Chu Teh, and Chen Yi virtually coauthors of Mao's speech, and to gloss over their differences. JMJP, 19 January 1981, p. 5, trans. in FBIS, No. 013, pp. L6-L9.
13. Whitson, p. 437.
14. Ying-mao Kao, The People's Liberation Army and China's National Development (White Plains, NJ: International Arts and Sciences Press, 1973), pp. xxiv-xxvii.
15. Whitson, pp. 439-449.
16. Reprinted in Kao Ying-mao et al., The Political Work System of the Chinese Communist Military (Providence, RI: Brown University, 1971).
17. Whitson, p. 454.
18. The author wishes to thank Harvey Nelsen for pointing this out.
19. Whitson, pp. 57-59 and 441.
20. Ibid., pp. 57-68.
21. All quotations in the following discussion are from an article by Yang Ch'eng-wu contained in a monograph about Lin Piao, printed by the Branch Detachment of the "Ching-Kang-Shan" Corps of Peking Industrial University, trans. in TCC:P&S, No. 406 (JPRS, No. 41, 801), pp. 18-24. Like many JPRS translations, this one is very poor. Yang presumably wrote this in 1966 or 1967.
22. Whitson, p. 71.
23. Mark Selden, The Yenan Way in Revolutionary China (Cambridge, MA: Harvard UP, 1971), pp. 188 ff.
24. The Mao-Liu alliance and its implications are treated at length in John W. Lewis and Leonard Schapiro, "The Roles of the Monolithic Party under the Totalitarian Leader," CQ, No. 40 (October-December 1969), 39-64; and in Stuart R. Schram, "The Party in Chinese Communist Ideology," CQ, No. 38 (April-June 1969), 1-26.
25. Lewis and Schapiro, p. 41.
26. Mao's classic statement on mass-line leadership is On Methods of Leadership (1943; reprint Peking: FLP, 1955), p. 1.
27. Chalmers A. Johnson, "Chinese Communist Leadership and Mass Response," in China in Crisis, I, Book 1, eds. Ho and Tsou (Chicago: University of Chicago Press, 1968), pp. 401-402.
28. Mark Selden, "Yenan Legacy: The Mass Line," in Chinese Communist Politics in Action, ed. A. Doak Barnett (Seattle: University of Washington Press, 1969), pp. 117-120; and Robert C. North, Moscow and the Chinese Communists, 2nd ed. (Stanford, CA: Stanford UP, 1963), p. 197.

29. Selden, "Yenan Legacy," pp. 108-109.
30. Chalmers A. Johnson, *Peasant Nationalism and Communist Power* (Stanford, CA: Stanford UP, 1962), p. 60.
31. Selden, "Yenan Legacy," p. 136; and John Gittings, *The Role of the Chinese Army* (New York: Oxford UP, 1967), p. 56.
32. Jerome Ch'en, *Mao and the Chinese Revolution* (London: Oxford UP, 1965), p. 249; and Mao Tse-Tung, *On Production Work by the Army for Its Own Support and On the Importance of the Great Movements for Rectification and for Production* (1945), in Vol. III, *Selected Works* (Peking: FLP, 1965), p. 326; the latter is cited hereafter as *SW* III.
33. Selden, "Yenan Legacy," p. 136.
34. This, and all the following quotations, are from Mao, *On Production Work*, pp. 60-61.
35. Selden, "Yenan Legacy," p. 145.
36. Boyd Compton ed., *Mao's China* (Seattle: University of Washington Press, 1952), p. xxxiii.
37. Johnson, *Peasant Nationalism*, pp. 253-254; and *The Chinese Communist Movement: A Report of the United States War Department, July 1945*, ed. Lyman P. Van Slyke (Stanford, CA: Stanford UP, 1968), pp. 49-50.
38. Franz Schurmann, *Ideology and Organization in Communist China*, pp. 415-416.
39. Ibid., p. 427.
40. Ibid., p. 416; also see Israel Epstein, *Unfinished Revolution in China* (Boston: Little, Brown, 1947), pp. 283 ff., for an excellent account of the "unity of arms and work" and its implementation.
41. Mao, *On Production Work*, p. 328.
42. Ibid., p. 325.
43. US War Department, *The Chinese Communist Movement*, pp. 54-58; John Gittings, *Role*, pp. 56-57; and Selden, "Yenan Legacy," p. 145.
44. Statistics on Red Army growth in 1937-46 are in Jerome Ch'en, pp. 246-252 and 365.
45. Whitson, pp. 79-83 and 86.
46. See, for example, K'o Shu, "The Ten Great Principles of Operation are Forever Radiant," *JMJP*, 23 August 1974, trans. in *SPRCP*, No. 5695, pp. 177-189.
47. Whitson, pp. 84 and 86.
48. Ibid., p. 87.
49. Whitson, p. 92; and Richard M. Bueschel, *Communist Chinese Air Power* (New York: Praeger, 1968), pp. 19-20.
50. Whitson, pp. 91-93.
51. Gittings, *Role*, Chapter I.
52. The best analysis of the Chinese intervention is still Allen S. Whiting, *China Crosses the Yalu* (New York: Macmillan, 1960).
53. *Ta P'i-p'an T'ung-hsun* [Big Criticism Bulletin] (Canton), 5 October 1967, trans. in *SCMP*, No. 4124, p. 2.
54. Gittings, *Role*, Chapter XI; Schurmann (pp. 267 ff.) contends that Kao represented a major challenge to Peking's rule.
55. Whitson, pp. 93-94 and 524.
56. Alexander George, *The Chinese Communist Army in Action* (New York: Columbia UP, 1967), passim, especially chapter 4.
57. Whitson, pp. 443-444 and 452.
58. Samuel B. Griffith, *The Chinese People's Liberation Army* (New York: McGraw Hill, 1967).

59. *Ta P'i-p'an T'ung-hsun* [*Big Criticism Bulletin*] (Canton), 5 October 1967, trans. in *SCMP*, No. 4124, p. 3.
60. Gittings, *Role*, Chapter IV; and Whitson, pp. 94-95 and 452.
61. Kao, p. xli; also see "Hold High the Great Red Banner of Mao Tse-tung Thought and Resolutely and Thoroughly Implement the Political Work Regulations," *CFCP*, 8 May 1963, trans. in Kao et al., pp. 83-84.
62. Bueschel, pp. 28-29.
63. Cheng Mien-chih, "The Organization and Equipment of the Chinese Communist Infantry," *I & S*, July 1967, p. 20.
64. Whitson, p. 473; Bueschel, p. 27; and refugee informant.
65. Borbrow, 151. (This article contains an excellent historical overview of officer's training and criteria up through 1964, and especially for the post-1949 period; pp. 143-152.)
66. "Wicked History of Big Conspirator, Big Ambitionist, Big Warlord P'eng Te-huai," compiled by Red Guards of Tsinghua University (November 1967), trans. in *CB*, No. 851 (26 April 1968), p. 10; and Whitson, p. 99.
67. Schurmann, p. 562.
68. Alice L. Hsieh, *Communist China's Strategy in the Nuclear Era* (New York: Prentice-Hall, 1962), p. 27.
69. James R. Townsend, "Intra-Party Conflict in China: Disintegration in an Established One-Party System," in *Authoritarian Politics in Modern Society*, eds. Samuel P. Huntington and Clement H. Moore (New York: Basic Books, 1970), pp. 303-304.
70. "Regulations on the Service of Officers," (8 February 1955), trans. in *CB*, No. 312 (15 February 1955).
71. Ellis Joffe, "The Conflict Between Old and New in the Chinese Army," *CQ*, No. 18, (April-June 1964), 121.
72. Translated in Kao et al., pp. 40-41.
73. "Hold High the Great Red Banner of Mao Tse-tung's Thought, Thoroughly Criticize and Repudiate the Bourgeois Military Line," *PR*, No. 32 (4 August 1967), 44.
74. Joffe, "Conflict," pp. 134-136; and Ellis Joffe, *Party and Army* (Cambridge, MA: Harvard UP, 1965), pp. 114 ff.
75. Peking Radio (8 October 1978), trans. in *FBIS*, No. 201, pp. E19-E20.
76. Gittings, *Role*, pp. 160-161.
77. Joffe, "Conflict," pp. 134-136; Griffith, p. 227; Joffe, *Party and Army*, pp. 114 ff.
78. Kao, p. xlii.
79. "The Revolutionary Significance of Cadres Working as Soldiers in the Armed Forces," *August First Magazine*, 3 (1959), trans. in Kao, pp. 97-101.
80. Bueschel, pp. 54-55.
81. Joffe, "Conflict," pp. 130-131; and *Union Research Service*, 21, No. 21, p. 229.
82. Harvey W. Nelsen, "Regional and Paramilitary Ground Forces," in *Military and Political Power*, p. 141; and *Kung-tso T'ung-hsun* [*Bulletin of Activities*] No. 4, trans. in *The Politics of the Chinese Red Army*, ed. J. Chester Cheng (Stanford, CA: Hoover Institution, 1966), pp. 117-125; hereafter cited as *KTTH*.
83. Nelsen, "Regional and Paramilitary," p. 141.
84. Griffith, p. 228.
85. Townsend, pp. 287 and 291; and Schurmann, pp. 55-56.
86. Thomas W. Robinson, "Lin Piao as an Elite Type," in *Elites in the People's Republic of China*, ed. Robert A. Scalapino (Seattle: University of

Washington Press, 1972), pp. 154-156; and Whitson, pp. 329-330. Robinson emphasizes Lin's long and generally harmonious relationship with Mao, whereas Whitson emphasizes their differences.

87. For recent complementary revelations, see "Commander P'eng Smiles in the Ninth Heaven...," *JMJP*, 29 November 1980, p. 4, trans. in *FBIS*, No. 247, pp. L15-L18; and "The Death of General P'eng Te-huai," *Ta Kung Pao* (Hong Kong), 13 December 1980, p. 3, trans. in *FBIS*, No. 247, pp. U4-U6. On "Hai Jui Dismissed from Office," see Thomas S. Fisher, "'The Play's the Thing:' Wu Han and *Hai Jui* Revisited," paper presented at the California Regional Seminar, Center for Chinese Studies, University of California, Berkeley, 1 December 1979.

88. For the "Maoist" case against P'eng, see two articles on the subject in *JMJP*, 27 August 1967, trans. in *SCMP*, No. 4027, pp. 10-16; "Wicked History of P'eng Te-huai"; and editorials from *CFCP* and *JMJP*, 16 August 1967, trans. in *SCMP* No. 4004, pp. 1-9.

89. Hsieh, p. 180.
90. Whitson, p. 330.
91. "March Under the Red Flag," *NCNA* (English), 29 September 1959.
92. This discussion is drawn from Hsieh, pp. 180-181; and Gittings, *Role*, p. 243.
93. *NCNA*, 21 November 1961, trans. in *SCMP*, No. 2540, pp. 1-3.
94. John W. Lewis, "China's Secret Military Papers," *CQ*, No. 18 (April-June 1964), 71.
95. *JMJP*, 20 July 1961, trans. in *URI*, 1961 ed., 2, p. 135-136.
96. A special rectification campaign was directed at officers and their dependents in the first half of 1961, stressing "democracy," political education, and the class background of officers. Political supervision of officers was steadily increased. Joffe, *Party and Army*, p. 140.
97. *URI*, 1961 ed., 2, p. 137.
98. Joffe, *Party and Army*, pp. 141 ff.
99. Richard E. Gillespie and John C. Sims, Jr., "The General Rear Services Department," in *Military and Political Power*, p. 200.
100. Bueschel, pp. 54-55 and 76-80.
101. Joffe, *Party and Army*, pp. 142-143.
102. Schurmann, pp. 504 and 532-533; Kao, p. xlvi; and Ralph L. Powell, "Commissars in the Economy," *AS*, 5, No. 3 (March 1965), 126-128 and 130 ff.
103. Whitson, p. 368.
104. Harvey W. Nelsen, "Military Forces in the Cultural Revolution," *CQ*, No. 51 (July-September 1972), passim.
105. *NCNA* (English), 15 September 1967, in *SCMP*, No. 4025, p. 8; and in *PR*, No. 32 (4 August 1967), 37.
106. "Basic Differences Between the Proletarian and Bourgeois Military Lines," *PR*, No. 48 (24 November 1967), 15.
107. *KTTH*, No. 2, pp. 35-36.
108. "Report of the CCP CC Work Group 'Concerning the Problem of Lo Jui-ch'ing's Mistakes,'" [*Chung-kung Chung-yung Kung-tso Hsiao-tsu 'Kuan-yu Lo Jui-ch'ing Tso-wu Wen-t'ite Pao-kao*], 30 April 1966, reprinted from Red Guard sources in *Yearbook '73*, Book II, Section 7, p. 16; hereafter cited as "Report on Lo's Mistakes"; and *PR*, No. 24 (14 June 1968), 18.
109. Trans. in Kao et. al.
110. Ch'en Hsi-to, "The Militia... in the 'Great Cultural Revolution,'" *FCYP*, 30 April 1970, trans. in *TCC*, No. 111 (JPRS, No. 50, 926), p. 11; also see *NCNA* (English), 12 October 1978, in *FBIS*, No. 199, p. E1.

111. "Report on Lo's Mistakes," p. 15.
112. Schurmann, pp. 555-557. The best discussion of the debate over China's Vietnam policy is Donald Zogoria, *Vietnam Triangle* (New York: Praeger, 1967).
113. "Report on Lo's Mistakes," pp. 16-19.
114. This was first pointed out by David P. Mozingo and Thomas W. Robinson in *Lin Piao on People's War* (Santa Monica, CA: RAND, 1965).
115. For example, see Chou En-lai's remarks quoted in *Wen-ke Fengyung* [*Cultural Revolution Storm*] (Canton), No. 2 (February 1968), trans. in *SCMP*, No. 4148, p. 5.
116. Bueschel, pp. 72-74.
117. Charles Horner, "The Production of Nuclear Weapons," in *Military and Political Power*, p. 246.
118. "Report on Lo's Mistakes," p. 117. See chapter 6.
119. Harry Harding, "The Making of Chinese Military Policy," in *Military and Political Power*, pp. 379-380.
120. Only after Mao Tse-tung's death did the PRC admit the existence of a new family of infantry weapons, a nuclear submarine, the Chinese-made MiG-21 (F7) fighter, or the Chinese-designed FANTAN aircraft, all designed in the 1960s.
121. Jonathan D. Pollack, "Chinese Attitudes Towards Nuclear Weapons, 1964-1969," *CQ*, 50 (April-June 1972), 244-271, especially 247.
122. The following draws heavily on Harding, p. 381.
123. Bueschel, pp. 82-84 and 89-90.
124. "Political Department of South China Sea Fleet Remarks on T'ien Ming," *Hung-ch'i Lien-wei* [*Red Flag United Forces*] (Canton), 12 February 1968, trans. in *SCMP*, No. 4133, p. 5.
125. *PR*, No. 36 (1 September 1967), 6.
126. *NCNA* (English) Nanning, 19 September 1967, in *SCMP*, No. 4026, p. 29: "U.S. Imperialist planes repeatedly intruded over Kwangsi, bombed and destroyed houses and the farmland of people's communes, killed draft animals and wounded commune members." Kwangsi is full of military targets, so why bomb a commune? The "bombs" were probably empty auxilliary fuel tanks.
127. Bueschel, pp. 90 ff.

3
"Maoism"

In the preceding chapter, we saw that Mao Tse-tung's vision of a highly politicized guerrilla army was by no means unchallenged prior to 1949. The development of the PLA was also shaped by leaders with more conventional military ideas. The interplay of these currents of military thought, and the vicissitudes of the 1927-49 period, produced various compromises. Mao's ideal was most closely approached during the Yenan period, while the civil war period (1945-49) saw a strong trend toward a more conventional "military line." The 1950s saw the latter trend reinforced by the Korean War, Soviet influence, the professionalizing influence of modern weapons, and the generally routinizing trend in Chinese government and society.

In 1959, with the replacement of P'eng Te-huai as Minister of Defense by Lin Piao, Mao began his counterattack against "revisionism." By 1964, the stage was set for the Great Proletarian Cultural Revolution (GPCR)—Mao's spectacular campaign to regain personal power and to rekindle China's social and political revolution. Chapter 4 will trace the role of the PLA in the GPCR. First, though, we must consider the "Maoism" of the GPCR and the issues it raised with respect to the military.

MAO AND "MAOISM"

"Maoism" has come to be identified with the radical rhetoric of the Red Guards and the official Chinese press during the Cultural Revolution (1965-69). Viewed from the outside world in the early 1980s, it is easy to dismiss "Maoism" as artificial and downright silly. It therefore might be appropriate to ask why the subject is addressed here at such length. The reason is that, while "Maoism" may seem phony to us, it was all too real to the Chinese, and to Chinese officers, during the Cultural Revolution. They experienced radical "Maoism" carried to its (il)logical extremes, and saw many die from its excesses. The depth of that trauma on China is still evident in the constant references to the "Malicious influence of Lin Piao and the 'gang of four.'" Like other relatively professional groups, the officer corps is particularly interested in erasing "Whateverism" (as it is now often called). There remains, in 1980, a genuine fear that if "Whateverists" got another chance (which is unlikely, but not impossible), they would reassert radically anti professional practices in the name of Mao Tse-tung. It is therefore useful to examine radical "Maoism" in order to fully appreciate the continuing concern, as well as the past trauma.

Of more immediate importance, lingering "Maoism" is officially, and quite correctly, recognized as an obstacle to the "four modernizations." The standards and terminology of "Maoism" were legitimately rooted in the revolutionary experience, and were reiterated long and loud from 1965 to 1976. They were ubiquitous and inescapable. Not even moderate, professionally oriented officers who were persecuted by the radicals were immune. In 1981, many officers still unconsciously tend to apply the standards of "Maoism" and think in its terms. This is the truth behind the rhetoric about the "lingering influence of Lin Piao and the gang of four."[1]

It is well to keep open the question of whether "Maoism" can rightly be identified as what Mao Tse-tung always thought, or ever thought. Mao's critics have often characterized him as impractical and dogmatic; yet he dealt with massive real-world problems for over six decades and was, at the end of his life, the most powerful and successful charismatic political leader in the world. It is, prima facie, erroneous and simplistic to label him "impractical" or "unrealistic."

Like the collected writings and sayings of other great men, the works of Mao can be selectively emphasized and interpreted. This is particularly true of Mao, because he lived so long, and did and said and wrote so much. He was faced with a wide range of concrete leadership problems which required flexible tactics and, often, doctrinal compromise. Precisely because he was a practical leader for so long, therefore, his works can be selectively quoted to justify virtually anything—even practical measures made wildly impractical by subsequent events. It is necessary, therefore, to try to distinguish the "Maoism" of the GPCR from what Mao himself really thought, and *when* he thought it. Even more importantly, we must compare what Mao the political philosopher said for the record with what Mao the practical politician did.

We are specifically concerned here with Mao's military thought. Since he was vitally concerned with military affairs throughout his career, the corpus of his military writings is quite substantial, spanning the years from the Autumn Harvest Uprising in 1927 to the mid-1970s. That period saw the military force at his disposal grow from a few peasants with spears and muskets to the largest army on earth armed with nuclear weapons. It is therefore quite easy to quote selectively from his military writings, because they addressed such a wide variety of problems and circumstances.

The spokesmen of radical "Maoism" during the GPCR (notably Lin Piao, Ch'en Po-ta, and Chiang Ch'ing) created a highly distorted version of Mao's earlier military and political thought. Mao himself encouraged this for tactical political reasons.

Discipline

An example of the distortion of Mao by "Maoism" is seen in the "Maoist" attitude toward military discipline. In November 1967, *CFCP* castigated the doctrine of "absolute subordination" to discipline, which Liu Shao-ch'i advocated in his *How to Be a Good Communist* (July 1939). True, said *CFCP*, the army and party must have discipline and avoid anarchy, and democracy must be under central guidance. But no one must ever obey "wrong" orders. The key is that any order not in accordance with Mao Tse-tung Thought must not be obeyed.[2]

In June 1968, a series of articles appeared in *Peking Review*, praising Men Ho, a "model" political commissar who had recently suffered a martyr's death. A former regimental staff officer recalled that in 1964, Men Ho had ignored the orders to emphasize Lo Jui-ch'ing's "crack fighter squad" training program, and had kept up heavy emphasis on political training instead. The 1968 articles praised Men Ho for this insubordination (which was "correct" in terms of 1968 politics), and for having refused, on occasion, to wear his officer's insignia.[3]

Even more extreme was the story, carried by *CFCP* in 1967, of a company political instructor named Liao Ch'u-chiang. In 1964 an investigating team reported that Liao's company was "backward" in military training, and ordered it to "rectify" itself by emphasizing "application." Instead of doing so, Liao and the company supposedly redoubled their political study and contemptuously denounced Lo Jui-ch'ing. Furthermore, the unit submitted a false report about its completion of the "rectification." "If you [Lo Jui-ch'ing] say this is 'fabrication,'" boasted the article, "Then this 'fabrication' is very fine!"[4]

Both of these stories were written after the purge of Lo, during the high tide of radical "Maoism," and, with the benefit of hindsight, were probably distorted considerably. The "Maoist" message, however, was clear: Disobedience of military orders is necessary when and if subordinates don't happen to think they conform to Mao's thought. Beyond that, Men and Liao—both of them officers, and political officers at that—were praised for holding the incumbent PLA Chief of Staff up to ridicule before their troops. This is surely as non-professional (and non-Leninist) an approach to military discipline as can be imagined.

Beyond mere disobedience, "Maoists" actively encouraged mutiny against allegedly "revisionist" military superiors. Mao himself was partly responsible for this search for "capitalist roaders" in the ranks of the PLA. For years his established strategy was to blame failures and problems on "internal enemies," a strategy being perpetuated by his successors. Lin Piao and the "gang of four" are only the latest in a long line of "internal enemies," "infiltrators," and "saboteurs" reaching back through Liu Shao-ch'i and Kao Kang to Wang Ming and Li Li-san.

Public denunciation of such persons has always been *post hoc*. No one below Central Committee level would dare to take the lead—especially not in the official press. It was one thing to describe, in 1968, having denounced and disobeyed Lo Jui-ch'ing, but it would have been something else indeed to have actually done so in 1964. All such tales must be taken with a large grain of salt: They reflect current politics, not real history. In 1975, for example, the official press asked us to believe that the brilliant conquest of Northeastern China in 1946-48 was carried out by the soldiers of the Fourth Field Army in defiance of the orders of their commander, Lin Piao, who was supposedly trying to sabotage the campaign.

There was always a contradiction between Leninist discipline and an anarchist conception of democracy in Mao's writings, and he was rather opportunistic in his emphasis. For example, emphasis on low-level initiative and on making adjustments to local conditions in implementing orders dates from May 1930—when he was in opposition to Li Li-san, the CC, and to his own generals. Mao's conception of decentralized execution gave military leaders a great deal of flexibility, but also helped give rise to "mountain-topism" (*shan-t'ou chu-yi*).[5] Whenever "mountain-topism" threatened Mao's own power, he reemphasized discipline, centralization, and organization.

Motivation

The "Maoism" of the Cultural Revolution held a similarly radical opinion on the motivation of the individual soldier. Lo and P'eng were denounced for believing that "the higher the level of one's technique, the greater one's courage," and that "combat effectiveness means weapons plus technique." This view of the sources of combat morale is truly professional, and has been confirmed repeatedly by studies of American, British, German, and Soviet soldiers. Confidence in one's weapons, and in the skill and dependability of one's leaders and comrades, has been found to be the universal basis of battlefield morale.

The "Maoist" view, however, was that "a high level of techniques stems from great courage. This courage attests the revolutionary fighters' boundless loyalty to Chairman Mao and their possession of ... high political consciousness."[6] Heroes in post-1949 Chinese literature reflect this "Maoist" vision. They are motivated almost exclusively by revolutionary passion and/or revenge.

During the 1960s, a principal device for creating high military and civilian morale was the "emulation campaign," which held up "model heroes" and "revolutionary martyrs" as inspirational examples. Typically, these heroes (like Lei Feng and Norman Bethune) gave up their lives to protect state property, fellow soldiers, or (most often) the common people. Mao himself originated hero emulation during the Yenan period, with his essays "In Memory of Norman Bethune" (December 1939) and "Serve the People" (September 1944). The new heroes introduced during the GPCR, however, often died needlessly—by disregarding safety precautions or simply by charging blindly into hopeless situations. Men Ho, for example, died in early 1968 when home-made rockets, being used in an attempt to seed rain clouds, exploded. His heroic sacrifice in muffling the explosion with his body was not at all overshadowed by his incompetence in firing the rockets in the immediate proximity of peasants who were mixing explosives and assembling more rockets. Any American or Soviet officer who caused such a stupid disaster and survived would be court-martialed. Perhaps even harder to accept is the "heroism" of a platoon of soldiers from PLA Unit 6011 who overloaded a leaky boat with themselves and a group of Red Guards and set out across the Yangtze River in 1967. When the boat began to disintegrate, and several Red Guards fell in, a number of soldiers, in a seizure of revolutionary fervor, jumped in to "rescue" them—disregarding the minor technicality that they (the soldiers) didn't know how to swim. Needless to say, several soldiers drowned. All became "model heroes"—including the platoon leader, who had been responsible for the safety of the Red Guards as well as his men; but had believed that Chairman Mao's Thought would calm the river, hold the boat together, and overrule Archemedes' principle. Several other units were even praised for dashing in under rock-slides and avalanches, though the only apparent results were several deaths.[7] The main characteristic of the "Maoist" hero of the 1960s was this foolhardy obsession with daring to face danger—even if for no good reason.

The tales of such heroes during the Cultural Revolution were undoubtedly the result of embroidering the facts in most cases. But it also appears that emulation campaigns did encourage such "heroics" by soldiers who wished to win fame and reputation.[8] We may well suspect that honorific titles and posthumous glory remain as desirable in Chinese society as they have been for centuries.

Mao himself never glorified useless sacrifice, however. On the contrary, he penned the dictum that all military principles "grow out of the one basic principle: to strive to the utmost *to preserve one's own strength*, and destroy the enemy."[9]

The "Magic Weapon of Mao's Thought"

"Maoism" also distorted Mao on the issue of "mind over matter." For example, Mao's teaching to "fight no battle unprepared, fight no battle you are not sure of winning," is excellent advice. Important military thinkers from Sun Tzu down to Liddel-Hart have all given the same counsel. Yet "Maoism" reduced preparation for battle to mental (i.e., ideological) preparation: One has only to convince oneself that he can overcome all material circumstances by ideological fervor, and the battle will be won by "the magic weapon" of Mao Tse-tung's Thought.[10]

It is true that Mao always emphasized the importance of politics, organization, tactics, and courage in offsetting the enemy's material superiority. He did so of necessity, because his soldiers almost never enjoyed even material parity with their enemies. But the extreme "mind over matter" doctrine of "Maoism" distorted Mao badly, making spirit so all-powerful as to nullify material conditions and to make good tactics unnecessary. A veteran of the 1969 border fighting declared:

> You [Soviet revisionists] fight with your "mechanization" and we with our revolutionization; you exert your superiority and we exert our superiority. No matter how many "tortoise shells" [i.e., tanks] the enemy has and no matter what superiority it may possess in "mechanization," it cannot escape being severely beaten like it was on the Chenpao Island! Courage and fearlessness in the face of death are an incomparably powerful spiritual atom bomb. It is the logic of history that revolutionization is bound to triumph over "mechanization!"[11]

Another soldier, a young recruit in March 1969, wrote:

> Facts proved that [with] the revolutionary spirit of fearing neither hardship nor death, new fighters who have never fought before and commanders who have had no experience in directing a battle can fight and direct a battle well. Some comrades asked us new fighters how was it that we were able to fight so brilliantly? Our answer was: Because we have a bitter hatred for Soviet revisionism and cherish boundless loyalty to our great leader Chairman Mao.[12]

Given such an attitude toward the inevitable victory of political ardor over weaponry, an obvious corollary is that military hardware and expertise are simply unnecessary. It was declared in 1969 that the Soviet Army "like all reactionary armies" has to rely on iron and steel to bolster its morale because it "has long since forfeited the political superiority of a proletarian army." It therefore has no choice but to "Have blind faith in 'tortoise shells' and make a fetish of weapons."[13]

One fairly consistent theme in the "Maoist" denigration of modern weapons and expertise was that they were "foreign." Even in cases involving aerial or naval combat, the assertion was frequently made that victory was achieved by "refuting the theory that weapons, foreign rules and regulations and 'experts' are all-powerful," and by ignoring "foreign" tactics, safety measures, and techniques. Instead, of course, Mao Tse-tung Thought was "placed in command." This usually meant charging in very close to the enemy while demanding more of weapons and equipment than they were designed to deliver. Sometimes, this attempt to use guerrilla tactics in the air and at sea worked, but the casualties were often high.[14] An air force pilot who downed a US plane in 1969 claimed that:

> All reactionaries make a fetish of weapons. They are advocates of the theory that weapons decide everything. With regard to the enemy's weapons and equipment, we must analyse them dialectically. Their radar can only detect things at a distance but not what is close. Their guided missiles can only attack far-off targets but not nearby targets. Their planes fly at high speeds but form a big angle when they turn. If we rush at an enemy plane, keep it in firing range, meet it face to face and bring our best close-range fighting skill into full play, then, in battle, when he has his way of fighting and we have ours, his guided missiles and radar will be ineffective .... Under such circumstances, his weapons will be nothing more than scrap-iron while we have our best skills in fighting close-range battles and battles of quick decision. With courage and a high level of skill, we will be able to give full play to our strong points of close-in fighting in the air and using them to attack the enemy's weak points. . . .

As Chairman Mao teaches us: "*Our chief method is to learn warfare through warfare,*" and therefore those who have no experience in fighting can win battles . . . . with Mao Tse-tung Thought as the spiritual atom bomb of infinite power, we can defeat all enemies. We will "*go all out and be sure to destroy the enemy intruders,*" whether they are the U.S. imperialists or the social-imperialists, whether they launch a conventional war or launch a large-scale nuclear war, whether they come by day or by night and whether they come by air or from the sea.[15]

The Universal Applicability of Mao's Thought

Another drastic departure of "Maoism" from Mao was the claim that Mao Tse-tung Thought was universally applicable. Mao himself always emphasized the necessity for each people to work out its own liberation based on its own situation. The "Maoist" claim of universality, however, was extended to quite specific aspects of the Chinese experience. The 1967 "Six-Day War" in the Middle East, for example, allegedly proved that reliance on conventional armies, weapons, and tactics is *never* correct:

> To defeat the armed attacks of imperialism and its lackeys, the oppressed nations and people can rely only on the theory, strategy and tactics of peoples war; no other strategy and tactics will work.
>
> This war against aggression proves that it will not do to place one's reliance on modern weapons. It will not do to rely on aircraft, tanks or long-range artillery. . . .
>
> In the past and today, military experts of the bourgeoisie and other exploiting classes have written volume after volume on military

science, but such books are of no use to the oppressed nations and people.[16]

Mao's *Problems of Strategy in China's Revolutionary War* (December 1936) was hailed as a great classic of military science which rendered all other thought on the subject obsolete, for it laid down "a complete set of invincible strategic and tactical principles." "The basic laws of China's revolutionary war," claimed *CFCP* in 1966, "Are also the universal laws of all revolutionary wars." Mao's military thought not only guided China's revolution, "but it is also the guiding principle for our future war against aggression."[17]

During the 1965-69 period, the Chinese press was filled with articles hailing the world-wide success of Mao's thought in guiding liberation movements. Guerrilla movements all over the world were credited with great victories, even in cases where the "movements" in question were so small as to be almost non-existent (as in Malaysia), or where they weren't even Marxist, let alone "Maoist" (as in northern Burma). History was rather boldly revised as well. The Malayan "Emergency" of the 1950s was defeated largely because the guerrillas were almost exclusively Chinese, while the Malays had backed the British authorities. According to the 1967 Chinese version, however, "people's war" had triumphed over imperialism in Malaya because all the people had supported the revolutionaries. Similarly, the official version of the Korean War was that, although the US "used every kind of modern weapon except nuclear weapons and bragged about their air and ground 'superiority' . . . the heroic Chinese People's Volunteers, together with the Korean People's Army, badly battered and routed them with rifles, bayonets, and hand grenades." Not only that, but the Chinese air force, armed with Mao's thoughts, had made US air superiority "a laughing stock."[18]

These extravagant claims must have been discomfiting to those Chinese who knew the true state of affairs in Korea, and who were aware that China was relatively weaker vis-a-vis the United States in 1969 than it had been in 1950-53.

People's War and the Revolutionary Army

If Mao Tse-tung's thought will guarantee victory in any kind of war against any enemy, it follows that the proper national defense strategy for China is guerrilla "people's war." There is little point in peacetime military training if "our chief method is to learn warfare through warfare." There is little reason to invest in modern weapons if one believes that "no matter how powerful the enemy's weapons are, they are not as powerful as Mao Tse-tung Thought." On the contrary, "the most effective weapon in defending the motherland and defeating the enemy is to persevere in arming the masses with Chairman Mao's thinking on people's war, make everyone a soldier and do a good job in building up a joint defense by both armymen and civilians."[19]

"People's war" is also the strategy best suited to the accomplishment of the army's non-military tasks. As we have seen, Mao emphasized the multi-functionality of the Red Army from the late 1920s on. It was to be a fighting force, a political force, and an economic production force. The need for tight political control followed from this. Military participation in political and economic work made day-to-day party direction imperative, above and beyond the obvious need to assure the army's loyalty. As in all of Mao's thinking, there is a "unity of opposites" in the way the military is to be run. A balance must be maintained between military expertise and political ardor. Deviation too far toward the "right," in the form of excessive concentration on the military role, is to be avoided. Similarly, "left" deviation toward excessive political or economic activity must be avoided. The optimum "red-expert" balance varies greatly according to circumstances, and the maintenance of a correct balance may be thought of as "civil-military relations" insofar as Mao envisioned "civil-military relations" at all.[20]

A totally "expert," apolitical army would always have been as inadmissible to Mao as would an army incapable of fighting. We have seen (Chapter 1) that a highly professional officer corps concentrates its energies on the management of violence, and leaves politics to civilians. It "stands ready to carry out the wishes of any civilian group which secures legitimate control within the state."[21] This was another reason for Mao to resist the professionalization of the Chinese officer corps. An apolitical officer corps would back any "revisionist" or reactionary group which gained control of China; and that was a possibility Mao could not tolerate. Furthermore, like all Marxists, he viewed an "apolitical" army as an impossibility.[22] From the very birth of the Red Army, he maintained that if the army were not "red," it would necessarily be controlled by counterrevolutionaries. According to an official statement of 1967, "In the final analysis, the struggle between the two miltiary lines ["red" and "expert"] is a struggle between the proletariat and the bourgeoisie for power over the armed forces."[23] Mao, like European aristocrats, American liberals, and Soviet communists before him, assumed that the only alternative to subjective civilian control by his party is subjective civilian control by his principal socio-political enemy.

Like Lenin and Trotsky before him (and much more persistently), Mao tried to minimize the distinction between the military and society. This was explicitly given as the reason for the abolition of insignias of rank in the PLA in 1965.[24] Edward Dreyer notes, in fact, that although most military officers continued to be promoted from within the PLA, the abolition of rank made officers theoretically interchangeable with the general body of cadres.[25] A logical corollary to Mao's 1958 slogan "Everyone a soldier" would be "Every cadre an officer."

A further reason why Mao insisted on the continuing politicization of the PLA is the military's role in politicizing the Chinese people. According to a 1967 statement in *CFCP*, the purpose of "giving prominence to politics" in the PLA "is definitely not confined to doing military and other work well [but rather is] revolutionizing people's thinking. . . ."[26]

Radical "Maoism" not only asserted that politics is prerequisite to technical expertise, but that technical training is of "secondary" importance. In its 1967 New Year's editorial, *CFCP* stated that the main criteria for PLA cadre promotion were (1) "Hold the great banner of Mao Tse-tung Thought high and be loyal to Chairman Mao and Mao Tse-tung Thought;" (2) "give prominence to proletarian politics and keep close contact with the masses;" and (3) "have revolutionary vigour and drive." The editorial added that "of course, the lesser points [e.g., expertise] must be taken note of, but the main thing is to judge by the essentials. . . ."

Those in China who questioned the doctrine of "giving prominence to politics" were under strong "Maoist" pressure after about 1958, and were denounced as "capitalist-roaders" during the Cultural Revolution. Throughout the tenure of Lin Piao as Minister of Defense (1959-71), there was continuous criticism of those (e.g., P'eng Te-huai and Lo Jui-ch'ing) who advocated the "bourgeois military line:" "They clamoured that if a person is good militarily, then he will naturally be good politically." Allegedly, "they openly put forward the absurd slogan 'let army headquarters handle outside matters,' in a vain attempt to abolish the leadership of the Party over the Red Army, do away with political organizations, negate politics and ideological work and lead the Red Army away from the leadership of the proletariat."[27]

"Capitalist-roaders," who hold that the army's primary concern should be military affairs, have clearly been numerous and influential since 1949. The remark, attributed to Lo Jui-ch'ing, that "politics cannot penetrate the skies or cross the seas,"[28] summarizes the attitude of many Chinese officers. There has been a strong and continuing consensus among a large proportion of the officer corps favoring modernization, regularization, specialization, and PLA disengagement from non-military activities.[29] In the 1960s, such ideas were considered to be fundamentally opposed to "The Military Thought of Chairman Mao":

> ... Our army is an armed body for carrying out the political tasks of the revolution and military affairs must be subordinated to politics. Our army is not only a fighting force. It is at the same time a working force and a production force.... In fighting our army must rely mainly on politics, on the consciousness and revolutionary spirit of man....[30]

In contrast to this "Maoist" doctrine, the "bourgeois military line" was closely identified with "Soviet revisionism." According to Lin Piao, "Their line in army building is the bourgeois line which ignores the human factor and sees only the material factor and which regards technique as everything and politics as nothing."[31]

The "Maoism" of the 1960s strongly implied that technical modernization necessarily means a drift toward "revisionism" and a loss of political purity. In fact, this notion was explicated at the time of the Sino-Soviet border clashes in 1969. Most of the official condemnation of P'eng Te-huai and Lo Jui-ch'ing, however, accused them of promoting the bourgeois military line "under the pretext of 'regularization' and 'modernization.'" This phraseology did not condemn regularization and modernization per se, but rather said that they had been misused, as a "pretext." Furthermore, modernization was a continuous trend during the Lin Piao years—all rhetoric to the contrary notwithstanding. Again, the dialectical relationship between politics and expertise seems to underlie the issue. Mao's military writings themselves have reflected the dialectical approach, emphasizing politics and "people's war" in times of military weakness (e.g., 1929-44) and emphasizing regularization in times of relative strength (e.g., 1946-49).

Just where Mao the philosopher stood on the issue is unclear; but as a practical matter, regularization and modernization in the PLA became politically sensitive only when they impinged on other and more fundamental questions of political power. In this regard, it is important to note that the overwhelming volume of criticism directed at P'eng Te-huai and Lo Jui-ch'ing did not come in 1959 and 1965, the years of their respective downfalls. Rather, it occurred in the summer of 1967, when Red Guards were attacking the PLA as a whole, in an attempt to impose a radical "Maoist" vision on Chinese society, and saw the PLA as the only remaining obstacle to that goal. Moreover, neither P'eng nor Lo was purged for advocating military regularization. P'eng challenged Mao's leadership over the Great Leap Forward. Lo attempted to undercut Lin Piao's authority as Minister of Defense, and challenged Mao's policies vis-a-vis the USSR and the American threat in

Vietnam.

Reliance on "people's war" in the 1960s gave rise to the assertion that "the focus of struggle between Chairman Mao's proletarian military line and the bourgeois military line is whether or not to rely on the masses in waging a revolutionary war."[32] Any suggestion that military technology and technique might be even equally as crucial to China's defense as "men armed with Mao Tse-tung's Thought" was denounced as "outright reactionary rubbish."[33]

This "mind over matter" approach of "Maoism" begs a brief comparison with fascism. Consider the following:

> Only by following Chairman Mao's instructions and putting "daring" and "doing" above everything else, and courageously plunging into the practice of war—tempering ourselves in the teeth of storm and learning to swim in swimming can we acquaint ourselves with the laws of war and master them.... On the basis of definite material conditions, we give full play to our subjective momentum. In this way we can become both courageous and wise heroes directing and staging a colourful and magnificent drama.[34]

Here we can identify several characteristic features of fascism: the glorification of action, and especially of battle, as opposed to reason; and the triumph of spirit and will ("subjective momentum") over material obstacles. Goebbels himself would have been hard-pressed to improve on this description of war as "courageous and wise heroes directing and staging a colorful and magnificent drama." In Cultural Revolution-style "Maoism" we also observe the deification of the "great leader," and a fixation on violence and glorious death bordering on nihilism.[35]

The fascistic complexion of "Maoism" was also evident in the belligerent foreign policy of the 1960s. In 1967, it was asserted that "From the point of view of class struggle, it is both natural and unavoidable that the US imperialists, Soviet Revisionists and reactionaries of all countries should unite and attack China." This situation was hailed as a "good thing," for it showed that China was pure and Red and revolutionary.[36]

> It is a great honour for the Chinese people that the U.S. imperialists, Soviet revisionists and the reactionaries of all countries—a handful of vermin—are wildly hostile to China and vainly try to "isolate" her.[37]

DOMESTIC ROLES OF A "MAOIST" ARMY

Mao's insistence that the army must be a "fighting force, a productive force, and a political force" implied important PLA domestic roles, even in peacetime. In some cases, this actually has resulted in unique military practices. In others, theory, propaganda, and practice have diverged considerably.

The Militia

Mao viewed the People's Militia as an integral part of China's defense forces, partly because it is necessary for "people's war."

To combine the building of a modern revolutionary army with

> large-scale militia training is a concrete application of the policy of "walking on two legs" toward the building of a national defense, a significant development of Chairman Mao's thought on the people's war under modern conditions.... Without a militia, our regular army would be like a river without a source, a tree without roots, or a general with only one arm, and thus could never fight a genuine people's war.[38]

Apart from this military role, the militia fills a number of others: It is useful as an "early warning net" along China's borders.[39] It also serves as a "shock force" for labor projects, and as a local security (i.e., police) force. Militarily, its value may be debatable (Krushchev is said to have described the Chinese militia as "a heap of flesh"), but its importance as labor pool and security force is undeniable.

The relationship of the PLA and the militia has varied considerably, but the militia has generally been an irritant to the regular army. From 1949 up to the Great Leap, the militia was under the direct control of local CCP committees at *hsien* (county) or *shih* (municipality) level. However, the PLA was responsible for providing arms and cadres for the People's Armed Departments (PADs), at the same administrative level. The PADs equipped and trained the militia, and supervised its military activities. During the Great Leap, the militia was heavily emphasized, and the PLA was ordered to divert massive resources to achieving the goal of "everyone a soldier." P'eng Te-huai and the army's commanders objected strenuously.

In April 1961, the PAD was placed officially under the dual control of the *hsien* (or *shih*) party committee and of the military subdistrict.[40] During the Cultural Revolution, the press generally referred to "the Liberation Army's militia units."[41] Indeed, it appears that most of the PADs, and therefore the militia, were solely responsible to the military regional commands from around 1966 or 1967 until at least 1973. The burden of militia work falls upon the miltiary regions and their forces. The burden of this task generally has been resented by PLA commanders, and the official press has constantly been at pains to defend the militia system.

A new phase of this ongoing controversy began shortly after the Tenth Party Congress in the fall of 1973. This controversy, described in chapter 5, revolved around the question of just who should control the People's Armed Departments: the local party committees or the regional PLA commands. The army's position reflected its perennial ambivalence toward the militia: It does not want to devote resources to the militia, but does want to maintain at least veto power over it.

If they had a choice, many PLA commanders would probably abolish the militia, and replace it with a modern-style system of military reserve forces. P'eng Te-huai attempted such a move in the 1950s. On the other hand, several very senior PLA leaders strongly reasserted the importance of the militia and of "people's war under modern conditions" during the summer of 1978.[42] This probably reflects an evolving divergence in view between the military-political "old warriors" in the MAC and their more professionalized subordinates in the operational units. As long as the defense of China may require a "luring deep" strategy (i.e., as long as the PLA lacks the power to stop a Russian invasion), the MAC still sees a need for militia. We shall return to this issue in a later chapter.

As long as the militia does exist, the PLA is anxious to prevent it from becoming a "counter-army army" like the Nazi SS or the Soviet KGB. It will therefore seek to maintain the control over the militia which it gained during the Cultural Revolution.

Socio-Cultural Roles

Militia work is not the only internal role of the PLA. Another is the political education and national "homogenization" of the soldiers. In an average year, some 900,000 people enter the PLA, while 900,000 others return to civilian life. They and their families are exposed to modern administration and organization, education, and technology. Soldiers are indoctrinated in the social and political values of the party, and learn to view the world from a Chinese national (rather than a regional) perspective. The PLA has spearheaded the regime's continuing drive for cultural unification. The national language (p'u-t'ung hua) is emphasized, for example—even in regional units. The impact of all this is carried back to civilian life by demobilized soldiers, who make up a substantial percentage of all civilian cadres.

The army's socialization role has been especially important—and difficult—in the strategically sensitive national-minority areas. The PLA and the media have long emphasized the importance of soldiers maintaining harmonious relations with the ethnic minorities along the borders. This is not only because the minorities are "class-brothers," but also for concrete military reasons. In border defense, "the most important thing is to do work with the fraternal non-Han nationalities," but "don't dominate by force."[43]

The PLA presence has been reinforced by the Production and Construction Corps (PCC) which has been mainly concentrated in national-minority areas. On the occasion of the establishment of the PCC of the Peking Military Region, the official communique stated one reason for doing so was to further unify the peoples of various nationalities.[44] Another stated mission of the PCC was to build a "strong political defense line" as well as a strong military defense. Both of these points can be interpreted to mean that the PCC, and the PLA generally, have an internal security mission vis-a-vis the minorities. In Inner Mongolia, "the development of the frontier regions" has meant, in practice, a massive influx of Han Chinese and their domination of the region. Apparently the military has been given a role in smoothing the way for Han civilians by pushing the acculturation of the Mongols, in addition to its more obvious police function. Both of these tasks must be handled delicately because "there is an important relationship between strengthening relations among nationalities and strengthening military-civilian defense" of the border.[45] Translated into practical language: If the Hans provoke too much resentment, there are forces beyond the border who stand ready to exploit it.

PLA Production: A Non-Issue

Conventional wisdom among western China scholars holds that economic production by the PLA has been a major bone of contention. Supposedly, military professionals have resisted this "Maoist" measure because it absorbs time and energy which could better be devoted to military training.[46] A close look at the evidence indicates that this is a non-existent issue.

To get a clear picture, we should distinguish several categories of PLA economic activity: PCC production, production for self-support, and assistance to the civilian economy.

The PCC (which is discussed in greater detail in chapter 5) consists mainly of civilians, who are organized along paramilitary lines and supervised by PLA cadres. It has three purposes: economic production, frontier defense, and the absorption of surplus labor from the cities. PCC units are controlled by the provincial governments and cadred by the Military Districts. They do absorb some PLA resources, but also provide a defensive screen along the border. The garrisoning of China's sparsely populated frontiers with self-sustaining military-agricultural communities is scarcely new. Chinese governments have practiced the system for centuries. In recent years, the regional PLA commands have been concerned mainly with the military aspects of the PCC, not its production work. PCC production is clearly not "PLA production" at all.

The second category of PLA economic activity is production for unit self-support. "Most field forces" reportedly produced enough meat and vegetables to feed themselves in 1967.[47] Many PLA organizations reportedly became self-sufficient in grain in 1968, while several even had surpluses.[48] In addition, it was claimed that "some are completely or mainly self-sufficient in grain, edible oil, coal, medicine and army horses."[49] This last claim is almost certainly true, since the PLA maintains a system of military stud-farms.

Self-sufficiency production is mainly directed at keeping the military budget down, just as it was in the early 1940s. "Maoists" claimed more for it than that, however: "Apart from supporting our state and easing the people's burden, this also speeds up the building of revolutionized and militant army units."[50]

When the Chinese press boasts about the PLA's contributions to the economy, the image projected is of neither the PCC nor self-support. Until recently, visitors to the 196th Infantry Division, the PLA's "show unit" near Peking, were shown shops where soldiers spent half their duty hours manufacturing electrical cable, while their dependents packaged pharmaceuticals. Clearly, such production is for the overall economy, not self-support. *Peking Review* and *China Pictorial* often picture rifles neatly stacked along a rice-paddy dike, while smiling soldiers, with sleeves and trousers rolled up, work shoulder-to-shoulder with smiling civilians. Many foreign observers have accepted this as an accurate picture of "typical" PLA economic production. It is the image Mao and his followers have cultivated since Yenan. It is a "Maoist" aspiration, however, not a fact.[51]

A careful examination of official statistics raises substantial doubt about the Maoist image (see Table 3.1). The highest official figure for PLA labor "furnished . . . to the economy" is 60 million man-days in 1958, the first year of the Great Leap. If we assume total PLA strength in that year to be 3.1 million men, and simply divide man-days by men, we arrive at a startling statistic: The average soldier devoted only 19.4 days to the economy in all 1958: That is the *highest* figure ever.

Peking's statistics are subject to further scepticism because, invariably, they are ambiguous about just what the overall figures include. Do they, for instance, include the PCC? It appears that they do not. If we assume that the PCC worked only a five-day work week in 1973 (which is *most* unlikely), it would have provided (3 million members times 260 days) 780 million man-days of labor. Since the official claim for "PLA labor" in the first half of 1973 was only 8.21 million man-days (and therefore presumably about 16.4 million for the full year), we must conclude the PCC labor is not included; since it was at least forty times the official claim for "PLA" labor.

What about production for self-support? Here, the claims are extremely ambiguous. Self-support production is, no doubt, beneficial to the economy; but it hardly jibes with the image projected by *China Pictorial*. Furthermore,

TABLE 3.1
Total PLA Economic Labor, 1957-79*

YEAR	MAN-DAYS (millions)	SECTOR OF ECONOMY	DAYS PER SOLDIER
1957	20	"furnished...to the economy"**	6.5
1958	60	"industry and agriculture"**	19.4
	59	"furnished...to the economy"**	19.0
1959	44	same	14.2
1960	46	same	14.8
1961	22	"industry and agriculture"***	7.1
	23	"furnished...to the economy"**	7.4
1963	8.5	"furnished...to the economy"**	2.74
1964-66	(nil)	same	(nil)
1967-72	---"Three Supports and Two Militaries" (see text)---		
1973	16.42	"local construction"****	5.4
1978	18-21(?)	Agriculture, Industry, and Disaster Relief	4-6(?)
1979	18-21(?)	same	4-6(?)
1949-79	15.3 avg.	"Agriculture production"*****	4.94 annually

Notes:
　　*Assuming 3.1 million men in PLA (excludes Production and Construction Corps)
　　**Ralph L. Powell, "Soldiers in the Economy," AS, 11, No. 8 (August 1971), 742-743.
　　***Ellis Joffe, "The Conflict Between Old and New . . .," CQ, 18 (April-June 1964), 137-138.
　　****"PLA Units Support . . .," PR, No. 35-36 (7 September 1973), 54.
　　*****NCNA, 28 September 1979, trans. in FBIS, No. 193, p. L26.

the figures presented in Table 3.1 hardly would account for "most" units being self-sufficient in anything, even if we assumed a very uneven distribution of labor among units. For the sake of discussion, let us assume that self-support labor is not included in the official claims either, and again consider the figures in Table 3.1. From a high of 19.4 days per soldier in 1958, PLA labor dropped to virtually none in 1964-66, and was only 5.4 days in 1973. Despite widespread calls to assist civilian production in 1978-79, scattered reports support estimates of only four to six workdays per soldier per year, at the very most.[52] In September 1979, NCNA officially claimed that since 1949, the PLA had contributed "more than 460 million workdays in support of agricultural production" (including machinery repair). Assuming average PLA strength of 3.1 million (which is charitably low), we derive an official claim to 15.3 million mandays per year, or only 4.94 workdays per soldier per year, on the average, in 1949-79 (see Table 3.1). Two striking conclusions are warranted:

1. PLA economic labor has never been very high—certainly nowhere near the "half-time production" claimed by the 196th Divison in 1967-76.
2. The steady decline after 1958 was not significantly reversed after the Cultural Revolution.

Still another problem is that in 1949-79, the PLA (on the average, and allowing for reorganizations), has had an average of about eleven divisions of railway construction troops, thirty-five regiments of combat and capital construction engineer troops, eleven regiments of telecommunications troops, and forty-two motor transport regiments.[53] Very conservatively, then, there are (assuming only 1,000 men per regiment and five regiments per division) at least 145,000 soldiers whose *primary mission* is economic production, construction, and services. If official statistics include engineer units constructing buildings, airfields, and highways; railroad troops building bridges and laying track; and telecommunications units erecting transmission lines, then PLA economic production claims are incredibly *low*.[54] If we again assume only a five-day work-week, these units alone would do (145,000 men times 260 workdays) 37.7 million man-days of work per year: over double the average claimed for the entire PLA. Even if these "productive" units devoted half their time to political and military training and administration, they could easily account for all of the PLA's economic contribution—and that is assuming only a five-day work-week in a country where civilians work six.

So, just to pursue the argument a bit further, let us not only exclude the PCC, but also the railroad and engineer and telecommunications and motor transport units. Further, let us assume the maximum published number of these "productive" troops: about 250,000 men.[55] That leaves (3.1 million minus 250,000) 2.85 million men in "non-productive" units: infantry and tank units, border guards, garrison troops, the air force and navy, etc. The results, which give the carefully nurtured "*China Pictorial* version" of PLA production the benefit of every possible doubt, are presented in Table 3.2. The smiling soldier worked shoulder-to-shoulder with the smiling civilian only 21 days in 1958, and an average of only 5.37 days annually since 1949.

Even here, we cannot leave the subject without mentioning two other problem areas: Several tens of thousands of PLA men and women are assigned to various research, development, and production facilities relating to military industry. Even more important, we should observe that a principal economic contribution of the PLA during the 1960s and 1970s has been in flood control and disaster relief.[56] Now, these are precisely the sorts of tasks that the engineering and transport units are most likely to be committed to, so their exclusion from the official figures seems unlikely. That means that the (lower) figures in Table 3.1 are probably much closer to actuality than those of Table 3.2.

During the period 1967-72, the PLA was heavily committed to "Three Supports and Two Militaries" (*san-chih liang-chun*) work. As many as two million soldiers were dispatched to schools, factories, communes, and governmental organs to support agriculture, industry, and the political "Left"; and to conduct military-political training and exercise military control. There are no figures available for PLA "economic labor" in those years. The overwhelming impression one gets from the literature of the period—both official and Red Guard—is that soldiers committed to the "Three Supports and Two Militaries" devoted virtually full time to military control, political

TABLE 3.2
Total PLA Economic Labor, 1957-79
(Excluding Railroad Engineers, Construction Engineers, Telecommunications Troops, and Motor Transport Units)*

YEAR	MAN-DAYS (millions)	SECTOR OF ECONOMY	DAYS PER SOLDIER
1957	20	"furnished...to the economy"**	7.02
1958	60	"industry and agriculture"***	21.05
	59	"furnished...to the economy"**	20.70
1959	44	same	15.43
1960	46	same	16.14
1961	22	"industry and agriculture"***	7.72
	23	"furnished...to the economy"**	8.07
1963	8.5	"furnished...to the economy"**	2.98
1964-66	(nil)	same	(nil)
1967-72	---"Three Supports and Two Militaries" (see text)---		
1973	16.42	"Local construction"****	5.76
1978	18-21(?)	Agriculture, Industry, and Disaster Relief	6.3-7.3(?)
1979	18-21(?)	same	6.3-7.3(?)
1949-79	15.3 avg.	"Agricultural production"*****	5.37 annually

Notes:
　　*Assumes 3.1 million men in PLA and 250,000 men in the excluded "productive" units. The latter figure, which is probably much too high, is derived from Leo Goodstadt, FEER, 29 November 1974, p. 30.
　　**Ralph L. Powell, "Soldiers in the Economy," AS, 11, No. 8 (August 1971), 742-743.
　　***Ellis Joffe, "The Conflict Between Old and New . . .," CQ, 18 (April-June 1964), 137-138.
　　****"PLA Units Support . . .," PR, No. 35-36 (7September 1973), 54.
　　*****NCNA, 28 September 1979, trans, in FBIS, No. 193, p. L26.

education, and peacekeeping. Here again, we have serious reason to wonder if the smiling soldier ever stacked his rifle, rolled up his sleeves, and went to work beside the smiling civilian (unless, of course, there was a photographer on the scene to coach him). In 1974, one of the author's colleagues interviewed over fifty refugees from the communes of Kwangtung province. *Not one* had ever *heard* of the PLA assisting in economic production.

Why then has so much been said and written about PLA production? The official line, that the PLA has made a substantial contribution to overall economic production, is clearly a myth—even if we give it every possible benefit of the doubt. In fact, since PLA labor has mostly been in the form of disaster relief and strategic construction, it has probably not differed significantly from similar military activities all over the world. The PLA simply does not devote much effort to assisting the civilian economy directly. It quite literally stays in garrison and tends its own garden. We may conclude that the great conflict over PLA economic production has been vastly overstated by foreign scholars who have uncritically taken Chinese propaganda at face value.

The PLA in Domestic Politics

An army oriented toward "people's war" is readily available for many civil roles. In Huntington's terms, it can be applied to "internal" and "situational" security tasks as well as external ones. In fact, far from being diversions from war preparation, many internal roles actually develop the very skills needed in the event the army must lead a protracted guerrilla war of resistance.[57] A 1970 Peking Review article pointed out that the "Three Supports and Two Militaries are the best preparation for a people's war."[58]

Ying-mao Kao has argued that Mao was bound to keep the PLA immersed in domestic politics so long as he insisted on "continuing revolution" in Chinese society. Continuing revolution is bound to provoke resistance from status quo elements ("revisionists," "class enemies"), so internal coercive power is a continuing necessity. The problem, says Kao, is to use the army without losing its loyalty or obedience.[59] The obvious solution, which Kao (and apparently Mao also) did not consider, is to establish an internal police force and leave the soldiers to soldiering. That is what Stalin did in the Soviet Union.

Mao drew the PLA into domestic affairs precisely because of its loyalty and discipline. Ironically, however, the more deeply it became involved in domestic politics, the more dangerously its loyalty and discipline were strained. Dreyer believes that this military dilemma is not new to China, but rather that it flows from the imperial past:

> As the PLA grows in power within the Chinese state ... its specifically military character becomes progressively diluted and increasing reliance is placed on the dogma of People's War and on the elements that constitute the imperial legacy. While the latter elements may also be traced to early Marxist military thinking, the Soviet Union and most other Communist countries have largely abandoned them in favor of a military system that provides for a great deal of professional autonomy. The survival of this institutional syndrome in China, therefore, indicates the strength of the Chinese historical tradition, which reinforces the Communist prejudice against a professional military .... [But] contemporary technology requires an expert, professional, and institutionally autonomous military establishment to provide effective defense.[60]

We have seen that "Maoism" was essentially a tactical device of the Cultural Revolution, which exaggerated and distorted much of Mao's military thought. However, the roots of "Maoism" were deep in the essential antimilitarism of Marx and Lenin, and in the Chinese tradition. Although the past few years have seen a strong repudiation of radical "Maoism," it is far too early to predict the abandonment of either Marxist-Leninist or traditional Chinese attitudes toward the military. Mao, Lin Piao, and the "gang of four" may be gone, but the leaders of China and of its army are still Marxists and still Chinese. Dreyer is quite right about the requirements of contemporary military technology, and also right about the significant political and cultural counterpressures.

NOTES

1. Peking Radio, 21 March 1981, trans. in *FBIS*, No. 056, pp. L8-L9.
2. *NCNA* (English), reprinted from *CFCP*, 3 November 1967, in *SCMP*, No. 4053, pp. 18-21.
3. *PR*, No. 24 (14 June 1968), 16-17.
4. *CFCP*, 28 October 1967, trans. in *SCMP*, No. 4056, p. 17.
5. Whitson, pp. 46-47.
6. "Heroic Air Force Man," *PR*, No. 31 (2 August 1968), 17.
7. For example, "Ten Devoted and Loyal Martyrs," *PR*, No. 14 (5 April 1968), 14-17.
8. *PR*, No. 35 (30 August 1968), 23-27.
9. Mao Tse-tung, *Problems of Strategy in the Guerrilla War Against Japan* (1938), in Vol. II, *Selected Works of Mao Tse-tung* (Peking: FLP, 1965), p. 81 (emphasis added); the latter is cited hereafter as *SW* II.
10. For example, "Chairman Mao's Military Thinking is the Magic Weapon in Defeating the Enemy," *PR*, No. 2 (9 January 1970), 15-17; and "Fearing Neither Hardship Nor Death," *PR*, No. 23 (6 June 1969), 12.
11. Huang Chuang-chih, "Defeat of 'Mechanization' by Revolutionization is the Logic of History," *PR*, No. 39 (26 September 1969), 35.
12. *PR*, No. 25 (20 June 1969), 15; and *PR*, No. 22 (30 May 1969), 13.
13. Huang Chuang-chih, pp. 34-35; and Hsu Lien-wen, "If They Insist on Fighting, We Will Keep Them company and Fight to the Finish," *PR*, No. 23 (6 June 1969), 16.
14. "Mao Tse-tung's Thought—The Invincible Weapon," *PR*, No. 30 (21 July 1967), 30-31; and Chang Yi-min, "Building the World's Strongest Navy," *PR*, No. 1 (3 January 1968), 41 and 43.
15. Sung Yi-min, "Mao Tse-tung's Thought Gives Us Exclusive Superiority," *PR*, No. 47 (21 November 1969), 11; "Fearing Neither Hardship Nor Death," p. 12; and "Heroic Air Force Men," p. 17.
16. Chou Tien-chih, "Lessons of the Arab War Against Aggression," *PR*, No. 37 (8 September 1967), 25 and 26; and "People's War is Invincible," *JMJP*, 7 July 1967.
17. "Study 'Problems of Strategy in China's Revolutionary War,'" *CFCP*, 29 December 1969.
18. For example, *PR*, No. 22 (30 May 1969), pp. 13-15.
19. Chien Hai-chin, "Infinite Might of Chairman Mao's Thinking on People's War," *PR*, No. 48 (28 November 1969), 8-9.
20. Kao, p. li.
21. Huntington, *The Soldier and the State*, p. 84.
22. *NCNA* (English), 15 September 1967, in *SCMP*, No. 4025, p. 10.
23. "Settle Accounts with P'eng . . . .," p. 15.
24. "Important Measure to Promote the Revolutionization of Our Army," *CFCP*, 25 May 1965, trans. in Kao, pp. 102-105.
25. Edward Dreyer, "Military Continuities: The PLA and Imperial China," in *The Military and Political Power in China in the 1970's*, p. 23.
26. This, and the following, is drawn from *NCNA* (English), 30 August 1967, trans. from *CFCP*, in *SCMP*, No. 4014, pp. 23-24.

27. Chang Hsu-chuan, "Advance Triumphantly Along Chairman Mao's Proletarian Line in Building the Army," PR, No. 42 (13 October 1967), 18.
28. Ibid., p. 19.
29. A good summary of the conflict between "Maoists" and "professionals" is in James Jordan, pp. 25-45; also see Borbrow; and Joffe, "Conflict."
30. "Hold High the Great Red Banner of Mao Tse-tung's Thought...," PR, No. 32 (4 August 1967), 43.
31. Lin Piao, "Long Live the Victory of People's War," reprinted in PR, No. 32 (4 August 1967), 32.
32. Chien Hai-chin, p. 9.
33. For example, Hung Tung-pin and Chi Yung-yao, "The Decisive Factor in War is People, Not Things," PR, No. 50 (12 December 1969), 22-24.
34. CFCP, 29 December 1966.
35. Huntington, The Soldier and the State, p. 92; and F.L. Carsten, The Rise of Fascism (Berkeley and Los Angeles: University of California Press, 1971), pp. 230-234.
36. "It's a Good Thing for Us that the Enemy Attacks China," PR, No. 35 (17 August 1967), 19-20. In the spring and summer of 1967 alone, PR reported official Chinese protests, warnings, and/or ultimata directed against the USA, the USSR, Burma, Thailand, Great Britain, the Ivory Coast, Nepal, Indonesia, India, Italy, Kenya, Israel, Czechoslovakia, Outer Mongolia, Japan, Ceylon, Yugoslavia, Malaysia, Greece, the Philippines, Tunisia, the UN, and the International Red Cross; plus dozens of nongoverning Communist parties.
37. PR, No. 22 (30 May 1969), 19.
38. "Fundamental Differences between the Proletarian ... and the Bourgeois Military Line," JMJP, 7 September 1967, trans. in Kao, p. 278.
39. "Army-People Joint Defense," [Chun-min lien-fang] HC, No. 10 (1973), 98-99.
40. KTTH, No. 19, p. 526.
41. For example, see the cases cited by Yu Yang, "People's Militia ...," FCYP, 9 (10 September 1968), 61-66, trans. in TCC, No. 33 (JPRS, No. 46, 920), pp. 1-12.
42. Nieh Jung-chen, "Speech to the National Militia Work Conference," (4 August 1978), in NCNA, 7 August 1978, trans. in FBIS, No. 154, pp. E1-E10; and Hsu Hsiang-ch'ien, "Heighten Vigilance, Be Ready to Fight," HC, No. 8 (1978).
43. "Army-People Joint Defense," p. 100; and "On the Grassands, Soldiers and Civilians are United as One," [Ts'ao-yuan Chun-min Hsin-hsin-hsiang-lien] HC, No. 2 (1973), 76-78.
44. Nei-meng-ku Jih-pao, 8 May 1969, in Chang Yun-t'ien, "The Establishment and Expansion of Communist China's 'Production and Construction Corps'...," CKYCYK, No. 3 (March 1970), 31-40, trans. in TCC, No. 108 (JPRS, No. 50, 719), p. 16.
45. "Army-People Joint Defense ...," p. 100. These themes were strongly reiterated in the official press in late 1980.
46. For example, Kao, p. xlii; and Gittings, Chapter VII.
47. NCNA (English), 30 December 1967, in SCMP, No. 4092, p. 28.
48. PR, No. 9 (27 February 1970), 29; and PR, No. 6 (23 February 1971), 18.
49. PR, No. 9 (27 February 1970), 29. Also see Peking City Service, 8 April 1979, trans. in FBIS, 20 April 1979, p. R1.
50. Ibid.

51. After a hiatus of several years, there was a reassertion of this myth in 1977-1980. See Foochow Radio, 30 July 1978, trans. in *FBIS*, No. 149, p. C2, and Haikow Radio, 1 August 1978, trans. in *FBIS*, No. 149, p. H8.

52. Tsinan Radio, 29 September 1978, trans. in *FBIS*, No. 191, p. G6; Changsha Radio, 29 July 1978, trans. in *FBIS*, No. 150, p. H5; Canton Radio, 28 July 1978), trans. in *FBIS*, No. 150, p. H2; Ch'ang-ch'un Kirin Prov. Svc., 11 February 1980, trans. in *FBIS*, No. 36, p. S2; Hangchow Chekiang Prov. Svc., 8 January 1980, trans. in *FBIS*, No. 007, p. O3; *NCNA*, 19 January 1980, trans. in *FBIS*, No. 015, p. O1; Taiyuan Shansi Prov. Svc., 18 February 1980, trans. in *FBIS*, No. 045, p. R1; Foochow Fukien Prov. Svc., 2 December 19079, trans. in *FBIS*, No. 240, p. O2; and Shenyang Liaoning Prov. Svc., 15 January 1980, trans. in *FBIS*, No. 015, p. S3.

53. These figures are, overall, a bit low.

54. Western observers in Peking in 1978 reported almost all major construction involved "military engineer" troops. *AFP* (Hong Kong), 4 October 1978), trans. in *FBIS*, No. 194, p. E13.

55. Leo Goodstadt, "Putting the Army in its Place," *FEER*, 29 November 1974, p. 30.

56. Ralph L. Powell, "Soldiers in the Economy," *AS*, 11, No. 8 (August 1971), 751: Kao, p. xlii; *NCNA*, 28 May 1978, trans. in *FBIS*, No. 105 p. E16; Tientsin Radio, 3 August 1978, trans. in *FBIS*, No. 154, p. K2; and Nanning Radio, 31 July 1978, trans. in *FBIS*, No. 148, p. H2.

57. Harding, pp. 364-365.

58. Chang Yuan-ho and Sun Hao-chen, "'Three Supports and Two Militaries' Make for the Best Army Building," *PR*, No. 3 (16 January 1970), 16.

59. Kao, p. lv; also see Whitson, p. 450, for a similar view.

60. Dreyer, p. 24.

4
Professionalism on Trial

INTRODUCTION

We have seen that much of the top leadership of the PLA was professionally inclined up to 1965, and that junior and middle-level officers (recruited after about 1945) had spent up to twenty years in a rather "professional" military setting—both in battle and in garrison.

In 1966-75, the PLA was put to its severest test since (at least) the Korean War—the Great Proletarian Cultural Revolution (GPCR).

In a domestic crisis involving illegal or extra-legal challenges to the authority of the state, a professional officer corps would be expected to avoid political involvement as much as possible. If it were forced to act, it could be expected to come to the defense of the status quo, and to try to disengage itself again as quickly as possible. Through it all, the officer corps would reiterate its primary concern with the military defense of the state, and its commitment to civilian control of the military.

This is generally how the PLA (i.e., its officer corps) did, in fact, behave in 1966-75. There were, however, deviations from this "model behavior," especially on the issue of disengagement. Ideally professional behavior was not possible owing to the recent historical proximity of the Chinese revolution, and the nature of the one-party state. For both reasons, the PLA high command was (and remains) dominated by men in whom political and military roles are merged.

The peak of the crisis came in August 1967. During that summer, the Chinese officer corps was confronted by virtually all of the conditions usually cited to justify military coups d'etat. Political factionalism had led to widespread civil disorder, the disruption of public services, economic stagnation, and the nearly total discrediting of civilian political institutions. As a result of these conditions, political power was falling into the hands of unstable radical groups who were fundamentally hostile to the established social and political order. Officers were alarmed at the disruption of defense industry and of strategic communications, and even more alarmed by radical attempts to undermine the discipline of the armed forces. All this was seen as laying the country open to external attack. In August 1967, a coup d'etat could have been justified, therefore, by all the familiar motives associated with "guardian" coups:[1]

1. Restoration of law and order.
2. Restoration of authoritative and orderly political processes.

3. Rescue of the nation from economic collapse.
4. Protection of the security of the state.
5. Suppression of irresponsible political radicalism.
6. Restoration of national unity.

Instead of staging a coup, however, the military high command made a compromise with Mao which labeled a conservative solution with a radical name. Revolutionary committees (RCs) were formed which, although supposedly products of "revolutionary seizures of power," generally were run by the same military power-holders from whom power had supposedly been seized.[2] Military control committees (MCCs) forced radical factions into "great alliances" which were, in turn, given only token representation on the RCs.

There were several reasons for reasserting order in this manner. Perhaps most important was the strong predilection of military commanders, especially in the main forces, to minimize political involvement. Main force commissars and commanders alike seem to have remained committed to the notion that the party and army needed each other, and that at least the appearances of party control had to be maintained. The enemies of order were the Red Guards and their radical sponsors in the Central Cultural Revolution Group (CRG). A coup would have been directed at the PLA's allies (the government and the party), not at its enemies.

Outright defiance of Central Committee (CC) orders was extremely rare among main force units. Military commitment to the CCP's leading role in the established order of things repeatedly surfaced in the tendency of military leaders to defend party leaders and organs from radical attack. That tendency only went so far, however. Most regional leaders preferred to act indirectly, neither openly flying to the aid of dismissed civil party leaders nor attempting to take advantage of their plight to set up military "empires." Most tried to maintain a balance between cooperation and competition with CCP bureaus and provincial committees with whom they had longstanding ties.

Leaders of military regional (MR) commands, because they occupied borderline positions between civil and military, were far more prone to defy CC orders if local interests appeared to be threatened. In addition, regional commissars were much more open to the temptation of attacking their commanders as a means of gaining local power and central favor. This was because regional commissars retained more clout than main force commissars, and also because the former were often "civilians in uniform," who had not served in the military at all during the 1950s.

A few very strong regional leaders (notably Ch'en Hsi-lien in Shenyang and Huang Yung-sheng in Canton) got into open conflicts, thereby exposing themselves to attacks from both "right" and "left." Both, especially Huang, paid the price in massive civil disorder and near personal disaster.[3] Another factor which may have operated in Shenyang and Canton was internal conflict within PLA organizations themselves. In a number of cases, commissars or junior officers of regional units attempted to unseat their own superiors in an effort to create "room at the top" within the hierarchy.[4]

Of the entire high command, those most prone to "warlordism" were MR commanders who, by concurrently holding key political posts, had dominated their regions for many years. They had made enough local enemies that they felt threatened by any disturbance in the status quo. Two particularly notable cases in point were Ulanfu in Inner Mongolia and Wang En-mao in Sinkiang, both of whom were simultaneously MR commander, MR commissar, and provincial CCP first secretary. Ulanfu was removed in May 1967, but his followers were not finally suppressed (by main force units) until September. Wang's grip on Sinkiang was so tight that he was able to suppress local radicals and the few "central support-the-Left" (main force) units in his domain. In the summer of 1968, the CC finally managed to force him into relinquishing his post as MR commander (only), and accepting a vice-chairmanship of the provincial RC.[5]

Yet even these two regional military leaders never seem to have contemplated secession from the PRC, nor the establishment of competing national governments—despite the fact that they were both in geographical positions to appeal for Soviet assistance. Wang and Ulanfu were guilty of disobedience and resistance, but not of rebellion.

This commitment to national and military unity appears to have been a crucial factor in the events of 1967. The high command realized that PLA unity could be preserved only by preserving central political authority. Without the latter, the army could easily have fragmented into a dozen or more regionally based factions. By mid-1967, the party apparatus was virtually non-existent, so the loss of unifying political symbols, and the uncertainty that loss would bring, would have meant an "every man for himself" situation in the main forces. That, in turn, would have meant civil war.

A coup d'etat would have been extremely costly, even if the PLA could have been held together. It is always easier and better to rule with symbols than with bayonets. In August 1967, the government and the CCP were at the nadir of their prestige. The PLA was the only organization with high prestige in the whole country. The only other prestigious "institution" was Chairman Mao himself. A coup would have pitted these two authoritative institutions against each other and damaged both terribly. It was therefore best to combine the two instead: to unite China under PLA control in the name of the venerable chairman. Apparently a secret inspection tour in late August convinced Mao that this was the only sensible course.

The period that followed (1968-73) is often described as one of "military control." In fact, the role of the PLA was essentially one of peacekeeping. Under the watchful eyes of soldiers, business was conducted much as usual by local civilian cadres from the discredited party and government organs. The return to civilian control was slowed, not so much by the army's unwillingness to yield power, as by continued infighting in Peking and by intra-military cleavages. Both of these factors contributed to the fall of Lin Piao in 1971. Thereafter, party rebuilding and the PLA's return to barracks progressed rapidly.

Overall, the behavior of the PLA main forces was very "professional" indeed, and regional force officers behaved far more "professionally" than might have been expected. Through it all, the vast majority of Chinese officers, especially at the lower and middle levels, adapted to circumstances and maintained discipline and loyalty to the PLA and to "the Center" in Peking—however indistinctly the latter often was defined.

THE PLA IN CRISIS: 1966-68

Between 1965 and 1969, the PLA came to dominate China. This was not so much an intentional climb to power as a continuation of trends already established in the early 1960s, and was due principally to the collapse of non-military political power.

Early PLA Involvement

We simply do not know just how and when Lin Piao became the conscious instrument of Mao Tse-tung in his struggle against "revisionism" in the civilian party and in society generally. Parris Chang argues that until late 1965 the army was just being used as an example to reform the CCP, and that it was only then that the PLA began to be used consciously by Mao to circumvent the party.[6]

The General Rear Services Department (GRSD) was the first military organization, as such, to become deeply involved in the Cultural Revolution. In 1966, masses of Red Guards began to travel about the country to "exchange revolutionary experiences," and the GRSD had to transport and feed them, while also dealing with their disruptive impact on China's transportation and communications systems. The GRSD gave a remarkably "red and expert" account of itself in this herculean task over the next three years. If the Cultural Revolution did nothing else, it proved that the PLA's logistical system, while it may have been relatively small and primitive, was run by capable, flexible, and imaginative soldiers.[7]

The first public notice that the Cultural Revolution would be carried into the PLA itself was the "May Sixteenth Circular" (1966) which referred to "bourgeoisie who have sneaked into ... the army."[8] This was the first indication that the PLA itself would have an internal Cultural Revolution.

A Central Committee decision of 8 August 1966 (the "Sixteen Points") contained two important provisions pointing toward continued PLA noninvolvement: Point twelve prohibited attacks on scientists, technicians, and their staffs. In effect, that placed defense R&D and military-industrial establishments off-limits to the Cultural Revolution. More important still was point fifteen, which provided that the GPCR would be carried out in the army, but that it would be conducted exclusively by the MAC, through the GPD. That effectively terminated the long-standing system of "dual control" which had theoretically placed PLA political work in the hands of the GPD and local civilian party committees. From that point on, even in theory, PLA politics was directed only through the military chains of command. The PLA's Cultural Revolution was to be entirely separate from the one in the rest of society.

Sometime in the early autumn of 1966, as civilian party authority began to crumble under the impact of Red Guard attacks, the PLA Cultural Revolution Group (CRG) was set up under Liu Chih-chien, who was also a member of the Central CRG. The officer corps became concerned, now that the GPCR had at last entered the army.[9]

The last months of 1966 witnessed a profusion of directives from various organs in Peking—some moderate, some radical, and some both at the same time. Red Guards "arrested," "dragged out," and "struggled" Lo Jui-ch'ing, P'eng Te-hui, and other military leaders.[10]

Pursuant to a CC circular of 31 December, the PLA began to dispatch "Mao Tse-tung Thought Propaganda Teams" to various civilian organizations to popularize Mao's works. These teams, varying in size from a handful to several hundred soldiers, became increasingly important as civilian political authority crumbled. By 1968 these teams, and "Three Supports and Two Militaries" teams, had become, largely by default, the final political authorities in most localities and organizations.

The "January Storm"

By the end of 1966, a number of top military commanders and their staffs had been dismissed, and the first wave of purges broke over the MAC itself. Resistance to the Cultural Revolution's encroachment on military discipline was being led by Ho Lung. It was becoming ever more necessary to insert the PLA into the civilian sector, where things were falling apart, but Ho strongly opposed such moves. A great many senior commanders backed his resistance, while some backed the radicals, and still others tried to stay on the fence. This period (December 1966 and January 1967) was truly a pivotal one, for sides were being chosen, whether the PLA liked it or not. Those who agreed with Ho were appalled by the armed civilian mobs, the breakdown of political authority, and the near anarchy. Others realized the upheaval was pregnant with opportunities for the clever and enterprising. The radically "Maoist" tone of the New Year's editorial in *CFCP* left no doubt about where the GPD (and Lin Piao) stood.

On 11 January 1967, the old PLA Cultural Revolution Group was dissolved. Ho Lung, Liao Han-sheng, Liu Chih-chien, and Su Chien-hua (political commissar of the navy) were purged. A new army CRG was formed, directly under the Military Affairs Commission where Lin Piao now had nearly absolute sway, and also under the Central CRG (headed by Chiang Ch'ing and Ch'en Po-ta). Chiang Ch'ing was named "advisor" to the new military CRG.[11]

The army was about to be thrust, officially, into the GPCR, but that had already been rendered inevitable by events in the vital defense industry—where government, PLA, and civilian educational institutions overlap. As early as 30 December, the National Defense Science and Technology Commission (NDSTC), which oversees all military research and development, was under attack by Peking Red Guards.[12] The first reported case of Red Guards attacking defense workers occurred at the Shenyang National Aircraft Factory about the same time.[13]

The PLA was pushed and pulled, willy-nilly, into the civilian Cultural Revolution through January 1967—usually to protect vital installations and preserve order.[14]

The radicals in the Central Cultural Revolution Group found themselves in a deepening quandary: They needed military backing to attack the party, and to maintain security and vital public services. Yet local military units were often siding with the local CCP cadres who were under radical attack. Left to their own judgment, most PLA commanders opted for order rather than "revolution."

Finally, on 23 January 1967, the CCP Central Committee, the Military Affairs Commission, the Central CRG, and the State Council issued the fateful joint directive "Concerning the Resolute Support of the PLA for the Revolutionary Masses of the Left."[15] This brief document raised more questions than it answered, for it called on the PLA to be all things to all people: "From now on, the demands of all true revolutionaries for support and assistance from the army should be satisfied. The so-called "non-involvement" is false, for the army was already involved long ago." That was certainly true enough, but exactly what was meant by "satisfying" (*man-tsu*) the demands of the revolutionaries? The directive explicitly voided all previous orders that had exempted individual units or localities from the Cultural Revolution—the whole PLA was now in, with both feet. Counterrevolutionaries were to be suppressed vigorously, and "when genuine proletarian Leftists ask the army for help, the army should send out troops to support them positively." The basic problem of figuring out just who the "genuine proletarian Leftists" were was left unanswered. That problem left every PLA commander in a "no-win" position. The obvious solution was to avoid getting involved at all, but that option was explicitly prohibited.

The authors of the 23 January directive also addressed a practice which had become fairly widespread: "The army must not be an air raid shelter for the handful of Party power-holders taking the capitalist road and diehards who persist in the bourgeois reactionary line." Local military commanders, more often than not, were protecting the very party cadres and organs that the "Maoists" were seeking to destroy. Despite the 23 January directive, this practice was to persist.

The "Black Wind"

To the dismay of the radicals, the intervention of the PLA to "Support the Left" backfired: A series of directives from the CC, the MAC, and the State Council began to moderate the 23 January directive almost immediately, and reversed its intent. The result came to be known (among "Maoists") as the "February Black Wind" (or "Adverse Current"). Chiang Ch'ing allegedly attempted, in February and March, to unseat the remaining "professionals" in the MAC (including Yeh Chien-ying, Nieh Jung-chen, and Chu Teh). She failed completely.[16]

Despite the supression of some radicals, disorder continued to spread: From 3 to 9 February no less than five directives had to be issued dealing with assaults on military region and military district (MD) headquarters.[17] In all cases, the central decision was to reimpose order at the expense of the Red Guards. The shift away from radicalism was dramatically symbolized on 24 February, when Mao told Chang Ch'un-ch'iao and Yao Wen-yuan that their "Shanghai Commune" bordered on anarchism, and was to be replaced by a revolutionary committee.[18]

Revolutionary committees were to be formed by means of a "three-way alliance"—an equal sharing of power, within each revolutionary committee, by (1) the PLA, (2) "revolutionary cadres" (which meant, in effect, any cadres still able to maintain power), and (3) the "revolutionary masses" (which meant, in effect, local Red Guard leaders). Implemented literally, it would have meant an impossible alliance among implacable enemies. In fact, it worked rather well, because the PLA dominated the "alliance" in virtually every case. In mid-January, the PLA had been ordered to dispatch work teams to carry out the "Three Supports and Two Militaries." These teams led the military penetration into civilian organizations, where they dominated the RCs. They were backed up by local force units, which enforced "revolutionary order."

In most areas, even a "three-way alliance" was not possible. In these areas, military control committees (MCCs) were established to maintain order. By the end of March 1967, all provinces, autonomous regions, and special municipalities (except the six which had RCs) were under the supervision of MCCs. MCCs were also established at lower levels of government, and in production units. Although evidence is not conclusive, Whitson theorizes that the MCCs were "little more than former military district party committees under a new name." He is probably right, for, as Nelsen points out, it was a practical impossibility for soldiers to assume all local governmental and economic functions in the country. They had to rely heavily on incumbent civilian officials and bureaucrats, who continued to do the work and therefore to shape the decisions. The typical MCC, then, was the same old governmental or CCP organization with a soldier or two at the top. The former civilian leader might be a member of the MCC, or might have been suspended or removed if the heat had been too intense.[19] In any case, the MCC often meant business as usual under PLA auspices.

As winter turned to spring, the radicals began to reassert themselves. The first step in any new wave of "revolution" had to be tightened central control over the local PLA commands, which controlled the MCCs. Accordingly, Peking began to transfer, dismiss, and suspend commanders and commissars on a large scale. By the end of June this had happened to the commanders of the Chengtu, Peking, Sinkiang, Lanchow, and Inner Mongolian Military Regions; and the Liaoning, Kirin, Honan, Shansi, Kingsu, and Chekiang Military Districts.[20] Still other MR and MD officers were called to Peking where they remained, in some cases for months at a time. On 6 April 1967, a MAC directive withdrew almost all powers of local discretion regarding the handling of Red Guard disruptions. This centralizing trend continued into the summer, and climaxed in Lin Piao's speech of 9 August, which virtually emasculated the MR commanders.[21]

As civil disorder spread in the spring and early summer of 1967, local military units received contradictory orders as to whether they could use force to restore order. For example, the 6 April directive was flatly contradicted by another of 6 June. That left local commanders vulnerable to charges of disobedience no matter what they did. Commanders all over China began resorting to a novel strategem: They organized "mass organizations" of their own, often packed with militiamen and even local security troops (in mufti). This expedient had been used, here and there, well prior to June 1967, but became widespread at that time. The beauty of the arrangement was that disorder could be suppressed, and the instigators arrested or killed, while still allowing local PLA commanders to disavow all responsibility if Peking subsequently disapproved. Peking's efforts, through the early summer of 1967, to tighten central control over the local forces only made the use of these "Red Guards" of the local establishments even more necessary.[22]

The radical Red Guards (who increasingly called themselves "Rebels" to differentiate themselves as "real" Maoists) usually fought back when the "establishment" Red Guards attacked them. As spring turned to summer, large-scale factional battles were being waged with firearms—including heavy weapons. In some areas, both sides actually used recoiless rifles, heavy artillery, and even tanks. The PLA was again allowed to defend arsenals forcibly after 6 June, but by then "Rebels" were well enough armed to conduct raids and to hijack arms shipments headed for Vietnam. Local forces reacted by arming "their" Red Guards more heavily, and an "arms race" of sorts resulted.

The Wuhan Incident

The process just described led to widespread violence in the city of Wuhan.[23] The local PLA built up an organization called the "Million Heroes," which included many older industrial workers and peasant militiamen from the surrounding countryside. The Wuhan case was typical of two phenomena which occurred all over China: the importation of peasant militia into cities to back the conservatives, and a factional alignment of proletarian and peasant conservatives versus student radicals.

Wuhan had experienced considerable turmoil as early as January, and, from February on, the "Million Heroes," with the backing of the Wuhan MR and Hupeh Provincial MD, had been forcibly suppressing radical "Rebels." Factional strife caused considerable bloodshed and industrial disruption through the spring and early summer. Robinson estimates "Rebel" strength at around 400,000. Since we know they were heavily outnumbered by the "Million Heroes," the huge scale of Wuhan's civil strife can be appreciated.[24]

A number of especially serious incidents took place in June. Chou En-lai went to Wuhan in the second week of July, investigated the situation, and issued his decision on the fourteenth: He endorsed the "Rebels," condemned the "Million Heroes" as conservatives, and rebuked the Wuhan MR commander, Ch'en Tsai-tao, for backing the latter. Then Chou flew back to Peking, leaving Wang Li and Hsieh Fu-chih to iron out the details. The next day, however, 500 soldiers of a local garrison unit (Division 8201) were apparently ordered to remove their uniforms and reinforce the "Million Heroes" in attacking "Rebels" who were demonstrating to welcome Wang and Hsieh.[25] By the evening of 19 July, Wuhan was effectively controlled by Unit 8201 and the "Million Heroes." Most of the population centers of Hupeh were also in the hands of sympathetic Red Guards, under the control of local garrisons and militia.

In the early hours of 20 July, a group of "Million Heroes" and two companies of 8201 soldiers entered the headquarters of the Wuhan MR, where Wang and Hsieh were staying. Wang was "arrested," while Hsieh escaped. Even though several of the Peking Red Guards acting as Wang's Bodyguards were killed, Ch'en Tsai-tao refused to intervene—supposedly because the "masses" were beyond his control.

The kaleidoscopic events of the next two days can only be generally, and tentatively, summarized. The "Million Heroes" and Division 8201 seized all strategic installations in the city. "Rebels" were attacked all over Wuhan, and there was considerable bloodshed and damage.

News of these events began to reach Peking on the morning of 20 July. The MAC, through Yang Ch'eng-wu, the acting chief of staff, ordered Ch'en Tsai-tao to release Wang and Hsieh, and to escort them to Peking. The East China Sea Fleet and the Fifteenth Airborne Corps were ordered to intervene.

The important distinction between the local forces and main forces of the PLA was clearly illustrated during the Wuhan Incident. It is especially interesting to note that Peking intervened principally with Fifteenth Corps, which is part of the air force.

Fifteenth Airborne Corps is stationed in the Wuhan area. As we saw in chapter 2, Lin Piao had made special efforts to tighten his grip on the air force in the early 1960s. The fact that Ch'en Tsai-tao acted as he did while literally surrounded by a corps of main force paratroopers gives strong credence to Robinson's theory that Ch'en felt sure he had, or could get, Lin Piao's personal approval for his handling of the situation in Wuhan. Ch'en had been associated with Lin for years.[26] Robinson also emphasizes the "combination of fatalism and the human propensity to misinterpret the signals of others. Both Centre and locality worked themselves into corners ... from which they found it difficult to extricate themselves." Ch'en had committed himself so fully to the "Million Heroes" (and more fundamentally to "law and order") that he had to impugn the credentials of Wang and Hsieh and "appeal over their heads to Mao and Lin." But Ch'en's actions smacked too much of "warlordism," and constituted an overt slap both at the radicals of the Central CRG, and at powerful moderates (especially Chou En-lai). "Peking probably felt it had no choice but to intervene militarily to make an example of that sort of behavior."[27]

The presence of Fifteenth Corps facilitated making an example in Wuhan (in Sinkinag, where Wang En-mao boasted that two rifle companies could "solve" the entire Lanchou Air Force, no such example could be made—although Wang's "warlordism" was far more blatant). On the afternoon of 20 July, paratroopers entered the city, rescued Wang and Hsieh, and began to supress Ch'en's forces and the "Million Heroes."

Peking's initial public reaction was surprisingly restrained. As Robinson suggests, that was partly because fighting in Wuhan continued, and Peking wanted to encourage "hoodwinked masses" and soldiers to surrender. For a week or so the leading slogan was conciliatory: "To be hoodwinked is no crime, to strike back is a merit."[28]

"Dragging Out" in the PLA: August 1967

Then, on 1 August (Army Day), the lead editorial in *Hung Ch'i* called for an all-out attack on "Ch'en Tsai-tao type persons" in the regional military commands.[29] The theme was picked up quickly by the rest of the official press. It has widely been assumed that the assault on "capitalist roaders" in the PLA was provoked by the Wuhan Incident. There is evidence to the contrary: *JMJP* had called for the "dragging out of bourgeois elements in the army" on 20 July—surely too quickly to have gotten such a major policy shift into print after the news arrived from Wuhan. Then, the call had been dropped completely for ten days.

Further evidence emerged in September (1967), when the pendulum swung back toward moderation: In attacking the "May Sixteenth" group, which became the official scapegoat for the radical excesses of August, it was acknowledged that ranking members of the *Hung Ch'i* editorial board had prepared the 1 August editorial well in advance. The individual personally saddled with the blame was Lin Chieh, a deputy editor who had been appointed to the Central CRG in July by Chiang Ch'ing. He allegedly proposed the slogan "drag out the handful in the army" at an editorial meeting on 19 July—the day before the Wuhan Incident began.[30] The incident provided an opportune excuse for the Central CRG to launch an attack on the PLA which was already in the works.[31] It appears, in fact, that the *JMJP* article of 20 July was the planned beginning of that attack, which was then suspended for over a week, while the dust settled in Wuhan. Then the attack was resumed, drawing added impetus from the Wuhan Incident.

"Rebels" all over China launched attacks at various military headquarters, while regional commanders were ordered to come to Peking and stay there. On 9 and 10 August, the latter were assembled, along with the Central CRG and the MAC, to hear two remarkable speeches by Lin Piao.

Lin's 9 August speech was the milder of the two.[32] Although he reassured his audience that civil order was necessary and that the army's primary mission was still war preparedness, published versions of the speech emphasized its radical content—and there was plenty of that. Its primary practical result was to deny the regional commanders any discretion at all, and thus to tie their hands.[33] Contrary to much published analysis, the speech was not a moderate one. It threw the door wide open to the radical excesses that were to follow. The state was "rotten" and was falling apart: "Let it fall!" said Lin, all "bad things" are going to be exposed and destroyed.[34] Furthermore, the PLA had made some mistakes—especially at the MR level:

"Cadres ... who have made mistakes should be sent to receive training in accordance with Chairman Mao's instructions, so that the revolutionary rebels may be their teachers and their own mistakes may be their teaching materials."

This directive for the PLA to "learn from the masses of the Left" was a new extreme in the radical tide, and was largely responsible for the August crisis. Up to 10 August, the PLA's Cultural Revolution was, at least officially, separate from the civilian one: Now the Army was told to "be humble and learn enthusiastically" from the slogan-screaming youngsters who were tearing Chinese society to pieces. Regional commanders were again forbidden to use force against mass organizations, regardless of provocation.

Lin's main point, however, which he emphasized repeatedly, was that PLA men were not to think or act on their own. They were to consult the Central Committee on even the smallest matters, and obey orders whether they understood the reasons or not.

The next day (10 August 1967), Lin delivered a violent attack on military cadres who were opposing Mao's line. He also criticized those who said that emphasizing politics meant falling behind in military preparedness: "This is an error. Military preparations and politics are not to be brought up together like that."[35]

Under heavy pressure from both the "right" and the "left," Hsiao Hua, director of the General Political Department of the PLA, was purged in mid-August. The entire GPD hierarchy dropped out of sight, and the organization entered a long period of limbo. No new director was named until 1969, and the GPD made no significant decisions or initiatives until 1975.[36]

The all-out attack on the PLA, which was made possible by Lin Piao's 9 and 10 August directives, was provided new ammunition on 16 August: *JMJP, CFCP,* and *NCNA* all published, for the first time, the complete text of the "Resolution of the [Eighth] Central Committee Concerning the Anti-Party Clique Headed by P'eng Te-huai." This was the first time the P'eng Te-huai affair was officially explained to the Chinese public—eight years (to the day) after the event. Accompanying editorials made the claim that both P'eng and Lo Jui-ch'ing had been agents of "China's Khrushchev" (Liu Shao-ch'i), and that their clique and the "bourgeois-military line" were still influential in the PLA.[37] Vilification of P'eng and Lo remained a major theme in the official press through the first week of September.[38]

The PLA was supposed to accept the criticism of the masses, while also helping to "forge alliances" among radical groups. Moreover, it was not to support some factions at the expense of others. Since only persuasion could be used to form alliances among warring factions, however, there were many factional clashes with the PLA caught defenseless in the middle. In some cases, PLA units and MCCs reportedly had to be protected by sympathetic Red Guards from other Red Guards who were intent on killing them. Exactly how many soldiers died trying to stop battles, or were simply murdered, is unknown, but the number was surely in the thousands.

Industry and transportation came to a virtual standstill by mid-August.[39] Revolt in the Foreign Ministry and Red Guard attacks on embassies in Peking made a shambles of China's foreign relations. On 20 August, the collapse of civil order was dramatized by the looting of eleven truckloads of secret documents from the Ministry of Chemical Industries. Fighting broke out in all twenty-six provinces, with the worst in Kwangtung,[40] Szechuan, and Sinkiang.[41]

Chou En-lai's prodigious efforts to mediate disputes and to defend local

PLA commanders were probably a major factor in averting complete chaos. Chou's personal defense of such commanders as Huang Yung-sheng and Ch'en Hsi-lien was in marked contrast to Lin Piao's abandonment of such old associates as Hsiao Hua. When the radical tide was finally turned, it was Chou En-lai, and not Lin, who held the IOUs for defending the PLA.[42]

The August crisis opened up deep divisions within the military. In Szechuan, PLA units reportedly battled each other with gunboats, tanks, and heavy artillery. In Sinkiang, an intermittent civil war broke out, with Production and Construction Corps (PCC) and MR units arrayed against the air force and some border defense units. The Wuhan Incident had been the first major armed clash between main force and local force troops, but it was far from the most serious, in terms of death and destruction.

Harvey Nelsen has detailed the political importance of the distinction between main forces and regional forces in the Cultural Revolution.[43] Initially, only token forces had been needed to back Red Guard "power seizures" in party and government offices, so local forces had been quite sufficient. Keeping the main forces out of the Cultural Revolution had also kept China's strategic defenses intact. Moreover, many PLA leaders evidently had been reluctant to approve military involvement at all, and had sought to minimize it once it was forced upon them.[44] In the spring of 1967, the advent of armed masses of conservative Red Guards made it difficult for local forces alone to act as the "Maoist" trump card, even when they wanted to—and as we have seen, they seldom did. Generally, the local forces and conservative Red Guards worked together, as in Wuhan. When removal of regional military leaders in the spring of 1967 failed to remedy this situation, the Central CRG was forced to play its last trump: PLA main force units were committed to support the radicals. Main force commanders had to choose between disobeying Peking's orders and fighting against their fellows in the regional forces.

By mid-1968, at least twenty of the thirty-six main force corps had been involved, at one time or another, as "central support-the-Left units."[45] Up to the Wuhan Incident, these main forces and their officers were not given important provincial or regional political responsibilities. In the first weeks of August 1967, however, main force units took over control of Kiangsi, Hunan, Hupeh, Anhwei, Chekiang, and Kirin. Nelsen presents evidence of at least eleven provinces being taken over by main force units in August 1967.[46] In addition, main force leaders were added to established revolutionary committees in at least seven provinces. Main force units took over countless smaller administrative units as well. For example, the 39th Corps took over Anshan (in Liaoning) and its vital iron and steel works. There was a "sweeping trend of politicizing main force leaders who had previously served in narrowly military functions." Unfortunately for the radicals, the main forces were nearly as ill-equipped, and hardly more willing, to push the Cultural Revolution through to a total "Maoist" victory.

Once the main forces did intervene, they too came under fire from the radical "left" for not pushing "revolution" hard enough. While the regional forces opposed them for being too radical, the "Rebels" attempted to "drag out" their alleged "bourgeois elements." In attempting to keep a lid on the situation, main force commanders were forced to disperse their troops ever more widely—thereby attenuating China's strategic defenses just as the US bombing offensive reached the borders of Kwangsi and Yunnan. Not only the main force corps, but also the centrally controlled administrative and specialized departments of the PLA, came under radical attack at the same time.[47] If the situation had continued for long, the People's Republic of China could easily have disintegrated into a chaotic jumble of warring factions. Whatever differences may have divided the high command, they agreed that the radical excesses had to stop.

The "Maoists" of the Central CRG had played their last card, and now faced the distasteful alternatives of losing the country or backing down on the Cultural Revolution. They wisely chose the latter course. Mao Tse-tung himself apparently made the decision to end the "dragging out" in the army in late August or early September. He made an unpublicized whirlwind "inspection tour" through eastern and central China, meeting with local military leaders, who impressed him with the seriousness of the situation. When news of Mao's tour finally broke in September, he was quoted as delivering a series of remarkably moderate "instructions."[48] By September 1st, a moderating tone was discernable in a *JMJP* editorial praising the "Great Chinese PLA."

The Turn of the Radical Tide

On 5 September 1967, the reversal of the radical line was announced by none other than Chiang Ch'ing, in a long speech to Red Guard representatives from Anhwei.[49] The same day, the official line was reversed (without admitting any change, of course) by an "Order ... Concerning the Prohibition of the Seizure of Arms, Equipment, and Other Military Supplies from the PLA."[50] The army was forbidden to hand over any such materials voluntarily, and was told to prevent their seizure—by force if necessary. All military equipment in civilian hands was to be returned at once. Failure to obey the order was to be considered a "counterrevolutionary act," and "dealt with as a case of violation of the State's law." This was the first official invocation of "law" since early June.

In addition, the 5 September order ended "dragging out" and the related line that the PLA was to "learn from the revolutionary masses of the Left." Henceforth, the military would carry on its own Cultural Revolution "stage by stage and place by place."

Portions of Chiang Ch'ing's speech sounded almost like a self-criticism, and its publication was followed by a radical retreat on all fronts. She and her followers were pushed into the background, and her Central Cultural Revolution Group was purged. By the end of October, the original membership of seventeen had been reduced to only four or five. In November, *Hung Ch'i* magazine was suspended, and a thorough purge of its editorial staff kept it closed until July 1968. It was also in November that Chiang Ch'ing went into seclusion for a seven-week "rest."[51]

In September 1967, the official press began a prolonged love affair with the PLA, which filled countless pages with effusive praises until 1971. This was necessary because the army was the only authoritative political institution left in China. Having retreated from the brink of the abyss, the Central Committee was anxious to bolster its only remaining instrument for enforcing civil order. The necessity for this was reflected by the serious civil disorders which continued to rock the country well into 1968.

"Rectification of Cadres" and the Restoration of Order

On 17 September, Chou En-lai summarized the official policies which would prevail, with a few lapses, through the Ninth Party Congress in April

1969. He began by again denouncing the slogan "drag out the handful in the army" which was, he declared, "a mistake in propaganda" which had led to "a height of frenzy in August."[52] In the remainder of 1967, said Chou, "power seizures" would be made by "great alliances" of all revolutionary groups and by the "three-in-one combination" of "revolutionary cadres," PLA, and "masses." The military control committees would continue to be the actual organizers of revolutionary committees. Chou optimistically said he expected that as many as twenty-five provincial-level RCs would be established by the end of 1967.

As for the army, it was not to "establish liaison with the local great proletarian cultural revolution," and was to cease doing so where it had. This was rather curious, considering that the PLA was obviously intended to dominate the "three-in-one combination" and deal directly and firmly with local factions to force them into "great alliances." In fact, the main thrust of the speech was that China's future was necessarily in PLA hands, at least until revolutionary committees had been formed. In context, Chou was protecting the army from civilian interference, rather than vice-versa, for he instructed soldiers to carry out internal "struggle-criticism-transformation" independently from the local "Left."

On 14 September, *JMJP* admitted that the proletariat had become factionalized, and called for "revolutionary great alliances." Henceforth, unity was to be regarded as the main goal of the Cultural Revolution.[53] The formation of "great alliances" proved to be a complex and frustrating business. On 26 October, for example, *NCNA* announced the formation, "after repeated consultations," of a "big alliance" in the Sixth Ministry of Machine Industry (Shipbuilding). There had been a great deal of disruption and conflict, but the PLA had enforced an "alliance," assisted by a good deal of pressure from "proletarian revolutionaries of many central government institutions [who] have gone to this Ministry to make a serious study of its experiences." (It will be noted that intervention by outsiders was quite all right, when they were helping to pressure radical factions into an "alliance"). Although conflicts still admittedly persisted, reported *NCNA*, Mao Tse-tung's thought prevailed, and there was "an atmosphere of militant solidarity in the Ministry."[54] The "alliance" broke up within a few weeks. It was not an easy time to be part of a PLA Mao Tse-tung Thought Propaganda Team in the Sixth Ministry of Machine Industry—or anywhere else.

The masses would no longer be allowed to "teach" the PLA, but military political work was to be intensified. The entire PLA was to undergo an intensive refresher course in Mao Tse-tung Thought, beginning with those units which had been most resistant to "power seizures." Cadres who had fallen victim to "power seizures" could be reinstated—but only after "rehabilitation." By the end of 1967, PLA "Mao Tse-tung Thought Study Classes" and "rehabilitation of cadres" had emerged as major new phenomena. Lin Piao ordered a massive campaign of reindoctrination courses for military cadres at all levels—starting with People's Armed Departments (PADs), Military Districts, and subdistricts. Ultimately, declared *CFCP*, "All our cadres need to study."[55]

Mao had called for "big study classes" as early as 13 July, and had repeatedly noted the recalcitrance of the PADs during his inspection tour in late August. One Red Guard source quoted his observation that: "The majority of the people's arms [sic] departments are good [but] many people in the military subdistricts have been hoodwinked."[56]

Military cadres from all over China began to pour into Peking for what were billed as "conferences of activists in the study of Mao Tse-tung Thought."

The "activists" were "military cadres from various provinces studying in the capital, and leading members of the PLA stationed in various provinces and regions"[57]—in other words, PLA regional cadres. Now that the revolutionary masses were no longer allowed to teach the PLA, thousands of cadres underwent one or two weeks of study in Peking. PAD cadres were followed by other regional cadres. Some time in late October, Mao delivered another of his "latest instructions": In addition to cadres, "fighters should be included in the study courses sponsored by the army," so that the cadres could "learn from the masses" of soldiers.[58] "Study conferences" began to assume gargantuan proportions. On 16 November, one "class" of 1300 men was received by Mao, Lin, and a galaxy of PLA big-shots. Another 1300-man class was convened the same day.[59] Entire units were evidently undergoing this "new stage of creative study and application" of Mao's thought as early as October.[60] By the end of November, the main forces were also sending "activists" to Peking,[61] and selected MRs began to conduct similar conferences on their own.[62] There, too, the emphasis was on unity and loyalty to the Chairman.

All this ideological training was not uniformly successful in teaching the PLA to "apply Chairman Mao's Thought in a living way." In December, for example, cadres from the 54th Corps came to Peking, studied Mao's thought, and showed "fine character." They reportedly reverted to their errant ways, however, upon their return to Szechuan.[63] The trouble was that China was still seething. As the drive to form RCs intensified, the army became increasingly high-handed with "Rebels" who refused to join "great alliances."[64] That provoked resistance, as for example in Canton, where violence continued into February 1968.[65] Armed conflict was endemic in many parts of the country. In January, during one of his continuing attempts to bring peace to the defense industry, Chou En-lai bluntly revealed that, "Because of factional outbursts some people seized weapons, rifles, cannon shells and other aid supplies for Vietnam. In an armed clash which broke out in a certain place, more than 10,000 shells [sic (*SCMP*)] were fired in the air instead of being given in support to Vietnam. Can this be making revolution while practicing economy?"[66]

The Fall of Yang Ch'eng-wu

As if there weren't enough to worry about already, the PLA was subjected to yet another trauma when, on 22 March 1968, Yang Ch'eng-wu was abruptly removed from his post as acting chief of staff. He was replaced by Huang Yung-sheng, the Canton MR commander.[67]

Yang had been acting chief of staff since the fall of Lo Jui-ch'ing, and had also replaced Ho Lung as vice-chairman of the MAC in January 1967.[68] He had played a relatively inconspicuous role in the tumultuous events of 1967, obeying orders, but exhibiting the same reticence toward "Maoism" typical of most career commanders. At a mass rally on 27 March 1968, however, he was accused of being both a "revisionist" and an "ultra-leftist."

It is not clear exactly what Yang had actually done, but he had probably overreached himself. As one of the central military leaders who had led the resistance to the Central CRG, Yang had survived the August crisis because he had the backing of the high command. The PLA was sufficiently crosscut by factions, however, that no top leader could afford to antagonize too many important groups at once. That was where Yang made his mistake. While continuing to resist the radicals, he began appointing many of his proteges to top positions, in effect undermining the very commanders who were his base of support. It was this ill-advised exercise in burning the candle at both ends which led to Yang's abrupt removal by a coalition of his old enemies on the "left" and his new enemies on the "right."[69]

The purge of Yang Ch'eng-wu, and the reappearance of Chiang Ch'ing, marked the beginning of a last attempt to swing the Cultural Revolution back to the "left." Although pale by comparison with the violent "revolution" of July-September 1967, this new phase saw the emergence of new slogans opposing "rightist reversals of verdict." This radical resurgence, such as it was, was possible only because the Central CRG could capitalize on the intra-military rivalries spawned the previous year.

One of the root causes of the PLA's internal conflict was a continuing debate over the proper role of the military in Chinese society in the aftermath of the Cultural Revolution. Lin Piao was clearly opposed to the "professionals" who apparently already were advocating a military withdrawal from civil politics. This group included Su Yü, Nieh Jung-chen, and Yeh Chien-ying. The August 1967 crisis had had a chastening effect, however, as Lin's downbeat handling of the Yang Ch'eng-wu affair demonstrated. He had to minimize internal stresses in the PLA in order to maintain his own overall control.

Serious disputes, often leading to bloodshed, continued to erupt between regional and main force units. Strife between 69th Corps and the Shansi MD,[70] between 38th Corps and the Hopeh MD,[71] and between the Lanchou Air Force and the Sinkiang MR,[72] were well-known examples.

The most serious breaches of the peace continued to be clashes between armed Red Guard factions backed by competing military units. On 6 June 1968, Canton was wracked by a major battle between rival groups armed with small arms and artillery. The conservatives, as usual, were backed by the military district, which had shown considerably more enthusiasm in disarming "Rebels."[73] Up the West River, in Wuchow, the radicals were much better armed, having looted PLA weapons and entire arms shipments bound for Vietnam. One radical source claimed that PLA troops were actively fighting on both sides. In any event, armed "Rebels" battled security troops of the Wuchow MCC in extended battles involving "mortars, field pieces, 60mm guns, 82mm guns, anti-aircraft guns, as well as heavy and light machineguns," explosives, and napalm. The fighting finally ended on 20-21 May, when the last "Rebel" resisters, hiding in the city's sewer system, were gassed out or buried alive by demolitions. Rail links with Vietnam were cut for weeks, and over 2000 buildings were razed. By the end of May, 40,000 people were homeless, 4000 imprisoned, and at least 500 dead—dozens of mutilated and bound corpses were carried down the river to the sea.[74]

THE PLA IN "CONTROL": 1969-71

By spring 1968, such outbreaks, while serious, were manageable because there was a clear national commitment to restoring order. More serious, from Peking's perspective, was the continued breakdown in central control, owing to the disruption of transportation and communications nets. Local military authorities presided over the formation of local RCs, generally drawing in the same people who had formed the old party committees. Military organs presided over the system, right down to the people's armed departments which controlled things at the lowest levels.[75]

The return to civilian control was slowed, not so much by the army's unwillingness to yield power, as by continued infighting in Peking and by intra-military cleavages. Both of these factors contributed to the fall of Lin Piao in

1971. Most of the high command was plainly unhappy about Lin Piao's policies, and by the strain continued civil strife was placing on the PLA. Whenever civil order began to break down in a given locality, and military intervention was required, an ad hoc "quick fix" was to dispatch yet another "Three Supports and Two Militaries" team. "Three Supports and Two Militaries" became the general heading used to refer to all PLA involvement in RCs, MCCs, Mao Tse-tung Thought Propaganda Teams, and militia work.[76] The impact of all this activity on China's defenses became extreme in mid-1968. Entire units were scattered, often across provincial and MR boundaries, in an effort to maintain civil order and to "forge revolutionary alliances." Even main force units were drained by the effort, as even specialists like submariners and pilots left their posts to help shoulder the burden.[77]

While the main forces carried a heavy load, the burden on the regional forces was absolutely staggering. Chou En-lai told Edgar Snow that two million PLA men had been committed to "Three Supports and Two Militaries" work. By subtracting the main force units committed (most of which have been identified) from the total, we conclude that well over a million troops were contributed by regional forces--virtually their entire strength. All told, according to Chou, the PLA suffered hundreds of thousands of casualties during the Cultural Revolution.[78] Heavy commitment to "Three Supports and Two Militaries" continued right up to the fall of Lin Piao in 1971, and remained a source of intra-military conflict.[79]

It is evident from military behavior during this period that, while insisting upon social order, PLA officers were not opposed to "revolutionary" innovation per se. The PLA seems to have cooperated fully in such radical developments as the revision of the educational system and the training and deployment of "barefoot doctors." There is little evidence, either, that the PLA attempted to impose any "military" complexion upon Chinese society beyond Mao's own continuing use of the army as a model of socialist rectitude.

Party Rebuilding: The Problem of "Many Centers"

In March 1969 fighting broke out along the Sino-Soviet border, precipitating a major international crisis. To a considerable extent, the Chinese closed ranks, and on 1 April 1969, the Ninth National Congress of the Communist Party of China convened. This is not to say that the Sino-Soviet fighting was entirely created for internal political purposes. The Chinese had been worried about the Soviet threat for years. But the timing of the 1969 fighting was no coincidence.[80] Accounts of the first major battle, on 2 March, are of course contradictory, but it probably began as an ambush, laid by Chinese troops, into which a Soviet patrol was lured by a group of Chinese "civilians." It is unreasonable to think that any local Chinese commander would have laid a bloody ambush, which was certain to provoke a major world crisis, without specific orders from the MAC.[81] There is no doubt that both sides deliberately built up for the 15 March battle, and it is certain that Peking was directly involved in the Chinese preparations.

Public reaction by both sides was belligerent, but the Soviets tried to initiate telephone consultations on 21 March. The Chinese refused to talk.[82] In his report to the Ninth Party Congress on 1 April, Lin Piao said that the Chinese position had "consistently" been willingness to negotiate the border disputes on the basis of the status quo and the "five principles of peaceful coexistence." It was only on 11 September, however, that Chou En-lai officially conveyed this policy to the Soviets. Negotiations began shortly thereafter, and the situation was defused. In retrospect, it appears that Chou offered the olive branch that ended a crisis Lin Piao had instigated. The Politburo may have planned it that way, but in the long run it provided ammunition for Lin's political enemies, who were able to cast him as a "left adventurist" and "desperado."[83] In view of Lin's uncertain political position, the allegations seem plausible.

The GPCR, the subsequent emphasis on reforging national unity, and the border fighting had all worked to place the PLA in a dominating position. It was hardly surprising, then, that nearly three-quarters of the delegates to the Ninth Party Congress wore uniforms. Despite this apparent homogeneity, however, the Party Congress met in secret on 1 April, and there was no public announcement until 14 April. At the opening session, Mao told the delegates, "We hope that the present congress will be a congress of unity and a congress of victory." Despite Mao's hope, and in contrast to past practice, the congress lasted twenty-four days. This strongly indicates that there was a great deal of horse-trading going on behind the scenes even after the congress finally convened. On 14 April the new CCP constitution was adopted. It then took another ten days of behind-the-scenes maneuvering before the Ninth Central Committee could be elected on 24 April, and then a further four days to elect a Politburo and Standing committee.[84]

All this delay, despite "PLA domination" of the proceedings, indicates that the remaining civilian radicals were not the only obstacles to unity: There was disagreement within the military itself, as to who would wield power and to what ends.

The dominance of the provinces by regional commanders became ever more evident as the new provincial party committees were formed in 1970-71. All eleven MR commanders, and at least 27 of the 29 MD-level commanders, became committee secretaries or higher. Twenty-six of the thirty-six first and second secretaries were soldiers (Table 4.1). Perhaps most significantly, only nine of the new first secretaries were career commissars, whereas thirteen were career troop commanders.[85] The preponderance of central military commanders in the Politburo, and of regional commanders in the CC, the RCs, and the new provincial-level CCP committees points toward four generalizations about the Chinese power structure in the 1969-71 period:

1. Regional political power had regained an importance not seen since the civil war.
2. Military men dominated the party and the state in Peking and at the provincial level.
3. Career troop commanders dominated the PLA. Political commissars had been eclipsed in the aftermath of the 1967 crisis.
4. Lin Piao's personal control of the People's Republic of China was not nearly so complete as most observers thought at the time.

The problem of regionalism was dramatized by the Peking press, in the months following the Ninth Party Congress, by intense criticism of the "theory of many centers" (*tuo-chung-hsin lun*). As Jurgen Domes has shown, regionalism strongly influenced the course and the timing of "party rebuilding." The last of the new provincial-level party committees was finally established, in Heilungkiang, on 19 August 1971. The whole process had been controlled by the regional military commands, so it is hardly surprising that *JMJP* greeted the formation of the Heilungkiang committee with still another attack on the

TABLE 4.1
Military Representation in the Chinese Power Structure, 1969-71[a]

POSITION	TOTAL	MILITARY MEN	PERCENTAGE MILITARY	REMARKS
Politburo[b,c]	25	13	52%	(9 Commanders 4 Commissars)
9th CC Full Members[d]	170	85	50%	(60 Commanders 25 Commissars)
9th CC Alternates	109	55	50%	
Provincial-level RC Chairmen[e]	29	20	69%	
Provincial-level RC Vice-Chairmen	290	100	34%	
First Secretaries of new CCP Provincial Committees	29	22	76%	(13 Commanders 9 Commissars)
1st & 2nd Secretaries of new CCP Provincial Committees	36	26	72%	
Secretaries & Deputy Secretaries of new CCP Provincial Committees[f]	158	98	62%	(51 Commanders 32 Commissars)
Ministers of the State Council[d]	29	20	69%	

Notes:
 a. Unless otherwise noted, data follows Ting Wang, p. 118. Various sources give somewhat different figures owing to differing interpretations of just what constitutes a "military man," but the same trend is clear. Also refer to Donald W. Kline and Lois B. Hager, "The Ninth Central Committee," CQ, No. 45 (January-March 1971), 37-56.
 b. Kao Ying-mao, p. xlii.
 c. Parris Chang, "Changing Patterns."
 d. Whitson, p. 549.
 e. For a concise survey of the RC Chairmen, see I and S, 1, No. 26 (16 October 1968), 24-28. Of the nine "revolutionary cadres" (e.g., civilians) serving as provincial RC Chairmen in 1969, six were or would become PLA regional political commissars: Chang Ch'un-ch'iao (Nanking MR), Liu Ke-p'ing (Peking MR), Li Hsueh-feng (Peking MR), Wei Kuo-ch'ing (Canton MR), Liu Chien-hsun (Honan MD), and Li Jui-shan (Shensi MD).
 f. Domes, Internal Politics, p. 210.

"theory of many centers" and a call for everyone to recognize the absolute leadership of the (central) party and Chairman Mao.[86]

Since the first "power seizure" in Heilungkiang on 21 January 1967, it had taken four and a half years to reestablish the provincial party committees, and over two years had elapsed since the Ninth Congress. A number of writers have attributed this long delay to "PLA footdragging,"[87] but that cannot be the whole story, since PLA men dominated the rebuilding of the party when it finally came. "Footdragging" was the result of intramilitary distrust, rather than PLA mistrust of civilians. Lin Piao wanted to legitimize his position, and extend his political base by quickly creating a strong and centralized CCP. This goal (if not Lin's motive) was shared by Mao, Chou, Chiang Ch'ing, and virtually the entire central leadership. The bitter criticism of "many centers" in the official press expressed their frustration at the way regional commanders first delayed, and then dominated, the rebirth of the CCP in the provinces.

It now appears that the regional commanders, for their part, were not really committed to maintaining regional autonomy, but were "footdragging" as a means of self-defense. They did not dare to let Lin and the radicals around Chiang Ch'ing control the new party, for their first move would surely be to purge the regional commands. Lin and Chiang Ch'ing had behaved too capriciously in 1967 to risk civil chaos again—let alone another open attack on the PLA. So, although everyone wanted to rebuild the party, no one was in any hurry because there were political opponents who would control significant parts of the new party machine. Something, or somebody, had to "give" before the CCP could be recentralized.

The Fall of Lin Piao

Almost inevitably, the impasse over "party building" between Lin Piao and the Peking radicals, on one hand, and the regional commands, on the other, worked against Lin. The longer the delay, the worse Lin looked, and the more dissatisfied the party chairman became. The MR commanders finally began to form provincial CCP committees which they, and not Peking, ultimately controlled.

Lin Piao had emerged as the number-two man in China because of Mao's personal backing, the support of Chiang Ch'ing and the CRG radicals, and because, as minister of defense, he commanded the main forces of the PLA. It appears that Mao attempted to begin pulling the main force corps out of politics as early as 1968, by ordering a large-scale geographical rotation of units. By 1974, however, only about half of them had moved, and these moves appear to have been mostly in response to the increased Soviet threat in the north and the US withdrawal from Indochina. Nelsen believes that Lin resisted the rotation policy in order to keep the corps in domestic politics.[88] If that was his intent, it didn't work very well, since main force officers seem to have been generally in sympathy with their regional comrades. For whatever reasons, Lin was unable to use the corps to keep the MR leaders in line when the final crunch came.

Lin's failure to get the party reorganized, and his jealousy of his newly-won power, displeased Mao. The chairman's turn back toward order and moderation increasingly found expression in his criticism of "arrogance"—a charge later leveled at Lin himself. Mao also began to criticize the idea that politics was everything while work-style was secondary—a notion by now closely associated with Lin Piao. In November 1969, Mao's criticism of the

PLA escalated, the Central CRG was abolished, and Ch'en Po-ta, the leading radical theoretician, was demoted. Investigation and criticism of the radical "May 16th" group was also intensified.[89]

Yet Lin's radicalism was not easily cast off. He had burned his ideological and personal bridges behind himself since 1959. He was personally identified with a stance of international belligerence and commitment to "self-reliance" (rejection of foreign trade and models). It was becoming evident that that policy condemned China to political isolation, economic stagnation, and military weakness. As Mao, and the political center of power, moved to the "right," Lin remained behind in a vulnerably "ultra-Leftist" position. His power base was too narrow and shaky to allow him to match Mao's shift back toward moderation. Too, Lin's acquiescence in the ruthless suppression of the Red Guards in 1967-68 had badly weakened the radicals surrounding Chiang Ch'ing. With this apparent betrayal, Lin had stayed in step with Mao momentarily, but he could never again count on the backing of the radicals in the CC. Thus, it is fair to date the beginning of the end of Lin Piao as early as 1967.

By 1969, Lin was isolated from the other CC radicals while he remained tied to radical policies. Mao's displeasure with "sham-Marxism" and "idealism" became ever more apparent through 1970, and was publicly proclaimed with the criticism and dismissal of Ch'en Po-ta after the Second Plenum at Lushan, in September.

Owing to his "ultra-Leftist" foreign policy, Lin opposed the shift toward detente with the United States—a shift Mao had initiated.[90] The 1 July 1971 editorial in *JMJP* stated that Chairman Mao's line on "proletarian internationalism" had been opposed by "interference" from the "Left." In August, *Hung Ch'i* said those opposing Mao's new policy toward the US were guilty of "subjectivism, dogmatism, and idealism"—all "Left" deviations later attributed to Lin Piao.

Franz Mogdis suggests that Lin's opposition to rapprochement with the US was also related to his power base within the PLA.[91] Rapprochement implied a reorientation away from naval and air power, needed to meet the American threat, toward greater emphasis on ground forces to fight the Soviets in northern and central Asia. The "steel versus electronics" controversy of 1971 also indicated a shift in priorities away from military industry. While the shift undoubtedly displeased military men in general, air force and navy men may have been particularly frustrated. Since Lin's main military support was in the air force, navy, and GRSD, the reduction of emphasis on these service branches hit directly at his power base. That the premier publicist of "people's war" should have had his principal backers in the air force and navy was still another of the ironies of the situation.

Lin had taken special efforts to assure the personal loyalty of the air force in the early 1960s. It is important to note that the navy, the air force, and the GRSD were generally much more politicized, technically oriented, and centralized than the rest of the PLA. They were also branches where a high level of frustration was evident among officers. By 1965, the relatively well-educated recruits of the early 1950s were field-grade officers, who found themselves blocked for further promotion by a hierarchy of more poorly-educated infantrymen who were as much as twenty years their seniors. This contributed to their relatively high level of radical activism during the GPCR, and to their continuing support of Lin Piao—who also opposed the old infantrymen of the MRs and the MF corps.

In addition to the air force, navy, and GRSD, and the occasional support of the radicals around Chiang Ch'ing, Lin also had the backing of some of the regional leaders who had, for one reason or another, become identified with radical "Maoism." Examples included Liu Feng (commissar of the Wuhan MR-- an air force man), Han Hsien-ch'u and Chou Chih-p'ing (Foochow MR commander and commissar), and Cheng Wei-shang and Li Hsueh-feng of the Peking MR.

On the other side of the hardening power lineup was "a much more amorphous group of officers composed of many powerful regional commanders" as well as professionally inclined officers in the main forces and in Peking. Many of these men had been attacked by radical Red Guards in the "heyday of the radical Left."[92]

Separating Lin from these "military moderates" were not only the issues of foreign policy and resource allocation, but also the grudges and fears accumulated over the years since 1959. Lin had risen at the expense of such respected commanders as P'eng Te-huai and Ho Lung. Moreover, there had been a number of occasions when Lin's associates had undertaken actions they thought Lin would back, only to be purged. Examples included Ch'en Tsai-tao and Hsiao Hua. This penchant for stabbing his supporters in the back had reduced Lin's roster of friends considerably by 1970. Nor had anyone forgotten that it was Lin who had opened the floodgates to Red Guard anarchy in August 1967. The moderates who had survived the "dragging out" episode owed no thanks to Lin, for it was Chou En-lai who had taken risks to protect them.

Still another bone of contention within the PLA was that of civil administration versus military preparedness. While Lin's backers relished their enhanced powers, more professionally inclined officers considered the administration of the country to be a dangerous and extraneous burden. They desired the reemergence of the civilian CCP so that the PLA could get back to soldiering. At a minimum, they wanted the main forces pulled out of domestic chores.[93] This widespread attitude was manifested in the lack of PLA support for Lin in 1971, and in the rapid surrender of PLA domestic power in the provinces in 1973-74.

The civilian moderates, led by Chou En-lai, found common cause with the military "professionals" on a number of issues. Both probably shared a certain desire to avenge the excesses of the GPCR, but more important was their desire to "break the deadlock which prevented the unequivocal enunciation of a moderate national policy."[94] That deadlock was bound to continue as long as Lin and his group were reinforced by the radicals around Chiang Ch'ing.

Robinson points out that Chou and Lin never seem to have disagreed over the years, and that Chou was hardly in a commanding position, himself, in 1969-71.[95] This is true, but Lin had changed since 1959, from a relatively professional soldier to a radical politican. Furthermore, Chou's moderate policies were widely shared among ground force commanders (and many commissars) in both the regional and main force commands. Too, Chou's tireless and courageous moderation during 1967-68 had won him considerable respect and gratitude among these officers.

As early as the end of 1969, then, Lin Piao's position was becoming tenuous. His positive support came from his personal following in the navy, air force, and GRSD, and from a few MR leaders. He could retain the support of the CC radicals only so long as he retained the chairman's personal backing. Arrayed against him was a solidifying coalition of civilian and military moderates, which included most of the MR leaders.

Mao's personal support, which was so crucial to Lin, had never been unconditional. Lin had little choice but to try all possible means to shore up his position. His base of support was so narrow and shaky, and his foes so many, that the withdrawal of the chairman's personal support would be disastrous. Yet every move Lin made to consolidate his power increased Mao's suspicion. That, in turn, made it even more critical for Lin to find other support. This vicious circle led to Lin's final downfall.

The details of Lin Piao's alleged coup d'etat and the flight to his death in September 1971 are too well known to require inclusion here.[96] The main political fact was that Lin's backing melted away, largely because most of the high command opposed his radical political line, and distrusted him personally.

THE PERENNIAL PROBLEMS: SUCCESSION AND REVISIONISM: 1971-75

The fall of Lin Piao reopened the question of succession and demonstrated that leadership relations were far from stable. It also raised anew the closely related problems of intramilitary conflict and the role of the PLA in civil society. However, Lin's removal also made it possible to begin resolving these problems. There was a gradual but accelerating reaction away from most of the radical policies of the GPCR. The PLA was mostly withdrawn from the civilian sector, while moderation and social discipline were reasserted. Most important, the machinery of both party and state were renovated, and CCP control of the PLA was reasserted. The military meanwhile reconcentrated its energies on military affairs to an extent not seen since the days of P'eng Te-huai.

Criticism of Lin Piao

From 1972 to 1975, a vehicle for this retrenchment was a massive campaign to criticize Lin Piao, who displaced Liu Shao-ch'i as the number one archvillain in Chinese propaganda. Upon his head was heaped the blame for every conceivable "deviation." He was accused of "rightist" crimes he never committed, while much of his "Left" radicalism was redefined as "revisionism."

In place of the traditional Army Day editorial, the 1 August 1973 issue of *Hung Ch'i* carried three articles praising Chairman Mao's correct military line, and attacking mistakes made by "swindlers of the Liu Shao-ch'i type" (read: Lin Piao) as far back as 1937. Lin was particularly taken to task for his faulty strategy and tactics, and for his disobedience to Mao during the civil war. Lin's error at that time was his refusal to build and hold base areas and to concentrate his troops for "battles of annihilation." In other words, he persisted in "guerrillaism" at a time when Mao and the rest of the high command were converting to conventional mobile warfare. In December 1947, Mao wrote "The Present Situation and Our Tasks"—in which he enunciated his "Ten Major Military Principles." These principles were applicable to the stage of mobile warfare, and to the capture and retention of territory, but Lin allegedly persisted in small-scale fighting to "route" (harass) the enemy, instead of massing for "battles of annihilation." Since no historical controversy is ever raised in a political vacuum in China, the message was pretty clear: In 1973, China's defensive strategy was shifting away from "guerrillaism" (e.g., "people's war") toward a more conventional defensive strategy.[97] Both the Chinese and the Soviets beefed up their border forces through 1973, and Chinese nuclear missiles were first targeted on Soviet cities, including Moscow.[98] Meanwhile, American forces formally withdrew from Indochina.

The reduced US threat helped enable Chou En-lai, and his allies in the central PLA organs and in the State Planning Commission, to press for a reorientation of China's defenses toward the Soviet threat.[99] An important new quotation from Chairman Mao began to appear everywhere: "Dig tunnels deep, store grain everywhere, and never seek hegemony." The development of Chinese MRBMs and IRBMs gave China a credible, if minimal, deterrent against the USSR. This fact was used to justify a reorientation of the economy away from further high technology military R&D, and toward a more even agricultural and industrial development. At the same time, the continuing attacks on Lin Piao's military errors pointed toward a more conventional defense of the Northeast in the event of a Soviet invasion. Such a strategy would require a more centrally controlled PLA. By mid-summer 1973, this strategy, and its inherent political-economic policies, were clearly identified with Premier Chou En-lai and Acting Defense Minister Yeh Chien-ying.

In the fall of 1973, after the Tenth CCP Congress, criticism of Lin was stepped up, and linked with criticism of Confucius.[100] The "P'i-Lin P'i K'ung" ("Criticize Lin, Criticize Confucius") campaign proved to be prolonged and intensive, continuing through the summer of 1975. It was, however, chronically ambivalent about whether to call Lin a left-wing "opportunist" or a right-wing "revisionist." Indeed, it is difficult to discern any clear trend in the emphasis placed on his alleged "Left" or "right" errors. In retrospect, the fact that Lin was alternately being condemned as a "rightist" and then as a "Leftist" was indicative of two groups which had very different goals and policy preferences. The moderates around Chou En-lai and Yeh Chien-ying were those who quite correctly associated Lin with radical distortions of Mao's ideas. The radicals who would come to be known as the "gang of four" voiced the accusation that he was a "rightist" who pursued the "bourgeois military line"--an accusation that was simply untrue by any theretofore accepted definition of that "line."[101]

Reassertion of civilian party control after Lin's demise was retarded by the simple fact that "party control of the PLA" can be meaningful only if the party is an essentially civilian organization. It was therefore necessary to civilianize the CCP as a first step toward reasserting party control over the military.

In 1971-73, there was much public emphasis on national unity, discipline, and obedience to the party. In particular, the PLA was admonished to observe the "three main rules and eight points for attention," to "learn from the fine work style of the party," and to "learn from the people of the whole country."[102] This was being published at the very time regional military leaders were at the pinnacle of their power. The purge of Lin and his group had left only three central military leaders on the Politburo, and one of them (Li Te-sheng) was concurrently an MD commander. That left the Politburo in the hands of MR leaders and civilian administrators, with both central PLA leaders and radicals as very small minorities.[103] Domes points out, however, that in at least one sense the MR leaders were conceding nothing to this sort of propaganda, for "exhortations to the military to 'accept the leadership of the local and regional (ti-fang) Party committees,' which dominated in the media between November 1971 and June 1972, for all practical purposes did not mean much more than a quest for the loyalty of the military rank-and-file to the regional military commanders."[104]

Even as they directed the gradual "return to barracks," the high command, in cooperation with moderate civilians, directed the moderating political trend which found expression in the new PRC constitution of January 1975. As Joffe suggests, the steady retreat from the "Maoism" of 1966-68 was the condition the PLA high command exacted in return for the military withdrawal from domestic affairs.[105] The three most dramatic trends in China between 1971 and 1975 were the reassertion of moderate politics, the disengagement of the PLA from the civilian sector, and the "rehabilitation" of virtually all of the "capitalist roaders" who fell victim to the GPCR and its aftermath. These three processes were apparent at provincial and local levels as well as in Peking. While the Lin Piao affair did not lead to a major purge of the regional military, a gradual withdrawal of ranking officers from provincial political posts took place through 1972 and the first half of 1973.

The revival of the civilian CCP was dramatically symbolized in May 1973 by the reappearance of Teng Hsiao-p'ing—the former CC general secretary who had been second only to Liu Shao-ch'i himself as an archvillain "capitalist roader" during the GPCR.[106] "Civilian control" was going to mean control by the moderate friends of the officer corps—men like Teng and Chou En-lai.

Even more remarkable than the reappearance of the civilian victims of the Cultural Revolution was the rapid "rehabilitation" of its military victims (Table 4.2).[107] Of all the rehabilitated soldiers, perhaps the most indicative of the direction events were taking was Ch'en Tsai-tao, the MR commander whose refusal to knuckle under to the CRG had provoked the Wuhan Incident. Ch'en's actions at Wuhan had been widely approved by PLA officers, and his purge had been a source of considerable irritation. Although, of course, Ch'en had supposedly studied Mao Thought, and had made several self-criticisms, his reinstatement was a milestone in the return to moderate politics, and a vindication of the PLA demand for social discipline and order.[108]

The Tenth Party Congress

Late in August 1973, the Chinese Communist Party convened its Tenth Congress, which ratified the new power alignments and strategies worked out since the fall of Lin Piao. The speeches of both Chou En-lai and Wang Hung-wen laid down the new line that Lin Piao had been a bourgeois-revisionist—and that revisionism was still China's "main danger." Recasting Lin as a rightist was clearly a concession to the CC radicals, and also marked a reassertion of Mao's own perennial concern with revisionism in the successor generation. It did not mark any appreciable return to radical politics, for a tone of moderation and orderliness ran through the entire congress.

The radicals were heavily outnumbered in the new Politburo Standing Committee. There was also a striking reduction in regional PLA representation. Of twenty-four full and alternate members, only three (four counting Li Teh-sheng) were career military men from regional posts.

More important than the headcount in the CC, however, was the spectacular disengagement of the regional PLA from non-military duties following the congress. The careful preparations for the Tenth Congress had been largely devoted to clearing the way for "demilitarization" at the local levels. The continuing presence of high-ranking military officers in the CC was (and is) to be expected; the unique "militarization" of China since 1967 had been the result of PLA penetration into politics and administration at the middle and lower levels. Immediately after the congress, military disengagement at those levels assumed impressive proportions.

In September 1973, "Three Supports and Two Militaries" was dropped from the official lexicon. All military officers of "Three Supports and Two Militaries" units were ordered to resign all local party and government posts. By the end of 1974, the last known MCCs had disappeared as well.[109] By mid-1974, most of the PLA "Mao Tse-tung Thought Propaganda Teams" had been

TABLE 4.2
Major "Rehabilitated" PLA Men: 1971-72*

NAME	FORMER POSITION	DATE PURGED	DATE REAPPEARED	NEW POSITION
Su Chien-hua	1st Political Commissar of Navy	January 1967	September 1971	Deputy Commander of Navy
Liu Tao-sheng	Political Commissar of Navy	January 1967	March 1972	Deputy Commander of Navy
Chang Tsung-shun	Deputy Chief of Staff	January 1967(?)	June 1972	Deputy Commander of Tainan MR
Yang Yung	Deputy Chief of Staff & Commander of Peking MR	January 1967	August 1972	(Named Commander of Sinkiang MR in August 1973)
Liao Han-sheng	Vice-MND & Political Commissar of Peking MR	January 1967	August 1972	(Public appearance)
Ch'en Tsi-tao	Commander of Wuhan MR	July 1967	August 1972	Deputy Commander of Foochow MR (?)
Chang Han-hua	Political Commissar of Wuhan MR	July 1967	August 1972	Deputy Political Commissar of Canton MR
Li Ta	Head of PLA Athletic Program	January 1967(?)	August 1972	Deputy Chief of Staff

*Data from C.P. Chang in I & S, 9, No. 4 (Janaury 1973), 6-8.

TABLE 4.3
Military Region Command Reassignments in December 1973-January 1974

MR	COMMANDER IN NOVEMBER 1973	COMMANDER IN FEBRUARY 1974	REMARKS
Tsinan	Yang Te-chih	Tseng Szu-yü	} trade
Wuhan	Tseng Szu-yü	Yang Te-chih	
Shenyang	Ch'en Hsi-lien	Li Teh-sheng	Li left GPD position
Peking	(vacant)	Ch'en Hsi-lien	
Canton	Ting Sheng	Hsu Shih-yu	} trade
Nanking	Hsu Shih-yu	Ting Sheng	
Foochow	Han Hsien-ch'u	P'i Ting-chun	} trade
Lanchou	P'i Ting-chun (acting)	Han Hsien-ch'u	
Sinkiang	Yang Yung	Yang Yung	Appointed August 1973
Ch'engtu	Ch'in Chi-wei	Ch'in Chi-wei	Appointed May 1973
Kunming	Wang Pi-ch'eng	Wang Pi-ch'eng	Appointed 1970 or 1971

withdrawn, or at least had been diluted by civilian cadres.

Travelers reported, in late 1974, that PLA uniforms were now completely missing from the revolutionary committees encountered during official tours. Everyone said that the "three-way alliance" referred to a combination of the "old, middle-aged, and young" (rather than PLA, cadres, and masses, as in 1967-68).[110] Owing to the sheer magnitude of the task, complete disengagement of the military probably lasted well into 1975, but the commitment was obviously made no later than August 1973.[111]

In late December 1973 and January 1974, the most spectacular single step was taken in the "demilitarization" of provincial politics: Eight of the eleven MR commanders were simultaneously ordered to new posts. In six cases, commanders actually traded places (Table 4.3). By mid-January, the only MR commander who had held his post for more than one year was Wang Pi-ch'eng, in Kunming. Of the eight commanders involved, six had been doubling as heads of provincial party committees—posts they all now gave up.[112] The Sinkiang, Ch'engtu, and Kunming MRs were reportedly reorganized as well, although their commanders remained in place.[113]

That these powerful men obediently allowed themselves to be reshuffled strongly supports the view that they were not bent on retaining civil power, and especially that there was no "balance of power" among the military regions. In 1967-73, the MR commanders had carefully hedged their positions against the threat of another outburst of radicalism. They had been reassured, however, by the return of domestic order and moderate foreign policy, by the purge of Lin Piao and Ch'en Po-ta, by the substantial weakening of Chiang Ch'ing and her remaining followers, by the "rehabilitation" of men like Teng Hsiao-p'ing and Ch'en Tsai-tao, and by the appointment of Yeh Chien-ying as defense minister.

Although there was agreement on party control of the PLA, there were still differences over the scope and nature of that control. Apparently, the crux of the matter was the institutional framework. As had happened so often before, the relationship of PLA units to local CCP committees became a bone of contention. In July, *KMJP* commended the "good experience" of a local regiment in the Northeast, which strictly observed the Three Rules and Eight Points, "conscientiously honored the *centralized leadership of the district Party committee*, and strengthened the solidarity of the army and the government, and of the army and the people."[114]

If the local CCP committees did not exert political leadership, of course, the only alternative had to be the internal military party organization, and the GPD commissar system, as had officially been the case since August 1966. The trouble was that the GPD had been in limbo since August 1967. PLA political work, especially in the regional forces, had been controlled mainly by military commanders, rather than commissars. During the tenure of Li Teh-sheng (a career commander) as GPD chief, the department had taken no initiatives. To the extent that it functioned at all, it was merely as a transmission belt for the directives of the MAC. With the GPD in eclipse and commanders in the ascent, the whole commissar system, as "institutional conscience," was severely limited.[115] The reassignment of Li Teh-sheng in January 1974 only served to cloud the situation further, for no new GPD chief was named for another year. During the period 1967-74, there had been a decline in formal PLA political work--especially after 1971. In 1974, Lin Piao's "Four-Good Company" and "Five-Good Soldier" programs were officially scrapped, as "disguised revisionism."[116]

There was also evidence that the moderate political trend contributed to further professionalization in the PLA. For one thing, a spate of articles on the subject of command responsibility versus collective leadership indicated that certain military officers were advocating a return to the "one-man command" system of the 1950s.[117] An indication of the strength of this view was the way reports about PLA units began to name unit commanders (but not commissars) and to credit them with unit achievements.[118]

October 1974 National Day festivities were highlighted by a hoard of newly "rehabilitated" civilian and military cadres--mostly "revisionist" victims of the Cultural Revolution. Most noteworthy of these were Hsiao Hua, the former GPD chief, and Fu Ch'ung-pi, the Peking Garrison Commander who ran afoul of Chiang Ch'ing in early 1968. Yang Ch'eng-wu and former PLAAF political commissar Yü Li-chin, both of whom had reappeared in August, were also present. Also appearing was Hsieh Ming, the widow of Ho Lung, the principal victim of the "January Storm" in 1967. This general "rehabilitation" of cadres made it ever more conspicuous that none of the radicals of Chiang Ch'ing's Central CRG (Ch'i Pen-yü, Wang Li, Kuan Feng, et al.) who fell in 1967-68, had reappeared (Table 4.4).[119]

There were still political problems within the high command in 1974. This was most obvious in the continuing failure to appoint new chiefs for the GRSD, GSD, and GPD, and commanders for the armored forces, telecommunications troops, and Peking Garrison. As Nelsen suggests, this was probably

TABLE 4.4[a]
Major PLA Figures "Rehabilitated" in 1973-74

NAME	FORMER POSITION	DATE PURGED	DATE REAPPEARED	REMARKS
Sung Jen-ch'iung*	1st PC Shenyang MR; 1st Secretary, CCP-CC Northeast Bureau	January 1968	October 1974	c
Ouyang Ch'in*	1st PC Heilungkiang MD; 1st Secretary, Heilungkiang CCP Committee	d	October 1974	c
Lin T'ieh*	1st PC Hopeh MD; 1st Secretary Hopeh CCP Committee	1967	October 1974	c
Yang Ch'eng-wu**	Acting Chief of Staff of PLA	March 1968	July 1974	Became Deputy Chief of Staff
Hsiao Hsiang-jung	Director, Admin. Office, MAC; Director, Admin. Office, MND	November 1966	October 1974	c
Wang Hsiang-jung**	Director, Operations, GSD	d	July 1974	c
Liu Shao-wen	Deputy Director, Intelligence, GSD	d	October 1974	c
Fu Ch'iu-t'ao	Director, Mobilization, GSD	d	October 1974	c
Hsiao Hua*	Director, GPD	August 1967	October 1974	c
Liu Chih-chien	Deputy Director, GPD	January 1967	October 1974	c

Liang Pi-yeh	Deputy Director, GPD	August 1966	May 1973	Became Deputy Director of GPD in 1975
Fu Chung	Deputy Director, GPD	d	October 1974	c
P'eng Ming-chih	Commander, Wuhan Garrison	October 1969	July 1974	c
Mou Li-shan	Commander, 38th Corps	1968	October 1974	Probably assigned to Second Artillery in 1975
Ulanfu*	Commander & 1st PC, Inner Mongolia MR; 1st Secretary Inner Mongolia CCP Committee	May 1967	August 1973	Full Member, 10th CC
Han Chen-chi	Deputy Director, GRSD	d	October 1974	c
Jao Cheng-hsi	Deputy Director, GRSD	d	October 1974	c
Li Hsueh-san	Deputy PC, GRSD	d	October 1974	c
Li Yao	Deputy PC, GRSD	d	October 1974	c
Yü Li-chin	PC, Air Force	March 1968	July 1974	c
Wang Hui-ch'iu	PC, Air Force	mid-1973	October 1974	c
Wu K'o-hua	Commander, Artillery	d	July 1974	c
Hsiang Shou-chih	Deputy Commander, Artillery (probable)	d	October 1974	c
Su Chin	Deputy Commander, Artillery	d	October 1974	c
Ouyang I	Deputy PC, Artillery	d	October 1974	c
Ch'eng Shih-ts'ai	Deputy Commander, Armored Corps	d	January 1974	c

(Table 4.4 continued on next page)

117

TABLE 4.4 (continued)

NAME	FORMER POSITION	DATE PURGED	DATE REAPPEARED	REMARKS
Chang Wen-chou	Deputy Commander, Armored Corps	d	October 1974	c
T'an Yu-lin	Deputy Commander, Engineer Corps	d	October 1974	c
Wang Shia-tao*	Heilungkiang MD Commander	September 1971	August 1973(?)	10th CC, Heilungkiang MD Commander again by March 1974
Li Shou-hsuan	Commander, Railway Corps	October 1969	January 1974	c
Kuo Wei-ch'eng	Deputy Commander, Railway Corps	d	October 1974	c
Ch'en Ho-ch'iao	2nd PC, Telecommunications Corps	d	October 1974	c
Li Chu-k'uei	PC, GRSD	d	July 1974	c
Chung Ch'i-kuang	Deputy Commandant, Higher Military College	d	October 1974	c
Chang T'ing-fa	Deputy Commander, Air Force	d	June 1973	Possibly a Deputy Chief of Staff and/or Deputy Commander of Air force in 1974
Chang Nai-keng	Director, Antichemical Corps	d	October 1974	c

Mo Wen-hua	Commandant, PLA Political Academy	d	July 1974	c
Liu Hsien-ch'uan	1st PC, Air Force	September 1971	August 1973	10th CC, Probably Commander of Railway Corps in 1974
Fu Ch'ung-pi	Commander, Peking Garrison	March 1968	October 1974	c
Huang Hsin-t'ing	Commander, Chengtu MR	May 1967	July 1974	c

Notes:
a. Data principally drawn from "1 October 1974 National Day Festivities," USCGDLO.
b. Full and Alternate Members of the Eighth CC are indicated with one and two asterisks, respectively.
c. No new position given as of October 1974.
d. Exact date of purge uncertain.

because the MAC was unable to agree on politically acceptable officers who were also widely acceptable to the officer corps.[120] The far-reaching "rehabilitation" of senior officers was certainly intended as a gesture toward the officer corps of the good faith of the MAC and CC. It is probably not true that all these top positions were being kept open as a means of enforcing MAC control: The burden on the MAC must have been terrific, and the appointment of Ma Ning to command the air force (in June 1974) indicated that the MAC was willing to fill vacancies if suitable officers were available.

The Radical "Backlash": 1974-75

One leftist theme in the press in 1974 persisted through 1975: All cadres must be willing to serve at "either higher or lower levels [and] work well as officials or as common people." This theme had first appeared in 1971, but received new emphasis, and was especially directed at the military, after mid-1973.[121]

In November 1974, Shensi Radio reported the most determined attack in fifteen years against the elite status of the PLA officer corps. It reported that large numbers of "selected cadres" from the Shensi MD had gone, on a rotational basis, to work on civilian communes "to unfold the campaign of learning from Tachai and to strengthen militia building." Beginning in August 1973, 1036 cadres, led by district deputy commanders, deputy commissars, the chief of staff, the director of the political department, and the director of logistics, had been "selected from the various organs and units subordinate to the districts and the various military subdistricts and county people's armed forces departments and dispatched to labor at 219 brigades on 216 communes. They labor ... for a period of one year ... and this system will be perpetuated." Of the second annual batch of cadres "sent down" in August 1974, "not a few ... are leading cadres at army [*chun*, corps], divisional, and regimental level." This indicates that main force units were involved, since there are no corps in the regional forces. Cadres reportedly "spent two-thirds of their time in labor" (and the rest, presumably, in militia work).[122]

This report was unique, in that no such movement to send PLA officers to labor in civilian communes has been reported before or since, in Shensi or elsewhere. Yet it had supposedly been underway since August 1973. It certainly appears to have been an even more extreme version of *hsia-fang* than the *hsia-lien tang-ping* movement of 1958-60. It not only reduced officers to the lowest level, but separated them entirely from the military. Furthermore, it required a full year of labor, as opposed to a few months. This movement apparently was dropped, but was replaced by a less extreme *hsia-lien* movement in 1975.

Although the general tenor of the Fourth National People's Congress (January 1975) was one of moderation, there were significant leftist countercurrents which directly affected the PLA. The appointment of Chang Ch'un-ch'iao as chief of the GPD was probably a real blow. Although Chang had been behaving much more moderately, he was still remembered as one of the leading radicals of the GPCR, and had few friends in the PLA high command. Under him, there was a distinctly leftist shift in PLA political work.

Shortly after the end of the National People's Congress, Chairman Mao called for a nationwide movement to "study the theory of the dictatorship of the proletariat." In the PLA, this meant heavy emphasis on CCP control, formal political work, and a renewed emphasis on the company-level party branches--much as in the early 1960s.[123] There was also a nationwide campaign against "bourgeois right," a term applied to all notions of private ownership, material incentive, and special status. Predictably, military rank was singled out as the most harmful manifestation of "bourgeois right" in the army. In July, *KMJP* spoke of the danger of incipient elitism among military cadres who consider themselves a "cut above" common soldiers.[124]

The Army Day 1975 editorial in *JMJP* was almost entirely devoted to officer-soldier "brotherhood," and the evil notions of "bourgeois right" and rank.[125] It also confirmed that a military *hsia-fang* movement was underway—strikingly similar to the *hsia-lien tang-ping* movement of 1958-63. Reportedly, company cadres all lived "in the squads," trained, studied, and worked alongside the soldiers.[126] In order to assure that cadres kept "the natural colors of an ordinary soldier," they took turns at "serving as ordinary soldiers or company leaders."[127]

It is unclear whether high-level officers were sent all the way "down" to be private soldiers, or whether they only went "down" to act as company-level cadres. It will be recalled that the former was the case in 1958-60, but that Lin Piao moderated the *hsia-lien* movement to the latter procedure in 1960-63. It appears that higher-ranking officers were mostly "going down" to act as company officers. However, there were also reports of the more radical procedure of literally "serving as a soldier": The logistics officer of a regional force regiment and the political commissar of a main force corps (the equivalent of a lieutenant general) reportedly both served as company cooks in July (cooks seem to have the lowest status of anyone in the PLA).[128] Whatever the requirements, the tone of the press coverage made it quite plain the PLA cadres were far from enthusiastic, but that, like good soldiers, they were obeying their orders while seeking to have them modified. It need hardly be added that Chang Ch'un-ch'iao made few new friends in the officer corps as a result of all this.

The Fourth National People's Congress and After

The National People's Congress of mid-January 1975, overall, appears to have been a major victory for Chou En-lai and the civilian moderates. One result was that the moderate coalition began to show signs of internal dispute over economic priorities. The PLA high command reportedly was in conflict with the civilian moderates over the decision to deemphasize military industry and R&D in favor of agriculture and capital construction.[129] With the exception of this disagreement over resource allocation, which is a common phenomenon in virtually any polity, the "professional" commanders of the PLA and the civilian moderates seemed to share views on most foreign and domestic issues.

The "rehabilitation" of purged "revisionist" PLA men was virtually completed when, on Army Day 1975, Lo Jui-ch'ing reappeared in Peking. Several important PLA vacancies were finally filled as well: Commanders were named for both the Railroad Corps (Liu Hsien-ch'uan) and the Telecommunications Corps (Chou Shih-chung). On Army Day, Chang Tsung-hsun was officially identified as head of the GRSD. The same *NCNA* name list made it clear that Yang Ch'eng-wu was, for all practical purposes, the acting PLA Chief of Staff, although Teng Hsiao-p'ing was officially named to that post at the NPC in January. Thus, two of the three principal departments of the PLA were now headed by commanders who had been purged for "revisionism" during the GPCR. The third (the GPD) was under Chang Ch'un-ch'iao, a civilian radical in uniform. Chang's background, and the unpopular *hsia-lien* movement, made his long-term prospects appear tenuous at best.

By mid-1975, the PLA had effectively "returned to barracks." The top military leaders were still deeply involved in the continuing competition among various groups within the CC, but that is inherent in the regime. Among these top leaders, the "military-civilian" distinction is simply inapplicable. But the army, as an institution, had withdrawn from domestic administration and police work, and was obediently carrying out the orders of the MAC, even when those orders were distasteful.

This "return to barracks" was possible only because the high command wished to keep the PLA out of politics, and because the vast majority of officers preferred to stick to soldiering. Despite the trauma of the GPCR and the Lin Piao affair, no known segment of China's junior and middle-grade officers had developed the "praetorian" mentality which has characterized so many twentieth-century officer corps. The authority of the party over the military had survived a severe and prolonged test.

The entire experience suggests that the PLA officer corps has always tended to trim its sails to the wind. Attempts to radicalize the officer corps have met with formal obedience, but also with subtle passive resistance. The officer corps has adapted itself to the rhetoric of the times and even assumed the superficial short-term guise of "politicalization," while maintaining a deeper conservatism and a long-range trend toward professionalism. Recent events have begun to expose an interesting anomaly, however. Officers in the operational units seem quite ready to discard "politicalization" completely. With the "old warriors" in the MAC, however, the story is different. Yeh Chien-ying, Nieh Jung-chen, Su Yü, et al., fought for moderation, "professionalism," and technological modernization throughout the long battle against radical "Maoism." Since Mao's death, however, they have made it plain that the are not about to discard the revolutionary heritage altogether.

MAO'S DEATH AND THE SUCCESSION

The following pages focus on the political events of 1976-81 and their impact on the PLA. Subsequent chapters will cover the same period, focusing on force structure and military capabilities (chapter 5), R&D and the defense industry (chapter 6), and PLA personnel management (chapter 7).

Perhaps the most controversial aspect of "demilitarization" was the movement to reassert local party control over the militia. This attempt, which was especially evident in Shanghai and Peking, began immediately after the Tenth Party Congress. A struggle soon developed between the regional PLA and civilian radicals over the issue.

In September 1973, the national media published calls to "learn from Shanghai in militia building." The movement was very clearly under the auspices of Chiang Ch'ing and the "gang of four." "Model" militia units in Shanghai reportedly trained themselves (i.e., without PLA involvement). Furthermore, they were described as being solely responsible to the local civilian party. The radicals also attempted to create a national militia command, directly responsive to themselves.[130]

While paying lip service to "learning from Shanghai," however, the regional PLA commands maintained a firm grip on most militia organizations. Their resistance to the "gang's" campaign was evidently successful. Chiang Ch'ing and her group allegedly began planning a coup d'etat as early as 1973, and supposedly attempted it in October 1976. Given the continued PLA influence in the militia, and the conservative nature of the militia itself, it is not surprising that the radical coup (if one was actually attempted) failed, even in Shanghai.[131]

Mao Tse-tung's death, in September 1976, was swiftly followed by the fall of the "gang of four" in early October. The details are not all known, but all accounts do agree that senior military men (most notably Yeh Chien-ying, Nieh Jung-chen, and Hsu Shih-yu) played instrumental roles.[132] Hua Kuo-feng has since claimed that in the crisis the "gang" could not get "even a single company" of the army to back them.[133]

Since the arrest of the "gang," the leading triumvirate has been Hua Kuo-feng, Teng Hsiao-p'ing, and Yeh Chien-ying, with the latter frequently appearing to arbitrate differences between the other two. The PLA role in smoothing the transition was so well played that it looked almost easy, viewed from the outside. Considering the traumatic succession crises that other Leninist states have experienced, and the post-Mao chaos that some had feared for China, the service the old soldiers did is hard to overestimate.

"Radical Revisionism" and the Revolutionary Tradition

1977-80 witnessed drastic "reversals of incorrect verdicts," and a movement to criticize the "gang of four" and remove their followers from the party. Foreign contacts suddenly proliferated. In 1978, the PRC began to solicit foreign loans and joint-management enterprises—two procedures that were officially denounced as recently as late 1977. In late 1978, a minister of the State Council held a western-style press conference, sporting a pin-stripe suit, silk tie, and digital watch.[134] P'eng Te-huai was "rehabilitated,"[135] and both the Great Leap forward and the Cultural Revolution have been repudiated. The status of Mao Tse-tung is now open to debate, and Liu Shao-ch'i has been posthumously "rehabilitated."[136] There has even been talk of a "fifth member of the gang of four"—presumably Mao himself.[137] Nothing, it appears, is sacred any more.

Though the policies of 1977-79 were widely characterized as "moderate," they were in fact nothing of the kind. The methods were vastly different, but the "new long march to the four modernizations" initially was cast in terms as flamboyant and optimistic as was the Great Leap Forward. The swing to the "right" was dramatic and uncompromising, and provoked deep anxieties. In 1978, a Hong Kong newspaper printed a letter from a young Chinese, speaking eloquently of the "collapse of the old faith."[138] At the practical level, the change in party line has been so drastic that all Chinese, and especially cadres, are "afraid of the big stick." Although the line moderated considerably in 1980-81, there is still a general hesitancy to commit oneself to the new line, because it is such a drastic reversal it seems likely to be reversed yet again. The witch hunt for followers of the "gang of four" serves to remind people what happens to those who exhibit too much zeal.

Since 1976, the PLA's "old warriors" have sought to defend some of the old faith, dampen the extremism of "modernization," and encourage constructive participation. In December 1978, for example, *CFCP* pleaded, "Implement the Principle of Not Seizing on Other's Faults, Not Slapping Labels on People and Not Wielding the Big Stick."[139] Otherwise, it said, "people will not speak their minds and consequently the true situation will remain exposed ... subjectivism and bureaucracy will prevail. People will live ... in fear that others may find fault with them while wisdom and talent will be suppressed."

On 11 December 1978, the GPD announced that the movement to criticize the "gang of four" would end in most military units at the end of the year, and the army's main energies would be devoted to training and modernization.[140] This preceded, by eleven days, a similar decision by the Third Plenum,[141] and may well have helped force it.

Throughout 1978-79, senior military leaders made statements and advocated policies which sounded "Maoist," or at least comparatively "revolutionary" in the traditional sense, thereby going against the "revisionist" tide. For example, Nieh Jung-chen, Lo Jui-ch'ing, and Yeh Chien-ying all made derogatory references to the way P'eng Te-huai opposed PLA political work, the "dual-command" (commissar) system, and the militia--all this in 1978, a year when no civilian criticized P'eng at all.[142]

Two major national conferences, one on PLA political work and the other on militia work, underscored the continuing PLA commitment to the revolutionary tradition in 1978. When Teng Hsiao-p'ing addressed the PLA Political Work Conference on 2 June, he stressed entirely predictable themes: "Seek truth from facts," root out the influence of the "gang of four," and work for the "four modernizations."[143] Similarly, Chairman Hua spoke to the conference about the importance of the new "Regulations on Cadres in Service" and "Regulations on PLA Political Work." These would provide a "fairly complete set of rules for all aspects of [PLA] work suited to the new historical conditions."[144]

When Yeh Chien-ying took the podium, however, it was to give a thundering reaffirmation of the faith: "Our army is the army of the party . . . political work is the source of our army's combat strength." The PLA, he said, must strengthen its political work. "Otherwise, it would face the danger of getting away from the party's leadership, of changing its proletarian character, of losing its combat strength and of having its leadership usurped by *bourgeois careerists*."[145]

The new PLA "Political Work Regulations" were promulgated in August. Judging from press reports, they contain remarkably little change, in tone or specifics, from the "Lin Piao regulations" of 1963 (except, of course, for references to the villainous Lin Piao and the idealistic, metaphysical, anarchical "gang of four").[146] As far as the "old warriors" are concerned, politics and expertise are still of equal importance: "The tendency to ignore politics must be criticized, and both armchair and misguided politicians must be opposed; it is necessary to prevent one tendency from concealing another."[147] The leading role of unit party committees, the commissar system, and the class brotherhood of officers and men were all reiterated in the same terms used in the early 1960s. To underscore this continuity with the revolutionary past, the 1944 "Report on Political Work by the Political Department of the Rear Detachment of the Eighth Route Army" was reprinted and widely circulated in August.[148] A spate of articles also appeared eulogizing the late Marshal Lo Jung-huan, chief of the GPD in the early 1960s.[149] This interesting stratagem made it possible to reassert Lin Piao's political reforms of that period, simply by attributing them to Lo (who was actually ill and inactive at the time).

Introduction of the air force's First Flight Division as a model had a three-fold significance. First, it was specifically the unit party committee that was singled out for emulation. Second, it represented the full "rehabilitation" of the air force, which has been under a cloud since the Lin Piao affair. Third, it made the point that traditional political work is entirely compatible with modernization, even in a high-technology setting.[150]

On 18 August 1978, the new "Regulations on the Service of Officers of the Chinese PLA" were ratified—but hardly any details were publicized.[151] It seems possible that the regulations contained provisions about which there were already second thoughts. Perhaps it is significant that although, in announcing ratification in August, NCNA used the English word "officer," the infrequent subsequent references to the regulations reverted to "cadre" (kan-pu).

In the first half of the year, it had appeared that the PLA would follow the lead of many civilian institutions and reintroduce a rank system. It was even officially confirmed that the 1975 attack on "bourgeois right" was indeed a "gang of four" plot.[152] When last "Regulations on the Service of Officers" were promulgated, in 1955, a system of ranks and differentiated uniforms was introduced. It was logical to expect the new regulations, in keeping with the new "Teng Hsiao-p'ing line," would reintroduce both. Indeed, the few provisions of the new Officer Regulations which have been announced are quite in step with the "four modernizations."[153] As early as May, foreign sources reported that the reintroduction of ranks and new uniforms was impending.[154] But it just didn't happen. Su Yü even went to the trouble of formally stating that the PLA "will never again take up the matter of restoring the rank system," because it would "only create gaps between the top and bottom...."[155] Yet it was further reported, in July, that the PLA was asking foreign attaches for sample foreign uniforms.[156] Apparently there are mixed opinions on the issue within the PLA—with senior leaders like Su resisting the inevitable.

Closely related to the rank issue is the fact that the army seems to be the only place in China where *hsia-fang* of cadres was practiced as late as 1978. "Going down to the companies" was ordered in a MAC resolution of 9 August, and was endorsed repeatedly by senior PLA leaders.[157] All this was in marked contrast to the growing elitism in the rest of society.

At the National Militia Work Conference in August, Yang Yung and Nieh Jung-chen attacked the "gang of four" for undermining militia work, and made it plain that the People's Militia is still vital to "people's war under modern conditions." According to Yang, "The militia system is something the people of our country like and want to keep."[158]

Nieh reiterated the time-honored formulas about "luring the enemy deep," but also said the PLA would "stop enemy penetrations" while the cities would be defended—mainly, it seems, by the militia. "The defense and security of cities is of great significance to stabilizing the war situation, preserving war potentials and supporting a protracted war."[159]

By means of "people's air defense" (e.g., "civil defense" in American terms) and "people's defense," the Chinese militia is expected to turn every Chinese city into a "Stalingrad-type city." *CFCP* has referred to "Stalingrad-type cities" since late 1977. The high command is clearly under no illusions about the PLA's ability to stop a Soviet invasion at the border. That being the case, "people's war" and the related political elan are still necessary.[160]

Initially, it was the shortage of foreign exchange which arrested China's swing toward the political and economic "right." During the brief war with Vietnam in early 1979, several foreign contracts were suspended, as were negotiations for large-scale technology imports. At the NPC session in June 1979, Hua Kuo-feng announced the new "eight character" policy (*t'iao-cheng, kai-ke, cheng-tuan, t'i-kao*: "Readjust, Restructure, Consolidate, Improve") for the economy. Under this policy, such "Maoist" economic slogans as "self-sufficiency" reappeared. By 1980, politics and ideology were following suit, with reassertion of many slogans and policies not seen since Mao's death. PLA spokesmen have been prominent in pacing this latest moderation of radical excess.

Some outside observers, especially in Hong Kong and Taiwan, have noted the reassertion of "revolutionary" slogans by military men in 1979-81, and have construed it as evidence of bitter conflict between the "Teng clique" and "the army."[161] PLA "radicalism" has been inferred only by highly selective use of the evidence, however. The main impulse for the retreat from extreme "revisionism" came from civilian economic circles. At this writing (spring 1981), civilians often sound more leftist than soldiers did in 1978. Writing in a Taiwan journal, Chu Liang notes that in September 1980, when Teng Hsiao-p'ing commented on the tragic sinking of the "Po-hai No. 2" oil rig (in November 1978), he criticized the overzealous incompetence of the responsible officials. He said their misconduct had resulted from an "ultra-leftist" attitude, justified by "Maoist" slogans like "fear neither hardship nor death." A few days later, CFCP ran an article entitled "For the Sake of the People, Fear Neither Hardship Nor Death."[162] Chu's conclusion: Teng and "the army" are in conflict over this slogan and the policy alternatives and attitudes it implies. Only a few months later, however, the civilian mass media were calling upon the people to renew their "spiritual" commitment to building socialism, invoking the "Yenan spirit," and urging them to "fear neither hardship nor death."[163] There seems to be little difference, even in emphasis, in the ideological pronouncements of military and civilian leaders in early 1981. The "radical revisionism" of 1977-79 has been reversed. The PLA high command surely welcomed and encouraged this, but that is hardly evidence of fundamental civil-military conflict—quite the contrary.

We have seen that the PLA high command was considerably to the "right" of the political mainstream during the Great Leap and the Cultural Revolution. In 1977-80, as in the early 1960s, however, senior soldiers emphasized many of the more "leftist" aspects of the revolutionary tradition. They have consistently tended toward a moderate course, balancing modernization and expertise with "people's war" and political work. They advocate this "red and expert" balance for two related reasons: The Chinese people, and especially middle-level cadres, will "fear the big stick" of retribution as long as the party line continues to oscillate violently. Even more fundamentally, the "old faith" must not be cast aside until and unless new myths and symbols replace the old ones.[164]

A "conservative" is one who defends the time-proven myths, symbols, and practices of his society against rapid or destabilizing change. The Chinese high command is not opposed to change per se. On the contrary, they are vitally concerned with technological progress. But they also understand the importance of a stable social base to maximum possible military preparedness. Accordingly, they continue to resist excessive zeal which threatens social, political, and economic stability.

The younger generations of Chinese officers, recruited after about 1945, lack the "old warriors'" revolutionary experience, and their military-political breadth of vision. The only experience these younger men have had with "politicization" has been the disaster of the Great Leap and the chaos of the Cultural Revolution. Furthermore, their battle experience has been relatively modern and conventional. They lack personal experience with "people's war." It is they who are now pressing hardest for guns instead of butter, for ranks and new uniforms, and for real professionalization. Yeh, Nieh, Su, Hsu Hsiang-ch'ien, and the other "old warriors" are now coming into conflict with these younger officers who have heretofore provided their bedrock support. Ironically, it is Teng Hsiao-p'ing, the septuagenarian civilian former commissar, who now speaks for the "professionals" of the PLA's post-1945 generations.

NOTES

1. On "guardian" coups, see Huntington, *Political Order*, pp. 225-226.
2. Jurgen Domes, "The Role of the Military in the Formation of Revolutionary Committees, 1967-68," *CQ*, No. 44 (October-December 1970), 144.
3. Harvey Nelsen, "Military Bureaucracy in the Cultural Revolution," *AS*, '4, No. 4 (April 1974), p. 379.
4. Harvey W. Nelsen, *The Chinese Military System* (Boulder, CO: Westview, 1977), pp. 148-149.
5. Domes, "The Role of the Military," pp. 122-123 and 140-141.
6. Parris Chang, "Changing Patterns of Military Roles in Chinese Politics," in *The Military and Political Power in China in the 1970's*, ed. William W. Whitson (New York: Praeger, 1972), p. 51.
7. Gillespie and Sims, p. 203.
8. "Circular of the CC of the CCP," 16 May 1966, in *CCP Documents of the Great Proletarian Cultural Revolution: 1966-67* (Hong Kong: URI, 1968), pp. 18 and 27-28.
9. Whitson, pp. 377-378.
10. Edward E. Rice, *Mao's Way* (Berkeley and Los Angeles: University of California Press, 1972), pp. 272-273; "Wicked History of P'eng Te-huai," pp. 17-18; and "The Death of General P'eng Te-huai," *Ta Kung Pao*, 13 December 1980, p. 2.
11. Rice, p. 301.
12. *Hung Ch'i* [*Red Flag*] (this is a Red Guard publication, not the *Hung Ch'i* published by the CCP Central Committee), Peking, No. 6 (18 January 1967), p. 4, trans. in *TCC:P&S*, No. 391 (*JPRS*, No. 40, 488), pp. 20-23.
13. Bueschel, p. 93.
14. "Some Regulations of the CCP CC and the State Council Concerning the Strengthening of Public Security Work in the GPCR," 13 January 1967, in *CCP Documents: 1966-1967*, pp. 173-177.
15. *CCP Documents; 1966-1967*, pp. 193-196.
16. See recently "revised" histories of the "Adverse Current" by Hsi Ch'en in *JMJP*, 26 February 1979, trans. in *FBIS*, No. 41, pp. E7-E20; and Chi Hsi-ch'en, *Cheng Ming*, Nos. 31, 32, 33 (May, June, July 1980), trans. in *China Report*, No. 105 (15 August 1980), 17-62.
17. *CCP Documents; 1966-1967*, pp. 227-254.
18. Rice, pp. 315-316. Rice's discussion of the events of January-March 1967 is excellent (pp. 302 ff.).
19. Nelsen, "Military Bureaucracy," pp. 391-392; Whitson, p. 388; and Ralph L. Powell, "Soldiers in the Economy," *AS*, 9, No. 8 (August 1971), p. 744.
20. Nelsen, "Military Forces in the Cultural Revolution," p. 454.
21. Nelsen, "Military Bureaucracy," p. 387.
22. See the excellent discussion on this in Rice, p. 394.
23. The following account draws on a variety of sources, many of which are mutually contradictory. The most detailed Red Guard source is *Wuhan Kang-erh-ssu* [*Wuhan Steel February Fourth*] (Huichow edition), No. 38 (22 August 1967), trans. in *SCMP*, No. 4073, pp. 1-18. Other sources include: *Wuhan Hsin Hua Kung* [*Wuhan New China Worker*] (16 September 1967), trans.

in *SCMP*, No. 4042, pp. 1-6; and *Ming Pao* [*Bright Daily*] (Hong Kong), 31 July 1967, trans. in *SCMP*, No. 3993, pp. 8-9. The best secondary accounts are: Thomas W. Robinson, "The Wuhan Incident," *CQ*, No. 47 (July-September 1971), 413-438; and Rice, pp. 398 ff.

24. Robinson, "The Wuhan Incident," pp. 418 and 421-423. One official statement reportedly placed the total number of participants at about 300,000: *KYODO* (English), 2 December 1978, in *FBIS*, No. 234, pp. El-E2.

25. "How Comrade Wang Li was Saved from Danger," *Wuhan Hsin Hua Kung* (K'ai-p'ing edition), 16 September 1967, trans. in *SCMP*, No. 4043, pp. 15-19.

26. Robinson, "The Wuhan Incident," pp. 422-423.

27. Ibid., p. 423.

28. *CFCP* editorial, reprinted in *NCNA*, 26 July 1967, trans. in *SCMP*, No. 3993, pp. 4-5.

29. *Hung Ch'i*, No. 12 (1 August 1967), quoted by Chang, "Changing Patterns," p. 58.

30. *Hung Tien-hsun* [*Red Telegram*] (Canton), No. 2 (March 1968), trans. in *SCMP*, No. 4143, p. 4.

31. Rice, pp. 401-402.

32. See a summary of Lin's speech in *Chu-ying Tung-fang hung* [*Pearl River Film Studio East is Red*] (13 September 1967), trans. in *SCMP*, No. 4036, pp. 1-6.

33. Whitson, p. 532; and Rice, pp. 413-415; both erroneously view Lin's 9 August speech as a moderate one.

34. This and all subsequent quotations in this discussion from Lin Piao's speech of 9 August 1967 are from *CYTFH* (13 September 1967), trans. in *SCMP*, No. 4036, pp. 2-6.

35. The following quotations are from the version of Lin Piao's speech of 10 August 1967, trans. in *TCC*, No. 140 (*JPRS*, No. 52,658), p. 16.

36. Nelsen, *The Chinese Military System*, pp. 104-105; and Paul Elmquist, "The Internal Role of the Military," in *Military and Political Power*, pp. 279-280.

37. *NCNA*, 16 August 1967, trans. in *SCMP*, No. 4004, pp. 1-9.

38. See articles on P'eng in *NCNA* 19 and 20 August 1967, trans. in *SCMP*, No. 4007, pp. 8-14.

39. Rice, pp. 401-412.

40. On the Cultural Revolution in Canton during August 1967, see *SCMP*, No. 4017, pp. 7 ff.; No. 4026, pp. 3-12; No. 4036, pp. 7-8; No. 4040, pp. 7-18; No. 4041, pp. 11-16; No. 4042, pp. 7-10; No. 4043, pp. 1-14; No. 4044, pp. 1-3 and 5-7; and No. 4045, pp. 8-12. Huang Yung-sheng was present at the signing of the "agreement" of 16 August (see *SCMP*, No. 4043, p. 8). These reports tell of over 1000 persons killed in Canton in 1967, including several dozen PLA soldiers. One radical source claimed that navy units backing "Rebels" fought against MR troops in early September. *CYTFH* (13 September 1967), trans. in *SCMP*, No. 4040, pp. 11-16.

41. "News from Sinkiang," *T'ienshan Feng-huo* [*Heavenly Mountains Beacon Fire*], Nos. 4 and 5 (15 January 1968), trans. in *CB*, No. 855, pp. 12-18. Also see another story on Sinkiang on pp. 5-8.

42. Ellis Joffe, "The Chinese Army After the Cultural Revolution," *CQ*, No. 55 (July-September 1973), p. 462.

43. Nelsen, "Military Forces in the Cultural Revolution," passim.

44. Nelsen, "Military Forces in the Cultural Revolution," p. 451, notes that, "On 12 April 1967, Madame Mao [Chiang Ch'ing] addressed the Central

Military Commission in her role as leader of the PLA Cultural Revolution Group. She stressed one theme repeatedly in her talk: PLA intervention was a necessity without which the Cultural Revolution would fail. Clearly, she was trying to convince her audience." The speech was first published by *CKYCYK* (June 1970), pp. 114-130. An English translation is in *TCC*, No. 115 (*JPRS*, No. 44,680), pp. 4-9.

45. The following draws heavily on Nelsen, "Military Forces in the Cultural Revolution," pp. 454-460.
46. Nelsen, "Military Forces in the Cultural Revolution," pp. 457-458 and 469-471.
47. *Chan Kuang-chou [Fighting Canton]*, No. 10 (30 September 1967), trans. in *SCMP*, No. 4068, p. 11.
48. *JMJP* finally broke the news of Mao's tour, with great fanfare, on 26 September 1967, trans. in *SCMP*, No. 4031, pp. 16-18; also see *Cheng-fa Hung-ch'i [Politics and Law Red Flag]* (Canton), Nos. 3 and 4 (17 October 1967), trans. in *SCMP*, No. 4070, pp. 8-9. It seems that Mao visited only the capitals of Hopeh, Honan, Hupeh, Hunan, Kiangsi, and Chehkiang, but the itinerary has never been published. See Rice's discussion, pp. 413-416.
49. "Important talk given by Comrade Chiang Ch'ing ...," 5 September 1967, in *CCP Documents: 1966-1967*, pp. 511-533; also see Rice, p. 418.
50. "Order of the CCP Central Committee, the State Council, the Central Military Commission and the Central Cultural Revolution Group ...," 5 September 1967, in *CCP Documents: 1966-1967*, pp. 505-510.
51. Chang, "Changing Patterns," p. 59; and Rice, pp. 419-420.
52. This and the following quotations are from Chou En-lai's speech of 17 September 1967, trans. in *SCMP*, No. 4066, pp. 3-5.
53. *JMJP*, 14 September 1967, trans. in *SCMP*, No. 4026, pp. 28-30.
54. *NCNA*, 26 October 1967, trans. in *SCMP*, No. 4050, pp. 30-31.
55. *CFCP*, 4 October 1967, trans. in *SCMP*, No. 4037, p. 21. Also see: *CFCP*, 20 October 1967, trans. in *SCMP*, No. 4047, pp. 11-12.
56. Mao quoted in *Cheng-fa Hung-ch'i [Politics and Law Red Flag]* (Canton), Nos. 3 and 4 (17 October 1967), trans. in *SCMP*, No. 4070, p. 8.
57. *NCNA*, 26 September 1967, trans. in *SCMP*, No. 4031, p. 1.
58. *NCNA*, 12 December 1967, trans. in *SCMP*, No. 4080, pp. 11-13. Also see: "Aways Remain Pupils of the Masses," *PR*, No. 52 (25 December 1967), 17-18.
59. *SCMP*, No. 4066, pp. 14 ff.; and *SCMP*, No. 4067, pp. 14 ff.
60. *NCNA*, 1 November 1967, trans. in *SCMP*, No. 4054, pp. 10-11; and *NCNA*, 24 October 1967, trnas. in *SCMP*, No. 4055, pp. 1-9.
61. Four thousand "activists" of the navy studied for 20 days in Peking in November: *NCNA*, 1 December 1967, trans. in *SCMP*, No. 4073, pp. 19-21. On a similar study session for air force troops, see "PLA Air Force Party Committee in Full Session," *PR*, No. 50 (8 December 1967), 11-12.
62. *NCNA* (Canton), 19 November 1967, trans. in *SCMP*, No. 4074, pp. 14-17; and *Wen-hui Pao* (Shanghai), 24 May 1968, trans. in *SCMP*, No. 4206, pp. 9-12.
63. Unidentified Red Guard source, translated in *SCMP*, No. 4181, p. 9.
64. Nelson, "Military Bureaucracy," p. 392.
65. *NCNA* (Canton), 19 November 1967, trans. in *SCMP*, No. 4065, pp. 4-5; and *SCMP*, No. 4082, pp. 1-16.
66. Chou En-lai quoted in *Wen-ko Feng-yun [Cultural Revolution Political Situation]* (Canton), No. 2 (February 1968), trans. in *SCMP*, No. 4148, p. 5.
67. "Important speeches by Central Leaders ...," *CYTFH*, No. 20

(Special Edition, April 1968), trans. in *SCMP*, No. 4172, pp. 1-10.

68. *Wan-shan Hung-p'ien* [*Ten Thousand Reddened Hills*], No. 1 (26 September 1967), trans. in *SCMP*, No. 4057, p. 5.

69. *Hung-ch'i T'ung-hsun* [*Red Flag Bulletin*] (Canton), No. 1 (mid-June 1968), trans. in *SCMP*, No. 4213, p. 3; *Chung-ta Chan-pao* [*Chung-ta Combat Bulletin*] (Canton), No. 47 (14 April 1968), trans. in *SCMP*, No. 4169, pp. 4-6; and "Yang Ch'eng-wu's 8 Major Crimes," Unnamed Tabloid dated May 1968, trans. in *SCMP*, No. 4186, pp. 1-5.

70. "Lin Piao's Important Directives...," *Pei-hang Hung-ch'i* [*Peking Aviation Red Flag*], No. 47, trans. in *F and F*, 1, No. 26 (16 October 1968), pp. 20 and 22-23.

71. CCP Committee of the Peking MR, "Resolutely Stop the Erroneous Words Harmful to the Reputation of the 38th Army," in *Tung-fang-hung Tienhsun* [*East is Red Telegram*], No. 2 (July 1968), trans. in *SCMP*, No. 4227, pp. 6-7.

72. *T'ien-shan Feng-huo*, Nos. 4 and 5 (15 January 1968), trans. in *CB*, No. 855, pp. 9-11.

73. *SCMP*, No. 4024, pp. 1-3.

74. *SCMP*, No. 4213, pp. 4-7; *SCMP*, No. 4220, pp. 7-13; and *Liuchow Kung-tsung*, No. 7 (12 July 1968), trans. in *SCMP*, No. 4226, pp. 1-3.

75. *JMJP*, 3 August 1968, trans. in *SCMP*, No. 4238, p. 5; Nelsen, "Military Bureaucracy," pp. 392-393; and Powell, "Soldiers in the Economy," pp. 743-745.

76. Refugee informant. "Mao Tse-tung Thought Propaganda Teams" might vary considerably in size. Some consisted of only a few soldiers, while the one at Ch'ing-hai University in 1968 equaled one soldier per student.

77. For example, see: "Resolutely Implement Chairman Mao's Line of Army Building, Penetratingly Carrying Out the Four-Good Company Movement," *KMJP*, 29 July 1968, trans. in *SCMP*, No. 4245, p. 13.

78. Edgar Snow, *The Long Revolution* (New York: Vintage, 1972), p. 103.

79. For two accounts of air force units still deeply involved in "Three Supports and Two Militaries" work in 1971, see *JMJP*, 22 September 1971, trans. in *SCMP*, No. 4990, pp. 99-102; and *JMJP*, 5 September 1971, trans. in *SCMP*, No. 4976, pp. 160-162.

80. The following is drawn from Thomas W. Robinson, "The Sino-Soviet Border Dispute," *APSR*, 64, No. 4 (December 1972), pp. 1175-1202.

81. Ibid., p. 1198. I disagree with Robinson's conclusion that the 2 March fighting was probably caused "directly" by a local commander "in response to changes in standing orders from Peking."

82. Lin Piao, "Report to the Ninth National Congress of the CCP," in *The Ninth National Congress of the... Party (Documents)*'(Peking: FLP, 1969), p. 96.

83. Robinson (Note, p. 1194) notes that Lin devoted a disproportionate amount of time to the March incidents, and suggests that, already in April, Lin was being criticized for his handling of the clashes—or even for starting them. See *Ninth Congress (Documents)*, p. 96.

84. Jurgen Domes, *The Internal Politics of China* (New York: Praeger, 1973), p. 207. See Domes' excellent discussion of the Ninth CCP Congress on pages 205-207.

85. Ibid., pp. 207-214.

86. *JMJP*, 27 August 1971.

87. For example, see Elmquist, p. 287.

88. Nelsen, *The Chinese Military System*, p. 139.
89. Philip Bridgeham, "The Fall of Lin Piao," *CQ*, No. 55 (July-September 1973), pp. 431-432.
90. Joffe, "The Chinese Army After the Cultural Revolution,"; and Bridgeham, p. 446.
91. Franz J. Mogdis, "The Role of the Chinese Communist Air Force in the 1970's," in *Military and Political Power*, p. 264.
92. Joffe, "The Chinese Army after the Cultural Revolution," pp. 467 and 463-464.
93. *CNA*, No. 830 (February 1971), 5; and Whitson, p. 547.
94. Joffe, "The Chinese Army After the Cultural Revolution," pp. 470-471.
95. Robinson, "Lin Piao," pp. 89-90.
96. On the "Lin Piao Incident," see: "Document concerning the Lin Piao Incident," *Cheng-fa*, No. 4 (1972), trans. in *I and S*, 8, No. 8 (May 1972), 78-79; and "Mao Tse-tung's Talks to Responsible Comrades in Nanking and Shanghai Areas . . .," abridged and trans. in *I and S*, 8, No. 10 (July 1972), 95-97; "Document No. 24 of the CCP Central Committee," *Cheng-fa*, No. 24 (2 July 1972), trans. in *I and S*, 9, No. 2 (December 1972), 92-96; "Document No. 12 of the CCP Central Committee," *Cheng-fa*, No. 12 (17 March 1972), trans. in *I and S*, 8, No. 12 (September 1972), 63-71; and Joffe, "The Chinese Army After the Cultural Revolution." These, and other documents, are collected by Micheal Y. M. Kao (ed.) in *The Lin Piao Affiar: Power Politics and Military Coup* (White Plains, NY: International Arts and Sciences Press, 1975). Although the Chinese press was filled with accounts of the Lin Piao affair during the "Gang of Four" trials in November-December 1980, there were few additional details and no surprises at all.
97. "Concisely Study Chairman Mao's Ten Major Military Principles," *HC*, No. 8 (1 August 1973), 43 ff., trans. in *SCMM*, No. 759, pp. 51-56.
98. Thomas W. Robinson, "China in 1973," *AS*, 14, No. 1 (January 1974), 19.
99. Whitson, pp. 556-557; and "Army-People Joint Defense Strengthens War Preparedness," *HC*, No. 10 (1973), 98-100.
100. Shih Lun, "On Worship of Confucianism and Opposition to Legalism," *HC*, No. 10 (1 October 1973), 33 ff., trans. in *SCMM*, No. 761, p. 46; "Chao Kao's Usurpation of Power and the Fall of the Ch'in Dynasty," *JMJP*, 8 September 1974, trans. in *SPRCP*, No. 5700, pp. 191-203; and *HC*, No. 12 (1 December 1973), 47 ff., trans. in *SCMM*, No. 766, pp. 51-53.
101. "Earnestly Study Chairman Mao's Military Writings," *HC*, No. 9 (1974), 5-7; *JMJP*, 23 August 1974, and *KMJP*, both trans. in *SPRCP*, No. 5695, pp. 177-186 and 187-189, respectively; "Lay Bare the Reactionary Essence . . .," p. 112; and *KMJP*, 20 July 1974, trans. in *SPRCP*, No. 5677, pp. 197-201.
102. For example, see *NCNA*, 15 January 1972, trans. in *FBIS*, 17 January 1972, pp. B1-B2; *SCMM*, No. 770, pp. 92-93; and "Important Teaching Materials," *HC*, No. 12 (1 November 1971), 7-11, trans. in *SCMM*, No. 717, pp. 5-6.
103. Domes, *Internal Politics*, p. 214. Also see "The Present Status of the Ninth CCP Central Committee," *I and S*, No. 1 (November 1972), pp. 29-34.
104. Domes, *Internal Politics*, p. 216.
105. Joffe, "The Chinese Army After the Cultural Revolution," p. 475.
106. *PR*, No. 18 (4 May 1973), 5. Teng first appeared on May Day, listed as the lowest of the vice-premiers.
107. *I and S*, 9, No. 4 (January 1973), 6-8.
108. *I and S*, 9, No. 3 (December 1972), 86-87.

109. Nelsen, *The Chinese Military System*, p. 142; and *HTJP*, 21 September 1973.
110. Information supplied in Hong Kong by Marie-Claire Bergere and Lucian Bianco after a tour in the PRC in September 1974.
111. A regiment of the Peking Garrison still had "102 cadres and fighters working in 68 primary and middle schools as political instructors" in July 1975. *NCNA*, 31 July 1975, trans. in *SPRCP*, No. 5912, p. 25.
112. *CSM*, 4 January 1974.
113. *I and S*, 10, No. 5 (February 1974), 11. See pp. 13-15 for a summary of MR personnel changes between 1971 and 1974. Not all of the CCP provincial committees reverted to civilian hands even then. In November 1974, eleven of the twenty-nine provincial-level first secretaries were still military men. As a general rule, however, once a PLA man vacated such a post, he was replaced (often after some delay) by a civilian. See *CN A*, No. 978 (1 November 1974), 2; and *CNS*, No. 533 (4 September 1974), 2.
114. *KMJP*, 30 July 1974, trans. in *SPRCP*, No. 5677, p. 200 (emphasis added).
115. Glen Dick, "The General Political Department," in *Military and Political Power*, p. 178; Nelsen, *The Chinese Military System*, pp. 104-106; and Whitson, pp. 549-550.
116. "Some Understanding from Criticizing Lin Piao's Bourgeois Military Line," *HC*, No. 8 (1 August 1974), trans. in *SPRCM*, No. 788, pp. 67-71; and *JMJP*, 23 October 1974, trans. in *SPRCP*, No. 5745, pp. 57-60.
117. "The Gun Must Forever . . .," p. 125.
118. For several good examples see *JMJP*, 23 October 1974, trans. in *SPRCP*, No. 5745, pp. 57-60.
119. "1 October 1974 National Day Celebrations," (Unclassified) USCGDLO, Hong Kong, p. 3 (cited hereafter as "1 October . . . Celrbrations").
120. Nelsen, *The Chinese Military System*, pp. 112-113.
121. For example: "Work Well at Either Higher or Lower Levels . . .," *HC*, No. 7 (1 July 1973), 22 ff., trans. in *SCMM*, No. 757, pp. 97-101.
122. "Shensi Army Cadres Rotated to Work . . .," Sian Shensi Prov. Radio, 15 November 1974, trans. in *FBIS*, 21 November 1974, p. M5.
123. For example: "Advance Along the Direction Charted by the Resolution Adopted at the Kut'ien Conference," *KMJP*, 19 December 1974, trans. in *SPRCP*, No. 5793, pp. 5-14.
124. "Officers and Soldiers are United and Fight in Unity," *KMJP*, 24 July 1975, trans. in *SPRCP*, No. 5912, pp. 6-7. Also see *JMJP*, 10 July 1975, trans. in *SPRCP*, No. 5916, pp. 190-193; and *KMJP*, 2 August 1975, trans. in *SPRCP*, No. 5918, pp. 96-99.
125. *JMJP*, 1 August 1975, trans. in *SPRCP*, No. 5918, pp. 44-50.
126. *KMJP*, 24 July 1975, trans. in *SPRCP*, No. 5912, p. 8.
127. *NCNA*, 6 August 1975, trans. in *SPRCP*, No. 5916, pp. 197-198.
128. *NCNA* (Lanchou), 4 August 1975, trans. in *SPRCP*, No. 5915, pp. 160-159 [sic].
129. *CSM*, 31 October 1975, p. 6.
130. "Failure of the "Gang of Four's' Scheme to Set up a 'Second Armed Force,'" *PR*, No. 13 (25 March 1977), 10-12.
131. Ibid., p. 12; and *PR*, No. 2 (7 January 1977), 31; also see Yang Yung, "Speech at the National Militia Work Conference," *NCNA*, 8 August 1978, trans. in *FBIS*, No. 156, pp. E1-E5.
132. Alan P. L. Liu, "The 'Gang of Four' and the PLA," *AS*, 19, No. 9 (September 1979), 829-837; and Andes D. Oanates, "Hua Kuo-feng and the

Arrest of the "Gang of Four,"' *CQ*, No. 75 (September 1978), 540-565. Also see *Cheng Ming* (Hong Kong), No. 12 (1 October 1978), 32-37; and Li T'ien-ming, "Marshal Yeh Chien-ying and Some Facets of the PLA," *I and S*, 14, No. 4 (April 1980), 32, for two colorful, if apocryphal accounts.

133. Quoted by *NCNA*, 3 June 1978, trans. in *FBIS*, No. 108, p. E9.
134. *CSM*, 28 December 1978, p. 3.
135. *NCNA*, 11 December 1978, in *FBIS*, No. 238, pp. E15-16.
136. *BR*, No. 12 (24 March 1980), 3.
137. *AKTIELT* (Copenhagen), 29 November 1978, pp. 10-11, extract translated in *FBIS*, No. 234, p. E2.
138. *Tung Hsiang* (Hong Kong), No. 2 (20 November 1978), p. 25, trans. in *FBIS*, No. 236, p. N7.
139. *CFCP*, 9 December 1978, trans. in *FBIS*, No. 241, p. E1.
140. *CFCP*, 12 December 1978, trans. in *FBIS*, No. 240, pp. E1-E3.
141. "Communique of the Third Plenary Session of the 11th Central Committee . . . (Adopted 22 December 1978)," *PR*, No. 52 (29 December 1978), 7.
142. Lo Jui-ch'ing's eulogy of Lo Jung-huan, *NCNA*, 12 August 1978, trans. in *FBIS*, No. 158, pp. E2-E4; and Nieh Jung-chen, "Speech to the National Militia Work Conference," (4 August 1978), in *NCNA*, 7 August 1978, trans. in *FBIS*, No. 154, pp. E1-E10.
143. *NCNA*, 5 June 1978, trans. in *FBIS*, No. 109, pp. E1-E10.
144. Quoted by *NCNA*, 3 June 1978, trans. in *FBIS*, No. 108, p. E6.
145. Yeh Chien-ying, "Speech at the All-Army Political Work Conference," (29 May 1978), in *NCNA*, 4 June 1978, trans. in *FBIS*, No. 108, p. E13 (emphasis added).
146. "Resolution of the MAC of the CC on Political Work," *NCNA*, 10 August 1978, trans. in *FBIS*, No. 156, pp. E13-E18.
147. *NCNA*, 9 August 1978, trans. in *FBIS*, No. 156, p. E20.
148. Reprinted in *FBIS*, No. 156S.
149. See Lo Jui-ch'ing's eulogy in *FBIS*, No. 158, pp. E2-E4; and "Our Good Director Lo Jung-huan," *HC*, No. 8, (1978).
150. *NCNA*, 24 June 1978, trans. in *FBIS*, No. 126, pp. E1-E2.
151. *NCNA* (English), 18 August 1978, in *FBIS*, No. 162, p. E4 and E6.
152. *NCNA*, 28 July 1978, trans. in *FBIS*, No. 152, p. E16.
153. Peking Domestic Service, 9 October 1978, trans. in *FBIS*, No. 200, p. E14.
154. For example, see *AFP* (Hong Kong), 5 May 1978, in *FBIS*, No. 88, pp. E23-E24.
155. *KYODO* (Tokyo), 22 May 1978, in *FBIS*, No. 99, p. E23.
156. *Air Force Times*, 14 August 1978, p. 16; and *CSM*, 27 July 1978, p. 4.
157. MAC Resolution, *NCNA*, 9 August 1978, trans. in *FBIS*, No. 156, pp. E18-E22; Li Te-sheng, *JMJP*, 9 September 1978, trans. in *FBIS*, No. 177, pp. E12-E17; and *CFCP*, 21 April 1978, trans. in *FBIS*, No. 79, pp. E14-E15.
158. Yang Yung, "Speech . . . at National Militia Work Conference" (n.d.) in *NCNA*, 8 August 1978, trans. in *FBIS*, No. 156, p. E4.
159. Nieh Jung-chen, "Militia Speech," p. E7.
160. The authoritative statement on "people's war under modern conditions" was Hsu Hsiang-ch'ien, "Heighten Vigilance, Be Ready to Fight," *HC*, No. 8 (1978).
161. Good examples include: Chu Liang, "*Ch'iang-kan-tzu yü cheng-ch'uan—Teng p'ai tui chun-tui te jang-pu* " ["The Gun and Political Power—The Teng Clique's concessions to the Army"], *CKYCYK*, 15, No. 1 (15 January 1981),

pp. 22-24; two stories by David Bonavia, "Mao's Ghost Faces the Final Downfall," *FEER*, 21 March 1980, pp. 8-9; and "The Army Stays the Gun," *FEER*, 16-22 January 1981, pp. 10-11. Also see *Cheng Ming*, No. 34 (1 August 1980), 10-11, in *FBIS*, No. 152, pp. U1-U2.

162. "*Wei Jen-min yi pu-p'a-k'u erh pu-p'a-szu,*" *CFCP*, 10 September 1980, cited by Chu Liang, p. 23.

163. For example: "Revolutionary Slogans Must Not be Criticized," Anhui Hofei Prov. Svc., 15 January 1981, in *FBIS*, No. 011, pp. O3-O4.

164. For the reported defense of Mao by Yeh Chien-ying and Hsiao Ch'ing-kuang, see *I and S*, 16, No. 6 (June 1980), 2-3.

5
The Force Structure

In the last chapter, we noted that the professionalizing trend of 1945-59 was paralleled by a declining percentage of military men on the CC. Even at its lowest (the Eighth CC, which was 23.7% PLA), however, PLA representation in the CC has been quite high. This is unlikely to change as long as the leaders of the revolution remain alive. For them, the distinction between military and civilian was largely meaningless up to 1949, and remains far from clear-cut. Even in the long run, though PLA representation on the CC may diminish, top officers will continue to sit at the innermost circles of power. Institutional arrangements at the top—especially the importance of the Military Affairs Commission (MAC) of the Central Committee in the making of national security policy—force PLA leaders to participate and compete at the apex of the political-military structure.

THE CENTRAL MILITARY STRUCTURE

Before the central military organs of the People's Republic of China are outlined, an important caveat is in order. Although a fairly straight-forward diagram is presented (Figure 5.1) depicting the relationship of these organs, it would be a serious error to take these neat lines of command too literally. There are several reasons for this, but the main one is the practice of multiple office-holding by military leaders. To give an example: Li Te-sheng currently sits on the Politburo of the Party Central Committee, is a member of the MAC, and is commander of the Shenyang Military Region (MR). Many similar examples could be cited, although it is now official policy that multiple office-holding is supposed to be phased out.

Since Mao's death, the top levels of the PLA seem to have been in transition to some still-undetermined pattern of office holding. The extensive reshuffling of the high command in January and February of 1980 rationalized the situation somewhat, but there were still top positions held by semiactive "elders" (e.g., Defense Minister Hsu Hsiang-ch'ien and GRSD Director Hung Hsueh-chih), while the actual work was done by senior assistants. This situation was further rationalized in March 1981 when Hsu was succeeded by Keng Piao.[1]

It is certain that the locus of military policy-making is the Military Affairs Commission (MAC) of the Party Central Committee. Its orders can bypass or override those of virtually any other organ. It is telling, in this regard, that when Mao sought to carry the Great Proletarian Cultural Revolution into the military in 1966, the "Cultural Revolution Small Group of

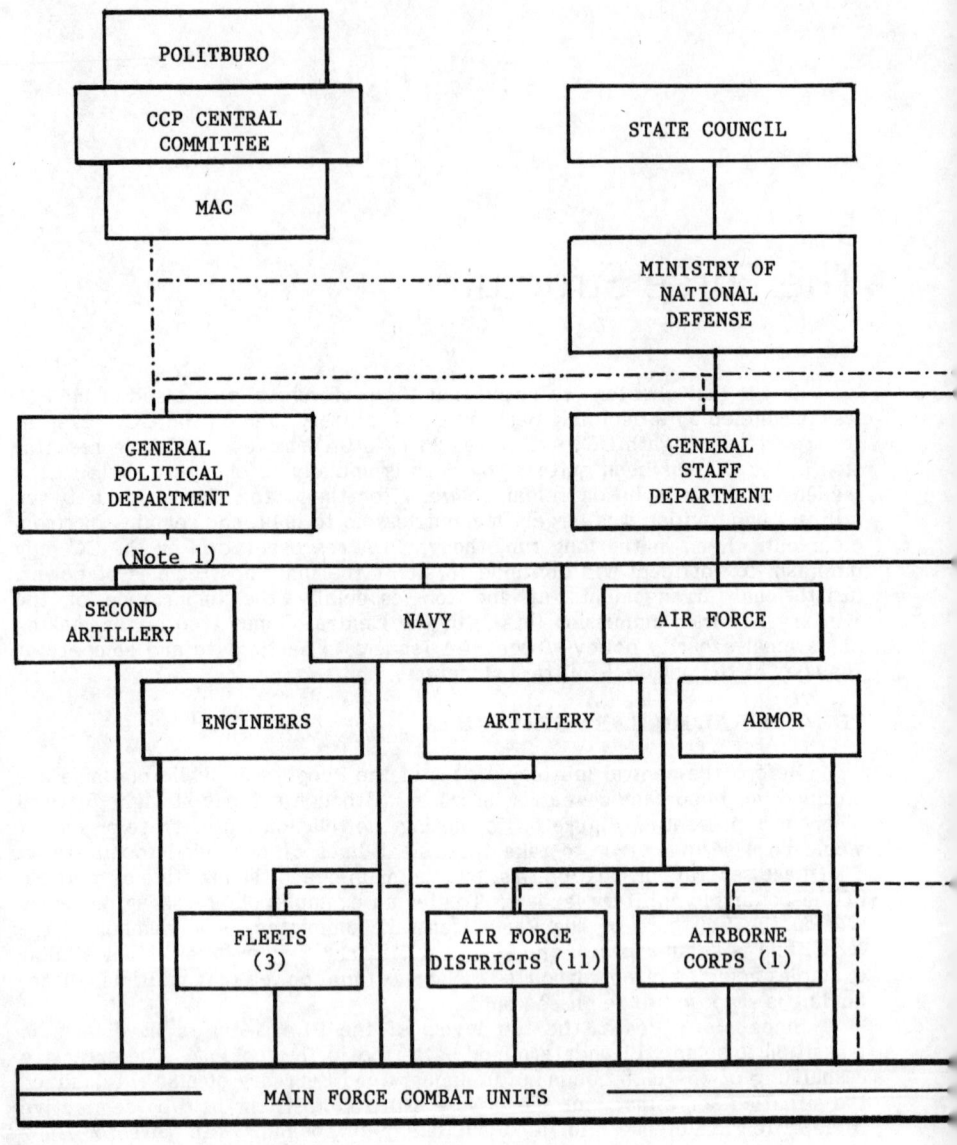

FIGURE 5.1
The Command Structure of the PLA: 1980

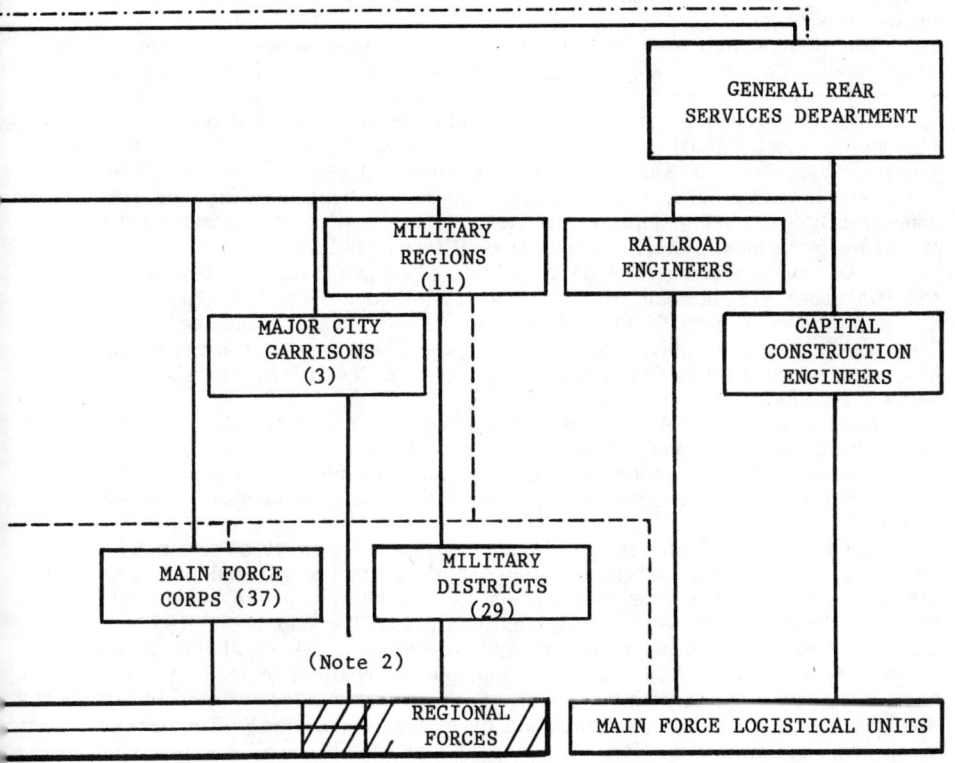

Notes:
  1. The political commissar system, under the GPD, parallels the military chain of command down to company level.
  2. The city garrisons of Peking, Tientsin, and Shanghai appear to control both regional and main force units.

the PLA" was grafted onto the MAC, rather than the Ministry of Defense or one of the PLA general departments. Furthermore, it is quite clear that the real power any given individual wields derives from his influence on the decisions of the MAC, rather than on hierarchical position per se.

The Military Affairs Commission

Until his death, Mao Tse-tung was chairman of the MAC, and Hua Kuo-feng assumed this position along with the party chairmanship. As the transition to a new national leadership has proceeded, the importance of the MAC has been underlined by changes in its membership. Wang Hung-wen and Chang Ch'un-ch'iao (of the "gang of four") have been removed, while Lo Jui-ch'ing (d. August 1978), Su Chien-hua (d. February 1979), Wang P'ing, Teng Hsiao-p'ing, and Keng Piao have been added.[2] Since Hua Kuo-feng has lost most of his political power through 1979-81, he will probably be replaced soon as MAC chairman.

The membership and workings of the MAC have never been clearly understood. The chairman, vice-chairmen, and about five senior officers currently constitute the Standing Committee of the MAC (*chun-shih ch'ang-hui*).[3] In the past, the first vice-chairman was normally the Minister of National Defense (MND), and the PLA chief of staff was MAC secretary-general. Vice-Premier Keng Piao became secretary-general when he joined the MAC in early 1979, however, and apparently continues in that post concurrently with being defense minister. In terms of formal position, this makes Keng the most powerful man in the military structure.

MAC vice-chairmen include CCP Vice-Chairman Teng Hsiao-p'ing and the PLA's four "old marshals" (Liu Po-ch'eng, Nieh Jung-chen, Yeh Chien-ying, and Hsu Hsiang-ch'ien). Chief of Staff Yang Te-chih is only a member of the Standing Committee. The membership of the MAC probably includes the commanders and first political commissars of the eleven MRs and the eight service branches.

Exactly how the MAC makes its decisions is not known, but is probably subject to complex personal interrelations and consensus-taking, rather than to hard-and-fast rules of procedure. It is evident that plenary sessions of the MAC are infrequent, because the MR commanders are seldom assembled in Peking.

During the Lin Piao years, the "Administrative Committee" of the MAC also became extremely powerful, especially after Lin reorganized it in July 1968. In April of that year, Chou En-lai referred to this same body as the "Business Unit" of the MAC.[4] Apparently, this small group (seven people in July 1968) presided over some sort of MAC secretariat. This "Administrative Commmittee of the MAC" was either Lin Piao's creation, or an established body which grew to inordinate power at his behest. At any rate, it was abolished after Lin's fall, and replaced by a "General Office."[5] The present size, membership, and functions of this new office are unknown.

In theory, the MAC sets policy on major issues of military policy, and on internal PLA matters of major importance, while these decisions are implemented by the Ministry of National Defense and the three general departments of the PLA. However, the dramatic events related to Mao's passing revealed the existence of "Unit 8341," directly under MAC control. "8341" provided guards for the political elite, and also apparently provided Mao with a nationwide network of informants. "8341" elements "stationed in Yunnan" were reported in October 1978. Some time in 1979, the unit was replaced, or absorbed, by a new unit designated "57003," which, unlike "8341," is subordinate to the Peking garrison.[6]

The Ministry of National Defense

Up until the death of Mao Tse-tung, the Minister of National Defense (MND) was generally the most powerful individual in the PLA. This was not necessarily because of the inherent power of that post, however. His power derived from his concurrent position as senior vice-chairman of the MAC. Moreover, an individual had to be well connected and widely acceptable to be appointed to the post of MND (presumably by the Politburo) in the first place. All defense ministers to date have been Politburo members—an arrangement likely to continue.

The importance of the defense ministry itself is uncertain, and may be at an all-time low. MND responsibilities and authority have varied considerably over the years. During the 1950s the ministry was quite important, generally controlling the military scientific and technological establishment, military schools, and the recruiting system. Yet the MAC often by-passed it to control the general departments, the navy, and the air force directly. The ministry was reorganized by Lin Piao in late 1959, and the general staff was clearly subordinated to it, as were all the service branches.[7] Despite that initial strengthening of MND power, the MAC gradually took control of research and development (R&D), schools, and even the general departments, as the 1960s progressed. After Lin Piao's fall, the MND seems to have reasserted control over schools and the "military-industrial complex" for a time. In 1977-79, the ministry once again yielded most of its authority to the MAC. The "center of gravity" of military authority thus seems to have oscillated over the years, between the MAC and the MND.

Currently, defense ministry functions are largely confined to administration, including such matters as finance, recruiting, and (possibly) personnel management. The MND probably houses the Academy of Military Sciences (AMS) as well.[8] This body is the PLA "think tank" concerned with military doctrine.

The MND no longer controls the three top military schools, which are now described as being "directly under the Military Commission."[9] The National Military Academy, the Political Academy, and the Logistics Academy are the highest-level military cadre schools. They were criticized as hotbeds of "revisionism" and "bourgeois military thinking" during the 1960s, were completely shut down sometime in the early 1970s, and only reopened in March 1978.[10] That they are now under the MAC indicates the very great prestige newly attached to the academies, as well as the reduced importance of the MND.

Defense-related R&D is supervised through the National Defense Science and Technology Commission (NDSTC) of the MAC. Defense industry is under no less than seven Ministries of Machine Industry, all of which are theoretically co-equal to the MND. Although precise relationships are unclear, the MAC coordinates all defense industry through its National Defense Industrial Committee (NDIC), probably through the National Defense Industrial Office (NDIO) of the State Council (see chapter 6).

With MND functions almost entirely confined to administration, the operational chain of command runs directly from the MAC to the general departments. Until 1978, the importance of the minister of defense as an individual was immense, however, owing to his formal position at the top of the uniformed PLA, and even more owing to his concurrent positions as first vice-chairman of the MAC and senior military spokesman on the Politburo. Moreover, he apparently appointed and dismissed the chiefs of the three general departments (with Politburo approval). He historically determined the overall direction of the general departments by appointing his own proteges and associates to these important posts. The appointment of Chang Ch'un-ch'iao as chief of the GPD in 1975 was unprecedented on this account, as well as others, since Chang and Yeh Chien-ying, the then current MND, had very different political affiliations and preferences. Chang was purged in 1976, as one of the "gang of four." This did not mark a reassertion of MND prerogatives, however, for Hsu Hsiang-ch'ien (MND March 1978-March 1981) was semiretired.

In early 1979, Keng Piao became the de facto defense minister, and then formally took over in March 1981. Keng once had quite a respectable military career (as a commander), but held no PLA post at all between 1949 and 1981. As the first "civilian" ever to hold the defense portfolio, he faces an unprecedented situation in PRC civil-military relations. As one of the "old warriors," he will probably be accepted by the high command, although the attitudes of younger officers are less certain. Keng will not only have to assert himself, but also convey the impression that he is standing up for PLA interests.

THE GENERAL DEPARTMENTS

The General Staff Department

The three general departments of the PLA must translate the policies of the MAC into action. Of the three, the General Staff Department (GSD) has far the heaviest responsibilities. It controls the main force combat units and (at least in theory) the military regions and their regional forces.

As a senior member of the MAC, the chief of staff plays a large role in the making of policy. In his capacity as chief of staff, he is the pivotal figure in turning policy into action. It is difficult and risky business: There have been nine chiefs or acting chiefs of staff since 1949, and nearly every one of them was fired, or at least left office under a cloud.[11] There has been considerably less turbulence at the MND level and in the service branches. The official report on the purge of Lo Jui-ch'ing illustrates the narrow path the chief of staff must tread between inaction and overstepping his prerogatives. Lo was accused of making decisions on his own and promulgating them as decisions of the MAC, the MND, the entire GSD, and even of the GPD. He was specifically criticized for promoting a batch of general officers without discussion or approval by the MAC Standing Committee.[12] Chiefs of staff have often spoken in the names of the MAC, the MND, and the GSD. It is evident that no chief of staff could fulfill his duties unelss he made far-reaching implementing decisions on behalf of the MAC—decisions which could come back to haunt him.

Since September 1971, only two men have actually held the title "Chief of Staff"—Teng Hsiao-p'ing (1975-76 and 1977-80) and Yang Te-chih (1980-). Until February 1980, the actual functioning of the GSD was usually in the hands of the senior vice-chief (P'eng Shao-hui 1971-75, Yang Ch'eng-wu 1977-78, and Yang Yung 1978-80). Apparently, this arrangement served to shield the uniformed general staff from political pressure, as much as to exert "civilian control." In either case, the failure to allow form to coincide with function emphasized the unsettled state of institutional civil-military relations. Part of the significance of Yang Te-chih's appointment lies in this: A career troop commmander is again fully in charge of the general staff.

The general staff directly controls the navy, air force, armored forces, artillery, the second artillery (strategic missiles), and engineers. It also controls the antichemical and signal subdepartments which have many of the functions of service branches.

Major subdepartments of the GSD are depicted in Figure 5.2. It is noteworthy that there are subdepartments for intelligence and mobilization (conscription and militia affairs). These functions were handled, historically, by the commissar system, and might have been expected to be under the GPD.[13] That the GSD has assumed both command and staff responsibility for these functions is indicative of its pre-eminence among the three general departments.

The General Political Department

The GPD is the highest political organ of the uniformed PLA, and is responsible for assuring party leadership of the military through a process known as "politicization." This process consists of two major elements: education and control. Corresponding roughly to these two functions are two distinct and separate organizational structures: party committees and political departments (Figure 7.1). Although the GPD exercises formal control over only the latter, the two hierarchies overlap considerably, and should be considered simultaneously. The system of political commissars, party committees, and political departments is detailed in chapter 7.

GPD history suggests that it is very closely controlled by the MAC and, to a lesser extent, by the MND and even by the chief of staff. In fact, command of the GPD has not been a particularly powerful post. Chang Ch'un-ch'iao was the only GPD chief ever to have markedly different political opinions than those of the MND and chief of staff. All other GPD chiefs appear to have tried very hard to stay in political step with both. Chang's purge, barely a month after the death of Mao Tse-tung, illustrated just how vulnerable he was, once deprived of the chairman's backing. It may safely be assumed that the GPD is now again under MAC control, and in step with both the MND and chief of staff.

The organization of the GPD is depicted in Figure 5.3. Of special interest is the mass work (*ch'un-chung kung-tso*) subdepartment, which is involved with PLA and militia economic work and disaster relief, and with civil defense (known in China as "people's air defense"). In addition, the GPD hierarchy is charged to "accept appeals and petitions from all servicemen."[14] This provides an alternative to command channels analogous to the inspector general system in the US Army.

The 1963 *Political Work Regulations* of the PLA required that the GPD "lead" the army "to investigate and study the condition of the enemy forces, and to administer prisoner work." Although the enemy affairs subdepartment of the GPD is responsible for collection, interrogation, and processing of prisoners of war, however, the GSD assumed overall responsibility for intelligence sometime after 1967.[15]

As we have already seen, and contrary to what might have been expected, the Cultural Revolution, which was intended to radically politicize the entire country, resulted in the decline of the GPD headquarters into virtual impotence between 1967 and 1975.[16] Even at the nadir of its influence,

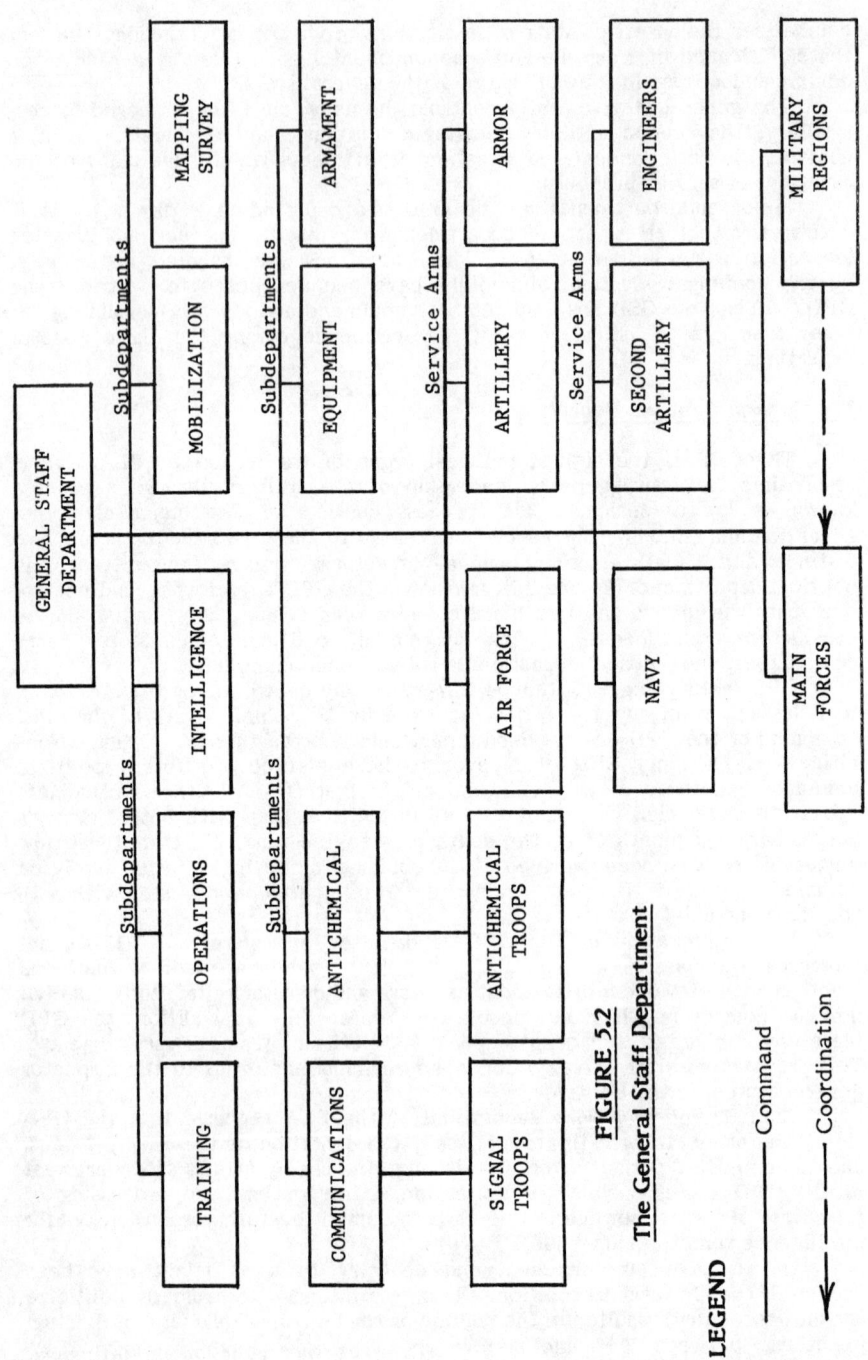

FIGURE 5.2
The General Staff Department

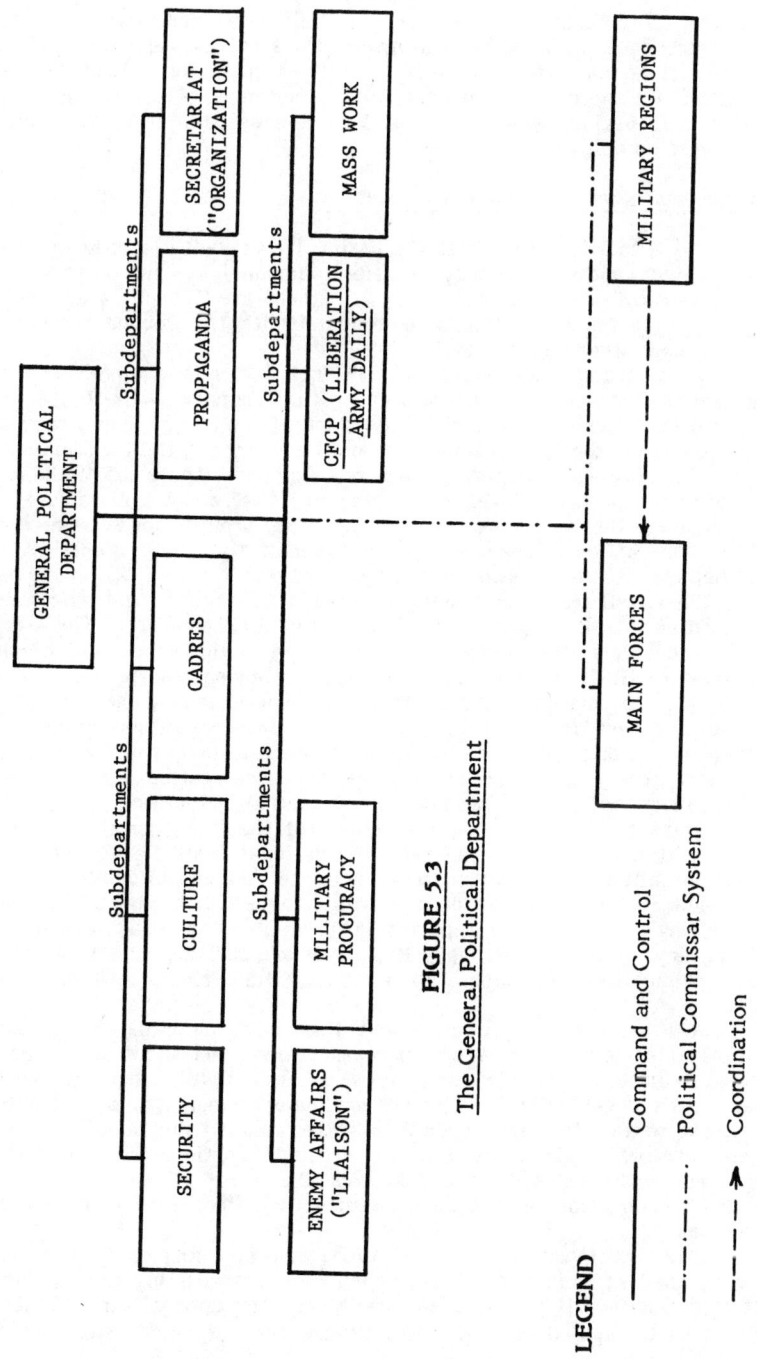

FIGURE 5.3

The General Political Department

however, the GPD structure within troop units remained intact and functioned in the areas of propaganda, culture, cadre selection, appeals, and military justice. It appears that the Administrative Committee of the MAC and the MR staffs (in the case of regional units) made most of the political decisions during that period, while GPD headquarters served, at best, merely as a "transmission belt."

The General Rear Services Department

The GRSD is charged, at the national level, with logistics planning and procurement, and with training logistical personnel, for the entire PLA. This role necessitates close coordination with the State Council (which has overall responsibility for production planning) and with the Second through Eighth Ministries of Machine Industry.[17]

GRSD headquarters supervises the logistical system which reaches down through the service arms, units, and military regions to the battalion level. This closely resembles the logistical system of the Soviet Army, upon which it was modeled in the 1950s. Unlike the political system, the logistical system is not an independent, competing chain of command. The chief of the logistical department at each level of command is directly subordinate to the commander. Unlike the practice in most other armies, however, he is not one of the staff officers supervised by the chief of staff. He is both the planner and implementor of logistics within the command.[18]

The GRSD trains logistical personnel and exercises staff supervision over the system. GRSD organization is depicted in Figure 5.4. The GRSD also directly controls certain specialized units and service arms. These constitute the bulk of GRSD manpower, and are actually engaged in moving, storing and accounting for materiel and in providing transportation and other logistical services. There are about forty-two motor transportation regiments in this category, although these are normally attached to main force units or to MRs. Similarly, the GRSD controls the capital construction engineers and the railroad engineers. These branches are discussed further below.

Transport is still a major weakness of the PLA, despite the efforts to upgrade it since 1949.[19] The available national truck fleet is currently just over one million, and roads in operation total 890,200 kilometers. there are now over 50,400 km of railroads as well. the GRSD has been instrumental in developing this national transportation system, and can draw on it in times of emergency. Despite this, many PLA units are still dependent on animals for tactical mobility and supply. In fact, the GRSD runs a system of breeding farms.

It is uncertain to what extent PLA doctrine calls for a centralized logistical system in the event of war. Under the constraints imposed by China's limited transportation network, the GRSD logistical system is necessarily decentralized. This system includes local storage facilities, and depends, to a certain extent, on local procurement from the civilian economy. These factors point to the MR as a critical logistical link between combat units and both local and national sources of materiel. Even air force and naval units rely on some MR support, despite their far more centralized supply systems.[20]

The GRSD has proven itself to be an extremely capable organization. During the GPCR, it kept rail lines open while transporting and feeding masses of Red Guards. It procured and transported millions of tons of materiel to North Vietnam, and transshipped millions more of Soviet aid. Its engineer

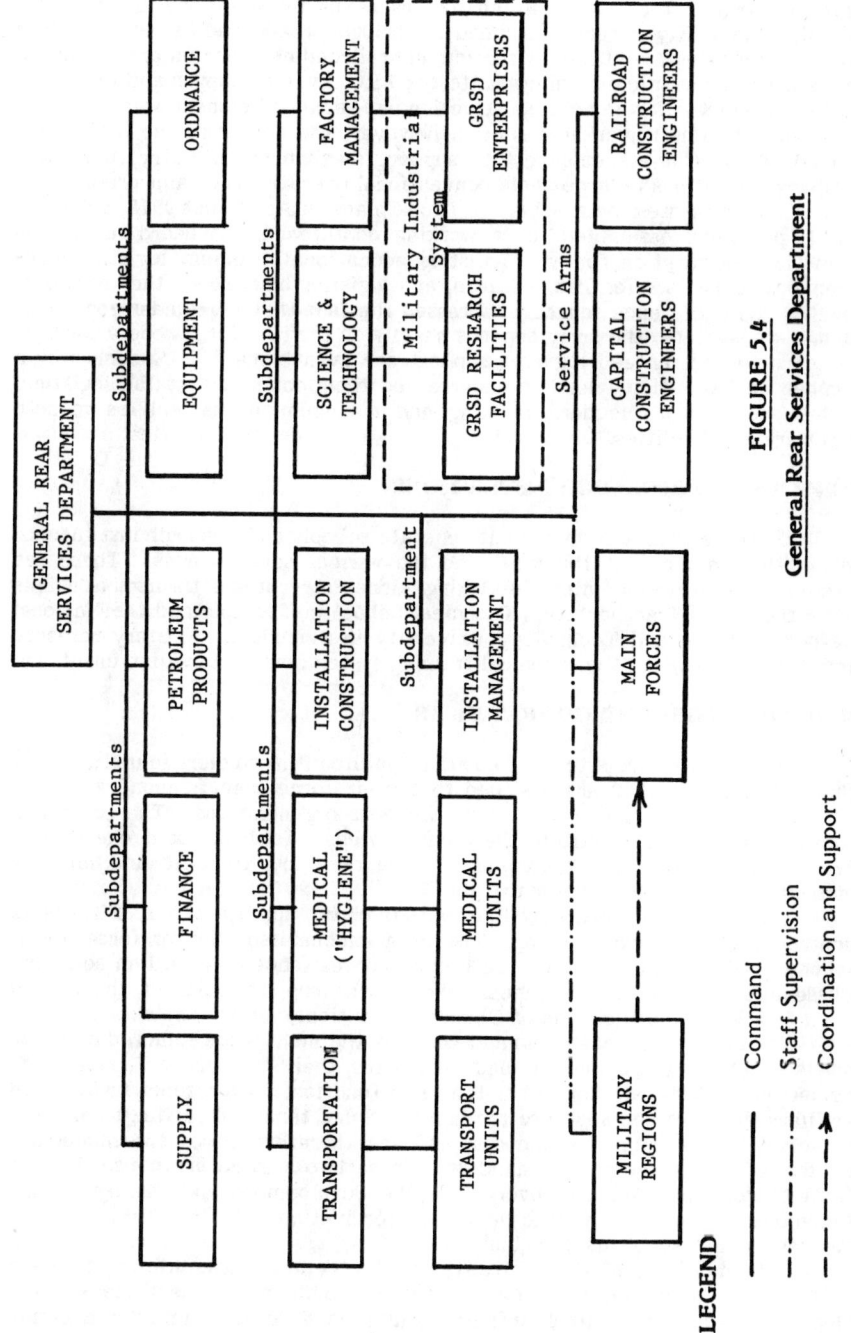

FIGURE 5.4

General Rear Services Department

units frustrated the American air offensive in Indochina by their nearly unbelievable ability to rebuild bombed-out bridges, roads, and rail lines. Under GRSD supervision, capital construction and railroad engineer units continue to make major economic contributions to the PRC, even as they maintain a high state of readiness for combat construction and repair missions in war.

Despite this remarkable record, however, the ability of the GRSD, and indeed of the Chinese economy, to support mechanized infantry, tank, and artillery formations in large-scale conventional operations remains problematical. A major reassessment apparently took place in April-June 1978, when top GRSD personnel assembled for a working conference. It heard reports on "logistical preparation for war, logistics educational training, logistics management, logistics scientific research, and logistics building at the grassroots level." The conference squarely addressed the fact that "... under conditions of modern warfare, the army depends heavily on the rear for its operations; its demands for guaranteed logistics support are even higher."[21] Speeches by a number of top national leaders underscored their concern that the logistical system needs more modern thinking and management, as well as modern hardware and facilities.[22]

SCHOOLS AND RESEARCH INSTITUTIONS

All three general departments operate schools and research institutions, in addition to those of the MAC and the various service arms. There are twenty "military academies" in Peking alone, plus others throughout China (e.g., the GRSD Transportation Technical School in T'ientsin and the National Defense Science and Technology University in Shanghai). Military research and development, and the technical training system, are discussed in chapter 6.

MAIN FORCE GROUND COMBAT UNITS

In 1981, there are a total of about 4.5 million PLA soldiers in uniform. Of these, perhaps 900,000 are assigned to the air force, navy, second artillery, various headquarters, and other miscellaneous organizations. The remaining three to six million constitute the ground forces, of which about one million are "regional forces" (RF, *ti-fang chun*) controlled by the MR and military district (MD) commands (refer to Table 5.1).[23]

The term "main forces" (MF, *cheng-kui chun*) applies to all PLA units controlled directly from Peking. The term encompasses the air force, navy, second artillery, and most of the ground forces (about 2.6 million soldiers). These infantry, artillery, engineer, and service support units of the ground main forces are the backbone of China's conventional military power.

The armored forces command controls the main force armored divisions and separate tank regiments, and supervises their training. The artillery command (or "first artillery") has the same functions with respect to the field artillery divisions and separate regiments. Some tank and artillery units are attached to the main force corps, and are therefore under the immediate control of various corps commanders. These two service arms also develop tactical doctrine, and are involved in the development and testing of new techniques and equipment (the latter in coordination with the GRSD and the relevant ministries of machine building).

It is indicative of the centrality of infantry in Chinese military thinking that there is no comparable "infantry forces command." The General Staff Department directly controls infantry training and develops infantry doctrine

TABLE 5.1
PLA Ground Forces Strength

I. PERSONNEL (3.6 Million)		Excludes AF paratroopers (about 29,000)
II. MAIN FORCE UNITS (About 2.6 Million)*		
Infantry Corps	37	Each corps normally has three divisions, plus support troops. There is an additional corps headquarters and three divisions of paratroops in the air force.
Separate Infantry Divisions	12	Total main force infantry and paratroop divisions: about 125.
Armored Divisions	11	The entire PLA has about 11,000 medium tanks of all types.
Tank Regiments (Separate)	a few	
Artillery Divisions (Gun, Rocket, and Antitank)	22	These are in addition to the artillery units organic to infantry and armored units, and do not include Anti-Aircraft Divisions, which are part of the air force.
Artillery Regiments (Separate)	12	
Motor Transportation Regiments	42	
Signal Regiments	11	
Combat Engineer Regiments	10	
Capital Construction Engineer Divisions	16	
Railroad Engineer Divisions	11	
Antichemical Regiments	a few	
III. REGIONAL AND LOCAL FORCES (About 1 million)		
Infantry-type Divisions	about 100	Including Garrison, Internal Defense, and Border Divisions.
Cavalry Regiments	12-16	Mainly horse-mounted.

*See Appendix A for details of organization and equipment.

Sources:
    Handbook on the Chinese Armed Forces, p. 1-11; M. G. MacLachlan, "China Report," Asian Defence Journal, No. 6178 (November/December 1978), pp. 62-64; Johnson with Yager, The Military Equation in Northeast Asia, quoted in CSM, 1 March 1979, p. 4; The Military Balance, 1978-79, 1979-80, and 1980-81 eds.

and equipment.

The Infantry Corps

The overwhelming majority of main force soldiers are assigned to the thirty-seven infantry corps (*chün*—this term is frequently and misleadingly translated as "army" or "field army"). Each full strength corps has a total manpower of about 4,500 cadres (officers) and 38,000 soldiers. It normally consists of a corps headquarters, three infantry divisions, and support units (see Appendix A). Additional tank, artillery, and service-support units frequently are attached, depending upon the corps mission. Like virtually all PLA units, the corps is "triangular" in structure—three divisions per corps, three regiments per division, three battalions per regiment, etc.

Standardization of ground forces equipment finally began to be achieved (with Chinese and Soviet designs) only in the 1960s. In 1967, the first infantry weapon of Chinese design—a good general purpose machinegun—entered service. Today, main force infantry weapons are only slightly below world standards—with two glaring exceptions: Most of the thousands of medium and long-range antitank (AT) weapons are obsolete. Even the PRC copy of the Soviet "SAGGER," which first entered service in 1978 or 1979, is primitive, compared to the Soviet "SPANDREL" or the US "TOW."

Anti-aircraft (AA) equipment is only slightly better. There are no known AA missiles in the ground forces, but there are many anti-aircraft machineguns and radar-controlled AA guns. These are relatively obsolescent, but the North Vienamese proved that such weapons still can be useful against modern aircraft.

The process of modernizing the PLA ground forces has been a slow and difficult one. Even today, there are considerable variations among the thirty-seven corps. They have been organized, trained, and equipped, not only depending upon equipment availability, but according to their assigned missions and the terrain upon which they operate. The Nationalists classify PLA infantry units as types "A," "B," and "C" corresponding to descending levels of modernization.[24] Even this, however, gives a much oversimplified impression of the actual variations involved. Generally speaking, more modernized forces are located in the north—especially in the northeast—and to a lesser extent opposite Taiwan and Vietnam. South of the Yangtze, and especially in mountainous interior regions with limited road nets, many main force units still depend on pack animals and human muscles for tactical and logistical movement. This may well be considered an advantage, actually making the PLA more mobile than would be a roadbound mechanized invader.

The "type A" infantry units depicted in Appendix A should be viewed as general, rather than exact, representations, because the degree of mechanization of even these units varies from complete to virtually none. Modernization has served to exacerbate variations among units because it requires a balance among many types of equipment. It is only marginally beneficial, for example, to provide armored personnel carriers for the infantry unless they can be supported by tanks, self-propelled artillery, and tactical air power. If only a limited amount of this hardware is available, any attempt to "spread it around" among different units would therefore be extremely wasteful.

Another, somewhat ironic, result of mechanization is that as tactical mobility has been improved by the addition of armored vehicles, *strategic* mobility has actually declined. China lacks both the rolling stock and the rail net to move large mechanized forces over long distances.[25]

Because of all these considerations, as well as the nature of the terrain and the strategic importance of the Northeast, the most modernized infantry units are heavily concentrated in the Peking and Shenyang Military Regions. There too are the best of the artillery units, most of the armored divisions, and most of the fighter-bombers of the PLAAF.

Another general pattern, with respect to modernization, is that the less complex a weapon or piece of equipment is, the more evenly and widely it is likely to be distributed through the ground forces. Thus, virtually all main force and many regional units now are armed with the new family of Chinese-made infantry weapons (see Appendix B). Modern artillery pieces and tactical radios are less evenly distributed, and heavier caliber field guns even less so. With tanks, the situation is quite uneven. Infantry divisions having their full tank regiments (the Nationalists' *sine qua non* of a "type A" division)[26] tend to be those in the north and Northeast. Even among these tank regiments, however, there are considerable variations, since some are equipped with ancient Soviet T-34/85 tanks, or with the Chinese Type-62 light tank, while still other regiments have a mixture of tanks and self-propelled guns. The only infantry units known to have large numbers of armored personnel carriers are those in the Northeast. In 1981, there are indications that entire infantry divisions in the Shenyang MR are being fully mechanized.

Since 1975, an increasing number of "type A" main force infantry divisions have been reported, which are not permanently assigned to corps. These "separate" divisions are also concentrated in the north and Northeast.[27]

The importance of the regimental level should be mentioned in passing. the regiment is the lowest level of command to have a full-fledged political office and political commissar. The tactical importance of the regiment is also seen in its organization. It is the smallest self-sustaining combat formation capable of independent operations. This is even more pronounced in the "type B" division, where the majority of available artillery is decentralized from divisional to regimental level. the commander of a "type B" division simply lacks the mobility, communications, and long-range firepower to influence the action throughout his sector, so he must rely very heavily on his regimental commanders.[28] As in Western armies, the traditions and *esprit de corps* of the PLA, at least from the perspective of the rank and file, are vested largely in regimental units.[29]

Armored Units

PLA tank forces have increased substantially since 1969, and there are now about 11,000 medium battle tanks—about as many as in the US Army. The standard Type-59 medium tank, however, is a modified version of the Soviet T-54, and is markedly inferior to both the American M-60 and the Soviet T-62. The newer, Chinese-designed, Type-60/63 amphibious tank and Type-62 light tank (the latter not to be confused with the Soviet T-62 medium) are both useful for reconnaissance purposes, especially in restricted terrain, although both are inferior to comparable Soviet and US types. Exactly how these two Chinese-designed tanks have been assigned is unclear, and the distribution shown in Appendix A is only an educated guess. It is certain that entire regiments of Type-62s were committed to the invasion of Vietnam in 1979.

Since 1969, several infantry divisions have been at least partially mechanized, and the tank regiments of many divisions have been filled out. Entire infantry divisions in the Shenyang MR currently are being fully mechanized. Armored divisions have increased from five to eleven. They are still weaker than comparable US or Soviet units, however—owing to the inferiority of PLA equipment.[30]

The Artillery

In addition to the "organic" artillery of infantry and armored units, there are about twenty-two divisions and twelve separate regiments of field artillery. There are extreme variations among these units. There are cannon, howitzer, rocket launcher, and AT divisions—and no two of the four AT divisions are nearly alike.

Chinese artillery is almost entirely of the towed variety, which is much less flexible and mobile, but somewhat more reliable, than the self-propelled type. On the other hand, the PLA actually equals the Soviet Army in numbers of field pieces, and outguns the US Army three to one.[31]

Communications

Tactical communications have been greatly improved over the past decade by the addition of many radio-equipped vehicles, and by the provision of excellent Chinese-designed man-portable radios down to platoon level. The PLA still uses telephones extensively, especially at higher levels of command. This appears to be a matter of choice (and security consciousness), since virtually all telephone nets are backed up by radio.[32] Tactical communications appear to be adequate, but not as extensive as in NATO or Warsaw Pact armies. One result, especially in the more poorly equipped "B" and "C" units, must necessarily be continued tactical decentralization and low-level initiative.

Logistics

Logistical support, even in "type A" units, is limited by a lack of trucks and by the poor road and rail nets (see the discussion of the GRSD, above). The drain on combat vehicles and manpower for logistical purposes is likely to pose a serious tactical constraint, unless combat commanders can draw on the labor and vehicles of the local population and/or the GRSD. Because of its much greater logistical requirements, a mechanized PLA task force may well be even more dependent on the logistical support of regional and militia forces than were the muscle-powered main force units of 1948-49. Until and unless this situation is remedied, PLA mechanized forces will lack the ability to carry sustained offensive operations beyond China's borders, and will necessarily remain on the strategic defensive. Logistical deficiencies hampered even the limited PLA operations in Vietnam in 1979.[33]

Chemical, Biological, and Radiological Capabilities

According to Nationalist sources, CBR training was neglected during the 1960s—a dangerous omission, considering that the Soviets have exhibited every intention of using chemical weapons in the event of war, and have a very strong capability to do so.[34] Most PLA chemical warfare equipment is of older Soviet design, although protective masks, clothing, and detection devices are now made in China.

In the past few years, CBR training has been very intensively emphasized, particularly passive defensive measures, detection, and decontamination.[35] Chinese offensive chemical and biological weapons are minimal, and tactical nuclear weapons are still under development. Vulnerability to Soviet (or Vietnamese) CBR attack is still a very serious PLA weakness.

Training and Tactics

According to Napoleon, "The first quality of a soldier is constancy in enduring fatigue and hardship." By that standard, the Chinese infantryman is among the best in the world. Although his equipment is inferior to his potential enemies, he is well-trained, highly motivated, and incredibly tough. His junior leaders are competent and imaginative tacticians. PLA training and tactics seek to capitalize on these qualities. They emphasize long forced marches, supply economy, astute use of terrain, careful camouflage, and the maximum use of deception, stealth, and surprise. The PLA is trained on the assumption that it must deal with enemies having air superiority and a big edge in firepower. Small unit tactics therefore seek to offset the enemy's firepower by "hugging" his positions. This tactic forces enemy commanders to risk killing their own troops if artillery and airpower are fully employed. Because of this emphasis on fighting at close quarters, the PLA has traditionally emphasized bayonet fighting.

PLA tactical, administrative, and logistical movement is usually conducted at night to help avoid air attack. The gigantic force of engineer troops is trained to repair or replace damaged roads, bridges, and installations in the dark, after air attack.

Mechanization of the main forces will not reduce the usefulness of deception, but must attenuate the emphasis on stealth, and especially on "hugging." Moreover, mechanization requires commanders and soldiers to master new skills with which they have no combat experience. The main forces train in a ten-month annual cycle, preceded by two months in the spring which are devoted to the absorption and basic unit training of the annual draft of recruits. The cycle begins with individual training, and progresses through small unit training to training tests and large-scale exercises in late autumn and winter. At least one-third of all training is at night.[36]

Ideally, training is supposed to maintain the high level of basic infantry skills while developing the new skills associated with mechanization. Especially at upper levels of command, however, complex logistics, maintenance, rapid movement, and enhanced firepower call for new tactical and professional conceptions as well as technical knowledge or skill. Combined arms training is now being emphasized all the way from the squad up to the corps and MR levels.[37] But the PLA is only beginning to develop doctrine and techniques which the Soviet, American, British, and German armies worked out during World War II.[38] Development of modern military doctrine is hampered by serious human and material deficiencies.

Material deficiencies are immense. The Chinese must develop truly modern doctrine which will become applicable as newer equipment becomes available. At the same time, they must develop interim doctrine to take maximum advantage of existing hardware under current conditions. This interim doctrine must combine the defense of strategic areas with various modifications of traditional guerrilla "people's war" elsewhere. In a major policy statement in October 1979, Defense Minister Hsu Hsiang-ch'ien directed that national defense be based on existing weapons, even as newer ones are developed. Moreover, he emphasized that the transitional period is likely to be lengthy.[39] Defense clearly has the lowest economic priority of the "four modernizations."

Human deficiencies are even more challenging. Hsu wrote that, "We will have a modern fighting force [only] when modern weaponry is combined with men who have advanced modern military thinking." The principle task of the PLA in 1979-81 has been "emancipating the mind" to overcome "ossified thinking"--especially among senior officers.[40] Veteran cadres evince a strong preference—officially denounced as "Leftist"—for the traditional PLA cadre who is "jack of all trades but master of none."[41]

"Ossification" could be dealt with by rapidly replacing all old cadres with well-trained younger men, but that is impossible for political and practical reasons. "Ossification" pervades the upper levels of the PLA, affecting men too numerous and too deeply entrenched to be eased out quietly all at once. Furthermore, there simply are too few well-trained younger men available. As a stop-gap measure, the general departments and MRs organized crash courses on "the technology and techniques of modern warfare for high and middle ranking officers" in late 1979.[42] These classes were extremely academic, being mostly lectures, discussions, and essay writing. New ideas are not being tested "on the ground," owing not only to the lack of equipment but to the apparent disinclination of some senior officers to try anything new. Passive resistance to change partly accounted for the endless discussions of "practice as the sole criterion of truth" in 1979. Still another problem is the advanced age of senior tactical commanders, many of whom are just not physically up to prolonged field duty.[43]

Even more serious, in the long term, is the low "cultural level" (literacy) of junior cadres and soldiers. A MAC directive on education and training, issued in May 1978, set off a major effort to encourage unit and individual "scientific and culture" study.[44] Unprecedented emphasis is also being accorded to formal schooling. Western-style military academies have resumed operation.[45] Cadres and soldiers are now being selected by upper levels for advanced schooling and subsequent reassignment. Both procedures will have far-reaching implications for PLA Personnel management, as well as military capability (see chapter 7).[46]

It will take a long time to train young cadres, to retrain or retire old ones, and to obtain really modern equipment. Meanwhile, China is militarily weaker, relatively, than it was thirty years ago.

Deployment

Harvey Nelsen has detailed the distinction and relationships between the main forces and the military regions.[47] The MRs have important logistical and administrative support responsibilities to the main force units located within their boundaries, and orders to the latter routinely pass through MR headquarters. Peking, however, can and does move main force units across MR boundaries at will. In early 1979, at least two corps were moved from the Foochow MR to the Vietnamese border. The national strategic reserve of up to four corps is located in the Wuhan MR. Main force deployment is depicted in Appendix C.

MAIN FORCE SUPPORT UNITS

The combat forces are supported by specialized service arms, which come under the command of the GSD or GRSD.

The Antichemical Troops

Once thought to be a separate service arm, the antichemical force is actually a subdepartment of the GSD. In addition to CBR training facilities, it controls a number of antichemical regiments. Their missions include smoke generating, monitoring and detection, technical advisory functions, and decontamination (see the discussion of CBR capabilities above).

Engineer, Telecommunications, Railway, and Capital Construction Troops

Until the mid-1970s, there were three PLA service branches concerned with capital construction: the Engineer Corps, the Telecommunications Corps, and the Railway Engineer Corps. The last, as the name implies, built and repaired rails, roadbeds, bridges, yards, etc. Similarly, telecommunications troops built much of the civil communications system, in addition to being responsible for military communications per se. Engineer troops built roads, bridges, airfields, and all kinds of public buildings and installations, but were also responsible for combat engineering tasks such as river crossing, demolitions, and fortifications. The latter two branches were further charged with training signal and engineer personnel for combat units.

All three of these service arms sent units to Indochina in 1965-73, where they performed commendably in their wartime mission of repairing bomb damage. As we have seen, this capability has been developed and maintained because the high command works on the assumption that, in any major conflict, the PLA will have to operate despite enemy air superiority.

Capital construction responsibilities overlapped considerably and diverted the resources of the engineer and telecommunications branches from their important combat support functions. Accordingly, a reorganization was initiated in 1966, with the establishment of the Capital Construction Engineering Corps. Reorganization proceeded sporadically, allegedly owing to interference by "the Lin Piao antiparty clique." Between 1971 and 1978, the new service arm took over the capital construction units and responsibilities of the engineer and telecommunications arms. Today, the latter retain responsibility only for combat engineering and military communications, respectively, including related training and R&D.[48]

The Railway Engineer Corps (apparently unaffected by the reorganization) and Capital Construction Engineer Corps continue to make substantial contributions to the national economy. This is particularly true in flood control and water conservancy, communications, and the opening up of new lands to economic exploitation. The construction of rail and telephone lines, and of roads, has been instrumental in tying the PRC together both economically and politically. Capital Construction Engineer units also work on steel mills, harbor installations, mines, geological survey, public buildings, the Peking subway, factories, airfields, and hydroelectric installations.[49] Although they may replace or supplement civilian labor anywhere, priority assignments for construction troops include those involving security considerations and projects in inaccessible areas and under severe conditions, where their superior discipline and special training make them more efficient.

Prior to the reorganization, the GRSD controlled all engineer and telecommunications troops. Today, combat engineer and signal units are under the GSD, the much reduced "signal corps" now being only the "communications subdepartment" analagous to the "antichemical force."[50] Railway and capital construction troops remain under the GRSD, which must coordinate their employment with the various ministries (of railways, chemical industry, coal industry, et al.). Construction units are administered, and probably sometimes controlled, by MR or MD commanders.

THE AIR FORCE

It is indicative of the extreme ground-force orientation of the PLA that, officially, the air force is just another of the eight service arms. Actually, the People's Liberation Army Air Force (PLAAF) enjoys a special status. It has a distinctive uniform (the PLA green jacket and cap with blue trousers), a separate personnel system, and a chain of command which is highly centralized and separate from that of the ground forces.

Organization

The PLAAF spans the country with a system of eleven Air Force Districts (AFDs), which coincide with the eleven Military Regions. While maintaining liaison with the local MR headquarters, AFDs must get clearance from PLAAF headquarters and/or the GSD for all but the most routine matters.[51]

Within each AFD are one or more "Air Armies" (*fei-hsing chün*). These are non-tactical organizations responsible for the administrative and logistical support of combat units. The AFDs control most combat air units, as well as the national air defense system, which includes radar, gun, and missile units (Table 5.2).

The largest tactical air units are the Air Divisions (*fei-hsing shih*), which are each assigned a specific mission or geographical area. Each division consists of two or (usually) three air regiments (*fei-hsing t'uan*). As in the ground forces, the regiment is the most important level of administration, political organization, and tactical command. Each air regiment contains three or four wings (*fei-hsing ta-tui*), each consisting of three or four squadrons (*fei-hsing chung-tui*).

The composition of the AFDs varies considerably, depending upon the perceived threat of air attack, and on the projected use of air power in defense of a given district. Most advanced air defense systems are concentrated around industrial and population centers. Most of the attack divisions equipped with the new A5 "FANTAN" fighter-bomber are normally concentrated in the critical Shenyang and Peking AFDs—where they can suppport the defense of the Northeast.

In addition to its air and air defense units, the PLAAF also has its own political and logistical systems. The Chinese have also chosen to make their airborne infantry units part of the air force. The 15th Airborne Corps, consisting of three paratroop divisions, is stationed in the Wuhan area, and is subordinate to the Wuhan AFD.[52] As part of China's strategic reserve, however, it could be moved elsewhere on short notice.

Equipment and Effectiveness

Although its manpower and equipment have increased steadily since 1950, the PLAAF remains heavily dependent on outdated equipment (see Appendix D).[53] The fighter-interceptor force primarily relies on obsolete F4 (MiG-17 "FRESCO") and obsolescent F6 (MiG-19 "FARMER") day fighters. There is a severe shortage of all-weather interceptors. Owing to the deficiencies of the

TABLE 5.2
PLAAF Strength: 1979*

AF Districts	11	Coincide with MRs.
Bomber divisions	5	AFD Control. Long-range units under Central control.
Fighter Divisions	24	AFD control
Fighter Regiments (Separate)	10-12	AFD control.
Attack Divisions	3	Fighter-bombers. AFD control.
Transport Divisions	2	Central control.
Reconnaissance Divisions	1	Central control.
Helicopter Divisions	1	Central control
Air Defense Divisions	11	One per AFD.
Airborne Infantry Corps	1	Three divisions of paratroops.
Total personnel	450,000	Including 220,000 air defense personnel and approximately 29,000 paratroops

*Some air units are understrength.

Sources:
Bueschel, Communist Chinese Air Power; Jane's Aircraft, 1978-79; The Military Balance, 1979-80 and 1980-81; Mogdis in Whitson, ed.,; "The PLA Air Force . . ."; I and S (August 1974); and Handbook on the Chinese Armed Forces, pp. 7-1 to 7-8.

Chinese-made F7 ("FISHBED" MiG-21), the all-weather version of the F6, a design over twenty years old, will remain China's best interceptor for several more years. Some interceptors mount "ATOLL" air-to-air missiles, but it is uncertain how successfully the Chinese have copied this design.[54] The newest aircraft in service is the "FANTAN," a Chinese design closely based on the F6. The entire bomber force is obsolete, and could not survive long against modern air defenses.
Since its inception, the PLAAF has been primarily a defensive force, built around its interceptors. Only in the past decade has it begun to equip and train itself to provide close air support for ground troops. Obsolete MiG-15 "FAGOT" fighters have been converted for use as fighter-bombers, and even interceptor pilots now receive some training in close support techniques. The survivability of even the "FAGOT" and "FANTAN" units against modern air defenses is problematical.[55]
The Sino-Soviet split, and the subsequent commitment to "self-reliance" resulted in the opening of a serious technological gap in the 1960s. The result is that, while the PLAAF is the world's third-largest air force, it is qualitatively inferior to the air forces of most of China's neighbors.
Supplies of aircraft repair parts are limited and unreliable, while PLAAF

maintenance management and training are only marginally effective. The result has been reluctance to fly in unclear weather or to take any risks or initiatives in the air, since the lack of even a worn-out seal might ground an aircraft for months. Operational aircraft tend to be regarded as too precious to fly.[56]

In 1977-78, there was reportedly an increase in flight training, but even then it was insufficient. The PLAAF planned for less than 100 annual flight hours per pilot in 1978. With the US Air Force flying less than at any time in its history, American transport pilots were getting 350-600 hours per year in 1978. That same year, one PLAAF transport unit proudly reported completion of a *three-year* flight training program in one year, for a grand total of less than 300 hours per pilot. If such unscheduled jumps in flight time were at all common, the PLAAF budget must have been a shambles. Flight training has been cut back drastically in 1980-81, owing to the reduced defense budget. Admonitions to make flight training "more intensive" and to "conduct hard ground training" will not alleviate the situation much.

Closely related to excessive caution is oversupervision. In one transport division, "Whenever three or more planes take off at the same time, they are led by a cadre of divisional or regimental level."[57] This practice, as well as others, deprives younger pilots of training and initiative.

The twenty-six regiments of air defense troops are organized into eleven divisions, one of which is assigned to each AFD. The Strength and equipment of these divisions vary considerably. They provide modest radar, gun, and missile protection to key industrial, communications, and political centers.

The only air-defense missiles are several hundred "Red Flag No. 4" (CSA-1, "GUIDELINE") missiles. This Chinese copy of the Soviet SA-2 was reasonably effective against American jets in Vietnam, although it is vulnerable to the constantly improving electronic countermeasures (ECM) of the two superpowers and their allies.[58]

China's air defenses are gradually improving, but are still far from adequate.[59] In 1965-70, a chain of air bases was built, in Manchuria and the Peking area, which now holds a major proportion of the PLAAF. Another chain of airfields, extending west from Hainan Island to Mengtze in Yunnan, was constructed to support the North Vietnamese and to beef up Chinese defenses in the south. Much of the PLAAF strength originally stationed at these bases was moved north after 1973, but was redeployed south as Sino-Vietnamese relations deteriorated in 1978-79. Between 1964 and 1970, the PLAAF posted a relatively poor record against American aircraft, considering the hundreds of intrusions that went undetected, or at least unchallenged, during that period. The PLAAF has also failed to deal with periodic intrusions by aircraft from India, the USSR, and Taiwan. Although this record is partly owing to intentional Chinese restraint and the wish to avoid incidents, it is quite clear that air defenses are inadequate. Detection of low-flying aircraft (under 5000 feet) is virtually nonexistent. Intercept capability is especially poor at night and in foul weather, even though some air units supposedly devote half their total flight time to night training.[60]

With the exception of a select few (discussed below, in the section on the navy), Chinese pilots seldom fly over open water. The Nationalists have been allowed to fly routine transport shuttles to Quemoy and Matsu, with almost complete impunity, since 1958.[61] There are two possible explanations for this: Most pilots may be forbidden to fly over the sea for fear of defection. More prosaic and more likely—given the PLAAF's mission to defend a huge land area with a wholly inadequate force—there is little justification for training and equipping more than a few units to fly beyond the coast.

Personnel

Air force personnel fall into a unique pattern compared to the rest of the PLA, because the PLAAF drew most of its original flight crews from among Nationalist defectors. Many of these men, and the slightly younger pilots trained during the Korean war, are still in the cockpit.[62] The purge of many younger pilots (because of a rash of defections) in the early 1960s exacerbated the situation, as did the failure to recruit or train any pilots at all during the GPCR. The age of most PLAAF pilots means that their long experience may well be accompanied by slowed reflexes and failing eyesight. They certainly provide a marked contrast to the "young hotshot" image projected by most of the world's military aviators.

The first pilots initially rose quickly through the ranks, but then ran into a barrier. Top positions are still occupied by old infantrymen (there is currently one PLAAF vice-commander who is a qualified pilot). Thus, although middle-grade air force officers are relatively young (compared to the ground forces), further promotion is denied them. This has created a good deal of frustration, which has probably contributed to the defection rate, as well as to the relatively radical behavior of the air force in 1967-71. A majority of pilots are still of urban bourgeois background, and therefore more subject to dissatisfaction with the regime's economic shortcomings. This factor was again underlined by the defection of an F6 pilot to Taiwan in July 1977. As recently as July 1975, wall posters alleged that Lin Piao's influence was still strong in the PLAAF—an accusation which probably reflects continuing frustration in the middle grades.[63]

Recent statements imply that the PLAAF is concerned about the age of its pilots,[64] although recruitment of young aviation candidates resumed in the early 1970s. The PLAAF is as badly afflicted by "ossified thinking" as the rest of the PLA, and it remains to be seen whether the infusion of young aviators at the bottom will affect the extreme centralization and excessive caution at the top.

Political restrictions habitually have been relaxed to allow defecting Nationalist pilots to be assigned as middle-grade officers in PLAAF units after brief periods of "reeducation," and to be back in the cockpit—usually as flight instructors. This tends to confirm the widely held opinion that PLAAF pilots are far inferior to their counterparts on Taiwan.

Many of the personnel factors which contributed to PLAAF political activism in 1967-71 are still operating, and could conceivably lead to renewed interservice strife. Air force frustration may be exacerbated by a continuing lack of modern equipment, and by the continued diversion of available resources to the ground forces and to the civilian sector. The long-range outlook is for only gradual improvement and expansion of air and air defense forces.

The Airborne Forces

PLAAF paratroop units have the best infantry weapons available, but are lacking in tanks and heavy artillery, which cannot be air-landed. There is little military justification for maintaining three airborne divisions, with all their special equipment and training requirements. The entire PLAAF would be hard-pressed to carry them, even if the civil air fleet were commandeered.

Moreover, a successful airborne assault would require the air force to gain and maintain local air superiority; a task it probably could not fulfill.

The existence of so many Airborne troops must therefore have a non-military explanation. The role of 15th Airborne Corps during the Wuhan incident suggests such an explanation: Although they are part of the PLA, and are a tiny minority of the total infantry force, paratroop units can serve as a highly mobile "fire brigade" force in the event of internal unrest or rebellion. Perhaps more importantly, they can bring major force quickly to bear against a rebellious military unit—anywhere in the country. By virtue of their separate chain of command, elite status, and mobility, airborne units thus fulfill something of the same "counter-military military" role as the Soviet KGB forces and Hitler's *Waffen SS*.[65]

Civil Aviation

The Civil Air Administration of China (CAAC) was modeled on *Aeroflot*, its Soviet counterpart, in the 1950s. It controls all civilian aviation, from international passenger service to crop-spraying. CAAC is controlled by the air force, is organized along military lines, and its personnel are trained in PLAAF schools. Moreover, CAAC and PLAAF operations overlap considerably even in peacetime. PLAAF "Tridents" sometimes fly scheduled CAAC domestic passenger runs, while military maneuvers use CAAC aircraft as tactical assault transports. Many air force and CAAC transports even wear nearly identical paint schemes, so they are easily "civilianized" or "militarized" with minor changes in their markings.[66]

NUCLEAR FORCES

China's strategic air force consists of about 90 B6 medium-range jet bombers. The B6, a copy of the Soviet Tu-16 "BADGER-A," is now used mainly for reconnaissance by the Soviets, who judge it obsolescent as a bomber. Its combat survivability is highly questionable.[67]

In September 1977 and March 1978, the Chinese tested nuclear devices of less than 20 kilotons (KT) yield.[68] This may well indicate that tactical-yield warheads are under development. If so, they presumably could be delivered by "FROG" missiles, the "FANTAN," or the ancient B5 (Il-28 "BEAGLE"). The advent of such weapons would necessitate a reassessment of the military balance in east Asia, but is probably still several years away.

Nuclear Missiles

Because the survivability of aircraft is questionable, ballistic missiles are China's most credible nuclear force. They are controlled by the Second Artillery Corps, which was formed in 1965. Details about this force are understandably lacking, so only an overview is possible. There is endless speculation and very little reliable data about Chinese missiles. In particular, figures diverge widely on ranges and numbers of launchers (see Appendix E).

The main nuclear strike force consists of 40-50 CSS-1 medium-range ballistic missiles (MRBMs), and 65-85 CSS-2 intermediate-range ballistic missiles (IRBMs), both of Chinese design. They carry warheads of about twenty kilotons and one megaton, respectively. There are a few CSS-3 "limited-range" intercontinental ballistic missiles (ICBMs), or perhaps improved IRBMs, which can threaten the European USSR and all of Asia (but not the United States).

After a decade of delay, on 18 and 23 May 1980 a "carrier rocket" (*yun-tsai huo-chien*), designated CSS-X-4 by NATO, was test-fired about 12,000 km (see chapter 6). An ICBM version is probably in production, and a few may already be deployed. It will put most of Europe and western North America within range of Chinese nuclear attack.[69]

Deployment

PLA Missiles are deployed in the north, northwest, and Tibet, and appear to be targeted almost exclusively on the Soviet Union. Beginning in 1967-68, these missiles were deployed at a very gradual rate, probably so as not to frighten the USSR into a "preemptive strike." They are widely dispersed, often installed in silos and man-made caves in mountainous terrain, and so carefully camouflaged that even satellite reconnaissance failed to discover them until 1973.[70] Pictures and stories released in 1979 indicate that some Chinese MRBMs are mobile (by road or rail). This makes a successful "first strike" very chancy. On the other hand, since all PLA ballistic missiles are liquid-fueled, reaction times are still measured in hours. Furthermore, there are very serious questions about the adequacy of targeting data, guidance, and warhead reliability.[71] Moreover, being generally close to Soviet territory, missile sites are vulnerable to conventional attack. In the event of a non-nuclear invasion, Peking very quickly must decide whether to initiate a nuclear war, or simply to allow much of its nuclear force to be overrun. Herein lies the strategic importance of the new CSS-X-4, which can be sited deep in the Chinese interior, safely beyond reach of such a conventional preemptive strike.

The second artillery has responsibilities in R&D work, and is involved in the PRC space program. It is almost certainly the proponent agency for Chinese reconnaissance satellites.[72] On 26 January 1978, booster components of the CSS-X-4 launched an earth satellite ("China-8") with an estimated weight of 1,250 kg. Four days later, a photographic data capsule was recovered from orbit.[73]

Personnel

Attesting to the extreme sensitivity of the second artillery is the fact that the core of its personnel was originally drawn from the public security forces of the Peking Garrison.[74] In this, the Chinese followed the Soviet example; the early custodians of Soviet nuclear weapons were taken from police units as well. For obvious reasons, the reliability of the troops, and especially of the officers, who man strategic nuclear weapons is of critical importance. It is therefore interesting to note that the GPCR hardly touched the second artillery. Even the Red Guard press made little mention of "struggle" within it—and absolutely none of second artillery soldiers "exchanging revolutionary experiences" with the "masses." Indeed, the second artillery appears to have been completely exempted from "Three Supports and Two Militaries" work which involved virtually everybody else in the PLA. It seems that no one was willing to either "radicalize" or distract the finger on China's nuclear trigger.

THE NAVY

Like the air force, the People's Liberation Army Navy (PLAN) is another of the eight service arms of the PLA. In addition to coastal defense, it is charged with policing and protecting the fishing fleet. Also like the air force, the navy has a special uniform, a highly centralized command structure, and a separate personnel system.

Organization and Equipment

The navy's equipment and organization reflect its defensive role.[75] Its seagoing forces are organized into three fleets. The North Sea Fleet, which is based primarily at Tsingtao and Lu Shun, is responsible for the Yellow Sea and the Sea of Japan, and is therefore concerned with the home waters of the Soviet Navy in the Western Pacific, as well as the considerable naval forces of the two Koreas and Japan. The East Sea Fleet is based at Shanghai and Chusan, and faces Taiwan. The South Sea Fleet, based at Chan Chiang and Huan Pu, is responsible for defense of Hainan and the southern coast. It also provides the military backing for Chinese claims to the Hsi-sha (Paracel), Nancha (Spratly), and other islands, against the claims of Vietnam, the Philippines, and Malaysia. This fleet has recently been reinforced in response to the growth of Vietnamese naval power and increased Soviet naval activity in the region.

The naval air force (PLANAF) is responsible for the air defense of much of the coast and for maritime reconnaissance (see Appendix F). Fighter units on Hainan Island, which engaged US air intruders in 1966-70, were entirely PLANAF. They earned a reputation for better-than-average equipment and skillful, aggressive airmanship. Unlike the air force, they can and do fly over water. Naval B6 patrol bombers range well out to sea, and there is also a force of B5 jet bombers which have been converted for use as torpedo planes. The PLANAF has the same general shortcomings as the air force; most notably poor maintenance management, limited training, and an inadequate foul-weather capability.[76]

The navy has air defense gun and missile units, which protect naval installations. Their equipment and capabilities are essentially the same as PLAAF air defense units. There are also naval radar units which support the fleet, the PLANAF, and naval air defense forces.

The navy's air and air defense forces are integrated into the national air defense system, which is, as we have seen, controlled by the air force. Exactly what command and liaison arrangements implement this joint system are unclear. Since air defenses are widely dispersed and contain large gaps, coordination is probably a relatively simple matter. It will become more complex as Chinese air defenses improve and the gaps are closed. The fleet has no operational air defense missiles, and therefore must remain close to shore-based protection.[77]

There are about 38,000 coastal defense infantry and artillery troops, which are also part of the navy. Although foreign sources often identify them as "marines," they have a primarily defensive mission. Several infantry regiments are trained amphibious landing forces, and could be delivered across landing beaches by the large (but obsolete) fleet of landing craft inherited from the Nationalists.

The largest Chinese surface vessels are "Lü Ta" class destroyers, which mount anti-aircraft guns, anti-submarine weapons, 130mm guns, and "STYX" surface-to-surface missiles (see Appendix F). The first of these destroyers became operational in 1971. There now are nine in service, plus a considerable number of missile-launching frigates and corvettes, which also entered service over the past decade. The fleet of high-speed guided missile and gun boats is now the largest in the world.

Currently, China's limited offensive naval capability resides primarily in the large force of conventionally powered patrol submarines. They are mostly Soviet designs which are, in turn, copies of late World War II German types. They were fine submarines in their day, but would not survive very long in the face of modern anti-submarine warfare (ASW) forces. Chinese electronics equipment is far inferior to that of the superpowers, even in the newest vessels.

The one "Han" class submarine is noteworthy for its nuclear power plant. Although it was launched in 1972, it still is not operational owing to propulsion problems. It is armed only with conventional torpedoes. A second attempt at building a nuclear submarine may now be underway.[78] Construction of the "Ming" class, a PRC modification of the Soviet "Whiskey," was discontinued after only two were completed.

There is one "Gulf" class submarine which has three vertical launch tubes for submarine-launched ballistic missiles (SLBMs). There is no evidence that the Chinese are trying to develop an SLBM, however.[79]

The light coastal defense boats are not only the most numerous in the world, but also are among the best. This is particularly true of the hydrofoils.[80] The problem with these small attack craft, as with larger vessels, is their primary weapon, a Chinese-made version of the Soviet "STYX" missile. That it can be effective was demonstrated in January 1974, when a South Vietnamese gunboat was sunk by a Chinese "STYX." On the other hand, the Egyptians, who fired about 100 Soviet-made "STYX" at Israeli ships in October 1973, were totally frustrated by ECM. The PLAN has deployed hundreds of these missiles, afloat and ashore, creating the possibility of "swamping" the sophisticated ECM defenses of an invader.[81] The "STYX" is also unreliable in bad weather, however.

From 1966 to 1971 there was a major push to expand the fleet of major surface combatants. Then, such construction was curtailed, only to resume again in 1978-80. Conversely, submarine and fast attack boat construction expanded rapidly in 1971-79, but has recently slowed. The current expansion of the surface fleet and PLANAF reflects China's concern with protecting her increasing maritime interests. In this regard, the merchant fleet has also expanded rapidly since 1972. In March 1981, it totalled over 400 vessels with a cargo capacity of about eight million tons.[82]

Training and Effectiveness

The navy trains in a ten-month cycle similar to the one in the ground forces. Considerable emphasis is given to night and foul-weather training, and to the use of large, high-speed formations of small craft. Because they stay close to the coast, they can be directed by shore-based radar. Nationalist ships have been subjected to well-coordinated sneak attacks, delivered from all quarters by torpedo and gun boats. This might be thought of as an adaptation of guerrilla tactics to naval warfare. Very high standards are demanded of naval personnel, especially radio operators and navigators.[83]

The expansion of PRC maritime commerce, conflicting national claims over South China Sea islands, and the drilling of offshore oil fields all require a strong PLA navy. An eighteen-ship task force supported the ICBM test in May 1980, cruising to the impact area 750 miles northwest of Fiji. They conducted underway-replenishment operations, flew a French-made Super-Frelon helicopter from shipboard, and held formation through a strong gale on the homeward voyage. It was an impressive show, which surprised foreign observers. Despite this evident capability, PLAN blue-water combat power is still quite limited. Even the capacity for coastal defense is limited by lack of shipborne anti-aircraft missiles, modern ASW systems, and EW gear, as well as the electronic vulnerability of the "STYX." Correcting these deficiencies will be very expensive, and their priority appears to be low. For the foreseeable future, China remains vulnerable from the sea.[84]

Personnel

The personnel situation in the PLAN is similar in many respects to that in the PLAAF. Experienced military seamen, like airmen, were drawn initially from among Nationalist deserters, and subsequently recruited from among the better-educated youth of the coastal cities. The civilian fishing fleet is also a major recruiting ground, to the extent that sufficiently educated men can be found. While it is advantageous to man the coastal defenses with locally recruited fisherfolk, the procedure has encouraged the persistence of local dialects in the navy—in marked contrast to the air force.

The navy has clung to the highest degree of rank-consciousness in the PLA. Even during the Lin Piao years, cadres and sailors wore different styles of shirts under their blue *Chung-shan* jackets. Shore-based naval personnel wear a uniform basically the same as the rest of the PLA, but all blue. In 1974, however, seagoing sailors appeared in new uniforms that closely resemble the Soviet-style ones rejected as "revisionist" in 1965. Blue in winter and white in summer, they are sharply differentiated between cadres (who wear peaked caps and *Chung-shan* jackets) and sailors (who wear traditional beribboned sailor caps and jumpers).

While the personnel of the PLAN and of the merchant marine are not interchangeable, merchant officers, seamen, and shore personnel are often former PLAN cadres or sailors. Since the PRC's seaborne commerce would probably cease in the event of a major war, the merchant marine would provide a reservoir of trained recruits for the navy.

THE MILITARY REGIONS

There are presently eleven military regions (MR,*chün-ta-ch'ü*), each consisting of one or more military districts (MD, *chün-ch'ü*). Twenty-two provinces and autonomous regions are coextensive with MDs, while the remaining four (Kwangtung, Tibet, Sinkiang, and Inner Mongolia) are subdivided (see maps in Appendix G).[85]

The three major city garrison commands (*wei-shu-ch'ü*) of Peking, Tientsin, and Shanghai have paramilitary and recruiting functions similar to the MDs, and are administratively under the Peking and Nanking MRs. They are directly under GSD control, however, and are nearly coequal in status with MRs. Indeed, the Peking garrison controls more and better troops than do several of the MRs.

Figure 5.5 depicts the estimated organization of a typical MR. An MR commander has a wide variety of military and paramilitary responsibilities. These include military training, command of the regional forces, logistical and administrative support of main force units, recruiting, and military command of the militia. The last two are accomplished through the MDs, military subdistricts (MSD, *chün-fen-chü*), and People's Armed Departments (PADs).

Training

Training is a major MR responsibility. PLA recruits generally receive their basic training in the replacement training divisions of the MRs within which they are recruited. Most are then sent to their assigned main or regional force units for on-the-job training, while a selected few receive further technical schooling.

MR schools also train both company-grade and field-grade officers.[88] It is unclear to what extent the MRs have a hand in running the specialized military training facilities of the service branches and general departments. It is not certain, for example, whether the armor training center at Hangchow is directly under the Armored Forces Command or the Nanking Military Region, or whether the Rear Services College in Peking is directly under the GRSD or the Peking Garrison. The situation with respect to the numerous training and research facilities (e.g., The Nanking Artillery Engineering Institute) is foggier still.

Logistics and Administration

Every installation, unit, or school within a given MR, whether main force or regional force, depends on the MR headquarters for support involving real estate, buildings, furniture, etc. In addition, as mentioned earlier, the MR is the crucial link in the GRSD supply system. These considerations make it clear why MR commanders must be kept abreast of all military activities in their regions, and explain why orders from Peking to the main forces normally flow through MR headquarters.

Regional Forces

The terms "regional forces" or "local forces" apply to a variety of military organizations directly under the command of regional military authorities. Some are controlled directly by MR commanders, while most are controlled through subordinate MDs and MSDs. Broadly defined, "regional forces" include the militia and the Production and Construction Corps (PCC), but these are sufficiently unique as to warrant separate consideration in the following sections. The present discussion is restricted to uniformed troops employed full-time in garrison, border, and/or internal security roles.

Most of these units are long-established in their localities, having originated as guerrillas during the anti-Japanese war.[87] In wartime, they are intended to serve three purposes: They defend their localities as units, provide cadres and "backbone" fighters for expanded militia forces, and provide a pool

FIGURE 5.5
Estimated Military Regional Organization

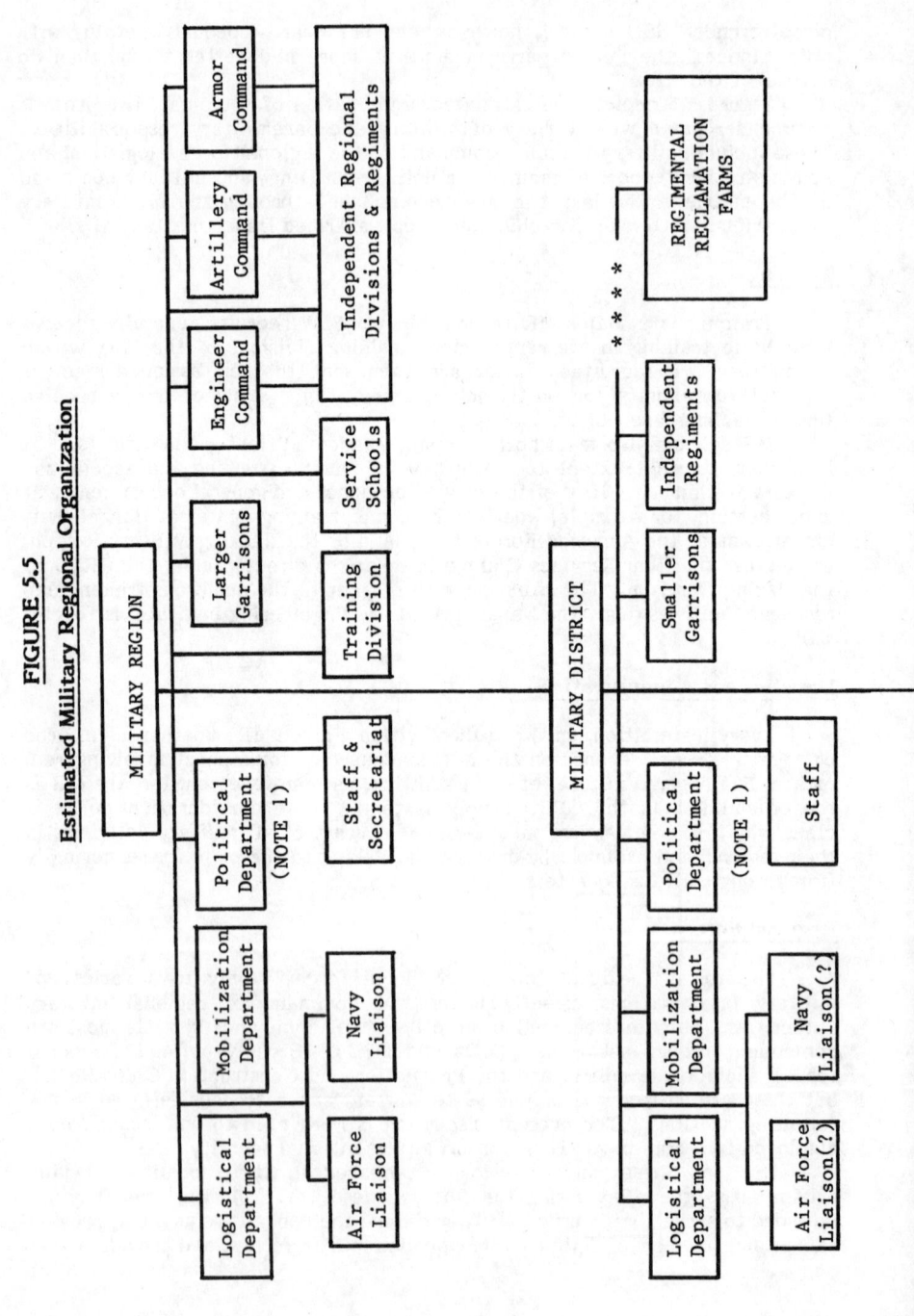

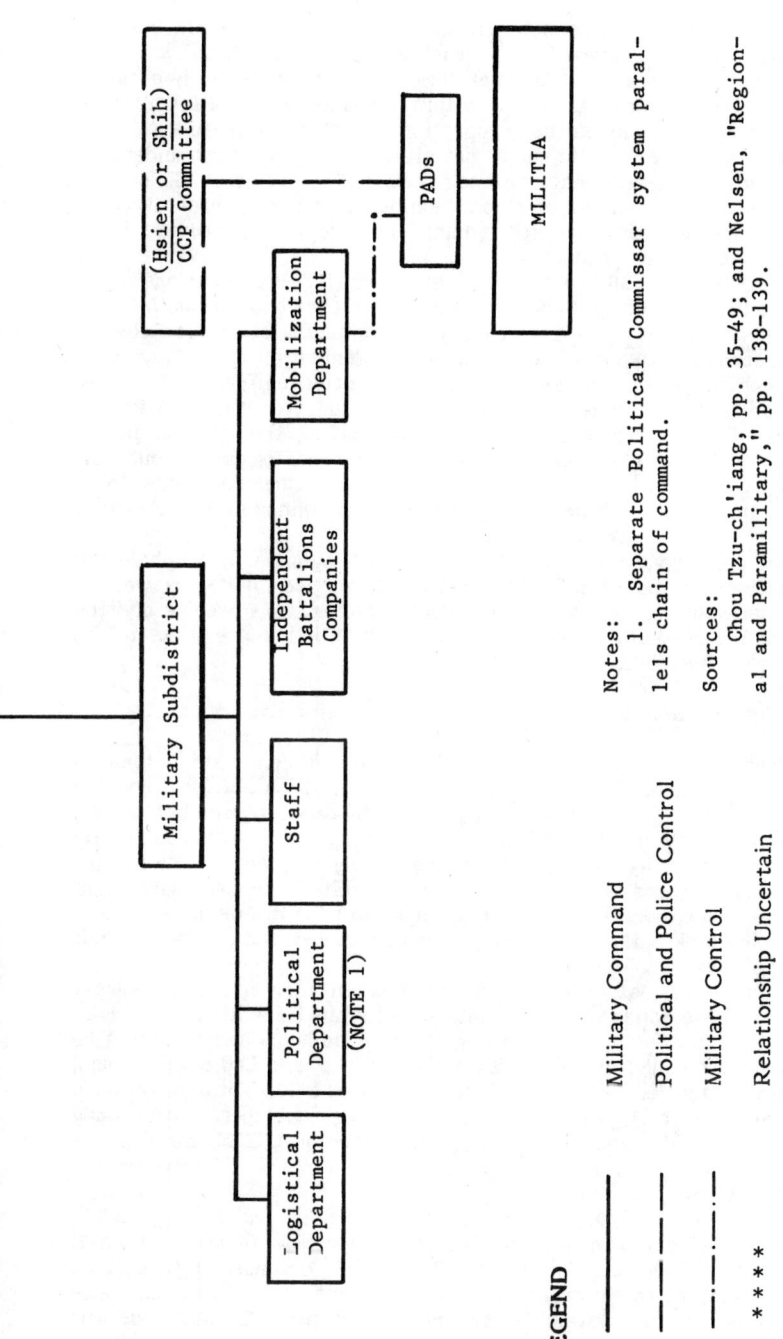

of units and individuals which can be "promoted" into the main forces. In peacetime, their primary concerns are internal and border security.

Since regional units are often much larger than their peacetime duties require, they frequently engage in agricultural production on "PLA farms," where they produce a substantial proportion of their own food.[88] In connection with this "self-sufficiency" activity, they sometimes undertake water-conservancy, land-reclamation, and small-scale industry. They also provide civil assistance in times of flood, famine, or other natural disaster. Propaganda to the contrary notwithstanding, however, they provide little direct assistance to civilian production.

Between 1958 and 1967, all police and security organizations were absorbed by the PLA. By early 1968, all these were in the hands of the MR and MD commands, and all wore PLA uniforms. The Ministry of Public Security (MPS) was apparently stripped of all its armed organizations. In May 1972, "People's Police" reappeared in Peking, with distinctive uniforms and under local civilian control.[89] Police reorganization apparently continued, with the MPS and local CCP committees regaining control of the various police organizations. In early 1981, there was a spate of press reports about new "people's armed police for border defense" in Yunnan and Chekiang, under local MPS organs.[90] On the other hand, border protection remained in PLA Hands in Kwangtung.[91]

All police units continue to use PLA political slogans and to uphold the "glorious traditions of the PLA." Moreover, PLA garrison units, as well as militia, still share public security duties with the police. If a precise division of labor has been worked out between army and police, it is not evident to the outside observer in mid-1981.

Training and Capabilities

Altogether, the various "independent" divisions, regiments, and battalions of the uniformed regional forces number about one million soldiers—roughly thirty percent of PLA ground force manpower. In terms of combat power, however, they are very much weaker. Generally speaking, they are lightly armed infantry, having little artillery and relatively few antitank weapons. Along the borders, there are regional cavalry units equipped with light howitzers, small arms, horses, camels, and a handful of motor vehicles. There are a few regional tank units in the north as well, although the quality of their equipment is poor (see Table 5.1).

Border units are better equipped and trained than internal security forces, but even these appear to be far inferior to main force units. A border guard who participated in the 1969 fighting at Ch'enpao Island testified that he had "never heard the sound of live artillery fire before, and had been through only one target practice." A recruit who entered the PLA in January 1979 went into combat on 17 February.[92] Even granting that these were young recruits, it is apparent that border units rely heavily on on-the-job training.

The Military Districts

MDs are charged with primary responsibility for frontier defense, "People's Defense," "People's Air Defense" (or civil defense, in American terms), maintenance of social order, military conscription, and war mobilization.[93] The conscription system is discussed in chapter 7. MDs and the

Military subdistricts (MSDs) exercise day-to-day control over most border and internal security units, although border units maintain direct communications with Peking, owing to the sensitivity of their mission.

Command of the militia is also exercised through the regional chain of command. In 1978-79, Peking vigorously reemphasized militia work, and specified that it is the main task of MDs and MSDs. The militia is controlled through the People's Armed Departments (PADs, also called People's Armed Forces Departments, *jen-min wu-chuang-pu*).

The People's Armed Departments

The PAD has both civil and military duties at the lowest levels. These duties include mobilization, recruiting, and militia work. Part of its personnel are civilian cadres, belonging to the local *hsien* or *shih* administration. Others are PLA men.

In April 1961, the militia, and presumably the PADs, were placed under the dual control of the *hsien* party committee and the MSD.[94] By 1963, the *PLA Political Work Regulations* referred to "the People's Armed Departments of the PLA," and greatly expanded the scope of PAD responsibilities.

In the early 1960s the PAD organization included a commander, deputy commander, and political commissar, and was large enough to include a political work section (or at least a political work cadre), and to have a full-fledged CCP committee of its own. A PAD at *hsien* level must therefore have consisted of at least twenty or thirty people, including both civilians and soldiers (see Figure 5.6).

The PAD may be thought of as the military staff of the *hsien* government, (in fact, this simile appears in official pronouncements). A PAD is probably too small to actually conduct large-scale military training. Therefore an important aspect of its training duties is to coordinate with locally stationed regional force units, and with the MSD and MD, for instructors, facilities, and equipment. In 1978-79, militia training was elevated to a "major task" of regional force units. Even main force units are involved in training the militia in such technical skills as anti-aircraft gunnery. This is the first main force involvement in militia work in at least two decades.[95]

Additional PAD duties involve the "community relations" of the PLA. It oversees such matters as the settlement of retired or disabled soldiers, the preferential treatment of servicemen's families, "the relationship between the army units stationed in the area and local party and government organs, and between such army units and the masses of the people."[96]

During the Cultural Revolution, largely by default, the PADs and the militia became the sole agencies able to carry out police functions. In 1967-73, the PADs and militia responded only to the military (MR-MD-MSD) chain of command. After the Tenth Party Congress (August 1973), the "gang of four" line was that the militia was the tool of the local CCP committee, and neither part of, nor subordinate to, the PLA. In practice, however, it continued to respond to orders from both the MSD and the local party.[97] As recently as August 1978, it seemed clear that the PLA (MR-MD-MSD) had the final word on use of the militia, and was not anxious to yield it up, despite the theory of "dual control."[98] Moreover, in its public security role, the militia theoretically answered to the local public security departments, as well as local MSDs and party committees.

Currently, militia work is undergoing yet another overhaul, based on

FIGURE 5.6
The Militia Administrative & Supervisory System: 1980

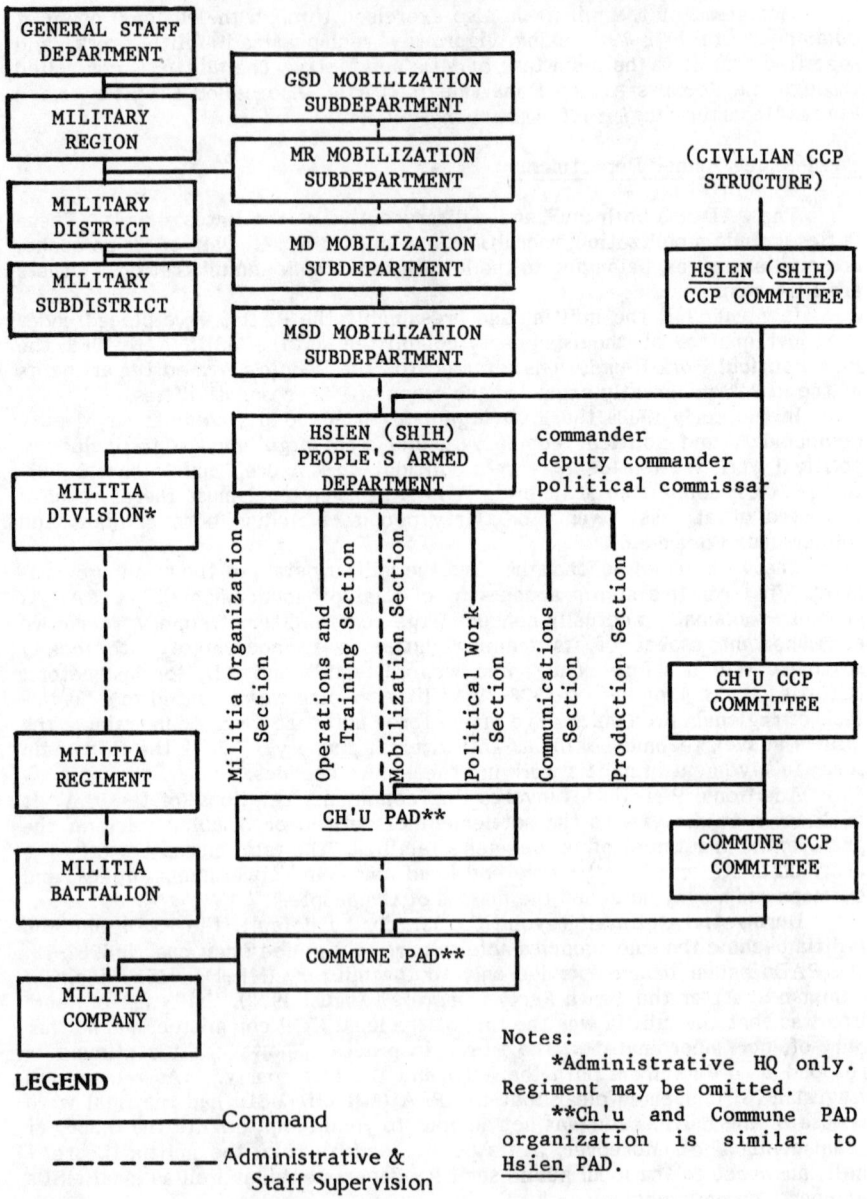

Adapted from Yu Yang

regulations and policies promulgated at the National Militia Conference of July-August 1978.[99] A major effort is underway to train the "full-time people's armed forces cadres" assigned to the PADs. While there is some evidence that these are demobilized PLA men, they are probably active-duty PLA cadres. Military control and expertise is also being strengthened by the requirement to assign recently demobilized soldiers as commanders of militia units.[100]

At the same time, local CCP control continues to be emphasized. It appears that civilians have been avoiding militia work for fear of appearing to infringe upon PLA prerogatives. 1978-79 has seen an intensive effort to reassert the "dual-control" system of PAD control by the MSD and the local CCP committees. An important aspect has been the insistence that party committees "include militia work in the agenda of every meeting." Another is the call for all party first secretaries to concurrently become first political commissars of MSDs, garrisons, and PADs.[101] Still another organizational measure has been the establishment of "People's Armed Forces Committees" by party committees at all levels (analogous to the MAC under the Central Committee).[102] The immense amount of media attention to militia reform suggests that civilian party leaders are still hesitant to get involved with the militia, while many soldiers still view militia work with distaste, and discount its military importance.

THE MILITIA

The militia (*min-ping*) has played an important role in the Chinese Communist movement for many decades, but its military usefulness and its control have been the subjects of a running controversy among CCP leaders. One of the "crimes" for which former Defense Minister P'eng Te-huai was purged was his contention that the militia was militarily useless, a waste of resources, and a potential source of disorder. In September 1973, the militia again became a major bone of contention between party radicals and the MRs.[103]

This round in the controversy began shortly after the Tenth Party Congress, with a national campaign to "Learn from Shanghai in Militia Building." The movement was very clearly under the auspices of Chiang Ch'ing and the "gang of four." "Model" militia units in Shanghai reportedly trained themselves (i.e., without PLA involvement). Furthermore, they were described as being solely responsible to the local civilian party. The radicals also attempted to create a national militia command, directly responsive to themselves.[104]

While paying lip-service to "learning from Shanghai," however, the regional PLA commands maintained a firm grip on most militia organizations. Their resistance to the "gang's" campaign was evidently successful, for not even the Shanghai militia backed the "gang" in October 1976.

Organization and Composition

The offical press has claimed that the militia numbers anywhere from thirty to a hundred million, or even "hundreds of millions."[105] The exact figure is uncertain and relatively unimportant. There are three distinct classes of militia, and the vast majority are "common militia" (*yi-pan ti min-ping*).[106] Theoretically comprised of all workers between the ages of sixteen and fifty, the "common militia," in fact, has little organizational structure, and amounts to little more than long lists of names. Its "members" are readily available for conscription, but have little or no military training. There may well be several hundred million of these.

Of considerably greater importance is the "basic" (*chi-pen* or *chi-kan*) militia which numbers twenty to one hundred million people between the ages of eighteen and forty. They are actually organized into units and receive several days of military training each year.

An elite subgroup of the "basic militia" are known as the "armed backbone militia" (*wu-ch uang ku-kan min-ping*), numbering from seven to eleven million. They are politically screened, relatively well trained, and carry weapons on a regular basis. They are supposed to get fifteen to twenty days of training annually, and are primarily concerned with border guard and public security duties. Of all militiamen, only the "armed backbone militia" receive material compensation (usually in the form of work points).[107] Although one-third of all militia are said to be women, and despite the existence of several highly publicized all-women militia units, the "armed backbone militia" is overwhelmingly male. There are substantial numbers of national minority militiamen. Their PAD, PLA, and party supervisors tend to be Han Chinese, although minority cadres are being recruited actively.[108]

Geographically, the armed militia appears to be concentrated along the borders and opposite Taiwan. That is to say, in these areas, the "armed militia" appears to constitute a relatively large percentage of the "basic militia." Because of their border security mission, these militia units have a much closer working relationship with the PLA (border units, MD, and MSD) than is the case in the interior or in the coastal cities.[109]

Traditionally, the militia was a light infantry force of peasants. The "gang of four's" emphasis on urban militia has been totally reconsolidated, but the urban militia continues to get unprecedented emphasis. "Militia divisions" now exist in many cities. Urban units receive considerable training in anti-aircraft defense, communications, antichemical warfare, etc. True, such specialties are also appearing in some rural units, but their heavy emphasis in cities points up the projected role for urban militia in "People's Defense" of "Stalingrad-type cities."[110]

In the past, the biggest militia organization to actually assemble and operate as a unit was the company, consisting of one or two hundred people. Militia infantry and artillery battalions reportedly participated in the 1979 "counterattack" on Vietnam,[111] however, and entire regiments now may assemble occasionally for training, especially in urban areas. Militia divisions exist on paper, and even have some assigned headquarters personnel, but are for strictly administrative purposes (refer to Figure 5.6). Although platoons and squads normally adhere to the same "triangular" structure as the PLA, higher echelons often depart from it.

Above the level of the militia "divisions," roughly at *hsien* level, all militia work is in the hands of the party and the PLA. Militia work at these higher levels consists mainly in coordination and policy making, plus some limited administrative and logistical support. Overall national supervisory responsibility for the militia is vested in the mobilization subdepartment of the GSD, which coordinates closely with the mass work subdepartment of the GPD.

In 1974-76, there were "militia commands" at provincial, municipal and national levels. This setup was part of the "gang of four's" attempted reorganization of the militia system, and has been abolished.

Roles and Missions

In wartime, militia missions include local defense and support of the regional and main forces of the PLA. This support includes the provision of guides, laborers, information, medical evacuation, and recruits. There has also been widespread consensus on some long-standing peacetime roles, such as border surveillance.

There has been considerable disagreement over other peacetime militia duties. There has been a trend over the past twenty years toward an increased militia role in internal security work. The "Learn from Shanghai" episode served to reinforce that trend, although urban militia are less involved in police work today than in 1975.

In peacetime, the primary task of each militia member is production. This simple proposition conceals yet another running controversy: Should militiamen just be exemplary workers in their civilian work places, or should militia units serve as "shock troops in socialist construction" under the supervision of higher authorities? The latter procedure, which has often been used for major construction projects, penalizes civilian work units by depriving them of their youngest and strongest workers, while requiring them to pay them (the militiamen) for labor performed elsewhere. In 1978-79, party and state officials were admonished to minimize militia unit labor, and to compensate work units for it.[112]

Equipment and Military Capability

Until recently, even the best militia units were equipped only as light infantry. As recently as 1970, published photographs—even those intended to convey maximum war preparedness—often showed militiamen armed with swords, spears, flintlocks, and even with no weapons at all.[113] In 1967, Mao himself was quoted as saying, "the militiamen have three million guns"[114]—not even enough for the "armed militia," let alone the rest. What militia weapons there were comprised of an incredible grab bag of types and calibers—manufactured virtually everywhere in the world, of every imaginable age, and in every possible state of condition. The militia was, as one expert noted, "a gun collector's paradise and an ammunition supply officer's nightmare."[115]

By 1974, the situation had changed dramatically. Most militia units were reequipped with standard Soviet and Chinese types and calibers. Furthermore, heavy weapons are much more in evidence. More and more militia units are now depicted manning anti-aircraft guns and field artillery, motorcycles, and telecommunications equipment. Militia military training is becoming regularized and specialized, while training of militia unit cadres and PAD cadres is emphasized as never before. The PLA high command plainly considers the militia to be a critical component of "people's war under modern conditions"—a strategy embracing much more than rural guerrilla warfare. Indeed, it appears that for the first time since 1949, top military leaders may attach more military importance to the militia than do civilians, who tend to give militia matters a low priority.

As with the regular army, the militia has been forced to curtail some training in 1981 owing to budget cuts.[116] Nevertheless, the dramatic improvement in militia armament, training, and logistics over the past five years has given the militia an unprecedented combat potential. Even if we accept a very conservative estimate of armed militia strength—say seven million—that still more than doubles the total ground forces of the PRC. At a bare minimum, they are a pool of seven million relatively well-trained and readily available recruits.

REGIMENTAL RECLAMATION FARMS

The Peking regime has continued the ancient Chinese practice of placing military-agricultural settlements along the Inner Asian border. The first of these was the Sinkiang Production and Construction Corps (PCC, *Sheng-ch'an chien-she ping-t'uan*), organized in 1954. During the Cultural Revolution, PCCs appeared in other areas, expanded until 1974 or so, and then declined after Mao's death. They have been reorganized recently as "regimental reclamation farms (*nung-k'en t'uan-chang*).

Purposes and Personnel

The PCC served a number of economic, military, and social purposes. It provided an enormous amount of economic production. In Sinkiang, where the PCC was most highly developed, it not only ran over 150 farms, but also grazing and fishing grounds, mines, and power generation plants. It also reportedly maintained over 500 factories of various sizes, which produced fertilizer, iron and steel, chemicals, and even tractors. Perhaps most important of all, in the long run, was its work in land reclamation, water conservancy, and aforestation. In the course of all this work, the Sinkiang PCC built and occupied many new border settlements.[117]

The military purpose of the PCC was border defense. Its members were organized along military lines, wore military-style uniforms, and received a modicum of military training. They were armed primarily with light infantry weapons, as well as a few armored cars and anti-aircraft weapons. In 1972, only about one-third of all PCC personnel had weapons.

The miltary effectiveness of the PCC was somewhat problematical owing to the make-up of its personnel. The first PCC consisted mainly of Nationalist troops who had surrendered in Sinkiang in 1948. To them were added demobilized PLA units and *hsia-fang* cadres. Later arrivals included social undersirables from the coastal cities, "labor-reform" prisoners, and "support the frontier intellectual youths." The PCC was made up of transplanted civilians, for it was much more than a military and economic organization—it was an important tool of social management.

For decades, excess urban workers were sent to remote areas as a means of alleviating unemployment and of developing new agricultural lands. A bonus effect was the infusion of huge numbers of Han Chinese into ethnic minority areas. The PCC was instrumental in the resettlement of Han people, not only in Sinkiang, but, in 1967-74, in other areas as well. The obverse of this social role of the PCC was the dispersion of socially disruptive elements. The major expansion of the PCC in 1968-70 was made possible (and necessary) by the forced exodus of tens of thousands of disillusioned Red Guards from the cities. In the 1970s, the PCC was a principal vehicle for the "rustification" of educated young people.[118]

The relationship of the PCC with the system of prison camps is unclear, but there is evidence of some connection. It may well be that many such camps were concealed within, and administered by, the PCCs of various MDs and MRs.[119] Martin K. Whyte's description of "free employees" in the labor-reform and labor-reeducation camps of Kwangtung in the early 1960s indicates remarkable similarities with the PCC.[120]

Size and Organization

The oldest, largest, and most economically diversified PCC was in Sinkiang. Beginning with about 200,000 people in 1954, it had grown to about 600,000 by 1970. It included ten "Agricultural Divisions" and three "Engineer Construction Divisions," plus at least three independent regiments.[121]

Beginning in 1969, new PCCs were established in most border areas, and in some interior provinces. By 1970, eleven PCCs were reportedly in operation. In 1970-74, there were thought to be up to three million people in the various PCCs. In 1979, there were reportedly five million educated youths resettled in the countryside, down from about twelve million in 1975.[122] There has been a massive return to the cities and curtailment of "rustification" since 1978, and, as a result, PCC strength fell considerably below the 1970-75 peak, even in Sinkiang. The 1979 total was probably less than one million, depending upon how the PCC was officially defined.

Until 1974, all PCCs were controlled by either an MD or MR headquarters. Typically, the commander of a given PCC was a deputy commander of the MD or MR in question. This arrangement persisted in Sinkiang, and possibly in Tibet and Inner Mongolia until 1979 or 1980. However, the PCCs of interior (Han) provinces were all reorganized and civilianized to the extent that they may now be indistinguishable from other state farms. Finally, in about 1980, even the Sinkiang PCC was reorganized as "regimental reclamation farms."

The regimental reclamation farms retain the economic roles of the PCC, and still "form a powerful reserve force" for the PLA, but they appear to be under civilian management. It may be significant that their personnel are no longer referred to as "members" (*yuan*), but as "staff and workers" (*chih-kung*)—a term normally applied to civilian enterprises.[123]

The PLA general staff was the central coordinating agency for the PCC beginning in the mid-1960s. It appears that the Ministry of State Farms and Land Reclamation assumed responsibility in 1976, at least for the interior provinces, and may now control all the regimental reclamation farms everywhere in cooperation with provincial civilian and military authorities.

Military Utility

Paramilitary agricultural settlements have enhanced border surveillance to some extent, merely by their presence, and have thereby freed some PLA border troops for more pressing tasks. The drain they impose on the MRs, in the form of cadres, weapons, and training facilities, appears to be minimal, considering the numbers of personnel. In any event, the economic and social usefulness of these settlements is so obvious that even the most professionally oriented officers must recognize them as a necessary concession to Chinese realities. In one form or another, they are likely to remain for the foreseeable future, as a paramilitary adjunct to the MR and MD commands along the Inner Asian border.

SOME OBSERVATIONS ON THE CHINESE MILITARY SYSTEM

The "Three-in-One" System

During the anti-Japanese war, Mao Tse-tung worked out the "three-in-one" military system of main forces, local forces, and militia. With the exception of the mid-1950s, when the Soviet model was being copied, this "three-in-one" system has characterized China's military structure ever since.

Without a militia, our regular army would be like a river without a source, a tree without roots, or a general with only one arm, and thus could never fight a genuine people's war.

Regional forces are the backbone for regional combat. They lead the broad masses of people to fight battles in consort [sic] with the main forces. They continually enlarge, elevate, and strengthen the main forces. With the help of the regional forces and the broad masses of militiamen in battles, the main forces can spare a free hand to form a powerful "fist," seeking and creating advantageous opportunities to fight concentrated battles of annihilation.[124]

One of the virtues of this system is that it allows for a good deal of flexibility. Emphasis can be shifted from the militia to the regional forces to the main forces, depending upon perceived needs at a given time. This can be done either by shifting the emphasis of their various missions (e.g., military preparedness, militia work, production, etc.), or simply by redistributing the defense budget. Exactly where to shift the emphasis can, of course, be a matter for disagreement in the MAC.

By observing the relative military importance the official press attributes to the regional forces and militia, we can make a rough evaluation of the emphasis of Chinese military policy at any given time. As long as the militia and RF remain large and important, China is likely to remain primarily concerned with economic production (especially agriculture), and with self-defense. On the other hand, if we were to see the militia being ignored, and regional units being absorbed into the main forces, this would indicate a higher degree of military separation from civil society, and possibly a more aggressive foreign policy.[125]

From even the most narrowly defined "military" viewpoint, the regional forces are useful as a manpower pool, a backup military reserve, and as a mobile labor force. Their economic and social value, in terms of disaster relief and internal security, is widely conceded as well. Moreover, regional units are relatively inexpensive to maintain, since they are partially self-supporting. Even in the event of foreign war, or of conventional or nuclear conflict in the north, the regional forces would remain quite useful.

Many regular PLA leaders have been considerably more skeptical about the militia. P'eng Te-huai plainly wanted to scrap it altogether and replace it with a Soviet-style system of reserve forces. Lo Jui-ch'ing and Lin Piao both have been accused of trying to downgrade the militia to little more than "pace-setters in production." The high comand seems to have been especially critical of the militia during those periods when it has been directly under the party, and not the military. P'eng allegedly believed the militia might become a source of social disorder. That allegation has been repeated frequently over the years—an indication that many PLA men still feel the same way. (Irving Horowitz's observation, that military men fear nothing so much as armed civilians, seems to hold true in the PRC.) One certain conclusion that can be drawn from the 1973-76 militia controversy is that if there is to be a militia at all, the army wants to control it.

As we have noted, some top military leaders currently are emphasizing the militia, perhaps more than at any time since 1949. This is clearly in recognition of the fact that "people's war under modern conditions" must remain China's basic defensive strategy for the foreseeable future. It also indicates that the militia is again under firm control. Even so, strong emphasis on the safeguarding of militia weapons indicates continuing military misgivings about armed civilians.[126]

The Military Command System

The system that controls the uniformed PLA reflects China's continuing preoccupation with internal political and economic matters. Peking's trump card in internal politics is its control of the main forces. This, in turn, means that whoever controls the MAC (and therefore the main forces), controls China. The experience of 1967-68 proved that rather conclusively.[127] The militia and police can exert only local, and very limited, power. Nationally, the overwhelming preponderance of the means of organized violence are still the main forces.

In the past, there has been one fairly dangerous source of potential internal defiance: the military regions. MR commanders have, on occasion, actually challenged the final authority of the Central Committee and the MAC—most notably during the Cultural Revolution. This problem of "warlordism" or "independent kingdoms" was surely a consideration when it was originally decided that all main force units would be kept under the direct control of PLA Headquarters in Peking.

This sytem places a very heavy burden on the PLA chief of staff, who must keep track of thirty-seven corps, twenty-two artillery divisions, eleven armored divisions, and about thirty separate regiments and divisions. A "span of control" of roughly a hundred major combat formations simply could not be managed if more than a handful were engaged by enemy forces.

In response to such a situation, one or two MRs could be constituted as a "Front," with an MR commander designated as Front commander.[128] He would be granted a considerable degree of authority over resident main force units, and become the overall commander of a multi-corps-sized force, composed of both regional and main force elements. This is exactly what happened in February 1979, when the Kunming and Canton MRs were designated the "Southern Front," and the Shenyang, Peking, Lanchow, and Sinkiang MRs were designated the "Northern Front."[129] Two or more "Army Groups" may also be constituted as intermediate command echelons between Front headquarters and the corps.

There are several problems with this procedure. It is a more or less ad hoc arrangement which requires precious time to "shake down," presumably amidst a military crisis. An even greater problem with the "Front" is that it is tied to a particular geographical area. This restricts maneuver and large-scale redeployment. In a purely defensive engagement, this might work out reasonably well. On the other hand, a large-scale war of movement, especially one beyond China's borders, would require reorganization of these MR-level commands into true "field armies," such as those used during the Korean war. As it stands, the MR system, and the lack of any comparable high-level main force command, ties the PLA to an essentially defensive, geographically oriented posture.[130] A further problem might well arise owing to friction and resentment generated by placing main force units under regional command, though there was no evidence of this in 1979.

It is, at best, a somewhat unwieldy system, but it has one overriding political advantage. No one in the PLA, short of the chief of staff—not even a service arm commander—has direct control of more than four or five combat divisions. The one possible exception is the commander of the Peking Garrison, which may consist of up to eight divisions. It is hardly surprising that the garrison commander is likely to be fired or transferred whenever the central leadership is undergoing an upheaval.[131]

The Real Power of the Regional Commander

Based on what we have learned about the structure of the PLA and its command system, we may question the conventional wisdom about the power of MR and MD commanders. It has long been assumed that their power, and the attendant problem of "warlordism" (or "mountaintopism," or "the theory of many centers," or "independent kingdoms"), derived from their military power. Yet in fact they control little real combat power. They do not control the main force units within their regions; on the contrary, the latter stand ready to enforce the will of the MAC upon the regions (as they did in August 1967).[132] Garrison, border, and security troops are widely scattered, lightly armed, and largely tied down with local duties, as is the militia. Regional commanders, *qua* military commanders, actually have relatively little usable military power at their disposal.

How then, can we explain the immense political power exercised by many MR and MD commanders during and after the Cultural Revolution? The answer lies in two factors. First, no powerful MR commander was *just* a military commander. Typically, he had held regional military, party, and governmental posts for many years. Thus, he had been able to create a military, political, and administrative grip on an entire geographical area. He not only controlled the regional armed forces and the militia (regardless of where organizational control of the militia lay at the local or national levels), but also controlled the civilian political and economic infrastructure. He had a geographical base of political and economic power, in addition to his military power.

The Cultural Revolution and its aftermath, especially the Lin Piao affair, substantially reduced this multi-faceted regional power. Two MRs were abolished outright, a number of MR and MD commanders were purged, others were coopted by transfer to central posts, and a few remained in place, but were forced to give up local party and governmental posts. Since 1972, various police units and, more recently, border guard units have been removed from MR and MD control, as well. The process has been long and painful, and probably never was conceived by anyone as a plan—but it has unquestionably been a major result of the Cultural Revolution.

Since the reshuffle of MR leaders in early 1974, regional military power has been further checked by occasional transfers of commanders, commissars, and staff officers (see chapter 7). An interesting example occurred in January 1979, when Yang Te-chih (Wuhan MR) and Wang Pi-ch'eng (Kunming MR) traded places in preparation for the invasion of Vietnam. This apparently was based mostly on military considerations, Yang being more active and more experienced in mountain warfare. A major reshuffle in early 1980 saw the appointment of eight new MR commanders and four new first commissars.

Rotation of ranking MR leaders cannot yet be termed a "system," but a system of periodic transfers does appear to be evolving. As members of the MAC, of course, the MR commanders continue to be heard in the inner circles of political and military power, but they have much less ability to defy those circles from without.

The second, and even more important, factor in explaining regional military power goes beyond the organizational perspective to the issue of political decisiveness in Peking. Perhaps the most crucial factor in the rise and fall of MR power during the Cultural Revolution was the will and ability of the CC and the MAC to use the main forces. A good deal of the chaos and uncertainty of the 1966-69 period resulted from erratic behavior at the center. Orders were often contradictory or ambiguous because the central leadership was divided against itself. Regional control devolved to the MRs and MDs by default. Once the main forces were committed (in August 1967), they faced the same problem of ambiguous and indecisive direction. The problem of central indecision persisted right down to the fall of Lin Piao--particularly with regard to rebuilding the civilian party apparatus. In the absence of a rebuilt party, the only alternative was continued rule by the regional commanders.

Since the Tenth Party Congress (August 1973), the central leadership has been at pains to maintain a stance of unity, authority, and consistency. Regardless of how the line may twist and turn, "The Party," conceived as a unity, leads the way in criticizing offending persons and heterodox tendencies. This has allowed the authority of the Central Committee and the government to survive the fall of Lin Piao, the recurrent disappearances and reappearances of T'eng Hsiao-p'ing, the death of Mao, and the fall of the "gang of four." The PLA, from the high command to the rank and file, can be expected to obey orders that are clear and decisive. By speaking with one voice, the central leadership (which may be deeply divided internally) is able to maintain the discipline of the armed forces, and therefore to control China. The crucial long-range question is whether the appearance of central unity can be maintained.

The PLA as a Modern Army

Since 1949, the PLA has been committed to battle in Korea (1950-53), on the borders of India (1962), the Soviet Union (1969), and Vietnam (1979), and in the Paracel Islands (1974). All of these engagements differed significantly from the revolutionary warfare in which the PLA developed. All were limited, both in geographical extent and in their political aims. They were almost exclusively military operations, as opposed to the military-political-social-economic warfare of earlier days. They generally were fought by regular PLA troops on the borders of China or even on foreign soil.

All things considered, the PLA acquitted itself well in these engagements, despite the unfamiliar conditions. Yet Chinese leaders and troops continued to show a preference for fluid, mobile warfare. Only during the later stages of the Korean fighting did the PLA adopt the strategy (as opposed to the tactic) of positional defense along a "front line."

Thus, the PLA is vastly less influenced by the experience of "front lines" and "rear areas" than are the armies of the West or the Warsaw Pact.

Furthermore, of necessity, the PLA has always trained and operated on the assumption of enemy air and firepower superiority. For these reasons, the PLA may well be better prepared, psychologically at least, for the highly fluid sort of operations that are envisioned on the nuclear battlefield.

On the other hand, the PLA is still woefully inferior to its potential adversaries on many counts. Logistics, CBR, EW, air defense, antitank defense, and naval and air power are the most glaring examples. As long as these shortcomings remain—*and they represent deficiencies in leadership, organization, and training, as well as material inferiority*—China simply will not represent a serious offensive threat to most of her neighbors, and certainly not to the US or the USSR.

According to Modelski, the "basic precondition for 'Great Power timber' is the possession of military power." Great Powers, "at least in principle . . . must be capable of fighting a major war. By derivation, the economic and industrial capability for raising, equipping, and sustaining a strong military force is also essential. More recently, nuclear capability has been the test of Great Power status. . . ." In the 1970s, "Through the mechanism of nuclear deterrence, a well-prepared nuclear state is in fact protected from attack by any other atomic power."[133]

This definition excludes China from "Great Power status" on several counts: Her nuclear deterrent vis-a-vis the Soviet Union is marginally effective, at least, and vis-a-vis the other nuclear powers it is still nonexistent. Her sea and air power are such that she probably is incapable of conquering Taiwan, even assuming no American (or Soviet) involvement.[134]

Any force attempting to invade China would be meeting the PLA on the latter's own terms, and could expect to suffer terrible losses. But whether northeastern China could be held, and its industrial production maintained, is highly problematical. Until the PLA can do that, it is simply unrealistic to think of the People's Republic of China as a "Great Power," in a military sense.

Prospects for Professionalism

Since military professionalism is tied closely to technological advance, it is most likely to continue developing where professionalism is already most evident—in the relatively modernized main forces. Professionalism in the regional forces will tend to remain low unless significant resources can be devoted to upgrading RF military capabilities. Closely related to that would be the disengagement of the PLA, and especially the regional forces, from police work and other quasi-civilian responsibilities. There appears to have been a trend in that direction over the past few years. Local police, and now border police, functions have been reverting to civilian institutional control. The PCC has apparently been "civilianized" as well. At this writing, there are rumors in Peking that the Capital Construction Engineer Corps and Railroad Engineer Corps, or at least some units thereof, also may be "civilianized."[135]

PLA uniformed manpower has declined significantly in late 1980 and 1981, after reaching a ten-year peak. The reduced military budget and a desire for improved equipment are clearly factors: It may well be that the decision has been made to create a smaller, but more militarily potent, army. A speculative report by *KYODO* recently spoke of a possible reduction down to 2.8 million soldiers, and a further consolidation of MRs.[136] All these measures would tend to enhance military professionalism and diminish the political importance of the regional commands. They also could result in the emergence of a separate body of police units—presumably under the Ministry of Public Security—analogous to Soviet MVD and KGB troops. This would allow much accelerated modernization and professionalization in the army, but would also create a "counter-army army," with far-reaching and unforeseeable political consequences.

NOTES

1. *NCNA*, 6 March 1981, in *FBIS*, No. 044, pp. L1-L2.
2. Keng Piao's appointment to the MAC was reported first by AFP, 3 February 1979. The MAC Standing Committee is listed by *NCNA*, 15 February 1980.
3. "Report on Lo's Mistakes," II, p. 18; Chang Kuo-hua's funeral notice (April 1974) named all the MR commanders as members of the MAC. Also see Fang Ching-yuan, "Problems of Military Leadership in Mainland China," *I and S*, 14, No. 11 (November 1978), 36-37; and *NCNA*, 17 March 1980.
4. *Ts'an-k'ao Tzu-liao* (Canton), No. 1 (July 1968), trans. in *SCMP*, No. 4222, p. 7. Chou's speech is given in a somewhat different version in *Tzu-liao Chuan-chi* (Canton) (undated-1968), trans. in *SCMM*, No. 631, p. 10.
5. Harvey Nelsen (private correspondence), drawn from Nationalist intelligence source.
6. Kunming Provincial Service, 6 October 1978, trans. in *FBIS*, No. 199, p. J4. *Ming Pao*, 7 February 1980, p. 1.
7. Hsieh, p. 180.
8. Yeh chien-ying, "Developing Advanced Military Science of Chinese Proletariat," *PR*, No. 12 (24 March 1978), 6-9; and Radio "Pa-yi," 16 October 1979, trans. in *FBIS*, No. 202, p. L23.
9. *NCNA*, 15 February 1979, trans. in *FBIS*, No. 34, p. E2.
10. *NCNA*, 1 August 1979, trans. in *FBIS*, No. 150, pp. L8-L9.
11. "Yang Ch'eng-wu—Newly Reinstated Cadre," *I and S*, 10, No. 13 (October 1974), 108-110. PLA chiefs of staff have been: Nieh Jung-chen (acting, 1949-51), Hsu Hsiang-ch'ien (1951-54), Su Yü (1954-58), Huang Ke-ch'eng (1958-59), Lo Jui-ch'ing (1959-65), Yang Ch'eng-wu (acting, 1966-68), Huang Yung-sheng (1968-71), [P'eng Shao-hui was senior vice-chief in 1971-74], Teng Hsiao-p'ing (1975-76), [Yang ch'eng-wu was senior vice-chief in 1975-77], Teng Hsiao-p'ing (1977-80), and Yang Te-chih (1980-).
12. "Report on Lo's Mistakes," II, p. 18.
13. The GPD still had explicit intelligence functions in 1963. See *Political Work Regulations for the Chinese PLA* (Peking: CC of the CCP, 27 March 1963), trans. in Ying-mao Kao, et al., *The Political Work System of the Chinese Communist Military* (Providence, RI: East Asia Language and Area Center, Brown University, 1971), II, 3, 1. Cited hereafter as *Political Work Regulations* (1963).
14. *Political Work Regulations* (1963), II, 3, f.
15. Ibid., II, 3, 1.
16. Nelson, *The Chinese Military System*, pp. 104-106; and Dick, p. 178.
17. See reports on the PLA Logistics Work Conference of 28 April to 5 June 1978. For example: *NCNA*, 6 June 1978, trans. in *FBIS*, No. 111, pp. E2-E4. Also see Gillespie and Sims, pp. 193-196.
18. Wang Shih-hung, "Inquiry into the Condition of Bandit Army Logistics and Supply [*fei-chün hou-ch'in pu-chi ch'ing-k'uang chih t'an-t'ao*]," *FCYP*, 23, No. 6 (December 1980), 44-51. This is the best recent study

on the GRSD.

19. The following statistics are from State Statistical Bureau figures published by *NCNA* (English), 22 September 1979, in *FBIS*, No. 186, p. L3. The figure for trucks is an estimate based on the above and on Fraser (p. 6) who estimated PLA trucks increased by eleven percent in 1963-73.

20. Gillespie and Sims, pp. 194-195.

21. *NCNA*, 6 June 1978, trans. in *FBIS*, No. 111, pp. E2 and E3.

22. For example, see Teng's references to the Logistics Conference in his speech to the PLA Political Work Conference on 2 June 1978. *NCNA* (English), 5 June 1978, in *FBIS*, No. 109, p. E10.

23. For a much higher CIA estimate (up to seven million uniformed PLA), see Ronald G. Mitchell and Edward P. Parris, "Chinese Defense Spending, 1965-78," in *Allocation of Resources in the Soviet Union and in China* (Washington, DC: GPO, 1979), p. 67.

24. Cheng Mien-chih, p. 21.

25. Heinlein, p. 166; and Nelsen, *The Chinese Military System*, p. 131. This problem was illustrated during the GPCR when 50th Corps was transferred from Kirin to Szechuan for political reasons, and had to leave its vehicles and artillery behind.

26. *PLA Unit History*, ed. William W. Whitson (Washington, DC: Chief of Military History, Department of the Army, n.d.); based on *History of Chinese Communist Infantry Units* (Taipei: MND, circa 1968), passim.

27. *Handbook on the Chinese Armed Forces* (Washington: DIA, 1976), p. 1-11.

28. "Type B" organization is depicted by Cheng Mien-chih, pp. 20-21.

29. That the regiment is the basic organizational building block of the PLA is also indicated by the numbering system. Corps, divisions, and regiments are numbered within the entire army, whereas lower units are numbered within their regiments.

30. Chin Chien-li, "A Look at Every Aspect of the Chinese Communist Armored Force" *HTJP*, 22 through 26 September 1971, trans. in *TPRC*, No. 165 (*JPRS*, No. 54, 447), p. 12; and *Handbook*, p. 1-11.

31. Admiral Thomas H. Moorer, "General Purpose Forces Compared," *Commanders Digest*, 15, No. 16 (18 April 1974), 8.

32. Angus M. Fraser, *The People's Liberation Army* (New York: Crane Russak, 1973), p. 24. Additional information provided by USCGDLO. Technical details (with some errors) are in Appendix 5 to Annex X of *Handbook*, pp. A-33 ff. For a survey of PRC communications, see Bruce Swanson, "An Introduction to Chinese Command, Control and Communications," *Signal*, 32, No. 8 (May-June 1978), 49 ff.

33. Harlan W. Jencks, "China's 'Punitive' War on Vietnam: A Military Assessment," *AS*, 19, No. 8 (August 1979), 813.

34. Lan Ching, "Chinese Communist Chemical Defense Force," *HTJP*, 25 through 27 August 1970, trans. in *TCC*, No. 132 (*JPRS*, No. 52, 264), pp. 1-13.

35. For an interesting example, see Nanking Kiangsu Prov. Svc., 11 April 1979, trans. in *FBIS*, No. 73, p. O2.

36. The present discussion draws heavily on the following: *Chün-shih Chi-pen Chih-shih [Basic Military Knowledge]* (Shanghai: People's Publishing House, 1974); Chang Yun-t'ien, "A Study of Training Work in the Chicom Military," *CKYCYK*, 5, No. 3 (10 March 1971), 71-81; and Dannen D. Mannschreck "Red and Expert," unpublished paper, pp. 15 and 21-26. The author wishes to thank Major Mannschreck for information shared in private

correspondence and conversations. On recent problems and procedures, see: *NCNA*, 7 November 1979, trans. in *FBIS*, No. 219, pp. L13-L14; Peking Domestic Svc., 1 September 1978, trans. in *FBIS*, No. 172, pp. E13-E14; *Ming Pao* (Hong Kong), 11 November 1979, p. 1; Foochow Fukien Prov. Svc., 30 March 1979, trans. in *FBIS*, No. 65, p. O4; and Canton Kwangtung Prov. Svc., 21 October 1979, trans. in *FBIS*, No. 207, pp. P5-P6.

37. Hsu Hsiang-ch'ien, "Strive to Achieve Modernization in National Defense—In Celebration of the 30th Anniversary . . . of the PRC," *HC*, No. 10 (2 October 1979), trans. in *FBIS*, No. 203, p. L16; *CFCP*, reported by Peking Dom. Svc., 12 May 1978, trans. in *FBIS*, No. 94, pp. E9-E12; Kunming Kweichow Prov. Svc., 21 October 1978, trans. in *FBIS*, No. 206, p. J2; Nanking Kiangsu Prov. Svc., 14 September 1978, trans. in *FBIS*, No. 182, p. G10; Peking Dom. Svc., 15 March 1979, trans. in *FBIS*, No. 54, pp. L9-L10; Peking Dom. Svc., 30 November 1978, trans. in *FBIS*, No. 234, p. K3; Peking Dom. Svc., 27 April 1978, trans. in *FBIS*, No. 84, pp. C1-C2; *NCNA*, 5 October 1979, in *FBIS*, No. 199, p. R4, and Nanking Kiangsu Prov. Svc., 11 April 1979, trans. in *FBIS*, No. 73, p. O2.

38. In excellent discussion of the problem of doctrine is Francis J. Romance, "Modernization of China's Armed Forces," paper presented at the Association for Asian Studies annual meeting, Los Angeles, 30 March-1 April 1979. Also see Jack M. Harris, "Enduring Chinese Dimensions in Peking's Military Policy and Doctrine," *I and S*, 15, No. 7 (July 1979), 77-88.

39. This discussion is based on Hsu Hsiang-ch'ien (2 October 1979), p. L13. also see the editorial in *CFCP*, 1 August 1979, trans. in *FBIS*, No. 150, pp. L1-L4; and *NCNA*, 28 January 1981, trans. in *FBIS*, No. 018, p. L10.

40. Sian Shensi Prov. Svc., 12 October 1979, trans. in *FBIS*, No. 204, p. T1; Ch'angch'un Kirin Pov. Svc., 13 March 1979, trans. in *FBIS*, No. 53, pp. L4-L5; Peking Dom. Svc., 18 October 1979, trans. in *FBIS*, No. 204, pp. R1-R2; and Peking Dom. Svc., 3 October 1979, trans. in *FBIS*, No. 172, pp. L12-L13.

41. PLAAF Commander Chang T'ing-fa, quoted by *NCNA*, 7 September 1979, trans. in *FBIS*, No. 177, p. L18.

42. *NCNA*, 1 August 1979, trans. in *FBIS*, No. 150, p. L8; Lanchow Kansu Prov. Svc., 4 September 1979, trans. in *FBIS*, No. 175, p. T1; Nanking Kiangsu Prov. Svc., 6 September 1979, trans. in *FBIS*, No. 177, pp. O5-O6; and Nanking Kiangsu Prov. Svc., 19 September 1979, trans. in *FBIS*, No. 185, p. O1.

43. *JMJP*, 22 October 1979, trans. in *FBIS*, No. 208, pp. L14-L15. On elderly commanders see: Ch'angch'un Kirin Prov. Svc., 12 November 1979, trans. in *FBIS*, No. 222, pp. S2-S3.

44. *NCNA*, 14 May 1978, trans. in *FBIS*, No. 94, p. E13; Peking Dom. Svc., 16 March 1979, trans. in *FBIS*, No. 56, p. S3; *NCNA*, 2 February 1979, trans. in *FBIS*, No. 33, p. E9; and Canton Kwangtung Prov. Svc., 25 March 1980, trans. in *FBIS*, No. 062, p. P3.

45. *JMJP*, 1 August 1979, trans. in *China Report*, No. 14 (7 September 1979), 16; *NCNA*, 1 August 1979, in *FBIS*, No. 152, p. L3; *NCNA*, 15 January 1981, trans. in *FBIS*, No. 011, pp. L10-L11; and *NCNA*, 23 January 1981, in *FBIS*, No. 017, p. L9.

46. *NCNA*, 23 April 1978, trans. in *FBIS*, No. 79, pp. E11-E14; *NCNA*, 29 December 1978, trans. in *FBIS*, No. 79, pp. E38-E39; Nanking Kiangsu Prov. Svc., 14 September 1978, trans. in *FBIS*, No. 182, p. G10; Nanking Kiangsu Prov. Svc., 24 September 1979, trans. in *FBIS*, No. 189, p. O3; Sian Shensi Prov. Svc., 10 September 1978, trans. in *FBIS*, No. 177, p. M1; Shihchiachuang Hopeh Prov. Svc., 27 October 1978, trans. in *FBIS*, No. 212, p. K1; and *NCNA*, 23 October 1979, trans. in *FBIS*, No. 207, p. L14.

47. Nelsen, "Military Forces in the Cultural Revolution," especially pp. 447, 467, and 472-474.
48. *NCNA*, 30 July 1978, trans. in *FBIS*, No. 152, p. E9; and Peking Dom. Svc., 25 April 1978, trans. in *FBIS*, No. 88, pp. E22-23. Note the reference to representatives of the Capital Construction Engineers and the Engineer Corps in Lanchow Kansu Prov. Svc., 27 July 1978, trans. in *FBIS*, No. 150, p. M1. On the Telecommunications ("Signal") Corps, see Nanking Kiangsu Prov. Svc., 27 September 1979, trans. in *FBIS*, No. 192, p. L28.
49. Peking Dom. Svc., 27 September 1979, trans. in *FBIS*, No. 192, p. L28; 21 July 1979, trans. in *FBIS*, No. 152, p. L3; 3 July 1979, trans. in *FBIS*, No. 130, p. L4; *NCNA*, 1 August 1978, trans. in *FBIS*, No. 152, pp. E14-E16; *NCNA*, 28 September 1978, trans. in *FBIS*, No. 193, p. L26; *NCNA*, 20 July 1979, trans. in *FBIS*, No. 151, p. L11; *AFP*, 4 October 1978, in *FBIS*, No. 194, p. E13; Peking City Service, 16 March 1979, trans. in *FBIS*, No. 54, p. R1; *NCNA*, 8 February 1979, trans. in *FBIS*, No. 55, p. R1; and *NCNA*, 6 July 1978, trans. in *FBIS*, No. 134, pp. E18-E19.
50. *USGDLO* document, 1 May 1980. On former GRSD control of engineers, see *NCNA*, 13 October 1967, trans. in *SCMP*, No. 4043, pp. 20-21.
51. This, and the following, draws heavily on Bueschel, pp. 32 ff. Also see the interesting but sometimes inaccurate description in "Chinese Air Force Equipment Special Edition," *Wu-chi Shih-chieh [Armaments World]*, No. 4 (October 1974), 5 and 7. I am also indebted to Harvey Nelsen for data on the "Air Armies." The Urumchi AFD was only organized in 1979.
52. During the GPCR, 15th Corps played a pivotal role in the "Wuhan Incident" of July-August 1967 (see chapter 4).
53. On PLAAF growth, see statistics in Mogdis, p. 256.
54. This, and the following, are drawn from *Jane's Aircraft*, "June 1979 Supplement," in *Air Force*, June 1979, pp. 87-88; *HTCS*, No. 30 (April 1979), 4 and 61; *HTCS*, No. 27 (January 1979), 64-65; "Chinese Air Power ... An Obsolescing Goliath," *Air International*, June 1979, pp. 273-277 and 306-308; *The Chinese War Machine*, ed. Ray Bonds (New York: Crescent, 1979), pp. 122-147; Hong Kong Television (courtesy Richard Latham and USCGDLO); and *Jane's Aircraft*, 1978-79 ed., pp. 29-30, 180-181, 641-642.
55. The PLAAF saw no combat action in the 1979 invasion of Vietnam: Jencks, "Punitive War," p. 808.
56. This, and the following, draws heavily on observations by CPT Tom Menza. Also see Peking Dom. Svc., 25 February 1981, trans. in *FBIS*, No. 038, p. L1; *NCNA*, 29 September 1979, trans. in *FBIS*, No. 192, pp. L29-L30; Kunming Yunnan Prov. Svc., 23 February 1979, trans. in *FBIS*, No. 39, p. J3; Shenyang Liaoning Prov. Svc., 14 October 1978, trans. in *FBIS*, No. 207, p. L7; *NCNA*, 15 October 1978, trans. in *FBIS*, No. 205, p. E5-E6; *NCNA*, 25 September 1979, trans. in *FBIS*, No. 188, p. L14; Peking Dom. Svc., 31 July 1979, trans. in *FBIS*, No. 150, pp. L9-L10; *NCNA*, 4 September 1979, trans. in *FBIS*, No. 175, pp. L7-L8.
57. *NCNA*, 24 July 1979, trans. *FBIS*, No. 155, pp. L10-L12; and *NCNA*, 14 November 1979, trans. in *FBIS*, No. 224, p. O1.
58. On PLAAF missiles, see *Ming Pao*, 8 March 1979, p. 1; Edward N. Luttwak, "Problems of Military Modernization for Mainland China," *I and S*, 14, No. 7 (July 1978), 59 and 62; Nanking Kiangsu Prov. Svc., 10 October 1979, trans. in *FBIS*, No. 199, pp. O1-O2; Tsinan Shantung Prov. Svc., 18 September 1978, trans. in *FBIS*, No. 185, p. O6; and *CFCHP*, No. 1 (1979), p. 2, trans. in *China Report*, No. 14 (7 September 1979).
59. The following is drawn primarily from Bueschel, pp. 56-60, 66, and

86; *PR*, No. 25 (21 June 1968), 28-29; and Admiral Thomas H. Moorer, "The Dynamic Balance of Strategic Power," *Commander's Digest*, 15, No. 15 (11 April 1974), 15.

60. Chang Yun-t'ien, "Study of Training Work," p. 80.
61. Bueschel, pp. 55-56.
62. Peking Radio to Taiwan, 1 June 1978, trans. in *FBIS*, No. 110, p. Cl.
63. Mogdis, pp. 264-265; and *CSM*, 5 July 1975, pp. 1 and 4.
64. See Tsinan Shantung Prov. Svc., 18 September 1978, trans. in *FBIS*, No. 189, p. G8; Peking Dom. Svc., 29 September 1979, trans. in *FBIS*, No. 192, p. L30; *NCNA*, 14 November 1979, trans. in *FBIS*, No. 224, p. O1; and Peking Dom. Svc., 20 March 1981, trans. in *FBIS*, No. 055, p. L21.
65. For a discussion of "counter-military military" forces under authoritarian regimes, see Van Doorn, p. 21.
66. See CAAC Mi-8s and An-26s carrying paratroopers in *HTCS*, No. 51 (February 1981), 2-3. I am grateful to MAJ Robert Walz for his observations. Also see *NCNA*, 21 April 1978, trans. in *FBIS*, No. 88, p. E24; Shanghai City Svc., 5 March 1979, trans. in *FBIS*, No. 52, p. G5; and Chengtu Szechuan Prov. Svc., 23 January 1979, trans. in *FBIS*, No. 24, p. J4.
67. Justin Galen, "US' Toughest Message to the USSR," *Armed Forces Journal*, February 1979, pp. 30-36. See pictures in *Tung Hsiang*(Hong Kong), No. 12 (September 1979), 14; and *PR*, No. 32 (10 August 1979), 3.
68. *London Times*, 16 March 1978; and *Chinese War Machine*, p. 174.
69. *Military Balance*, 1979-80 ed., claims that a few ICBMs are "probably operational."
70. Gerard H. Corr, *The Chinese Red Army* (Berkshire, England: Osprey, 1974), p. 165; and Harvey Nelsen (private correspondence) drawn from Taiwan MND sources. Also see *NCNA*, 23 September 1978, trans. in *FBIS*, No. 186, pp. E3-E4; Peking Dom. Svc., 4 October 1979, trans. in *FBIS*, No. 205, pp. L16-L21.
71. Jonathan D. Pollack, "The Logic of Chinese Military Strategy," *Bulletin of the Atomic Scientists*, January 1979, p. 26; Peking Dom. Svc., 21 September 1979, trans. in *FBIS*, No. 186, pp. L15-L16; Ling Yü, p. 25; *Ming Jen Ch'ung K'an [Famous Persons Series]*, No. 4 (May 1979), 28-31; *Chieh Fang Chun Wen Yi [Liberation Army Literature]*, No. 3 (1 March 1978), 20-26, trans. in *China Report*, No. 11 (16 August 1979), 44-56; and Galen, p. 31.
72. *Jane's Aircraft*, 1975-76 ed., p. 644; *Newsweek*, 1 March 1976, p. 65; Peking Dom. Svc., 4 January 1979, trans. in *FBIS*, No. 8, pp. E11-E13; and *Chieh Fang Chun Wen Yi*, No. 4 (1 April 1979), 54-57; trans. in *China Report*, No. 11 (16 August 1979), 25-31.
73. Russel Spurr, "Stepping up the Space Race," *FEER*, 13 October 1978, p. 14. Also see *Military Balance*, 1979-80 ed.; Charles H. Murphy, "China's Nuclear Deterrent," *Air Force*, 55, No. 4 (April 1972); Ling Yü, "China's Offensive Nuclear Missiles," *Kwang Chiao Chi [Wide Angle]* (Hong Kong), No. 82 (16 July 1979), 24-26.
74. Horner, p. 246; and *Tung Hsi Feng* (Hong Kong), No. 8 (10 August 1979), 65, trans. in *China Report*, No. 22 (9 October 1979), 38.
75. The following draws heavily on *Jane's Ships*, 1977-78 ed. and 1975-76 ed.; *Military Balance*, 1979-80 ed. and 1980-81 ed.; *HTCS*, No. 28 (Feb. 1979), 40-44; *Yearbook '73*, II, p. 54; *Handbook*, pp. 4-48 through 4-50 and 6-2; and Moorer, "General Purpose Forces," p. 13.
76. This is implied in Haikow Hainan Is. Regional Svc., 17 February 1979, trans. in *FBIS*, No. 37, p. H3.
77. *Chinese War Machine*, pp. 120 and 162.

78. *Jane's Ships,* 1975-76 ed., p. 81; *Yearbook '73,* II, p. 54; *Chinese War Machine,* p. 158; and *Military Balance,* 1980-81 ed.
79. *Jane's Ships,* 1973-74 ed., p. 149; Moorer, "Dynamic Balance," p. 15; and *Military Balance,* 1980-81 ed.
80. *Jane's Ships,* 1975-76 ed., pp. 82-83; and *Jane's Surface Skimmers,* 1974-75 ed., p. 206.
81. *CSM,* 21 January 1974, p. 2; *Chinese War Machine,* p. 162; *BR,* No. 40 (5 October 1979), 30.
82. *Jane's Ships,* 1975-76 ed., p. 79; Moorer, "General Purpose Forces," p. 13; *CSM,* 27 March 1979, p. B19; *Chinese War Machine,* p. 166; *NCNA,* 21 September 1979, trans. in *FBIS,* No. 186, p. L2; Mitchell and Parris; and *NCNA,* 7 March 1981, trans. in *FBIS,* No. 048, p. L19.
83. Chang Yun-t'ien, "A Study of Training Work," p. 81; *Handbook,* p. 6-2; *NYT,* 12 May 1965, p. 83; and *NYT,* 7 August 1965, p. 4.
84. *HTCS,* No. 43 (June 1980), 13-15; Canton Kwangtung Prov. Svc., 8 March 1981, trans. in *FBIS,* No. 045, p. P3; Desmond Wettern, "PRC Navy Close-Up," *US Naval Institute Proceedings,* March 1981, pp. 123-125; *AFP,* 18 May 1980, in *FBIS-ASIA* and *PACIFIC,* No. 098, p. M1; Luttwak, p. 61; and*Chinese War Machine,* pp. 162 and 166.
85. The former Sinkiang MR was reorganized into the Urumachi MR in 1979: *KYODO,* 5 February 1979, in *FBIS,* No. 25, pp. E5-E6; and Urumachi Rgnl. Svc., 15 August 1979, trans. in *FBIS,* No. 161, p. T1. The Inner Mongolia MD is still defined by the 1969-79 regional political boundaries.
86. In the summer of 1974, a "Military and Political School for Cadres" was established by the Ch'engtu MR, and an "Intermediate Political and Military School" by the Kunming MR. It appears that more important MRs already had such schools: Ch'engtu Szechuan Prov. Svc., 2 August 1974, trans. in *FBIS,* 5 August 1974, pp. J2-J3; and Kunming Yunnan Prov. Svc., 9 June 1974, reported by USCGDLO.
87. Whitson, p. 92. See *KMJP,* 30 July 1974, trans. in *SPRCP,* No. 5677, pp. 197-20., for the history of a typical regional unit, the "T'aishan Hero Regiment."
88. Nelsen, *The Chinese Military System,* pp. 143-145.
89. Ralph L. Powell and Chong-kun Yoon, "Public Security and the PLA," *AS,* 12, No. 12 (December 1972), 1098-1099; "The People's Police," *CP,* No. 1 (1974), 32-33; *Handbook,* pp. 2-13, 10-10, and 10-12; Nelsen correspondence; Chengtu Szechuan Pov. Svc., 6 October 1978, trans. in *FBIS,* No. 199, p. J5; and Lanchow Kansu Prob. Svc., 11 April 1979, trans. in *FBIS,* No. 74, p. T1.
90. See the following reports by Kunming Yunnan Prov. Svc.: 4 February 1981, trans. in *FBIS,* No. 024, p. Q4; 15 February 1981, trans. in *FBIS,* No. 031, pp. Q3-Q4; 22 February 1981, trans. in *FBIS,* No. 037, pp. Q5-Q6; and 27 February 1981, trans. in *FBIS,* No. 043, p. Q5. Also, Hangchow Chekiang Prov. Svc., 20 December 1980, trans. in *FBIS,* No. 249, pp. O8-O9.
91. Canton Kwangtung Prov. Svc., 28 January 1981, trans. in *FBIS,* No. 022, p. P1.
92. *PR,* No. 25 (20 June 1969), 14; and *NCNA* (English), 25 February 1979, in *FBIS,* No. 39, p. A17.
93. *Political Work Regulations* (1963), XV, 2. None of these responsibilities was specified for any military echelon other than the MD. The present discussion is based on these regulations, and on information supplied by a refugee who was a PSF officer in the 1950s. On "People's Air Defense," see Nanking Kiangsu Prov. Svc., 16 October 1979, trans. in *FBIS,* No. 206, pp. O3-O4.

94. *KTTH*, No. 19, p. 526; and Yu Yang, p. 7.
95. On RF militia tasks, see Tsinan Shantung Prov. Svc., 29 September 1979, trans. in *FBIS*, No. 191, pp. G5-G6. On main force involvement, see *Tientsin Jih-pao*, 20 August 1979, p. 3; Tsinan Shantung Prov. Svc., 29 September 1978, trans. in *FBIS*, No. 191, p. G5; and Nanning Kwangsi Rgnl. Svc., 11 September 1979, trans. in *FBIS*, No. 182, p. P13.
96. *Political Work Regulations* (1963), XVI, 9-12.
97. "Uphold the Centralized Leadership of the Party and Strengthen the Solidarity of the Army and the Government," *JMJP*, 31 July 1974, trans. in *SPRCP*, No. 5673, pp. 1-3.
98. Tsinan Shantung Prov. Svc., 22 August 1978, trans. in *FBIS*, No. 165, p. G3; and Hsing Chun, "It is Forbidden to Employ the Militia Armed Forces to Handle Contradictions Among the People," Sian Shensi Prov. Svc., 27 August 1978, trans. in *FBIS*, No. 169, p. M4.
99. The principle documents are "Speech by Yang Yung at National Militia Work Conference" (n.d.), in *NCNA*, 8 August 1978, trans. in *FBIS*, No. 156, pp. E1-E13; and Nieh Jung-chen, Speech to the National Militia Conference (4 August 1978), in *NCNA*, 7 August 1978, trans. in *FBIS*, No. 154, pp. E1-E10. An excellent study is Sh'iu Shih-tung, "The Current Phase of Chinese Communist Militia Work," *I and S*, 15, No. 6 (June 1979), 81-97.
100. In a speech, Kirin MC commander Ho Yu-fa implied a difference between "full-time armed forces cadres" and "active service armed forces cadres." The latter were to be trained by the MSDs and the MD. Ch'angch'un Kirin Prov. Svc., 16 September 1978, trans. in *FBIS*, No. 184, p. L4.
101. For example: Lanchow Kansu Prov. Svc., 1 April 1979, trans. in *FBIS*, No. 65, p. T1; Nanking Kiangsu Prov. Svc., 10 October 1979, trans. in *FBIS*, No. 199, p. O1; Tientsin City Svc., 6 September 1979, trans. in *FBIS*, No. 177, pp. R5-R6; and Wuhan Hupeh Prov. Svc., 25 August 1979, trans in *FBIS*, No. 170, pp. P4-P5.
102. Nanking Kiangsu Prov. Svc., 10 October 1979, trans. in *FBIS*, No. 199, p. O1; and Wuhan Hopeh Prov. Svc., 25 August 1979, trans. in *FBIS*, No. 170, p. P4-P5.
103. See especially: Yu Yang, passim; and Ch'en Hsi-to, pp. 7-21.
104. "Failure of the 'Gang of Four's' Scheme to Set Up a 'Second Armed Force,'" *PR*, No. 13 (25 March 1977), 10-12.
105. Jen Wu-chun, "Hold Aloft the Great Red Banner of Chairman Mao's Thinking on People's War and ... Militia," *PR*, No. 6 (6 February 1970), 7-9. US Senator Henry Jackson was told, in August 1979, that the PRC can mobilize 200 million militia. *Tung Hsiang*, No. 12 (September 1979), 15.
106. The following draws on Nelsen, "Military and Paramilitary," p. 136; Yu Yang; and Yang Yung's Militia Speech of August 1978, pp. E8 and E12-E13.
107. Foochow Fukien Prov. Svc., 22 September 1978, trans. in *FBIS*, No. 186, p. G5; and Haikow Hainan Is. Rgnl. Svc., 24 September 1979, trans. in *FBIS*, No. 188, p. P9.
108. William R. Heaton, "The Minorities and the Military in China," paper presented at the Conference on the Military in Communist Societies, Maxwell AFB, November 1975, pp. 4-5; and Dawa Norbu, "Strategic Development in Tibet," *AS*, 19, No. 3 (March 1979), 254-256.
109. Urumchi Sinkiang Rgnl. Svc., 17 October 1974, claimed that in the Akeu region, 25.2 percent of the entire population were militiamen: *CNS*, No. 543 (13 November 1974), 7. On militia in various border areas see: *NCNA* (Harbin), 2 February 1975, trans. in *SPRCP*, No. 5793, pp. 19-20; *PR*, No. 35 (29 August 1969), 8-10; Ch'angch'un Kirin Prov. Svc., 17 October 1978, trans. in

FBIS, No. 205, p. Ll; "Army-People Joint Defense," pp. 98-99; and *Hsin-hua Yueh-pao*, No. 5 (1979), 38-39.

110. Tsinan Shantung Prov. Svc., 24 January 1979, trans. in *FBIS*, No. 40, p. G8; *Chieh-fang Jih-pao* [*Liberation Daily*] (Shanghai), 24 September 1979, trans. in *FBIS*, No. 198, p. O8; Nanking Kiangsu Prov. Svc., 12 April 1979, in *FBIS*, No. 73, pp. O2-O3; *Tientsin Jih-pao*, 20 April 1979, p. 3; *Chieh-fang Jih-pao*, 6 June 1979, p. 1, trans. in *China Report*, No. 9 (13 August 1979), 16; Ch'angch'un Kirin Prov. Svc., 16 September 1978, trans. in *FBIS*, No. 184, p. L4; Nanking Kiangsu Prov. Svc., 1 March 1979, trans. in *FBIS*, No. 43, pp. G5-G6; Harbin Heilungkiang Prov. Svc., 25 August 1979, trans. in *FBIS*, No. 167, pp. S2-S3; and Nanning Kwangsi Rgnl. Svc., 29 September 1978, trans. in *FBIS*, No. 194, p. E6.

111. *NCNA*, 18 March 1979, trans. in *FBIS*, No. 54, p. P3; *NCNA*, 17 March 1979, trans. in *FBIS*, No. 56, p. E5; Peking Dom. Svc., 28 March 1979, trans. in *FBIS*, No. 65, p. E5; Changsha Hunan Prov. Svc., 27 August 1979, trans. in *FBIS*, No. 170, p. P7.

112. Hsing Chun, pp. M2-M4; and Ch'angch'un Kirin Prov. Svc., 16 September 1978, trans. in *FBIS*, No. 184, p. L4.

113. See, for example, *Down With the New Tsars!*, pp. 62-63.

114. Quoted in *SCMP*, NO. 4070, p. 10.

115. W.H.B. Smith and Joseph E. Smith, *Small Arms of the World*, 10th ed. (New York: Galahad, 1973), pp. 296-297 and 299a.

116. Hofei Anhui Prov. Svc., 17 March 1981, trans. in *FBIS*, No. 052, p. O1.

117. *NCNA* (Urumachi), 19 August 1974, trans. in *SPRCP*, No. 5686, pp. 127-128; *NCNA* (Urumachi), 11 September 1974, trans. in *SPRCP*, No. 5702, pp. 79-80; and *NCNA* (Urumachi), 16 December 1974, trans. in *SPRCP*, No. 5762, p. 16. The most complete study of the *PCC* is Chang Yun-t'ien, ". . . the 'Production-Construction Corps.'"

118. *NCNA* (Urumachi), 19 August 1974, trans. in *SPRCP*, No. 5686, p. 127.

119. A Red Guard tabloid of 1968 claimed that the 23rd Rgt. of the 8th Agricultural Division of the Sinkiang PCC was being used as a "concentration camp" by MR commander Wang En-mao. "News from Sinkiang," pp. 508. Chang Yun-t'ien (p. 29) reports a "reform through labor" agency was absorbed into the Inner Mongolian PCC in 1969.

120. Martin K. Whyte, *Small Groups and Political Rituals in China* (Berkeley and Los Angeles: University of California Press, 1974), pp. 195, 204-205.

121. This, and the following, is drawn from Chang Yun-t'ien, ". . . the 'Production-Construction Corps;'" and Ting Wang, "The Emergent Military Class," in *Military and Political Power*, p. 128. The Sinkiang PCC was observed by Fredric Moritz, *CSM*, 16 July 1979, p. 3.

122. Peking Dom. Svc., 2 November 1979, trans. in *FBIS*, No. 217, pp. L12-L13.

123. See Wang Chen's speech in Sinkiang in *JMJP*, 16 October 1980, p. 2.

124. "Fundamental Differences," pp. 279-280. The Three-in-One System was authoritatively reaffirmed by Hsu Hsiang-ch'ien in *HC*, No. 10 (2 October 1979), 29.

125. Nelsen, "Regional and Paramilitary," p. 147-148.

126. Tsinan Shantung Prov. Svc., 20 September 1978, trans. in *FBIS*, No. 187, p. G5; Peking Dom. Svc., 24 September 1978, trans. in *FBIS*, No. 189, p. L10; Ch'angch'un Kirin Prov. Svc., 16 September 1978, trans. in *FBIS*, No. 184, p.

L4; and Shanghai City Svc., 21 February 1981, trans. in *FBIS*, No. 035, p. O3.
   127. Nelsen, "Military Forces in the Cultural Revolution," p. 466.
   128. *Handbook*, pp. 2-1, 3-1, and 3-2.
   129. Jencks, pp. 805-806.
   130. Heinlein, p. 161.
   131. Michael Pillsbury, "Patterns of Chinese Power Struggles," Paper delivered to Seminar on Modern China, Columbia University, 27 March 1974, passim.
   132. Nelsen, "Military Forces in the Cultural Revolution," passim. An important exception was Sinkiang, where there were so few main force units in 1967 that Peking attempted to intervene with the Lanchow AFD headquarters. That Wang En-mao was able to defy Peking in 1967-68 was attributable to the chaotic situation in the entire country, which made it difficult to intervene in Sinkiang with large main force units. As the situation elsewhere settled down, Wang finally was forced to give up his grip on Sinkiang.
   133. George Modelski, *Principles of World Politics* (New York: Free Press, 1972), p. 149.
   134. Luttwak (passim, especially p. 65) makes a plausible case that China cannot afford to reach "minimum levels of adequacy" against the Soviet threat for the foreseeable future.
   135. *KYODO*, 20 January 1981, in *FBIS*, No. 013, p. L1.
   136. *KYODO*, 20 February 1981, in *FBIS*, No. 034, pp. L3-L4.

6
The Military Industrial System

INTRODUCTION

Although still a poor country, the PRC has achieved a decent, if austere, standard of living for most of its people, produced a wide variety of industrial goods, extended communications and tranportation lines to all parts of the country, and equipped its armed forces with domestically produced weapons.[1] Nevertheless, Chinese science and technology still lag many years behind those of such highly industrialized countries as Japan and the US. Nor has China been gaining on these industrialized countries, despite her declared intention to do so.

Until 1962, economic emphasis was on heavy industrial and military production and development. This has resulted in an overall growth rate of about eight percent per annum for industry since 1949, as compared with only two percent for agriculture. Stress was shifted to agriculture in 1962, after the Great Leap Forward resulted in the "three bad years" of hunger (1959-61). Industrial investment in the production of fertilizer, trucks, tractors, synthetic fiber, etc., increased substantially. The primacy of agriculture was reemphasized in 1971, with heavy new investment and foreign purchasing in agriculture-related industries. Chinese economic planners clearly recognize today that "agricultural production and its relation to population is still the basic problem" they face.

In 1974, the US Central Intelligence Agency (CIA) predicted the long-range growth rate of China's GNP at four to five percent per annum—a rate that would support the population at a slowly rising standard of living and support expanding industrial capacity while providing a gradually improving inventory of modern weapons to the military. Like all competent projections of the Chinese future, the CIA report added the caveat that unpredictable political upheavals make "straight-line projections of economic policy and growth prospects" very uncertain. "Nevertheless, periods of political turbulence probably will have a smaller impact than in the past, because ... economic organizations, controls, and priorities will be more resistant to change."[2]

The economic impact of China's domestic political movements has been widely noted. The Cultural Revolution was particularly disruptive,[3] but the "gang of four period" (1971-76) also saw considerable disruption.[4] It remains to be seen whether the purge of the "gang of four" and the ascendance of moderate economic policies will result in the improved long-range stability the CIA predicted in 1974. It is quite clear that the immediate prospects are for more work, more planning, and less official political activism.

Priorities

This is not to say that the economy will not be subject to a continuing push and pull over priorities. It seems clear now that Lin Piao and others in the military disputed the 1962 decision to emphasize agriculture at the expense of heavy industry. Despite the "people's war" rhetoric of the 1960s, there was large-scale development and production of improved types and large quantities of military equipment. Moreover, a steady stream of news releases hailing advances in electronics emphasized what was already obvious from the spectacular advances in Chinese missiles, aircraft, and nuclear weapons: The electronics industry, half to two-thirds of whose production was devoted to the military, was receiving disproportionately high capital investment.[5]

In the summer of 1971, the question of priorities was raised anew in the "steel versus electronics" debate. In the West, this debate has been subject to three major interpretations:

1. The electronics industry was very weak, and was therefore receiving disproportionate emphasis, which resulted in a shortage of iron and steel.[6]
2. The navy and air force (electronics) were disputing military priorities with the ground forces (steel).[7]
3. The issue was over the primary thrust of economic development, pitting military modernization (electronics) versus general industrial and agricultural growth (steel).

The first hypothesis may be helpful, but it is clearly oversimplified. It may be that steel suffered somewhat owing to large investment in electronics, but steel production made great strides through the 1960s. Press reports of new achievements by the steel industry were nearly as prominent as those in electronics.[8]

The second hypothesis is widely held by those who note that the debate took place just as Mao and his supporters were preparing to purge Lin Piao. Lin, whose base of support was in the air force, supposedly emphasized electronics for political reasons. The assumption is that while missiles and aircraft require advanced electronics, ground force equipment merely requires massive amounts of steel. This is fallacious on both counts: The shortcomings of Chinese military aircraft have been as much attributable to inferior metallurgy as to primitive electronics.[9] The deficiencies of the Chinese-made F7 "FISHBED" fighter, for example, are widely attributed to inferior steel. Conversely, the next generation of Chinese ground weapons will require extensive electronics applications in those areas where the PLA is now most lacking: antitank and anti-aircraft weapons, fire control, surveillance, target acquisition, and electronic warfare.

After the fall of Lin Piao (in September 1971), military procurement dropped precipitously (Figure 6.1) while agricultural mechanization was given renewed emphasis. Chairman Mao's formulation that "agriculture is the foundation" has continued to receive heavy emphasis ever since.[10]

Since 1973, the Chinese have also sought to make a virtue of necessity by identifying large military industry with imperialism and revisionism. The USSR has allegedly "militarized" its economy since the death of Stalin (!), in order to pursue its imperialist goals and compete with the US as a superpower.

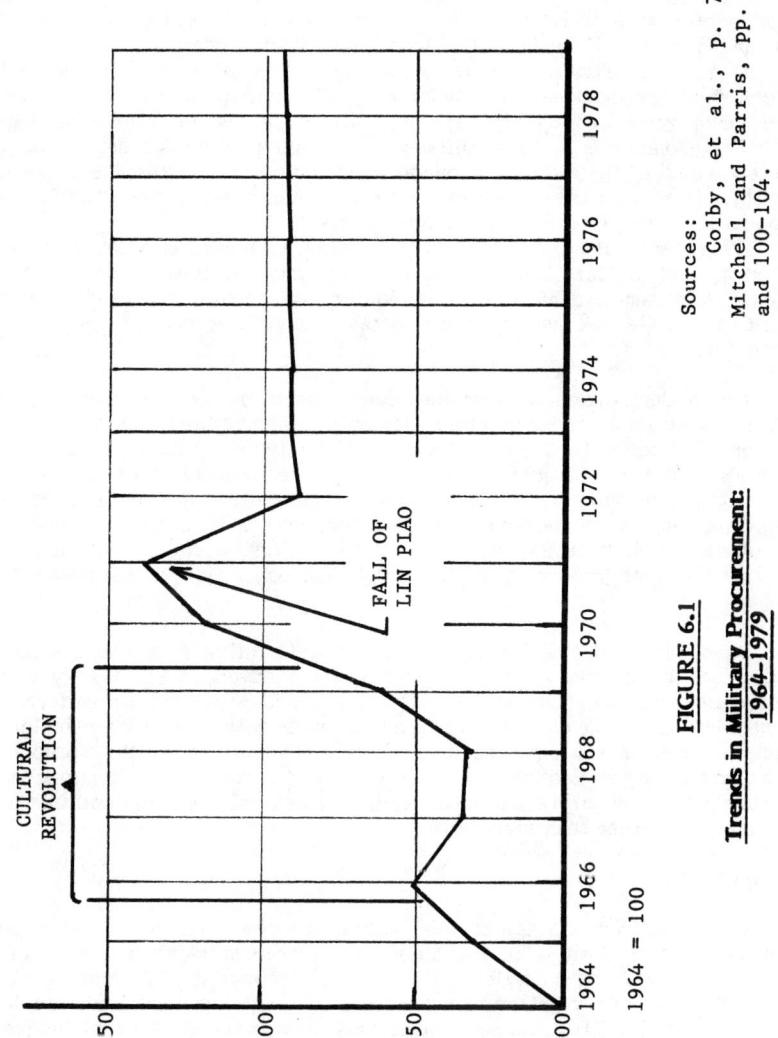

FIGURE 6.1

Trends in Military Procurement: 1964-1979

Sources:
 Colby, et al., p. 77; and
 Mitchell and Parris, pp. 66-72
 and 100-104.

The result, say the Chinese, has been the decay of the Soviet economy, and of socialism itself. Decadence and bourgeois revisionism, we are told, are the inevitable results of a national economy subordinated to military production.[11]

With the demise of the "gang of four," the debate over productivity versus revolutionary purity finally may be at an end. But China's leaders still may disagree on the relative importance of military modernization, civilian industry, and agriculture.[12] Clearly, there are important advocates of military modernization in the Eleventh Politburo. In January and February 1977, four major conferences were held on various aspects of national defense, and chairman Hua himself spoke on the need for military modernization.

A major reassessment of the economy in the spring of 1979 resulted in the policy of "readjustment, restructuring, consolidation, and improvement" (t'iao-cheng, kai-ke, cheng-tuan, t'i-kao). Under this "eight character slogan" the entire economy is to be stabilized and rationalized before any major new initiatives begin. Meanwhile, announced priorities are: (1) agriculture, (2) light industry, (3) mining, transportation and communications, and (4) development of modern science, technology, and management.[13]

The absence of heavy industry from this list leaves little doubt as to the low priority of military industry in the short term. Lest there be any doubt, Defense Minister Hsu Hsiang-ch'ien explicated it in the October 1979 issue of *Hung Ch'i*. While acknowledging the pressing need for modern weapons, Hsu stressed that:

> The modernization of national defense cannot be divorced from the modernization of agriculture, industry, science and technology, and, in the final analysis, is based on the national economy . . . . we must first of all guarantee the high-speed development of the national economy. Blindly pursuing large-scale and high-speed development in building national defense will invariably and seriously hinder the development of the national economy and harm the base of the defense industry. Subsequently, "haste makes waste."[14]

It appears that the Chinese will attempt to follow a balanced economic strategy of steady but gradual improvement in advanced technology and in capital construction, financed by agriculture and exports.[15] "By foregoing massive military programs now, and addressing directly the tasks of building a solid modern industrial base, the Chinese will develop the ability to produce in future much larger and more modern military systems."[16] The long-range strategy is to allow military industry to follow general economic and industrial development, rather than vice versa.

Foreign Trade

It is clear that "China's oft-stated goal of self-sufficiency in industry and technology is not likely to be attained in the foreseeable future." Nor, in the short run, is total self-sufficiency necessarily a good idea. China can continue to benefit from her "relative backwardness by obtaining plant and equipment abroad on which R&D costs have been paid off and technical problems ironed out."[17] This is true of some military technology as well. Specific examples will be discussed in the following sections.

Although foreign trade is a relatively small proportion of China's economy, it is, and will remain, crucial to the realization of Chou En-lai's vision of a modern industrial society by the year 2000. It is clear that the post-Mao leadership recognizes the ironic fact that imported technology holds out China's only realistic hope for achieving genuine economic independence.[18]

China's own production of machinery and equipment is now so large that imported technology represents only a small fraction (perhaps six to eight percent) of its overall technology accretion. In qualitative terms, however, technology imports are still a key factor in the development of the more sophisticated sectors of China's industrial production system.[19]

Human Capital

In the long run, the most serious brake on China's economic and industrial development will probably prove to be a self-inflicted one. From 1966 to 1976 radical politics dealt repeated setbacks to the educational system which must produce scientists, engineers, managers, technicians, and skilled laborers. "Maoist" worship of the "wisdom of the masses" produced a strong tendency to undervalue formal education, and to view foreign intellectual or technical influence as unnecessary or outrightly treasonous:

> The conscious emphasis, especially during the Cultural Revolution, on practical experience, on "learning by doing"; closing universities for several years, and the proletarianizing reforms of tertiary education (reducing admission standards, shortening curriculum) could not help but retard the development of a technical labor force with skills and educational standards comparable to those of the Western world. It takes decades to develop such a force ....[20]

Repair of the damage has only begun. Scientific and technical publications, which ceased entirely in 1967, only fully resumed in 1979. Until late 1977, entry into universities was based mainly on political criteria. Higher education in foreign countries was extremely rare, and politically suspect. Likewise, the need to train skilled modern managers was virtually unacknowledged.[21]

Instead, the state and party attempted to produce technicians and engineers right in the factories, on a part-time basis. They also encouraged "mass technical innovation drives." "Three-in-one technical innovation groups" (of workers, cadres, and technicians) were credited with working out "all industrial designs," and with developing thousands of "innovations."[22] The overall result has been a chronic tendency to refine existing products rather than to come up with new ones. Even military industry tends to produce too much too late, rather than really to innovate.

National leaders now openly admit that the scientific gap between China and the "advanced world level has widened," and call urgently for education of a new generation."[23] Meanwhile, the PRC continues to rely on some 10,000 aging qualified engineers and scientists. In 1977, China had, altogether, "fewer qualified scientific and technical personnel than are routinely employed by a single major industrial corporation in the United States."[24] Many of these have not been properly utilized in their specialties since 1966, owing to radical political measures such as *hsia-fang*. To meet this problem, a nationwide survey of scientific and technical personnel was announced in September 1978.

It was found that 196,000 such persons were "out of work," yet only twenty percent of them had been returned to useful scientific and technical work by late 1980. This continued waste of China's scarcest resource is officially blamed on bureaucratism and a generalized suspicion of intellectuals by older cadres.[25]

DEFENSE INDUSTRY

In the aftermath of the Cultural Revolution, virtually all of China's industry was under some degree of military control.[26] As recently as 1975, PLA officers were still in charge of some "civilian" ministries.[27]

Overall, defense production is thought to absorb twenty-five percent of China's total industrial capacity, and to produce about ten percent of GNP. The total system is similar to the Soviet model, being a functionally divided series of semi-autonomous "corporations," with powerful coordinating links to resolve conflicts. The system includes parts of some "civilian" ministries (e.g., Chemical Industry and Metalurgical Industry), as well as the military machine-building ministries.

The Ministries of Machine Industry

Most of China's military industry is under the Second through Eighth Ministries of Machine Industry (MMIs). All of these are formally under the State Council, and are theoretically co-equal with the Ministry of National Defense (MND).

Since 1949, the number of MMIs has varied from one up to eight. The current system emerged with a reorganization begun in 1960. By 1965, there were seven MMIs, only one of which (the First—1MMI) was concerned with civilian production. Lines of responsibility are not rigid, and there is some overlapping. Computers, for example, are produced under the supervision of several different ministries.[28]

An Eighth MMI, charged with agricultural machinery, was formed in the mid-1960s, but was consolidated with the 1MMI, which was responsible for all civilian machine-building, in 1970.[29] In September 1979, a new 8MMI, completely unrelated to the previous one, was formed (see below).

In the following pages, the defense industrial and scientific systems are examined. It must be kept in mind, however, that a reorganization of the entire machine-building industry began in 1978—an effort expected to take from three to five years to complete. We shall first address the past and present before returning to the shape of things to come.

The seven military-related MMIs and their responsibilities are shown in Table 6.1. It will be noted that most produce some products for civilian use as well (e.g., light aircraft from the 3MMI, merchant ships from 6MMI shipyards, etc.). Exactly how funding and coordination of this "civilian" production are arranged is unknown. Indeed, there are many unanswered questions regarding the interrelationships of the MMIs, the MND, the State Council, the Military Affairs Commission of the Party Central Committee (MAC), and the uniformed PLA.[30]

The Second MMI (atomic energy) was the first defense industrial ministry to be charged with one general product line, an institutional arrangement later extended to all defense industry. The 2MMI's early separation, only months after the withdrawal of Soviet advisors, reflected the importance the Chinese attached to developing their own nuclear technology. They successfully tested

TABLE 6.1
The Ministries of Machine Industry—1981

Ministry	Responsibility	Year Assumed Present Responsibility	Current Minister	Former Ministers
Second	Atomic Energy	September 1960	Liu Wei (Brig-Gen)	Sung Jen-ch'iung (Col-Gen) Liu Chieh Liu Hsi-yao
Third	Aircraft and Air-to-Air Missiles	1963-65	Lü Tung	Chang Lien-kuei Sun Chih-yuan Li Ch'i-t'ai (AF Maj-Gen)
Fourth	Electronics	May 1963	Ch'ien Min	Wang Cheng (Lt-Gen)
Fifth	Ordnance (Conventional weapons, etc.)	September 1963	Chang Chen	Ch'iu Chuang-ch'eng (Lt-Gen) Li Ch'eng-fang (Gen)
Sixth	Shipbuilding	September 1963	Ch'ai Shu-fan	Fang Ch'iang (V-Adm) Pien Chiang
Seventh	Ballistic Missiles	January 1965	Cheng T'ien-hsiang	Wang Ping-chang (AF Lt-Gen) Wang Yang (Gen) Sung Jen-ch'iung (Lt-Gen)
Eighth	Tactical Missiles (all guided missiles except air-to-air)	September 1979	Vacant?	Chiao Jo-yü

Sources:
Latham, "China's National Defense Industrial System" (June 1975); NCNA, 18 January 1975, trans. in SPRCP, No. 5783, p. 98; Chinese Communist Biographical Directory (Chung Kung Jen Ming Lu) (Taipei, 1978); China Handbook (Chung Kuo Shou Ts'e) (Hong Kong, 1979); NCNA, 23 February 1979.

a twenty-kiloton (KT) atomic bomb on 16 October 1964, and a megaton (MT) range thermonuclear bomb on 17 June 1967. The PRC thus made the transition from fission to fusion in less than three years, showing a first-rate research, development, and production capability.

A gaseous diffusion plant at Lanchow has been producing weapons-grade U-235 since 1963, and a reactor complex at Yumen has produced plutonium since 1967.[31] Fissile material is not a serious constraint on Chinese warhead production. Relatively small ("less than twenty-KT") test explosions in September 1977 and March 1978 indicated that R&D is proceeding on low-yield tactical nuclear warheads.[32]

The nuclear weapons and missile programs (the latter under the 7MMI) are exceptions to the general observations on PRC defense industry which follow. These programs have enjoyed very high prirority in funding, resources, and talent, and have been shielded from political disruption during all but the most chaotic months of 1967-68. The spectacular progress of these programs have been made at the expense of other military and civilian needs.

The 3MMI was responsible for all military machine industry (less nuclear) in 1960-63, but between 1963 and 1965 most product lines were reassigned to the new Fourth through Seventh ministries, leaving the 3MMI responsible only for aircraft and aerodynamic missiles.[33] Most of the latter were reassigned to the new 8MMI in 1979 (see below). The aircraft industry is the most studied and best understood part of the defense industrial system, and exhibits most of its characteristic problems.

PRC aircraft production began at Shenyang in the 1950s with massive Soviet assistance.[34] Since the designs were all Russian, Chinese R&D was confined to making and improving existing products rather than designing new ones. In 1959-60, construction of large aircraft complexes began at Sian and Chengtu.[35]

The Sino-Soviet split and the abrupt withdrawal of Soviet advisors in 1960 left the Chinese defense industry with half-built factories, partly-completed assembly lines, blueprints without prototypes, and prototypes without blueprints. Production lines for a copy of the MiG-19 "FARMER" fighter (called the "Shenyang F6") were still incomplete. Despite the setback, F6 production began in the early 1960s and continues to this day. After nearly twenty years of incremental improvement, the F6 is surely the most highly perfected obsolescent fighter on earth—vastly better than the best Soviet MiG-19, but two generations behind current technology.

The Soviets also left behind two examples of the MiG-21F "FISHBED-C." After a herculean effort of "reverse engineering," a Chinese copy, called "Shenyang F7," flew in late 1964, and entered service in 1965. It was subsequently improved by reference to the MiG-21PF, copies of which the Chinese misappropriated on their way to North Vietnam in 1966-67. The Chinese "have made a number of innovative changes to the MiG-21's cockpit avionics and developed reconnaissance versions," and have exported the F7 to Albania, Tanzania, and Egypt.[36] Nevertheless, production has repeatedly been interrupted by problems with engine metallurgy, and fewer than 100 "FISHBEDs" are currently in PLAAF service.[37]

The PLAAF needed a better fighter and a fighter-bomber, but China simply could not design a new aircraft. The interim solution was the "FANTAN," obviously an extensively modified F6 (so much so that some purists insist on designating it "F6bis"). The "FANTAN" apparently exists in a fighter version called "F9" (*Chien-tou-chi Chiu-shih*), but the fighter-bomber version, called "A5" (*Ch'iang-chi-chi Wu-shih*) is far more common. The "FANTAN" is a fairly impressive achievement, with afterburners, a host of modifications and improvements, and (in the fighter-bomber version) an internal weapons bay. Yet it still relies on the technology of the 1950s, is somewhat underpowered for its mission, and is reportedly plagued by engine problems.[38]

The situation with bombers is even worse. The Soviet Il-28 "BEAGLE," a design dating from the 1940s, is still in frontline service in its Chinese-made version (called "B5"). The Soviet Tu-16 "BADGER-A" medium-range bomber was supplied to the PLAAF in the 1950s. "Reverse engineering" began in 1962, and after considerable resource expenditure, production of the Chinese version (called "B6") began in 1968. Then, in 1972, the Chinese discovered that their newly purchased Boeing 707 airliners were far more sophisticated than the B6, which was evidently more obsolescent than they had ever suspected. Nevertheless, limited production apparently continues. Reportedly, a few were sold to Pakistan, and spare parts have been supplied to Egypt.[39]

The 3MMI also produces a copy of the Soviet "ATOLL" air-to-air missile, and is reportedly developing at least two new air-to-air missiles.[40]

It will be seen that all aircraft in production incorporate outdated technology. The Chinese have sought to palliate the problem by constant improvement of performance and detail. This extends right into the operational squadrons of the PLAAF, which are requried to "remodel" frontline aircraft, incorporating new improvements.[41]

The approach to helicopters and transports has been rather different, and has produced somewhat better results. With relatively light, simple types, a number of Soviet and two Chinese Designs have been produced in substantial numbers. More sophisticated types, such as recent-model helicopters and commercial airliners, needed in only limited quantities, have simply been purchased abroad, even during the Cultural Revolution. This met PRC air transport needs without expending scarce design and production resources. It has also meant exposure to new technology (such as the turbofan engines and inertial navigation system of the 707).[42] Further access to foreign technology was recently gained by a 3MMI contract to produce landing gear doors for the American McDonnell-Douglas DC-9.[43]

Even in the transport field, the limits of "reverse engineering" may have been reached. While the Soviet An-12 "CUB" apparently has been copied successfully, the Boeing 707 has not. The 707 project reportedly began in 1972-73, but repeatedly failed to get a much revised prototype (designated "C10") even to fly until September 1980. The C10 is reportedly powered by Pratt and Whitney JT3D-7 turbofan engines purchased as spares for the Boeing originals.[44]

By 1973, the civil air fleet was considerably more up-to-date than the air force, whose newest machines were products of the evidently inefficient "reverse engineering" process. Foreign transport and helicopter purchases continued through the 1970s while the Chinese began shopping for a Western European fighter and an advanced jet engine. In December 1975, they signed a contract with Rolls Royce for PRC production of the RB168-25R Spey Mk 202M afterburning turbofan engine. This engine, to be produced in Sian, is the specifically military Spey. It is a design dating from the early 1960s, but still represents a "quantum increase in production capability," and a "jumping off point for modern aviation systems at minimum expense in manpower investment and gestation time."[45] The first two Speys were trial-produced at Sian in late 1979, while over 700 Chinese were in training at Rolls Royce in England.[46] Series production of the Spey was expected to begin in 1980, but did not. For reasons which remain unclear at this writing, the Sian Spey project seems to be in abeyance. Meanwhile, some of the technological and managerial lessons learned reportedly will be applied to the main aircraft building complex at Shenyang.[47]

The Spey project has provoked speculation as to just what the Chinese plan to do with it. It will not fit either the "FARMER" or "FANTAN," but might be used to upgrade the "FISHBED." Several "new" Chinese designs are also said to be intended for mating with the Spey: intercepters tentatively identified as "F-8" and "F-10," and a more advanced multi-role combat aircraft designated "F-12."[48]

Whatever their plans for the Spey, the Chinese have also expressed interest in a number of foreign fighters, including the Swedish "Viggen," the French "Mirage," and the American F-15 and F-16. By far the most publicity has been generated by the extended negotiations with Hawker-Siddley for the "Harrier" vertical and short take-off and landing (VSTOL) fighter-bomber. The Chinese were reportedly set to sign a contract for up to 90 "Harriers" early in 1979, but the invasion of Vietnam and the economic retrenchment of February-March seem to have delayed it indefinitely.[49]

In the course of all this "shopping," the Chinese have learned a great deal. In fact, some Europeans have become irritated by the numerous PRC technical missions since 1978, "which do little more than examine equipment. Some even suggest China is seeking cheap consultancy advice and has little intention of buying."[50]

Another indirect source of modern technology continues to be the USSR. Since about 1976, China and Egypt have engaged in the symbiotic exchange of Chinese aircraft and spare parts (for Egypt's Soviet-made air force), in exchange for sample late-model Soviet weapons from Egypt to the PRC. The 3MMI has thus acquired examples of the sophisticated swing-wing MiG-23 ("FLOGGER-E") fighter. MiG-23 technology reportedly will be used in the Chinese F12.[51]

The situation with respect to electronics, the purview of the 4MMI, is similar to that in aviation. The PLA still depends largely upon copies and adaptations of Soviet military electronics. Compared to aviation, however, PRC electronics have not fallen quite so far behind. In the 1970s, a few really new systems were developed, including long-range secure voice communications, large-scale integrated circuits, laser applications, and computers.[52] A laser rangefinder has evidently been fielded on PLA tanks.[53]

Although some of these developments are said to be up to world standards, the PLA is far behind in most areas. Deficiencies in the field of electronic warfare are especially severe. Even the air force seems to have done little in this field until quite recently. In September 1979, for example, one surface-to-air missile (SAM) unit conducted its first ever firing exercise against electronic countermeasures (ECM)—resorting to a primitive manual guidance system against only minor "jamming."[54] The same month, a PLA electronics engineering college was opened. Speaking at the opening ceremony was Vice-Chief of Staff Wu Hsiu-ch'uan, who implied the General Staff's grave concern with the backward state of PLA ECM capabilities.[55]

"The PRC is attempting to catch up with computer technology too. While it is currently developing a Chinese third-generation computer capable of one million operations per second, the PRC is also purchasing more advanced computers" abroad.[56] Computers have been purchased in Japan and the US, as have COMSAT and INTELSAT stations. The widely heralded purchase of LANDSAT-D ground equipment from the US remains hung up by its high asking price.[57]

In 1978, RCA, Hitachi, and Toshiba were negotiating for color television manufacturing plants in China, which would involve export of integrated circuit printing technology. The US also approved export of sophisticated oil exploration gear. These are examples of "gray area" or "dual-use" technology which, though ostensibly "peaceful," can readily be applied to military purposes.[58] The oil exploration technology, for example, can be used in antisubmarine warfare (ASW) systems.

It is not certain that 4MMI production will continue to go mainly to the military, nor that imported technology will necessarily be put immediately to military uses. Non-military modernization presently has clear priority, and electronics is seen as a leading factor in developing the civilian economy. In any event, whenever and however the PLA is truly modernized, electronics will be required in virtually every sort of equipment, from nuclear missiles to ASW to infantry weapons.

The 5MMI produces all conventional weapons, munitions, and fighting vehicles. A variety of artillery pieces, several armored vehicles, and assorted small arms are currently in production[59] (Appendix B). Most are copies or modifications of Soviet types. Only at the least-sophisticated levels have the Chinese kept up with world standards: The service rifles, machineguns, and light antitank weapons used in PLA rifle companies are only a few years behind current US and Soviet standards. Even so, the PLA has reportedly shown some interest in recent European assault rifle design.

Although practically all PLA guns, munitions, and vehicles are obsolescent, the Chinese seem most interested in acquiring a new main battle tank. PLA delegations have been "browsing" in Europe, but have given no strong indication of readiness to buy.[60] The Egyptians have also provided at least two Soviet T-62 tanks to China, although the PLA reportedly captured several in the 1969 border clashes. 5MMI products presently have an even lower priority than aircraft, with respect to research and development, so it is likely that the PLA will have to "make do" in most categories, for the foreseeable future. The exception might be a "new" tank incorporating T-62 technology.

The 6MMI is responsible for both merchant and naval shipbuilding. Here, too, the general pattern applies with respect to military production. Nearly all PLA Naval vessels are copies or modifications of early post-war Soviet designs. Small coastal-defense craft are a partial exception, however. Without known foreign assistance, the Chinese have developed two fast hydrofoils, the "Huch'uan" class torpedo boats and "Haitao" class missile boats.[61]

Certainly the most impressive recent strides in the field of transportation have been in merchant shipbuilding. Perhaps uniquely, these appear to have been "spin-off" from the military shipbuilding program begun in the 1950s. Civilian shipbuilding really hit its stride only in 1968, with the launching of two freighters of 19,000 tons each. Both were hailed as victories of self-reliance over the "slavish worship of foreign 'experts.'"[62] Reflecting another specialized technology, a 3,200 ton icebreaker was launched in December 1969. Surely the most important additions to the merchant fleet have been Chinese-built oil tankers, the first of which was also launched in 1969.[63] In 1970-79, the 6MMI built nearly one hundred merchant ships totalling about a million gross tons.[64] In 1980 alone, an additional 818,000 tons were reportedly produced. A new class of 10,000-ton supply ships has also been developed for the navy, which will enable the PLAN to remain longer and further at sea.[65]

Nevertheless, shipbuilding, especially military shipbuilding, is quite outdated, so European and Japanese expertise is being studied.[66] In 1978, the

PRC purchased a number of British diesel engines for naval vessels.[67] Such a purchase, rather than acquisition of production rights, appears to indicate limited needs and low priority in naval construction.

The 7MMI was once thought to produce all aircraft and missiles, but disruptions during the GPCR revealed that it is concerned only with ballistic missiles.[68] Thus it produces the strategic missiles of the Second Artillery and the launchers for the Chinese space program. As we noted above, ballistic missile research and production enjoy a very high priority, along with nuclear weapons.

Beginning with a few Soviet missiles, and a cadre of Western-trained scientists, the Chinese launched their first ballistic missile in 1960.[69] By the end of the 1970s, the Second Artillery had three operational ballistic nuclear missiles, with a maximum range of about 6,000 km (see Appendix E). All of them still reportedly suffer from poor navigation and guidance systems and only marginal reliability. All are liquid-fueled, and hence subject to serious limitations with respect to preparation time, site hardening, and other considerations. (See the discussion of the Second Artillery in chapter 5).

1979 saw a flurry of missile tests, and at least one unsuccessful satellite launch (in July).[70] Indian sources claimed development has begun of a solid fuel ICBM, as well.[71]

A large rocket, identified by NATO as "CSS-X-4," has launched recent PRC satellites, and was the basis of the two ICBMs test-fired into the Pacific in May 1980. These test shots traveled about 12,000 km. Presumably, the Second Artillery now can deploy a few ICBMs, targeted on European Russia, deep inside China, well away from Soviet ground attack.[72]

While missiles have apparently achieved the necessary "throw weight" capability, they are still thought to be deficient in reliability, survivability, and such electronics-related aspects as targeting and guidance. Many of these faults could be rapidly improved, using commercially available "gray area" foreign technology. According to Justin Galen, "Improved relations with the US are thus worth years and billions of dollars to the Chinese strategic effort."[73] The accuracy of the two 1980 test shots, however, indicates that guidance may already be fairly well advanced. Like most foreign observers (including this author), Galen may have underestimated Chinese progress in this area, but his conclusion probably remains valid.

In September 1979, the new 8MMI was split off from the 3MMI. The 8MMI is responsible for "tactical missiles"—a category including all guided aerodynamic missiles, except air-to-air rockets, which remain within the domain of the 3MMI.[74] The 8MMI has inherited production responsibility for copies of the Soviet SA-2 "GUIDELINE" surface-to-air missiles (SAM) which the Chinese call "Red Flag No. 4," and the Soviet SS-N-2A "STYX" naval surface-to-surface cruise missile. Both designs date from the 1950s, but have been modified and improved in China.

Creation of the 8MMI in a time of industrial retrenchment indicates the high priority the PLA places on tactical missile development. The navy needs a better cruise missile than the "STYX," if it is to become a really credible force. Even more critical is the need for modern tactical air defense and antitank (AT) missiles. The Egyptians have supplied copies of at least two Soviet SAMs (SA-3 "GOA" and SA-6 "GAINFUL") and the AT-3 "SAGGER" AT missile. Additional examples of the "GAINFUL" and "SAGGER," as well as the hand-held SA-7 "GRAIL" were reportedly captured from the Vietnamese in 1979.[75]

In 1978-79, the Chinese also generated immense excitement by shopping for anti-aircraft and antitank weapons. They expressed interest in practically every such system in Western Europe—most notably the French "Crotale" and French-German "Roland" air-defense missiles, and the "HOT" and "MILAN" antitank missiles. Notwithstanding premature reports to the contrary, however, no contracts have been signed for supplies of, nor production rights to, any of these. Again, the economic retrenchment of 1979, as well as European compunctions arising from the Chinese invasion of Vietnam, seem to have ended negotiations indefinitely.

Instead, in 1979, the Chinese went into production with a copy of the "SAGGER," a design that entered Soviet service in 1965 and is now being replaced by improved missiles. The PLA is still behind in AT weapons, but will have closed the gap significantly when and if the "SAGGER" is deployed in quantity.[76] Continued R&D on AT missiles remains a high priority.

Development of a new SAM is proceeding with even less success. In 1979, after years of delay, a naval SAM, vaguely resembling the "GUIDELINE," appeared on the PLAN's two "Kiangtung" class frigates.[77] A recent observer, however, reports these SAM mounts had been removed again by early 1981.

The defense MMIs appear to be "vertically integrated," which is to say they include every sort of installation from mines to factories to research institutes. A 1967 circular stated that "the factories and mines, scientific research and planning organizations, and capital construction units of the Second, Third, Fourth, Fifth, Sixth, and Seventh Ministries of Machine Building Industry are important secret state organs."[78] This pattern of organization is highly inefficient from the perspective of the overall economy, and may well be changed by the current reorganization, to which we shall return at the end of this chapter.

Geographical Dispersion

Despite thirty years of proclamations, planning, and construction, China's industrial centers are still essentially where they were in 1949: the urban centers of Manchuria and the coast. The few inland industrial centers established by the PRC include Wuhan (begun before World War II by foreign capital) and Pao-t'ou in Inner Mongolia. Lanchow and Sian have also been developing, as have Chengtu and Loyang.

Geographical dispersion of industry remains official policy for reasons of military defense as well as socio-economic balance. Dispersion can help minimize China's vulnerability to bombing, and facilitate "people's war" in the event of invasion. James Blaker has found, however, that in the early 1970s only five or six of the PRC's eleven military regions (MRs) had the capability of producing a wide range of modern weaponry. Furthermore, only the Shenyang, Peking, and Nanking MRs (which embrace the long-established industrial centers) could produce a full range of conventional weapons on a self-sustaining basis. Blaker also found that complex end-items (e.g., tanks and aircraft) were often assembled in only one complex, or even in one factory, in the entire country. With the possible exceptions of the Shenyang, Peking, and Nanking MRs, then, no MR was capable of self-sufficiency in military industry.[79] This situation remains essentially unchanged in 1981.

The small arms situation is much different. There are factories capable of making pistols, rifles, machine guns, and their ammunition in every province. The problem here is the reverse of the over-centralized production of tanks, aircraft, and missiles. As with railroad rolling stock, tractors, and trucks, many localities are self-sufficient in light infantry weapons, but their parts are not always interchangeable from factory to factory. Standardization and quality control tend to suffer in such highly decentralized industries.[80]

Separation of military from civilian industry extends even to such items as bedding and clothing, which are produced for the PLA by plants under GRSD or MR supervision.[81]

Managing Agencies: The NDIO and NDIC

In order to coordinate the defense industry, a National Defense Industrial Office (NDIO) was organized under the State Council in the 1950s. Premier Chou was its first director.[82] The relationship of the NDIO to the State Planning Commission and to the MND was, and remains, somewhat ambiguous. As a practical matter, the NDIO probably has been most responsive to the PLA viewpoint, because its leading cadres mostly have been career soldiers. Chou was succeeded by Chao Erh-lu, formerly head of the ordnance subdepartment of the army's GRSD. He was succeeded in 1963-64 by PLA Chief of Staff Lo Jui-ch'ing. During the same period, Marshal Ho Lung was a deputy director of the NDIO as well as Chairman of the National Defense Industrial Committee (NDIC) of the MAC. The NDIC, as a MAC organ, presumably was, at least up to 1979, the ultimate policy authority over military industry. In 1967, General Su Yü took over as head of both the NDIO and NDIC, and retained both positions until the late 1970s.[83]

The NDIO probably coordinates the flow of products among MMIs (e.g., 5MMI guns and 4MMI electronics to the 6MMI, for installation on ships). As overall supervisor of the defense industry, the NDIO reaches into every province and municipality to control the manufacture of every subcomponent of military hardware.[84]

RESEARCH AND DEVELOPMENT

The entire industrial sector has been plagued by the problem of integrating production with research and development (R&D). In the decade following liberation a variety of institutional arrangements were tried and then dropped. They all tended to keep research so separated from production that "research priorities ... did not necessarily coincide with the needs of industrial customers. To a great extent industry [got] what science thought industry needed."[85] A State Science and Technology Commission (SSTC) was charged with integrating R&D with production from 1958 to about 1972, when it was replaced by a smaller "Science and Education Group," also under the State Council. The SSTC was restored by the Fifth NPC in March 1978, and is chaired by Vice-Premier Fang Yi.[86]

The NDSTC

The National Defense Science and Technology Commission (NDSTC) was formed sometime in the mid-1950s, but rose to importance with the withdrawal of Soviet aid in 1960.[87] One response to that trauma was to strengthen the NDIO, which hastened to consolidate control of the defense industrial ministries. The latter all must have been clamoring for the R&D personnel, budgets, and facilities needed to pick up the pieces left behind by the Soviet departure. This pressure must have been especially strong in view of the unsatisfactory input industry had already been getting from outside research facilities.

The problems might have been solved by allowing each defense industrial ministry or plant to set up its own R&D facilities, staffed by its own research personnel. Might have been, that is, but for the severe shortages of money, material, scientists, and technicians. The only alternative was to pool those resources, and centrally dictate the priorities to which they would be devoted. The NDSTC was charged with that task.

The NDSTC's primary function is to see that the policies of the MAC and the Party CC are supported by the R&D effort. In 1975, Latham noted that most known NDSTC leaders have had backgrounds as military political commissars, rather than in science or industry.

> In general terms ... an officer assigned to the NDSTC as a vice-chairman or "responsible" person typically will be an army general officer, will represent the PLA rather than industry, will not have a technical background, will likely have been a political commissar, and will remain in the Commission for only a few years. Additionally, his duties may be so light that he can hold other positions some distance from Peking.[88]

NDSTC management is probably much more concerned with setting politically dictated priorities than with technical details.

A logical extension of the above function is the planning of future R&D programs. These plans, once approved by the MAC, determine the allocation of resources for years in advance. In this regard, the NDSTC monitors and controls the importation of foreign technology and technical personnel, acting as the political, as well as economic and technical, watchdog. Another function is to oversee the development of the R&D facilities which actually implement planned projects. It is apparent that whatever else the NDSTC may do, it does not represent the perspective of the MMIs, but rather of the PLA high command and the service branches. NDSTC control precludes the MMIs and even the large research institutes from setting their own priorities. "In short, the Commission controls the defense industries by controlling the size of the defense R&D base and the areas in which it will be expended. That is to say, the defense industries can only build what the NDSTC allows the research academies and institutes to design and develop."[89]

If we assume that the NDSTC works roughly like the SSTC did prior to 1972, it functions something like this: Annually or semi-annually, research institutes submit status reports, problems, and suggestions; the PLA service branches and general departments submit ideas and requirements for new equipment or materiel. All this is then evaluated by the NDSTC, in the light of MAC policies and long-range plans. Decisions are made to begin, combine, continue, terminate, expand, or disapprove the various projects or proposals. Duplication is eliminated, and construction or collateral research is authorized if necessary. Finally, manpower and equipment are allocated or redistributed. After review by the MAC these decisions are promulgated to the research establishments and the MMIs. The latter are solicited for feedback on the practicability of the new programs, and any problems they may engender.

The advantage of this system—indeed, its *raison d'etre*—is that it eliminates duplication and assures maximization of China's limited technical manpower and facilities. Another result, especially up to 1968, was that the system prevented the MMIs from initiating R&D projects on their own. In top priority areas, like nuclear weapons and ballistic missiles, the NDSTC has allotted the necessary funds, personnel, and flexibility. In most areas, however, bureaucratic delay, lack of technical expertise on the commission, and lack of resources have all contributed to a generally plodding and unimaginative quality in Chinese military R&D.

Chairman of the NDSTC from its inception until 1975 was Nieh Jung-chen, the most widely traveled and well-educated marshal of the PLA. He has been an advocate of professional management, technical specialization, and the adaptation of foreign technology for many years. As chairman of both the NDSTC (1958?-75) and the SSTC (1958-72?) his personal influence over scientific and technical affairs has been immense. There was probably more than a grain of truth in the Red Guard accusation that Nieh had created a "personal kingdom" in science and technology by 1968.[90]

As the most influential individual in the setting of R&D priorities, Nieh inevitably came into conflict with the MMIs, the NDIO, and the NDIC. Lo Jui-ch'ing reportedly criticized the NDSTC because research work went "from data to data, from design to design, without completing anything."[91] Lo was apparently backed on this issue by Ho Lung, the Chairman of the NDIC. They and several defense industrial ministers spoke out for greater integration of production and research, and less PLA involvement in the defense industry. They seem to have advocated a system in which the MMIs would have more say in the development of new products.[92]

When both Lo and Ho fell early victims of the GPCR,[93] Nieh and the NDSTC won the R&D controversy more or less by default. Ho's and Lo's position was labeled as "reactionary" mainly just because it had been *their* position, and the existing NDSTC system was officially vindicated.[94] One of the many ironies of the Cultural Revolution, then, was the triumph of an institutional setup which favors advanced research rather than "practical" development. It is ironic because the thrust of technological innovation, for a variety of other reasons, has been "practical" rather than theoretical.

R&D Institutions

The exact organization of R&D in China is difficult to delineate owing to frequent reorganizations and official secrecy. The following description, gleaned from official and Red Guard publications, must be considered tentative (Refer to Figure 6.2). Associated with MMIs are at least fourteen numbered research institutes. Each seems to be associated with a specific MMI. In 1968, for example, the First, Second, and Third Institutes (with a total of 12,000 employees) were associated with the 7MMI, and the Seventh Institute was associated with the 6MMI. These particular institutes were centers of Red Guard conflict in 1968, a condition Chou En-lai partly attributed to their simply being too big. He called for reduction in the staffs of all the MMI research institutes. Whether or not this was done is unknown.[95] In 1978, the Second and Tenth Institutes were associated with the 7MMI.[96]

These institutes, while supposedly engaged in "scientific research," are in fact concerned with technological development, and are closely related to experimental factories. It is mainly these institutes where production plans, final prototypes, and product improvements are worked out. The institutes are funded by, and belong to, the MMIs, but the NDSTC is the "broker" which determines which institutes are funded, and for what purposes. "They seem to be administratively subordinate to the MMIs and operationally subordinate to the NDSTC."[97] One step further away from production are the research academies of the MMIs. These are technical schools where research and limited experimental fabrication work complement the training of scientific

FIGURE 6.2

The Chinese Military-Industrial and Research System: 1979

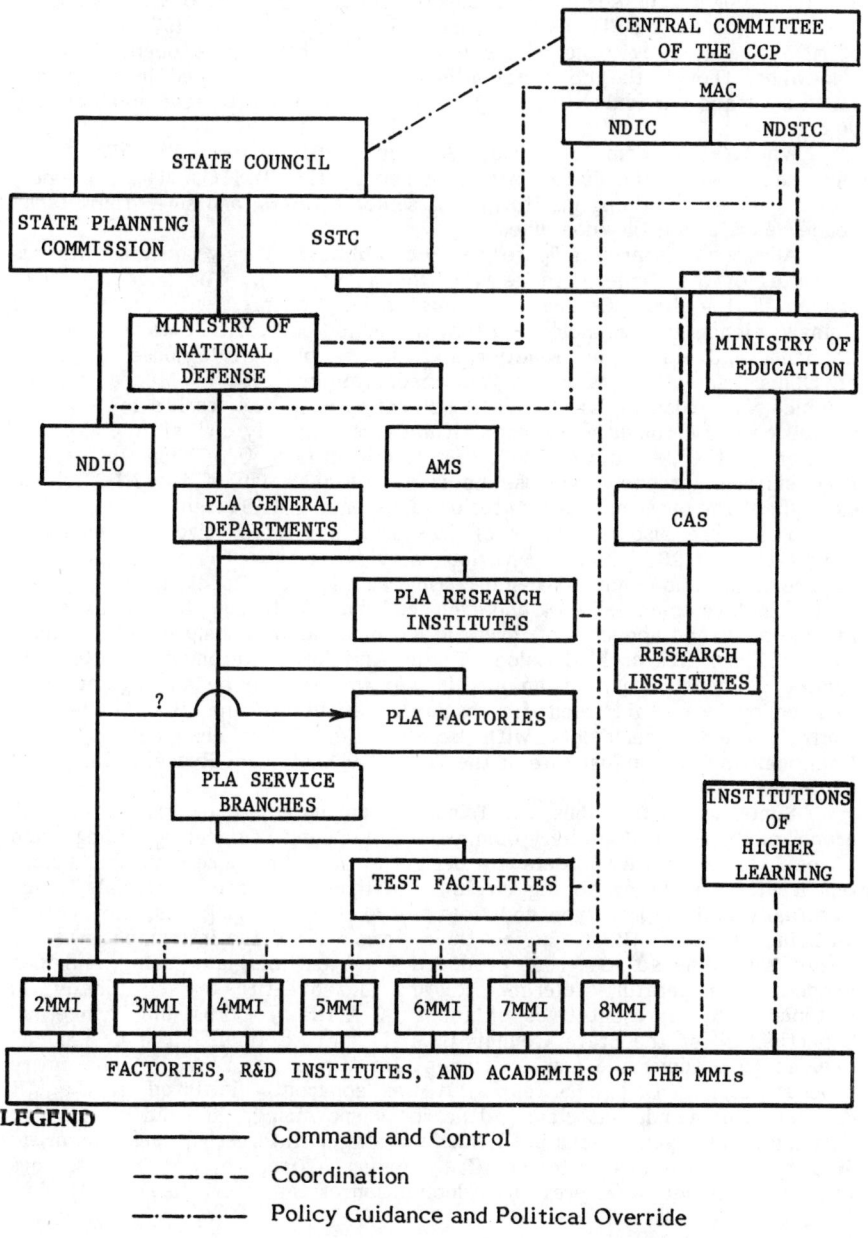

LEGEND
———— Command and Control
— — — — Coordination
—·—·—·— Policy Guidance and Political Override

and technical students. Many of these academies maintain ties with two or more MMIs.[98]

During the Cultural Revolution, the NDSTC, as an organ of the MAC, controlled virtually all schools even remotely connected with defense science and technology. The academies probably occupied the same position vis-a-vis the MMIs and the NDSTC as the research institutes.[99] Since 1971, the degree of NDSTC control over the relatively "civilian" schools has probably lessened somewhat, though the commission is probably still involved in manpower allocations and curriculum planning. MMI affiliations with academies clearly do continue.[100]

When the Academy of Military Science (AMS) was formed in 1958, it may have had most of the duties later assumed by the NDSTC. The AMS now serves only as a training institution for senior officers, and as a "think tank" concerned with military doctrine.[101]

Advanced research in "pure" science is almost entirely under the various institutes of the Chinese Academy of Sciences (CAS). The academy is an agency of the State Council, and was initially charged with managing all China's science and technology—a task it bungled badly.[102] It was stripped of its managerial and military functions in 1956, but continues to house the cream of China's scientific talent. The academy's Institute of Mechanics, for instance, is headed by Dr. Ch'ien Hsueh-sen, one of the world's leading jet-propulsion and aeronautics experts. While it is primarily civilian in character, the work of the CAS is often defense-related. In 1979, Dr. Ch'ien was seen in PLA uniform (probably because he is a vice-chairman of the NDSTC)—an example of the quasi-military status of some leading CAS scientists.

There are also a number of "research institutes" directly under the army's GSD, GRSD, and the various service arms. These provide "user requirements" and conduct service testing, as might be expected, but they also engage in developmental work and even trial manufacturing. Recent examples include published accounts of construction of a rapid decompression chamber by the Third Research Division of the Air Force Aeromedical Research Center,[103] construction of an auxiliary power system by an engineer unit assisted by "a certain scientific research institute of the PLA Engineering Corps,[104] and experiments with beach solidification chemicals by "The Chemical Application Institute of the Technical Equipment Research Institute" of the GRSD.[105]

Sometime in the 1950s, the Tsinan MR set up an ad hoc "triune research group" of the regional artillery command, Hua Chung Engineering College, and a local factory, with orders to design a new fire direction instrument (apparently a sight or aiming circle). "Without reference materials," they eventually built a prototype and field-tested it. Following this, they visited units in four other MRs "to solicit their views." Told the instrument was too heavy, this same ad hoc group produced a lighter fiberglass casing, and then conducted temperature tolerance testing and live-fire tests. Finally, in October 1978, representatives of the PLA Artillery Corps and "concerned departments" of the State Council (MMIs?) met to finalize the design and decided to produce the new instrument for the entire PLA.[106] The entire process took *at least twenty years*. It was apparently initiated by the MR Artillery Command, was clearly done "on a shoestring," and did not involve national-level organizations until the final stage. Interesting questions arise: Was this project allocated to the MR by Peking? If so, why were no resources allocated? If not, what prevented duplication of the effort elsewhere? How typical is this case?

A similar project involved development of a remote control system for an anti-aircraft gun. In this case, however, the task was assigned to an individual technician in an MR signal battalion. Though he initially knew nothing about the gun, he did have technical references, access to manufacturing facilities, and could travel widely to consult experts. When he finally succeeded in 1979, "his superiors dubbed it the '601' system and bestowed on him the honor of first class meritorious service."[107] There was no indication whether the entire PLA (or any part of it) adopted the system, however.

At still lower levels of command is true "mass innovation." A widely publicized recent example was an antitank rifle grenade developed by the "deputy chief of the ordnance section" of a regimental-level unit in the Lanchow MR. After two years of work, his prototype attracted attention, funding, and assistance from MR headquarters.[108] In 1979, the grenade was pronounced a success, and the inventor rewarded.

In all these cases, it appears the PLA personnel involved were working part-time, in ad hoc groups, on local initiative. The inevitable duplication of effort by countless unit-level "research" groups would seem to be inefficient, and their "innovations" are generally variants on existing designs rather than technical breakthroughs. Moreover, "mass innovation" smacks of radical "Maoism." The system (or rather, lack of a system) has produced unknown numbers of bizarre contraptions, which are used (if at all) only in their units of origin.[109] These must greatly complicate both logistical support and tactical employment. Despite these drawbacks, the GRSD launched a "major campaign to make full use of ... PLA unit innovations" in 1979.[110] This can only be attributed to persistence of the "walking on two legs" tradition, and to the generally low level of PLA technology.

THE IMPACT OF POLITICS

The early 1950s were devoted to reconstruction and the start of forced industrialization. The emphasis on heavy, and especially military, industry was urged both by the Korean War and by the influence of Soviet aid and advisors. There was remarkable progress, accompanied by an intensifying search for organizational forms more suited to Chinese society and ideology than the simple copying of Soviet experience.

As is well known, industrial production was badly disrupted by the Great Leap Forward. Moreover, considerable loss of producers' goods resulted from misuse and lack of proper maintenance. This, plus the diversion of capital and materials to such abortive schemes as the famous "backyard" blast furnaces, contributed to the economic disaster which forced a retreat to more moderate policies by 1961. Unlike industry, R&D was relatively immune from political interference during the GLF, and military R&D continued to advance. Military industry achieved remarkable results in the early 1960s.

The Great Proletarian Cultural Revolution

Defense industry and R&D were initially shielded from the Cultural Revolution, as well. As late as August 1966, a Central Committee directive specifically exempted scientific and technical personnel from the GPCR. Scientists were praised, even as other intellectuals were being assaulted. In 1967, however, the push from the radical left led to attacks on "bourgeois revisionism" in scientific work. Leading scientists were criticized for their foreign educations and their alleged reliance on foreign books and techniques, as well as their resistance to ideological control.

By mid-1967 the NDSTC and Nieh Jung-chen were under attack from two quarters. In August, the radicals of the Central Cultural Revolution Group sponsored a "Conference of Criticism and Struggle Against Revisionism" in the NDSTC as part of the attack on "capitalist roaders in the army." Despite an apparent "power seizure" in the NDSTC in January,[111] the commission had continued "business as usual" to the extent of actively recruiting aircraft and rocket designers and engineers in Germany.[112] The radicals could make a good case for claiming that Nieh was "suppressing class struggle" in the NDSTC.[113]

Taking advantage of the radical ideologues' offensive against the NDSTC, various interests in the defense MMIs, with Red Guard factions of their own, launched an attack on Nieh and the R&D system he dominated. Radical ideology and bureaucratic competition became entangled in a welter of factionalism, especially in the research institutes, academies, and experimental factories of the Sixth and Seventh MMIs. There was relative calm both in the large factories and in the "pure science" facilities. This isn't too surprising, since young intellectuals, universally the most volatile and factious elements in the GPCR, were concentrated in the institutes and academies. In April 1968, Chou En-lai told representatives of 7MMI factions, "You young intellectuals must learn to temper yourselves a bit in the revolutionary movement."[114]

This April 1968 conference was one of several which Chou and other top leaders held through the first half of the year, in a frustrating effort to bring peace and restored productivity to the defense industrial and scientific system. Despite such efforts, turmoil continued well into the summer. "Revolutionary Great Alliances" of all the factions in a particular organization were repeatedly formed at conferences in Peking, only to dissolve within hours of the representatives' return home. Published transcripts of these conferences leave no doubt that defense production suffered extensively (see Figure 6.1).[115] In May, armed clashes in a number of R&D academies in Peking reportedly claimed a number of lives.[116]

Defense Industry and R&D Since the Cultural Revolution

As we have already noted, one early result of the Cultural Revolution was that, in 1967, Su Yü took over both the NDIC and the NDIO. By the end of 1968, Nieh Jung-chen had clearly won out against the MMI factions. Su and Nieh, who now dominated defense science and industry, shared a perspective which soon became evident. By 1971, even *Hung Ch'i* was praising the achievements of highly specialized reseach personnel.[117] The controversy over the relationship of R&D versus production should have ended there. It did not, however, owing to the worsening shortage of technical manpower, on one hand, and the continuing demands of radical ideology, on the other.

Concentration of R&D work in the hands of a technical elite remained ideologically suspect. Moreover, the Cultural Revolution, which hailed the creative wisdom of the laboring masses, had resulted in the suspension of virtually all educational activities in China. When schools finally began to reopen, the ever-increasing need for scientists and technicians was to be met by a "revolutionized" educational system. Political, rather than academic, criteria determined which students went to college, while curricula were abbreviated and skewed toward "practical" low-technology skills.

Despite the institutional pre-eminence of the NDSTC since the GPCR, the trend until 1977 was away from advanced R&D, toward more production-related developmental work in the institutes, academies, and factories of the MMIs. "Three-in-one" teams of workers, cadres, and technicians in the factories were credited with most "new" products. Factories were expected to train their own technicians from among their own workers.[118] Moreover, schools and colleges were exhorted to set up factories and "undertake production tasks."[119]

Already by 1975, it required more trained personnel than were available just to absorb the technology that was then being purchased abroad. Even the internal expansion of industry was forcing the state to "rob Peter to pay Paul." Cadres from local government and the PLA were transferred to industrial enterprises, where they were admittedly "technically inexperienced," but had "high political consciousness and work very hard." Established factories were levied for veteran technicians and workers who served as "cadres of worker-teachers" in new ones.[120] To what extent these practices persist is not clear.

The worship of politics, production, and "practical" skills exacerbated the tendency to refine proven products, while failing to make really new technical departures. Pioneering breakthroughs in the US and USSR typically originate from "pure research." Yet that sort of research, by definition, is "divorced from production," and therefore was ideologically suspect up to 1977. Moreover, there are few qualified scientists who can undertake "pure research"—and those few are mostly foreign-trained and aging.

The educational and research systems atrophied badly from 1965 to 1976. Under such conditions, the science and technology situation only could have gone from bad to worse. The new leadership clearly recognized this, because in the fall of 1977 it initiated a complete reversal in the educational system: Competitive examinations were reinstated, and the requirement for labor between middle-school and college was dropped. But even this new commitment to education and research cannot begin to show results for several more years. Meanwhile, the narrow base of technical manpower will be China's most serious and inflexible military and economic constraint.

CURRENT DEVELOPMENTS AND THE FUTURE

R&D Reorganization

At the National Science Conference in March 1978, Teng Hsiao-p'ing spoke on a number of basic issues and outlined science and technology policies. There is a persistent anti-intellectualism in China, he said, but science and technology workers are *real* workers and are to be respected as such. Scientific and technical education is vital to China's future and is to be heavily emphasized. While the party committees of R&D organizations are still to "lead," they must recognize that the current stress is on modernization and defer to qualified experts on technical issues. An atmosphere of "letting a hundred flowers bloom" is to be encouraged in scientific and technical work and in "academic matters." A system of individual responsibility is to be instituted in R&D work, while organizations will be judged by their *results*, and by the technical personnel they train.[121]

Based on Teng's guidelines, reorganization of R&D institutions began, but has met resistance, particularly with respect to political interference by party committees.[122] Teng's critique, addressed to the internal reorganization of the institutes, apparently did not go far enough. In September 1979, *KMJP* complained that the entire R&D system needed consolidation. There is "organizational overlapping, duplication of research topics and many other questions .... China's 6000 [sic] independent research institutes, treble the 1965 figures ... should now consider readjustment to improve the work."[123]

Consolidation and coordination are intended to extend to defense-related R&D organizations. Military research units have better facilities and more qualified personnel, but have used excessive security measures as an excuse to avoid sharing data and coordinating and communicating with civilians. Now, maximum possible "civilian" work, as well as application of military research results to civilian purposes, is desirable.[124] Another aspect of the consolidation effort is in education, where some military technical schools (The National Defense College of Science and Technology, for example) are participating in the "key institutes admission [testing] program."[125]

One aspect of Chinese research work appears to be unchanged: "Research institutes should deal with topics within their specialty that serve production and bring economic results."[126] This emphasis on immediate "payoffs" is understandable in an underdeveloped economy, but produced the generally plodding and non-innovative quality of PRC technology in the 1960s and 1970s. Now that foreign trade is expanding, the "productive" emphasis makes more sense, since China can benefit from its status as a late-comer, especially in non-military and "gray area" technologies.

We can only speculate on the repercussions of the R&D reorganization at the top. As we have seen, the NDSTC system has favored advanced research from the beginning. Since military-related institutes will continue some advanced R&D (e.g., nuclear weapons) which cannot be imported, the overall shape of the system may not change drastically. Nieh Jung-chen was succeeded as director of the NDSTC in about 1975, by PLA Deputy Chief of Staff Chang Ai-p'ing, also a career commander. On the other hand, consolidation and increased coordination among military and civilian institutes will require more technical expertise and detailed management by the NDSTC, and closer coordination with the SSTC. In fact, Fang Yi, who is a full member of the Politburo and President of the CAS as well as Minister in Charge of the SSTC, now may have final authority over all research—military as well as civilian.

Industrial Reorganization

In August 1978, a National Machine Building Conference was convened to attack the inefficiencies of the "Maoist" structure of PRC industry. It was frankly admitted that industry was twenty to thirty years out of date, and that a primary reason was the inefficient "vertical" structure of countless small-scale "comprehensive" industrial enterprises. Managers were specifically criticized for "toying with the ideal of not having to ask for outside help."[127] That, of course, is what Maoist "self-sufficiency" was all about. Whether "big and comprehensive" or "small and comprehensive," such enterprises were "incapable of meeting the needs of modernized mass production."[128] The machine-building sector had a tremendous capacity which was being wasted because of "restricted small-scale production" and "managerial methods that are endemic in handicraft undertakings ... peasant economy and even peculiar to feudal bureaucracy."[129] The overall system, the delegates were told, was unplanned, inefficient, and "loose":

> Anyone can do whatever he pleases and do it his own way. The leadership is split. Each leader has his own policy. Each level makes additions to plans from higher levels. Each level withholds

some materials needed to fulfill production plans. Some leading departments even issue output targets which can never be fulfilled. There are too many makes and models of machinery.[130]

A related problem was only implied: The existing machine industry was organizationally ill-suited to the adaptation of foreign technology.

Chairman Hua's "instruction" for the conference neatly summarized the major reorganization that was to begin at once: "Be organized in accordance with the principle of coordination between specialized departments."[131] "Consolidation and centralization" are to displace "self-sufficiency" and decentralization. The implications are clear and far-reaching: Many plants will be closed or reorganized for more narrowly specialized production. Inevitably, bureaucratic oxen are being gored. Even within enterprises that survive consolidation, "jack-of-all-trades" cadres are to be replaced by "modern managers." Stiff resistance to industrial "readjustment" continues, despite determined efforts by the central authorities. A March 1981 report from Szechuan describes exactly the same problems the National Machine Building Conference decried in 1978.[132]

"Specialization" means increased movement of parts and subassemblies among plants, which requires much better standardization and quality control. October 1978 was designated "quality month" in support of the reorganization. By December, the farm machinery and automobile industries reportedly had completed the reorganization. It was estimated that three to five years would be required for the entire machine-building industry, however. It is indicative of the realism of this project that by 1985, it is planned that "most of the products will attain the world's technical and economic standards of the 1970s."[133] That is to say, they will be ten to fifteen years out of date, instead of twenty or thirty.

Such a comprehensive reorganization necessarily involves the defense industrial system. The self-contained "vertical" structure of the defense MMIs is precisely the sort of inefficient organization that is to be abolished. Hence, the coordinating and controlling functions of the NDIO must be greatly expanded, while some State Council-level authority must now enforce much closer interaction between defense and civilian enterprises. Such an authority was apparently created at the Fifth Plenum in February 1980. Po Yi-po was appointed to head the new State Machine Building Industry Commission, which will direct and coordinate all machine building and oversee the work of the eight MMIs.[134] Additional organizational groundwork was already laid at the Fifth NPC in March 1978, with the restoration of the SSTC and designation of several new defense MMI ministers. Some sort of high-level PLA reorganization is suggested by one reference to the "fourth department of the headquarters" of the General Staff—which seems to be related to military industry.[135] In a name-change which may be significant, the NDIO is now sometimes called the "Second Office of National Defense." Sometime before August 1978, Su Yü was succeeded as head of the NDIO ("Second office") by Hung Hsueh-chih, who was GRSD director in the 1950s.[136]

There is already a discernably new look to the defense MMIs (refer to Table 6.1): In the 3MMI, air force General Li Ch'i-ta'i was replaced (in March 1978) by Lü Tung, a civilian industrial manager. In the 4MMI, General Wang Cheng, who died in August 1978, was replaced by Ch'ien Min, a party bureaucrat from Szechuan. In the 5MMI, General Li Ch'eng-fang was replaced (March 1978) by Chang Chen, former Vice-Minister of Petroleum Industry. In the 6MMI, Admiral Fang Ch'iang was replaced (1977) by Pien Chiang, a civilian who had been vice-minister since 1963. In March 1978, Pien was replaced by Ch'ai Shu-fan, whose career has been in the State Planning Commission and foreign trade. In the 7MMI, General Sung Jen-ch'iung was replaced (23 February 1979) by Cheng T'ien-hsiang, a municipal party and government cadre from Peking. The new 8MMI, established in September 1979, was headed by Chiao Jo-yü, former ambassador to North Korea and a civilian cadre from Liaoning. Chiao left the 8MMI to become Mayor of Peking in March 1981. No successor has been identified.

The pattern is starkly clear: Military men have been replaced by career civilians, three of whom (Ch'ien Min, Cheng T'ien-hsiang, and Chiao Jo-yü) do not even have any background in industrial or economic work. Virtually the only common denominator of the new men is a record as effective administrators.

Only in the highly sensitive 2MMI is there still a minister from the army (General Liu Wei), and he may be in trouble: In February 1979, *AFP* erroneously (it seems) reported Liu being replaced by Liu Hsi-yao, the civilian Minister of Education who was also Liu Wei's predecessor in the 2MMI. In November 1979, there was a fascinating detailed report of unresolved political and administrative turbulence in the Shanghai Atomic Nuclear Research Institute, carried in *Wen Hui Pao*.[137] Problems were said to include lack of leadership in "professional matters," "no knowledgeable leader," and "factionalism" in the party committee. Publicizing such unresolved problems may well have been part of an effort to ease Liu Wei out in favor of a more technically expert minister. Moreover, recent PRC interest in nuclear power generation indicates the purely military character of the 2MMI is changing.[138]

Reassessment and Reconsolidation

Within the machine-building industry, the "eight character slogan," announced in mid-1979, reaffirmed the reorganization and goals announced in August 1978, but the priority of military industry was clearly lowered. Moreover, military plants were ordered to devote productive capacity in excess of PLA needs to the production of goods for civilian consumption and export, and were told to assist civilian industrial and agricultural units. This measure to "turn deficits into profits" in the usually under-utilized defense factories will go far to break down the long-standing separation of the military and civilian industrial sectors.[139] The next logical step would be to reassign redundant PLA plants to the relevant civilian ministries (e.g., transfer GRSD textile plants to the Textile Industry Ministry). There is no evidence that this has been attempted—the PLA still maintains its own independent but wasteful light industrial capacity. The NDIO may well come under closer supervision by the State Planning Commission, as well, probably through the new State Machine Building Industry Commission. Military research institutes also have been ordered to contribute to the development of the civilian sector.[140]

In such a context, it would be reasonable to expect a heated debate over economic and military priorities, but there has been little public evidence of one. While there are undoubtedly differences over details, the general course for the next few years is reasonably clear. For the foreseeable future, the PLA will have to make do with what it has, plus a few new high-priority items needed to meet the Soviet threat.[141]

The projected cost of bringing the PLA up to par with the Soviet Army is awesome. Edward Luttwak estimates it would cost five to seven billion US dollars to reequip the PLA with a modern main battle tank. "Commensurate" personnel carriers, mobile artillery, etc. would cost that much again.[142] In view of the revised 1980 defense budget of roughly sixteen billion yuan (about US $9.5 billion), it is clear that defense spending would have to double for even those first steps.[143]

Development of a domestic capability to produce a full range of up-to-date arms would cost much more, at least initially—to say nothing of the economic braking effect on the rest of the economy, to which Hsu Hsiang-ch'ien referred in the quotation above. In the long run, a self-sufficient national defense industry is still the Chinese goal, however. The "catalytic role" of foreign technology is officially recognized, and small purchases continue.[144]

Meanwhile, the Chinese are willing to acquire military technology anywhere they can—even in the United States. In April 1979, Teng told a US Congressional delegation that the PRC "would have the courage to buy modern weapons from the US if the US had the courage to sell them."[145] Constraints on foreign arms purchase, on the Chinese side at least, are no longer political, only economic and technical.

In the near future, there is prospect for only gradual improvement in PLA equipment. That prospect is bound to be a source of continued frustration for the military modernizers and "professional" defense planners. Moreover, the paucity of really advanced equipment will tend to slow the growth of PLA professionalism. Barring some unforeseen escalation in the perceived Soviet threat, the "old warriors" of the high command are intent upon this course. As they pass from the scene, however, there is likely to be an increasingly open "guns versus butter" debate between civilian economists and the post-1945 generations of the PLA officer corps.

NOTES

1. This discussion draws heavily on Arthur G. Ashbrook, ". . . An Economic Overview," in US Congress, Joint Economics Committee, *China: A Reassessment of the Economy*, 94th Congress (Washington, DC: GPO, 10 July 1975), pp. 20-51; and William Colby, et al., *Allocation of Resources in the Soviet Union and China* (Subcommittee on Priorities and Economy in Government of the Joint Economics Committee, US 93rd Congress, 2nd Session, Washington: GPO, 1974), pp. 44-77 ff.

2. Colby, et al., p. 43; and *CSM*, 22 August 1977, p. 11.

3. Sources on the economic impact of the Cultural Revolution are voluminous, but of varying reliability. Two Taiwan sources, despite the usual bias to show the PRC in the worst possible light, provide generally reliable data, if not interpretation: Ch'eng Chih-yuan, "Communist China's Transportation and Communications," *FCYP*, 2, No. 5 (1 July 1968), 81-83, trans. in *TCC*, No. 30 (*JPRS*, No. 46, 645), pp. 1-7; and Chi I-chai, "Influence of the Cultural Revolution's Impact on Industrial and Mining Enterprises" (three parts), *FCYP*, 2, Nos. 1, 2, and 3 (March, April, and May 1968), trans. (poorly) in *TCC*, No. 5 (*JPRS*, No. 45, 417), pp. 1-2, *TCC*, No. 18 (*JPRS*, No. 45, 741), pp. 12-29, and *TCC*, No. 19 (*JPRS*, No. 45, 823), pp. 22-42.

Red Guard sources, often quoting central leaders, reported damage, stoppages, and slowdowns. For example: "Premier Chou's Important Speech" (Excerpts), *Hsiao Ping [Little Soldier]* (Canton) No. 22 (17 February 1968), trans. in *SCMP*, No. 4134, pp. 3-4; *Kuan-yin Hung-ch'i [Kuan-yin Red*

Flag] (Canton), No. 5 (March 1968), trans. in *SCMP*, No. 4162, p. 9; and *Ta-ch'ing Kung-she [Ta-ch'ing Commune]* (Peking), 24 February 1967, trans. in *TCC:P&S*, No. 397 (*JPRS*, No. 41, 249), pp. 1-7.

The official press generally reported only in ambiguous terms, such as "an acute and fierce struggle" in an electronics plant (*JMJP*, October 1967, trans. in *SCMP*, No. 4039, p. 28). Occasionally, especially in retrospect, it has been more candid: *JMJP*, 25 July 1971, trans. in *CNA*, No. 854, p. 3, reported on the Fukien Provincial "San Ming" Iron and Steel Works as follows: "Before the establishment in December 1968 of the plant's revolutionary committee, this plant had been severely damaged by the counterrevolutionary revisionist line. Two high furnaces were out of action for a long time; the coke conversion installation was completely destroyed; nine of the ten chimneys fell down." Revelations in 1979-81 indicate this sort of destruction was not uncommon.

4. *Time*, 3 February 1975, p. 30; *Newsweek*, 3 February 1975, p. 29; "China's Capitalist Problems," *CSM*, 27 August 1975; *JMJP*, 15 July 1975, trans. in *SPRCP*, No. 5916, pp. 186-189; *PR*, No. 46 (12 November 1976), pp. 11-12; *KMJP*, 12 September 1974, trans. in *SPRCP*, No. 5710, pp. 7-8; *CSM*, 18 May 1977, p. 3; *CSM*, 7 June 1977, p. 34; *CSM*, 11 November 1977, p. 31; *CSM*, 31 December 1976, p. 26; *CSM*, 4 January 1977, p. 4; and *JMJP*, November 1976 (the last admitted unrest in factories in Fukien).

5. *K'o-hsueh T'ung-pao [Science Bulletin]*, No. 10 (1965), 875: "The technology of electronics . . . is first of all to satisfy the demands of national defense." Also see: *NCNA*, 13 October 1967, trans. in *SCMP*, No. 4043, p. 28; *NCNA*, 30 November 1967, trans. in *SCMP*, 4072, p. 20; *NCNA*, 22 June 1968, trans. in *SCMP*, No. 4207, pp. 20-21; *NCNA*, 3 September 1974, trans. in *SPRCP*, No. 5696, p. 23; and *CNA*, No. 976 (11 October 1974), p. 4.

6. *CNA*, No. 854 (10 September 1972), 1-2. For a typical article, see "Criticism of 'The Supremacy of Electronics,'" *JMJP*, 12 August 1971, p. 2.

7. For an example of this hypothesis, see Whitson, p. 552.

8. For example: *NCNA* (Shenyang), 31 December 1967, trans. in *SCMP*, No. 4092, p. 35; and *CNA*, No. 976 (11 October 1974), p. 4. For steel production statistics, see *CSM*, 10 March 1976, p. 3; *CSM*, 19 August 1977, p. 14; and A. H. Usack and J. D. Egan, "China's Iron and Steel Industry," in *China: A Reassessment . . .*, p. 276.

9. Wu Hsiu-ch'uan, a PLA Deputy Chief of Staff, told Drew Middleton of the *NYT* that, "The PLA lags behind the equipment used by the West and the Soviet Union because industry is backward. We do not have first-grade steel." *NYT*, 1 December 1976, p. A16.

10. "Building Up Agriculture in Line with Chairman Mao's Thinking," *HC*, No. 7 (1975).

11. *PR*, No. 20 (17 May 1974), 15-18.

12. See the discussion of this point in Jack H. Harris, "Politics of National Security in China," *Problems of Communism*, 28, No. 2 (March-April 1979), 65.

13. Hsu Ti-hsin (Director of Institute of Economics of the Chinese Academy of Social Sciences), colloquium at University of California, Berkeley, 12 December 1979. Also see *AFP*, 8 March 1979, in *FBIS*, No. 48, pp. A18-A19; and *CSM*, 27 March 1979, p. B14.

14. *HC*, No. 10 (2 October 1979), 28-33, trans. in *FBIS*, No. 203, p. L13.

15. See three thoughtful studies on the economics of military development in Section IV of *China: A Reassessment . . .*, Also see a CIA report cited in *CSM*, 30 August 1977, p. 2.

16. Angus M. Fraser, "The Utility of Alternative Strategic Postures to the People's Republic of China," in *China: A Reassessment*..., p. 457.
17. Colby, et al., p. 43.
18. Usack and Egan, p. 284; Hsu Ti-hsin; and *CSM*, 10 November 1976, p. 9.
19. Hans Heymann, "Acquisition and Diffusion of Technology in China," in *China: A Reassessment*..., p. 679.
20. Ibid., p. 705. On the persistence of anti-intellectual attitudes in 1979, see *NCNA*, 23 November 1979, in *FBIS*, No. 227, pp. L8-L9. For an excellent study on the human and managerial aspects of "modernization," see Richard P. Suttmeier, "Politics, Modernization, and Science in China," *Problems of Communism*, 30 (January-February 1981), 22-36.
21. On management problems, see: *CSM*, 30 August 1977, p. 2; and *CSM*, 27 October 1977, p. 5.
22. For example: *NCNA*, 23 July 1974, trans. in *SPRCP*, No. 5667, p. 183; and *NCNA*, 19 and 20 March 1975, trans. in *SPRCP*, No. 5822, pp. 56-60.
23. For example: see *KMJP*, 24 August 1978, trans. in *FBIS*, No. 174, pp. E13-E14.
24. Barry A. Walrath, *China: Defense Industrial Capabilities and Limitations* (Air Command and Staff College Research Study, May 1977, reprinted by US Defense Logistics Agency, September 1977), pp. 16-17.
25. *JMJP*, 3 September 1978, trans. in *FBIS*, No. 178, pp. E28-E29; and *JMJP*, 28 October 1980, p. 3, trans. in *FBIS*, No. 222, pp. L7-L8.
26. James R. Blaker, "The Production of Conventional Weapons," *The Military and Political Power in China in the 1970's*, ed. Whitson (New York: Praeger, 1972), p. xxix.
27. Li Shui-ch'ing was Minister of Light Industry until 17 January 1975, when he was reassigned as Political Commissar of the Nanking Military Region. Chang Wen-pi was Minister of Water Conservancy and Power until the same date. He was reassigned as Commander of the Chehkiang Military District.
28. Richard J. Latham, "China's Defense Industrial System: Order or Disorder?" Paper presented to Asian Studies on the West Coast 1975 Conference, Honolulu, June 1975, pp. 1-4. I am grateful to Richard Baum for information on MMI overlapping.
29. *China Science Notes*, 1, No. 2 (September 1970), 2.
30. As early as spring 1965, the director of the political department of the 7MMI attended a working conference of political commissars called by the PLA General Political Department. This indicates that the uniformed PLA controlled political work in the MMIs prior to the GPCR. *TFYL*, 1 May 1967, trans. in *SCMP*, NO. 4005, pp. 1-8.
31. Kenneth R. Whiting, *The Chinese Communist Armed Forces*, (Maxwell AFB, AL: Air University, 1974).
32. For a complete list of PRC nuclear tests through 1978, see *Chinese War Machine*, p. 174. The official PRC list (*NCNA*, 24 September 1979, in *FBIS*, No. 186, p. L15) omits three tests, two of which were known to be partial failures. On tactical nuclear weapons, see Gerald Segal, "China's Nuclear Posture for the 1980s," *Survival*, 23, No. 1 (January-February 1981), 11-12; and William T. Tow and Douglas T. Stuart, "China's Military Turns to the West," *International Affairs* (Spring 1981).
33. There is a persistent misconception that the 3MMI produces "munitions," which apparently originated with Chu-yuan Cheng, in "Growth and Structural Change in the Chinese Mainland Machine-Building Industry, 1952-

1966," *CQ*, No. 41 (January-March 1970), 26-57. Despite Latham's 1975 evidence to the contrary (p. 4), Chu's error was perpetuated by Bohdan and Maria Szuprowicz, in their *Doing Business with China* (New York: John Wiley, 1978). A Chinese aviation industry delegation to England was led by 3MMI Minister Lü Tung: *NCNA* (English), 13 December 1978, in *FBIS*, No. 241, p. A22. Also note *CSM*, 8 February 1977, p. 4.

34. The following draws upon the excellent summary in Nikolai Cherikov, "The Shenyang F-9 Combat Aircraft," *International Defense Review*, 9, No. 5 (October 1976), p. 714; and the more detailed but less reliable accounts in "Chinese . . . Goliath," especially p. 307; Bueschel, passim; and *HTCS*, No. 49 (December 1980), 8-10. For pictures of aircraft production lines, see *CFCHP*, No. 7 (1980), 14-17, in *China Report*, No. 113 (5 September 1980), 14-21.

35. Hans Heymann, Jr., *China's Approach to Technology Acquisition: Part I—The Aircraft Industry*, Rand Report R-1537-ARPA (Santa Monica, CA: Rand, February 1975). Micheal Westlake points out that the "Soviet designs" copied by China in the 1950s were themselves largely outdated copies of Western designs: "How do you update copies of a copy of a copy?" *FEER*, 7 March 1980, pp. 61-62.

36. Until 1979, Western observers erroneously identified the Chinese "FISHBED" as "F8." See *AWST* (10 Setpember 1979), p. 19.

37. A variety of dates have been reported for suspension of PRC "FISHBED" production: 1966 ("Chinese . . . Goliath"); 1970 and 1974 (*Jane's Aircraft*, 1978-79 ed.); 1971 (*World Combat Aircraft Directory*, William Polmar, ed. [Garden City, NY: Doubleday, 1976], p. 19).

38. Ibid. See pictures in *CP*, No. 1 (1979), 40-41; *Chinese War Machine*, pp. 122 and 139; and *HTCS*, No. 30 (April 1979), 4.

39. Indian military sources reported Chinese-made "BADGERs" in Pakistani service in 1973. *Jane's Aircraft*, 1978-79 ed., p. 29 claims limited production of both the "BADGER" and "BEAGLE" continues. Also see "Chinese . . . Goliath," p. 306. On parts for Egypt, see *HTCS*, No. 49 (December 1980), p. 8 of Supplement.

40. US Defense Secretary Brown was told the PRC "ATOLL" was copied from an American "Sidewinder" captured from Taiwan (*Newsweek*, 21 January 1980, p. 51). The Soviets copied their "ATOLL" from a "Sidewinder" stolen in Germany. On current developments, see *HTCS*, No. 49 (December 1980), 14-15.

41. Peking Dom. Svc., 31 July 1979, trans. in *FBIS*, No. 150, pp. L9-L10.

42. Walrath, pp. 19-20.

43. The contract was signed in October 1979, and the first doors delivered in February 1981. *NCNA* (English), 25 February 1981, in *FBIS*, No. 037, p. B3.

44. "Boeing, Going . . . Gone," *FEER*, 26 October 1979, p. 5; *HTCS*, No. 44 (July 1980), 8; *HTCS*, No. 49 (December 1980), 9; and *AFP* (Hong Kong), 15 January 1981, in *FBIS*, No. 010, p. L8.

45. Walrath, pp. 20-21. On the Spey engine, see *Jane's Aircraft*, 1971-72 ed., p. 633; *Jane's Aircraft*, 1978-79 ed., p. 29; *AWST*, 19 January 1976, p. 19; and *AWST*, 12 July 1977, p. 16.

46. *NCNA* (English), 31 October 1979, in *FBIS*, No. 213, p. G2.

47. *Ming Pao* (Hong Kong), 14 April 1981.

48. Cherikov, p. 716; "Chinese . . . Goliath," p. 306; and *Jane's Aircraft*, 1978-79 ed., p. 29. Also note plans to manufacture "a new jet aircraft" near Peking, in Peking Dom. Svc., 16 October 1979, trans. in *FBIS*, No. 205, p. L15; *HTCS*, No. 49 (December 1980), 14-15; *China Business Review*, 7, No. 4 (July-

August 1980), 25; and *FEER*, 7 March 1980, p. 64.

49. *The Times* (London), 17 August 1978, p. 15; *CSM*, 20 November 1978, p. 11; *NCNA*, 6 December 1978, in *FBIS*, No. 236, p. A16; *AFP*, 25 February 1979, in *FBIS*, No. 39, p. A32; *CSM*, 6 March 1979, p. 6; *FEER*, 16 November 1979, p. 21; and *FEER*, 7 March 1980, pp. 62-63.

50. *FEER*, 16 November 1979, p. 21. For an excellent analysis, see Tow & Stuart, "China's Military Turns to the West."

51. *HTCS*, No. 26 (December 1978), 13-18; *CSM*, 19 January 1978, p. 2; *AWST*, 10 September 1979, p. 19; *Financial Times* (London), 21 September 1979, p. 1. It is possible that China has obtained a MiG-25 "FOXBAT" from Libya: Tom Weber, "The Strange Capital of World Terrorism," *San Francisco Chronicle*, 9 October 1978, pp. 1, 6, and 7.

52. Bruce Swanson, "An Introduction to Chinese Command, Control and Communications," *Signal*, 32, No. 8 (May-June 1978), 50 and 52; and *Handbook*, pp. A-33 to A-35 (the latter is not wholly accurate). On recent developments of large-scale integrated circuits, see *NCNA*, 30 October 1980.

53. *HTCS*, No. 30 (April 1979), 6-7 and 61.

54. Tsinan Shantung Prov. Svc., 18 September 1979, trans. in *FBIS*, No. 185, p. O6.

55. Hofei Anhui Prov. Svc., 18 September 1979, trans. in *FBIS*, No. 184, p. O1.

56. Swanson, p. 53.

57. *CSM*, 26 September 1980.

58. Ibid.; *CSM*, 25 October 1979, p. 9; Banning Garrett, "China Policy and the Strategic Triangle," in *Eagle Entangled: American Foreign Policy in a Complex World* (Longman, May 1979), pp. 234-235; *FEER*, 29 December 1978, pp. 42 and 44; and Karen Berney, "Dual-Use Technology Sales," *China Business Review*, 7, No. 4 (July-August 1980), 23-26.

59. For a brief illustrated survey of 5MMI production, see *HTCS*, No. 51 (February 1981), 8-11.

60. *FEER*, 14 July 1978, p. 26.

61. *HTCS*, No. 27 (January 1979), 34; *Chinese War Machine*, p. 121; *HTCS*, No. 28 (February 1979), 38.

62. *PR*, No. 3 (19 January 1968), 15-17; and *NCNA* (Shanghai), 14 May 1968, trans. in *SCMP*, No. 4182, pp. 24-25.

63. *PR*, No. 16 (18 April 1969), 34-35; *NCNA* (Shenyang), 11 August 1974, trans. in *SPRCP*, No. 5680, pp. 115-116; and *NCNA* (Shenyang), 4 September 1974, trans. in *SPRCP*, No. 5697, pp. 66-67.

64. *NCNA*, 11 January 1974, trans. in *SCMP*, No. 5539, p. 51; *Jane's Ships*, 1975-76 ed., p. 79; *Chinese War Machine*, p. 166; *Aktuelt* (Copenhagen) 10 August 1978, p. 14, trans. in *FBIS*, No. 57, p. A28; *NCNA*, 19 August 1978, in *FBIS*, No. 175, p. A20; *NCNA*, 10 August 1974, trans. in *SPRCP*, No. 5680, p. 114; and *NCNA*, 21 September 1979, trans. in *FBIS*, No. 186, p. L2.

65. Communique on 1980 by the State Statistical Bureau, *NCNA*, 29 April 1981, trans. in *FBIS*, 29 April 1981, p. K8; and *FEER*, 7 November 1980.

66. *AFP*, 14 October 1978, in *FBIS*, No. 201, pp. A14-A15. On a recent deal involving German technology in Shanghai shipyards, see Peking Radio, 18 January 1981, in *FBIS*, 21 January 1981, p. G6.

67. Harry Harding, *China and the U.S.* (New York: Foreign Policy Association, 1979), p. 25.

68. Two major rival Red Guard factions within the 7MMI published the tabloids *Fei Ming Ti* and *Tsao-fan Yu-li*. These provided a wealth of information on the missile industry and the entire military industrial and research

system. Both appeared frequently in *SCMP* in 1967-68.

69. Peking Dom. Svc., 4 January 1979, in *FBIS*, No. 8, p. E11. Typically, PRC sources refer to military rockets as "guided missiles," even when they are actually ballistic. For a thoughtful summary of the PRC strategic missile program, see *Jane's Weapons Systems*, 1977 ed., pp. 3-4.

70. *Tung Hsiang [The Trend]*, No. 12 (September 1979), 14-15; *KYODO*, 2 October 1979, in *FBIS*, No. 192, pp. L34-L35; and *Ming Pao*, 20 December 1979, p. 1.

71. *United News of India*, cited in *KYODO*, 7 September 1978, in *FBIS*, No. 174, p. E4. Development of a solid fuel suitable for strategic missiles was announced in Ch'ang Ch'un Kirin Prov. Svc. (28 December 1979), trans. in *FBIS*, No. 002, p. L20. This has been announced before, and should be taken with a grain of salt.

72. On the Chinese space program, see *FEER*, 13 October 1978, pp. 13-14; *NCNA* (English), 24 September 1979, in *FBIS*, No. 186, p. L14; *AFP*, 22 February 1979, in *FBIS*, No. 38, p. E2; *AFP*, 24 July 1979, in *FBIS*, No. 144, p. L9; *AFP*, 30 October 1979, in *FBIS*, No. 193, p. L27; *KYODO*, 11 November 1979, in *FBIS*, No. 220, pp. L22-L23; and *Kwang Chiao Chi [Wide Angle]*, No. 82 (16 July 1979), 24-26. On the May 1980 tests, see *JMJP*, Extra 18 May 1980; *KYODO*, 31 May 1980, in *FBIS*, No. 108, p. L13; *CSM*, 22 May 1980, p. 2; *NCNA*, 23 May 1980, in *FBIS*, No. 103, p. L8; *AFP*, 18 May 1980, in *FBIS-ASIA AND PACIFIC*, No. 98, p. M1; *HTCS*, No. 43 (June 1980), 13-15; and *HTCS*, No. 48 (November 1980), 41-44.

73. Justin Galen, "U.S.'s Toughest Message to the USSR," *Armed Forces Journal*, February 1979, p. 32.

74. *NCNA*, 13 September 1979, trans. in *FBIS*, No. 180, p. L1; and *China Business Review*, 7, No. 4 (July-August 1980), 25.

75. *Ming Pao*, 8 March 1979, p. 1; and *HTCS*, No. 30 (April 1979), 58-61.

76. *CFCHP*, No. 9 (1979), 6-9, trans. in *China Report*, No. 39, pp. 54-56. For details see my "New Chinese Sagger," *Infantry*, 71, No. 1 (January-February 1981), 11-13.

77. *HTCS*, No. 41 (April 1980), 54-55.

78. "Circular of the State Council and the Central Military Commission Forbidding Exchange of Revolutionary Experience in . . . the Industrial System for National Defense" (4 February 1967), reprinted in *CCP Documents: 1966-67*, pp. 231-232.

79. Blaker, pp. 223-226.

80. For the economics of this, see Nicholas R. Lardy, "Economic Planning in the PRC: Central-Provincial Fiscal Relations," in *China: A Reassessment* . . . , pp. 94-115. My personal experience with Chinese small arms in Vietnam was that parts often were not interchangeable.

81. *NCNA*, 1 August 1978, trans. in *FBIS*, No. 150, pp. L10-L11.

82. "Comrade Chou En-lai—Faithful Executor of Chairman Mao's Military Thinking," *JMJP*, 30 July 1978, excerpted in *NCNA*, 30 July 1978, trans. in *FBIS*, No. 152, p. E10.

83. Chou En-lai (20 April 1968) said Lin Piao had ordered Su Yü to "handle all defense production." Chou also identified Su as head of NDIO. *Tzu-liao Chuan-chi* (Canton) n.d. (1968), trans. in *SCMM*, No. 631, pp. 1-27.

84. Walrath, pp. 10-11. See references to provincial and municipal NDIO branches in: Wuhan Hupeh Prov. Svc., 11 October 1979, trans. in *FBIS*, No. 199, p. P3; Sian Shensi Prov. Svc., 21 October 1978, trans. in *FBIS*, No. 206, pp. M2-M4; and *China Report*, No. 14 (7 September 1979), p. 10.

85. This discussion draws from Latham, pp. 6-10. The quotation is from

p. 8.
86. *CQ*, No. 74 (June 1978), 463; and *DPA* (Hamburg), 18 August 1978, trans. in *FBIS*, No. 161, p. A27.
87. Existence of the NDSTC was revealed only in 1966, so the exact year of its creation (circa 1958-61) is uncertain. This discussion draws on Latham, pp. 9-16.
88. Latham, p. 16.
89. Ibid., p. 11.
90. *Tzu-liao Chuan-chi* (Canton), n.d. (1968), trans. in *SCMM*, No. 631, pp. 1-4.
91. "Report on Lo's Mistakes," II, p. 17.
92. "Counter-Revolutionary . . . Defense Research Repudiated," *NCNA,*, 27 August 1967.
93. Lo was officially purged on 16 May 1966. Ho was a victim of the "January Storm" in 1967. The history of Lo's role in R&D and military industry was rewritten (favorably) in honor of his funeral: *KMJP*, 13 August 1978, trans. in *FBIS*, No. 162, pp. E19-E20; and *NCNA*, 17 August 1978, in *FBIS*, No. 161, pp. E2-E3.
94. *Tzu-liao Chuan-chi* (Canton), n.d. (1968), trans. in *SCMM*, No. 631, pp. 25-26.
95. Ibid., pp. 19-26; USCGDLO; and *TFYL* (12 May 1967), trans. in *SCMP*, No. 4007, pp. 10-11.
96. *NCNA*, 29 May 1978, in *FBIS*, No. 106, pp. E18-E22.
97. Latham, p. 13.
98. For example, the Harbin Military Engineering College was identified with the 7MMI during the GPCR. Its commandant in 1968 was Liu Chu-ying, a naval officer. The college probably is connected with the 6MMI, as well. For a partial listing of academies and their MMI affiliations, see my *The Politics of Chinese Military Development: 1945-1977* (Ph.D. dissertation, University of Washington, 1978, reprinted Ann Arbor, MI: University Microfilms, 1979), p. 565.
99. Chou En-lai referred to schools "under" the NDSTC in *TCC:P&S*, No. 391 (*JPRS*, No. 40, 488), pp. 20-23.
100. *NCNA*, 19 August 1978, in *FBIS*, No. 162, p. E3.
101. Latham, p. 10 and private correspondence. Also see Yeh Chien-ying, in *PR*, No. 12 (24 March 1978), 6-9.
102. Latham, pp. 6-7.
103. Peking Dom. Svc., 27 September 1979, in *FBIS*, No. 192, pp. L28-L29; and Peking Radio to Taiwan, 1 June 1978, trans. in *FBIS*, No. 110, p. C1.
104. Peking Dom. Svc., 25 April 1978, trans. in *FBIS*, No. 88, pp. E22-E23.
105. *NCNA*, 2 August 1979, in *FBIS*, No. 155, p. L17.
106. Peking Dom. Svc., 25 October 1979, trans. in *China Report*, No. 33 (14 November 1979), 28-29.
107. *CFCHP*, No. 1 (1979), p. 2, trans. in *China Report*, No. 14 (7 September 1979), p. 24.
108. *JMJP*, 4 September 1979, p. 1, trans. in *FBIS*, No. 178, pp. L16-L17; Peking Dom. Svc., 18 August 1979, trans. in *FBIS*, No. 167, p. L19; and *HTCS*, No. 44 (July 1980), pp. 6-7.
109. For two good examples, see the self-propelled anti-aircraft gun in *AFV-G2 Magazine*, 5, No. 12 (May-June 1977), 14-16; and the double-barreled perversion of the Type-69 ATGL in *CP*, No. 8 (1977), 31.
110. Peking Dom. Svc., 17 December 1979, trans. in *FBIS*, No. 245, pp.

L7-L8.
111. *Hung Ch'i [Red Flag]* (the Red Guard tabloid) (Peking), No. 6 (18 January 1967), 4, trans. in *TCC:P&S*, No. 391 (*JPRS*, No. 40, 488), pp. 20-23.
112. Bueschel, p. 98.
113. *Chung-hsueh Hung-wei-ping [Middle School Red Guard]* (Canton) No. 8 (July 1968), trans. in *SCMP*, No. 4326, pp. 1-2.
114. Quoted in *Tzu-liao Chuan-chi* (Canton), n.d. (1968), trans. in *SCMM*, No. 631, pp. 19-20.
115. See numerous examples in ibid.; *Hsiao Ping* (Canton), No. 22 (17 February 1968), trans. in *SCMP*, No. 4134, pp. 1-5; and *Chiu-i-liu T'ung-hsun [916 Bulletin]* (Canton), August 1968, trans. in *SCMP*, No. 4240, p. 9.
116. For a recently published version of such events, see Sian Shensi Prov. Svc., 21 October 1978, trans. in *FBIS*, No. 206, pp. M2-M4.
117. *HC*, No. 11 (1 October 1971), 61 ff.
118. *KMJP*, 24 December 1973, trans. in *SCMP*, No. 5538, pp. 1 ff.
119. *China Science Notes*, 1, No. 4 (September 1970), 1.
120. *NCNA*, 19 March 1975, trans. in *SPRCP*, No. 5822, p. 60.
121. *PR*, No. 12 (24 March 1978), 9-18.
122. *KMJP*, 13 September 1978, p. 1, trans. in *FBIS*, No. 185, pp. E1-E2.
123. Translated by *NCNA*, 26 September 1979, in *FBIS*, No. 188, p. 11.
124. *KMJP*, 22 July 1979, p. 2, trans. in *FBIS*, No. 154, pp. L17-L19.
125. *Wen-hui-Pao*, 31 August 1979, trans. in *FBIS*, No. 184, p. L9.
126. *KMJP*, trans. in *NCNA*, 26 September 1979, in *FBIS*, No. 188, p. 11; and Peking Dom. Svc., 10 January 1981, trans. in *FBIS*, No. 008, p. L15.
127. Peking Dom. Svc., 13 October 1978, trans. in *FBIS*, No. 201, p. E12.
128. *NCNA*, 19 September 1978, trans. in *FBIS*, No. 185, p. E4.
129. *NCNA* (English), 20 September 1978, in *FBIS*, No. 185, p. E8.
130. Ibid., p. E6.
131. Quoted by *NCNA*, 20 September 1978, trans. in *FBIS*, No. 185, p. E6.
132. Chengtu Szechuan Prov. Svc., 7 March 1981, trans. in *FBIS*, No. 045, p. Q1. Also see Peking Dom. Svc., 13 March 1981, trans. in *FBIS*, No. 050, p. L7.
133. *PR*, No. 48 (1 December 1978), 19.
134. *China Business Review*, 7, No. 2 (March-April 1980), 42 and 45.
135. Wang Cheng, the 4MMI Minister who died in 1978, was also director of this "fourth office": *NCNA*, 19 August 1978, in *FBIS*, No. 168, p. E3.
136. *NCNA*, 25 February 1979, in *FBIS*, No. 39, p. A33; and *NCNA*, 20 December 1979, trans. in *FBIS*, No. 250, p. L14. On Hung Hsueh-chih, see Whitson, p. 99.
137. *Wen Hui Pao*, 28 November 1979, p. 1, trans. in *FBIS*, No. 249, p. O4-O9.
138. *CSM*, 5 December 1978, p. 11; *CSM*, 15 December 1978, p. 11.
139. *NCNA*, 30 July 1979, trans. in *FBIS*, No. 152, pp. L2-L3; *NCNA*, 1 August 1979, trans. in *FBIS*, No. 150, pp. L10-L11; Shenyang Liaoning Prov. Svc., 31 July 1979, trans. in *FBIS*, No. 155, p. S4; Kunming Yunnan Prov. Svc., 20 August 1979, trans. in *FBIS*, No. 166, pp. Q1-Q2; *NCNA*, 6 September 1979, in *FBIS*, No. 176, pp. L15-L17; *NCNA*, 19 September 1979, trans. in *FBIS*, No. 189, p. P6; *NCNA*, 4 October 1979, trans. in *China Report*, No. 29 (29 October 1979), 55-56; Wuhan Hopeh Prov. Svc., 11 October 1979, trans. in *FBIS*, No. 199, p. P3; and *NCNA*, 3 February 1981, trans. in *FBIS*, No. 022, p. L22.
140. *KMJP*, 22 July 1979, trans. in *FBIS*, No. 154, pp. L17-L19.
141. Deputy Chief of Staff Wu Hsiu-ch'uan, cited in *AFP*, 3 May 1979, in *FBIS*, No. 88, p. G1; and *Mainichi Shimbun* (Tokyo), 9 September 1979, p. 4.

142. Costs are in 1978 dollars. Edward N. Luttwak, "Problems of Military Modernization for Mainland China," *I and S*, 14: No. 7 (July 1978), pp. 60 and 65.

143. The original 1980 defense budget was 19.3 billion yuan: See Wang Ping-chien's "Report on Financial Work" to the 3rd Session 5th NPC in *BR*, No. 39 (29 September 1980), pp. 11-23. "Defense, administration, and nonprofitable enterprises" were cut by an additional 6.4 billion yuan in March 1981: See Yao Yi-lin's report to the NPC Standing Committee in *NCNA*, 7 March 1981, trans. in *FBIS*, No. 045, p. L11 ("nonprofitable enterprises" include heavy industry). On the question of what the defense budget does and does not include, see *Military Balance*, 1979-80 ed., p. 61. For an interesting discussion of this point, and other issues raised in this chapter, see Angus M. Fraser, "Military Modernization in China," *Problems of Communism*, 28, Nos. 5-6 (September-December 1979), 34-49.

144. In January 1980, the PRC reportedly purchased five Field Artillery Control Equipment systems from a British firm, for about one million pounds: *Business China* (Hong Kong), 19 January 1980, p. 2.

145. Quoted in Robert N. Gainsburgh, "China Touches the Tigers' Bottoms," *Air Force*, June 1979, pp. 41-45.

7
Personnel Management in the PLA

INTRODUCTION

Having considered the organization and armament of the PLA, and its prospects for further technological modernization, we now turn to its personnel. This chapter briefly examines recruiting, promotion, assignment, motivation, and the command system. We will analyze some of the interrelationships among these factors. Finally, recent trends in personnel management are assessed, and some projections of the future of the Chinese officer corps are offered.

PERSONNEL MANAGEMENT

Recruiting

The PLA normally demobilizes twenty to twenty-five percent of its personnel annually and recruits commensurate replacements.[1] The exact number of recruits is determined not only by PLA needs, but by China's overall economic, social, and political situation. Until March 1978, the Military Service Law of 1955 was the legal basis for conscription, although there were significant deviations from it in practice. The "Decision on the System of Military Service" of 7 March 1978, which modified the 1955 system, is currently in force.[2]

The Ministry of National Defense (MND) supervises the annual draft, which takes place from November through February.[3] The total national quotas for the ground forces, certain police units,[4] navy, and air force are determined by the MAC and the State Council, and are subdivided among the provinces. These provincial quotas are generally prorated on the basis of military-aged population, but may be modified to account for pertinent demographic variations. For example, quotas were disproportionately large in national minority areas in 1975-76 because of a drive to recruit more minorities. Air force quotas tend to be higher in urban areas owing to high educational standards, etc. The quotas are broken down and assigned, in turn, to communes.[5] MR commanders sometimes specify additional requirements or standards for their regions, supplementing those of the MND.

Initial selection is outside direct military control. In 1949-79, PLA service was highly regarded throughout China and was sought after. There was little difficulty in finding volunteers. In fact, there was a continuing problem of some parents helping "their sons and daughters enlist in the army through private connections [*kuan-hsi*]," a practice known as "entering by the back door." The problem faced by local party committees was not recruiting, but screening. In the early 1970s, communes in Kwangtung, for example, had to present only five or ten candidates per year, of whom only two or three were eventually inducted.[6]

In the 1979 and 1980 conscription periods, however, volunteers have not been so forthcoming nor as enthusiastic. This is partially because PLA prestige has diminished somewhat, but is also owing to the increased attractiveness of civilian careers, especially in science and technology. The PLA no longer automatically attracts the brightest and best of Chinese youth. Among peasants, a disincentive in 1980-81 is the new "responsibility system" of rural production. Peasant households now stand to profit in direct proportion to their own production. Moreover, there is a wide-spread suspicion that the "responsibility system" will cause a breakdown in the communal welfare system which heretofore guaranteed "preferential treatment" to "military families." For the head of a peasant household, there is now a strong economic incentive to keep a strong young son at home. It is indicative of the diminished attractiveness of military service that Changsha Radio reported, in October 1980, that, "Many cadres have taken the lead in encouraging and supporting their sons and daughters to report for enlistment."[7] Thus, PLA enlistment is viewed as something of a noble sacrifice for a cadre's child, whereas four years ago it was an advantage to be sought "by the back door."

This new situation should not be exaggerated. While the army's prestige, and the attractiveness of military service, are significantly lower than they were a few years ago, both remain incomparably higher, especially among peasants, than in Western Europe or North America. PLA service is still the best hope for an ambitious peasant to escape the village, learn a skill, join the party, and/or become a cadre. Military academies offer opportunities to educated youngsters, as well. The army could undoubtedly find plenty of enthusiastic volunteers, but for the requirements to maintain regional balance and to get sufficiently educated people. The conscription quota system requires a certain number of recruits from areas where military service is no longer highly regarded. Well-educated urban youths, in particular, now tend to avoid the PLA in favor of college and civilian careers.

The People's Armed Department (PAD) of the administrative unit, working through the party committee, publicizes the conscription drive and investigates prospective recruits. Those whom they select are then given a stringent physical examination by a PLA doctor. Final selection is made by the Military Subdistrict (MSD) headquarters. After formal approval by the Military District (MD), the MSD actually inducts those selected into the military.

Terms of service have been altered from time to time, whenever manpower needs or the political/economic situation have required.[8] Currently, service in the ground forces is generally for three years, but is four years for persons with special skills. Service in the air force is generally for four years, and in the navy, five years.

Some eighteen million Chinese reach military age (eighteen) each year. Of the nine million males, about ten percent (900,000) are actually inducted, along with fewer than 10,000 women. Specific nationwide selection standards are set each year by the MND, with guidance from the MAC, and take into account both PLA needs and the overall economic, political, and social situation. Physical, political, and "cultural" (literacy) standards are high relative to the overall population. During the GPCR, at least, quotas for social origin and occupation were specified as well.

The most detailed single source on PLA conscription standards and quotas is the alleged "Decision on Kwangtung's 1968 Conscription Work." While this document is almost certainly a Hong Kong forgery, it is probably of Nationalist origin and based on KMT intelligence. Refugee informants and several members of the US intelligence community have assured the author that the figures are "about right." The data in Table 7.1 is presented with this caveat.

Conscription and retention standards are such that the PLA is not a cross section of the population. Physically, recruits are the "cream of the crop." Their educational levels are considerably above average, particularly for the air force. Although peasants are still the large majority, the social makeup of the PLA runs disproportionately to urban students and workers. Even the rank and file are somewhat better educated and more urban-oriented than the population at large. The long-standing recruiting bias against relatively less-educated peasants, especially in the air force, helps explain the relatively high degree of politicization among Chinese soldiers. The sense of elitism and radicalism of the air force has already been noted. As the technological level of the PLA improves, the antipeasant bias will probably increase still further. In 1979 or 1980, the PLA began discharging many soldiers up to six months before their enlistments were up. These were soldiers judged unable to "master modern science and technology." These are most likely to be peasants.

In the competition to enter military service, the children of serving PLA cadres have always had a distinct advantage, and disproportionate numbers are accepted. While soldiers' sons tend to become soldiers in most of the world's armies, this has been at least partially the result of "entering by the back door" in China.

Cadres and Their Careers

Prior to his demobilization, a soldier may volunteer for extended service. This normally will be permitted only if he has special skills or if he is judged to be cadre material. In some cases, specialists are retained involuntarily. Again, peasants are the least likely to be retained. Personnel on exended active duty (officially known as "volunteers" as distinguished from "conscripts") are thought to total twenty to twenty-five percent of the PLA.[9]

The decision to retain a soldier on active duty is probably made at regimental level, and is based upon unit personnel needs. There is evidence that technically specialized units, like naval vessels and even tank companies, are considerably overmanned with "volunteers"—possibly at double the manpower actually needed to crew existing equipment. Apparently this is done to keep trained crewmen available in case of national emergency. If there were a burst of emergency military equipment production, trained crews would already be available.[10]

Luck plays an important role in a cadre's career from the outset. There has long been a *de facto* quota of about twenty CCP members per company. If an infantryman happens to be in a company with a full quota of party members or a full complement of cadres, he is unlikely to be retained and his career is nipped in the bud. Here again, personal and family connections often come into play, however.

Military "cadres" (*kan-pu*), strictly speaking, are assistant platoon leaders and up, about the same as the officer corps in other armies. Squad leaders

TABLE 7.1
Kwangtung Provincial Conscription Quotas: 1968[1]

SERVICE	NUMBER MEN	NUMBER WOMEN	OCCUPATIONS					"CULTURAL LEVEL"		
			Students[2]	Industrial workers	Peasants	Cadres	"Social Youths"[3]	Senior middle school and up	Junior middle school and up	Grammar School and higher
ARMY	41,968	3,649	30%	21%	19%	5%	25%	--	35%	65%
NAVY	20,386	849	30%	21%	19%	5%	25%	--	40%	60%
AIR FORCE	11,798	none	60%	15%	1%	2%	22%	65%	35%	none
TOTALS	74,152	4,498								
	78,650									

OTHER STANDARDS: Unmarried. Aged 18-20 years. "Primarily" children of workers and poor and lower-middle peasants. None from classes above middle peasant. None who are sole supporters of dependents. "Clean in political profile." "Sound ideology and physique."

Comment: These standards were written in late 1967 and are more "egalitarian" than they are today. The "class" standards no longer apply, but the others do.

Notes:
 1. Source: "Decision on Kwangtung's 1968 Conscription Work" (November 1967). See Text.
 2. Includes school graduates still unemployed within a year after graduation.
 3. Unemployed urban youths. In common parlance, this term (she-hui ch'ing-nien) has a pejorative connotation which is not intended here.

(who would be NCOs in any other army) are treated as cadres in certain respects, and bear some responsibility. Similarly, "political activists" in the ranks, and many specialists (office workers, aircraft ground crews, etc.) have a status greater than "fighter" (*chan-shih*), but less than "cadre." In practice, an individual is known and addressed by his position (e.g., "Platoon Leader Wang," "Squad Leader Chieh"). This, along with personal recognition, alleviates the ambiguities of NCO-level status. In any event, the line between cadre and fighter is clearly drawn, and PLA squad leaders do not enjoy many of the privileges associated with NCO status in the West.

In the 1950s, despite regulations which provided for NCO ranks and which centralized the commissioning of officers in the MND, one became an officer more or less automatically if one was accepted for extended service. Formal officer training, though required by regulation, sometimes was neglected entirely.[11] In the 1960s and 1970s, it has been possible for an infantryman to become a "volunteer" and spend a relatively short career (four or five additional years) as a squad leader. If, in that time, he has not become a cadre, he will usually be discharged.

Generally speaking, PLA cadres rise from the ranks. The system of 1955-65, under which officers were commissioned straight out of colleges and academies, was abolished in 1965, but has been partially restored since 1978. Civilian middle-school graduates are now entering PLA "specialized technical academies and command academies" by competitive examination.[12] In 1979, civilians admitted to academies were required to spend a largely symbolic period of "service in the ranks" of the PLA prior to actually entering the academies as cadets. This period seems to be a year or less, although practice may vary.[13]

In addition to this new system, recruitment from the ranks into officer training schools continues, as in 1965-78. A high percentage of those chosen in 1979 had distinguished themselves in the "counterattack" on Vietnam.[14] Formal schooling for these officer candidates, as well as for squad leaders and middle-level cadres, is provided by the MR commands. Centrally controlled schools and academies train specialists and higher-ranking officers.

Since 1979, there has been a massive new emphasis upon formal schooling for cadres and specialists. Schools under the general departments, service arms, MRs, and MDs expanded, while many new ones were established.[15] Training of instructors and development of teaching methods has been emphasized. The keynote is "modernization," which includes "overcoming ossified thinking" among older officers, as well as learning technical specialties and combined-arms tactics.

In November 1980, regulations were promulgated specifying the educational levels and training diplomas to be required for all cadres and staff personnel, from company up through corps levels. Appended to these impressively high standards, however, was a "supplemental explanation" that:

> The majority of commanding cadres at and above battalion level have not received academy education. Therefore, when it is time to promote regimental and corps-level cadres, interim procedures may be adopted, until 1985, when the system of posts corresponding with diplomas (*chih-wei yü hsueh-tzu p'ei-he ti chih-tu*) will be fully implemented.[16]

It remains to be seen whether these ambitious standards can be met in 1985, or later. Senior and middle-grade cadres recruited before 1954, and ground forces cadres generally, are overwhelmingly of peasant origin and seldom have more than middle school educations. In fact, a recent circular from the general departments noted there are "cadres [?below] regimental level whose level of education is lower than junior middle school," and that there are still illiterate soldiers in the ranks.[17]

Considering salaries, allowances, and fringe benefits, PLA officers and their families live well by Chinese standards. There are twenty-four pay grades from assistant platoon leaders (level 24) to the top generals (level 1). In 1975, the former made base pay of 40 yuan per month, and the latter a princely 270 yuan. In addition, longevity pay adds five percent for five years service, ten percent for ten years service, etc. There are also family subsistence allowances, and substantial perquisites at upper levels. Officer salaries had been somewhat higher, but were "voluntarily" reduced by about one-third during the GPCR.[18] They were reportedly increased again in 1979.[19]

According to the 1955 "Regulations on the Service of Officers" (articles 14, 25, and 27), officer promotion was generally supposed to be one step at a time, and to be based on "political quality and professional ability," and "on the basis of vacancies in personnel organization and according to the order of promotion." Under some circumstances, combat heroes and specialists might receive accelerated promotions (article 16). In practice, however, seniority and the availability of a vacancy in one's own unit have been the overriding determinants of PLA promotion since the Civil War. Schooling, professional expertise, and other qualifications have been relatively unimportant. Even political factors have had relatively little importance, except during and just after the Cultural Revolution.

The MAC clearly intends to change that situation. New "Regulations on the Service of Officers" were adopted in August 1978. Published commentaries on these as yet unpublished regulations indicate they contain provisions for tying cadre promotion to individual performance in the new "yearend review and examination" system.[20]

The time limits for promotion and the age limits for active service set forth in the 1955 "Regulations on ... Officers" were inoperative from the outset. Under those regulations even a colonel had to retire if he failed to be promoted after four years in grade (articles 15, 17, and 32). In fact, promotion stagnated, while the PLA officer corps became one of the most aged in the world. The 1978 Regulations contain similiar provisions. It appears they are being enforced for company-grade cadres, but not among older and more senior ones. PLA units above battalion level frequently have one or several old "deputy commanders" who are merely occupying sinecures, for all practical purposes.

In mid-1981, there still appears to be no centralilzed cadre career management system. A man is promoted when and if a vacancy appears in his own unit. Thus, there are few career options and little "room at the top." A cadre must wait for one of his superiors to die, be promoted, or (rarely, at higher levels) to retire. A company commander will normally be promoted to the battalion headquarters which controlled his company, and so on up the line. The vast majority of officers spend their entire careers within the same regiments they joined as recruits.[21]

> At army corps level, opportunities widen. A corps commander might become a district commander. Later still, he could be promoted to a responsible position at military region level. Relatively few troop commanders are assigned to the PLA administra-

tive network below the level of military district. Missions assigned to subdistricts and people's armed departments (e.g., militia work and conscription) are not well suited to the talents and training of unit commanders, so those posts usually go to political officers. Thus, the political commissariat system offers somewhat more career opportunities through lateral transfer than does the command chain.[22]

This system has certain advantages. It eliminates the need for a centralized promotion system and a bureaucracy to run it. It also simplifies unit personnel record-keeping, because those with promotion authority are personally familiar with their junior cadres. Since officers and men train together for long periods in highly stable organizations, experience and unit proficiency can accumulate. This promotes *esprit de corps* and close relationships among cadres and soldiers.

There are also major drawbacks: There is little incentive to innovate, and such stability can lead to stagnation. Units and individuals sometimes become so comfortable in one location that they resist transfer.[23] This problem is particularly serious among more senior officers, who may rise to command regiments or divisions, and still lack knowledge or experience in the employment of supporting arms and services. The nearly universal tendency of armies to "prepare for the last war" is therefore exacerbated in the PLA. An inevitable, and undesirable, corollary of unit *esprit de corps* is "mountaintopism." A unit comes to reflect its commander to a high degree, and tends to become his "personal kingdom"—a situation the party has always abhorred.

Inevitably, the system generates frustration among ambitious young officers. During the 1974-75 campaign against status-consciousness in the officer corps, *NCNA* approvingly cited a squad leader in the Honan regional forces who had served in the same company for twenty-three years, never complaining about his lack of promotion.[24] This presumably extreme "good example" was clearly addressed to PLA cadres who were not so patient.

Harvey Nelsen has detailed the way this frustration manifested itself during the GPCR in radical political activity among many junior officers, especially in the regional forces.[25] They either spurred their superiors into political adventures or attempted to "seize power" from them—creating "room at the top" for themselves either way.

Another consequence of the narrowly restricted promotion system is the importance of "*kuan-hsi*." An ambitious cadre, if he is lucky, can escape the frustrations of slow promotion by catching the eye of a powerful patron. This results in an even more important sort of "mountaintopism," for it generates "vertical cliques which compete with each other for high-level positions."

> The higher the echelon, the more important this nascent factionalism becomes, because top-level leaders have a long string of subordinates with whom they have served, and the power to promote and transfer these trusted associates. Thus, the top men on the [MAC], general staff, political, and rear service departments have their own mental or real "black books" of men they know and trust and would like to promote to responsible positions. As a result, high-level appointments tend to precipitate political struggles and are a potential source of disunity in the PLA.[26]

While these vertical cliques are significant, their importance has been overstated by the Chinese Nationalists and by certain Americans, notably William Whitson.[27] For one thing, the PLA is hardly unique with respect to senior officers advancing their proteges. In the US Army, for example, General Marshall promoted Eisenhower and Stillwell, over dozens of their seniors, the very day he became chief of staff. More recently, the "Airborne Club," centered on Generals Taylor, Gavin, and Ridgeway, dominated the army well into the 1970s. William Parrish has shown that cliques are indeed widespread in the PLA, but that Whitson's "Field Army Elite" theory focuses on one set of cliques while ignoring other cross-cutting ones.[28]

Nelson suggests that the personal relations factor may have been partially legitimated in the upper levels by a "recognized system of sponsor/guarantor and protege relations." He goes on to stress that the guarantor-protege system has a long tradition in China. In imperial times, an official being promoted to a high post had to be sponsored by one or more higher-ranking officials, who were held responsible for his behavior in office.[29]

Such "vestiges of feudalism" are now officially recognized as such, and a full-scale campaign was launched in 1980 to eliminate "feudal remnants" like the personal patronage system, and especially the "system of lifelong tenure in office for leading cadres."

> As cadre positions have become an "iron rice bowl," some cadres are encouraged to drift along and gain seniority. There is less and less revolutionary vigor, but more and more bureaucratic airs, apathy, arrogance, and finicky airs.
>
> Particularly because there cannot be normal replacement of the old by the new in the cadre ranks, the result is that some people, although incompetent, continue to hold high office, while truly talented, competent people are unable to play their proper roles.[30]

The overriding importance of seniority and unit vacancy in promotion was partially disrupted by the Cultural Revolution. Political "redness" became, at least officially, the leading promotion criterion in early 1967. With a few highly publicized exceptions, however, this criterion was not widely applied even then.

The strict seniority system was never fully restored, either. In the mid-1970s there were cases of politically active young cadres being elevated over several intermediate levels. The obvious drawback to these accelerated promotions, within the overall framework of the old unit-oriented seniority system, was that the more senior cadres who were by-passed must have felt more frustrated and resentful than ever.

A regularized system of officer rotation may finally be evolving. Of ninety-four new assignments of ranking PLA men during the first tenure of Teng Hsiao-p'ing as chief of staff (January 1975 to April 1976), fifty-four were transfers from one region to another (thirty-one cases) or from a central military organ to a region (twenty-three cases). At least among high-level officers, a full-fledged system of periodic rotation of individuals similar to that in the American military seems to have been initiated.[31] In the major reshuffle of MR and PLA headquarters leaders of early 1980, many older men were replaced by younger ones, and others are simply moved to counter "mountaintopism." A Central Committee document on "transfer of high-level cadres" to "end the lifelong tenure system" was reportedly issued in January 1981.[32]

As we saw in chapter 5, higher-level headquarters are now selecting cadres from subordinate units, ordering them to formal schools, and routinely reassigning them after graduation. Thus, changes of unit assignment are on the increase among lower ranks as well. The system of merit promotion, based on annual examinations, is bound to have the same effect, since some units will have more openings than promotable cadres, while others will have an excess of the latter. The results of this increased cadre circulation are likely to be far-reaching (see the concluding section, below).

In 1979-81, the press has been filled with articles urging the importance of promoting young and middle-aged cadres to leading posts. The "most urgent task" in military modernization is said to be the selection and training of younger successors.[33] A corollary of promoting younger cadres is retiring older ones. Teng Hsiao-p'ing (aged seventy-six) set the example in February 1980, by replacing himself as chief of staff with Yang Te-chih (who is merely seventy).

The post of "advisor" has been created for "veteran cadres [who] have been relieved of their executive duties . . . because of their advanced age or ill health. They will be required to inspect work and propose ways of improving it. They will continue to draw their original salaries."[34] This delicate handling of older cadres is necessitated by the resistance and resentment that forced retirement has provoked. How successful it will be remains to be seen. "Advisors" and even "advisory groups" now exist down as low as regimental level.

There have been recent "good examples" of ranking cadres who took "the whole nation's situation in mind[,] . . . went along with the organizational arrangement in all respects," and retired.[35] There has also been resentment and resistance, especially among cadres below division level, who evidently are not as carefully handled. There have been reports of suicides, and of riots by demobilized soldiers and cadres, who sometimes find themselves unhonored, unemployed, and unwelcome.[36]

Nor is lack of civilian employment the only reason for resisting retirement. Another is the new policy that "demobilized soldiers from rural areas should return to rural areas [and] settle down to agricultural production work." One of the chief attractions of PLA service has always been that it offered a good chance of working in the city after demobilization. The new policy is regarded as a betrayal of that expectation. Closely related is the poor treatment veterans and their families may receive because of high unemployment in cities and the "responsibility system" in rural production.

> . . . we strengthened the work of supporting the army and giving preferential treatment to military dependents and arrangements for the placement of retired soldiers . . . . However, in a few places or units we still underestimate and pay less attention to the demobilized retired soldiers' active role. A few cadres even regard retired comrades as a "burden" and are not willing to actively and warmly accept their placement . . . ."[37]

A retired cadre thus stands to lose both his "rice bowl" and his accustomed honored status.

MOTIVATION

It is a truism of the military art that the personal motivation of soldiers and officers—their morale, dedication, and self-discipline—are critical components of an army's fighting capacity.

The PLA employs many of the same means of motivating its soldiers that are used in other armies. Though hardly a "spit and polish" army in the conventional sense, the PLA recognizes and exploits military music, pageantry, and unit tradition. While today's PLA uniform may appear drab to our eyes, it serves the same purposes in China as elsewhere. It sets its wearer apart as one with a special role in society and special duties to the state. The Chinese soldier is proud of his uniform, for it marks him as part of a select and prestigious institution.

Individual and collective merit is recognized by various awards and commendations. The actual wearing of medals was discontinued in 1965, but was reinstated in March 1979. Individuals may be awarded the "Heroic Model's Medal" (in two classes) or the "Order of Merit" (in three classes) for anything from extreme heroism to the conscientious performance of routine duties. Campaign medals were also reinstituted in 1979.[38] Special titles may be conferred upon individuals whose conduct is judged worthy of emulation (e.g., "Model Soldier in Helping the Left," "Model Cadre in Cherishing the Soldiers"). Individual commendations and citations by higher military and party organs are also awarded.

A unit may be awarded a Collective Order of Merit or, in exceptional cases, a special title (e.g., "Heroic Sea Eagle Air Regiment," "Model Company in Fighting Earthquake Effects and Cherishing the People"). In the latter case, a red citation banner with a gold inscription is awarded by the MAC.

Although Lin Piao's "Five-Good Soldier" and "Four-Good Company" movements were officially junked in the early 1970s,[39] units and individuals are still being awarded such titles as "Advanced Company" and "Pacesetter" for excellence in political and military training.

Military tradition is preserved in many of the ways seen in other armies. Units maintain museums and official histories, and sons are often assigned to their fathers' former regiments. The emulation campaigns described in chapter 3 are somewhat less prominent than during the GPCR, but martyrs like Lei Feng are still honored, much as are the fallen heroes of other military forces.

In 1979-80, there were indications of new efforts to improve morale by improving PLA food and housing, and to assist soldiers with their personal (especially family) problems.[40] At the same time, there has been renewed emphasis on strict military discipline, which deteriorated somewhat since the Cultural Revolution—largely, it seems, because of the pampered status of the PLA. Nationwide emphasis on the rule of law in 1979-80 was accompanied by an unprecedented emphasis on, and publication of, formal military laws and regulations.[41] The system of military courts and procuratorates, which was allgedly "dismantled" by Lin Piao and the "gang of four," was officially revived on 20 October 1978.[42]

Loyalty oaths are sworn by soldiers in virtually all the world's armies. Revolutionary Chinese soldiers took various oaths before 1949, but then the practice was discontinued. In February 1981, a new PLA oath was promulgated, to be taken by recruits and by all serving cadres and fighters. Oath-taking ceremonies all over the country were publicized in March.[43] Although military oaths are taken almost universally, some PLA cadres have evidenced uneasiness and resentment. They seem to sense that their loyalty somehow has been impugned by the very existence of a new requirement to swear to it.

It is noteworthy that, in contrast to the Soviet Army oath, which is sworn to the Soviet state, the PLA oath swears loyalty to both the state and the party. It also pledges support for two current political campaigns: the "four modernizations" and "socialist spiritual civilization." Everyone expects these slogans and campaigns to fade away just like all the others have. "Socialist spiritual civilization," in particular, will probably fade fairly soon. When that happens, the PLA loyalty oath itself will become outdated. It will have to either be revised or fall into disuse. Either way, the importance of the oath will be denigrated. Thus, although the new oath is intended to inspire stability and solidarity, it may turn out to be counterproductive.

Political Work

As we noted at the end of chapter 4, the PLA Political Work Conference of May-June 1978 underscored the continuing commitment of the high command to some aspects of the revolutionary tradition. Yeh Chien-ying emphasized that "political work is the source of our army's combat strength."[44]

New PLA "Political Work Regulations" were promulgated in August 1978. The full text has not been published but, judging from published commentaries, they contain remarkably little change, in tone or specifics, from the "Lin Piao regulations" of 1963.[45] The leading role of unit party committees, the commissar system, and the class brotherhood of officers and men are all reiterated in the same terms used in the early 1960s.

The 1978 Political Work Regulations set out the purposes of political work. Among these are: to uphold Mao Tse-tung's thought, assure the CCP's "absolute leadership over the army," educate the PLA ideologically and maintain its "proletarian nature," "implement the party's program, line, principles, and policies," safeguard military unity, centralization, and discipline," "raise the army's combat strength," and "lead and ensure the fulfillment of all tasks entrusted to our army by the party and state."[46]

"Political work" includes everything from political agitation to literacy classes to recreation. Activities include publication of unit newspapers, maintenance of reading rooms and recreational centers, organizing sports, "cultural activities," schools, and spare-time study.

One major aim of this activity is the enhanced performance of military duties. This theme has been strongly reemphasized since the PLA Political Work Conference of January 1981.[47] This is in contrast to the "Maoist" view that political work ought to be mainly concerned with developing political consciousness per se, on the explicit theory that military efficiency, good citizenship, and high productivity follow more or less automatically from a correct political orientation. This view prevailed during the Lin Piao years (1959-71), and was the justification for many of the political work themes and movements which were noted in chapters 2 and 4. Since Lin's fall in 1971 there has been a marked reversal, and Lin is criticized for "criminal acts in standing military affairs against politics and sabotaging army building."[48] In the 1970s, PLA political work increasingly was justified as being a means to the ends of courage, skill, and efficiency.[49]

A related question is how much time ought to be devoted to formal political work. "Maoists" felt it should take up several hours per day, while professionally inclined soldiers maintain that mission-oriented work and training should take up the vast majority of a soldier's time. Troop leaders are currently faced with the dilemma of being ordered to make "strenuous efforts to ... promote ideological work" while simultaneously readjusting "the proportions between military training and political education ... thus increasing all units' military training. . . ."[50]

A traditional aspect of political work is the promotion of "solidarity" and manipulability by means of small group study and discussion—particularly the practice of "criticism and self-criticism." The psychological dynamics of the technique have been treated at length by Robert J. Lifton, and the actual practice by Martin K. Whyte.[51] Roman Kolkowicz has examined the impact of criticism and self-criticism on the Soviet officer corps.[52] It appears that, as in the Soviet case, criticism and self-criticism in the PLA is practiced with varying intensity depending upon the overall political situation. Kolkowicz found that in the mid-1960s officers were subjected to criticism by their military subordinates; whereas we saw that this was not the case in 1973 (chapter 1). Similarly, this particular aspect of "military democracy" was emphasized during the early Lin Piao years, but was not universally practiced during the GPCR. The movement in 1967-69, to build unity by means of "unity-criticism-transformation" was the last major drive to promote criticism and self-criticism, but it continues to be a standard component of PLA "politicization." Its actual practice presumably has paralleled the ups and downs of "military democracy" versus command authority which we examined in chapter 4.

Whyte writes that small-group political rituals and self-criticism are most likely to be effective in organizational settings where individuals live and work together, where they have high prestige, do clearly important work, and where they are subject to close control and a steady high volume of orthodox political information.[53] On all counts, the PLA is virtually ideal.

Since an "apolitical military" is intolerable in an authoritarian society, politics is always "in command," in fact. It is therefore important to keep soldiers well informed on the twists and turns of the party line. Despite unstinting efforts to keep the PLA "current" in this regard, it is inevitable that varying interpretations, distorted communictions, and time delays sometimes cause what appear to be conflicts between political work themes in different units. (To be sure, some such conflicts may be quite real). The point is that "political work" is largely devoted to keeping soldiers informed on the constantly changing "party line," and trying to get them to "unlearn" yesterday's verities. As in the rest of society, this often means overcoming severe anxiety induced by the "obsessive lingering fear" of still further changes tomorrow, and the consequent disgrace or punishment of anyone who was too enthusiastic about the party line today.[54]

Partly as a result of this, Lifton, Whyte, and others have noted that recurring drives for political participation and self-criticism tend to encourage a drift toward ritualized behavior. Confession, criticism, slogan shouting, and even essay writing become almost theatrical. The PRC terms for this include "formalism," and "mechanical reproduction." A 1978 report claimed that a political movement in the navy had "completely changed" the "situation of the movement's starting out with intensity, then slowing down due to laxity and finally becoming a mere formality, as happened in the past."[55] We may well be sceptical about this "complete change."

COMMAND

Military science recognizes "unity of command" as essential to effective operations. Most military forces seek to assure unity of command by means of a hierarchy of authority and clear-cut lines of command. Every unit, from a field army to a typing pool, has one individual who is "in command," which is to say, personally responsible for everything his unit does or fails to do. Commensurate with his responsibility, he is officially endowed with full authority over his subordinates. Each individual knows what individual is his immediate commander and obeys his orders; in turn, he expects the obedience of his own subordinates. In practice, it has long been recognized that there must be some compromise with this ideal, for absolute command authority would be open to terrible abuse. Accordingly, the power of commanders has been limited by laws and customs which provide recourse for subordinates. In general, however, one-man command has been adopted as the basic, if not absolute, principle.

For a variety of reasons, which we examined in chapter 2, the PLA is an important exception. In principle, every unit from company up is commanded not by one but by two coequal commanders. In Chinese usage these two, the military commander and the political commissar, are commonly referred to as the "commanders" of the unit.

Even this dual-command system is compromised. "Work teams" can be dispatched by party or military organs to any subordinate military unit, where they may stay for any length of time, intervene in the minutest affairs, submit reports, or merely observe for short periods. These *ad hoc* teams bear resemblances both to the old imperial censorate and to the inspector general system in the US military. Work teams were dispatched in unprecedented numbers in 1978-80 as part of the campaigns to "overcome the remnant influence of Lin Piao and the 'gang of four,'" and to "shift the focus to modernization."[56]

Temporary political conditions have sometimes disrupted the command system drastically. In 1967, a centralized and cumbersome system was instituted, whereby orders from a higher to a lower headquarters had to be confirmed by the next higher still. That system denied subordinates the slightest flexibility or exercise of initiative, and was discontinued after the GPCR. In direct contradiction to this overly centralized practice, the GPCR also saw the very principle of obedience called into question on the theory that every soldier had the duty to decide whether or not his orders were sufficiently "correct" politically to be obeyed. This notion, discussed in chapter 3, contributed to the disruption of discipline in some units. This political justification of insubordination ceased in late 1967, and since has been repudiated by an almost continuous emphasis on unity and discipline.

Command authority is also compromised by the Chinese Communist Party, of which two segments need to be distinguished—the civilian CCP and the military party structure. The former has, on occasion, been able to intervene in military affairs, especially in the regional forces. As we saw in chapters 2 and 4, the degree of control over local PLA units by civilian party committees has varied considerably over time and space. After being emphasized in the official press in 1974-75, local civilian party "criticism and supervision" seems to have been relegated to discussing common problems and complaints with military leaders.[57] The one important exception is MD, MSD, and PAD militia work, over which local party control has been strongly reemphasized (chapter 5).

"Democratic Centralism"

Owing to the welter of institutional constraints upon PLA commanders, an essential fact is sometimes overlooked: The PLA is a well-disciplined military force. The existence of party committees within units, and the practice of "democracy" within them, in no way hinders military discipline—

quite the contrary. The essentials of "mass-line" leadership were worked out by Mao Tse-tung during the Yenan period, based in turn upon the Leninist doctrine of democratic centralism (chapter 2). The opinions and reactions of the masses are constantly solicited, and party policy at both the local and national levels has been considerably influenced by popular opinion. But this should not obscure the fact that it is the leading cadres who make the decisions and the masses who obey. When the higher level issues an order, "democracy" at the lower level is directed toward working out and popularizing the best way to implement that order; there is never any question or discussion as to whether or not it shall be obeyed.

The focus of "democratic centralism" in the PLA is the unit party committee.

> The Chinese Communist Party shall organize Party Committees at various levels of the ... Army to serve as the nucleus of unified leadership and solidarity in the Army units. The system of division of work and responsibility among individual leading officers under the unified collective leadership of Party committees is the fundamental system for implementing Party leadership in the Army. Except for emergency situations, in which the leading officers shall take appropriate actions, all important issues ... must be referred to the Party committees for discussion and decision *in accordance with the principle of democratic centralism.* In matters pertaining to military work, organization and implementation shall be the responsibility of the military commanders, and in matters pertaining to political work, organization and implementation shall be the responsibility of the political commissars. Both the ... commissars and the ... commanders are the leading officers of the Army units, jointly responsible for the Army's work. Under normal conditions, the *political commissars are also the directors of daily work of the Party committees.* The Party shall organize Party branches at the company level ... [which] are the basic tie linking the Party to the vast masses of officers and men.[58]

It should be noted that, in accordance with normal CCP practice, consulting with the "party committee" almost always means consulting with its standing committee, a group which seldom numbers more than ten people, even at very high levels of command. CCP branches and committees normally supervise Communist Youth League (CYL) organizations in their units. They also organize the same internal organs as civilian party committees (e.g., a discipline inspection commission, security commission, etc.).

In addition to the CCP committee, each unit above battalion level has a political department or office, which is part of the PLA structure and is manned by personnel of the GPD (See Figure 7.1). The unit commissar controls this department, normally through a designated Political Department Director. This department seems to be necessary because the political commissar, unlike the military commander (whose orders come only from the military commander at next higher headquarters), receives his guidance from many sources—the CC, the MAC General Office, the GPD, the unit party committee, and "the Party committee, commander, commissar, and political department at the next higher level. For problems created by multiple channels of communication and influence, the typical solution appears to be the meeting. One device

FIGURE 7.1

PLA POLITICAL ORGANIZATION

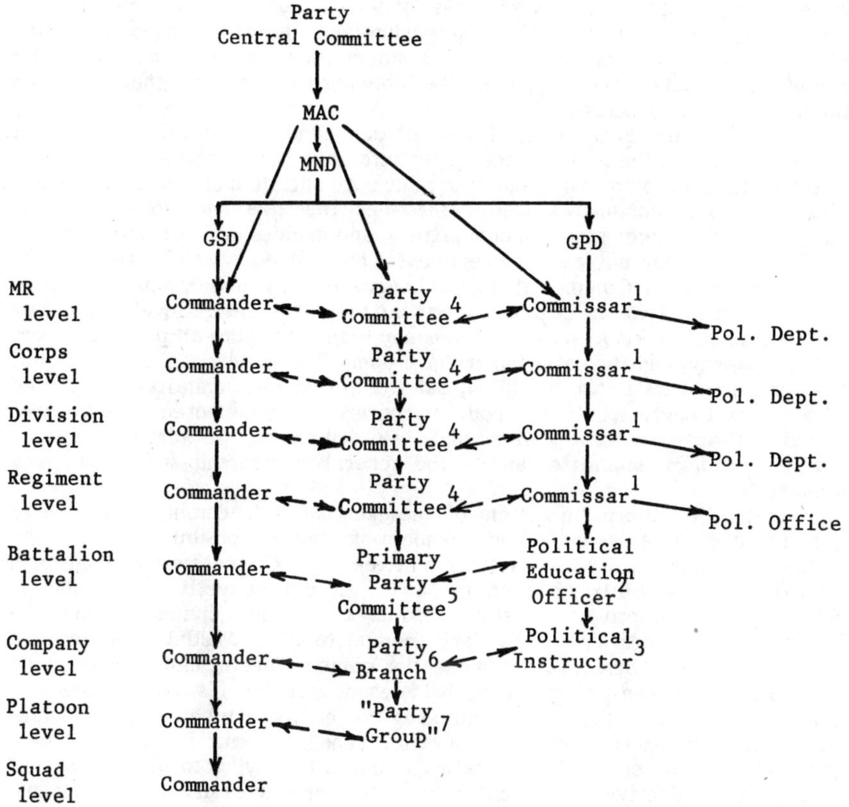

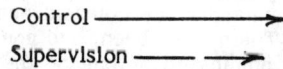

LEGEND

Control ⎯⎯⎯⎯⎯→
Supervision ⎯ ⎯ ⎯→

Notes:
1. Political Commissar (cheng-chih wei-yuan).
2. Political Education Officer (cheng-chih chiao-tao-yuan).
3. Political Instructor (cheng-chih chih-tao-yuan).
4. Elected by a "Party Congress" of the unit.
5. Directly elected by all CCP members in battalion.
6. Includes all CCP members in company.
7. Semi-official grouping consisting of all CCP members in platoon.

that clears the air on a nationwide scale is the telephone conference."[59] Normally, however, the political department keeps track of all the orders from above, and handles the massive paperwork entailed.

When a unit party committee meets, debate, while often lively, is not culminated by a vote, but rather arrives at a consensus. Depending on the issue at hand, there may be a good deal of leeway possible in the committee's decision, and the opinions of the membership (and, through them, of the unit's rank and file) are frequently, and quite sincerely, taken into account. If no consensus is reached, the matter may be tabled or referred to higher levels for further guidance or decision.[60]

The regiment is the critical level of command in political, as well as in military, organization. It is the regimental party committee which must approve the election of party secretaries at both battalion and company levels. The regimental committee also determines the size and composition of company party branch standing committees, and decides whether new company branches may be organized. The regimental committee must also approve the establishment of a Communist Youth League branch in a company.[61] It is hardly surprising that the regimental committee is the lowest level committee with bolshevized membership. The company branch includes all party members in the company, and the battalion primary committee is directly elected by all the party members in the battalion, but the regimental committee is elected by a "Party Congress." It is a body of representatives elected by a body of representatives and has powers that are denied to the directly elected battalion primary committee and to the general membership in the company branch.[62]

In theory, "the basic system of the exercise of leadership by the Party over the army is a system of commanders sharing responsibilities under the collective leadership of the Party committee .... Collective leadership and individual responsibility go hand in hand ..., but collective leadership is primary .... Collective leadership would never weaken individual responsibility under the leadership of the Party committee."[63] Making this work, in practice, is tricky business, for while the commanders cannot appear to be dictatorial, they know they will be held responsible for mistakes. Moreover, actually consulting with the party standing committee can be extremely time-consuming and become very bureaucratic. The PLA, and indeed the entire governmental and economic apparatus, is currently trying to devise ways of reconciling "collective leadership" with modern principles of management and leadership. Clearly, it is not going to be easy.

Since Lin Piao strengthened the commissars and reestablished the party committee system in the early 1960s, the normal command situation has been that the commanders (military commander and political commissar) of a unit dominate their party committee. There have been, and continue to be, cases where a given unit committee is dominated by one or the other of the two commanders, to the virtual exclusion of the other. Rarely, and only during the GPCR, some unit party committees actually challenged the commander's authority. This was usually possible only because the unit committee had outside support from civilian party organs, the Central Cultural Revolution Group, or Red Guards. In extremely rare instances, military subordinates actually attempted to "seize power" from their commanders. Such challenges were apparently restricted to regional commands and units.

There were common themes among those struggles: ... *They were fought out in the Party committee meetings* of the military regions. *After this approach proved fruitless*, the challengers aligned themselves with one or more mass organizations seeking to discredit the regional military leadership. . . . Such political ploys were uniformly unsuccessful, and in all cases except Tibet, the challengers were purged. The end of the GPCR wrote finis to any further overt attacks by subordinates against their superiors.[64]

Even during the Cultural Revolution, then, PLA party committees were unable to overrule their unit commanders. In practice, the "leadership" of the party committee means "democratic" participation and input, but it does not compromise command authority or discipline. Buried in the 1963 *Political Work Regulations* (X.4.a.) is the crucial admonition that "the Party branch should respect the functions and powers of the company cadres and fully develop their active role."

This is not to say that the CCP committees serve no purpose. They provide information, make suggestions, advise, and communicate criticisms, complaints, and suggestions from the soldiers. They serve a "backbone" role in agitation and propaganda, both in military training and in political work. PLA commanders can do a more effective job by listening to and utilizing their unit party committees.[65]

Commanders and Commissars

Because the military commander and the political commissar dominate the unit party committee, there is no real conflict between the commanders' "individual responsibility" and the committee's "collective leadership." The latter is advisory and symbolic. Between the two commanders, however, there is room for conflict. They are jointly responsible for the unit, yet receive their orders through different channels and tend to have different priorities and perspectives.

So much indoctrination, political evaluation, political counterintelligence, and record-keeping is required that "political work" long ago became a . . . specialty. There are a series of political staff schools that train officers for this activity; officers choosing this branch of service are normally expected to continue in it throughout their careers.[66]

The commissar controls the unit political department or office, and is usually, but not always, the "elected" first secretary of the unit party committee. The commander is normally "elected" second secretary. There are exceptions to this pattern at the MR and MD levels, where, frequently, the commander is first secretary if the commissar is basically a "civilian." It is noteworthy that the *ad hoc* Northern and Southern Fronts, set up in February-March 1979, had no designated commissars at all. At these levels, we are talking about MAC members, who (collectively) make their own rules.[67]

The original Whampoa system of "party representatives" was essentially a "defensive" means of gaining and assuring obedience to the party to "inspire sacrifice, and create ideological and institutional means to measure loyalty, reward its expression, and punish its absence."[68] This restricted role of "institutional conscience" has remained relatively unchanged in the Soviet Army. By the beginning of the Long March in 1934, however, Chinese commissars had already acquired a multitude of other tasks, many of which would be considered the normal purview of the commanders in other armies.[69]

The 1963 *Political Work Regulations* specified that commissars must give political lectures and lead discussions; organize newspaper reading, broadcast listening, and the preparation of wall posters; conduct political campaigns; lead tours and visits to factories, mines, museums, etc.; invite heroes, model workers, and soldiers' families to make reports; and generally to take charge of "ideological education through cultural and artistic activities" (article IX). In addition to these clearly "political" activities, the *Regulations* (II, IV, and IX) also specified many others which overlap or duplicate those of the military commander:

1. Arrangements for the dead and wounded.
2. "Assist the ... commander in making adjustments in the administrative structure in good time" to meet combat conditions.
3. Psychological operations against the enemy.
4. Handling prisoners of war.
5. Safety, health, and welfare work and the prevention of desertion or dereliction of duty.
6. Security and counterintelligence.
7. Intelligence.
8. Cadre and personnel evaluation, assignment, training, and transfer.
9. Work and contacts with the local population.
10. Relations with soldiers' families.
11. Discipline.
12. Investigation and complaints.

A few of these deserve comment:

It appears that the GSD took over all intelligence functions from the GPD during the 1960s. Presumably, this was reflected, at unit level, in the transfer of primary intelligence responsibilities to the commander. The commissar's continuing roles in PW handling and counterintelligence necessarily mean he remains part of the intelligence effort.[70]

Political departments, under commissar direction, continue to direct internal security work and to handle major disciplinary problems. Commissars control the military procuracy and the system of courts martial.[71] The GPD system also administers the award of medals and commendations.[72]

In addition to these duties, commissars are required to share "responsibility with the military commander of the same level for formulating programs of combat training, supply, and construction of Army units, and to countersign orders to be issued" (IV.3.).

It can be seen that the workload on a PLA commissar is immense. In addition to strictly political work, he bears primary responsibility for personnel administration, "civil affairs," psychological operations, and security. He shares important responsibilities for intelligence, operations, training, and logistics. A cooperative and hardworking commissar is a real asset to a military commander, for he relieves the latter of most of his administrative burden.

The existence of such a harmonious division of work between the two "commanders" appears to be fairly widespread. The trouble is that this relegates the commissar to the role of administrative assistant, which is contrary to the fundamental intent of the system. Political organs and personnel are not supposed to deal with general administration, a point the leadership has had to stress repeatedly over the years.[73]

The commander-commissar division of labor, which has never been clear-cut in the PLA, is becoming increasingly blurry in 1980-81:

> The political work cadres at various levels have also been studying the art of war in a sincere effort to change from nonprofessionals into experts in this field. Such efforts make political work an organic part of military training. Nowadays many political instructors and supervisors have become excellent training officers in military subjects .... Soldiers say: "In the past, the instructor just looked on while the company commander labored, with political work appearing to be peripheral .... However, things have now changed with the instructor really coming to grips with essentials. Every word he now says strikes a chord in our hearts."[74]

Increasing the military expertise and role of the commissar is now a national policy.[75] As we saw in chapter 1, it was precisely this process which blurred the distinction between commander and commissar in the Soviet Army in the 1930s, and ultimately led to abolition of the commissar system. It would be premature to predict that this is what will happen in China, but it could certainly contribute to a trend in that direction.

As we have stressed in earlier chapters, the relationship between commander and commissar varies from unit to unit, and over time, owing to personality differences and the overall political climate. Institutional arrangements at different levels of command also affect the relationship. With respect to his last factor, military commanders of squads, platoons, companies, and battalions (the lowest-level units, and those closest to the rank and file) enjoy distinct advantages over commissars. At the lowest levels, neither a squad leader nor a platoon leader has a political "co-commander" at all.

We have already seen that the company "party branch" does not have the prerogatives of a full-fledged "party committee," and the company "political instructor" lacks the powers of a fully qualified commissar. Similarly, at battalion level, the "Primary party committee" and the "political education officer" lack certain powers which are reserved to the full-fledged party committees and political commissars at and above regimental level. The 1963 regulations (IX.10.) give commissars final authority in the event of disagreement between the commander and commissar at the next level down. That final authority is not granted to the battalion political education officer, however. It does not appear that the 1978 Political Work Regulations have changed any of this.

As is indicated by these limitations upon their authority and by their unique titles, the company political instructor and the battalion political education officer are still "apprentices," and don't have the full powers of true commissars. Nor do they, like true commissars, enjoy the staff support of a political office or department. It may therefore be concluded that the military commanders of companies and battalions enjoy "one-up" positions vis-a-vis their political "co-commanders."

At and above regimental level, the organizational cards seem to be stacked in favor of the commissars.

> Both the political commissar and the military commander are the leading officers of any Army unit. Under normal conditions, the

> ... commissar is also the director of the daily work of the Party committee.... In Party and political work he shall obey the political commissars and political organs of the higher levels; in military work, he shall obey the military command, *political commissars*, and military organs of higher levels.[76]

Note that while the higher-level commissar can intervene in military matters, the higher commander cannot intervene in political affairs. In the event of commander-commissar disagreement, they are to refer the issue to their party committee for discussion or to the next higher level for decision. Again, the higher-level commissar has the last word:

> In emergency conditions, matters pertaining to combat actions and military work shall be determined by the military commander; and matters pertaining to Party policy and political work ... by the political commissar. But both should submit reports afterwards to the Party committee and higher-level *commissars* and accept inspection.[77]

Other advantages the commissar enjoys are his more ready access to the multiple sources of political direction and his control of the unit political office. These factors, plus the fact that he is usually the first secretary of the unit party committee, gave him a considerable edge in controlling the committee's decisions.

It is also significant that, in the absence of the assigned commissar or political officer, his responsibilities are to be assumed by his political assistant, and not by the military commander (as is the case in the Soviet Army). Thus, a military commander supposedly is not permitted to assume concurrent military and political leadership of a unit. On the other hand, there is no explicit prohibition against the commissar doing so.

In practice, it is well known that commanders can and do assume concurrent commissar positions, and vice versa. This gap between legal theory and practice is characteristic of a society where personalized and *ad hoc* procedures still moderate legalistic rule-following. The relative authority of commissars vis-a-vis commanders has waxed and waned over the decades. Since 1976, the reaction against the radical "gang of four" presumably has been accompanied by a tendency toward commander ascendency. Again, however, it is premature to predict anything so drastic as the official, or even *de facto*, abolition of the commissar system, or even a major modification of its workings. Indeed, all available evidence on current practice, and on the 1978 PLA Political Work Regulations, indicates the provisions of the 1963 regulations regarding political work and the commander-commissar relationship remain in effect.

There are both historical and functional reasons for conflict between commanders and commissars. The former have tended to see the latter as a challenge to command authority and military effectiveness, whereas commissars see themselves as guardians of political purity and of central authority over the military. Commanders tend to be governed by an "operational ethic" which is skeptical of the need for the "institutional conscience" of the commissariat.[78] Whitson writes that this skepticism is especially strong among commanders recruited during and since the civil war. These men, who spent their first decade or more of service fighting mobile and conventional wars, and serving in a Soviet-style garrison army in the mid-1950s, are now regimental and divisional cadres. Their turn to run the PLA high command is still a decade or more away. For the foreseeable future, the Chinese army and state will continue under the guidance of the "old warriors," who entered the PLA before 1945, and tend not to draw a sharp distinction between "political" and "military." They still appear to be committed to the commissar system.

It appears that the role of the commissar at unit level and the role of the GPD in the high command are not equally important. Commissars continued to function at and below division level throughout the period (1967-74) that the GPD headquarters in Peking was in disrepute and disuse.[79] As we observed in chapter 5, the GPD is not a rival to the MAC nor even to the GSD—of the three general departments, the general staff is clearly *primus inter pares*. The MAC can take over all GPD functions and directly control the commissars. The GPD only facilitates that, just as the GSD facilitates troop command.

The unit commissar system is far more important, and is not so easily dispensable. The dual-command system helps assure loyalty to the party Central Committee, and to guarantee the obedience of the army. It is, in effect, a "checks and balances" system which is likely to be retained as long as there remain doubts and fears of "mountaintopism" or "warlordism." Beyond its political importance, however, the commissar system continues to be integral to the normal functioning of command in the PLA.

Superiors and Subordinates

Leadership in the PLA has traditionally been characterized by flexibility and a willingness to allow the exercise of initiative by subordinates. This tradition was forced upon the Red Army by the fluid and decentralized nature of the warfare of 1927-49. Since the Korean War, there has been emphasis on detailed planning at higher levels, but flexibility and initiative in execution, and in the face of the unexpected, are still encouraged. This is in marked contrast to the extreme emphasis on obeying orders to the letter, no matter what, which we noted in the Soviet military (chapter 1).

PLA doctrine also emphasizes physical leadership and example. The recent emphasis on cadre training has quite frankly been based on the belief that good leadership will necessarily result in good soldiers and good results. This is an article of faith to professional soldiers everywhere.

In the early days of the Chinese Red Army, leaders participated in "company democratic conferences" and in "Chu-ko Liang meetings" to discuss military matters and to enlist the soldiers' ideas. As the allusion to Chu-ko Liang (a hero of *The Romance of the Three Kingdoms*) indicates, this practice had traditional as well as doctrinal roots. The "Chinese peasant military tradition" tended to cast a military leader as either a father figure or, better yet, a "sworn brother."[80] This latter role emphasized a horizontal bond of comradeship, and involved a high degree of personal interchange and mutual obligation. PLA leaders are still expected to treat soldiers as "class brothers." It appears that the ideal of "class brotherhood" is most closely approximated at and below company level, but that "commandism" and status-consciousness raise their ugly heads at higher levels. In a 1967 speech to a PLA cadre conference, Chang Ch'un-ch'iao stated the problem quite frankly:

> Chairman Mao ... said that our company commanders and political instructors are in regular contact with the rank and file, but once they become battalion cadres they estrange themselves from them.[81]

The PLA has been tilting with the windmill of rank-consciousness and privilege all of its institutional life. Mao's 1929 Kutien Speech castigated it, the 1942-44 rectification campaign sought to stamp it out; the *hsia-lien tang-ping* movement of 1958-61 was directed against it. The "abolition of explicit differentials of rank" in 1965 was intended "to remove the conditions that foster the ideas of rank, fame, and personal interest"; and to help cadres "to regard themselves more consciously, as ordinary soldiers and ordinary workers and to reform themselves ideologically"; and to further strengthen "the ideology of serving the people wholeheartedly."[82]

Again in 1974-75, the nationwide campaign to abolish "bourgeois-right" was expressed in the PLA as a new *hsia-lien* campaign.[83] Despite the stated object of the movement, it appears that many of the "sent-down" officers continued to "bear themselves as leaders" and to expect, and receive, treatment as special guests. Many reportedly "behaved like oil floating on the surface of water." *Hsia-lien* continued in the PLA right up to the eve of the invasion of Vietnam—long after it had been discontinued everywhere else.[84] Since then, "going deep into basic-level units" as members of work groups is still said to help high-ranking cadres "change their work style and improve their work methods."[85]

The problem evidently remains unresolved, for the press has been filled with accounts of abuse of privilege, especially by higher ranks.[86] In September 1979, Ch'en Tsai-tao, of "Wuhan Incident" fame, drew a stinging public rebuke for allegedly ordering a nursery school dismantled to make way for building a private house.[87] The new Discipline Inspection Commissions in the party also have been organized in the PLA party system. They are specifically intended to root out such "feudal" abuses of privilege as extravagance, "going in the back door," favoritism for cadres' families, and undisciplined behavior by their children.[88] All these same problems, we should note, are concurrently under attack throughout civilian society.

CONCLUSIONS AND PROJECTIONS

It appears that, as Chang Ch'un-ch'iao indicated in 1967, the problem of "estrangement from the masses" applies equally to commanders and commissars. This is by no means the only area in which they seem to act and react the same way.

Whitson suggests that commissars have always been more "Bonapartist" than commanders, pressing the PLA into the civil sphere, and into politics generally.[89] While this has been true, especially during the Cultural Revolution, it has only been *regional* commissars who were grasping civil authority. Main force commissars were just as hesitant at becoming involved in civil politics as their commanders, and relinquished power just as readily in 1968-69. This was true even among cadres at higher levels of command. At lower levels, even Whitson recognizes that, beginning with the "sixth generation" of PLA cadres (recruited in 1945-50), both commanders and commissars tend to have great respect for military professional standards and goals, and "evidently experience some discomfort in a nonprofessional or semi-professional context...."[90]

Recent events in China support the conclusion that there are few commissars with radically "Maoist" sympathies. The evidence for this is negative, but persuasive: since October 1976, purges of cadres who were adherents of the "gang of four" have been spreading through the government and party like ripples in a pool, but there have been relatively few purges in

the army. Those who have been removed have as often been commanders as
political commissars. Moreover, official statements claim that when the "gang
of four" attempted to "encourage ultra-democracy" and "ferret out capitalist-
roaders" in the army in 1976, they met with solid resistance from all ranks at
all levels.[91] There appear to be virtually no radical Maoists (or "Whateverists,"
as they are currently called) among either commanders or commissars,
especially in the main forces.

Perhaps the key to major change in the PLA will prove to be the adoption
of a system of periodic rotation of individual cadre assignments. Just how far
down into the cadre ranks this system will reach is still uncertain. Indeed, it is
not certain that the system will survive at all. If it does, a centralized
promotion system will have to be set up, since the old informal personalized
system of promoting unit members into unit vacancies will no longer operate.

There would be other important consequences as well, most of which
would tend to engender increased professionalism in the officer corps. Cadre
rotation would necessarily weaken the role that commissars and unit CCP
committees currently play in the selection and promotion of cadres.[92] The
functioning of the current system is illustrated in the following:

> Early this year [1974] when the [regimental] Party committee was
> discussing the appointment of a new commander for the second
> company, Tu Sung-p'ing [apparently a high-ranking officer of the
> regiment] held that the cadres of this company were relatively new
> and suggested that a cadre with more experience and of greater
> seniority be transferred from another unit [in the regiment] to take
> up the post. But the majority of the comrades favored the
> promotion of the deputy commander of the company as commander
> . . . . Tu Sung-p'ing respected their view and the Party committee
> unanimously approved the promotion of the deputy company
> commander as commander of the second company.[93]

"Promotion, schooling, transfer, demobilization, and reward and punishment of
cadres" are still specified as CCP committee decisions in 1981.[94] If cadres
were habitually reassigned among units, this important party committee role
would be virtually eliminated.

Periodic cadre rotations would certainly enhance the overall experience
level of PLA officers, by exposing them to different types of units, differing
terrain and equipment, etc. It would also be much easier to eliminate elderly
officers who were no longer physically up to the demands of active service.
Just as a formal system of military schooling may contribute to the emergence
of cadre rotation, so, too, will rotation further promote formal schooling. An
officer could attend school between assignments, and would not have to be
pried away from his unit.

Circulation of officers would enhance the sense of the PLA being a
national institution by helping break down cliques and regionalism. By the
same token, rotation of assignments would reinforce the self-consciousness of
the officer corps as a corporate entity. Helping to reinforce this would be the
almost inevitable return to badges of rank.

Since 1965 there has been no formal system of insignia of rank or
position, except that cadres have four pockets on their jackets, while fighters
have only two. A fairly complex informal system has evolved, however,
whereby an individual's status can be determined fairly closely by the number
and quality of pens in his breast pocket, the presence of a wristwatch and/or

leather shoes, and the cut and material of his uniform. Still, it is an awkward system which makes exact recognition of relative authority virtually impossible. It works well enough today because officers and men recognize each other through constant contact. If new cadres were periodically joining units, at all levels of command, personal recognition would have to be supplemented by recognizable insignia. The new (1974) naval uniforms, which sharply distinguish between cadres and fighters, presage similarly differentiated uniforms in the rest of the PLA, and eventually badges of rank as well. The implementation of a system of cadre rotation would provide justification for such changes.

It will be recalled that in 1978 the promulgation of new "Regulations on the Service of Officers," and a flurry of other activities, indicated that the PLA was about to adopt new uniforms and reintroduce a system of rank and insignia (chapter 4). Su Yü, however, said the PLA would "never again take up the matter of restoring the rank system" because it would "only create gaps between the top and bottom."[95] It appears that Su and some of the other "old warriors" would like to preserve the rankless revolutionary tradition.

Nevertheless, speculation currently abounds that new uniforms and ranks soon will appear (the date August First, 1982, is often mentioned). The step is virtually inevitable, but it could be delayed considerably by the "old warriors'" resistance. Another practical reason for the delay might be that the new officer regulations contain stringent time-in-grade standards. Once in force, these would mandate the removal of numerous "deputy commanders" who are way overage for their rank-levels. The current retirement drive may be partly intended to clear the way for the new regulations. If so, continued resistance to retirement could lead to further delay of the officer regulations, the uniforms, and the rank system. Here again, T'eng Hsiao-p'ing and Keng Piao seem to be more closely attuned to the desires of young and middle-aged cadres (who want these reforms) in opposition to the pre-1945 generations.

How a formal rotation system would affect the distinction between regional and main forces would depend upon whether or not officers were freely transferred between the two components. Currently their cadres are on separate career tracks, and seldom cross the line, except when main force officers are "retired" to work with the militia. Currently, such transfers are regarded as irreversible demotions,[96] and both local force and militia cadres tend to be frustrated by dead-end career patterns even more than are main force officers.[97]

The impact of a rotation system on political commissars' careers would probably be about the same as on commanders. Although they do have somewhat more lateral mobility in the local forces, commissars in the main forces appear to be subject to the same career platterns and frustrations as other officers. It is virtually certain that, with rare exceptions, commissars will continue to be part of a distinct career progression under the GPD, however.

Cadre rotation will tend to lower the relative importance of commissars, if we are correct in thinking that it will reduce the role of unit party committees. Increased formal schooling and more widespread experience with modern weapons systems will also increase the emphasis upon technical expertise. This, in turn, will increasingly call into question, especially in the minds of the post-Yenan generations of cadres, the value of commissars in a modern army.

NOTES

1. *Handbook*, pp. 5-1 and 5-25; and D. Gordon White, p. 366.
2. *PR*, No. 11 (17 March 1978), 4; and "The Military Service System in China," *China Reconstructs*, 29, No. 7 (July 1980), 43.
3. The following discussion is based on: "Military Service Law of the PRC" (30 July 1955), trans. in *CB*, No. 344 (8 August 1955), 4-11; Ch'iu Shih-tung, "Current Military Service on the Chinese Mainland," *I and S*, 10, No. 10 (July 1974), 64-70; *Handbook*, p. 5-21; and "Decision on Kwangtung's 1968 Conscription Work," (November 1967). See text regarding this last source.
4. Some "People's Police" are "enlisted through compulsory military service." *NCNA*, 18 December 1979, trans. in *FBIS*, No. 247, p. L1.
5. According to the "Decision on Kwangtung's 1968 Conscription Work," the quota for that province (population approximately 40 million) was 78,650. This was about 7.2 percent of the national quota. The latter was therefore about 1,092,000, which was nearly one-third of PLA strength. This figure is plausible, considering that the PLA was expanding, and that there had not been any draft in 1966-67. Annual draft calls have ranged from 800,000 up to 1.2 million (Ch'iu Shih-tung, p. 65).
6. This information was provided by Marc Blecher and Harvey Nelsen, based on refugee interviews in 1974. Also see *Political Work Regulations* (1963) (XVI.8.); and *NCNA*, 13 December 1967, trans. in *SCMP*, No. 4081, p. 21. On "entering by the back door," see: *PR*, No. 16 (15 April 1977), 28.
7. Changsha Hunan Prov. Svc., 31 October 1980, trans. in *FBIS*, No. 214, p. 4.
8. *Handbook*, p. 5-21. From 1965-69, terms of service were temporarily extended to four years in the infantry; five years in the air force, public security, and certain special units; and six years for fleet sailors. From 1968 to 1974 terms were shortened to two years for ground forces and three years for the navy and air force (Ch'iu Shih-tung, pp. 66-67).
9. *Handbook*, pp. 5-21 and 5-25.
10. Wettern, pp. 124-125; and Chin Chien-li, "Armored Forces."
11. Interviews with two refugee informants (1974); and "Regulations on the Service of Officers," article 18.
12. *JMJP*, 1 August 1979, p. 1, trans. in *China Report*, No. 14 (7 September 1979), 16. Also see: Nanking Kiangsu Prov. Svc., 14 September 1978, trans. in *FBIS*, No. 182, pp. G9-G10; *NCNA*, 1 August 1979, in *FBIS*, No. 152, p. L3; *Wen Hui Pao*, 31 August 1979, trans. in *FBIS*, No. 184, p. L9; Hofei Anhui Prov. Svc., 18 September 1979, trans. in *FBIS*, No. 184, p. O1; and *NCNA*, 13 October 1979, trans. in *FBIS*, No. 202, p. F3.
13. I am grateful to LCDR Jerry Fletcher for this information.
14. *NCNA*, 23 October 1979, trans. in *FBIS*, No. 207, p. L14; Nanchang Kiangsi Prov. Svc., 24 September 1979, trans. in *FBIS*, No. 189, pp. O3-O4; and *NCNA*, 23 January 1981, trans. in *FBIS*, No. 017, p. L9.
15. This discussion draws on Hsu Hsiang-ch'ien, *HC*, No. 10 (1979); *NCNA*, 1 August 1979, trans. in *FBIS*, No. 150, pp. L8-L9; *NCNA*, 14 January 1980, in *FBIS*, No. 010, p. E4; Shihchiachuang Hopeh Prov. Svc., 27 October 1978, trans. in *FBIS*, No. 212, p. K1; Sian Shensi Prov. Svc., 10 September 1978, trans. in *FBIS*, No. 177, p. M1; *CFCP*, 1 January 1980, trans. in *NCNA*, 1 January 1980, in *FBIS*, No. 001, p. L5; Peking Dom. Svc., 26 September 1979, trans. in *FBIS*, No. 189, p. L5; *NCNA*, 9 September 1979, trans. in *FBIS*, No. 176, pp. L13-L15; *CFCP*, 1 August 1979, p. 1, trans. in *FBIS*, No. 150, pp. L1-L4; *NCNA*, 23 April 1978, trans. in *FBIS*, No. 79, pp. E11-E14; *NCNA*, 7 September 1979, trans.

in *FBIS*, No. 177, pp. L16-L18; Peking Dom. Svc., 30 November 1978, trans. in *FBIS*, No. 234, pp. K3-K4.

16. These regulations are reproduced in full by Tang Chi-ming in "Military Affairs in 1980 [*i-chiu-pa-ling-nien ti chung-kung chün-shih*]," *CKYCYK*, 15, No. 1 (15 January 1981), 71-72. For two recent works on the PLA academy system, see William R. Heaton, "Professional Military Education in China: A Visit to the Military Academy of the PLA," *CQ*, No. 81 (March 1980), 122-128; and Wang Yong-yeh, "Inquiry Regarding the Current Situation of Chinese Communist Military Academies [*tui chung-kung chün-shih yuan-hsiao hsien-k'uang chih t'an-t'ao*],"*CKYCYK* , 14, No. 12 (15 December 1980), 84-90.

17. Peking Domestic Svc., 25 February 1981, trans. in *FBIS*, No. 038, p. L18.

18. Nelsen, *The Chinese Military System*, p. 146.

19. Takashi Oka, *CSM*, 8 January 1980, p. 3.

20. *NCNA*, 7 November 1979, trans. in *FBIS*, No. 219, pp. L13-L14; and *CFCP*, 9 October 1979, cited by Peking Dom. Svc., 9 October 1979, trans. in *FBIS*, No. 200, p. E14.

21. In 1970, Edgar Snow interviewed a regimental commander and one of his officers, both of whom had joined the same *squad* in 1933, and had served together in this same regiment ever since (*The Long Revolution*, pp. 112-113). Such cases are still fairly typical.

22. Nelsen, *The Chinese Military System*, pp. 150-151.

23. *NCNA*, 24 November 1979, trans. in *FBIS*, No. 228, p. P1. In the mid-1970s, an RF division in Hangchow was ordered to relocate. Many soldiers refused to go because their wives, who were all Hangchow natives, refused to accompany them. The unit finally moved after being ordered three times, wrecking its barracks on the way out. (I am grateful to Roger Garside for this story.)

24. *NCNA* (Chengchow), 1 December 1974, trans. in *SPRCP*, No. 5753, p. 232.

25. Nelsen, *The Chinese Military System*, pp. 148-150.

26. Ibid., p. 152.

27. In *The Chinese High Command*, Whitson argued that a "balance of power system" among "field army elites" controlled China from 1949 through at least 1970.

28. William L. Parrish, "Factions in Chinese Military Politics," *CQ*, No. 56 (October-December 1973), 667-699.

29. Nelsen, *The Chinese Military System*, pp. 155-156. This "phenomenon" in the PLA is admitted in *HC*, No. 8 (1978), trans. in *FBIS*, No. 150, p. E14.

30. *CFCP*, 11 December 1980, quoted by Peking Dom. Svc., 19 December 1980, trans. in *FBIS*, No. 247, p. L32. Also see *CFCP*, cited in *JMJP*, 21 November 1980, p. 5, trans. in *FBIS*, No. 230, pp. L17-L19.

31. USCGDLO.

32. *Wen Wei Pao* (Hong Kong), 14 January 1981, trans. in *FBIS*, No. 009, p. U3; and *Tung Hsiang* (Hong Kong), No. 18 (16 March 1980), pp. 8-10, trans. in *China Report*, No. 75 (8 April 1980), p. 44.

33. Wang En-Mao, cited by Ch'angch'un Kirin Prov. Svc., 12 November 1979, trans. in *FBIS*, No. 222, pp. S2-S3; Yeh Chien-ying, cited by *CFCP*, 10 August 1978, trans. in *FBIS*, No. 156, p. E25; *CFCP*, 7 October 1979, quoted by *NCNA*, 8 October 1979, trans. in *FBIS*, No. 198, pp. L17-L19; Shenyang Liaoning Prov. Svc., 27 February 1980, trans. in *FBIS*, No. 042, p. S2; and Canton Kwangtung Prov. Svc., 25 March 1980, trans. in *FBIS*, No. 062, p. P3.

34. *NCNA*, 19 December 1979, in *FBIS*, No. 246, p. R2; and *JMJP*, 18

November 1979, p. 3, trans. in *FBIS*, No. 239, pp. L4-L6.

35. *NCNA*, 28 February 1981, trans. in *FBIS*, No. 041, p. O2; and Lanchow Kansu Prov. Svc., 28 April 1980, trans. in *FBIS*, No. 084, p. T1.

36. Such a riot on Hainan, in December 1980, reportedly led to a bloody clash with security troops: *KYODO*, 20 February 1981, in *FBIS*, No. 034, pp. L3-L4. Numerous suicides by cadres were alleged by Soviet-run "*Pa Yi* [August First] Radio," 14 January 1980, trans. in *China Report*, No. 54 (25 January 1980), 24-25. For a Nationalist study see Tsou Szu-yuan, "Survey of Bandit Army Discharge and Retirement in 1981 (*yi-chiu-ba-yi nien-tu fei-chün t'u-wu t'ui-wu kai-k'uang*)," *FCYP*, 23, No. 8 (February 1981), 54-59.

37. *NCNA*, 10 December 1980, trans. in *FBIS*, No. 240, p. L13.

38. *KMJP*, 31 March 1979, p. 1. On medal awards in 1979, see examples in *NCNA*, 21 January 1980, trans. in *FBIS*, No. 016, p. L2; *NCNA*, 16 March 1979, trans. in *FBIS*, No. 56, p. E5. On the pre-1979 system, see *Handbook*, pp. 10-13 and 10-14; *PR*, No. 25 (20 June 1969), 15-16; *PR*, No. 35 (30 August 1968), 23-27; *PR*, No. 15 (12 August 1968), 5; and *PR*, No. 39 (26 September 1969), 12-13.

39. *JMJP*, 23 October 1974, trans. in *SPRCP*, No. 5745, pp. 57-60.

40. Kunming Yunnan Prov. Svc., 6 November 1979, trans. in *FBIS*, No. 218, p. Q3; Peking Dom. Svc., 19 October 1979, trans. in *China Report*, No. 33 (14 November 1979), 31-32; and Kunming Yunnan Prov. Svc., 4 January 1981, trans. in *FBIS*, No. 002, p. Q1.

41. Shenyang Liaoning Prov. Svc., 15 January 1980, trans. in *FBIS*, No. 015, pp. S5-S7, especially p. S7; Shih-chia-ch'uang Hopeh Prov. Svc., 27 January 1980, trans. in *FBIS*, No. 024, pp. R3-R4; Canton City Svc., 1 February 1980, trans. in *FBIS*, No. 024, p. P1; Foochow Fukien Prov. Svc., 8 August 1979, trans. in *FBIS*, No. 160, p. O9; *NCNA*, 20 May 1978, trans. in *FBIS*, No. 99, pp. E1-E2; and Kunming Yunnan Prov. Svc., 18 January 1980, trans. in *FBIS*, No. 015, p. Q5.

42. *NCNA*, 6 December 1978, trans. in *FBIS*, No. 237, pp. E21-E22.

43. *NCNA*, 2 March 1981, trans. in *FBIS*, No. 041, pp. L3-L4; Shanghai City Svc., 13 March 1981, trans. in *FBIS*, No. 050, p. O6; Peking Dom. Svc., 21 March 1981, trans. in *FBIS*, No. 056, p. L10; and Nanking Kiangsu Prov. Svc., 26 March 1981, trans. in *FBIS*, No. 059, p. O1.

44. Yeh Chien-ying, "Speech at the All-Army Political Work Conference," (29 May 1978), in *NCNA*, 4 June 1978, trans. in *FBIS*, No. 108, p. E13. Also see *CFCP*, 10 August 1978, quoted by *NCNA*, 10 August 1978, trans. in *FBIS*, No. 156, pp. E23-E26.

45. ["Central Committee Issues Regulations on PLA Political Work"], *NCNA*, 10 August 1978, trans. in *FBIS*, No. 156, pp. E13-E18 (cited hereafter as Political Regulations—1978"); and Peking Dom. Svc., 25 September 1978, trans. in *FBIS*, No. 193.

46. "Political Regulations—1978," p. E5. See similar provisions in *Political Work Regulations* (1963) (I.1-5).

47. *JMJP*, 24 January 1981, trans. in *FBIS*, No. 021, p. L14. Two especially clear statements on current political work themes are by Yin Fa-t'ang (Tibet MD) in Lhasa Tibet Radio, 21 February 1981, trans. in *FBIS*, No. 035, pp. Q2-Q3; and by air force commander Chang T'ing-fa in *NCNA*, 26 March 1980, trans. in *FBIS*, No. 061, pp. L2-L5.

48. *JMJP*, 23 October 1974, trans. in *SPRCP*, No. 5745, p. 57.

49. For examples, see: *NCNA* (Canton), 14 August 1971, trans. in *SCMP*, No. 4964, pp. 181-182; *JMJP*, 11 January 1974, trans. in *SCMP*, No. 5548, pp. 134-136; *KMJP*, 31 July 1974, trans. in *SPRCP*, No. 5688, pp. 56-58; *NCNA*, 2 August 1974, trans. in *SPRCP*, No. 5674, p. 79; *CFCP*, 1 August 1978, trans. in

FBIS, No. 148, p. E17; and Sining Tsinghai Prov. Svc., 2 August 1978, trans. in *FBIS*, No. 152, pp. E12-E13.

50. Peking Dom. Svc., 2 January 1980, trans. in *FBIS*, No. 005, p. R3.

51. Robert J. Lifton, *Thought Reform and the Psychology of Totalism* (New York: Norton, 1961); and Martin K. Whyte, *Small Groups and Political Rituals in China* (Berkeley and Los Angeles: University of California Press, 1974).

52. Kilkowicz, pp. 94-96.

53. Whyte, Chapter X.

54. On "lingering fear," see Chang T'ing-fa in *NCNA*, 22 September 1978, trans. in *FBIS*, No. 187, p. E9.

55. *NCNA*, 5 September 1978, trans. in *FBIS*, No. 174, p. E3.

56. *NCNA*, 28 June 1978, trans. in *FBIS*, No. 126, p. E3; Foochow Fukien Prov. Svc., 30 March 1979, trans. in *FBIS*, No. 65, p. O4; Canton Kwangtung Prov. Svc., 6 December 1978, trans. in *FBIS*, No. 240, p. E12; Wuhan Hupeh Prov. Svc., 19 April 1979, trans. in *FBIS*, No. 80, p. P4; *NCNA*, 5 Setpember 1978, trans. in *FBIS*, No. 174, p. E3; and *NCNA*, 16 October 1979, trans. in *FBIS*, No. 204, p. L13.

57. Canton Kwangtung Prov. Svc., 1 February 1980, trans. in *FBIS*, No. 024, p. P1.

58. *Political Work Regulations* (1963) (I.3.) (emphasis added).

59. Elmquist, p. 279.

60. For an interesting account of company-level political work and "democratic life" in the PLA, see: *NCNA*, 3 August 1975, trans. in *SPRCP*, No. 5914, pp. 108 ff. Also see *KMJP*, 20 July 1974, trans. in *SPRCP*, No. 5679, pp. 57-61; *NCNA*, 2 November 1978, trans. in *FBIS*, No. 217, pp. K2-K4.

61. *Political Work Regulations* (1963) (X.3.).

62. Ibid. (III. and X.3.). The term "party committee" (*Tang Wei-yuan-hui*) is used only at and above regimental level (III.1.).

63. "The Gun Must Forever Be Kept in the Hands of the Party and People," *JMJP*, 13 November 1974, trans. in *SPRCP*, No. 5737, p. 125.

64. Nelsen, *The Chinese Military System*, p. 149 (emphasis added).

65. For examples, see *NCNA*, 29 January 1980, trans. in *FBIS*, No. 023, pp. O1-O2; Kunming Yunnan Prov. Svc., 23 February 1979, trans. in *FBIS*, No. 39, p. J3; Huhehot Inner Mongolia Regional Svc., 28 October 1979, trans. in *FBIS*, No. 212, pp. K1-K2; and *NCNA*, 27 May 1978, trans. in *FBIS*, No. 107, pp. E7-E8.

66. Dick, p. 175.

67. This discussion was prompted by Harvey Nelsen's observations in private correspondence. On the Northern and Southern Fronts in 1979, see Jencks, "Punitive War," pp. 805-807.

68. Whitson, p. 437.

69. For a discussion of early commissar roles, see Ying-mao Kao, pp. xxiv-xxvii.

70. On Chinese handling of PWs, see *CSM*, 28 March 1979, pp. 1 and 9.

71. *NCNA*, 6 December 1978, trans. in *FBIS*, No. 237, pp. E21-E22; Kunming Yunnan Prov. Svc., 18 January 1980, trans. in *FBIS*, No. 015, p. Q5; Peking Dom. Svc., 7 December 1978, trans. in *FBIS*, No. 237, pp. E22-E23; *NCNA*, 20 May 1978, trans. in *FBIS*, No. 99, p. E2.

72. *KMJP*, 31 March 1979, p. 1.

73. "Hold High . . . the Political Work Regulations," *CFCP*, 8 May 1963, trans. in Ying-mao Kao; and *NCNA*, 25 May 1978, trans. in *FBIS*, No. 107, p. E2.

74. *JMJP*, 24 January 1980, trans. in *FBIS*, No. 021, p. L15.

75. Wuhan Hupeh Prov. Svc., 26 January 1980, trans. in *FBIS*, No. 021, p. P2; and *NCNA*, 15 October 1978, trans. in *FBIS*, No. 205, p. E6.
76. *Political Work Regulations* (1963) (IV.2.) (emphasis added).
77. Ibid. (IV.4.) (emphasis added).
78. Whitson, especially pp. 439-449.
79. Dick, pp. 176-177.
80. Whitson, p. 20. On "Chu-ko Liang meetings," see Ying-mao Kao, p. xxiv. "Chu-ko Liang meetings" in the PLA were reported in the early 1970s.
81. Quoted in *Hung Chan-pao* (Canton), No. 10 (10 October 1967), trans. in *SCMP*, No. 4072, p. 3.
82. "Important Measure to Promote Revolutionization of our Army," *CFCP*, 25 May 1965, trans. in Ying-mao Kao, pp. 102-105.
83. This, and the following, is drawn from: "Transfer of Army Cadres to Lower Ranks," *JMJP*, 19 July 1975, trans. in *SPRCP*, No. 5925, pp. 144-147. Also see chapter 4.
84. See the MAC Resolution cited in *NCNA*, 9 August 1978, trans. in *FBIS*, No. 156, p. E22; and *JMJP*, 9 September 1978, p. 2, trans. in *FBIS*, No. 177, p. E12.
85. Foochow Fukien Prov. Svc., 30 March 1979, trans. in *FBIS*, No. 65, p. O4.
86. Teng Hsiao-p'ing, Speech to the All-Army Political Work Conference (2 June 1978), trans. in *NCNA*, 5 June 1978, in *FBIS*, No. 109, pp. E9 and E10; Lanchow Kansu Prov. Svc., 10 December 1979, trans. in *FBIS*, No. 002 (1980), p. T8; Chengtu Szechuan Prov. Svc., 23 December 1979, trans. in *FBIS*, No. 006 (1980), p. Q5; *CSM*, 24 June 1977, p. 12; *Pei-ching Jih-pao [Peking Daily]*, 30 July 1979, p. 4, trans. in *China Report*, No. 46 (7 January 1980), 65-66.
87. *Shih-k'an [Poetry]*, No. 8 (1979), 50-55. Also reprinted in *Wen-hui Pao*, 8 September 1979, trans. in *FBIS*, No. 207, pp. L14-L18.
88. *NCNA*, 12 December 1980, trans. in *FBIS*, No. 246, p. L13; Canton Kwangtung Prov. Svc., 25 January 1981, trans. in *FBIS*, No. 018, pp. P1-P2; and *NCNA*, 29 January 1981, trans. in *FBIS*, No. 020, pp. L1-L2.
89. Whitson, p. 368, also see pp. 414 and 431.
90. Ibid., pp. 445-446.
91. *PR*, No. 10 (4 March 1977), 10-11.
92. The roles of the unit party committee in cadre selection, evaluation, and assignment are specified in *Political Work Regulations* (1963) (I.5.g. and X.4.a.).
93. *JMJP*, 23 October 1974, trans. in *SPRCP*, No. 5745, pp. 56-60.
94. Canton Kwangtung Prov. Svc., 25 January 1981, trans. in *FBIS*, No. 018, p. P1.
95. *KYODO*, 22 May 1978, in *FBIS*, No. 99, p. E23; and *Mainichi Shimbun* (Tokyo), 9 September 1978, p. 4.
96. Such "transfers" are provided for in *Political Work Regulations* (1963) (XVI.5-7). For two examples of frustrated former regular officers assigned to PAD duty, see: *JMJP*, 25 August 1975, in *SPRCP*, No. 5948, pp. 188-190.
97. Nelsen, *The Chinese Military System*, p. 151.

8
Conclusion

This final chapter attempts to draw together the various threads of this study. We will briefly recall the professionalizing trend in the PLA since the civil war and the resistance of the officer corps to involvement in the GPCR and to radical "Maoism," the rapid "return to barracks" after the fall of Lin Piao, and the behavior of the PLA in the events surrounding Mao's death and since.

Some current trends will be discussed, in the areas of defense strategy, organization, non-military activities, and the military personnel system.

Finally, we will suggest some projections of the future of the Chinese officer corps.

THE DEBATE OVER MILITARY LINE

In chapters 2, 3, and 4, we traced a controversy over "military line" which is older than the PLA itself. This running debate was long represented in the official press as an ideological one. Yet ideology is not always an unambiguous guide to action, and certainly has not been in this matter. Any attempts to describe the debate simply in terms of "reds versus experts," for example, overlooks such vital factors as regionalism, civil-military relations, and bureaucratic politics. Modernization and regularization of the PLA have not been fundamental issues in the top echelon power struggles of the CCP. These issues at the operating level of national military security policy have become controversial only when they have impinged on other, more fundamental operating issues (such as national resource allocations and alliance arrangements), and even more basic issues at the institutional level.

It is especially important to distinguish debates about military ethic and style from power struggles. P'eng Te-huai, Lo Jui-ch'ing, and Lin Piao were all purged when they lost out in struggles for political power, and only incidentally, if at all, because they advocated particular "military lines." In all three cases, too, an erroneous "military line" was attributed to the purge victim only years after the fact—and always in the context of a renewed struggle for political power. It is telling that Lin Piao's military line was attacked from both the "red" and "expert" sides of the policy debate in 1974-75. "Reds" accused him of opposing "people's war" and "politics in command," while "experts" accused him of "subjectivism," "idealism," and "metaphysics"—both labeled his alleged errors the "bourgeois military line." In the PRC, one might define the "bourgeois military line" as "any military policy advocated by a political opponent."

Having said this, it must be added that, to the extent power struggles have involved actual ideological differences over the current and future shape of Chinese society, military policy has been one component of the debate. As we stressed in chapter 1, the military is intimately and inevitably related to the society it serves. The point here is just that "military line," per se, has never been fundamentally at issue in a power struggle.

Mao Tse-tung was closely identified with the ideal of the military as a multifunctional tool of the party (a "fighting force, a political force, and an economic production force"). Closely correlated was the strategy of "people's war," which was based on the assumption of military weakness vis-a-vis China's enemies. In opposition, men like Chu Teh, P'eng Te-huai, Yeh Chien-ying, Liu Po-ch'eng, Su Yü, and Nieh Jung-chen advocated armed forces devoted primarily to military operations with the most advanced weapons available. This implied the necessity to strive for industrial, scientific, and military modernity.

Clearly, different times and circumstances favored different military policies, and the history of the communist movement has seen different blendings of these two. Mao's "people's war" ideal dominated during the anti-Japanese war. During the civil war, and especially after 1949, there was a trend toward more conventional and professional military operations and policies. After 1949 there was also a marked tendency toward bureaucratic routinization and professionalization in all segments of the regime, and the PLA officer corps emerged as a separate and relatively self-conscious opinion group. It developed routines, career patterns, and preferences. One preference was the avoidance of non-military activity, rather narrowly construed. Mao opposed this PLA withdrawal from politics. He was interested in using the army as a militant arm of the CCP in the mobilization and transformation of society—a role the PLA under P'eng Te-huai avoided.

The irony of the situation was that party control over the PLA was probably stronger in the 1950s than at any time before or since.[1] This was precisely because the army confined itself to military affairs. Over the years, the PLA has intervened most in nonmilitary activities whenever politics has been "in command." That aspect of the Maoist model which requires a multifunctional army tends to contradict the other major aspect of party control.

Because the party controlled "the gun" in 1959, P'eng could not challenge Mao from a power base in the PLA. It was doubly ironic, then, that Mao and Lin Piao immediately proceeded to repoliticize the army so that they could use it to overthrow the "revisionist" party. In the 1960s, Mao himself successfully regained control of the party with "the gun." Supposedly, a "Maoist" army is highly responsive to the party because of control at the top and by local party committees at the unit level. The events of the late 1960s demonstrated that such close lateral ties can just as well facilitate military control of the party. It is surely no coincidence that Mao first called for "politics in command" of the army (at Kutien in 1929) when he was trying to gain control of Li Li-san's Central Committee. Then, as later, the civilians who dominated the CCP wanted to confine the army to purely military work, partly, at least, so as to prevent a military-based challenge to the political status quo. In the 1960s, it was quite true, as Mao and his followers constantly asserted, that Liu Shao-ch'i, Teng Hsiao-p'ing, et al., wanted the PLA to confine itself to the business of national defense and to leave politics to civilians. At that time, Liu wanted the "party to control the gun," and Mao did not.

Having regained control of the party by 1969, Mao moved to control the monster he had created. Allied with Chou En-lai and the moderates, he labored in the early 1970s to divest the PLA of most of the domestic political power he (Mao) had thrust upon it in the 1960s. After the fall of Lin Piao in 1971, this task proved remarkably easy.

PERSISTENT "PROFESSIONALISM"

It is a basic contention of this study that Chinese officers, especially those below corps level, are strongly disinclined toward political involvement. They resisted being forced into the GPCR, and speedily withdrew from politics in the 1970s because they preferred to do so. In chapter 1, we saw that professional soldiers value order, hierarchy, division of labor, public safety, and strong civil authority. They wish to concentrate their own energies upon the specialized problems of military security and, therefore, to avoid non-military affairs. The Chinese officer corps has exhibited these "professional" preferences to a remarkable degree over the past three decades, most notably when the PLA was thrust into the Cultural Revolution.

The Cultural Revolution

The PLA's progress from political dominance in the early 1960s to military intervention in 1967-68 resulted from pressure by "Maoists" to expand the military role, and from the crisis in the civilian sector which required the PLA to intervene to maintain order. China's post-1949 history has demonstrated Huntington's point that the scope and level of internal military political power is an inverse function of the stability and strength of civilian political institutions. It was the breakdown and turmoil of the GLF and the ideological and political conflict within the party CC which first caused the PLA to reverse the professionalizing trend in the late 1950s. As the conflict between Mao and Liu Shao-ch'i intensified, the army was thrust ever more deeply into non-military activities. CCP leadership over military and bureaucratic institutions had been thorough and sufficient until the CCP began to disintegrate.

Even at the height of the crisis, troop commanders persisted in the "bourgeois military line" that soldiers ought to devote their energies to soldiering. Subordinates were still being told to "let army headquarters handle outside (civilian) matters."[2] To be sure, there were some in the PLA who were more anxious to avoid politics than others. Many regional commissars, in particular, were quite willing to act as a political "priesthood" for both the PLA and for civilian society. Whitson writes that in 1963-64, these men became involved in civilian political work.[3] In fact, it was rather the reverse: As Harvey Nelsen writes, "Regional commissars did not become involved in civilian work—they were already civilians. It would be more correct to say that Party secretaries became involved in military affairs."[4] Some of these regional commissars were radical "Maoists" (e.g., Chang Ch'un-ch'iao), but others were not. Very often, they held common cause with the regional military commanders and CCP cadres, both of which groups wished to keep the PLA out of the Cultural Revolution.

Among PLA main force officers (commissars included), the disinction between military and civilian was much more clear, and they overwhelmingly attempted to minimize their involvement in the GPCR and to maintain their purely military status.

As regional units were forced into action through the spring of 1967, they continued to opt for social order and to suppress radical Red Guards. This situation led up to the great crisis in late July and August: The "Wuhan Incident" of late July appeared to be a challenge to central party control over the PLA. The radicals in the Central Cultural Revolution Group exploited the incident with their attack on "capitalist roaders in the army." These events forced the MAC to commit main force units extensively to maintain order. These units were often forced to intervene against regional forces while simultaneously being attacked by radical Red Guards.

By mid-August 1967, PLA commanders faced virtually all the conditions that so often provoke coups d'etat in other countries, but there was no coup. Instead, the central and regional commanders exerted their considerable influence in a direct appeal to Mao to restore centralized control and order. Mao turned the GPCR away from "rebellion" and "power seizure," toward "unity," "revolutionary order," and "Great Alliances." The PLA, both main and regional forces, acted decisively to restore order.

"Party rebuilding" gathered momentum in 1968, and found expression in the formation of the provincial-level revolutionary committees (RCs) by early September. Veteran civilian cadres and military commanders, many of whom had been criticized by the Red Guards, controlled most of the RCs. Below the level of the RCs, PLA "Three Supports and Two Militaries" teams controlled much of China's government and economy.

There is a long tradition of CCP involvement with the PLA, and of PLA involvement in the civilian sector. John Simmonds goes so far as to claim that since the PLA parallels the party and government, from top to bottom, it has always existed as an alternate means for governing communist-controlled China. He goes on to say that the military is not designed to rule anything but itself, so it can overthrow existing bureaucratic elites, but only rule for a while. The problem, according to Simmonds, is that once the PLA assumes civil power, it may become "civilianized" and not give its power up again. This view is wrong on several counts. First of all, Simmonds implies that the party is thoroughly "civilian." As we have repeatedly emphasized, this is just not so: Most of China's top leaders have held both military and civilian posts, and make little distinction between "military" and "civilian" perspectives. The remarkable fact is not that top PLA leaders ended the GPCR with great political power, for they had always held substantial power. What was significant was the resistance of even most of the very top soldiers to involving military units and organizations in civil politics. Simmonds assumes that there is (or was) a top leadership with the power to "shift gears" (his metaphor) from civil bureaucracy to PLA, and back again, in order to carry on "permanent but controlled revolution."[5] In fact, despite the PLA tradition of political involvement, most of the PLA high command resisted the "shift" to PLA control, and acted rapidly to facilitate the return to orderly civilian party leadership. Moreover, PLA officers below the level of corps or MD commander—men who had held little political power before the Cultural Revolution—strongly resisted the very involvement which gave them enhanced power, and they "returned to barracks" with remarkable speed after 1971.

The "Return to Barracks": 1969-74

At the climax of the GPCR, in the late summer of 1967, Mao and the military high command made a compromise that shaped the events of the years that followed. Social order and control were reestablished in the name of "Mao Tse-tung's Thought." Military leaders (as opposed to the PLA as a monolithic institution) dominated China in the following years. MR commanders, in particular, were so powerful they had to be consulted in the reconstruction of the political order. Accordingly, they were heavily represented in the Ninth Central Committee, elected in April 1969.

Although the party center was still engaged in infighting while the regional commanders held unprecedented power, the latter never defied Peking openly. The main forces could not have suppressed the regions, had all or even most of them rebelled. The regional commanders remained basically loyal to party and state, however, "despite the centrifugal tendencies inherent in their newly attained power."[6] Although they were anxious to reestablish the party and orderly political processes, they acted to protect themselves from any recurrence of radical civilian attack and from internal PLA rivals. MR leaders therefore maintained control of revolutionary committees and of the later provincial party committees. The chief obstacle to real reunification of the CCP was internal PLA rivalry, and the chief obstacle to PLA unity was Lin Piao.

As we saw in chapter 4, Lin was promoting his own power, rather than the PLA's. He had relatively little military backing, having alienated much of the high command during the Cultural Revolution. He had risen because of Mao's support, and the withdrawal of that support in 1970-71 made his fall inevitable.

He had been the leading spokesman for the military aspects of radical "Maoism" during the 1960s. The fall of Lin and his group ended the apparent influence of soldiers who actively sought to inject the PLA, as an institution, into non-military activities. Since September 1971 there has been little evidence of political radicalism in the PLA.

William Whitson was certainly on the mark, in 1972, when he predicted that, just as in Kiangsi in 1929-31, it would be Chou En-lai and Yeh Chien-ying who again would be the "professionals" who would step in to reverse a Mao-initiated trend toward excessive military involvement in civil affairs.[7] Yeh and Chou indeed were the architects of the post-Lin Piao return to normalcy in the PLA and the country. They seem to have had the active cooperation of the regional PLA commanders, who proved quite willing to return to a separation of military and party functions after 1971.

The army had entered the political and economic arena at the expense of the moderate civilian party and governmental bureaucrats who were the main targets of the Cultural Revolution. Military officers generally sympathized with these civilian cadres, however, and very often supported and protected them. This collusion between military and civilian cadres was a natural result of their complementary views on the separation of military and civilian functions. Military men, especially commanders, took common cause with "revisionist" cadres because the latter were (and are) necessary to the governing of the stable, disciplined, productive society which is a precondition for an effective modern military defense establishment.

In 1972-74, the PLA pulled out of most non-military activity. Following the Tenth Party Congress, the highly symbolic reshuffling of MR commands in late 1973 and early 1974 broke up the regional bases for "independent kingdoms" (and administered the *coup de grace* to the "field army balance of power" theory).

Transition: 1974-77

Through 1974-75, PLA subordination to the party was strongly emphasized with little apparent resistance. In 1974-76, two spheres of activity were noticeable exceptions to the re-emerging party-army separation of function: The militia and the PLA's General Political Department (GPD)—institutions wherein the "gang of four" retained considerable influence. After the Tenth Party Congress, and especially after the Fourth National People's Congress (January 1975), Chiang Ch'ing and her radical followers saw the handwriting on the wall: Once Mao was gone they were doomed unless they rapidly could build up a base from which to oppose the civilian and military "revisionists" led, respectively, by Chou En-lai and Yeh Chien-ying.

The radicals had two major assets: A geographical power base in Shanghai and control of the leading press and propaganda organs.[8] Moreover, they could count on Mao's personal support on certain issues. Once Mao was gone, however, they were quickly purged, despite their alleged attempt to stage a counter-coup with the Shanghai militia.[9]

As we have seen, the militia has been, and is likely to remain, a source of civil-military friction. How, or indeed whether, the problem of the militia can be solved, remains to be seen. One solution would be the one P'eng Te-huai attempted after 1954: Outright abolition of the militia in favor of a PLA reserve system. That would be a relatively drastic measure since it would require practical adjustments (e.g., more police units for public security duties) as well as a break with Mao's "three-in-one" military system. Meanwhile the militia appears to be back to the status of 1960-65: Under joint party-army control.

At this writing, all indications point toward a more "professional" PLA. Some fundamental attitudes seem to prevail among Chinese officers which make Mao's ideal of an obedient and politically activist PLA impossible. Always excepting the top layer of military-political "old warriors," Chinese officers apparently wish to avoid civilian politics so as to concentrate on national defense. The entire officer corps, even including the top echelon, is far more committed to specialization, efficiency, and national security than to revolutionary ideology.

This is not to say that ideology is no longer relevant, but that we are now more likely to see ideology modified to fit policy than vice versa. The beginning of that more pragmatic line was already evident in the redefinition of "Chairman Mao's Military Thought" after the fall of Lin Piao. Mao's longtime advocacy of careful and cautious planning, flexibility, and discipline were reemphasized, while "politics in command" was relegated to being a slogan rather than a "spiritual atomic bomb." We have also noted that the "old warriors" still persist in certain "Maoist" practices, such as the lack of rank titles and insignias. This is not because they are "Whateverists" (i.e., "Maoists"), but because they see value in these traditional PLA practices, and seem to fear psychological upset if they were too heedlessly cast aside. It is quite plausible that, as is rumored, Yeh Chien-ying and other "old warriors" are holding out against further "de-Maoification" for the same reason.

TRENDS

China's defensive strategy is in transition away from "people's war" toward a somewhat more conventional defense, capable of holding ground against foreign invasion. However, Chinese military leaders recognize their country's relative technical, economic, and military backwardness. Since that same recognition was a component of Mao's military and political thought, certain "Maoist" aspects of Chinese military doctrine and action will continue to be evident. Certain aspects of China's politics and armed forces provide indications of trends in military thinking and, in turn, influence the future of civil-military relations. These aspects include national security strategy, organization, nonmilitary activities, the commissar system, and the military personnel system.

National Security Strategy

In the 1960s, Defense Minister P'eng Te-huai embarked on a program of modernization which was heavily dependent on Soviet assistance. The dependency was not only distasteful but also risky, since Russian support might not be forthcoming in a crunch. When the Soviets failed to back China in the 1958 "Straits crisis" and then reneged on the nuclear sharing agreement in 1959, P'eng's vision of high-speed military modernization was doomed.

In the early 1960s, a "balanced" approach was adopted which entailed continued force modernization, but more slowly and on a self-sufficient basis, combined with an overall security strategy of "people's war." This strategy accentuated China's assets: people and political organization. Like Soviet "unified strategy" in the early 1920s, it reflected military weakness and thus envisioned a defensive strategy of mass mobilization.[10] "People's war" must remain the cornerstone of Chinese defense as long as the PRC remains technologically backward.

The "balanced" approach also accommodated the fact that PRC strategic security policy was and is subject to factional debate.[11] For example, Lin Piao's *Long Live the Victory of People's War*, and the "people's war" line generally, were aimed largely, if not primarily, at Lin's domestic opponents, especially Lo Jui-ch'ing (chapter 2).

"People's War" is a broad outlook rather than a particular tactical plan. It is not limited war but a *total mobilization* approach to defense. Thus, the current term "people's war under modern conditions" is not really new, since the concept has always been flexible enough to encompass nuclear missiles and aircraft just as well as "rifles plus millet." "What is central to the doctrine of people's war is its resort to *mobilization,* its use of *protraction,* and its decidedly *defensive* flavor. And those three characteristics are consistent with a wide variety of weaponry, tactics, and political ideologies."[12] From 1965 until quite recently, however, even the Chinese themselves narrowly conceived of "people's war" in terms of "luring deep" and guerrilla tactics. This was partly the influence of radical "Maoist" rhetoric, but was also owing to the fact that in the early 1960s, "people's war" offered a "quick fix" solution to China's technological backwardness[13] and has come to be associated with that condition.

Conceived in this way, "people's war" has serious shortcomings as a defensive strategy:

> The protracted war of annihilation against invading enemy forces "lured deep" into Chinese territory ... does not constitute worst case thinking. Rather, it is best case thinking—depicting a form of warfare that no reasonable or rational military adversary would possibly contemplate or undertake. Inasmuch as no opposing army since the 1930s has been foolish enough "to dare to go deep into our country," it is a non-existent category of defense planning, comprehensible only as one component of a larger effort to deter war. As a means of instilling confidence ... its efficacy has been undeniable. But it reveals little about how Chinese decision-

makers intend to deal with a range of more limited—and far more probable—threats to the nation's security.[14]

The most dangerous and probable Soviet military actions against China would be short-range armored thrusts into the north and Northeast, or bombardment of industrial and military centers, or both. Guerrilla warfare would be useless in the face of either. Hence, the current emphasis on conventional defense in the north and the concern with air defense. Nobody has yet spelled out just what is meant by "people's war under modern conditions," but it plainly involves more flexible strategic thinking within the limits imposed by current weaponry.[15]

Mao Tse-tung clearly wanted nuclear technology and realized what immense political leverage a nuclear capability would give China on the world stage—to say nothing of the national pride that nuclear-power status would engender internally. But he was unwilling to pay the price of Soviet domination or of an end to China's social revolution. He was faced with the dilemma that plagued him to the end of his days: He wanted the benefits of modern technology, but was unwilling to see the emergence and growth of the technical, educational, and managerial elites which always accompany technological development. Nuclear development would require a stable, modernizing economy, and (as P'eng Te-huai pointed out at Lushan in 1959) that meant no more chaotic political-economic experiments like the Great Leap Forward. Since Mao needed PLA backing in his campaign to unseat Liu Shao-ch'i, he had to proceed with military industrial development in any case. The "balanced strategy" therefore included an accelerated nuclear program.

The "balanced strategy" has remained in effect since the Cultural Revolution, with the emphasis shifting steadily toward modernization of the regular forces. A great virtue of the policy was, and is, that it can encompass such shifts. These affect the militia and the ground forces more than the more technically sophisticated branches of the PLA, which are more constrained by long lead times in weapons programs. That such long-term programs continued through the 1960s refutes the notion that "luring deep" was ever taken seriously as a long-term strategy—even during the Cultural Revolution.

Lin Piao was the spokesman—if not indeed the architect—of the "balanced policy." In the late 1960s, however, he did not take advantage of the flexibility the policy afforded. Rather, he belligerently accused the United States and the USSR of forming an anti-Chinese "Unholy Alliance,"[16] and he provoked the 1969 border fighting. This "adventurist" foreign policy reflected Lin's preoccupation with internal politics. Here, as in other ways we examined in chapter 4, Lin was unable to adjust to changing conditions because of his narrow political base.

Already in 1968, as the first nuclear weapons approached operational status, Mao and the moderates had begun to tone down their revolutionary rhetoric and to repair diplomatic contacts.[17] The very possession of nuclear weapons induced caution. Belligerent "Maoist" rhetoric steadily dissipated as Chinese nuclear strike capability increased. The official line squarely faced the fact that as the Americans and Russians became more frightened by China, the possibility of pre-emptive attack increased. As a result, the Chinese were careful not to make explicit threats about their nuclear weapons capability.

Furthermore, no open Chinese source has ever suggested that nuclear arms would allow the PLA to pursue a bolder tactical line. Interestingly, the secret 1961 *Work Bulletins* [*Kung-tso T'ung-hsun*] indicate quite matter-offactly that, even then, PLA commanders recognized that they might well obtain and use tactical nuclear weapons. However, the Chinese have chosen to publicise their weakness, especially to foreigners. Harvey Nelsen has also pointed out the slow and extremely secretive deployment of nuclear missiles in 1966-74. The reason, he argues, is that the Chinese were anxious not to provoke Soviet overreaction by disturbing the status quo too quickly or unexpectedly.[18]

Two important phenomena of the 1970s seem to have followed from the increased sense of China's vulnerability. One was the widely noted movement to prepare for nuclear attack, under Mao's slogan of "dig tunnels deep, store grain everywhere, [and] never seek hegemony." The Chinese sought to reassure foreigners of their peaceful intentions while maintaining the "state of siege" mentality in a new guise. The second result was the rapprochement with the United States in 1971-72.

Inherent in the "balanced" security strategy was a balanced military acquisition policy, which has accomodated the economic and industrial fluctuations we examined in chapter 6. Since 1977, Chinese leaders have debated defense and economic priorities more openly than at any time since the 1950s. It is hardly surprising that it has been lower-ranking PLA spokesmen who advocate "accelerated" military modernization—even if at the expense of the rest of the economy.[19] On the other hand, top-level military/civilian leaders like Hua, Yeh, Hsu, and Teng are advocating the "balanced" economic approach which emphasizes long-range growth and future self-sufficiency. The very vastness of China's economy helps moderate the problem of resource allocation, however. As Angus Fraser points out, although China is a poor country, it is a big poor country.[20] That fact allows a certain flexibility in the application of resources to social and security needs. It will help China avoid the fate of so many small impoverished states, whose soldiers have taken over so as to guarantee themselves the lion's share of hopelessly inadequate economies.

The debate between younger, more "professional" officers and the more economically minded "old warriors" has been over pace and magnitude, not over the perceived need. The debate has been "acute but not acrimonious," and no one appears to have been fired or transferred as a result of it. Moreover, the "gap was significantly narrowed by what seemed to be a compromise rather than a complete rejection of the [younger] officers' views."[21] While equipment modernization will have to proceed slowly, human modernization has been given high priority. "Ossified thinking" is under attack by means of modern professional training in combined arms operations and various technical specialties. Among older cadres, "ossified thinking" is being eliminated by retraining and by forced retirement.

If modern military thinking really takes hold, it will upset the institutional conservatism of the PLA. One important kind of "ossification" has been identified by Whitson as a "ground forces syndrome," which has inhibited strategic thinking as well as equipment development, and has been expressed in domination by the ground forces. Closely related is an "infantry weapons syndrome." Most commanders have had personal experience only

> ... with the strategic deployment of infantry small arms and the notion of firepower projections over a battle area extending no further than the several thousand yards covered by field artillery. This perception['s] ... persistence ... among most senior Chinese commanders at the corps and military-regional levels deserves

wider consideration by students of contemporary strategy in Asia, since it implies, among other things, that the Chinese high command remains preoccupied with a space-time strategic stage that is oriented to the thirty-miles-per-day foot march; it hardly suggests global offensive.[22]

For the foreseeable future, the ground forces, and their less-educated peasant officers, will continue to dominate the PLA. This will be true even as the post-1945 generations take over the high command. Even if these younger men develop new conceptions of modern warfare and overcome the "infantry weapons syndrome," a somewhat updated "ground forces syndrome" will remain. Interservice rivalries seem likely to intensify as the passing years bring more advanced naval, air, and missile forces which attempt to erode ground force dominance.

In terms of China's strategic policy, increased PLA professionalism, for reasons we examined in Chapter 1, will tend to reinforce the highly realistic and non-ideological foreign policy which has emerged under the current leadership.

It will take several more decades for the industrial base to become capable of providing the quality, quantity, and variety of modern arms needed to put the PRC in the military "big leagues." Meanwhile, the military deterrent depends upon the possibility that the Chinese might get off a few nuclear warheads in retaliation. The principal means of deterrent will have to be diplomacy and deception. By understating and concealing the strength they do have, the Chinese leave it up to the military professionals in the US, USSR, and elsewhere to overestimate PLA power. Partly by denying that they are, or ever will be, a great power, the Chinese have managed to convince a great many foreigners, who ought to know better, that China actually is a great power.

For the foreseeable future, there is likely to be little work on developing a capability to project military power beyond China's borders, except for a small but credible nuclear deterrent. Despite nuclear and conventional weapons advances, the PLA will remain technologically inferior to the US and Soviet armed forces for decades to come, and will continue to plan and operate on that assumption. It is unlikely that this could or would change even once China has really operational nuclear strike forces (including both tactical and intercontinental ones)—which are still years away.[23]

External factors may cause modifications in China's essentially defensive "balanced" strategy, but only a really drastic turn of events could lead to its abandonment. One very dangerous possibility does exist: PRC leaders are increasingly amenable to military cooperation with Japan and the NATO countries,[24] and have even indicated a desire to purchase American weapons.[25] If, in an ill-advised effort to scare the Russians, the United States or its allies were to furnish significant military aid to the PRC, it might cause a jump in *perceived* Chinese military power. That, in turn, might contribute to a more aggressive Chinese foreign policy. Even more likely, it could provoke some sort of "pre-emptive" action by the Soviet Union, which is already concerned with the essentially non-existent "Chinese threat." In either event, such Western action would prove to be both unnecessary and dangerous.

Organization

In addition to economic limitations and the "ground forces syndrome," China's geography and inadequate transportation net require a strategy of regional defense rather than centralized national defense. As we saw in chapter 5, this strategy is expressed in the concentration of the PLA's most modern units in northeastern China. In that area—with its important industrial and political centers—the main forces will attempt to defend some territory with more-or-less conventional tactics. Elsewhere, the reliance will continue to be largely upon foot infantry and "luring deep."

Regional units and the militia, which are most susceptible to sudden change, are apt to be the most sensitive indicators of Chinese military priorities. As long as they continue to be emphasized at the current levels, it will indicate that the PRC remains committed to economic development and self-defense of large areas by "people's war." On the other hand, the reduction of regional or militia forces, or the integration of the former into the main forces, would indicate a more conventional defensive strategy and possibly even a more aggressive foreign policy (the latter because it would enhance the capability for military action beyond China's borders). Complete abolition of the regional forces is unlikely, for they can serve usefully even in conventional or nuclear war, and are not a major economic drain.

Other organizational changes which might herald departures in military policy would be those affecting the military regional system. Further consolidation of the MRs would undoubtedly indicate a more centrally coordinated conventional defense of those areas involved. Such a redrawing of boundaries would have to be preceded by improved internal communications and transportation to facilitate large scale maneuver and redeployment. The MRs are now about as big as geography and current mobility and logistics permit.

There are current indications that the PLA is going to become smaller, but better trained and (to the extent possible) better equipped.

Nonmilitary Activity

The PLA still engages in several nonmilitary duties. Self-sufficiency production is perhaps the most widely noted. This PLA tradition, practiced mainly by the regional forces, makes good economic sense. By feeding themselves, regional soldiers substantially reduce their burden on the national economy. Self-sufficiency production continues to be publicized—which points up its domestic propaganda value. The fact that the army works to support itself is of symbolic importance in a society where everyone is asked to make sacrifices. As was indicated in chapter 3, PLA commanders have not voiced much opposition to self-sufficiency production by the regional forces. We also noted that the conventional wisdom, that professional officers object to PLA productive labor in the civilian economy, is a moot point. Official PRC statistics indicate that, in fact, such PLA labor is minimal.

Of continuing political importance is the interface of MR, MD, and MSD organs with those of provincial and local government and party, and the presence of PLA cadres in the PADs. As has been observed, militia control, and indeed the continued existence of the militia, remains an irritant to harmonious civil-military relations.

Although the militia system appears to remain unchallenged at this writing, there are clear indications of a general disengagement of the army from other nonmilitary and some paramilitary activities. Police functions (both internally and along the borders) gradually are being "civilianized," and the PCC has been abolished. PLA construction troops may well be "civilianized" next.

All such steps will tend to enhance the professionalism of the Chinese officer corps—its military expertise, its exclusively military responsibility, and its corporative self-awareness as a separate body.

The GPD and the Commissars

As we saw in chapters 5 and 7, the GPD is very much under the control of the MAC, and to a lesser extent of the MND and general staff. The direction of PLA political work will continue to be dictated by the MAC—not by an autonomous GPD system. Wei Kuo-ch'ing, currently head of the GPD, is a "civilian" in that his post-1949 career has been mainly in the government and civilian party. At MR and MD levels, a majority of commissars are also "civilians" in that sense—in keeping with past practice. This points up the continuing "borderline" character of the regional commands, which are responsible for coordinating military and civilian political affairs.

In troop units, however, and especially in the main forces, PLA political work is almost exclusively in the hands of career military commissars. They appear to be well established as part of the PLA command system (chapter 7). While enhancing "mass-line" leadership and morale, they are also supposed to serve as a check on their military "co-commanders." To what extent they do so is debatable. If the events of the Cultural Revolution (chapter 4) are any indication, the perspectives of commanders and commissars coincide to a considerable degree. The post-Mao leadership is instituting more bureaucratically regularized procedures in the army and directing PLA energies to more purely military matters. Both actions will encourage the further merging of commander and commissar perspectives. As the younger officers in the troop units enter the high command over the next decade, their relative professionalism will become increasingly apparent.

On the other hand, there is still a strong tradition of commander-commissar division of function, and of political work and organization. This is clearly seen in the continuity of the 1978 Political Work Regulations with the 1963 Regulations (chapter 7).

Personnel

PLA officers above company grade are among the oldest in the world, on the average. As we have suggested, this encourages institutional conservatism and frustrates ambitious young officers. We also observed in chapter 7 that, as death and senility claim most of the high command over the next few years, a flurry of promotions will be necessary to fill the vacancies thus created. There may well be a period of uncertainty as the new high command settles in and as the first of the post-1945 military generations makes itself felt.

We have also noted that the PLA is gradually instituting a regularized system of cadre rotation. If the system takes hold, career patterns will be very different than heretofore. *"Kuan-hsi"* and factionalism will become less important, and the influence of CCP committees on cadre affairs will be reduced. Promotion will probably speed up, technical proficiency improve, and the frustration of junior officers decline.

Rhetoric about being a people's army notwithstanding, we have noted the elite quality of the PLA. Military service is still a relatively accessible and attractive route by which to rise in Chinese society, so the ranks continue to be filled with ambitious, politically aware, and relatively well-educated volunteers. Both the PLA and society will continue to feel the results. Soldiers of all ranks are seen, and see themselves, as a national elite. The army has always been part of the hard core of the communist movement, but its ever-increasing educational and technical eliteness may well engender new behavior patterns, though how and to what extent is uncertain. Just as society gives many of its brightest and most active youth to the PLA, so does the military return many thousands of experienced cadres, technicians, and political activists to civilian society. Thus, without compromising its professional autonomy the PLA will continue to function as an institutional means of national unification and modernization. Consequently, however, PLA personnel actions such as draft calls, demobilization, and contraction or expansion cannot be taken without careful regard for their social and economic repercussions.

In chapter 7 we considered the status of officership in China and the significance of such overt symbols as uniforms and badges of rank. Chinese officers enjoy higher pay and status than enlisted soldiers, and very considerable perquisites in the way of food, housing, transportation, and other amenities. Neither the Cultural Revolution nor the recurrent campaigns to promote "class brotherhood" seem to have much abated the status-consciousness of Chinese officers. Foreign visitors who meet PLA cadres are invariably made aware that, "In your army, Comrade So-and-so would be a colonel," or "I am the equivalent of a brigadier general." The rest of the PLA will probably follow the navy's lead in adopting uniforms that differentiate officers from enlisted personnel. Some sort of rank system, with insignia, will almost certainly be reintroduced within the next year or two.

A self-conscious profession of officership is now emerging with official encouragement. In 1979, high officials began to call for the development of both military and civilian "professionals" (*chuan-yeh jen-ts'ai*) and to say that these "professionals" should be in charge of work.[26] The distinction between "professional" and "expert" (*chuan-chia*) appears to be clear and intentional. Chinese officers are beginning to expand their contacts with the officers of other countries. The PLA has even joined the International Council of Military Sports (CISM). Delegations and other military exchanges are expanding constantly, and it seems only a matter of time before PLA and foreign military schools begin student and faculty exchanges.

UNRESOLVED ISSUES

A number of unresolved issues remain which cloud China's prospects for achieving stable civil-military relations, despite the trend toward relatively professional military ethic and style.

For one thing, there is the debate over budgets and priorities. This debate is a common one, and is not an insuperable problem. China's resources are adequate to support effective military forces. An acceptable mechanism for resource allocation depends on a stable, authoritative government.—the single issue which is most critical in the PLA's future, and to China's future.

A more important problem is the internal unity of the PLA itself.[27] Irreconcilable cleavages within the military will inevitably lead military men to attempt to gain advantage through political maneuvering. Potential areas for such discord include regionalism, personal cliques, generational conflicts, grudges engendered by the Cultural Revolution, resource allocation within the PLA, foreign policy, and the proper scope of military-political activities. The last two issues—again—would be eliminated by strong, stable, civilian authority. It is nearly impossible to assess the seriousness of any of the above issues as causes for PLA disunity. It is harder still to guess what sorts of factions might arise from them, owing to the crosscutting nature of different issues. It can only be observed that the PLA has given a fairly convincing impression of internal unity since 1971, and especially since Mao's death and the purge of the "gang of four."

Another factor in the future of China's civil-military relations is the long tradition of military involvement in politics. Twentieth-century Chinese politics have had a "winner-take-all" quality that has forced military officers to be involved out of simple self-preservation. Protecting oneself from domestic political opponents has been a continuing consideration of CCP leaders. The result has been that China's external defense has been informed by internal political considerations (a phenomenon which is hardly unique to this century). If China's future military leaders are to refrain from political activism prompted by fear—yet again—a strong, stable, authoritative civilian government is the precondition.

The current high command (Whitson's first through fifth "military generations"), for whom the distinction between party and army has never been clear, will continue to participate in policy making and political competition at the center. Although they have exhibited a strong preference for an autonomous military chain of command which will keep the PLA, as an institution, largely out of political conflict, the notion of an apolitical army is entirely foreign to their experience. Indeed, it is foreign to all Chinese soldiers. At least in theory, the Marxist tenet that the army is a tool of class struggle must remain as long as China is a Marxist state.

If this makes high-level PLA political involvement inevitable, it also provides the logical focus for PLA loyalty and for central authority: the communist party. The CCP provided the single recognized source of legitimate authority over the military right up to the Cultural Revolution. The People's Republic of China was, in Townsend's phrase, a "viable one-party system." A crucial problem facing today's Chinese leaders is whether or not that system has been, or can be, fully reestablished after the trauma of the GPCR. The party structure has been rebuilt, but it remains to be seen whether the authority of the party and its representative can ever again be as secure as they were before 1966.

THE FUTURE

The army has a great stake in the answer to that question. Moreover, the chronically unsettled state of power arrangements at the top of the party hierarchy is a major factor in the future of China's civil-military relations. The problem is not so much who wins, but how long it takes. Huntington and Brzezinski have noted the propensity of Soviet power struggles to emphasize differences and to produce abrupt, radical policy initiatives by the contestants.[28] In China, this sort of polarization seems to have operated in the Mao-Liu struggle of the late 1950s and 1960s, the Mao-Lin Piao struggle of 1968-71, and the "moderates" versus "gang of four" conflict of the 1970s. Teng Hsiao-p'ing's conflict with remnant "Whateverists" in 1976-79 produced policies which have been characterized as "moderate" in the West, but in fact are nothing of the kind. The swing to the "right," especially in 1977-78, was dramatic and uncompromising. Teng seems determined to commit China irrevocably to his policies, so that they will live beyond him. For about twenty years now, China has been dominated by very old men, and has been caught in a perpetual succession crisis. There is a constant possibility that the maximum leader is about to die, and therefore constant jockeying for position and a constant tendency toward radical policy initiatives.

The military high command has consistently sought to moderate this tendency toward extremism, which endangers China's military autonomy. As Perlmutter writes:

> Institutional security depends on stable order and legitimacy, derived from normative compliance. Not until the problems of legitimacy are settled and the transfer of power institutionalized in the Soviet [or Chinese] system can institutional autonomy be achieved for the military or any other group except the fountainhead of legitimacy—the party.[29]

The technological state of the PLA also contains contradictions which are fraught with political ramifications. Relative to the experience of the Chinese population it is highly complex, technically, yet much of the army is almost primitive by world standards. Small arms and obsolescent artillery constitute the overwhelming weight of its firepower. Only a handful of PLA soldiers deal with really modern technology—a situation that will persist so long as the nation's scientific and industrial capacity remains low. In technological terms, Chinese leaders are speaking literal truth when they say China is a developing third-world country. Most Chinese officers are aware of this and are dissatisfied with reduced defense budgets and the low priority of arms aquisition. Younger officers, who will begin to assume PLA executive and policy positions in the coming decade, lack the military-political breadth of vision of the current high command and will probably press for higher military priorities.

This "guns versus butter" issue, of course, is a common one, since officers everywhere urge the priority of military preparedness. It has often contributed to civil-military strife in other developing countries, and to the emergence of praetorianism among junior and middle-grade officers. A common result is that governments purchase modern weapons they cannot afford, and often do not need, in hopes of keeping their officers occupied and (therefore) out of politics.

By according very high prestige to modern technology, the "Four Modernizations" policy may be contributing to such a situation in China. "Maoism," whatever its other failures, effectively prevented it by according high prestige to the army while denigrating the importance, and even the desirability, of high technology hardware. Over the coming ten to twenty years, the CCP-PLA partnership might break down, if party policy too long continues to hold out high hopes for modernization while denying the military the new equipment it wants and needs and the prestige associated with it.

A frustrated and discontented PLA, in and of itself, would probably not threaten the political order as long as the Communist Party remained strong and authoritative. Under such conditions, the officer corps, however, would not be capable of moderating civilian politics, and might be disinclined to do so. Moreover, if a new wave of radicalism were to weaken the party, and create a political vacuum, PLA praetorianism would be the likely result. Rather than striving to rescue the party, as it did in 1967-68, the officer corps, or elements of it, would be tempted to seize power.

In much of the third world, military leaders see themselves as the self-evident leaders of their countries. Because of their discipline, organization, and (often foreign) education, officers are thought to be the leading "modernizing elites." This is not the case in China. It is the party which organized and disciplined the society which Sun Yat-sen despairingly likened to a heap of loose sand. The PLA has long recognized its own stake in strong and effective party leadership. One very professional aspect of the Chinese officer corps is this evident recognition that a strong state needs strong civilian political institutions. Officers therefore have taken common cause with "revisionist" civilians who share their bureaucratic, technical, and functionally specific orientation.

At this writing, civilian and military men who share that "revisionist" perspective appear to be in unchallenged control of China. This is not to say that they may not quarrel over power or over specific policies or priorities. Making predictions with respect to individuals is hazardous and, for our purposes, unnecessary. Regardless of what *personalities* end up on the Politburo, the general *policies* will be of the sort long identified with such figures as Chou En-lai, Teng Hsiao-p'ing, Yeh Chien-ying, P'eng Te-huai, and Nieh Jeng-chen.

Assuming that the national leadership remains reasonably stable, the future of the PLA will be shaped by the pace and nature of force modernization; not only in terms of hardware, but of organization, training, personnel management, etc. None of this will alter the political role of the current high command. They will remain as politically active as ever. By pushing military modernization, however, they are creating successors who, while still loyal to the CCP regime, will regard themselves as professional officers rather than as revolutionary successors.

In chapter 1, we examined a possible approximation of the PLA's future. The Soviet officer corps enjoys great privilege and a considerable degree of professional autonomy. On the other hand, it is subject to tight subjective civilian control by the CPSU. Top Soviet military leaders wield considerable political clout—especially when the civilian leadership falters. That general sort of future probably awaits the PLA, modified, of course, by the relatively slow pace of modernization, and by the unique political and cultural characteristics of China.

NOTES

1. Whitson, pp. 450-453.
2. This slogan was allegedly spread in the PLA in 1967. Chang Hsu-chuan, p. 13.
3. Whitson, p. 451.
4. Nelsen, private correspondence. James Townsend also pointed this out in discussion.
5. John D. Simmonds, "The New Gun-Barrel Elite," in *Military and Political Power*, pp. 105-106.

6. Joffe, "The Chinese Army after the Cultural Revolution," pp. 458-459.
7. Whitson, p. 551.
8. In 1977, the official press asserted that the "gang of four" controlled the press in 1974-76. See, for example: "The 'Gang of Four' Sabotaged News Coverage of Mourning the Late Premier Chou," *PR*, No. 4 (21 January 1977), 14-17.
9. See the discussion of the militia and the "gang of four" in chapter 5. An excellent analysis of the October 1976 leadership crisis is: Ting Wang, "Leadership Realignments," *Problems of Communism*, July-August 1977, pp. 1-17.
10. Whitson, p. 15.
11. Jack H. Harris, "Politics of National Security in China," *Problems of Communism*, 28, No. 2 (March-April 1979), 64-66.
12. Ibid.
13. Heinlein, p. 166; also see Harding, p. 382.
14. Jonathan D. Pollack, "China's Changing Polity . . .," Paper presented to the Workshop on Security and Arms Control in the Pacific, Aspen Institute for Humanistic Studies, Aspen, Colorado, August 1977, pp. 12-13.
15. Ellis Joffe, "The Army After Mao," *International Journal*, 34 (Autumn 1979), 584. The closest the Chinese have come to a comprehensive statement on the subject is in Hsu Hsiang-ch'ien's "Heighten Vigilance, Be Ready to Fight," *HC*, No. 8 (August 1978), trans. in *FBIS*, No. 148, pp. E10-E13.
16. The term "Unholy Alliance" first appeared in 1969. "Soviet Revisionism is U.S. Imperialism's No. 1 Accomplice," *PR*, No. 12 (12 March 1969), 25-26.
17. See Jonathan D. Pollack, "Chinese Attitudes Toward Nuclear Weapons, 1964-1969," *CQ*, 50 (April-June 1972), pp. 262-265, for an excellent discussion of this point.
18. Harvey Nelsen (private correspondence), based on KMT intelligence sources.
19. See "Launch a Mass Movement to Learn from the 'Hard-Bone' Sixth Company," *CFCP*, 25 February 1977; "It Is Imperative to Modernize Our National Defense," Peking Dom. Svc., 10 April 1977, trans. in *FBIS*, 15 April 1977, pp. E22-E24; "Improvement of Weaponry is a Prerequisite for Greater Combat Effectiveness," Peking Dom. Service, 10 April 1977, trans. in *FBIS*, 14 April 1977, pp. H1-H2; and "A Great Call for Accelerating the Revolutionization and Modernization of Our Army," *CFCP*, 5 June 1977.
20. Angus M. Fraser, *The People's Liberation Army* (New York: Crane Russak, 1973), p. 22.
21. Joffe, "The Army After Mao," p. 579.
22. Whitson, pp. 460-463.
23. Pollack, "Chinese Attitudes Toward Nuclear Weapons," pp. 260-261.
24. Peking Dom. Svc., 19 December 1979, trans. in *FBIS*, No. 247, p. A2; *NCNA*, 9 January 1980, in *FBIS*, No. 007, pp. B3-B4; and David Bonavia, "All Anti-Moscow Men are Brothers," *FEER*, 22 February 1980, p. 37.
25. *AFP*, 19 April 1979, in *FBIS*, No. 78, p. B1; and Robert N. Ginsburgh, "China Touches the Tigers' Bottoms," *Air Force*, June 1979, pp. 41-45.
26. For example: *NCNA*, 26 March 1980, trans. in *FBIS*, No. 61, p. L2.
27. This discussion is inspired by Joffe, "The Chinese Army after the Cultural Revolution," pp. 463-464.
28. Zbigniew Brzezinski and Samuel P. Huntington, *Political Power: USA/USSR* (New York: Viking, 1967), pp. 266-267 and 270.
29. Perlmutter, p. 84.

Appendix A:
Organization and Equipment of Type "A" Units of the PLA

The following data is intended to illustrate the organizational principles of PLA units. Some main force units approach these "ideals" fairly closely in manpower, weapons, and equipment. Others, however, vary considerably from them. In general, the PLA does not adhere as closely to formal tables of organization and equipment as do either the Soviet or US armies.

A-1: Major Items of Equipment and Weapons, Type "A" Corps

ITEMS*	CORPS TOTAL	CORPS ARTY CMD	INFANTRY DIV (3)	INFANTRY RGT (9)	INFANTRY BN (27)	INFANTRY CO (81)	INFANTRY PLAT(243)	INFANTRY SQD(729)	TANK RGT (3)
Pistol	10,000	A	A	235	49	9	A	A	182
Assault Rifle	17,000	A	A	817	221	49	A	A	233
Carbine	17,000	A	A	1,398	361	82	A	A	165
LMG (7.62mm)	1,087	A	339	99	30	9	3	1	A
HMG (7.62mm)	200+	B	B	18	6	–	–	–	35
HMG (12.7mm)		B	B	6	–	–	–	–	35
AAHMG (14.5mm)	46	10	12	–	–	–	–	–	–
AT Launcher (40mm)	1,558+	A	516+	156	36	9	–	–	–
Mortar (60mm)	168	–	54	18	6	2	–	–	–
Mortar (82mm)	243	–	81	27	6	–	–	–	–
Mortar (120/160mm)	36	–	12	4	–	–	–	–	–
AA Gun (37/57mm)	79	25	18	–	–	–	–	–	–
Recoiless Gun*** (57/75mm)	162	–	27	9	3	–	–	–	–
Recoiless Gun*** (75/82mm)		–	27	9	–	–	–	–	–
Assault Gun (SP) (76/85/100mm)	30	–	10	–	–	–	–	–	10
140/130mm	18	18	–	–	–	–	–	–	–
Multiple RL									

107mm Multiple RL	54	–	18	–	–	–	–
Field Gun (76/85/100mm)	54	–	18	–	–	–	–
Field Gun (122/130mm)	10	10	–	–	–	–	–
Howitzer (122mm)	46	10	12	–	–	–	–
Howitzer (152mm)	10	10	–	–	–	–	–
Flame Thrower	81	–	27	–	–	–	–
Medium Tank	96	–	32	–	–	–	32
Armored Recon Vehicle/Light Tank	27	–	6	–	–	–	3
APC	0–200**						
Jeep	apx 270	A	A	A	A	–	7
Truck (Cargo/Prime Mover)	1,464	100	373	30	–	–	29
Artillery Tractor/Prime Mover	24	24	–	–	–	–	–
Draft Animals	378+	–	126+	42+	14+	–	–
Motorcycle (and sidecar)	132+	A	44+	3	–	–	12
Armored Recovery Vehicle	6	–	2	–	–	–	2

*See Appendix B for data on individual items.
**Armored Personnel Carriers are held in special transportation units at corps, division, and regimental levels, and assigned as needed. Each APC carries one infantry squad (12 men).
***Recoilless guns are being replaced/supplemented by SAGGER AT missiles.
A. Data cannot be determined, and/or subject to wide variation.
B. Number of heavy machineguns varies with number of armored vehicles.

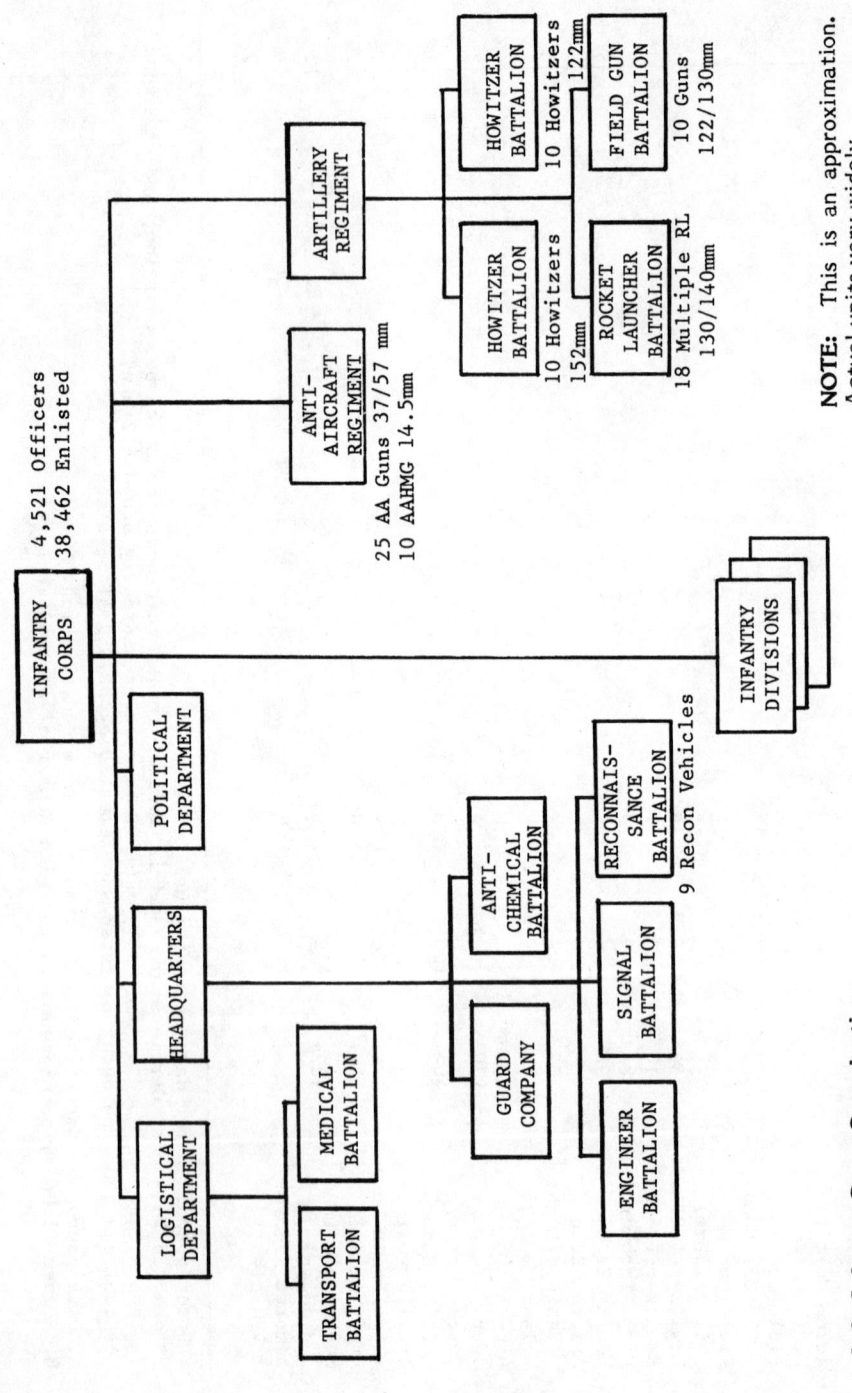

A-2: Infantry Corps Organization

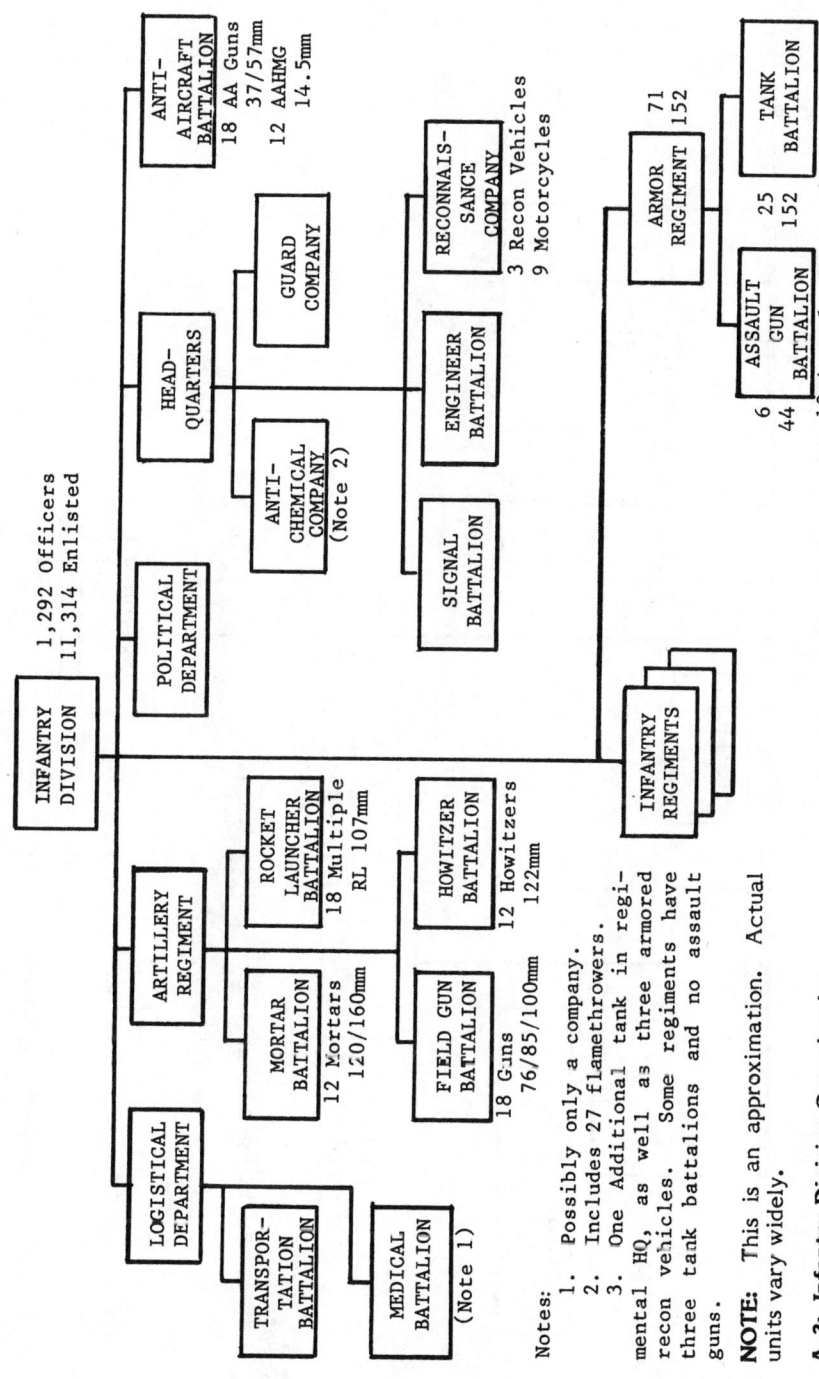

Notes:
1. Possibly only a company.
2. Includes 27 flamethrowers.
3. One additional tank in regimental HQ, as well as three armored recon vehicles. Some regiments have three tank battalions and no assault guns.

NOTE: This is an approximation. Actual units vary widely.

A-3: Infantry Division Organization

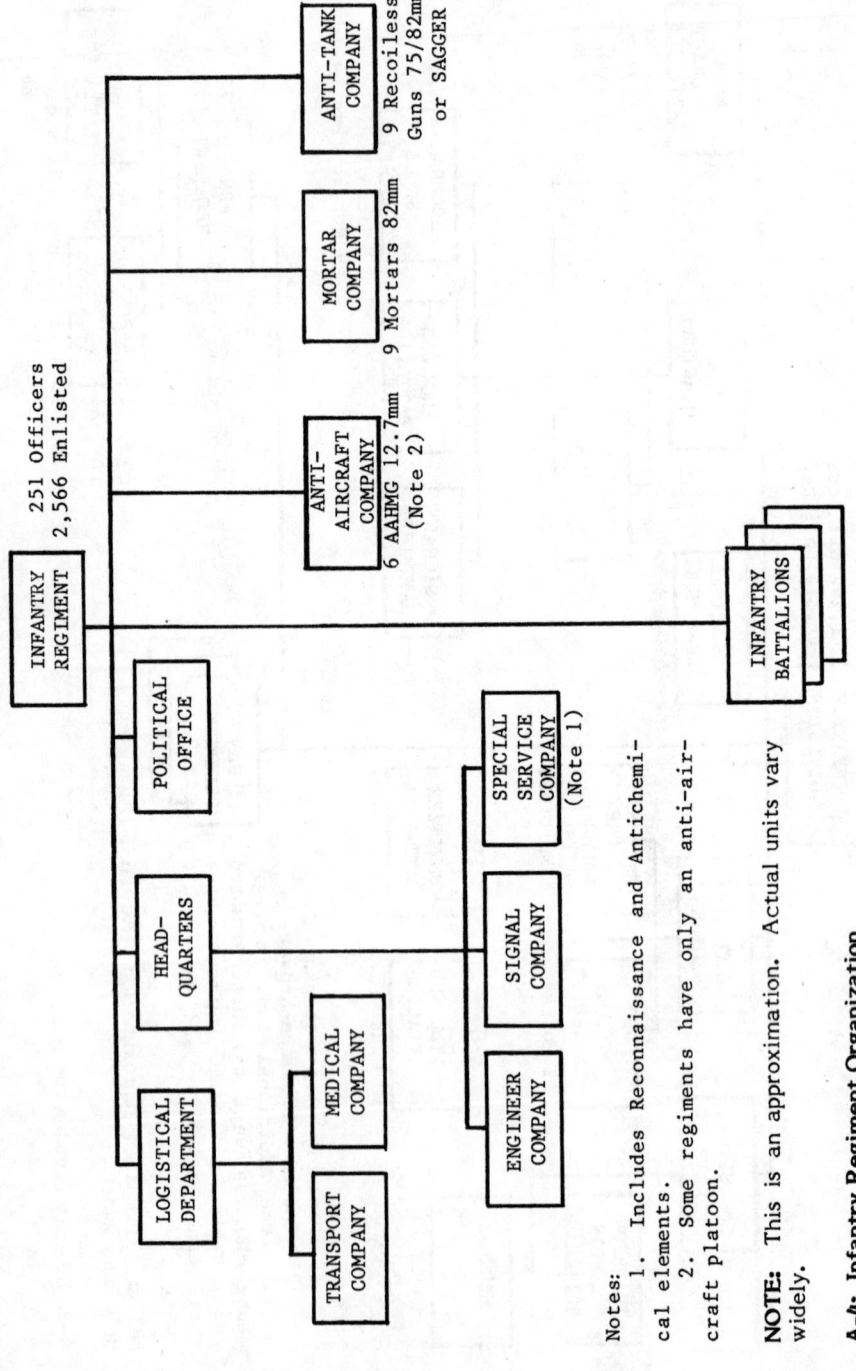

Notes:
1. Includes Reconnaissance and Antichemical elements.
2. Some regiments have only an anti-aircraft platoon.

NOTE: This is an approximation. Actual units vary widely.

A-4: Infantry Regiment Organization

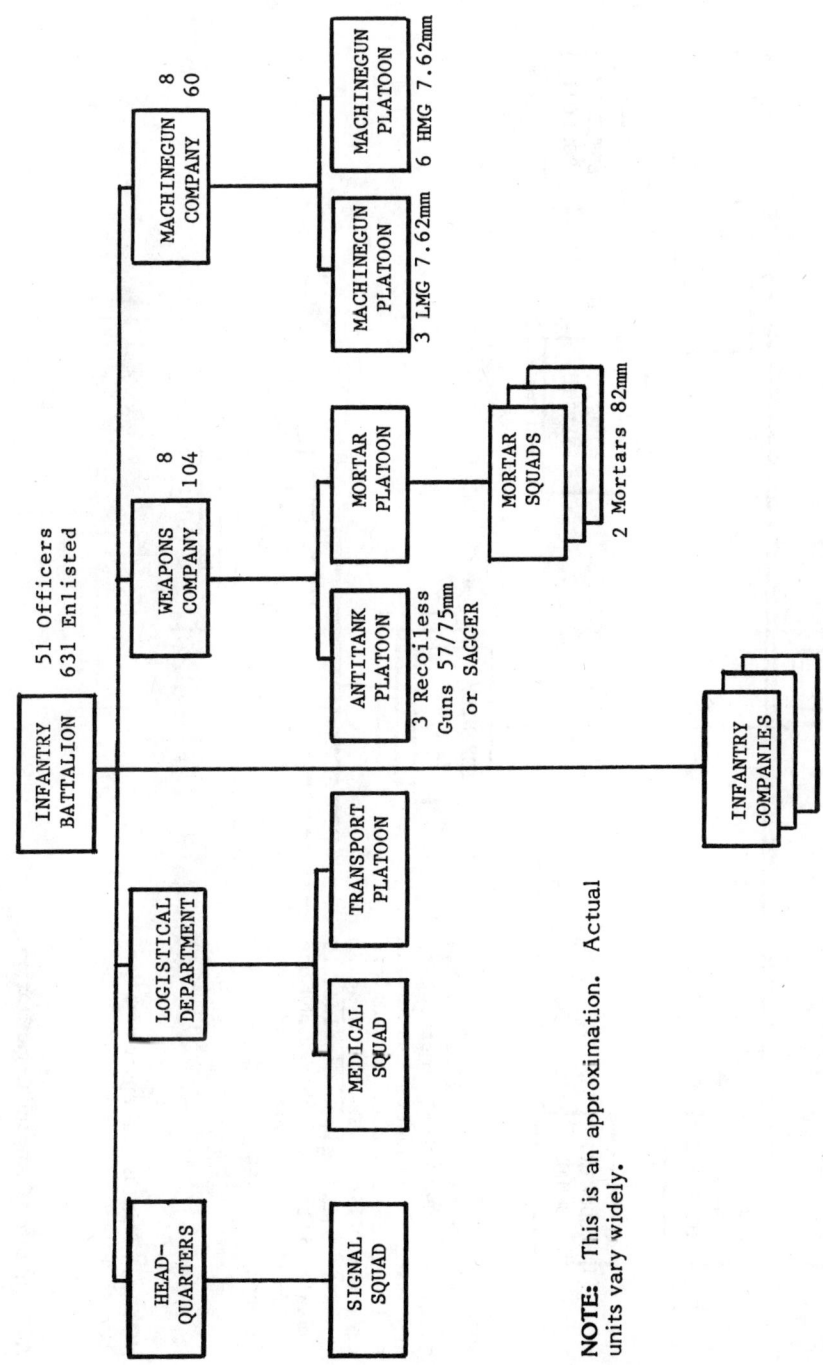

NOTE: This is an approximation. Actual units vary widely.

A-5: Infantry Battalion Organization

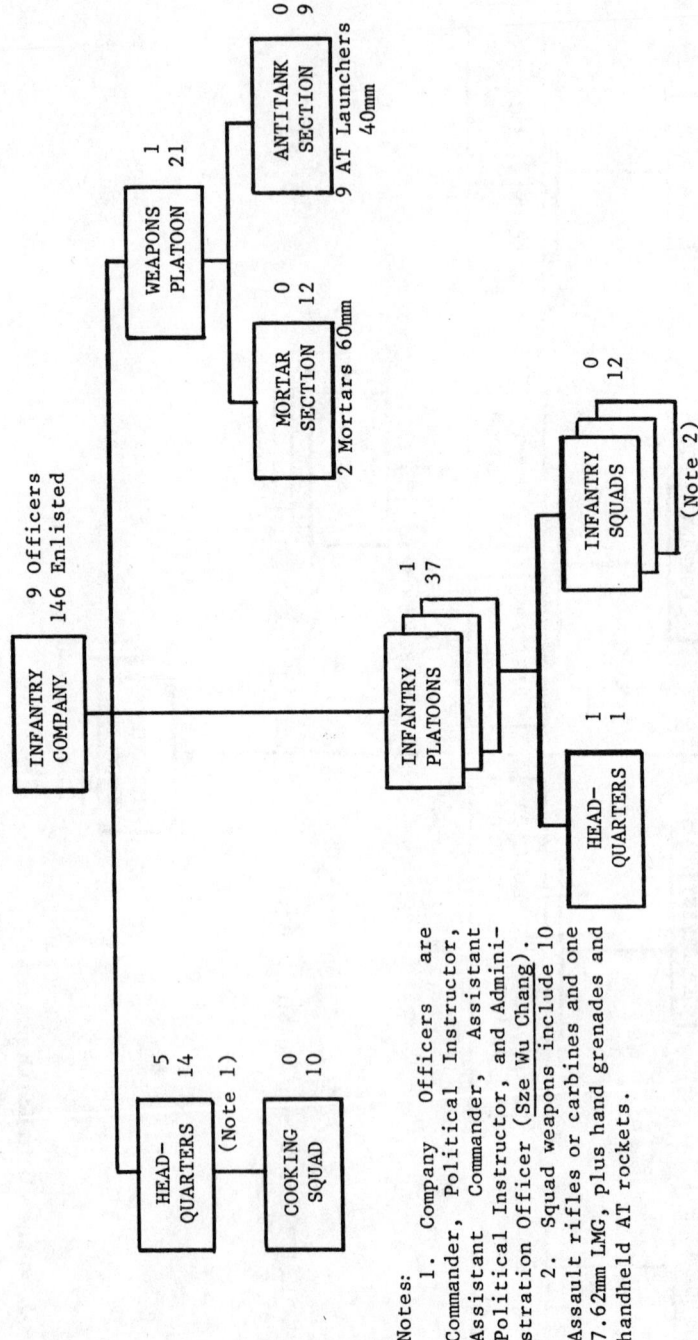

A-6: Infantry Company Organization

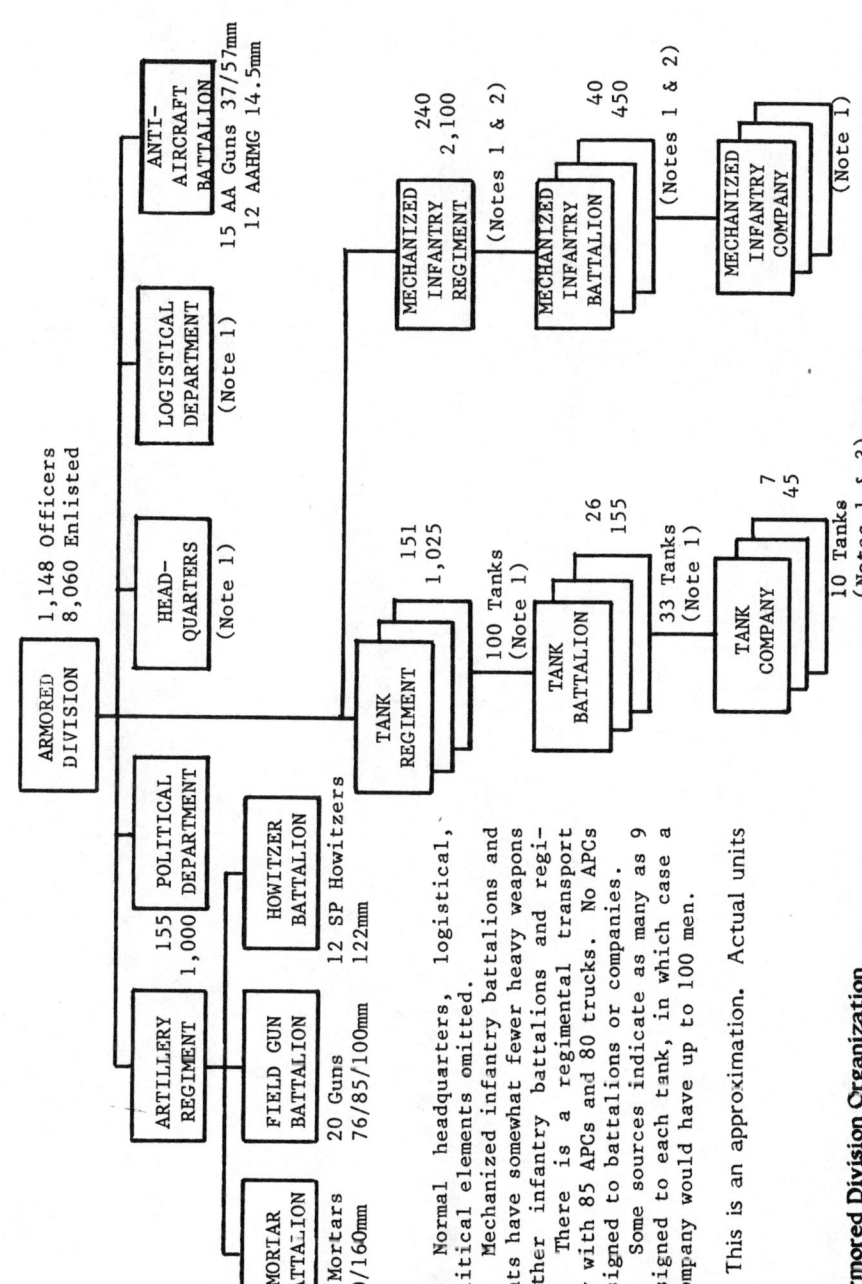

Notes:
 1. Normal headquarters, logistical, and political elements omitted.
 2. Mechanized infantry battalions and regiments have somewhat fewer heavy weapons than other infantry battalions and regiments. There is a regimental transport company with 85 APCs and 80 trucks. No APCs are assigned to battalions or companies.
 3. Some sources indicate as many as 9 men assigned to each tank, in which case a tank company would have up to 100 men.

NOTE: This is an approximation. Actual units vary.

A-7: Armored Division Organization

Appendix B:
PLA Ground Forces Weapons and Equipment in Service

I. Infantry

Weapons	Nomenclature	Remarks**
Pistol	7.62mm, Types 51 & 54*	Copy of the Soviet 7.62mm Tokarev TT33.
	9mm, Type 59*	Copy of the Soviet 9mm Makarov Pistol.
	7.65mm, Type 64/67, Silenced*	<u>Chinese design</u> and manufacture, fires only the 7.65x17 rimless cartridge.
Submachine-gun	7.62mm, Type 50	Copy of the Soviet 7.62mm Model PPSh-41.
	7.62mm, Type 43, Copy	Copy of the Soviet 7.62mm Model PPS-43.
	7.62mm, Type 64, Silenced	<u>Chinese design</u> and construction, 7.62x25 cartridge.
Carbine/Rifle	7.62mm, Type 53, Carbine	Copy of Soviet 7.62mm Model 1944 Carbine.
	7.62mm, Type 56, Carbine	Copy of the Soviet 7.62mm SKS.
	7.62mm, Type 56, Assault Rifle*	Copy of 7.62mm Soviet AK-47. Late versions have permanently attached folding spike bayonet.
	7.62mm, Type 56-1, Assault Rifle*	Copy of the folding stock Soviet 7.62mm AK-47.
	7.62mm, Type 63, Rifle*	<u>Chinese design</u> combining features from the Type 56 Carbine and the Type 56 Assault Rifle. Formerly identified erroneously as Type 68.
	7.62mm, Type-?, Rifle*	<u>Chinese design</u>. Improved version of Type 63.

281

Weapons	Nomenclature	Remarks**
Machinegun, Light	7.62mm, Type 53	Copy of Soviet 7.62mm DPM.
	7.62mm, Type 56-1	Copy of Soviet 7.62mm RPDM.
	7.62mm, Type 58	Copy of Soviet 7.62mm RP-46.
	7.62mm, Type 67*	Chinese designed, replacing Type 53 and Type 58 MGs.
Machinegun, Medium	7.62mm, Type 57*	Copy of Soviet 7.62mm SGM.
	7.62mm, Type 53	Copy of Soviet 7.62mm SG-43.
Machinegun, Heavy	12.7mm, Type 54*	Copy of Soviet 12.7mm Model 38/46 DShK.
Grenades	RG-42 Antipersonnel	Soviet design.
	F1 Antipersonnel	Soviet design.
	RGD-5 Antipersonnel	Soviet design.
	RPG-6 Antitank	Soviet design.
	RKG-3 Antitank*	Soviet design.
	RDG-2 Smoke*	Soviet design.
	Type 73 AP Rifle/Hand*	Chinese design.
	Type-? AT Rifle Grenade*	Chinese design. Introduced in 1979.
Mortars, Light	60mm, Type 31	Copy of the US Mortar 60mm M2.
	60mm, Type 63	Chinese design.
Mortars, Medium	82mm, Type 53*	Copy of the Soviet 82mm M 1937 (new version).
Mortars, Heavy	120mm, Type 53*	Copy of the Soviet 120mm M1943.
	160mm, Type 56*	Copy of the Soviet 160mm M1943.
Antitank Weapons	70mm?, Type-?, Hand-held AT Rocket*	Chinese design. Introduced 1979.
	40mm, Type 56	Modification of the Soviet RPG-2.
	40mm, Type 69*	Modification of Soviet RPG-7V.
	57mm, Recoilless Gun, Type 36	Copy of the US M18A1.
	75mm, Recoiless Gun, Type 52	Copy of the US 75mm M20.
	75mm, Recoiless Gun, Type 56	An improvement on the Type 52.
	90mm Antitank Rocket, Type 51	A copy of the US 3.5in. M20 "Bazooka."
	82mm Recoiless Gun, Type 65*	Improved version of Soviet B-10.
	SAGGER wire-guided AT missile. Type-?*	Copy of Soviet AT-3. Introduced 1979.

II. Artillery Weapons

Weapons	Nomenclature	Remarks**
Antitank Weapons	57mm Gun, Type 55	Copy of Soviet M1943 (ZIS-2).
	76mm SP Gun, SU-76	Soviet mfg.
	85mm Gun, Type 55	Copy of Soviet D-44.
	85mm SP Gun, SU-85	Soviet mfg.
	100mm SP Gun, Type-?*	Copy of Soviet SU-100.
	100mm Gun, Type-?	Copy of Soviet M55.
Anti-aircraft Weapons	14.5mm Heavy MG, Types 56 & 58*	Copy of Soviet KPV 14.5mm (mounted on copies of Soviet ZPU-4 & ZPU-2, respectively).
	37mm, Type 55*	Soviet design M1939. Single & dual.
	37mm SP, Type 63?	Twin mount on T-34 tank chassis.
	57mm, Type 59*	Soviet design, Radar aimed S60.
	85mm, Type ?*	Soviet designed, Radar aimed KS-18.
	100mm, Type 59*	Soviet designed, Radar aimed KS-19.
Bombardment Weapons	70mm Howitzer	Japanese-made circa WWII.
	75mm Pack Howitzer	US-made circa WWII.
	76.2mm Gun & Gun/Howitzer*	Chinese copies & variations of Soviet M1942 (ZIS-3).
	107mm Multiple RL, Types 63 & 63-1*	Chinese designs. Towed or jeep mounted.
	122mm Rocket*	Copy of Soviet DKZ-B.
	122mm SP Gun JSU-122	Soviet-made.
	122mm SP Howitzer, Type-?*	Chinese design.
	122mm Howitzer, Type 54*	Copy of Soviet M1938.
	122mm Gun, D-30 & D-74	Soviet-made.
	122mm Gun, Type 60*	Chinese design, probably based on Soviet D-74.
	130mm Gun M46	Soviet-made.
	130mm Gun, Type 59-1*	Modified Soviet M-46 mated to D-74 carriage.
	130mm Multiple RL, Type 63*	Chinese design.
	132mm Multiple RL, BM-13	Soviet mfg. "Katyusha." Fires Chinese-designed rockets with scatterable AT mines.

Weapons	Nomenclature	Remarks**
	140mm Multiple RL, Type-?	Copy of Soviet BM-14.
	152mm Howitzer, Type 56	Copy of Soviet M1943.
	152mm Gun/Howitzer, Type 66*	Copy of Soviet D-20.
	203mm Gun/Howitzer, M55	Soviet mfg.

III. Armored Vehicles

Weapons	Nomenclature	Remarks
Armored Personnel Carrier	Type 531*	Previously identified variously as "M1967," "M1970," and/or "K-63." <u>Chinese design</u>. Amphibious. 12.7mm HMG.
	Type 56	Copy of Soviet BTR-152.
	BTR-60	Soviet, poss. Chinese copy.
Reconnaissance Car	Type 55	Copy of Soviet BTR-40 (BRDM), Amphibious.
Amphibious Tank	Type-?	Copy of Soviet PT-76, 76mm Gun, 7.62mm Coax MG.
	Type 60 & 60/63*	<u>Chinese design</u>, 85mm Gun, Type 54 HMG, 7.62mm Coax MG.
Tank, Light	Type 62*	<u>Chinese design</u>, 85mm Gun, Type 54 HMG, 7.62mm Coax MG.
Tank, Medium	T-34/85	Soviet-made, 85mm gun.
	T-54/55	Soviet-made, 100mm gun, Type 54 HMG, 7.62mm Coax MG.
	Type 59*	Chinese version of T-54/55, same armament.
Tank, Heavy	JS-2	Soviet-made, 122mm gun.

---

*Weapons probably in current production.
**Where foreign designs have been copied, substantial numbers of the foreign originals are also in service.

Sources:
 Chin Chien-li, "Survey of Chinese Communist Artillery. . . .," <u>HTJP</u> (1 January 1971); Defense Liaison Office, USCG, Hong Kong; Fraser, p. 5; <u>Jane's Infantry Weapons</u>, 1975 and 1977 eds.; <u>Jane's Weapon Systems</u>, 1969-70 ed., 1971-72 ed., 1973-74 and 1977 eds.; Smith and Smith, <u>Small Arms of the World</u>, 10th ed.; <u>Handbook on the Chinese Armed Forces</u>, pp. A-24 to A-39.; <u>HTCS</u>, No. 33 (July 1979), 35; <u>HTCS</u>, No. 36 (October 1979), 6-7; <u>HTCS</u>, No. 38 (January 1980), 1-2; and <u>HTCS</u>, No. 44 (July 1980), 1-2 and 6-7.

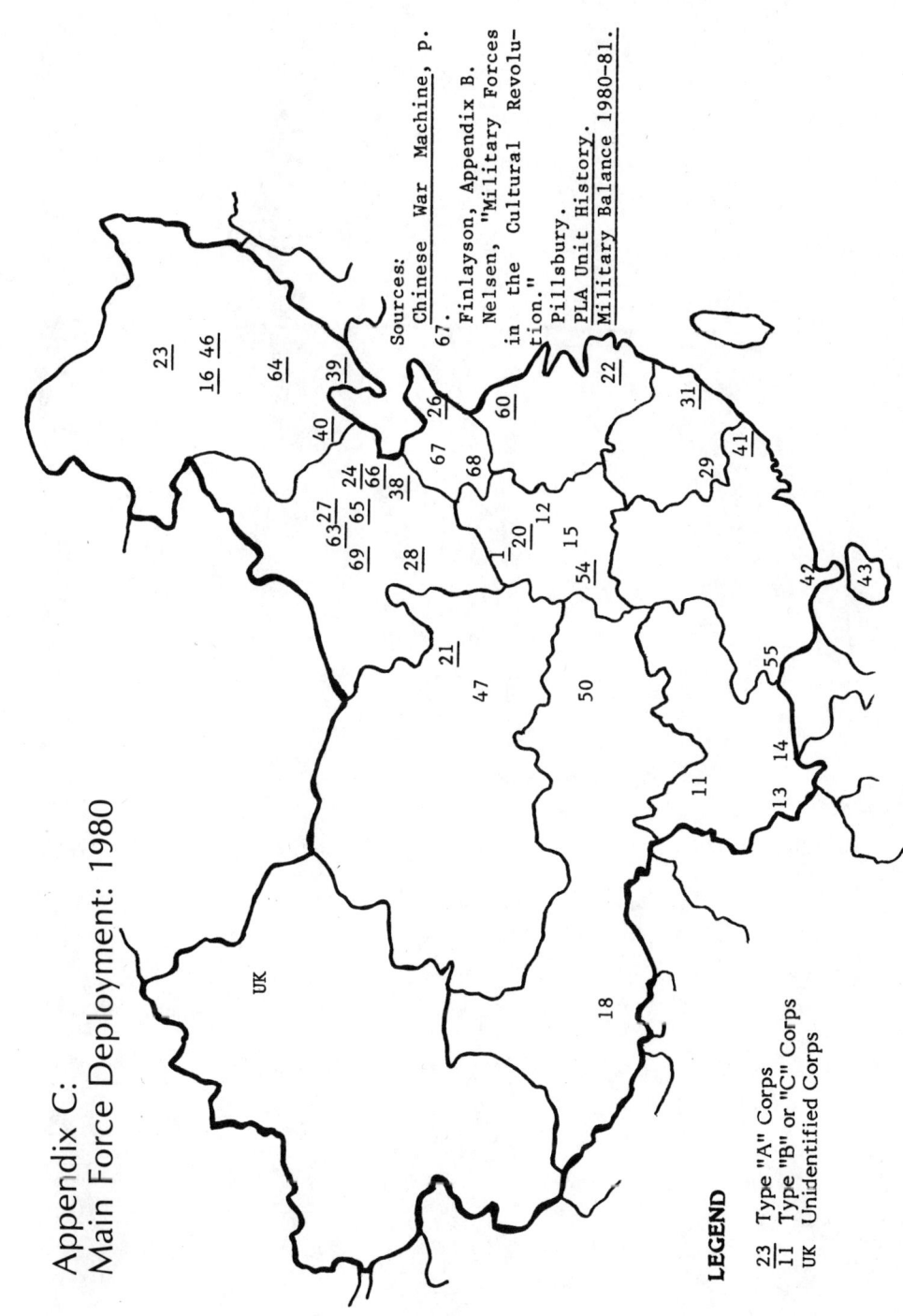

Appendix C:
Main Force Deployment: 1980

Appendix D:
PLA Air Force Equipment

FIGHTERS

AIRCRAFT*	NUMBER IN PLAAF	MAX. SPEED mph (km/h)	SERVICE CEILING ft (m)	ARMAMENT/CARGO	YEAR FIRST FLOWN	REMARKS
MiG-15 (F2) [FAGOT]	100	668 (1,075)	51,000 (15,545)	1x37mm cannon 2x23mm cannon 2x250Kg bombs	1947	OBSOLETE. Now used as fighter-bomber. Only the trainer version MiG-15UTI was built in China.
MiG-17 F&PF (F4 & F5) [FRESCO]	1,700	711 (1,145)	54,460 (16,600)	same	apx 1951	OBSOLETE. There is a unique PRC two-seat version.
MiG-19 (F6) [FARMER]	1,900	920 (1,480)	58,700 (17,900)	3x30mm cannon or 2x30mm cannon & 2 ATOLL air-to-air missiles	1955	First F6 delivered 1961. An unknown number have all-weather intercept capability. OBSOLESCENT.
MiG-21 (F7) [FISHBED]	80-100	Mach 2	59,050 (18,000)	2x30mm cannon & 2 ATOLL air-to-air missiles	1956	F7 first flew in 1964. In service 1965. Production interrupted repeatedly. Previously misidentified as F8.

AIRCRAFT*	NUMBER IN PLAAF	MAX. SPEED mph (km/h)	SERVICE CEILING ft (m)	ARMAMENT/CARGO	YEAR FIRST FLOWN	REMARKS
(A5 & F9) [FANTAN]	400+	Mach 2		2x23mm cannon & up to 1,000Kg bombs and/or rockets. Fighter version probably armed with 2-4 ATOLL missiles.	1970?	Chinese-designed fighter-bomber based on F6. Probably called "Type 5 Attack Plane" (Ch'iang chi-chi). Also variously identified as F9, F6bis, and F6B. Fighter-bomber has internal weapons bay. Fighter has nose radar of unknown type.

BOMBERS

AIRCRAFT*	NUMBER IN PLAAF	MAX. SPEED mph (km/h)	SERVICE CEILING ft (m)	ARMAMENT/CARGO	YEAR FIRST FLOWN	REMARKS
IL-28 (B5) [BEAGLE]	400	559 (900)	40,355 (12,300)	2,000Kg bombs 4x23mm cannon	1947	Max. range (empty) is 3,540Km. OBSOLETE.
TU-16 (B6) [BADGER]	90	620 (998)	43,000 (13,000)	9,000Kg bombs 7x23mm cannon	1954	PRC production began in 1968. Max. range 4,800Km. Useful for reconnaissance. Obsolete as a bomber.
TU-4 [BULL]	few	375 (600)	35,000+ (10,770+)	10,000Kg bombs	apx 1945	Soviet copy of Boeing B-29. Reportedly refitted with turboprop engines by PRC in 1960s.

						OBSOLETE.
TU-2 [BAT]	90	340 (547)		2,700Kg bombs	1948	Twin piston engines. OBSOLETE.
TRANSPORTS and UTILITY AIRCRAFT**						
LI-2 [CAB]	100			medium cargo	apx 1942	Soviet copy of US Douglas DC3/C-47. Some US originals also in service.
YAK-16 [CORK]	some	190 (305)		light cargo	1946	
(C11)	few	136 (220)		800Kg or 14 passengers	1977	Chinese design. Two piston engines.
AN-2 (C5, Feng-shou 2) [COLT]	5,000+	160 (258)	14,425 (4,400)	1,310Kg or 14 passengers	1947	Produced in PRC since 1957. Extremely efficient.
(Chinese-made light aircraft of various models)	1,000±					Training, liaison, light transport, etc.
IL-12 [COACH]	100+			4,000Kg cargo	1944	
IL-14M [CRATE]	30			4,990Kg cargo	1953	Standard PLA transports.
IL-18 [COOT]	15	419 (675)	33,000 (10,000)	110 passengers	1957	Four turboprop engines. 6,500Km range.

AIRCRAFT*	NUMBER IN PLAAF	MAX. SPEED mph (km/h)	SERVICE CEILING ft (m)	ARMAMENT/CARGO	YEAR FIRST FLOWN	REMARKS
IL-62 [CLASSIC]***	5	560+ (900+)	40,000 (12,192)	23,000Kg cargo	1962	Four jet engines. 8-10,000Km range.
AN-12 [CUB]	30+	482 (777)	33,500 (10,200)	20,000Kg 2x23mm cannon	1960	Four turboprop engines. 3,600Km range. PRC copy in production.
AN-24 [COKE]	20?	290 (467)	27,560 (8,400)	5,500Kg or 44 passengers	1960	Two turboprop engines. 2,400Km range. Possible PRC copy.
AN-26 [CURL]	30+	290 (467)	24,935 (7,600)	5,000Kg or 44 passengers	1968	Two turboprop engines & one aux. turbojet. 2,500Km range. Probable PRC copy.
AN-30 [CLANK]	few				1975?	Aerial survey and mapping aircraft.
TU-70 [CART]	few	298 (480)		110 passengers	1949	
TU-124*** [COOKPOT]	few	603 (970)	33,000 (10,058)	6,000Kg or 56 passengers	1960	Two turbojet engines. 3,000Km range.
707	10					US-made, four turbojets. PRC copy under development.
747 SP***	3					US-made, four turbojets.
Herold	2					UK-made, piston engines.

⎫
⎬ commercial airliners operated mainly by CAAC
⎭

Aircraft	Number	Speed (mph/km/h)	Ceiling ft (m)	Capacity	Year	Notes
Trident	37					UK-made, three turbojets.
Viscount	6					UK-made, four piston engines.

HELICOPTERS**

Aircraft	Number	Speed	Ceiling	Capacity	Year	Notes
MI-1 [HARE]	some	105 (170)		1 passenger	1950	Light utility.
MI-4 (H5, Hsuan-feng 25) [HOUND]	300-350	130 (210)	18,000 (548)	1,740Kg or 14 passengers	1952	Chinese version flew in 1959. 160-mile range.
MI-6 [HOOK]	some	186 (300)	14,730 (4,500)	12,000Kg or 65 passengers	1957	Heavy transport helo. 640Km range. Possible PRC copy.
MI-8 [HIP]	20+	155 (260)	14,760 (4,500)	4,000Kg or 28 passengers	1960	480Km range. Possible PRC copy.
Allouette III	15	131 (210)	19,700 (6,000)	7 persons (including crew)	1959	Purchased from France in 1967. Excellent at very high altitudes.
Super Frelon SA 321	10	171 (275)	10,325 (3,150)	27 passengers or 4,090Kg cargo (5,000 Kg slung)	1967	Purchased from France in 1967.

Various other Western helicopters were purchased in small numbers in 1978-79. These included the West German "Puma" and BO-105, and the American Bell Textron 212.

AIRCRAFT*	NUMBER IN PLAAF	MAX. SPEED mph (km/h)	SERVICE CEILING ft (m)	ARMAMENT/CARGO	YEAR FIRST FLOWN	REMARKS
AIR-TO-AIR MISSILES						
K-13 AA-2, CAA-1, [ATOLL]						Soviet copy of the US "Sidewinder" infrared homing missile. Also copied in the PRC. Significant numbers mounted on PLAAF FARMERs and FISHBEDs, and possibly on some FRESCOs and FANTANs.
[AA-1, ALKALI]						Soviet radar beam-riding missile, reportedly furnished to PLAAF in 1950s. Few, if any, remain in service.
SURFACE-TO-AIR MISSILE						
V750VK (Hung Ch'i 4) [SA-2, CSA-1, GUIDELINE]	several hundred		55,000 (16,760)	130Kg HE warhead	early 1960s	Chinese copy of Soviet design in production since late 1960s. Slant range 45Km. Approaching obsolescence.

RECAPITULATION:

Total Fighters:	4,200	
Total Bombers	600	Includes fighter-bombers. Apx. 100 bombers have piston engines.
Total Combat Aircraft:	apx 4,800	
Heavy and Medium Transports:	apx 500	Many are operated by CAAC.
Light Transports:	6,000±	Includes CAAC and PLAAF.
Helicopters:	400+	Many operated by CAAC.

Notes:
 *Designation given first is that in country of origin. In parentheses is PRC designation of the Chinese-made copy/modification, if any. NATO code identifiers, if any, are in brackets.
 **Includes aircraft operated by the Civil Air Administration of China (CAAC).
 ***All may be in CAAC.

Appendix E:
Missiles of the Second Artillery Command

NATC DESIG- NATION	NATO CODE NAME	NUMBER OPERA- TIONAL	PROPULSION	LAUNCH WEIGHT	RANGE	GUIDANCE	REMARKS
A. Short-Range Tactical Missiles							
--	FROG	100+	Solid	3,000kg	25-65km	Unguided	Obsolete, Soviet-made, Nuclear or HE.
SS-1	SCUD-A		Liquid	4,500kg	100+km	Radio Command	Soviet-made, Nuclear or HE.
B. MRBM							
SS-2	SIBLING	few	One-stage, liquid	26,000kg	800–1,200km	Radio Command	Obsolete, Soviet-made.
SS-3 ("Shuang-ch'eng-tzu")	SHYSTER						
CCS-1	--	40-50	One-stage, liquid	27,000kg	1,100km	Probably inertial	Similar to Soviet SANDAL; Chinese-made; Deployed apx. 1970; 20KT warhead.
C. IRBM							
CSS-2	--	65-85	One-stage, storable liquid	40,000kg	3,000km	UK	Tested 1970; Deployed 1973. Probably launched first earth satellite. 1MT warhead.

APPENDIX E (continued)
MISSILES OF THE SECOND ARTILLERY COMMAND*

NATO DESIG- NATION	NATO CODE NAME	NUMBER OPERA- TIONAL	PROPULSION	LAUNCH WEIGHT	RANGE	GUIDANCE	REMARKS
D. "Limited-Range ICBM"**							
CCS-3	--	a few	Multi-stage, liquid	UK	6,000km	UK	Tested late 1970. Possibly deployed 1975. Can reach European USSR and all Asia. 3MT warhead.
E. ICBM							
CSS-X-4	--	a few possible	Three-stage, liquid	200,000kg?	12,000+km	UK	Satellite launch vehicle. ICBM version tested May 1980. Possibly called "New Long March No. 3."

*Data is principally taken from: The Military Balance, 1977-78, 1978-79, 1979-80, 1980-81 eds.; Jane's Weapon Systems, 1971-72, 1973-74, and 1977 eds.; HTCS, No. 34 (August 1979), 34; Chin Chien-li, "Survey of Chinese Communist Artillery and 'Second Artillery,'" p. 4; Ta Kung Pao, 13 August 19719; USCGDLO, Hong Kong; USAF Attache Office, Taipei; and HTCS, No. 43 (June 1980), 13-15.

**This May be upgraded version of the IRBM (line C).

Appendix F:
The PLA Navy and Its Equipment

I. PERSONNEL: 360,000 (including 38,000 in the PLANNAF and 38,000 "Marines").

II. FIGHTING SHIPS AND BOATS:

	ACTIVE	(UNDER CONSTRUCTION)	REMARKS
Destroyers	13	(?)	Includes 9 "Lü Ta" class of Chinese design, and 4 Soviet ex-"Gordy" class. All are armed with STYX missiles.
Frigates	15	(?)	Includes 2 "Kiangtung" class, 5 "Kiangnan" class, 3 "Kianghu" class, 5 "Ch'engtu" (modified ex-"Riga") class. "Kianghu" and "Ch'engtu" mount STYX missiles. "Kiangtung" may mount SAMs.
Corvettes	46	(?)	Includes 20 "Krondstadt" class of Soviet design and PRC mfg. and 25 "Hainan" class of PRC design.
Patrol Escorts	9	(?)	
Minesweepers	21+	(0)	Soviet T-43 class. Mostly built in PRC.
Fleet Submarines	0	(2?)	"Han" class. First was launched in 1972. Nuclear powered. Not active owing to propulsion problems. Second attempt reportedly underway.
Missile Submarines	1	(0)	"Golf" class of Soviet design and PRC mfg. Has launch tubes for three SLBMs. PLAN has no known SLBM for this sub to carry.
Patrol Submarines	95-100	(?)	2 "Ming" class of PRC design. 21 Soviet "Whiskey" class. 50-68 "Romeo" class of Soviet design and PRC mfg. All under construction are "Romeo."

	ACTIVE	(UNDER CONSTRUCTION)	REMARKS
Fast Attack Craft (Missile)	180	(20+)	Includes 40 "Osa" class, of Soviet design, and 50 PRC varients designated "Hola" class (total 90). Also includes Soviet-designed "Komar" class, and PRC varients designated "Hoku" class and "Homa" class (total 80), and 10 PRC-designed "Haitao" class hydrofoils. All carry STYX missiles. "Haitao" and "Hola" under construction.
Fast Attack Craft (Gun)	500+	(20?)	375 "Shanghai" class (Types I, II, III, IV), 80-90 "Swatow" class, 30 "Huangpu" class, 2 "Shantung" class, and 6 "Haikou" class. All of PRC design.
Fast Attack Craft (Torpedo)	250	(?)	120 P4/P6 class and 130 "Huchuan" hydrofoils.

III. AIRCRAFT OF THE PLANNAF:

	ACTIVE		REMARKS
Fighters	575-600		FRESCOs and FARMERs, plus a few FANTANs and possibly a few FISHBEDs.
Torpedo Bombers	130		All are BEAGLEs.
Light Bombers	a few		Tu-2 BAT (Probably only used for training).
Flying Boats	20		BE-6 (NATO code: "MADGE"). Soviet built; Obsolete (1947); can fly 3000+ miles at 250 mph.
Helicopters	50		HOUND.
Auxilliary and Transport	some		Miscellaneous types.

Patrol Bombers: 12? BADGERS. Possibly armed with KENNEL antishipping missiles.

IV. MISSILES:

"Red Flag No. 4" (CSA-1, SA-2, GUIDELINE) — Air defense. Some are controlled by PLANNAF. Soviet design and PRC mfg. Obsolescent.

(SS-N-2A STYX) — Soviet design, PRC mfg. Obsolescent. Solid fuel; two-stage; cruises apx. Mach 0.9. Range 40km; launch weight apx. 1000-1500kg; radiolink inertial guidance; radar homing. A PRC modification reportedly is mounted on "Lü Ta," "Kianghu," and "Haitao" classes.

(AS-1 KENNEL) — Soviet design, possible PRC mfg. Reportedly carried by Tu-16 bombers of PLANNAF. Turbojet engine; subsonic; range apx. 150km; radio command link guidance; passive or active radar homing. Obsolete.

Surface-to-Air Missile, Type? — Chinese design. Possibly mounted on "Kiangtung" class frigates. Still under development.

---

*Sources: Chinese War Machine, passim; Military Balance, 1978-79 ed., 1979-80 ed., 1980-81 ed.; Jane's Fighting Ships, 1973-74 ed., 1974-75 ed., 1975-76 ed., 1977-78 ed.; Jane's Weapon Systems, 1971-72 ed., 1977 ed.; Yearbock on Chinese Communism (1973), pp. II 54-55; Bueschel, p. 75, 114-115; Fraser, p. 10; Harvey Nelsen, private correspondence; Flight International, 118, No. 3679 (22 September 1979), 959; HTCS, No. 40 (March 1980), 35; HTCS, No. 41 (April 1980), 54-55; Wettern, pp. 123-125.

Appendix G:
The Military Regions and Districts

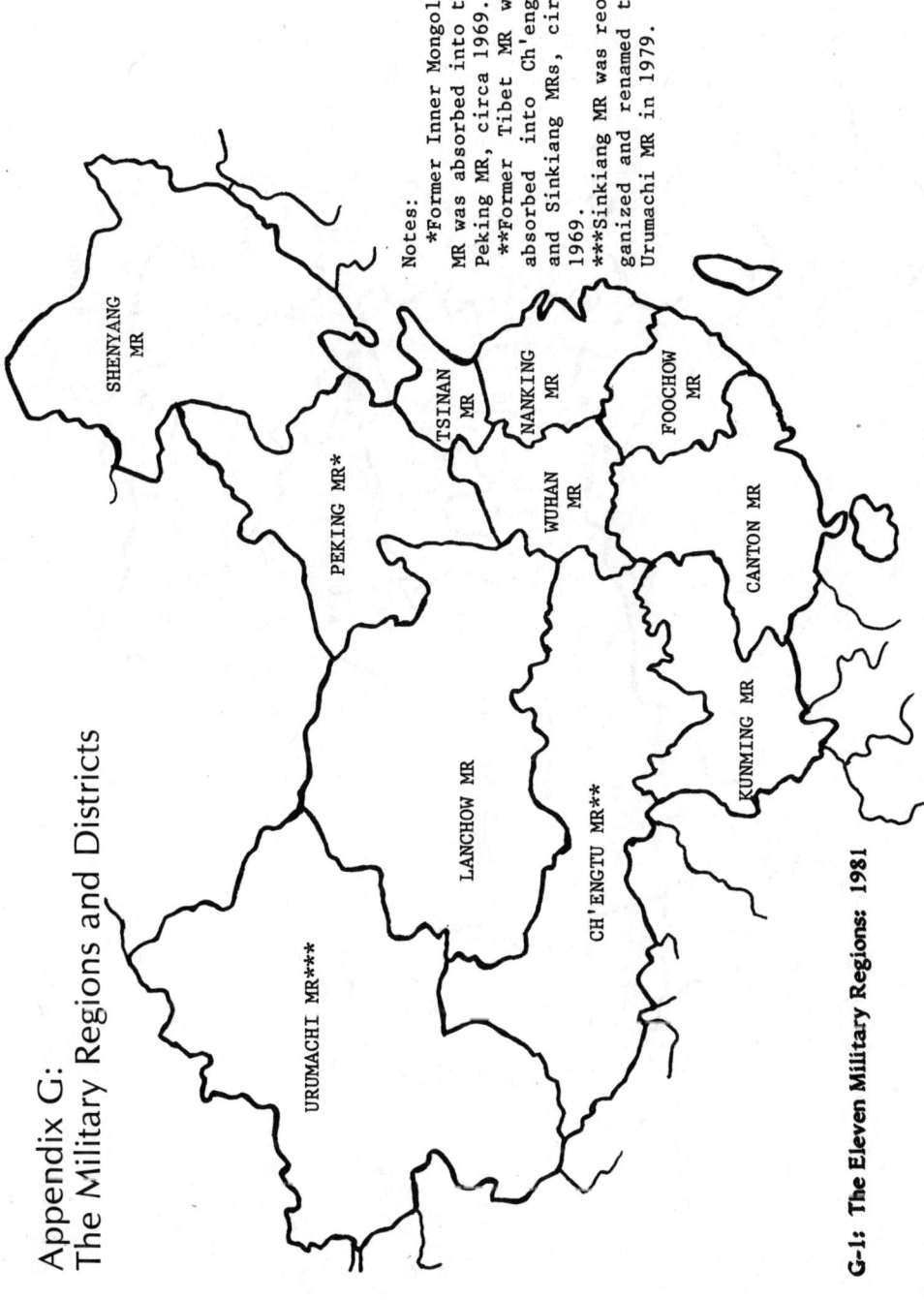

G-1: The Eleven Military Regions: 1981

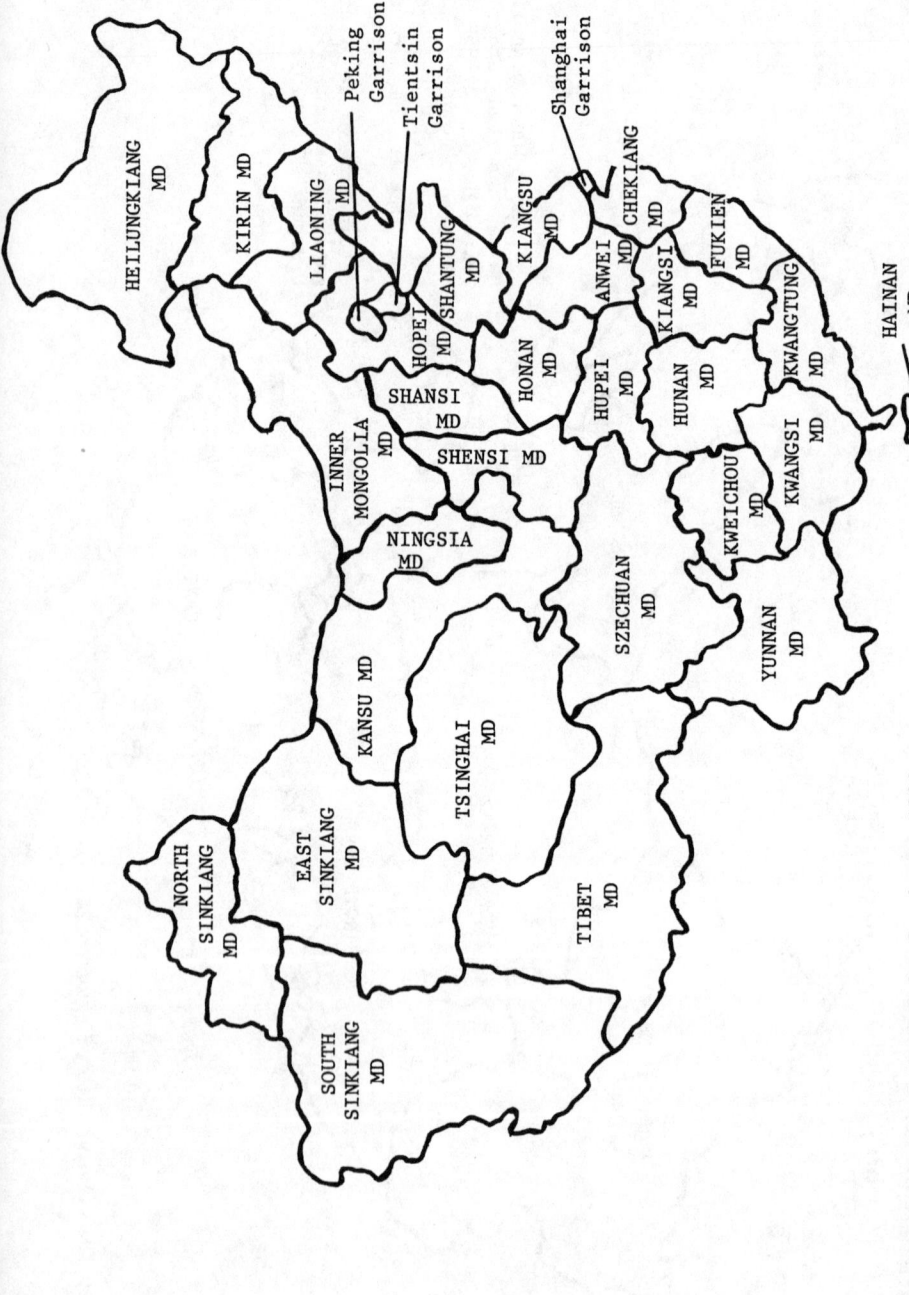

G-2: Military Districts and Major Garrisons: 1980

Selected Bibliography

All abbreviations are in the glossary, which begins on page xxi.

Adelman, Jonathan R. "Origins of the Difference in Political Influence of the Soviet and Chinese Armies: The Officer Corps in the Civil Wars." *Studies in Comparative Communism*, 10, No. 4 (Winter 1977), 347-369.
"Army-People Joint Defense . . . [chun-min lien-fang . . .]." *HC*, No. 10 (1973), 98-99.
"Basic Differences Between the Proletarian and Bourgeois Military Lines." *PR*, No. 48 (24 November 1967), 11-16.
Basic Military Knowledge [chun-shih chi-pen chih-shih]. Shanghai: People's Publishing Agency, 1974.
Bobrow, Davis B. "The Good Officer: Definition and Training." *CQ*, No. 18 (April-June 1964), 141-152.
Borisov, B. and V. Ryabov. *The Soviet Army*. Moscow: FLPH, n.d. (about 1960).
Bridgham, Philip. "The Fall of Lin Piao." *CQ*, No. 55 (July-September 1973), 427-449.
Brown, General George S. "Testimony Before the Senate Armed Services Committee." 5 February 1975.
Bueschel, Richard M. *Communist Chinese Air Power*. New York: Praeger, 1968.
CCP Documents of the Great Proletarian Cultural Revolution: 1966-1967. Hong Kong: URI, 1968.
["Central Committee Issues Regulations on PLA Political Work"]. *NCNA*, 10 August 1978. Trans. in *FBIS*, No. 156, pp. E13-E18.
Chang, Parris H. "Political Rehabilitation of Cadres in China: A Traveller's View." *CQ*, No. 54 (April-June 1973), 331-340.
Chang Yi-min. "Building the World's Strongest Navy." *PR*, No. 1 (3 January 1968), 40-43.
Chang Yuan-ho and Sun Hao-chen, "'Three Supports and Two Militaries' Make for the Best Army Building." *PR*, No. 3 (16 January 1970), 16.
Chang Yun-t'ien. "A Study of Training Work in the Chicom Military [chung-kung chun hsun-lien kung-tso chih yen-chiu]." *CKYCYK*, 5, No. 3 (10 March 1971), 71-83.
Chang Yun-t'ien. "The Establishment and Expansion of Communist China's 'Production-Construction Corps': A Study of Its Conditions and Functions." *CKYCYK*, 4, No. 3 (March 1970), 31-41. Trans. in *TCC*, No. 108, *JPRS* No. 50,719, pp. 12-34.

Ch'en, Hsi-to. "The Militia of Communist China in the 'Great Cultural Revolution.'" *FCYP* (30 April 1970), pp. 61-66. Trans. in *TCC*, No. 111, *JPRS* No. 50,926, pp. 7-21.

Cheng, J. Chester. "Problems of Chinese Communist Leadership As Seen in the Secret Military Papers." *AS*, 4 (June 1964), 861-872.

Cheng Mien-chih. "The Organization and Equipment of the Chinese Communist Infantry." *I and S*, 3, No. 10 (July 1967), 18-25.

Chi I-chai. "A Study of the Cultural Revolution's Impact on Industrial and Mining Enterprises (Part I)." *FCYP*, 2, No. 1 (1 March 1968), 78-87. Trans. in *TCC*, No. 5, *JPRS* No. 45,417, pp. 1-20.

Chi I-chai. "Influence of the Cultural Revolution on the Communist Industrial and Mining Enterprises (Part II)." *FCYP*, 2, No. 2 (1 April 1968), 63-71. Trans. in *TCC*, No. 18, *JPRS* No. 45,741, pp. 12-29.

Chi I-chai. "Influence of the Cultural Revolution on the Communist Industrial and Mining Enterprises (Part III)." *FCYP*, 2, No. 3 (1 May 1968), 61-72. Trans. in *TCC*, No. 19, *JPRS* No. 45,823, pp. 22-42.

Chin Chien-li. "A Look at Every Aspect of the Chinese Communist Armored Force." *HTJP*, 22, 23, 24, 25, 26 September 1971. Trans. in *TPRC*, No. 165, *JPRS* No. 54,447, pp. 4-23.

Chin Chien-li. "Survey of Chinese Communist Artillery and 'Second Artillery.'" *HTJP*, 29, 30, 31 December 1970 and 1 January 1971. Trans. in *TCC*, No. 134, *JPRS* No. 52,417, p. 1-21.

"Chinese Air Force Equipment Special Edition [*chung-kuo k'ung-chun chan-chi t'e-chi*]." *Wu-chi Shih-chieh* (Hong Kong), No. 4 (October 1974).

"Chinese Air Power . . . An Obsolescing Goliath," *Air International*, June 1979, pp. 273-277 and 306-308.

Chinese War Machine, The. Edited by Ray Bonds. New York: Crescent Books, 1979.

Ch'iu Shih-tung. "Current Military Service on the Chinese Mainland." *I and S*, 10, No. 10 (July 1974), 64-70.

Ch'iu Shih-tung. "The Current Phase of Chinese Communist Militia Work." *I and S*, 15, No. 6 (June 1979), 81-97.

Chou En-lai. "Premier Chou's Important Speech" (at Reception for Representatives of Universities and Colleges in Peking on 17 September 1967). *CYTFH* (1 October 1967). Trans. in *SCMP*, No. 4066, pp. 1-6.

Chou En-lai. "Premier Chou's Important Speech (Excerpts)" (undated—possibly 17 January 1968). *Little Soldier [Hsiao Ping]*. Canton, No. 22 (17 February 1968). Trans. in *SCMP*, No. 4134, pp. 1-5.

Chou En-lai. "Premier Chou's Latest Important Instructions on Relevant Questions—relayed on June 2 by Comrade Su Yu in an interview with the 'September 16' Corps of the Seventh Ministry of Machine Building." *Battle Flag of the Third Headquarters [San-szu Chan-ch'i]*. Canton, No. 2 (mid-June 1968). Trans. in *SCMM*, No. 622, p. 2.

Chou En-lai. "Premier Chou's Talk at a Reception for Revolutionary Masses of XX Industrial Systems." *Cultural Revolution Storm [Wen-ko Fengyun]*. Canton, No. 2 (February 1968). Trans. in *SCMP*, No. 4148, pp. 3-9.

Chou En-lai. "Speech by Chou En-lai at Interview with Some Representatives of the Scientific and Technological Commission for National Defense, the Congress of Students, the Military Control Committees, the Revolutionary Mass Organizations of the Seventh Ministry of Machine Building, and the Academia Sinica" (20 April 1968). *Special Collection of Materials [Tzu-liao chuan-chi]*. Canton (undated—1968). Trans. in *SCMM*, No. 631, pp. 1-27.

Chou Tzu-ch'iang. *I and S*, 8, No. 5 (February 1972), 35-49.
Colby, William, et al. *Allocation of Resources in the Soviet Union and China*, Hearings before the Subcommittee on Priorities and Economy in Government of the Joint Economics Committee, US 93rd Congress, 2nd session. Washington, DC: GPO, April 1974.
"Comrade Chou En-lai—Faithful Executer of Chairman Mao's Military Thinking." *JMJP*, 30 July 1978. Trans. excerpts in *NCNA*, 30 July 1978. In *FBIS*, No. 152, pp. E5-E11.
Condition of the Mainland Communist Bandits' Aircraft Industry [*ta-lu kung-fei hang-k'ung kung-yeh kai-kuang*]. Taipei: Ministry of Economics, 1970.
Corr, Gerard H. *The Chinese Red Army: Campaigns and Politics Since 1949*. Berkshire, England: Osprey Publishing, 1974.
"Criticism of 'The Supremacy of Electronics' [*'tien-tze chung-hsin lun' p'i-p'ing*]." *JMJP*, 12 August 1971, p. 2.
"Decision on Kwangtung's 1968 Conscription Work." Canton: Provisional Conscription Work Committee of Kwangtung, November 1967. Trans. in *TCC*, No. 28, *JPRS* No. 46,324, pp. 3-12. NOTE: The CIA is virtually certain this document is a clever Hong Kong forgery. See text in chapter 7.
Directory of Officials of the People's Republic of China (Reference Aid) A (CR) 75-16. Washington, DC: CIA, April 1975.
Directory of Officials of the People's Republic of China (Reference Aid) A (CR) 78-16506. Washington, DC: CIA, November 1978.
Domes, Jurgen. *The Internal Politics of China*. Trans. R. Machetzki. New York: Praeger, 1973.
Domes, Jurgen. "The Role of the Military in the Formation of Revolutionary Committees, 1967-68." *CQ*, No. 44 (October-December 1970), 112-145.
Doorn, Jacques van. "Political Change and the Control of the Military: Some General Remarks." In *Military Profession and Military Regimes: Commitments and Conflicts*. Edited by Jacques van Doorn. Paris and The Hague: Mouton, 1969, pp. 11-31.
Down with the New Tsars! Peking: FLP, 1969.
Etzold, Thomas H. "Analyzing Military Modernization: The State of the Art, 1978." *I and S*, 14, No. 7 (July 1978), 66-74.
"Excerpts from Premier Chou En-lai's Comment on the Situation in N.E. China" (to Red Guard representatives on 28 September 1967). Trans. in Chien Yu-shen. *China's Fading Revolution: Army Dissent and Military Divisions, 1967-68*. Hong Kong: Centre of Contemporary Chinese Studies, 1969, pp. 318-327.
"Failure of the 'Gang of Four's' Scheme to Set Up a 'Second Armed Force.'" *PR*, No. 13 (25 March 1977), 10-12.
Finlayson, A. R. "Command and Control in the Chinese People's Liberation Army." Unpublished paper prepared for the Modern China Seminar, Columbia University, 2 May 1975.
"Firm Pillar of the Dictatorship of the Proletariat." *PR*, No. 31 (2 August 1968), 5-8.
Ford, Harold P. "Modern Weapons and Sino-Soviet Estrangement." *CQ*, No. 18 (April-June 1964), 160-173.
Fraser, Angus M. *The People's Liberation Army: Communist China's Armed Forces*. New York: Crane, Russak, 1973.
Garrett, Banning. "China Policy and the Strategic Triangle." In *Eagle Entangled: American Foreign Policy in a Complex World*. New York: Longman, 1979, pp. 228-263.

George, Alexander. *The Chinese Communist Army in Action.* New York: Columbia UP, 1967.
Gittings, John. "The 'Learn from the Army' Campaign." *CQ,* No. 18 (April-June 1964), 153-159.
Gittings, John. *The Role of the Chinese Army.* New York: Oxford UP, 1967.
"Great Chinese PLA, The—Reliable Pillar of Our Proletarian Dictatorship and Great Proletarian Cultural Revolution." *PR,* No. 36 (1 September 1967), 5-6.
Griffith, Samuel B. *The Chinese People's Liberation Army.* New York: McGraw Hill, 1967.
"Gun Must Forever Be Kept in the Hands of the Party and People, The." *JMJP,* 13 November 1974. Trans. in *SPRCP,* No. 5737, pp. 120-127.
Handbook on the Chinese Armed Forces (DDI-2680-32-76). Washington, DC: Defense Intelligence Agency, July 1976.
Harding, Harry. "China After Mao." *Problems of Communism* (March-April 1977), pp. 1-18.
Harris, Jack H. "Enduring Chinese Dimensions in Peking's Military Policy and Doctrines." *I and S,* 15, No. 7 (July 1979), 75-88.
Harris, Jack H. "The Politics of National Security in China." *Problems of Communism,* 28, No. 2 (March-April 1979), 64-66.
Herspring, Dale R. "Technology and the Changing Political Officer in the Armed Forces: The Polish and East German Cases." *Studies in Comparative Communism,* 10, No. 4 (Winter 1977), 370-393.
Heymann, Hans. "Acquisition and Diffusion of Technology in China." US Congress, Joint Economics Committee. *China: A Reassessment of the Economy, 1975.* Washington, DC: GPO, July 1975, pp. 678-729.
"Hold High the Great Red Banner of Mao Tse-tung's Thought, Thoroughly Criticize and Repudiate the Bourgeois Military Line." *PR,* No. 32 (4 August 1967), 42-45.
Hsieh, Alice Langley. *Communist China's Strategy in the Nuclear Era.* Englewood Cliffs, NJ: Prentice-Hall, 1962.
Hsin Feng. "Mighty Ideological Weapon in the Struggle Against Revisionism." *PR,* No. 20 (17 May 1974), 15-18.
Hsu Hsiang-ch'ien. "Heighten Vigilance, Be Ready to Fight." *HC,* No. 8 (August 1978). Trans. in *FBIS,* No. 148, pp. E4-E15.
Hsu Hsiang-ch'ien. "Strive to Achieve Modernization in National Defense—In Celebration of the 30th Anniversary of the Founding of the People's Republic of China." *HC,* No. 10 (October 1979), 28-33. Trans. in *FBIS,* No. 203, pp. L12-L19.
Hua Kuo-feng. Speech at the PLA Political Work Conference (29 May 1978). Trans. in *NCNA,* 3 June 1978. In *FBIS,* No. 108, pp. E5-E12.
Huang Chen-hsia. *Mao's Generals (chung-kung chun-jen chih).* Hong Kong: Research Institute of Contemporary China, 1968.
Hung Chuang-chih. "Defeat of 'Mechanization' by Revolutionization is the Logic of History." *PR,* No. 39 (26 September 1969), 34-35.
Huntington, Samuel P. *Political Order in Changing Societies.* New York: Yale UP, 1968.
Huntington, Samuel P. *The Soldier and the State.* New York: Vintage, 1957.
Jane's All the World's Aircraft. Various editions. London: Jane's Yearbooks, 1969-80.
Jane's Fighting Ships. Various editions. London: Jane's Yearbooks, 1969-79.
Jane's Infantry Weapons. Various editions. London: Jane's Yearbooks, 1975-78.

Jane's Weapons Systems. Various editions. London: Jane's Yearbooks, 1971-79.
Janowitz, Morris. *The Professional Soldier.* New York: Free Press, 1960.
Jencks, Harlan W. "China's 'Punitive War' on Vietnam: A Military Assessment." *AS,* 19, No. 8 (August 1979), 801-815.
Joffe, Ellis. "The Army After Mao." *International Journal,* 34 (Autumn 1979), 568-584.
Joffe, Ellis. "The Chinese Army After the Cultural Revolution: The Effects of Intervention." *CQ,* No. 55 (July-September 1973), 450-477.
Joffe, Ellis. "The Conflict Between Old and New in the Chinese Army." *CQ,* No. 18 (April-June 1964), 118-140.
Joffe, Ellis and Gerald Segal. "The Chinese Army and Professionalism." *Problems of Communism,* 27 (November-December 1978), 1-19.
Kao Ying-mao, et al. *The Political Work System of the Chinese Communist Military.* Providence, RI: East Asia Language and Area Center, Brown University, 1971.
Kao Ying-mao. *The People's Liberation Army and China's National Development.* White Plains, NY: International Arts and Sciences Press, 1973.
Kau, Michael Ying-mao. *The Lin Piao Affair: Power Politics and Military Coup.* White Plains, NY: International Arts and Sciences Press, 1975.
K'o Shu. "The Ten Great Principles of Operations Are Forever Radiant." *JMJP,* 23 August 1974. Trans. in *SPRCP,* No. 5695, pp. 177-186.
Kolkowicz, Roman. "The Impact of Modern Technology on the Soviet Officer Corps." In *Armed Forces and Society: Sociological Essays.* Edited by Jacques van Doorn. Paris and The Hague: Mouton, 1968, pp. 148-168.
Kolkowicz, Roman. *The Soviet Military and the Communist Party.* Princeton, NJ: Princeton UP, 1967.
Kung-tso T'ung-hsun [Bulletin of Activities]. Peking: General Political Department of the PLA, 1961. Trans. J. Chester Cheng. In *The Politics of the Chinese Red Army.* Stanford, CA: Stanford UP, 1966.
Lan Ching. "Chinese Communist Chemical Defense Force." *HTJP,* 25, 26, 27 August 1970. Trans. in *TCC,* No. 132, *JPRS* No. 52,264, pp. 1-13.
Latham, Richard. "China's National Defense Industrial System: Order or Disorder?" Paper presented at Asian Studies on the West Coast Conference, University of Hawaii, June 1975.
Lewis, John W. "China's Secret Military Papers: 'Continuities' and 'Revelations.'" *CQ,* No. 18 (April-June 1964), 68-78.
Lewis, John W. and Leonard Schapiro. "The Roles of the Monolithic Party Under the Totalitarian Leader." *CQ,* No. 40 (October-December 1969), 39-64.
Lin Piao. "An Important Speech by Vice-Chairman Lin at Reception of Army Cadres on March 25." *Kung-lien.* Canton. (Special Issue, April 1968). Trans. in *SCMP,* No. 4173, pp. 1-5.
Lin Piao. "Deputy Commander Lin's Important Directive" (9 August 1967). Summarized in *CYTFH* (13 September 1967). Trans. in *SCMP,* No. 4036, pp. 1-6.
Lin Piao. "Heighten Our Vigilance, Defend the Motherland." *PR,* No. 31 (7 August 1970), 6-7 and 23.
Lin Piao. "Long Live the Victory of People's War! " (3 September 1965). Trans. in *PR,* No. 32 (4 August 1967), 14-35.
Lin Piao. Speech of 10 August 1967 (Excerpts). Trans. in *TCC,* No. 140, *JPRS* No. 52,658, pp. 15-16.
"Lin Piao's Important Directive to the Army" (6-9 April 1968). *Peking Aviation College Red Flag [Pei-hang Hung-ch'i],* No. 47 (n.d.). Trans. in *F and F,*

1, No. 26 (16 October 1968), 19-23.
Liu, Alan P. L. "The 'Gang of Four' and the Chinese People's Liberation Army." *AS*, 19, No. 9 (September 1979), 817-836.
Luttwak, Edward N. "Problems of Military Modernization for Mainland China." *I and S*, 14, No. 7 (July 1978), 53-65.
Mao Tse-tung. *Basic Tactics*. Trans. S. Schram. New York: Praeger, 1966.
Mao Tse-tung. *On Guerilla Warfare*. Trans. S. B. Griffith. New York: Praeger, 1961.
Mao Tse-tung. *Selected Military Writings*. Peking: FLP, 1967.
Mao Tse-tung. *Selected Works*. Vol. I. Peking: FLP, 1967.
Mao Tse-tung. *Selected Works*. Vols. II and III. Peking: FLP, 1965.
Mao Tse-tung. *Selected Works*. Vol. IV. Peking: FLP, 1961.
"Mao Tse-tung's Talks to Responsible Comrades in Nanking and Shanghai Areas During His Inspection of the Troops." Trans. and abridged in *I and S*, 8, No. 10 (July 1972), 95-97.
"Mao Tse-tung's Thought—The Invincible Weapon." *PR*, No. 30 (21 July 1967), 30-34.
Meyer, Alfred G. "Theories of Convergence." In *Change in Communist Systems*. Ed. Chalmers A. Johnson. Stanford, CA: Stanford UP, 1970, pp. 313-341.
Military Balance, The. Various editions. London. International Institute of Strategic Studies, 1975-81.
"Military Service Law of the PRC" (30 July 1955). Trans. in *CB*, No. 344, pp. 4-11.
Mitchell, Ronald G. and Edward P. Parris. "Chinese Defense Spending, 1965-78." In *Allocation of Resources in the Soviet Union and China, 1979*. Hearings before the Subcommittee on Priorities and Economy in Government of the Joint Economics Committee, US Congress. Washington, DC: GPO, 1979, pp. 66-72.
Moorer, Admiral Thomas H. "The Dynamic Balance of Strategic Power." *Commanders Digest*, 15, No. 15 (11 April 1974), 1-16.
Moorer, Admiral Thomas H. "General Purpose Forces Compared." *Commanders Digest*, 15, No. 16, (18 April 1974), 1-20.
Mozingo, David P. and Thomas W. Robinson. *Lin Piao on People's War: China Takes a Second Look at Vietnam*. Santa Monica, CA: RAND, 1965.
Murphy, C. H. "Mainland China's Evolving Nuclear Deterrent." *Bulletin of the Atomic Scientists*, 28, No. 1 (January 1972), 28-35.
Nelsen, Harvey W. *The Chinese Military System: An Organizational Study of the Chinese People's Liberation Army*. Boulder, CO: Westview Press, 1977.
Nelsen, Harvey W. "Military Bureaucracy in the Cultural Revolution." *AS*, 14, No. 4 (April 1974), 372-395.
Nelsen, Harvey W. "Military Forces in the Cultural Revolution." *CQ*, No. 51 (July-September 1972), 444-474.
Nieh Jung-chen, Speech at the National Militia Conference (4 August 1978). Trans. in *NCNA*, 7 August 1978. In *FBIS*, No. 154, pp. E1-E10.
Ninth National Congress of the Communist Party of China (Documents), The. Peking: FLP, 1969.
Parrish, William L. "Factions in Chinese Military Politics." *CQ*, No. 56 (October-December 1973), 667-699.
"Party Committee of a Certain Regiment of the Peking Units Persevere [sic] in Implementing Democratic Centralism, Strengthening the Centralized Leadership of the Party and Deepening the Development of Criticism of

Lin Piao and Confucius." *JMJP*, 23 October 1974. Trans. in *SPRCP*, No. 5745, pp. 57-60.

"Party Leadership is the Basic Guarantee for the Victory of Our Army." *KMJP*, 30 July 1974. Trans. in *SPRCP*, No. 5677, pp. 197-201.

Perlmutter, Amos. *The Military and Politics in Modern Times: On Professionals, Praetorians, and Revolutionary Soldiers*. New Haven and London: Yale UP, 1977.

Pillsbury, Michael. "Patterns of Chinese Power Struggles." Unpublished paper delivered to the Seminar on Modern China, Columbia University, 27 March 1974.

"PLA Air Force and Its New Commander, Ma Ning, The." *I and S*, 10, No. 11 (August 1974), 96-103.

PLA Unit History. Edited by William W. Whitson. Washington, DC: Chief of Military History, n.d. Based on *History of Chinese Communist Infantry Units*. Taipei: Ministry of National Defense, n.d. (1968?).

Political Work Regulations for the Chinese People's Liberation Army. Peking: CC of the CCP, 27 March 1963. Trans. in Ying-mao Kao. *The Political Work System of the Chinese Communist Military*. Providence, RI: East Asia Language and Area Center, Brown University, 1971, pp. 215-323. A Chinese text is in *Fei-chun cheng-chih kung-tso tiao-li*. Taipei: Ministry of Defense, 1965.

Pollack, Jonathan D. "China's Changing Polity: New Directions in Peking's Military and Foreign Policy." Paper presented at Workshop on Security and Arms Control in the Pacific, Aspen Institute for Humanistic Studies, Aspen, CO, August 1977.

Pollack, Jonathan D. "Chinese Attitudes Towards Nuclear Weapons, 1964-69." *CQ*, No. 50 (April-June 1972), 244-271.

Pollack, Jonathan D. "The Logic of Chinese Military Strategy." *Bulletin of the Atomic Scientists*, 35, No. 1 (January 1979), 22-33.

Pollack, Jonathan D. "The Study of Chinese Military Politics: Toward a Framework for Analysis." In *Political-Military Systems: Comparative Perspectives*. Edited by Catherine McArdle Kelleher. Beverley Hills and London: Sage Publications, 1974.

Powell, Ralph L. "Commissars in the Economy: The Learn from the PLA Movement in China." *AS*, 5, No. 3 (March 1965), 125-138.

Powell, Ralph L. Soldiers in the Economy," *AS*, 11, No. 8 (August 1971), 742-760.

Powell, Ralph L. and Chong-kun Yoon. "Public Security and the PLA." *AS*, 12, No. 12 (December 1972), 1082-1100.

"Press Communique of the Tenth National Congress of the Communist Party of China." *PR*, Nos. 35-36 (7 September 1973), 5-7.

"Proletariat Must Take a Firm Hold of the Gun, The." *PR*, No. 32 (4 August 1967), 36-39.

Ralston, David B., ed. *Soldiers and States*. Boston: D. C. Heath, 1966.

"Regulations on Militia Work" (1978), *I and S*, 16, No. 2 (February 1980), 76-86.

"Regulations on Militia Work" (1961), *I and S*, 16, No. 2 (February 1980), 86-95.

"Regulations on the Service of Officers (8 February 1955). Trans. in *CB*, 312.

"Report of the CCP CC Work Group 'Concerning the Problem of Lo Jui-ch'ing's Mistakes' [*chung-kung chung-yung kung-tso hsiao-tzu 'kuan-yu Lo ... tso-wu wen-t'i' pao-kao*]" (30 April 1966). Reprinted from Red Guard sources in *Yearbook '73*, Book II, Section 7, pp. 14-21. An English translation is in Kao, pp. 286-313. (Also see *SCMP*, No. 4046, pp. 1-12 for essentially the same story.)

"Resolutely Observe the Three Main Rules of Discipline and the Eight Points for Attention." *HC*, No. 2 (1 February 1974), 72 ff. Trans. in *SCMM*, No. 770, pp. 90-95.

"Revolutionary Students Unite, Crush the Counterrevolutionary Organization—the 'May 16' Sinister Corps." A pamphlet compiled in September 1967 by Revolutionary Rebel Commune of the Peking College of Iron and Steel Industry of the Red Guard Congress of the Capital. Trans. excerpts in *CB*, No. 844, pp. 1-30.

Rice, Edward E. *Mao's Way*. Berkeley and Los Angeles: University of California Press, 1972.

Robinson, Thomas W. "The Sino-Soviet Border Dispute: Background, Development, and the March 1969 Clashes." *APSR*, 66, No. 4 (December 1972), 1175-1202.

Robinson, Thomas W. "The Wuhan Incident: Local Strife and Provincial Rebellion During the Cultural Revolution." *CQ*, No. 47 (July-September 1971), 413-438.

Romance, Francis J. "Modernization of China's Armed Forces." Paper presented at Association for Asian Studies annual meeting, March 30-April 1, 1979. Los Angeles, CA.

Schram, Stuart R. "The Party in Chinese Communist Ideology." *CQ*, No. 38 (April-June 1969), 1-26.

Schurmann, Franz. *Ideology and Organization in Communist China*. 2nd ed. Berkeley and Los Angeles: University of California Press, 1968.

"Settle Accounts with P'eng Te-huai for his Heinous Crimes of Usurping Army Leadership and Opposing the Party." *PR*, No. 36 (1 September 1967), 12-15.

Shiffrin, Harold Z. "Military and Politics in China: Is the Warlord Model Pertinent?" *Asia Quarterly*, 3 (1975), 193-206.

Smirnov, Colonel Y. "The Soldier and Politics." *SMR*, No. 12 (December 1973), 6-7.

Smith, W. H. B. and Joseph E. Smith, eds. *Small Arms of the World*, 8th ed. Harrisburg, PA: Stockpole, 1966.

Smith, W. H. B. and Joseph E. Smith, eds. *Small Arms of the World*, 10th ed. New York: Galahad, 1973.

Snow, Edgar. *The Long Revolution*. New York: Vintage, 1973.

Sokolvsky, Marshal V. C., ed. *Military Strategy: Soviet Doctrines and Concepts*. Moscow, September 1962, rpt. New York: Praeger, 1963.

"Strongest Pillar of the Proletarian Dictatorship, The." *PR*, No. 32 (4 August 1967), 40-42.

Sulimov, Major General V. "Principles of Development of the Soviet Armed Forces." *SMR*, No. 3 (March 1973), 12-14.

Tang Chi-ming, "Military Affairs in 1980 [*yi-chiu-pa-ling-nien ti chung-kung chun-shih*]," *CKYCYK*, 15, No. 1 (15 January 1981), 70-80.

Teng Hsiao-p'ing. Speech at the All-Army Political Work Conference (2 June 1978). Trans. in *NCNA*, 5 June 1978. In *FBIS*, No. 109, pp. E1-E10.

T'ien chun. "Our Policy is that the Party Commands the Gun [*wo-men-te yuan-tse shih tang chih-hui ch'iang*]." *HC*, No. 9 (1974), 49-54.

Tsou Sze-yuan, "Summary of Bandit Army Demobilization and Retirement in 1981 [*yi-chiu-pa-yi nien-tu fei-chun t'ui-wu t'ui-hsiu kai-k'uang*]," *FCYP*, 23, No. 8 (February 1981), 54-59.

US Congress, Joint Economics Committee. *China: A Reassessment of the Economy, 1975*. Washington, DC: GPO, July 1975.

Wang Shih-kung. "Inquiry into the Condition of Bandit Army Logistics and

Supply [*fei-chun kou-ch'in pu-chi ch'ing-k'uang chih t'an-t'ao*]," *FCYP*, 23, No. 6 (December 1980), 44-51.
Wang Yung-yeh, "Inquiry Regarding the Current Situation of Chicom Military Academies [*tui chung-kung chun-shih yuan-hsiao hsien-k'uang chih t'an-t'ao*]," *CKYCYK*, 14, No. 12 (15 December 1980), 84-90.
Wettern, Desmond. "PRC Navy Close-Up." *US Naval Institute Proceedings*, March 1981, pp. 122-127.
Whiting, Alan. *China Crosses the Yalu.* New York: Macmillan, 1960.
Whitson, William W. *The Chinese High Command.* New York: Praeger, 1973.
Whitson, William W., ed. *The Military and Political Power in China in the 1970's.* New York: Praeger, 1972.
Who's Who in Communist China. Hong Kong: URI, 1966.
Who's Who in Communist China. Rev. ed. 2 vols. Hong Kong: URI, 1969.
"Wicked History of Big Conspirator, Big Ambitionist, Big Warlord P'eng Te-huai." A pamphlet compiled by Red Guards of Tsinghua University in November 1967. Trans. in *CB*, 851.
Wu Yun-kuang. "Study of Communist China's Artillery No. 2." *FCYP* (September 1967), pp. 67-70. Trans. in *TCC*, No. 3, *JPRS* No. 44,680, p. 409.
"Yang Ch'eng-wu—Newly Reinstated Cadre." *I and S*, 10, No. 13 (October 1974), 107-110.
Yang Yung. "Speech . . . at National Militia Work Conference" (n.d.). *NCNA*, 8 August 1978. Trans. in *FBIS*, No. 156, pp. E1-E13.
Yearbook on Chinese Communism [*Chung-kung nien-pao*]. Taipei: Chung-kung Yen-chiu magazine publishers, August 1973.
Yeh Chien-ying. Speech at the All-Army Political Work Conference (29 May 1978). Trans. in *NCNA*, 4 June 1978. In *FBIS*, No. 108, pp. E12-E21.
Yepishev, General of the Army Andre. *The Party's Powerful Weapon: Some Problems of Party-Political Work in the Army and Navy.* Moscow: Military Publishing House, 1973.
Yu Yang. "People's Militia Powerful in Cultural Revolution." *FCYP*, 10 (10 September 1968), 61-66. Trans. in *TCC*, No. 33, *JPRS* No. 46,920, pp. 1-12.
Zagoria, Donald. *Vietnam Triangle.* New York: Praeger, 1967.

Name Index

Blücher, V.K., 17, 38
Ch'ai Shu-fan, 195, 211
Chang Ai-p'ing, 210
Chang Chen, 195, 211
Chang Ch'un-ch'iao, 94, 106, 120, 121, 138, 140, 141, 243, 244, 255
Chang Han-hua, 113
Chang Kuo-t'ao, 39, 40
Chang Lien-kuei, 195
Chang T'ing-fa, 118
Chang Tsung-hsun, 113, 121
Chao Erh-lu, 202
Ch'en Hsi-lien, 90, 99, 114
Ch'en Po-ta, 70, 93, 108, 115
Ch'en Tsai-tao, 96, 97, 109, 112, 113, 244
Cheng T'ien-hsiang, 195, 212
Cheng Wei-shang, 109
Ch'eng Shih-ts'ai, 117
Ch'i Pen-yü, 115
Chiang Ch'ing, 70, 93, 94, 97, 100, 103, 107-109, 115, 122, 128, 129, 169, 258
Chiang K'ai-shek, 45, 46
Chiao Jo-yü, 195, 212
Ch'ien Hsueh-sen, 206
Ch'ien Min, 195, 211, 212
Ch'in Chi-wei, 114
Ch'iu Chuang-ch'eng, 195
Ch'iu Hui-tso, 55
Chou Chih-p'ing, 109
Chou En-lai, 18, 39-41, 47, 55, 96, 98-102, 104, 105, 107, 109-112, 121, 138, 192, 202, 204, 208, 254, 257, 258, 268
Chou Shih-chung, 121
Chu Teh, 39, 41, 45, 46, 51, 94, 254
Clausewitz, Karl von, 3, 4, 25, 30
Fang Ch'iang, 195, 211
Fang Yi, 202, 210
Fu Ch'ung-pi, 115, 119
Frunze, M. V., 17, 18, 23, 38
Han Hsien-ch'u, 109, 114
Ho Lung, 55, 93, 102, 109, 115, 202, 204
Hsiao Ch'ing-kuang, 18
Hsiao Hua, 55, 59, 99, 109, 115, 116
Hsien Fu-chih, 96, 97
Hsu Hsiang-ch'ien, 18, 37, 46, 126, 135, 138, 140, 151, 152, 192, 213, 261
Hsu Shih-yu, 114, 123
Hua Kuo-feng, 123-125, 138, 192, 261
Huang Yung-sheng, 90, 99, 102
Hung Hsueh-chih, 135, 211
Kao Kang, 46, 71
Keng Piao, 135, 138, 140, 246
Khrushchev, N. S., 24, 26, 79
Kuan Feng, 115
Lenin, V. I., 15-17, 21, 25, 51, 76, 85; See also Leninism
Li Ch'eng-fang, 195, 211
Li Ch'i-t'ai, 195, 211
Li Hsueh-feng, 106, 109
Li Jui-shan, 106
Li Li-san, 71, 254
Li Shou-hsuan, 118
Li Ta, 113
Li Te-sheng, 111, 115, 135
Li Teh (Otto Braun), 41
Liang Pi-yeh, 117

Liao Han-sheng, 93, 113
Lin Chieh, 97
Lin Piao, xvii, xviii, 18, 27,
  41, 45, 47, 54-62, 69-71, 76,
  77, 85, 91-93, 95-98, 101-105,
  107-112, 115, 121, 122, 124,
  138, 139, 153, 157, 174, 176,
  177, 190, 191, 232-235, 238,
  253-255, 257-260, 266
Lin T'ieh, 116
Liu Chieh, 195
Liu Chien-hsun, 106
Liu Chih-chien, 92, 93, 116
Liu Hsi-yao, 195, 212
Liu Hsien-ch'uan, 119, 121
Liu Ke-p'ing, 106
Liu Po-ch'eng, 29, 49, 53, 138,
  254
Liu Shao-ch'i, 18, 42, 46, 54,
  57, 58, 60, 70, 98, 110, 112,
  123, 254, 255, 260, 266
Liu Tao-sheng, 113
Liu Wei, 195, 212
Liu Ya-lou, 62
Lo Jui-ch'ing, 55, 58-62, 70,
  71, 76, 77, 92, 98, 102, 121,
  124, 138, 140, 174, 204, 253,
  259
Lo Jung-huan, 55, 124
Lü Tung, 195, 211
Ma Ning, 120
Mao Tse-tung, 19, 28-31, 37-46,
  48, 53-56, 58, 60, 61, 63, 69,
  70, 73, 74, 77, 78, 81, 85, 90-
  92, 98, 100-102, 104, 105, 107-
  112, 120, 122, 123, 125, 135,
  138, 139, 141, 171, 172, 174,
  177, 190, 193, 236, 243, 244,
  253-258, 260, 261, 264, 266;
  See also Mao Tse-tung's
  Thought; "Maoism"
Nieh Jung-chen, 18, 29, 39, 46,
  53, 61, 94, 103, 122-126, 138,
  204, 208, 210, 254, 268
Ouyang Ch'in, 116
P'eng Shao-hui, 140, 179
P'eng Te-huai, xviii, 29, 39, 41,
  45-55, 58, 61, 62, 69, 71, 76,
  77, 79, 92, 98, 109, 110, 123,
  124, 169, 174, 253, 254, 258,
  259, 260, 268
P'i Ting-chun, 114
Pien, Chiang, 195, 211
Po Yi-po, 211
Sokolovsky, V. D., 25
Stalin, J. V., 18, 24, 26, 48,
  51, 85
Su Chien-hua, 93, 113, 138
Su Yü, 29, 53, 56, 61, 103, 122,
  125, 126, 202, 208, 211, 246,
  254
Sun Chih-yuan, 195
Sung Jen-ch'iung, 116, 195, 212
T'an Yu-lin, 118
Teng Hsiao-p'ing, 18, 30, 37, 57,
  112, 115, 121, 123-126, 138,
  140, 177, 209, 213, 230, 231,
  246, 254, 261, 267, 268
Ting Sheng, 114
Trotsky, L. D., 15-18, 30, 76
Tseng Szu-yü, 114
Tukhachevsky, M. N., 17, 18, 22
Ulanfu, 90, 91, 117
Wang Cheng, 195, 211
Wang En-mao, 90, 91, 97, 187
Wang Hung-wen, 138
Wang Li, 96, 97, 115
Wang Pi-ch'eng, 114, 176
Wang P'ing, 138
Wang Ping-chang, 195
Wei Kuo-ch'ing, 106, 264
Wu K'o-hua, 117
Wu Hsiu-ch'uan, 198
Yang Ch'eng-wu, 41, 96, 102, 103,
  115, 116, 121, 140
Yang Te-chih, 114, 138, 141, 176,
  177, 231
Yang Yung, 113, 114, 125, 140
Yao Wen-yuan, 94
Yeh Chien-ying, 18, 28-30, 37,
  41, 45, 46, 48, 49, 53, 94,
  103, 111, 115, 122-124, 126,
  138, 140, 233, 254, 257, 258,
  261, 268
Yü Li-chin, 115, 117
Zhukov, G. K., 24, 48

Subject Index

Academy of Military Sciences, 49, 139, 205, 206
Academies, Military. See Schools
Aid, Chinese military, 62, 197. See also Vietnam, Chinese support for
Aircraft
 in service with the PLA, 154-158, 162, 190, 196-198, 259, 287-293, 298, 299
 production and development, 48, 61, 93, 190, 194-201, 208
Air defense, 62, 63, 147, 148, 154-157, 160-162, 167, 170-172, 178, 190, 198, 200, 201, 207, 260, 272, 274-276, 279, 283, 299
Air force, 24, 27, 46, 48, 49, 53, 55-57, 61-63, 74, 75, 96, 97, 99, 103, 108, 109, 115, 117-120, 124, 136, 139, 141, 142, 144, 146, 147, 149, 154-158, 160, 162, 178, 190, 196-198, 206, 223-225, 262, 287-293
 airborne troops, 96, 97, 136, 147, 154, 155, 157, 158
 Air Force District(s) (AFD), 136, 154-156, 187
Anti-aircraft. See Air defense
Antichemical troops, 118, 141, 142, 147, 148, 170, 274-276. See also Chemical, biological, and radiological (CBR) capabilities
Antisubmarine warfare (ASW), 161, 162, 199
Antitank (AT) units and equipment, 147, 148, 150, 166, 178, 190, 199-201, 207, 272, 276-278, 282, 283
Armored forces and equipment, 115, 117, 118, 136, 141, 142, 146-150, 163, 164, 166, 175, 198, 199, 201, 212, 225, 272, 273, 275, 279, 284
Artillery forces and equipment, 117, 136, 141, 142, 146-149, 160, 163, 164, 166, 170, 171, 175, 206, 213, 261, 267, 272-275, 279, 283, 284. See also Second Artillery
Atomic Energy. See Nuclear weapons

Budget, Chinese military, 156, 171, 174, 178, 202, 213, 265, 267

Cadres, 41, 42, 44-46, 56, 59, 76, 91, 99, 101, 114, 115, 143, 144, 152, 156, 162, 163, 167, 169-172, 194, 202, 209, 211, 224-232, 236, 239-241, 243-246, 255-257, 261, 263-265. See also Officer corps, Chinese
Capital Construction Engineer Corps, 83, 84, 137, 144-147, 153, 154, 178, 264
Chemical, biological, and radiological (CBR) capabilities, 150, 151, 153, 178. See also Antichemical troops
Cheng-feng (rectification) campaign(1942-44),30,42-44, 244

Chief of staff. See General Staff Department (GSD)
Chinese Academy of Sciences (CAS), 205, 206, 210
"Chu-ko Liang meetings," 39, 243
Civil aviation, 157, 158, 197, 289-291, 293
Civil-military relations, 5, 7-9, 12-14, 26, 27, 76, 122, 126, 135, 140, 141, 244, 253, 255-259, 264-268
  civilian control of the military, 4, 5, 10-12, 17, 22, 23, 76, 89, 110-112, 140, 242, 244, 254, 256, 268
Civil war, Chinese (1945-49), 45-48, 110, 253, 254
"Collective leadership" in the PLA, 238, 239
Command authority, xviii, 234, 235, 239-243, 246
Commissars and political officers, 13, 25, 26
  in the PLA, 25, 38-41, 44, 45, 47-52, 54, 55, 57, 58, 71, 90, 105, 106, 109, 113, 115-121, 124, 126, 137, 138, 141, 143, 149, 165, 167-169, 176, 177, 203, 229, 233, 236-246, 254, 255, 259, 264, 278
  in the Soviet army, 16-19, 22, 25-27, 39, 51
Communications, 149, 150, 154, 168, 170, 171, 189, 198, 263. See also Signal troops; Telecommunications troops
Communist party, 30, 38
  of China (CCP), 28, 30, 37, 40-46, 48-58, 77, 79, 90-95, 99, 100, 103-107, 109-112, 114-117, 120, 122-124, 126, 135, 136, 138-141, 165-171, 174-177, 193, 194, 203, 205, 207, 209, 211, 212, 224, 225, 229, 230, 233, 235-239, 241-246, 253-257, 263-268
    Ninth Party Congress (1969), 100, 104-107, 257
    Tenth Party Congress (1973), 111, 122, 167, 169, 177, 257, 258
  of the Soviet Union (CPSU), 19-24, 27, 268

Communist Youth League (CYL) of China, 56, 236, 238
Conscription. See Recruiting and conscription
Convergence theory, 29-31. See also Revisionism
Corps (chun) of the PLA, 99, 103, 107, 108, 117, 120, 137, 146-149, 151, 152, 155, 158, 175, 227, 228, 237, 255, 256, 261, 272-274, 285. See also Main forces
"Counter-army armies," 24, 79, 158, 179
Cultural revolution. See Great Proletarian Cultural Revolution
Cultural Revolution Group (CRG)
  Central, 90, 92, 93, 97, 99, 100, 102, 103, 107, 108, 112, 115, 208, 238, 256
  of the PLA, 92, 93, 129, 135, 137

Demobilization. See Retirement and demobilization
Democratic centralism, 42, 70, 235, 236. See also "Mass line"
"Dual command" system. See Commissars and political officers; One-man command

Economic production by the military
  in China, 43-45, 55, 75, 77, 78, 80-85, 141, 153, 154, 166, 254, 263. See Self-support production in the PLA
  in the Soviet Union, 17, 20
Egypt, Chinese military relations with, 196-200
8341 Unit of the PLA, 138, 139
Electronics and electronic warfare (EW), 156, 161, 162, 178, 190, 195, 198-200. See also "Steel versus electronics"
Engineer troops, 83, 84, 118, 136, 141, 142, 144, 146, 151, 153, 164, 206, 274

Families of PLA members, 52, 80,

81, 167, 224, 225, 228, 231, 232, 240, 244
"Field army elites" thesis, xvii, 9, 46, 47, 114, 230, 257
"Five-good soldier" movement, 56, 115, 232
"Four-firsts" movement, 56
"Four-good company" movement, 56, 115, 232
"Four modernizations," 69, 123-125, 151, 152, 233, 267

"Gang of four," xviii, 69-71, 85, 111, 122-125, 138, 140, 167, 169, 170, 177, 189, 192, 232, 235, 242, 244, 245, 258, 266, 267
Garrisons, major city, 137, 147, 162, 164, 166, 169, 302
  Peking garrison, 115, 119, 137, 139, 159, 162, 163, 176, 302
  Shanghai garrison, 137, 162, 302
  Tientsin garrison, 137, 162, 302
General Political Department (GPD), 55-57, 59, 92, 93, 98, 114-116, 120, 121, 123, 124, 136, 137, 140, 141, 143, 144, 170, 229, 236, 237, 240, 243, 246, 258, 264. See also Commissars and political officers
General Rear Services Department (GRSD), 55, 92, 108, 109, 115, 117, 118, 121, 135, 137, 144-146, 150, 152, 153, 163, 202, 206, 207, 211, 212, 229. See also Logistics
General Staff Department (GSD), 46, 48, 49, 55, 58, 60, 112, 115, 116, 118, 121, 136, 138-142, 146, 152-154, 163, 168, 170, 173, 175, 176, 179, 198, 202, 206, 211, 229-231, 237, 240, 243, 264
"Generations" of PLA officers, xvii, xviii, 1, 2, 37-39, 126, 127, 213, 244, 246, 264, 266
Great Leap Forward (GLF), 42, 49, 52-55, 56, 79, 123, 126, 189, 207, 255, 260
Great Proletarian Cultural Revolution (GPCR), xvii, 15, 30, 42, 55, 58, 62, 63, 69-76, 78-80, 83, 85, 89-105, 109, 110, 112, 115, 120-123, 126, 129, 135, 141, 157, 159, 167, 172, 175-177, 189, 191, 193, 194, 197, 200, 204, 206-208, 224, 228-230, 232, 234, 235, 238, 239, 244, 253, 255-257, 260, 264-266
Guerrilla warfare, 21, 41, 45, 63, 69, 75, 110, 151, 162, 163, 171, 259, 260. See also People's war

"Hai Jui Dismissed from Office," 55
Hsia-fang ("sending down"), 31, 120, 125, 172, 193
Hsia-lien tang-ping ("go down to the companies and soldier"), 52-55, 120-122, 125, 244

Industry, military, 51, 53, 60, 61, 83, 92, 93, 102, 108, 111, 121, 139, 145, 178, 189, 190, 192-213, 260, 262, 267
Infantry units and equipment, 146-151, 157, 158, 160, 166, 170, 171, 199, 201, 225, 227, 261-263, 272-279, 281-282
Intelligence, military, 47, 141, 142, 240
"Iron rice bowl," 52, 230

Japan, war against (1937-1945), 39, 41-46, 163, 174, 254

KGB, 24, 79, 158, 179
Korean war (1950-1953), 28, 29, 38, 46-48, 55, 69, 75, 157, 176, 177, 207, 243
Kuomintang (KMT), 43, 225
Kutien speech (1929), 39, 40, 244, 254

Leninism, 15, 42, 71, 236
Local forces of the PLA. See Regional Forces
Logistics, 26, 45, 47-49, 92,

144-146, 150-152, 154, 163-165, 170, 171, 178, 207, 240, 263, 274-277, 279. See also General Rear Services Department
Lushan Plenum
  August 1959, 53, 54, 260
  September 1970, 108, 112

Main forces of the PLA, 24, 55, 59, 90, 91, 96, 99, 102-104, 107-109, 120, 121, 136, 137, 140, 142-149, 151, 152, 163, 166, 167, 171, 174-178, 187, 244-246, 255-257, 263, 264, 271, 285. See also Corps
Main Political Administration (MPA) of the Soviet Army, 19, 23, 27
"Many centers," theory of, 104, 105, 107, 176
"Maoism," xix, 25, 26, 30, 38, 41, 51, 57-59, 69-81, 85, 93, 94, 99, 100, 102, 109, 111, 122, 124-126, 193, 207, 233, 244, 245, 253-255, 257-260, 267. See also Mao Tse-tung, military thought of
Mao Tse-tung, military thought of, 37-39, 41, 44, 45, 57-60, 63, 69-81, 85, 101, 102, 110, 112, 233, 256-258
Mao Tse-tung thought propaganda teams, 92, 101, 104, 112
Marxism regarding the military, 15, 30, 39, 85, 266
"Mass line," 42, 57, 236, 264. See also Democratic centralism
Mechanized combat units, 146, 148-151, 279
Medical units, 145, 274-277
Military Affairs Commission (MAC), 45, 46, 50, 55, 59, 60, 79, 92-97, 102, 104, 115, 116, 120, 122, 125, 129, 130, 135, 136, 138-141, 144, 146, 152, 169, 174-177, 194, 202, 203, 205, 206, 223, 224, 228, 229, 232, 236, 237, 239, 243, 256, 264
Military Control Committee(s) (MCC), 90, 94, 95, 98, 101, 103, 104, 112
Military District(s) (MD), 54, 81, 94-96, 101, 103, 105, 111, 116, 118, 120, 137, 146, 154, 162-168, 170, 172, 173, 176, 177, 224, 227-229, 235, 239, 256, 263, 264, 301, 302
Military justice. See Procuracy, military
"Military Line." See Security policy, military; "Military line, bourgeois"
"Military line, bourgeois," 15, 19, 30, 31, 39, 54, 58, 59, 76-78, 98, 111, 139, 253, 255
Military policy. See Security policy, military
Military Region(s) (MR), 24, 79-81, 90, 91, 94-99, 102, 104, 105, 107-109, 111-114, 116, 117, 119, 122, 135, 137, 138, 140, 142-146, 149, 151, 152, 154, 155, 162-164, 166-169, 173, 175-178, 201, 202, 206, 207, 223, 227, 228, 230, 237-239, 244, 255-257, 261, 263, 264, 301
Military subdistrict(s) (MSD), 79, 101, 120, 163, 165, 167-170, 224, 229, 235, 263
Militia, 26
  Chinese people's, 24, 43, 44, 49, 51, 53-55, 58, 59, 62, 78-80, 95, 96, 104, 120, 122, 124, 125, 141, 150, 163, 165-172, 174-176, 229, 235, 246, 258, 260, 263, 264
  in the Soviet Union, 16, 17, 26
Ministries of machine industry (MMI), 139, 144, 146, 194, 195, 201, 203-206, 208, 209, 211
  first, 194
  second, 194, 195, 201, 205, 212
  third, 194-196, 198, 200, 201, 205, 211
  fourth, 195, 198, 199, 201, 202, 205, 211
  fifth, 195, 199, 201, 202, 205, 211
  sixth, 101, 194, 195, 199, 201, 202, 204, 205, 208, 211
  seventh, 195, 200, 201, 204,

205, 208, 212
  eighth, 194-196, 200, 205, 212
Ministry of National Defense (MND), 51, 54, 55, 59, 60, 115, 116, 135, 136, 138-141, 192, 194, 202, 205, 223, 224, 227, 237, 264
Ministry of Public Security (MPS), 55, 58, 166, 178, 179
Missiles, strategic, 158, 190, 195, 196, 199, 200, 203, 259, 262, 295, 296
  ICBM, 158, 159, 162, 200, 296
  IRBM, 111, 158, 295
  MRBM, 111, 158, 159, 295
  SLBM, 161, 297
Model heroes, 70-72, 232
Motivation of soldiers
  in the PLA, 71, 72, 151, 223, 231, 232
  in the Soviet army, 19, 20
"Mountaintopism," 71, 176, 229, 230, 243

National Defense Industrial Committee (NDIC), 139, 202, 204, 205, 208
National Defense Industrial Office (NDIO), 139, 202, 204, 205, 208, 211
National Defense Science and Technology Commission (NDSTC), 61, 93, 139, 202-206, 208, 210
National People's Congress, Fourth, 120, 121, 258
National minorities and the PLA, 80, 170, 172, 223
Navy (PLAN), 55, 108, 109, 113, 136, 139, 141, 142, 144, 146, 160-162, 164, 178, 190, 199, 223-225, 234, 246, 262, 265, 297-299
  air force, naval (PLANAF), 160, 161, 297-299
  fleets, 96, 160
Noncommissioned officers in the PLA, 227
Nuclear weapons, 26, 27, 49, 52, 53, 55, 56, 59-62, 70, 74, 110, 111, 151, 158, 159, 178, 190, 194-196, 199, 200, 203, 210, 212, 259-263, 295, 296

Oath of loyalty, PLA, 232, 233
Officer corps, 9, 10, 14, 47, 255
  corporativism of, 4, 5, 12-14, 29, 245, 264, 265
  Chinese, xviii, xix, 1, 25, 27-29, 30, 38, 45, 48-54, 56, 59, 69, 70, 76, 77, 81, 89, 91-93, 98, 99, 102, 104, 105, 107-109, 111, 115, 120-122, 124-126, 152, 159, 163, 194, 203, 206, 223, 225, 227-231, 233, 236, 239, 241, 244-246, 253-258, 261-268, 278. <u>See also</u> Cadres
  Soviet, xviii, 21-23, 25-28, 30, 31, 234, 268
"Old warriors" of the PLA, 18, 27, 28, 79, 123, 124, 126, 140, 213, 243, 246, 258, 261
One-man command, 17, 18, 21, 22, 26, 51, 52, 115, 234, 235
Ossification of thinking," 152, 157, 227, 261

People's air defense, 125, 141, 166
People's Armed Department(s) (PAD), 79, 101-103, 120, 163, 165, 167-171, 224, 229, 235, 263
People's defense. <u>See</u> People's war
People's war, 17, 26, 45, 60-62, 74, 75, 77-79, 108, 110, 125, 126, 151, 166, 170, 171, 174, 175, 190, 201, 253, 254, 258-260, 263
Police units and functions in China, 166, 167, 175, 176, 178, 223, 258, 264
Political departments in PLA units, 236-242, 274-279
Political work
  in the PLA, 40, 41, 44, 47, 48, 54-59, 70, 71, 76, 77, 80, 92, 101, 102, 115, 120, 124, 126, 141, 166-168, 232-234, 236, 239-242, 264
  in the Soviet army, 19
Practorianism, 10, 12-14, 122, 267, 268
Procuracy, military, 143, 144, 232, 240

Production and Construction Corps (PCC), 80, 81, 99, 163, 172, 173, 178, 264. See also Regimental reclamation farms
Professionalism, military, 1-7, 10-12, 14, 15, 76, 89, 225
  ethic of, 5-7, 19, 242, 253, 265, 267
  in the PLA, xvii-xix, 1, 2, 9, 11, 15, 25, 27, 28-31, 37-39, 48, 49, 51-53, 55, 56, 58, 63, 69, 70, 72, 77, 79, 80, 89, 91, 94, 103, 109, 115, 121, 122, 126, 127, 135, 151, 173, 178, 179, 213, 228, 233, 241, 243-245, 253-255, 257, 258, 261-265, 268
  in the Soviet army, xviii, 18, 19, 23-28, 30, 31, 85, 262, 268
  and technology, xviii, 1, 2, 12, 13, 15, 25-29, 31, 45, 46, 49, 50, 53, 54, 63, 69, 85, 86, 126, 152, 178, 213, 246, 268
  in the West, 3-7
Promotion of PLA officers, 50, 53, 76, 108, 140, 157, 223, 228-231, 245, 265
Public Security Forces (PSF), 46, 55, 159, 258. See also Police units and functions; Regional Forces
"Purely military approach." See "Military line, bourgeois"

Railroad Engineer Corps, 83, 84, 118, 119, 121, 137, 144-147, 153, 178
Rank, military, 5
  in the PLA, 49-52, 60, 71, 76, 121, 125, 126, 162, 244-246, 258, 265
  in the Soviet army, 18, 22, 23
Reassignment of cadres. See Rotation and transfer of cadres
Recruiting and conscription, 16, 48, 49, 139, 141, 151, 157, 162, 163, 166, 167, 170-172, 223-226, 229, 265
"Red-expert," 38, 54, 76, 126, 253

Red guard(s), xvii, 58, 69, 72, 77, 90, 92-103, 108, 109, 144, 159, 172, 204, 208, 238, 255, 256
Regimental reclamation farms, 164, 172, 173. See also Production and Construction Corps
Regional commands of the PLA. See Military Regions
Regional Forces (RF) of the PLA, 46, 53, 55, 57-59, 79, 80, 91, 95, 96, 99, 103, 104, 107, 115, 120, 121, 137, 140, 144, 146, 147, 149, 150, 163-167, 171, 174-176, 178, 229, 235, 246, 256, 263
Regulations on the Service of Officers of the PLA
  of 1955, 50, 51, 125, 228
  of 1978, 124, 125, 228, 246
Rehabilitation of cadres, 101, 112, 115, 116, 123
Research and development (R&D), 61, 92, 93, 111, 139, 145, 146, 153, 159, 192, 196, 198, 199, 201-210. See also Weapons and equipment, production and development of
Reserve military forces
  in China, 49-51, 53, 79, 174, 258
  officers, 10
Retirement and demobilization, 80, 152, 167, 169, 223, 225, 228, 231, 245, 246, 261, 265
Revolutionary Servicemen's Committees, 56
Revisionism, 30, 31, 57, 69, 71, 76, 77, 85, 92, 110-112, 115, 121, 123, 124, 126, 139, 162, 190, 192, 207, 208, 254, 255, 257, 258, 268
Revolutionary committee(s) (RC), 90, 91, 94, 99, 101, 103-106, 114, 256, 257
Rotation and transfer of cadres, 152, 229-231, 240, 245, 246, 264

Salaries in the PLA, 50, 51, 228, 231
Schools, military, 3, 45, 46, 49,

53, 60, 118, 119, 139, 146, 152, 158, 163, 164, 224, 227, 228, 231, 233, 239, 245, 246, 265. See also Whampoa Military Academy
Second Artillery, 117, 136, 141, 142, 146, 158, 159, 200, 295, 296
Security policy, military, xviii, 8, 19, 27, 28, 47, 49, 60, 61, 69, 75, 76, 108-111, 115, 135, 174, 175, 200, 253-255, 258-263
Self-support production in the PLA, 80, 81, 166, 174, 263
Ships and boats of the PLA navy, 161, 162, 199-201, 225, 297, 298
Signal troops, 141, 142, 147, 153, 207, 274-277, 279. See also Telecommunications troops
Sino-Soviet relations. See Soviet Union, relations with PRC
Soviet Army, 7, 15-28, 31, 72, 73, 148, 150, 151, 232, 243. See also Officer corps, Soviet
aid and influence in the PLA, 15, 16, 37-39, 46, 48, 49, 51-54, 56, 60, 69, 144, 158, 159, 162, 174, 194, 198-201, 207, 239, 242, 259, 281-284, 287-293, 295
Soviet Union, relations with PRC, 46-49, 53, 54, 60-62, 77-79, 85, 91, 104, 105, 107, 110, 111, 125, 150, 151, 155, 156, 158-160, 177, 178, 196, 198, 200, 202, 212, 213, 260-262
State Council, 93, 94, 106, 123, 136, 139, 144, 194, 202, 205, 206, 211, 223
State Machine Building Industry Commission, 211, 212
State Planning Commission, 110, 202, 205, 212
State Science and Technology Commission (SSTC), 202-205, 210, 211
"Steel vesus electronics," 108, 190
Strategy
"integral," 18, 38, 41, 45, 49
"unified," 17, 18, 38, 45, 259. See also People's war
Strategy and tactics, 38, 41, 45, 47-49, 73-75, 110, 151, 161, 162, 175, 177, 207, 227, 259-263
combined arms tactics, 26, 37, 151, 261
Submarines, 161, 297

Tactics. See Strategy and tactics
Tanks and tank units. See Armored forces and equipment; Weapons and equipment
Taiwan, xvii, 46, 53, 57, 148, 156, 157, 160, 170, 178
Technology
education, 152, 193, 198, 204-206, 208-210, 227, 265. See also Research and development
importation of, 125, 192, 193, 197-201, 203, 204, 207, 209-211, 213, 262
innovation, 193, 207, 209
Telecommunications troops, 83, 84, 115, 118, 121, 153, 154. See also Signal troops
"Three rules of discipline and eight points for attention," 39, 111, 115
"Three Supports and Two Militaries," 82-84, 92, 94, 104, 112, 159, 256
Training, military, 54-56, 58, 59, 71, 80, 142, 144, 146, 148, 150-153, 156, 157, 160, 161, 163, 164, 166-172, 178, 225, 227, 232-234, 239-241, 243, 261, 263, 268
Transportation and transportation units, 144, 146, 147, 155, 156, 263, 273-277, 279. See also Logistics

Uniforms, PLA, 60, 125, 126, 154, 160, 162, 166, 232, 245, 246, 265
United States, PRC relations

with, 48, 53, 60-63, 69, 77, 78, 99, 107, 108, 110, 146, 156, 159, 160, 178, 197-200, 213, 260-262, 290, 291

Vietnam
 Chinese support for (1960-1975), 60-62, 78, 95, 102, 103, 144, 153, 156, 196, 198
 Chinese conflict with (1975-81), 125, 148-152, 156, 160, 170, 176, 177, 200, 201, 227, 244

Weapons and equipment of the PLA
 importance of, 25, 56, 59, 72-75, 78, 254, 259, 260, 267
 production and development, 48, 61, 62, 189, 190, 192, 194, 197-204, 207, 212, 213, 225, 260-262, 267, 281-284, 287-293, 295-299
 in service, xviii, 49, 70, 142, 145, 148-152, 154-157, 160-162, 166, 171, 172, 190, 201, 207, 259, 267, 271-284, 287-299
Whampoa Military Academy, 17, 18, 38, 39, 41, 239
"Whateverism," 69, 245, 258, 267. See also "Maoism"
Wuhan incident (1967), 95-97, 99, 112, 244, 256

Zampolit. See Commissars and political officers, in the Soviet Army